SQL SERVER 2000

A Beginner's Guide

DUŠAN PETKOVIC

Osborne/**McGraw-Hill**
Berkeley New York St. Louis San Francisco
Auckland Bogotá Hamburg London Madrid
Mexico City Milan Montreal New Delhi Panama City
Paris São Paulo Singapore Sydney
Tokyo Toronto

Osborne/**McGraw-Hill**
2600 Tenth Street
Berkeley, California 94710
U.S.A.

For information on translations or book distributors outside the U.S.A., or to arrange bulk purchase discounts for sales promotions, premiums, or fund-raisers, please contact Osborne/**McGraw-Hill** at the above address.

SQL Server 2000: A Beginner's Guide

1234567890 AGM AGM 01987654321

Book P/N 0-07-213118-7 and CD P/N 0-07-213117-9
parts of
ISBN 0-07-212587-X

Publisher
Brandon A. Nordin
Vice President and Associate Publisher
Scott Rogers
Editorial Director
Wendy Rinaldi
Associate Acquisitions Editor
Ann Sellers
Project Editor
Patty Mon
Acquisitions Coordinator
Tim Madrid
Technical Editor
Mark Linsenbardt
Copy Editor
Dennis Weaver
Proofreader
Brian Galloway
Indexer
Valerie Robbins
Computer Designers
Gary Corrigan & Melinda Moore Lytle
Illustrators
Michael Mueller & Beth Young
Series Design
Peter Hancik
Cover Design
William Voss

This book was composed with Corel VENTURA™ Publisher.

CONTENTS

ABOUT THE AUTHOR

Dušan Petkovic is a professor in the Department of Computer Science at the Polytechnic in Rosenheim, Germany. He is the author of *SQL Server 7: A Beginner's Guide* and a frequent contributor to SQL Server magazine.

ACKNOWLEDGMENTS

I would like to thank my wife Sibille for her support in the last 12 years of working with database systems. Her patience with me during this time allowed me to concentrate on my job and on writing books.

It gives me great pleasure to thank Christian Unterreitmeier and Elke Hansel. Christian encouraged me to start this project, while Elke was of great help in the early phase of planning the book.

I would also like to thank all reviewers for many valuable ideas, which significantly improve the quality of the book. My friend Wolfgang Stein read several chapters of the book and made a number of corrections, which certainly make some topics of the book easier to understand. Two of my former students—Christian Unterreitmeier and Thomas Kammerloher—read selected chapters of the book and made several important suggestions concerning performance and data warehousing issues.

Finally, I would like to thank my acquisitions editor Ann Sellers and project editor Patty Mon for their extraordinary support during the work on this book.

INTRODUCTION

Relational database systems (RDBMS) are the most important database systems used in the software industry today. One of the most outstanding systems is MS SQL Server. There are a couple of reasons why SQL Server is the best choice for a broad spectrum of end users and database programmers building business applications. SQL Server is certainly the best database system for Windows NT/2000 and Windows 9*x*, because it is tightly integrated with those two operating systems. The number of installed Windows NT/2000 and Windows 9*x* systems is increasing rapidly, and due to the best integration (and low pricing, too), SQL Server is really a big database system!

Second, SQL Server is the easiest database system to use: in addition to the well-known user interface, Microsoft offers several different tools to help you create database objects, tune your database applications, and manage system administration's tasks. For example, SQL Server 2000 includes *dozens* of wizards for almost everything (database creation, maintenance, alerts, security, data replication, and many more tasks).

Third, bundling two products in one—SQL Server itself and Analysis Services—also brings the overall system to the winning position. The ability to use one system for operational tasks as well as for mission-critical applications is all that users want and need.

Goals of the Book

Generally, all *new* SQL Server users, who want to get a good understanding of this database system and to work successfully with it, will find this book very helpful. The special group of users, which this book addresses, are MS Access users who want to use another (more powerful) database system other than Access but stay with the known operating system and Windows user interface.

The book also addresses *all* users of the SQL Server system. For this reason, it is divided into several parts: end users will find the first two parts of the book the most interesting, while the third part provides know-how for database and system administrators. The second part of the book is dedicated to database application programmers, while several chapters address the special task facing them: tuning database applications. The second to the last part of the book provides insight for users who want to use decision support components of the system.

For all these reasons, the book gives you an overall introduction to the complete SQL Server system. In contrast to SQL Server Books Online (BOL), which are very voluminous and hence often not easy to use, the book teaches you all topics of this database system and especially provides explanations for connections between different topics.

Working with the Sample Database

An introductory book like this one requires a sample database that can be easily understood by each reader. For this reason, I used a very simple concept for the sample database: it has only four tables with several rows each. On the other hand, its logic is complex enough to demonstrate the hundreds of examples within the text of the book. The sample database that you will use in this book represents a company with departments and employees. Each employee belongs to exactly one department, which itself has one or more employees. Jobs of employees center around projects: each employee works at the same time for one or more projects, and each project engages one or more employees.

The tables of the sample database are shown here:

The **department** table

dept_no	dept_name	location
d1	Research	Dallas
d2	Accounting	Seattle
d3	Marketing	Dallas

The **employee** table

emp_no	emp_fname	emp_lname	dept_no
25348	Matthew	Smith	d3
10102	Ann	Jones	d3
18316	John	Barrimore	d1
29346	James	James	d2
9031	Elisa	Bertoni	d2
2581	Elke	Hansel	d2
28559	Sybill	Moser	d1

The **project** table

project_no	project_name	budget
p1	Apollo	120000
p2	Gemini	95000
p3	Mercury	185600

The **works_on** table

emp_no	project_no	job	enter_date
10102	p1	Analyst	1997.10.1 00:00:00
10102	p3	Manager	1999.1.1 00:00:00
25348	p2	Clerk	1998.2.15 00:00:00
18316	p2	NULL	1998.6.1 00:00:00
29346	p2	NULL	1997.12.15 00:00:00
2581	p3	Analyst	1998.10.15 00:00:00
9031	p1	Manager	1998.4.15 00:00:00
28559	p1	NULL	1998.8.1. 00:00:00
28559	p2	Clerk	1999.2.1 00:00:00
9031	p3	Clerk	1997.11.15 00:00:00
29346	p1	Clerk	1998.1.4 00:00:00

You can download the sample database from the Osborne/McGraw-Hill Web site at (www.osborne.com).

Organization of the Book

The book's 30 chapters are divided into five different parts. The first part of the book (Chapters 1 and 2) describes the notion of database systems generally and SQL Server in particular; the second part (Chapters 3 through 15) is intended for end users and application programmers, while the third part (Chapters 16 through 25) describes all objectives of SQL Server system administration.

The fourth part of the book contains three chapters that are dedicated to the Microsoft Analysis Services. MS Analysis Services allow users to analyze and query data in data warehouses and data marts. Finally, the last part of the book describes different application tools that are also part of the overall system.

The first chapter discusses databases in general and SQL Server in particular. The notion of normal forms and the sample database are also presented here. The chapter also introduces the syntax conventions that are used in the rest of the book.

In the second chapter, you can find the description of two SQL Server client components—SQL Server Enterprise Manager and SQL Server Query Analyzer. The goal of this presentation at the beginning of the book is to give you the ability to create database objects and to query data without knowing the SQL database language.

Chapter 3 begins a new part of the book and describes one of the most important parts of an RDBMS—a database language. For all RDBMS, there is only one language that counts, and that is SQL. In this chapter, all components of SQL Server's own database language—called Transact-SQL—are described. You can also find the basic concepts and existing data types of SQL in this chapter. Finally, all functions and operators are described.

Chapter 4 begins a new part of the book. It describes all data definition language (DDL) statements of Transact-SQL. At the beginning of the chapter, all DDL statements are divided into three groups. The first group contains all forms of the CREATE statement that are used to create database objects. A modification of the structure of some database objects is executed using the Transact-SQL statements from the second group. Finally, the third group contains all forms of the DROP statement, which is used to remove different database objects.

Chapters 5 and 6 discuss the most important Transact-SQL statement—the SELECT statement. These chapters introduce to you how data in a database can be retrieved and describe the use of simple and complex queries. Each clause concerning SELECT is separately defined and explained with reference to the sample database.

In Chapter 7, we discuss the four Transact-SQL statements for updating data—INSERT, UPDATE, DELETE, and TRUNCATE TABLE. Each of these statements is explained through the use of numerous examples.

Transact-SQL is complete computational language. This means all procedural extensions are an inseparable part of the language. Chapter 8 describes those extensions that can be used to create powerful scripts called batches and stored procedures (scripts that are stored on the server and can be reused). Some stored procedures are written by users, and others are provided by Microsoft and are referred to as system stored procedures. The creation and execution of the user-defined stored procedures are also discussed in this chapter.

Every user (especially database applications programmers) can tune their applications to get better system response and therefore better performance. The first and most powerful method is the use of indices. The first part of Chapter 9 describes the creation of indices, while the second part discusses the overall possibilities to achieve better performance.

Chapter 10 introduces the notion of a view. This chapter explains all Transact-SQL statements concerning views, using numerous examples. Also, an important new feature of SQL Server 2000—materialized views—is explained in this chapter. At the end of the chapter, you will find a discussion of the existing restrictions concerning updating of views.

One of the most important parts of an RDBMS is a system catalog. The system catalog contains all the information concerning database objects and their relationships. The most important system tables belonging to the SQL Server system catalog are described in Chapter 11, and examples concerning querying those tables are given. SQL Server supports system procedures, which make possible an alternate (and easier) way to query the system catalog. The final part of this chapter describes the numerous system procedures.

In Chapter 12, you will find the answer to two primary questions concerning protection of data in the database against unauthorized access. These questions concern authorization (which user has been granted legitimate access to the database system) and permissions (which access privileges are valid for a particular user). Three Transact-SQL statements are discussed in this chapter—GRANT, DENY, and REVOKE. They provide the access privileges of database objects against unauthorized access. The use of views and stored procedures for the same purpose is also explained.

There are two ways of keeping SQL Server databases in a consistent state with respect to the constructs specified in the database—procedural and declarative. After the definition of declarative integrity constraints in Chapter 4, Chapter 13 describes the implementation of procedural integrity constraints using triggers. Each example in this chapter concerns an integrity problem that you can meet in your everyday life as a database application programmer.

Chapter 14 describes the concept of a transaction and the Transact-SQL statements that control a transaction. Locking as a method to solve a problem of concurrency control is discussed further. At the end of the chapter, you can learn what isolation levels and deadlocks are.

In Chapter 15, some internal and external issues concerning SQL Server 2000 are discussed. System databases and system architecture are two different internal facilities of the SQL Server system. Utilities like **osql**, **isql**, and **bcp** allow users to execute certain database operations like interactive queries and data load. At the end of this chapter, we describe Unicode, which allows the use of different languages within the SQL Server system and supports their specific properties.

The third part of the book describes system administration issues and starts with Chapter 16, which is an introduction to the system administrator's tools and tasks. This short chapter lists all existing SQL Server components, which will be explained in detail in the following chapters.

The first system administration task is the installation of the SQL Server system. Although the system installation is a straightforward task, there are certain steps that need explanation. We handle all of these steps in Chapter 17.

Chapter 18 deals with storage management responsibilities of the system administrator. This includes how to create databases and their transaction logs using SQL Server Enterprise Manager, how to expand the size of databases and logs, and also how to drop databases.

Chapter 19 addresses the issues concerning system and database access. It covers the discussion and the implementation of system security modes (Windows NT and Mixed Mode). This chapter also discusses creating and managing the different types of user accounts, including SQL Server logins and roles.

Chapter 20 provides an overview of the SQL Server fault-tolerance methods used to implement a backup strategy using either SQL Server Enterprise Manager or corresponding Transact-SQL statements. (There is also a discussion of using wizards for this task.) The first part of the chapter specifies the different methods used to implement a backup strategy. The second part of the chapter deals with the restoration of databases. We describe methods for recovery of user-defined databases and transaction logs as well as recovery of system databases.

Data transfer issues are covered in Chapter 21. Transferring data can involve exporting data from a database, importing data into a database from other sources, and also modifying data in between. The most important SQL Server component for these tasks—Data Transformation Services (DTS)—is explained in this chapter.

SQL Server is one of a few RDBMS that includes the facilities to automate certain system administration jobs, such as backing up data and using the scheduling and alert features to notify operators. A SQL Server component called SQL Server Agent schedules and automates such problems. This component, together with the SQL Server Services, is described in Chapter 22.

SQL Server provides two sources—Windows NT event log and SQL Server error log—that give the system administrator the ability to react to system warnings and failures. Chapter 23 covers those components and describes their benefits and disadvantages.

Chapter 24 provides an overview of the monitoring and tuning tasks that a system administrator performs using SQL Server Query Analyzer. At the beginning of the chapter, different factors that influence the overall performance of a system are listed and explained. In the second part of the chapter, SQL Server Query Analyzer is used to show how a query execution plan of SQL Server can be modified to improve performance of a query.

Chapter 25 provides an introduction to data replication, including notions such as the publisher and subscriber. The different models of replication are shown as well as the installation of publishers and subscribers using SQL Server Enterprise Manager.

The fourth part of the book is dedicated to Microsoft Analysis Services. Chapter 26 introduces to you the notion of data warehousing. In the first part of the chapter, the differences between the online transaction processing on one side and the data warehousing on the other side are explained. The data store for a data warehousing process can be either a data warehouse or a data mart. Both types of data store are discussed, and their differences are listed in the second part of the chapter. The data warehouse design is explained at the end of the chapter.

In contrast to Chapter 26, which describes general properties of data warehousing systems, Chapter 27 discusses specific properties of MS Analysis Services. At the beginning of the chapter, the architecture of Analysis Services is described. The second part of the chapter discusses several main components of Analysis Services, such as the repository and Analysis Manager.

Chapter 28 describes client components for MS Analysis Services. For this version of Analysis Services, there are three groups of components: the Transact-SQL extensions (such as ROLLUP and TOP n statements), Excel 2000, and several third-party client software systems.

The last part of the book begins with one of the most important new topics in SQL Server 2000—XML. Chapter 29 first shows you all the preliminary steps that you have to undertake before you can use Internet Information Server to execute queries, which results are displayed in XML form. Also, this chapter discusses the different XML modes using numerous examples.

Data warehousing is not the only area that is supported with one of SQL Server's integrated components. If you want to do full text search (as a part of your Internet solution, for example), you can use the full text search feature, which is also an integral part of SQL Server 2000. Chapter 30 explains how to enable databases and tables for a full text search and how to populate the implicitly created full text index.

Almost all chapters include at the end numerous exercises, which you can use to improve your knowledge concerning the chapter's content. Appendix A comprises all solutions to the given exercises.

Conventions Used in this Book

The following conventions are used in this book:

UPPERCASE indicates Transact-SQL keywords.

Boldface indicates names of database objects (database itself, tables, columns) in the text.

Italics indicates new terms or items of emphasis. (This and other syntax conventions are described in detail at the end of Chapter 1.)

PART 1

SQL Server: Basic Concepts

CHAPTER 1

Database Systems and SQL Server

MS SQL Server is a database management system (DBMS) developed and marketed by Microsoft. This system is the most important part of Microsoft Back Office, an enterprise suite of client/server applications. (In addition to SQL Server, Microsoft Back Office includes Windows NT Server, SNA Server, Systems Management Server, Exchange Server, Microsoft Transaction Server, Internet Information Server, and MSMQ Server.)

MS SQL Server runs exclusively under Microsoft operating systems Windows NT/2000 and Windows 9*x*. Microsoft's decision to concentrate on only two of their own operating systems has a lot of benefits and one disadvantage. The most important benefits are as follows:

- MS SQL Server works as a natural extension of Windows NT/2000 (i.e., Windows 9*x*), because it is so closely integrated with this operating system. As such, the user does not have to learn another user interface to work with this database system.
- MS SQL Server has the same easy setup and maintenance of Windows NT/2000. This unity is accomplished through easy installation of the system, elimination of many complicated tasks concerning database administration, and, generally, using a graphical computing environment for every system administration task.
- MS SQL Server uses the services of Windows NT/2000 to offer new or extended database capabilities, such as sending and receiving messages and managing login security.

On the other hand, by focusing only upon Microsoft operating systems, SQL Server cannot benefit from the advanced properties of an operating system such as UNIX, which, in some areas like enhanced parallel architectures or enterprise computing, still has advantages over Windows NT/2000.

The most important aspects of SQL Server are as follows:

- SQL Server is easy to use.
- SQL Server scales from a mobile laptop to symmetric multiprocessor (SMP) systems.
- SQL Server provides data warehousing features that until now have only been available in Oracle and other more expensive DBMSs.

Almost all relational DBMSs originated under the UNIX operating system. The consequence is that existing user interfaces provided by these systems are rather difficult to use. Microsoft's goal is to make SQL Server the easiest database system for implementing and managing database applications. One way SQL Server helps to further this goal is by providing wizards for almost all administrative tasks.

Scalability means that the same DBMS runs on mobile laptop computers, single-processing systems, and multiprocessing hardware systems. One of the goals of such a

DBMS is to scale from the single-processing computer to an SMP if the DBMS becomes CPU-bound because of CPU-intensive database applications.

Microsoft bundled the Analysis Services with SQL Server to create a comprehensive approach to the process of data warehousing. The goal of Analysis Services is to make it easier to build data warehousing and data mart solutions using Microsoft's new OLAP technology as well as the existing technology of other data warehousing software companies. Part IV will provide additional detailed information on the data warehousing features of MS SQL Server.

NOTE: The SQL Server database system was originally developed and implemented by Sybase Inc. Microsoft licensed this DBMS in 1988 for the OS/2 operating system and began the implementation of it for Windows NT/2000 in the early 1990s. At almost the same time, the further development of SQL Server for OS/2 was canceled. In April 1994, Microsoft ended their cooperative agreement with Sybase Inc.

SQL Server was, from the beginning, designed as a client/server DBMS. The client/server architecture has been developed to manage a large number of different computers (PCs, workstations, and SMP machines), which are connected using a network. The functionality of SQL Server is divided between clients and server(s). A client provides one or more different user interfaces that are used to formulate a user request to a DBMS. The server (i.e., DBMS) processes this request and sends the result back to the client.

NOTE: The client/server architecture does not necessarily include a DBMS. It is also possible to have other exclusively specialized servers, such as a print server and computing server, in such an environment. However, a DBMS is almost always a part of client/server architecture.

DATABASE SYSTEMS: AN OVERVIEW

A database system is an overall collection of different database software components and databases containing the following parts:

- Database application programs
- Front-end (i.e., client) components
- Database management system(s)
- Databases

A database application program is special-purpose software that is designed and implemented by users or implemented by third-party software companies. In contrast, front-end components are general-purpose database software designed and implemented by a database company or delivered as third-party software. By using database application programs and front-end components, users can manage and query data within the database.

The task of a database management system is to manage data stored in a database. In general, a database can be viewed from at least two perspectives: the user's and a DBMS's. Users view a database as a collection of data that logically belongs together. For a DBMS, a database is simply a series of bytes, usually stored on a disk.

Although these two views of a database are totally different, they do have something in common. The database system not only needs to provide interfaces that enable users to create databases and retrieve or modify data, but it also needs to provide system components to manage the stored data. A database system must provide the following features:

- Variety of user interfaces
- Physical data independence
- Logical data independence
- Query optimization
- Data integrity
- Concurrency control
- Backup and recovery
- Security and authorization

The following sections briefly describe these features.

Variety of User Interfaces

Most databases are designed and implemented for use by many different types of users with varied levels of knowledge. For this reason, a database system should offer many distinct user interfaces. These interfaces include query by example, natural language, and forms for end users, as well as interactive query language for experienced users.

Physical Data Independence

Physical data independence means that the database application programs are not dependent on the physical structure of the stored data in a database. This important feature makes it possible to make changes in the stored data without having to make any changes in database application programs. For example, if the stored data is previously ordered using one criterion, and if this later should be changed using another, the modification of the physical data should not affect the existing database applications or the existing database *schema* (a description of a database generated by the data definition language of the DBMS).

Logical Data Independence

In file processing (using traditional programming languages), the declaration of a file is done in application programs, so any changes to the structure of that file usually require the modification of all programs using it. Database systems provide logical data independence—in other words, it is possible to make changes in the logical structure of the database separately from the database application programs. For example, if the structure of an object named PERSON exists in the DBMS and we want to add an attribute to PERSON (say the address), only the logical structure of the database has to be modified, and none of the existing application programs requires changing.

Query Optimization

Every database system contains a subcomponent called an *optimizer* that considers a variety of possible execution strategies for querying the data and then selects the most efficient one. The selected strategy is called the *execution plan* of the query. The optimizer makes its decisions using considerations such as how big the tables are that are involved in the query, what indices exist, and what Boolean operator (AND, OR, or NOT) is used in the WHERE clause. (Indices and query optimization are discussed in detail in Chapter 10.)

> ***NOTE:*** In some legacy database applications, which were implemented using lower-level database languages concerning network and hierarchical database systems, the programmer chooses the query execution plan.

Data Integrity

One of the tasks of a DBMS is to identify logically inconsistent data and reject their storage in a database. (The date February 30, and the time 5:77:00 P.M. are two examples of such data.) Additionally, most real-life problems that are implemented using database systems have *integrity constraints* that must hold true for the data. (One example of an integrity constraint might be the company's employee number, which must be a five-digit integer.) The task of maintaining integrity can be handled by the user in application programs or by the DBMS. As much as possible, this task should be handled by the DBMS. (Data integrity is discussed in two chapters of this book: declarative integrity in Chapter 4 and procedural integrity in Chapter 13.)

Concurrency Control

A DBMS is a multiuser software system, meaning that many user applications access a database at the same time. Therefore, each DBMS must have some kind of control mechanism to ensure that several applications, trying to update the same data, do so in some controlled way. The following is an example of a problem that can arise if a DBMS does not contain such control mechanisms:

1. The owners of bank account 4711 at bank X have an account balance of $2,000.
2. The two joint owners of this bank account, Mrs. A and Mr. B, go to two different bank tellers, and each withdraws $1,000 *at the same time.*
3. After these transactions, the amount of money in bank account 4711 should be $0 and not $1,000.

All DBMSs have the necessary mechanisms to handle cases like this example. Concurrency control is discussed in detail in Chapter 14.

Backup and Recovery

A DBMS must have a subsystem that is responsible for recovery from hardware or software errors. For example, if a failure occurs while a database application updates a hundred rows of a table, the recovery subsystem must roll back all previously executed updates to ensure that the corresponding data is consistent after the error occurs. (See Chapter 20 for further discussion on backup and recovery.)

Security and Authorization

Security means that the data stored in a database is protected against any kind of unauthorized user or against a misuse. For example, access to the data item **salary** containing employee salaries of a company should be allowed only to authorized persons. Additionally, some users may have only read access to the data, whereas others may have read and write access to the same data.

Each DBMS provides some kind of authorization control by means of *user accounts* that grant and revoke privileges to the users of the system. Chapter 12 discusses this topic in detail.

RELATIONAL DATABASE SYSTEMS

MS SQL Server is a relational DBMS. The notion of relational database systems was first introduced by E. F. Codd in his article "A Relational Model of Data for Large Shared Data Banks" in 1970. In contrast to earlier database systems (network and hierarchical), *relational database systems* are based upon the relational data model, which has a strong mathematical background.

> ***NOTE:*** A *data model* is a collection of concepts, their relationships, and their constraints that are used to represent data of a real-world problem.

The central concept of the relational data model is a relation—that is, a table. Therefore, from the user's point of view, a relational database contains tables and nothing but tables. In a table, there are one or more columns and zero or more rows. At every row and column position in a table there is always exactly one data value.

Working with the Book's Sample Database

The sample database that we will use in this book represents a company with departments and employees. Each employee belongs to exactly one department, which itself has one or more employees. Jobs of employees center around projects: each employee works at the same time for one or more projects, and each project engages one or more employees.

The data of the sample database can be represented using four tables:

- department
- employee
- project
- works_on

Tables 1-1 through 1-4 show all the tables of the sample database.

The table **department** represents all departments of the company. Each department has the following attributes:

department (dept_no, dept_name, location)

dept_no represents the unique number of each department. **dept_name** is its name, and **location** is the location of the corresponding department.

The table **employee** represents all employees working for a company. Each employee has the following attributes:

employee (emp_no, emp_fname, emp_lname, dept_no)

emp_no represents the unique number of each employee. **emp_fname** and **emp_lname** are the first and last name of each employee, respectively. Finally, **dept_no** is the number of the department to which the employee belongs.

Each project of a company is represented in the table **project**. This table has the following columns:

project (project_no, project_name, budget)

project_no represents the unique number of each project. **project_name** and **budget** specify the name and the budget of each project, respectively.

dept_no	dept_name	location
d1	Research	Dallas
d2	Accounting	Seattle
d3	Marketing	Dallas

Table 1-1. The Table **department**

emp_no	emp_fname	emp_lname	dept_no
25348	Matthew	Smith	d3
10102	Ann	Jones	d3
18316	John	Barrimore	d1
29346	James	James	d2
9031	Elke	Hansel	d2
2581	Elsa	Bertoni	d2
28559	Sybill	Moser	d1

Table 1-2. The Table **employee**

The table **works_on** specifies the relationship between employees and projects. It has the following columns:

works_on (emp_no, project_no , job, enter_date)

emp_no specifies the employee number and **project_no** the number of the project on which the employee works. The combination of data values belonging to these two columns is always unique. **job** and **enter_date** specify the task and the starting date of an employee in the corresponding project, respectively.

project_no	project_name	budget
p1	Apollo	120000
p2	Gemini	95000
p3	Mercury	185600

Table 1-3. The Table **project**

emp_no	project_no	Job	enter_date
10102	p1	Analyst	1997.10.1 00:00:00
10102	p3	Manager	1999.1.1 00:00:00
25348	p2	Clerk	1998.2.15 00:00:00
18316	p2	NULL	1998.6.1 00:00:00
29346	p2	NULL	1997.12.15 00:00:00
2581	p3	Analyst	1998.10.15 00:00:00
9031	p1	Manager	1998.4.15 00:00:00
28559	p1	NULL	1998.8.1. 00:00:00
28559	p2	Clerk	1999.2.1 00:00:00
9031	p3	Clerk	1997.11.15 00:00:00
29346	p1	Clerk	1998.1.4 00:00:00

Table 1-4. The Table **works_on**

Using the sample database, it is possible to describe some important properties of relational database systems:

- Rows in a table do not have any particular order.
- Columns in a table do not have any particular order.
- Every column must have a unique name within a table. On the other hand, columns from different tables may have the same name. (For example, the sample database has a column **dept_no** in the table **department** and a column with the same name in the table **employee**.)
- Every single data item in the table must be single valued. This means that in every row and column position of a table there is never a set of multiple data values.

- For every table, there is at least one identifier (i.e., a combination of columns with the property that no two rows have the same combination of data values for these columns). In the relational data model, such an identifier is called a *candidate key*. If there is more than one candidate key within a table, the database designer designates one of them as the *primary key* of the table. For example, the column **dept_no** is the primary key of the table **department**; the columns **emp_no** and **project_no** are the primary keys of the tables **employee** and **project**, respectively. Finally, the primary key for the table **works_on** is the combination of the columns (**emp_no, project_no**).
- In a table, there are never two identical rows. (This property is only theoretical; SQL Server and all other relational database systems generally allow the existence of identical rows within a table.)

SQL: A RELATIONAL DATABASE LANGUAGE

The SQL Server relational language is called Transact-SQL. It is a dialect of the most important database language today: SQL, an abbreviation for Structured Query Language. The origin of SQL is closely connected with the project called System R, which was designed and implemented by IBM in the early 1980s. This project showed that it is possible, using the theoretical foundations of E. F. Codd, to build a relational database system. SQL was built in the project's first phase, the goal of which was to implement a prototype with only limited functionality.

After the success of System R, a lot of new companies built their own relational database systems using SQL as the language of choice. All these implementations were expanded dialects of the language, as every company implemented its own extensions. For this reason, the American National Standards Institute (ANSI) and the International Standards Organization (ISO) founded a committee in 1982 with the goal of designing a standard version of SQL. The first standard of SQL, which was based primarily on the IBM dialect of this language, was released in 1986. After the release of an intermediate standard in 1989, a much more voluminous standard called SQL92 was developed and finally released in December 1992. In the last years, both standards organizations developed a new standard—SQL3—which encompasses several new database concepts, including triggers, stored procedures, and numerous object-oriented concepts. The main parts of the SQL3 standard were released in September 1999. (For this reason, the synonym for SQL3 is SQL99.)

In contrast to traditional languages like C, C++, and Java, SQL is a set-oriented language. (The former are called record-oriented or record-at-time languages.) This means that SQL can query many rows from one or more tables using just one statement. This feature is one of the most important advantages of SQL, allowing the use of this language at a logically higher level than procedural languages.

Another important property of SQL is its nonprocedurality. Every program written in a procedural language (C, C++, Java) describes *how* a task is accomplished, step by step. In contrast to this, SQL, as any other nonprocedural language, describes *what* it is that the user wants. Thus, the system is responsible for finding the appropriate way to solve users' requests.

SQL, like all database languages, contains two sublanguages: a data definition language (DDL) and a data manipulation language (DML). DDL statements are used to describe the schema of database tables. The DDL contains three generic SQL statements: CREATE object, ALTER object, and DROP object. These generate, alter, and remove database objects such as databases, tables, columns, and indexes. These statements are discussed in detail in Chapter 4. In contrast, the DML encompasses all operations that manipulate the data. There are always four generic operations for manipulating the database: retrieval, insertion, deletion, and modification. The retrieval statement SELECT is described in Chapters 5 and 6, while the INSERT, DELETE, and UPDATE statements are discussed in detail in Chapter 7.

Syntax Conventions

In this book, we will use the conventions shown in Table 1-5 for the syntax of the Transact-SQL statements and for the indication of the text.

Convention	Indication
Italics	New terms or items of emphasis.
UPPERCASE	Transact-SQL keywords, for example, CREATE TABLE. Additional information about Transact-SQL keywords can be found in Chapter 2.
lowercase	Variables in Transact-SQL statements—for example, CREATE TABLE tablename. (The user must replace "tablename" with the actual name of the table.)
var1 | var2	Alternative use of the items **var1**, **var2**. (You may choose only one of the items separated by vertical bar.)
{ }	Alternative use of more items. Example: { expression | USER | NULL }
[ ]	Optional item(s) are written in brackets. Example: [FOR LOAD]
{ } ...	Item(s) in braces can be repeated any number of times. Example: {, @param1 typ1} ...
bold	Name of database object (database itself, tables, columns) in the text.
<u>Default</u>	The default value is always underlined. Example: <u>ALL</u> | DISTINCT

Table 1-5. Syntax Conventions

NOTE: In contrast to brackets and braces, which belong to syntax conventions, parentheses (and) belong to the syntax of a statement and must *always* be typed!

DATABASE DESIGN

Designing a database is a very important phase in the database life cycle, which precedes all other phases except the requirements collection and the analysis. If the database design is created merely intuitively and without any plan, the resulting database will most likely not meet the user requirements concerning performance. Another consequence of a bad database design is superfluous data redundancy, which in itself has two disadvantages: the existence of data anomalies and the use of an unnecessary amount of disk space.

Normalization of data is a process during which the existing tables of a database are tested to find certain dependencies between the columns of a table. If such dependencies exist, the table is restructured into multiple (usually two) tables, which eliminates any column dependencies. If one of these generated tables still contains data dependencies, the process of normalization must be repeated until all dependencies are resolved.

The process of eliminating data redundancy in a table is based upon the theory of functional dependencies. A *functional dependency* means that by using the known value of one column, the corresponding value of another column can always be uniquely determined. (The same is true for column groups.) The functional dependencies between columns A and B is denoted by A → B, specifying that a value of column A can always be used to determine the corresponding value of column B. ("B is functionally dependent on A.")

The following example shows the functional dependency between two attributes of the table **employee** in the sample database.

▼ EXAMPLE 1.1

emp_no → emp_lname

By having a unique value for the employee number, the corresponding last name of employee (and all other corresponding attributes) can be determined. (This kind of functional dependency, where a column is dependent upon the key of a table, is called *trivial* functional dependency.)

Another kind of functional dependency is called *multivalued dependency*. In contrast to the functional dependency just described, the multivalued dependency is specified for multivalued attributes. This means that by using the known value of one attribute (column), the corresponding *set of values* of another multivalued attribute can be uniquely determined. The multivalued dependency is denoted by →→.

The next example shows the multivalued dependency that holds for two attributes of the object BOOK.

▼ EXAMPLE 1.2

ISBN →→ Authors

The ISBN of a book always determines all of its authors. Therefore, the attribute **Authors** is multivalued dependent on the attribute **isbn**.

Normal Forms

Normal forms are used for the process of normalization of data and therefore for the database design. In theory, there are at least five different normal forms, of which the first three are the most important for practical use. The third normal form for a table can be achieved by testing the first and second normal forms at the intermediate states, and as such, the goal of good database design can usually be fulfilled if all tables of a database are in the third normal form.

> ***NOTE:*** The multivalued dependency is used to test the fourth normal form of a table. Therefore, this kind of dependency will not be used further in this book.

First Normal Form

First normal form (1NF) means that a table has no multivalued attributes or composite attributes. (A composite attribute contains other attributes and can therefore be divided into smaller parts.) All relational tables are by definition in 1NF, because the value of any column in a row must be *atomic*—that is, single valued.

We will demonstrate the first normal form using part of the **works_on** table from the sample database (Table 1-6). The rows of the table **works_on** could be grouped together, using the employee number. The resulting Table 1-7 is not in 1NF because the column **project_no** contains a set of values (p1,p3).

emp_no	project_no	....
10102	p1	....
10102	p3	....
....	....	....

Table 1-6. Part of the Table **works_on**

emp_no	project_no	....
10102	(p1, p3)	....
....	....	....

Table 1-7. This "table" is not in 1NF

Second Normal Form

A table is in second normal form (2NF) if it is in 1NF and there is no nonkey column dependent on a partial key of that table. This means if (A,B) is a combination of two table columns building the key, then there is no column of the table depending either on only A or only B.

For example, let us take a look at Table 1-8, which is identical to the table **works_on**, except for the additional column **dept_no**. The primary key of this table is the combination of columns (**emp_no**, **project_no**). The column **dept_no** is dependent on the partial key **emp_no** (and is independent of **project_no)**, so this table is not in 2NF. (The original table **works_on** is in 2NF.)

> ***NOTE:*** Every table with a one-column primary key is always in 2NF.

emp_no	project_no	job	enter_date	dept_no
10102	p1	Analyst	1997.10.1 00:00:00	d3
10102	p3	Manager	1999.1.1 00:00:00	d3
25348	p2	Clerk	1998.2.15 00:00:00	d3
18316	p2	NULL	1998.6.1 00:00:00	d1
....	....	....		....

Table 1-8. **The Table works_onl**

Third Normal Form

A table is in third normal form (3NF) if it is in 2NF and there are no functional dependencies between nonkey columns. For example, Table 1-9, which is identical to the table **employee** except for the additional column **dept_name**, is not in 3NF, because for every known value of the column **dept_no** the corresponding value of the column **dept_name** can be uniquely determined. (The original table **employee**, and all other tables of the sample database, are in 3NF.)

Entity-Relationship (ER) Model

The data in a database could easily be designed using only one table that contains all data. The main disadvantage of such a database design is its high redundancy of data. For example, if your database contains data concerning employees and their projects (assuming each employee works at the same time for one or more projects, and each project engages one or more employees), the data stored in a single table contains a lot of columns and many rows. The main disadvantage of such a table is that data is difficult to keep consistent because of its redundancy.

The ER model is used to design relational databases by removing all existing redundancy in the data. The basic object of the ER model is an *entity*, that is, a real-world object. Each entity has several *attributes* that are properties of the entity and therefore describe it. Based on its type, an attribute can be

- Atomic (or single valued)
- Multivalued
- Composite

emp_no	emp_fname	emp_lname	dept_no	dept_name
25348	Matthew	Smith	d3	Marketing
10102	Ann	Jones	d3	Marketing
18316	John	Barrimore	d1	Research
29346	James	James	d2	Accounting
....	....	....	....	....

Table 1-9. The Table **employeel**

An attribute is called atomic if it is always represented by a single value for a particular entity. For example, a person's marital status is always an atomic attribute. Most attributes are atomic attributes. A multivalued attribute may have one or more values for a particular entity. For example, **Location** as the attribute of an entity called ENTERPRISE is multivalued, because each enterprise can have one or more locations. Composite attributes are not atomic because they are assembled using some other atomic attributes. A typical example of a composite attribute is a person's address, which is composed of atomic attributes, such as **City**, **Zip**, and **Street**. The entity PERSON in Example 1.3 has several atomic attributes, one composite attribute, **Address,** and a multivalued attribute, **College_degree**.

▼ EXAMPLE 1.3

PERSON (Personal_nr, F_name, L_name, Address(City,Zip,Street),{College_degree})

Each entity has one or more key attributes that are attributes (or a combination of two or more attributes) whose values are unique for each particular entity. In Example 1.3, the attribute **Personal_nr** is the key attribute of the entity PERSON.

Besides entity and attribute, *relationship* is another basic concept of the ER model. A relationship exists when an entity refers to one (or more) other entities. The number of participating entities defines the degree of a relationship. For example, the relationship **works_on** between entities EMPLOYEE and PROJECT has degree two.

Every existing relationship between two entities must be one of the following three types: 1:1, 1:N, and M:N. (This property of a relationship is also called cardinality ratio.) For example, the relationship between the entities DEPARTMENT and EMPLOYEE is 1:N because each employee belongs to exactly one department, which itself has one or more employees. A relationship can also have its own attributes (see Figure 1-1). Figure 1-1 shows an example of an ER diagram. (The ER diagram is the graphical notation used to describe the ER model.) Using this notation, entities are modeled using rectangular boxes, with the entity name written inside the box. Attributes are shown in ovals, and each attribute is attached to a particular entity (or relationship) using a straight line. Finally, relationships are modeled using diamonds, and entities participating in the relationship are attached to it using straight lines. The cardinality ratio of each entity is written on the corresponding line.

OVERVIEW OF MICROSOFT SQL SERVER

The most important benefits of Microsoft SQL Server are as follows:

- SQL Server works as a natural extension of Windows NT/2000 and Windows 9*x*.
- SQL Server is relatively easy to manage through the use of a graphical computing environment for almost every task of system and database administration.
- SQL Server uses services of Windows NT/2000 to offer new or extended database capabilities, such as sending and receiving messages and managing login security.

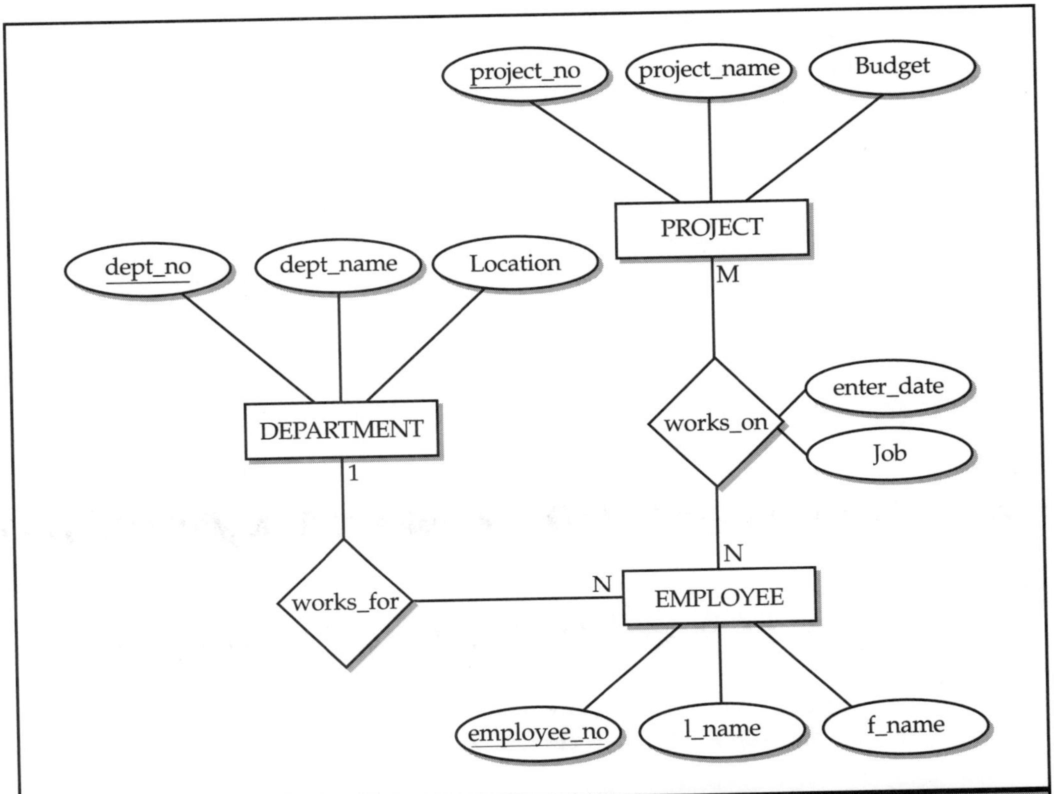

Figure 1-1. Example of an ER diagram

- SQL Server is easy to use.
- SQL Server scales from a mobile laptop to symmetric multiprocessor systems.
- SQL Server provides data warehousing features that up until now have only been available in Oracle and other more expensive DBMSs.

CONCLUSION

SQL Server is a relational database management system for distributed client/server computing. Like all other database management systems, it provides the following features:

- Variety of user interfaces
- Physical data independence
- Logical data independence
- Query optimization

- Data integrity
- Concurrency control
- Backup and recovery
- Security and authorization

The next chapter introduces the two most important SQL Server tools: SQL Server Enterprise Manager and SQL Server Query Analyzer. SQL Server Enterprise Manager is a system administration tool for managing almost every task concerning database systems. On the other hand, SQL Server Query Analyzer is an end-user tool for executing and analyzing ad hoc queries. Chapter 1 and Chapter 2 form the introductory part of this book.

EXERCISES

▼ E.1.1

What does "data independence" mean and which two forms of data independence exist?

▼ E.1.2

Which is the main concept of the relational model?

▼ E.1.3

What does the table **employee** represent in the real world? And what does the row in this table with the data for Ann Jones represent?

▼ E.1.4

What does the table **works_on** represent in the real world (and in relation to the other tables of the sample database)?

▼ E.1.5

Let **book** be a table with two columns: **isbn** and **title**. Assuming that **isbn** is unique and there are no identical titles, answer the following questions:

A. Is **title** a key of the table?

B. Does **isbn** functionally depend on **title**?

C. Is the table **book** in 3NF?

▼ E.1.6

Let **order** be a table with the following columns: **order_no, customer_no, discount**. If the column **customer_no** is functionally dependent on **order_no** and the column **Discount** is functionally dependent on **customer_no**, answer the following questions and explain in detail your answers:

A. Is **order_no** a key of the table?

B. Is **customer_no** a key of the table?

▼ E.1.7

Let **company** be a table with the following columns: **company_no, location**. Each company has one or more locations. In which normal form is the table **company**?

▼ E.1.8

Let **supplier** be a table with the following columns: **supplier_no, article, city**. The key of the table is the combination of the first two columns. Each supplier delivers several articles and each article is delivered by several suppliers. There is only one supplier in each city. Answer the following questions:

A. In which normal form is the table **supplier**?

B. How can you resolve the existing functional dependencies?

▼ E.1.9

Let R(<u>A</u>, <u>B</u>, C) be a relation with the functional dependency: B -> C. (The attributes A and B build the composite key and the attribute C is functionally dependent on B.) In which normal form is the relation R?

▼ E.1.10

Let R(<u>A</u>, <u>B</u>, C) be a relation with the functional dependency: C -> B. (The attributes A and B build the composite key and the attribute B is functionally dependent on C.) In which normal form is the relation R?

CHAPTER 2

SQL Server Enterprise Manager and Query Analyzer

SQL Server provides a number of tools that serve different purposes, such as installation, database query, and replication. All these tools have user-friendly graphical interfaces. This chapter examines first the **Start** menu and discusses briefly Books Online, the online reference source with all necessary information concerning SQL Server. After that, two of the most important SQL Server front-end components are introduced: SQL Server Enterprise Manager and SQL Server Query Analyzer. By the end of this chapter you should be able to create and manage database objects using SQL Server Enterprise Manager. You will also learn all the Query Analyzer functions necessary for creating and executing any other Transact-SQL statements.

NOTE: This chapter is dedicated to the activities of the end user. Therefore, only the functionality of Enterprise Manager with respect to the creation of database objects is described in detail. All administrative tasks will be discussed later, beginning in Chapter 16.

THE SQL SERVER PROGRAM GROUP AND BOOKS ONLINE

To see the SQL Server program group (see Figure 2-1) you have to click **Start** | **Programs** and, finally, **Microsoft SQL Server**. The SQL Server program group comprises all applications you will use during your work with SQL Server. In this chapter we will look only at particular applications, starting with Books Online (BOL).

Books Online

Books Online is the online documentation that is delivered with the SQL Server software. All components of Book Online can be installed either on the disk (in the Books directory, by default) or installed and run from CD. In the latter case, the installation process creates a **Start** menu shortcut to run the online documentation from the SQL Server disc.

NOTE: To run Books Online from the SQL Server disc requires about 2MB of disk space, while installing it on a hard disk requires about 15MB. Installing Books Online on the hard disk gives you faster performance.

The **Books Online** dialog box contains in the left part of the detail pane four different tabs:

- Contents
- Index
- Search
- Favorites

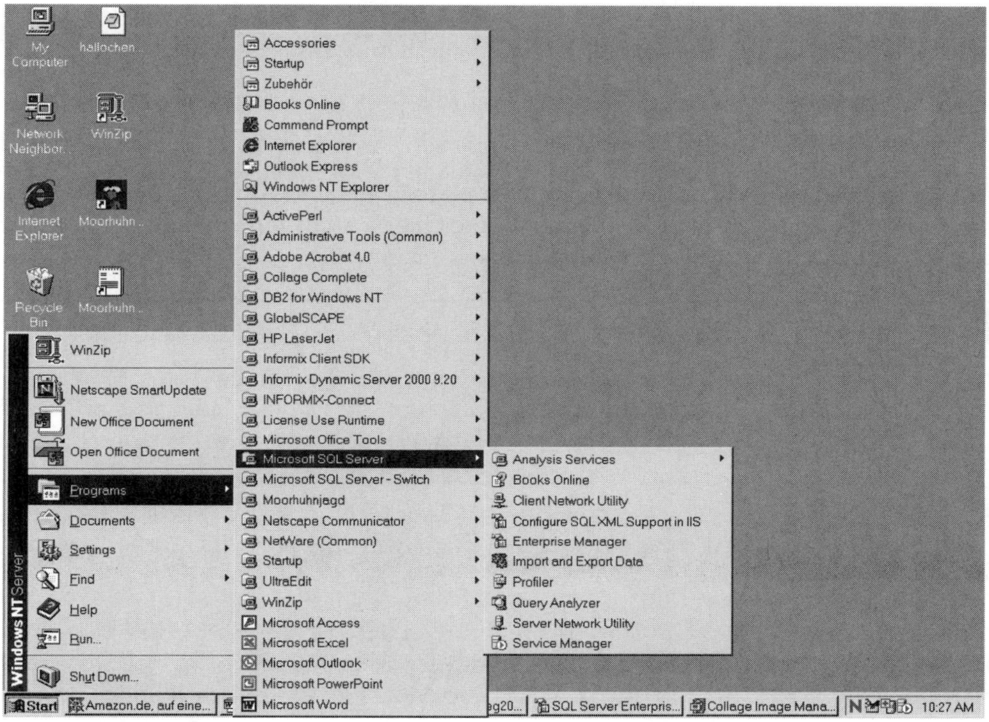

Figure 2-1. SQL Server program group

If you click the **Contents** tab, you will see the content of the whole online documentation divided into different books. Each specific topic (such as Installing SQL Server, for instance) is divided into subtopics, which can be opened by clicking the corresponding plus (+) symbol. You can view the content of each subfolder in the same way—that is, by clicking the + symbols of the corresponding book and all superfolders of that folder.

The **Index** tab is an alphabetically sorted sequence of each keyword that appears in the online documentation. There are two ways to select one of the keywords: by double-clicking the keyword in the list or by typing the starting letters of it. In the latter case, the system selects (and highlights) the alphabetically first keyword in the list that has the typed letters at its beginning.

The next tab, **Search**, is the most used tab of all. It allows you to type a phrase (or a single word) that is then used in the search process to display all topics, where they appear. (SQL Server uses its own Full Text Search component to support this process.) The results of the search process are displayed in the left part of the default pane. After double-clicking one of the entries, the corresponding content appears in the left part of the pane. In the lower part of the dialog box, you can select one or more of the options that influence the search process. For instance, if you check the **Search only title** check box, the search will be reduced only to the existing titles in the online documentation. This is recommended if you expect that there will be too many results in your search.

The **Favorites** tab allows you to store selected keywords (and phrases). To select again one of stored topics, double-click the entry in the list of your favorites.

INTRODUCTION TO SQL SERVER ENTERPRISE MANAGER

The SQL Server administrator's primary tool for interacting with the system is Enterprise Manager. Both administrators and end users can use Enterprise Manager to administer multiple servers, develop databases, and replicate data, among other things.

NOTE: Enterprise Manager is integrated with the Microsoft Management Console (MMC), which is becoming the standard user interface for all Windows administration tools. The user interface of MMC is similar to Windows Explorer.

To open this tool, click the **Start** menu and then **SQL Server Enterprise Manager** in the SQL Server program group. Every user with access to SQL Server can also use Enterprise Manager. Figure 2-2 shows a server group contained in a folder, which allows the logical organization of different servers. To open a folder, click the server's plus (+) symbol (or double-click the folder, or press the RIGHT-ARROW key while the folder is selected). After the click, Enterprise Manager shows all objects at the next lower logical level. The direct subobjects of the server **NTB11901**, and therefore of every server, are (among others) the group of front-end components such as SQL Server Agent, and the groups for databases and security.

NOTE: You will find that there will often be several ways of accomplishing the same task within Enterprise Manager. This chapter will indicate more than one way to do things; later, only a single method will be given. Different people prefer different methods (some like to double-click, some like to click the +/- signs, some like to right-click, others like to use the pull-down menus, others like to use the keyboard as much as possible). Experiment with the different ways to navigate Enterprise Manager, and use the methods that feel most natural to you.

A subobject appears only if you click the plus sign of its direct predecessor. A right-click on an object displays the properties of that object. The minus (-) sign indicates that an object is currently expanded (for example, server). To compress all subobjects of an object, click its minus sign (or double-click the folder, or press the LEFT-ARROW key while the folder is selected).

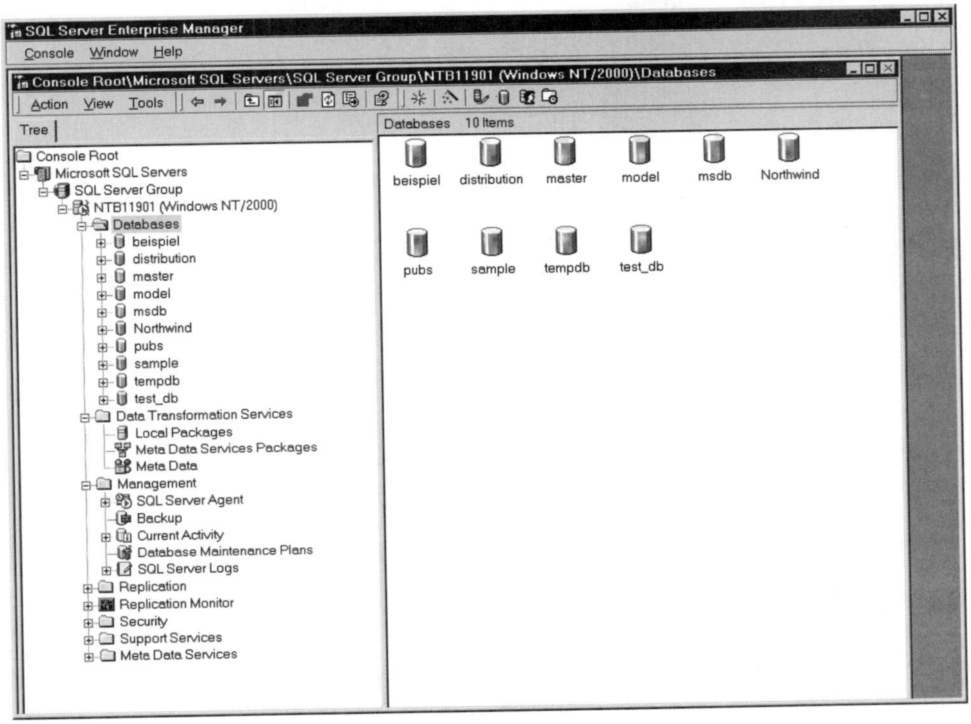

Figure 2-2. SQL Server Enterprise Manager

Using Enterprise Manager

Enterprise Manager has two main purposes:

- Administration of the database server
- Management of database objects

The administration tasks, which can be started using SQL Server Enterprise Manager, are as follows, among others:

- Management of several servers on one computer
- Registration of servers
- Starting and stopping SQL Server
- Addition of new server groups

- Database management
- Login security management
- Job management
- Display of server properties

The following tasks concerning database objects can be performed:

- Creation and modification of database objects without using the Transact-SQL language
- Management of database objects and their usage
- Generation and execution of SQL statements

Enterprise Manager allows you to administer multiple database engines (called instances) on one computer. (This is a new feature in SQL Server 2000.) Each instance of SQL Server has its own set of database objects (system and user databases) that are not shared between different instances. The installation and management of SQL Server instances will be discussed in detail in Chapter 16.

Every server (local or remote) must be registered before use. A server can be registered during the first execution of Enterprise Manager or later. To register a server later, you can do any of the following: select either the **Microsoft SQL Servers** folder, or a server group folder, or a server, and then click the **Action** button in the toolbar and select **Register SQL Server** from the pull-down menu; or click the **New** button from the toolbar while a server is selected; or click the **Register Server** button from the toolbar. You'll find that the choices under the **Action** menu and the object added by the **New** button change depending on what object is selected. Additionally, you can right-click an object to get the same choices in a pop-up menu as you would get by clicking the **Action** button on the toolbar while that object is selected.

SQL Server can be started and stopped automatically each time Windows NT/2000 starts and stops or by using SQL Server Enterprise Manager. Right-click the selected server and click **Start** in the pull-down menu. The pull-down menu also contains the corresponding **Stop** function that stops the activated server. The additional **Pause** function pauses the whole system, which means that new users are not allowed to log into the system.

To create a new server group using Enterprise Manager, right-click the **SQL Server Group** (or click the Action button on the toolbar when one of these is selected), click **New SQL Server Group**, and select the group level (top-level group or subgroup under an existing group). Yet another way to add a new server group is to click the **New** button on the toolbar while a server group or the **Microsoft SQL Servers** folder is selected.

SQL Server supports the creation of a new database using Enterprise Manager or Transact-SQL. (The next section discusses database creation and modification using Enterprise Manager. Database creation using the Transact-SQL language will be discussed in Chapter 4.)

Managing login properties is similar to managing databases, and it can be done using either Enterprise Manager or Transact-SQL. To create a new login using Enterprise Manager, click the **New Login** button in the toolbar (or right-click the **Logins** subfolder in the **Security** folder of the corresponding instance and choose **New Login**) and fill in the SQL Server **Login Properties** sheet.

Repetitive processes, such as database backup, can be managed using jobs. *Jobs* are a SQL Server feature that allows the scheduling of different database and server procedures. Enterprise Manager supports the creation of jobs. You can click the **New Job** button in the toolbar and specify the properties (name and category, for example) of the new job.

To view the server properties, right-click the server and click **Properties**. Then select the tab containing the property you are interested in. Figure 2-3 shows the general properties of the server **NTB11901**.

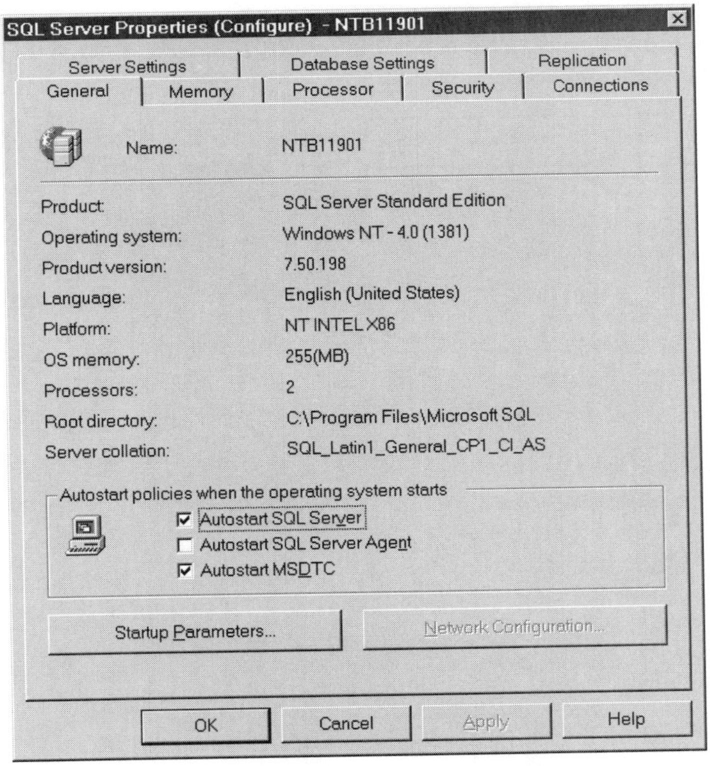

Figure 2-3. General properties of the server NTB11901

Managing Databases and Database Objects

One of the first tasks you perform when using SQL Server is the creation of a new database. SQL Server provides three different ways to create a new database:

- Use the Create Database Wizard
- Use SQL Server Enterprise Manager
- Use the Transact-SQL language

The Create Database Wizard guides you through the process of creating a database. To use the wizard, click the **Run a Wizard** button in the Enterprise Manager toolbar (or choose **Wizards** from the Help menu), select **Database** folder, and double-click the corresponding wizard.

To create a database using Enterprise Manager, click the **New Database** button in the toolbar (note that the Create Database Wizard as well as the **New Database** button only appear if you have selected a server or one of its child entities). Alternatively, you can right-click the **Databases** folder (which appears under the server level) and select **New Database**. Use the **Database Properties** dialog box (Figure 2-4) to display or set all the properties of the new database.

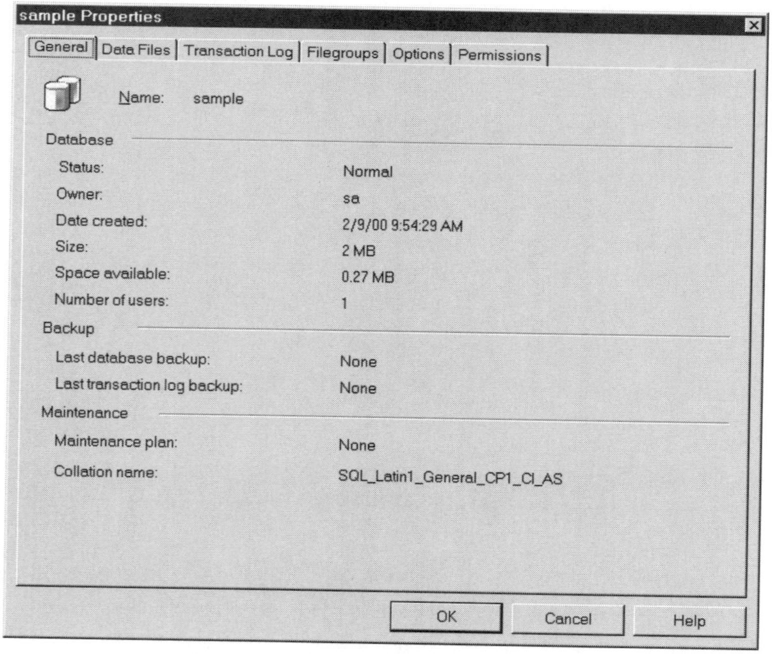

Figure 2-4. Database Properties dialog box

Database properties (for an existing database) can be divided into six groups:

- General properties
- Data file properties
- Properties of the transaction log
- File group properties
- Database options
- Permissions

Each property group has a corresponding tab in the **Database Properties** dialog box.

General properties of the database (Figure 2-4) include, among others, the database name, the owner of the database, its size, and the space available. The properties in the **Data Files** tab (see Figure 2-5) comprise the name and initial size of the file, where the database will be stored, and the type of the file (PRIMARY, for instance). A database can be stored in multiple files.

NOTE: Since Version 7, SQL Server has dynamic disk space management. This means databases can be set up to automatically expand and shrink as needed. The **Automatically grow file** (see Figure 2-5) check box should be checked to allow the database to autogrow. Each time there is insufficient space within the file when data is added to the database, the server will request the additional space from the operating system. The amount (in megabytes) of the additional space is set by the number in the **File growth** frame of the same dialog box. Similarly, freed space is given back to the operating system if the corresponding configuration parameter is activated.

Properties of the transaction log of the database include the name and the initial size of the log file. Similar to the database file, the log file can be set up to autogrow and autoshrink. (Transactions and log files will be discussed in detail in Chapter 20.)

The **Filegroups** tab contains name(s) of the file group(s) to which the database file belongs, the art of the file group (default or nondefault), and the allowed operation on the file group (read/write or read only).

All database-level options can be displayed and modified by clicking the **Options** tab in the **Database Properties** dialog box (Figure 2-6). Three options concern access to a database:

- **Restrict access (Members of db_owner, dbcreattor or sysadmin)** Restricts the use of the database to database owners (DBOs) and system administrators. This option will usually be used for maintenance of the database.
- **Restrict access (single user)** Restricts the use of the database to one user at a time.
- **Read-only** Allows only read access to the database. This prohibits users from modifying any data.

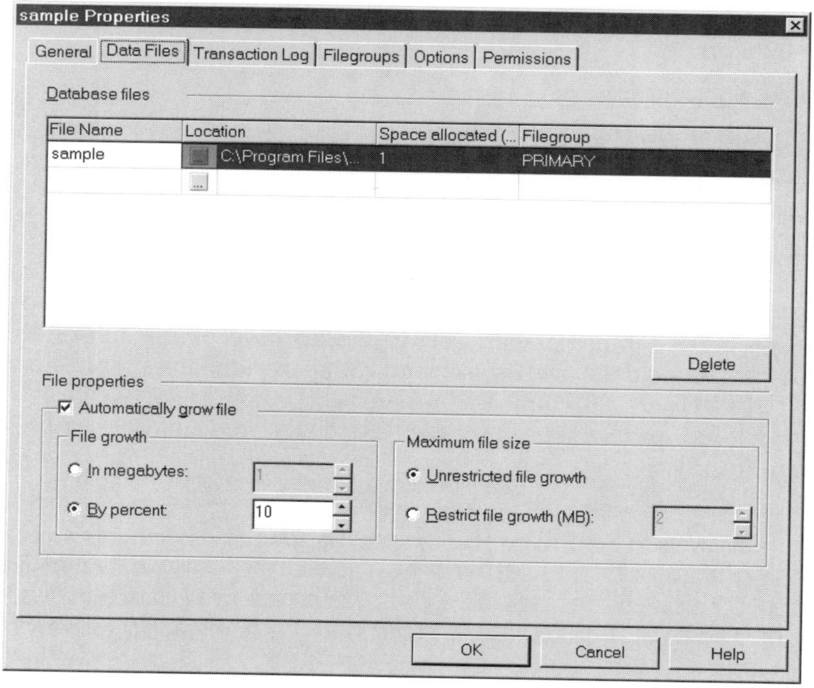

Figure 2-5. The Data Files Properties dialog box

NOTE: The **Restrict access (Members of db_owner, dbcreattor or sysadmin)** option allows the use of the database by more than one DBO (or system administrator) at a time, while the **Single user** option restricts the use to any single user.

If you click the **Permissions** tab, SQL Server will display the corresponding dialog box with all users and roles along with their permissions concerning statement permissions. (For the discussion of permissions, see Chapter 12.)

Enterprise Manager and the Transact-SQL language can also be used to modify an existing database. To modify a database using Enterprise Manager, right-click the database name and select **Properties**. The properties that can be modified are, for example, the names of the database and log files, the file growth, and its maximum size. (A list of all properties that can be modified is given with the definition of the CREATE DATABASE statement in Chapter 4.) Additionally, it is possible to activate or deactivate all database options and to add or modify statement permission options.

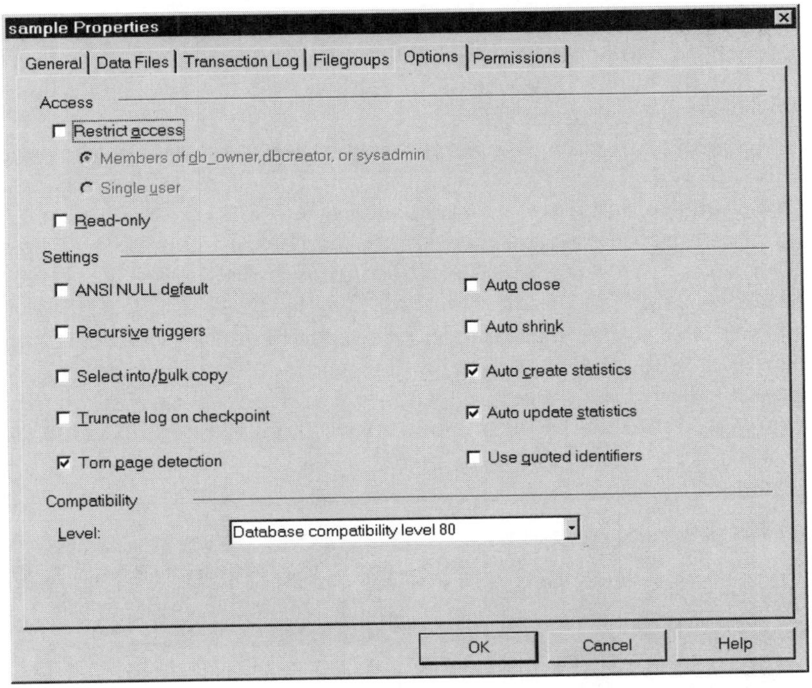

Figure 2-6. The Options tab with database options

NOTE: Only the system administrator or the database owner can modify the database properties mentioned above.

To delete a database using the Enterprise Manager, right-click the database name and choose **Delete**.

Managing Tables Using Enterprise Manager

The next task after the creation of a database is the creation of all tables belonging to it. Again, you can create tables by using either Enterprise Manager or Transact-SQL.

To create a table using Enterprise Manager, right-click the database name, click **New**, and then click **Table**. The other possibility is to click the database folder, right-click **Tables**, and select **New Table**. (You might try to see how many other ways you can find to do this.) The creation of a table and all other database objects using the Transact-SQL language will be discussed in detail in Chapter 4.

To demonstrate the creation of a table using Enterprise Manager, the **department** table of the sample database will be used as an example. Enter the names of all columns with their properties in the **New Table** dialog box. Column names, their data types, and lengths, as well as the NULL property of the column, must be entered in the two-dimensional matrix, as shown in Figure 2-7.

All data types supported by SQL Server can be displayed (and one of them selected) by clicking the arrow sign in the **Data Type** column (the arrow appears after the cell has been selected). Subsequently, you can type entries in the **Length**, **Precision,** and **Scale** columns for the chosen data type (See Figure 2-7, below). Some data types, such as CHARACTER, require a value for the **Length** column, and some, such as FLOAT, require a value in the **Precision** and **Scale** columns. On the other hand, data types such as INTEGER do not need any of these entries to be specified. (The valid entries for a specified data type are highlighted in the list of all possible column properties.)

The **Allow Nulls** column must be checked if you want a table column to permit null values to be inserted into that column. Similarly, if there is a default value, it should be

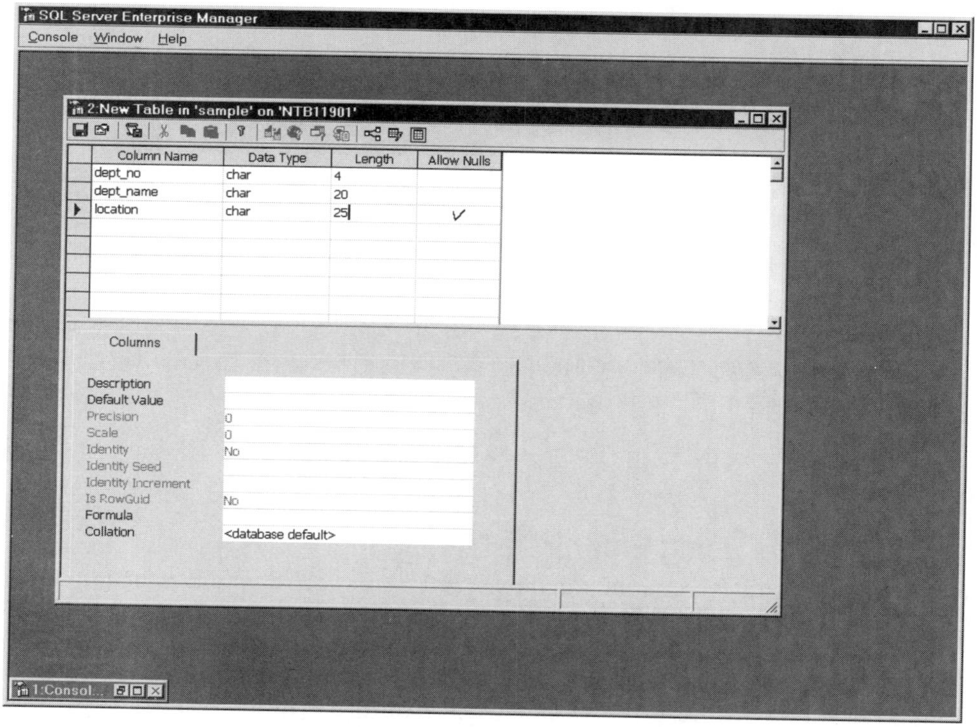

Figure 2-7. Creating the table **department** using the Enterprise Manager

entered in the **Default Value** column. (A default value is a value that will be inserted in a table column when there is no explicit value entered for it.)

The column **dept_no** is the primary key of the **department** table. (For the discussion of primary keys of the sample database, see Chapter 1.) To specify a column as the primary key of the table, you must first mark the column and then choose **Select Primary Key** in the toolbar of the **Create Table** dialog box. Finally, enter the name of the new table in the **Choose Name** dialog box.

To view the properties of an existing table, first double-click the folder of the database to which the table belongs. Subsequently, double-click **Tables**, and then double-click the name of the table. Figure 2-8 shows the **Table Properties** dialog box for the **department** table.

One way to remove a table is to double-click the **Tables** folder in the database to which the table belongs. The table can then be deleted in the usual way, by selecting the table name and using the DELETE key (or the standard **Delete** button from the toolbar).

If you create all four tables of the sample database (**employee**, **department**, **project**, and **works_on**) you can use another existing feature of Enterprise Manager to display the corre-

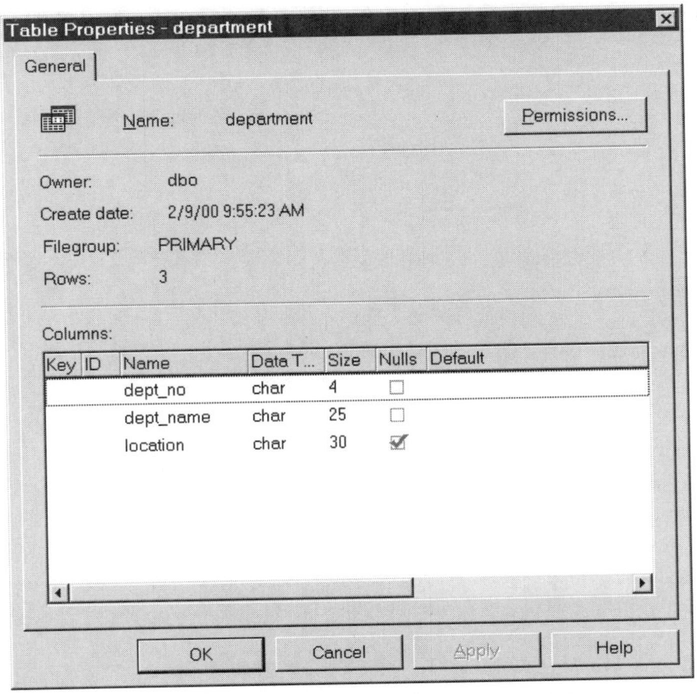

Figure 2-8. Table Properties dialog box for the **department** table

sponding E/R diagram of the sample database. (The process of converting the existing tables of a database into the corresponding E/R diagram is called reverse engineering.)

To see the E/R model of the sample database, right-click the **Diagrams** subfolder of the sample database folder and select **New Database Diagram**. The Create Database Diagram Wizard helps you to create the E/R model for specified tables or add new tables to an existing diagram. The first (and only) step is to select tables that will be added to the digram. After adding all four tables of the sample database, the wizard completes the work and creates the diagram (see Figure 2-9).

The diagram in Figure 2-9 is not the real E/R diagram of the sample database, because it shows all four tables with their columns (and the corresponding primary keys) but does not show any relationship between the tables. A relationship between two tables is based on the primary key of one table and the (possible) corresponding column(s) of the other. (For a detailed discussion of these relationships and referential integrity, see Chapter 4.)

There are exactly three relationships between the existing tables of the sample database. First, the tables **department** and **employee** have a 1:N relationship, because for each value in the primary key column of the **department** table (**dept_no**) there is one or more

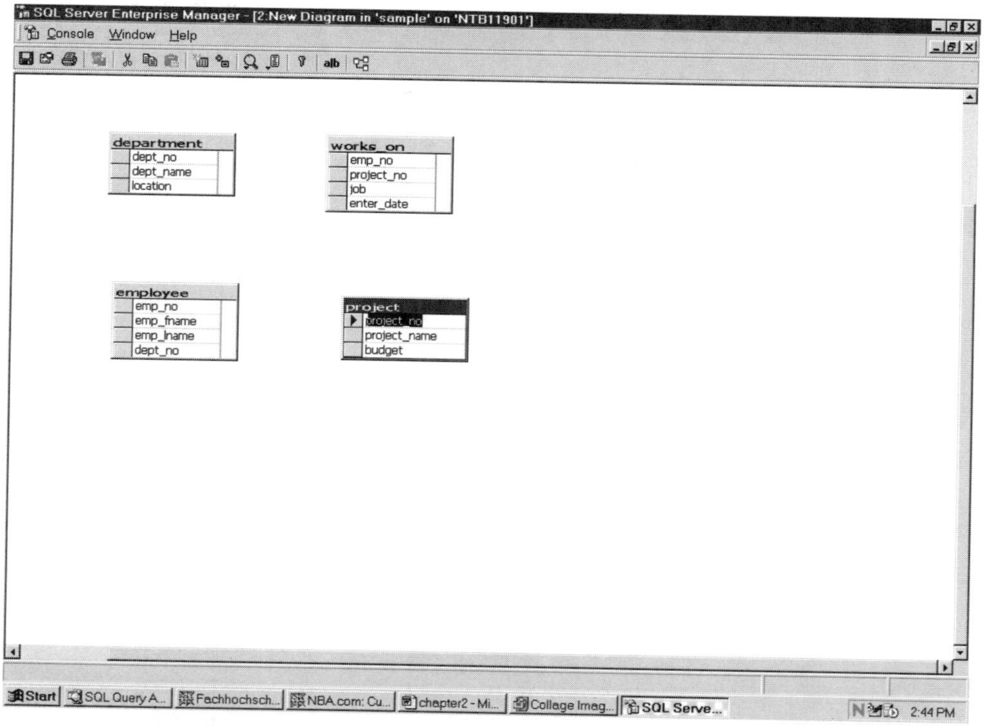

Figure 2-9. First diagram of the sample database

corresponding values in the column **dept_no** of the **employee** table. Analogously, there is a relationship between the tables **employee** and **works_on**, because only those values that exist in the primary key of the **employee** table (**emp_no**) appear also in the column **emp_no** of the **works_on** table. (The third relationship is between the tables **project** and **works_on**.)

To create each of relationships described above, you have to redesign the table with the column that corresponds to the primary key column of the other table. (Such a column is called a foreign key.) To show this, you can use the **employee** table and define its column **dept_no** as the foreign key of the **department** table.

Click **Tables** in the sample database folder, right-click the **employee** table in the detail pane, and select **Design Table**. In the toolbar of the **Design Table** dialog box, click **Table and Index Properties** and select the **Relationships** tab in the **Properties** dialog box. Figure 2-10 appears.

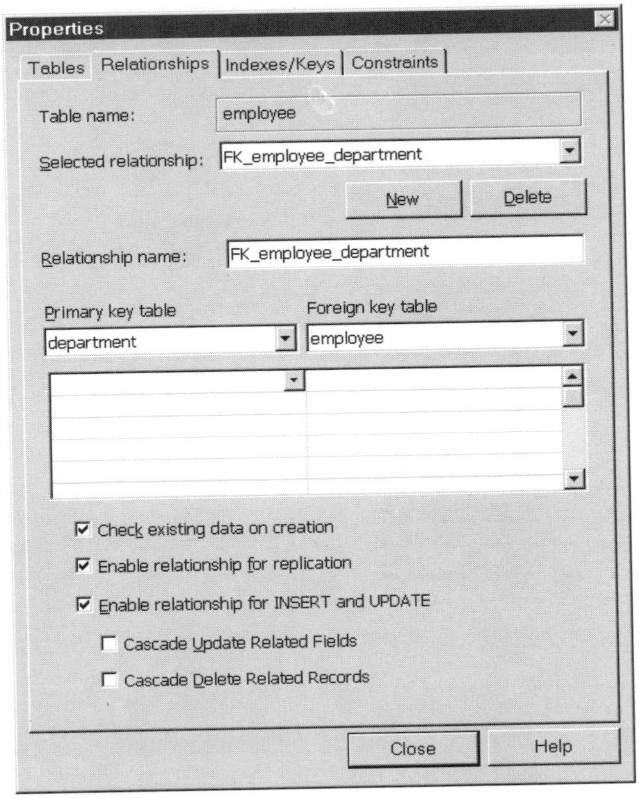

Figure 2-10. The Properties dialog box after selection of the Relationships tab

In the **Primary key table** field, choose the **department** table and select **dept_no** in the list of all columns of this table. Analogously, choose **employee** in the **Foreign key table** field (on the right side) and its column **dept_no** as the column with the corresponding foreign key. Close the dialog box and save the modified **employee** table.

Figure 2-11 shows the E/R diagram after all three relationships described above between tables in the sample database have been created and the tables **employee** and **works_on** have been modified.

NOTE: If you take a closer look at the diagram in Figure 2-11 of this chapter, you will see a lot of differences in E/R notation in both of them. The reason for these differences is that the E/R notation is not standardized at all. Therefore, there exist several different ways to design the main concepts (entities, attributes, and relationships) in this model.

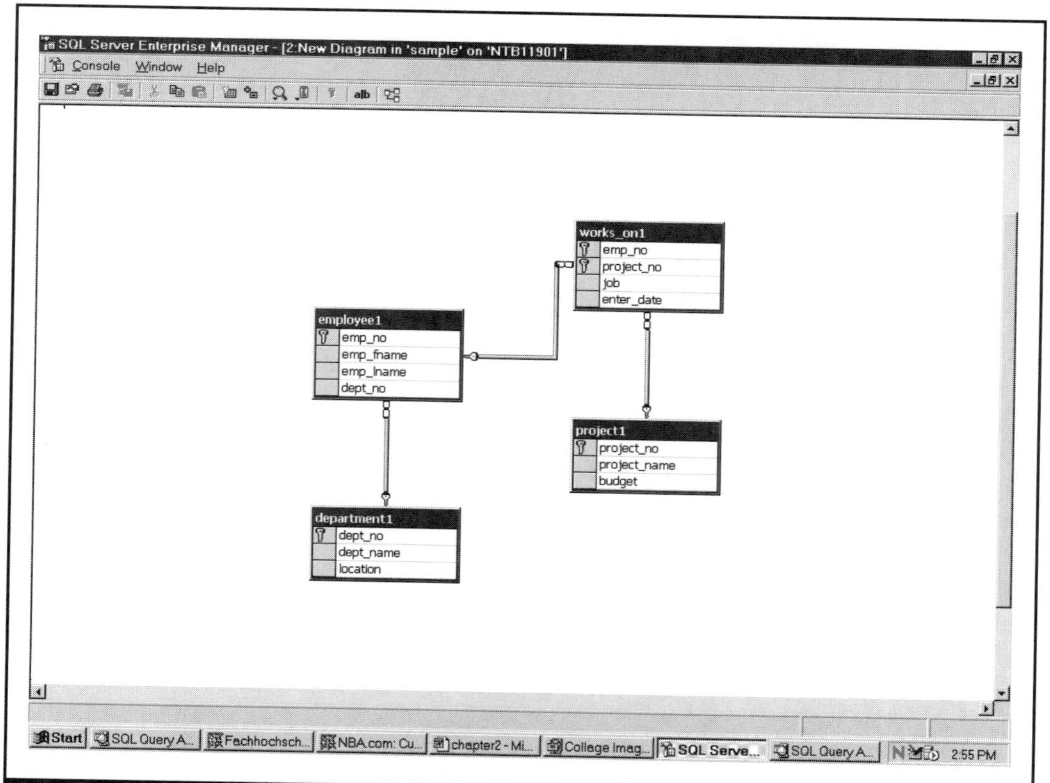

Figure 2-11. The modified E/R diagram of the sample database with all existing relationships between tables

INTRODUCTION TO SQL SERVER QUERY ANALYZER

SQL Server Query Analyzer is the most important user interface for running Transact-SQL statements and stored procedures. There are a lot of new features that were implemented for SQL Server 2000. These are, among others: two new tools (Object Browser and Object Search), and a toolbar that can be configured by user. This interactive component of SQL Server can be used by end users for the following tasks:

- Generating and executing Transact-SQL statements
- Storing the generated Transact-SQL statements in a file
- Analyzing execution plans for generated queries
- Graphically illustrating the execution plan for a selected query

Connection to SQL Server

You open this SQL Server front-end component via **Start | Programs | Microsoft SQL Server | Query Analyzer**, or via the **Tools** menu of Enterprise Manager. Before opening the SQL Server component, you have to identify yourself and the server instance you want to use in the **Connect to SQL Server** dialog box (see Figure 2-12).

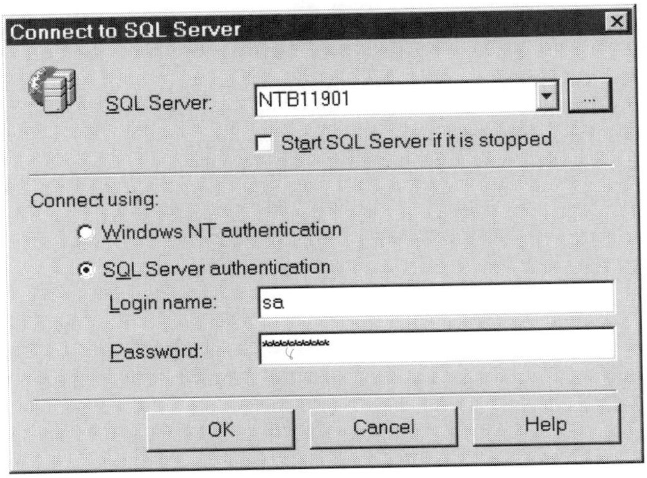

Figure 2-12. Connect to SQL Server dialog box

NOTE: **The Connect to SQL Server** dialog box can be also accessed from the toolbar and using the **Connect** option in the **File** menu.

First, in the SQL Server box, enter the name of the database server to which you want to connect. To select the default server, choose (or type) **local**. If you want to specify another server (or another instance of an active server), click **...** on the right side of the box to display a list of all active servers with their instances. (Each entry appears in the form **server_name\instance_name**.)

The next connection information concerns the authorization issue. If you select **Windows authorization**, you will be connected to SQL Server using your Windows account. If you select the other option (**SQL Server authentication**), SQL Server uses its own authentication. For this reason, the former option is much simpler, while the latter enhances SQL server security with an additional security level. (For more information concerning SQL Server security, see Chapter 12.)

After typing the valid login name and the corresponding password, the **Query Analyzer** window appears (see Figure 2-13). There are several possible reasons if you view an error window instead of the Query Analyzer component. The error window that you will see most often is the **Login Failed** window that is shown in Figure 2-14. The reason for this error is usually a mistyped password. (Another reason could be that your login name does not exist or is mistyped.)

Query Analyzer Editor

Query Analyzer contains an internal text editor and a selection of buttons in its toolbar. The main window is divided into a query pane (upper) and a results pane (lower) (see Figure 2-13). Users enter the Transact-SQL statements (queries) that they want to be executed into the query pane, and after the queries have been processed by SQL Server the output is displayed in the results pane.

Using an example you will see how queries are entered and processed by SQL Server. If you type the two Transact-SQL statements shown in Figure 2-15 and press either the **Execute Query** button in the toolbar or the F5 key, the results of these statements are shown in the results pane of Query Analyzer. (Note that Figure 2-15 shows two different windows—that is, two different connections to SQL Server. You create new connections by clicking the **New Query** button in the toolbar.)

NOTE: The first statement in Figure 2-15, USE, specifies the **Northwind** database as the current database. The second statement, SELECT, displays all the rows of the **orders** table, which belongs to the **Northwind** database.

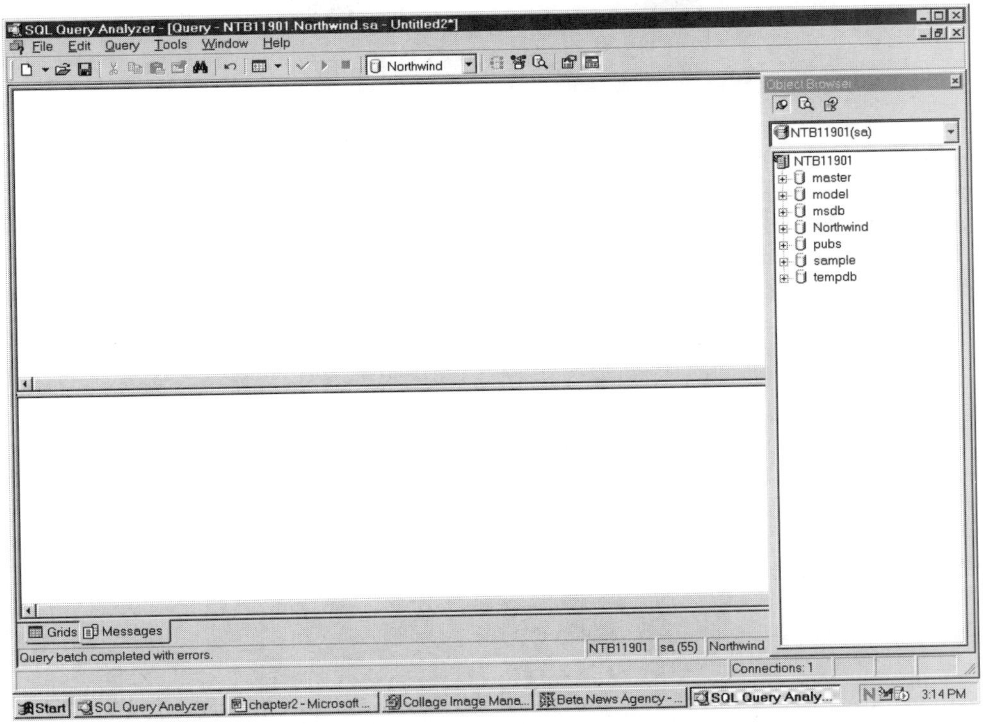

Figure 2-13. SQL Server Query Analyzer

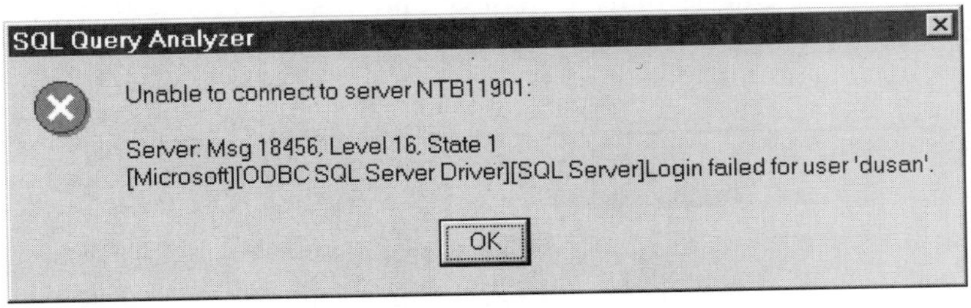

Figure 2-14. The Login Failed window

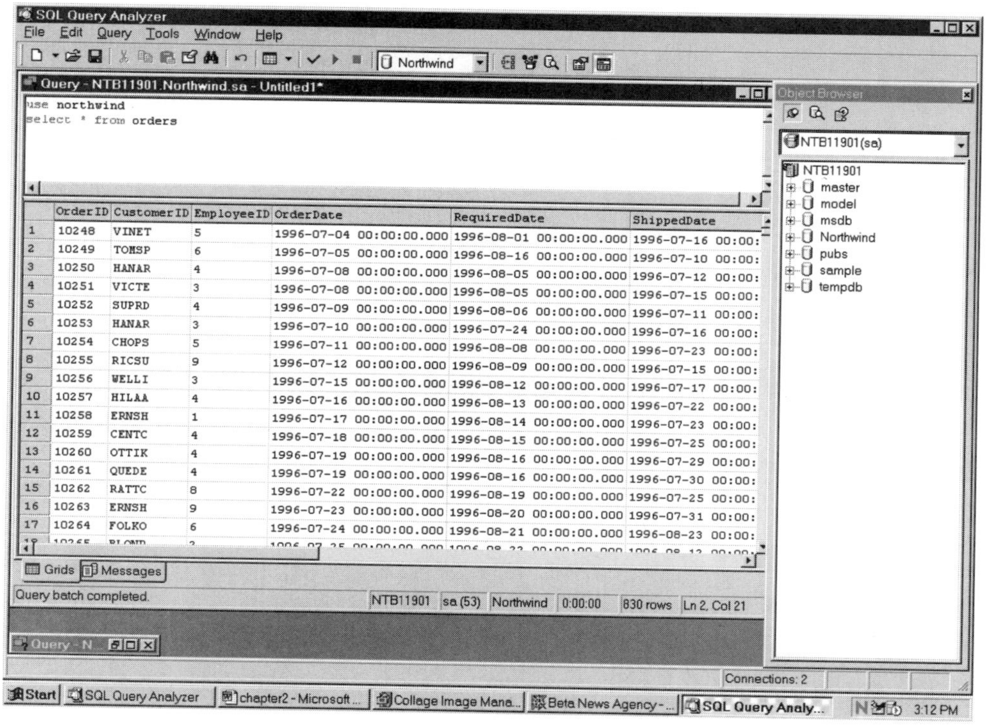

Figure 2-15. Query Analyzer with a query and its results

The buttons in the Query Analyzer toolbar and their functionality are described in Table 2-1.

Button	Functionality
New Query	Opens a new Query window—that is, a new connection to SQL Server for writing one or more Transact-SQL statements.
Load SQL Script	Opens a file that contains the Transact-SQL statements.

Table 2-1. Buttons on the SQL Server Query Analyzer Toolbar

Button	Functionality
Save Query/Result	Allows the saving of either Transact-SQL statements or the output from them. Transact-SQL statements are saved by default with the suffix .sql, while the corresponding output usually has the suffix .rtp.
Clear Query Window	Clears the content of the editor of the current Query Analyzer window.
Execute Mode	This button gives you a way to select how the results of your query will be displayed (see also Table 2-2).
Execute Query	Executes the Transact-SQL statements, which appear in the query pane, and displays the result in the results pane.
Parse Query	Parses the Transact-SQL statements, which appear in the query pane—that is, checks their syntax—without executing them.
Cancel Query Execution	Cancels the current query. (The red light in the square indicates that there is currently a query executing that could be canceled.)
Display Estimated Execution Plan	Displays the graphic of the execution plan of the query.
Object Browser	Displays Object Browser in Query Analyzer. (Object Browser is explained later in this section.)
Connect	Displays the **Connect to SQL Server** dialog box (see Figure 2-12).
Show Results Pane	By clicking this button, Query Analyzer shows you either both the query and results panes or the query pane alone.
Object Search	Displays the **Object Search** dialog box.
Current Connection Properties	Shows the valid connection properties for the current Transact-SQL statement.

Table 2-1. Buttons on the SQL Server Query Analyzer Toolbar *(continued)*

Clicking the **Execute Mode** button, the menu with six options appears. The first three options are related to the display of query results, while the last three allow you the enhanced analysis of statements in the Query Analyzer editor. Table 2-2 describes all these options with their functionality.

Option	Functionality
Results in Text	The result of a query is displayed as a text in the results pane.
Results in Grid	The result of a query is displayed in a grid in the results pane.
Results to File	The result of a query is saved in a file.
Show Execution Plan	Displays the graphic of the execution plan of a query.
Show Server Trace	Displays information concerning the trace of a query (database ID, start time, and CPU usage).
Show Client Statistics	Displays information concerning client side statistics for execution of a query. (For more information about statistics, see Chapter 9.)

Table 2-2. Options of the Executive Mode menu

SQL Server 2000 enhances also the information that is displayed in the status bar of the **Query Analyzer** windows. The following information is displayed:

- The status of the current operation (in the left corner of the window)
- Database server name
- Current user name and server process ID
- Current database name
- Elapsed time for the execution of the last query
- The number of retrieved rows
- The current position of the cursor in the **Query Analyzer** window

SQL Server 2000 allows you to customize the Query Analyzer toolbar according to your needs. To configure the toolbar, right-click anyplace on it. In the **Customize Toolbar** dialog box (Figure 2-16), add or remove the buttons to be displayed on the toolbar. You can also rearrange the order of the buttons in the toolbar using the **Move Up** and **Move Down** buttons. If you want to restore the toolbar to the default form, click **Reset**.

Query Pane

One of main properties of SQL Server is ease of use. This general idea is also applied to the Query Analyzer component. Query Analyzer supports a lot of features that make coding of Transact-SQL statements easier. First, SQL Server uses a color-coded editor to

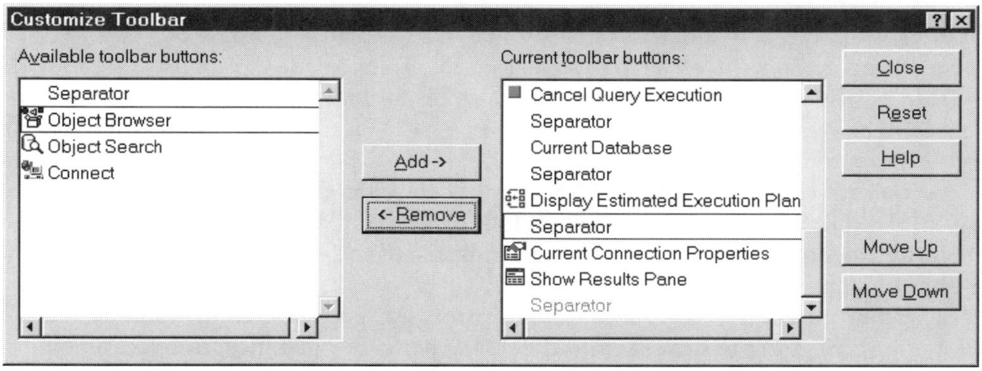

Figure 2-16. The Customize Toolbar dialog box

improve the readability of Transact-SQL statements. It displays all reserved words in blue, all variables in black, and strings in red. (For a discussion of reserved words, see the next chapter.)

There is also context-sensitive **Help** that allows you to get help on a particular statement. If you do not know the syntax of a statement, just highlight that statement in the editor and select the **Transact-SQL Help** option on the **Help** menu. (The alternative way is to use SHIFT-F1.)

SQL Server 2000 added some new enhancements concerning coding. You can find all of them by clicking the **Advanced** option on the **Edit** menu. Table 2-3 shows all options with their functionality.

Option	Functionality
Make Selection Lower Case	Makes selected text lowercase
Make Selection Upper Case	Makes selected text uppercase
Increase Indent	Applies indentation on a block of text
Decrease Indent	Removes indentation from a block of text
Comment Out	Comments out a block of text
Remove Comments	Removes comments from a block of text

Table 2-3. The Advanced Options of the Edit Menu

Object Browser

Object Browser is a new tool that allows you to edit and add database objects of your database server to code as well as to execute queries. To open the Object Browser tool, click the **Object Browser** button in the Query Analyzer toolbar. (Two alternative ways are to select **Object Browser** in the **Tools** menu or press F2.) Figure 2-13 shows the **Query Analyzer** window with Object Browser.

As you can see from Figure 2-13, the displayed tree in Object Browser shows all databases of the database server called **NTB11901**. Each database object you want to use can be selected by expanding the corresponding database and expanding the folder to which the object belongs.

To add an object to a code using Object Browser, you have to navigate to it and by clicking and dragging to move it into the query pane. For instance, to select all columns for the Transact-SQL statement in Figure 2-15, select **Northwind** | **User Tables** | **Orders** and click the **Columns** folder and drag it into the query pane. (If you want to select a particular column, expand further the **Columns** folder and click and drag that column.)

You can use the Object Browser tool to query all rows of a table. To execute the query shown in Figure 2-15, expand the **Northwind** database, expand **User Tables**, right-click the **Orders** table, and click **Open**. The same query results as in Figure 2-15 should be displayed in a separate results window.

You can also modify or drop database objects using Object Browser. For the former operation, right-click the object you want to modify and select **Edit**. Object Browser displays the ALTER statement for that object in the query pane. This statement must be further enhanced and then executed. (All forms of the ALTER statement are discussed in detail in Chapter 4.) To delete an object, select **Delete** after clicking the object you want to drop.

NOTE: The functionality of Object Browser differs during the modification and deletion of an object. The selection of the **Delete** option does not generate a corresponding Transact-SQL statement in the query pane. Instead, you will be asked to confirm that you want to delete the object.

Object Browser can be used to execute or modify an existing stored procedure. For more information on this tool feature, see Chapter 8.

Object Search

The Object Search tool has a similar functionality to the **Search** option of Windows NT/2000 Explorer. In contrast to the latter, which searches files and file directories, Object Search allows you to find database objects of your database server. To open Object Search, click the **Object Search** button in the Query Analyzer toolbar. (Two alternative ways are to select **Object Search** in the **Tools** menu or press F4.)

To search for an object in the **Object Search** dialog box, type the name of the object in the **Object name** box, select the server name and database name in the **Server** and **Database** list, respectively, select one or more database object types in the **Object type** check box(es), and click **Find Now** (see Figure 2-17). The results of the Object Search component can be limited by entering the maximum number of search hits in the **Hit limit** box.

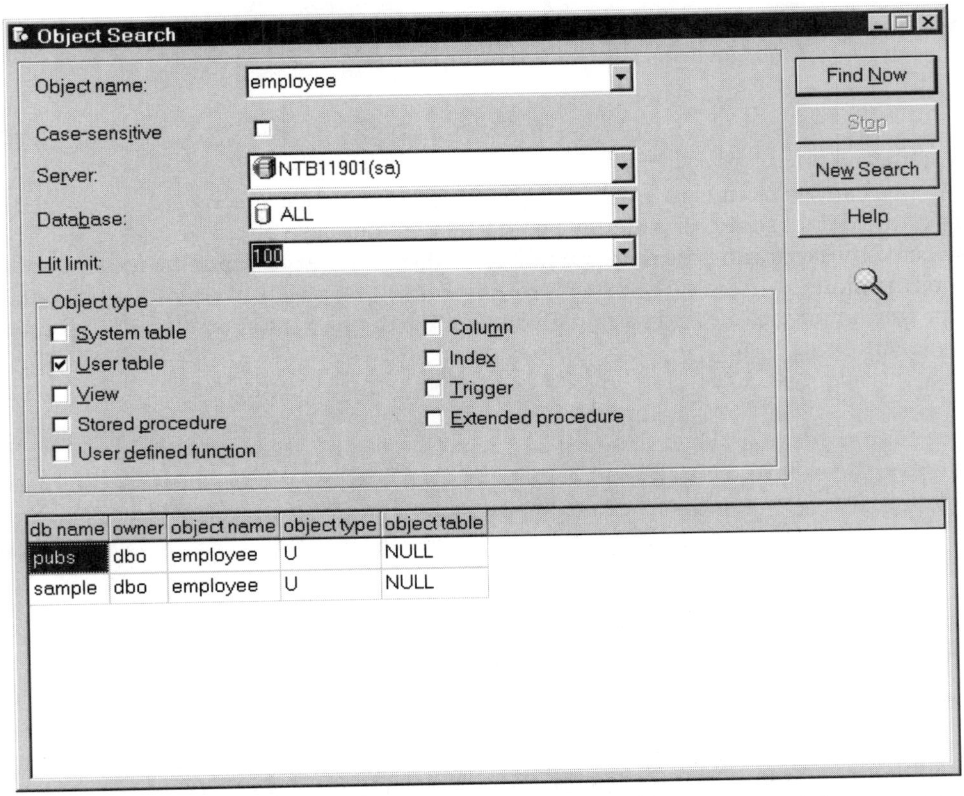

Figure 2-17. Using the Object Search tool to find all tables named **employee**

CONCLUSION

This chapter covers two SQL Server front-end components, both of which are very useful for end users and administrators. The first, SQL Server Enterprise Manager, allows many administrative functions to be performed. These are touched on here, but are covered in more detail later in the book. The most important functions of the Enterprise Manager concerning end users—database and table creation—are discussed in more detail in this chapter.

The second interactive SQL Server front-end component, Query Analyzer, allows end users to generate, execute, and store Transact-SQL statements. Additionally, it provides the ability to analyze queries by displaying the execution plan and to create suggestions with respect to index creation. For more information on index creation and the query execution plan, see Chapter 10.

The next chapter introduces the Transact-SQL language and describes its main components. After introducing the basic concepts and existing data types, the chapter also describes system functions that Transact-SQL supports.

EXERCISES

▼ E.2.1

Using Enterprise Manager, create a database called **test**. The database is stored in the file named **testdate_a** of the directory C:\tmp and the space allocated is 10MB. The file in which the database is located should grow with portions of 2MB and should not be larger than 20MB.

▼ E.2.2

Using Enterprise Manager, change the transaction log for the **test** database. The initial size of the file is 3MB, with growth of 20 percent. Allow the file for the transaction log to autogrow.

▼ E.2.3

Using Enterprise Manager, allow the use of the **test** database only to the database owner and system administrator. Is it possible that several users could use the database at the same time?

▼ E.2.4

Using Enterprise Manager, create all four tables of the sample database (see Chapter 1) with all their columns. (The **test** database is the current database.)

▼ E.2.5

Using Enterprise Manager, view which tables the **Northwind** database contains. After that, choose the **orders** table and view its properties.

▼ E.2.6

Using Query Analyzer, type the following Transact-SQL statement:

```
CREATE DATABASE test
```

Explain the error message shown in the result pane.

▼ E.2.7

Store the Transact-SQL statement in E.2.6 in the file C:\tmp\createdb.sql.

▼ E.2.8

Using Query Analyzer, how can you make the **test** database the current database?

▼ E.2.9

Using Query Analyzer, make the **Northwind** database the current database and execute the following Transact-SQL statement: SELECT * FROM orders

Stop the execution of that statement. How can you do it?

▼ E.2.10

Using Query Analyzer, change the output of the SELECT statement (E.2.9) so that the results appear as the text (and not as the grid).

PART II

Transact-SQL Language

CHAPTER 3

SQL Components

This chapter introduces the elementary objects and basic operators supported by SQL Server. First, the basic language elements, including constants, identifiers, and delimiters, are described. Every elementary object has a corresponding data type, and the subsequent section discusses data types in detail. Additionally, all existing operators and functions of SQL Server are explained. At the end of the chapter, NULL values are introduced.

SQL'S BASIC OBJECTS

The language of SQL Server, Transact-SQL, has the same basic features as other common programming languages:

- Constants or literal values
- Delimiters
- Identifiers
- Reserved keywords

A *literal* value is an alphanumerical, hexadecimal, or numeric constant. A string constant contains one or more characters of the SQL Server character set enclosed in two single straight quotation marks or double straight quotation marks (single quotation marks are preferred due to the multiple uses of double quotation marks, as discussed in a moment). If you want to include the single quotation mark within a string delimited by single quotation marks, use two consecutive single quotation marks within the string. Hexadecimal constants are used to represent nonprintable characters (and other binary data). Each hexadecimal constant begins with the characters "0x" followed by an even number of characters or numbers. Examples 3.1 and 3.2 illustrate some valid and invalid string constants and hexadecimal constants.

▼ EXAMPLE 3.1

Some valid string constants and hexadecimal constants:

'Philadelphia'
"Berkeley, CA 94710"
'9876'
'Apostrophe is displayed like this: can''t ' (note the two consecutive single quotation marks)
0x53514C0D

▼ EXAMPLE 3.2

The following are *not* string constants:

'AB'C' (odd number of single quotes)
'New York" (same type of quotation mark—single or double—must be used at each end of the string)

Beginning with SQL Server Version 6.0, double quotation marks have had two meanings. In addition to enclosing strings, quotation marks can also be used as delimiters for so-called *delimited identifiers.* Delimited identifiers are a special kind of identifier usually used to allow the use of reserved keywords as identifiers and also to allow spaces in the names of database objects.

NOTE: Differentiation between single quotes and quotation marks was first introduced in the SQL92 standard. In the case of identifiers, this standard differentiates between regular and delimited identifiers. Two key differences are that delimited identifiers are enclosed in quotation marks (Transact-SQL also supports the use of square brackets: [identifier]) and are case sensitive. Single quotes are only used for delimiting strings. Generally, delimited identifiers were introduced to allow the specification of identifiers, which are otherwise identical to reserved keywords. Specifically, delimited identifiers protect you from using names (identifiers, variable names) that could be introduced as reserved keywords in one of the future SQL standards. Additionally, delimited identifiers can contain characters that are normally illegal within identifier names, such as blanks.

In SQL Server, the use of quotation marks is defined using the QUOTED_IDENTIFIER option of the SET statement. If this option is set to ON, an identifier in quotation marks will be defined as a delimited identifier. In this case, quotation marks cannot be used for delimiting strings. By default, quotation marks can be used in the same way as single quotes for delimiting strings. However, to avoid ambiguity, the use of single quotes for string constants is preferred.

The numeric constants include all integer, fixed-point, and floating-point values with and without signs (see Example 3.3).

▼ EXAMPLE 3.3

The following are numeric constants:

130
-130.00
-0.357E5 (scientific notation—nEm means n multiplied by10^m)
22.3E-3

A constant always has a data type and a length, and both are dependent on the format of the constant. Additionally, every numeric constant has a precision and a scale factor. (The data types of the different kinds of literal values are explained later in this chapter.)

Comments

There are different ways to specify a comment in a Transact-SQL statement. The pairs of characters **/*** and ***/** mark the enclosed text as a comment. In this case, the comment may extend over several lines. Furthermore, the characters **--** (two hyphens) indicate that the remainder of the current line is a comment (see Examples 13.1 and 13.2 for the use of comments). (The two characters **--** comply with the ANSI SQL standard, while **/*** and ***/** are the extensions of the Transact-SQL language.)

Identifiers

In Transact-SQL, identifiers are used to identify database objects such as tables and indices. They are represented by character strings that may include up to 128 characters and can contain letters, numerals, or the following characters: _ , @, #, and $. Each name must begin with a letter or one of the following characters: _ , #, or @. The character # at the beginning of a table or stored procedure name denotes a temporary object, while @ at the beginning of a name denotes a variable. As indicated earlier, these rules don't apply to delimited identifiers (also known as quoted identifiers), which can contain, or begin with, any character (other than the delimiters themselves).

Reserved Keywords

Each programming language has a set of names with reserved meanings, which must be written and used in the defined format. Names of this kind are called *reserved keywords*. Transact-SQL uses a variety of such names, which, as in many other programming languages, cannot be used as object names (unless the objects are specified as delimited, or quoted, identifiers, but the use of reserved words as object names is not recommended). For a list of all reserved keywords, please refer to the Appendix of this book.

NOTE: In Transact-SQL, the names of all data types and system functions, such as CHARACTER and INTEGER, are not reserved keywords. They can therefore be used for denoting objects. (Do not use reserved words as object names! Such a use makes Transact-SQL statements difficult to read and understand.)

DATA TYPES

All the data values of a column must be of the same data type. Transact-SQL uses different data types, which can be categorized in the following way:

- Numeric data types
- String data types
- Data types for date and/or time
- Derived data types

Numeric Data Types

Numeric data types are used to represent numbers. Transact-SQL uses the following numeric data types:

Data Type	Explanation
INT	Represents integer values, which can be stored in 4 bytes. INT is the short form for INTEGER.
SMALLINT	Represents integer values, which can be stored in 2 bytes. (The range of values of the SMALLINT data type is therefore between -32768 and 32767.)
TINYINT	Represents non-negative integer values, which can be stored in 1 byte. (The range of values of the TINYINT data type is between 0 and 255.)
BIGINT	Represents integer values, which can be stored in 8 bytes. The range of values of the BIGINT data type is therefore between -2^{63} and $2^{63} - 1$. (BIGINT is a new data type in SQL Server 2000.)
DECIMAL(p,[s])	Describes fixed-point values. The argument **p** (precision) specifies the total number of digits with assumed decimal point **s** (scale) digits from the right. (DECIMAL values are stored, depending on the value of **p**, in 2 to 17 bytes. DEC is the short form for DECIMAL.)
NUMERIC(p,[s])	Synonym for DECIMAL.
REAL	Used for floating-point values. The range of positive values is approximately from 2.23E – 308 through 1.79E + 308, and the range of negative values is approximately from -2.23E – 308 through - 1.79E + 308 (the value zero can also be stored).
FLOAT[(p)]	Represents floating-point values, like REAL. **p** defines the precision with **p** < 25 as single precision (4 byte) and **p** >= 25 as double precision (8 byte).
MONEY	Used for representing monetary values. MONEY values correspond to 8-byte DECIMAL values and are rounded to four digits after the decimal point.
SMALLMONEY	Corresponds to the data type MONEY but is stored in 4 bytes.

String Data Types

There are three types of string data types: character strings, binary strings, and bit strings. The following character string data types are used:

Data Type	Explanation
CHAR[(n)]	Represents a string, where **n** is the number of characters inside the string. The maximum value of **n** is 8000. CHARACTER(n) is an additional equivalent form for CHAR(n). If **n** is omitted, the length of the string is assumed to be 1.
VARCHAR[(n)]	Describes a string with varying length ($0 < \mathbf{n} \leq 8000$). In contrast to the CHAR data type, the values for the VARCHAR data type are stored in their actual length. This data type has two synonyms: CHAR VARYING and CHARACTER VARYING.
NCHAR[(n)]	The NCHAR data type stores fixed-length Unicode character data. (Unicode will be discussed in detail in Chapter 15.) The main difference between the CHAR and NCHAR data types is that each NCHAR character is stored in 2 bytes, while each CHAR character uses 1 byte of storage space. The maximum number of characters in a column of NCHAR data type is 4000 because each character is stored in two bytes.
NVARCHAR[(n)]	The NVARCHAR data type stores Unicode characters of varying lengths. The main difference between the VARCHAR and the NVARCHAR data types is that each NVARCHAR character is stored in 2 bytes, while each VARCHAR character uses 1 byte of storage space. The maximum number of characters in a column of NVARCHAR data type is 4000.
TEXT[(n)]	Defines a fixed-length string up to 2GB. (This data type is described later in the chapter, as is the data type IMAGE.)
NTEXT[(n)]	The NTEXT data type stores large character data of varying length. The maximum number of bytes in a column of NTEXT data type is $2^{31} - 1$. This data can be a sequence of single-byte or multibyte characters. The main difference between the TEXT and the NTEXT data types is that each NTEXT character is stored in 2 bytes, while each TEXT character uses 1 byte of storage space.

NOTE: VARCHAR denotes a string of variable length, which can contain printable and nonprintable characters as well as null values. The data type VARCHAR is identical to the data type CHAR except for one difference: if the content of a CHAR(n) string is shorter than **n** characters, the rest of the string is padded with blanks. (A value of the VARCHAR data type is always stored in its actual length.)

Binary data types describe data objects being represented in the internal format of the system. The binary string data types are described here:

Data Type	Explanation
BINARY[(n)]	Specifies a bit string of fixed length with exactly **n** bytes ($0 < \mathbf{n} \leq 8000$).
VARBINARY[(n)]	Specifies a bit string of variable length with up to **n** bytes ($0 < \mathbf{n} \leq 8000$).
IMAGE[(n)]	Specifies a bit string of fixed length with nearly unlimited values. (The limit lies at 2^{31} bytes.)
BIT	Used for specifying the Boolean data type with three possible values: false, true, and NULL. Each value of this data type is stored in 1 bit. Columns of type BIT cannot be indexed.

NOTE: The previously mentioned string data type TEXT, together with the data type IMAGE, constitutes the text/image data type. Data objects of the type IMAGE can contain any kind of data (load modules, audio/video), while data objects of the data type TEXT can contain any text data (i.e., printable data).

Text/image data are stored separately from all other values of a database using a b-tree structure that points to the fragments of text/image data. For each table that contains more than one column with text/image data, all values of the columns are stored together.

Specifying Date and Time

SQL Server supports the following date and time data types:

Data Type	Explanation
DATETIME	Specifies a date and time with each value being stored as an integer value in 4 bytes.
SMALLDATETIME	Specifies a date and time with each value being stored as an integer value in 2 bytes.

The data types DATETIME and SMALLDATETIME are stored as numeric values. The date value is stored in the first 4- or 2-byte field as the number of days starting from January 1, 1753 (DATETIME) or January 1, 1900 (SMALLDATETIME) and ranging through December 31, 9999 (DATETIME) or June 6, 2079 (SMALLDATETIME). The time value is stored in the second 4- or 2-byte field as the number of three-hundredths of a second (DATETIME) or minutes (SMALLDATETIME) having passed since midnight.

The date value in the Transact-SQL language is by default specified as a string in a format like "mmm dd yyyy" (e.g., 'Jan 10 1993') inside two single quotes or double quotation marks. (Note that the relative order of month, day, and year can be controlled by the SET DATEFORMAT statement; additionally, SQL Server recognizes numeric month values with delimiters of / or -). Similarly, the time value is specified in the format 'hh:mm AM' or 'hh:mm PM' (e.g., '11:31 PM'). See Examples 3.4 and 3.5 for possible date and time entries.

NOTE: SQL Server supports a variety of different input formats for date and time values. Both objects are identified separately, thus date and time values can be specified in any order or alone. If one of the values is omitted, SQL Server uses the default values. (The default value for time is 12:00 AM, and the default date is January 1, 1900.)

▼ EXAMPLE 3.4

The following date descriptions can be entered:

'28/5/1959' (with SET DATEFORMAT dmy)
'May 28, 1959'
'1959 MAY 28'

▼ EXAMPLE 3.5

The following time expressions can be used:

'8:45 AM'
'4 pm'

Derived Data Types

SQL Server supports two data types that can be derived from simple data types: TIMESTAMP and SYSNAME.

Data Type	Explanation
TIMESTAMP	Specifies a column being defined as VARBINARY(8) (or BINARY(8), depending on nullability of the column). The system maintains a current value (not a date or time) for each database (accessible via @@dbts), which it increments whenever any row with a timestamp column is inserted or updated (and sets the timestamp column to that value). Thus, timestamp columns can be used to determine the relative time when rows were last changed.
SYSNAME	Specifies the name of database objects in the system catalog (defined as NVARCHAR(128)).

New Data Types in SQL Server 7 and SQL Server 2000

SQL Server 7 supports two data types, which do not belong to any of the data type groups described previously. They are:

- CURSOR
- UNIQUEIDENTIFIER

The data type CURSOR allows for the creation of a cursor variable in a stored procedure. (Cursors allow processing data one row at a time. The description of cursors is beyond the scope of this book.) This data type cannot be used as the data type for a column in a table.

As its name implies, UNIQUEIDENTIFIER is a unique identification number stored as a 16-byte binary string. This data type is closely related to the GUID (globally unique identifier), which is used for data replication (see Chapter 25). The initialization of a column or a variable of type UNIQUEIDENTIFIER can be provided using the function NEWID or with a string constant written in a special form using hexadecimal digits and hyphens.

Besides the data type BIGINT that is described together with other numeric data types, there are two other data types in SQL Server 2000 that do not belong to any of the groups described previously:

- SQL_VARIANT
- TABLE

The SQL_VARIANT data type can be used to store values of various data types at the same time, such as numeric values, strings, and date values. (The only types of values that cannot be stored are text/image and TIMESTAMP.) Each value of a SQL_VARIANT column has two parts: the data value and the information that describes the value. (This information contains all properties of the actual data type of the value, such as length, scale, and precision.) SQL Server 2000 supports the SQL_VARIANT_PROPERTY function, which displays the attached information for each value of a SQL_VARIANT column.

NOTE: Declare a column of a table using the SQL_VARIANT data type only if it is really necessary. A column should have this data type if its values may be of different types or if it is not possible to determine the type of a column during the database design process.

The TABLE data type specifies what its name says: the data type that can store rows with several and different values. Such a data type can be used in many useful cases. However, SQL Server 2000 restricts its use to two areas:

- As a local variable
- As a return value of a user-defined function. (Local variables, as well as user-defined functions, are defined in Chapter 8.)

The use of the TABLE data type is shown in Example 8.10.

PREDICATES

A *predicate* defines a logical condition being applied to rows in a table. The common logical conditions with two values (true, false) are extended in the SQL language by a third value (unknown or not applicable).

The Transact-SQL language supports the following predicates, described in detail in Chapter 5:

- All relational operators
- BETWEEN operator
- IN operator
- LIKE operator
- NULL operator
- ALL and ANY operators
- EXISTS function

AGGREGATE FUNCTIONS

Aggregate functions are applied to a group of data values (in other words, from multiple rows) from a column. Aggregate functions always return a single value. The Transact-SQL language supports five aggregate functions:

- AVG
- MAX
- MIN
- SUM
- COUNT_BIG

AVG (short for *average*) calculates the arithmetic mean of the data values contained within a column. The column must contain numeric values. MAX calculates the maximum, and MIN the minimum, data value of the column. The column can contain numeric, string, and date/time values.

SUM calculates the total of all data values in a column. The column must contain numeric values. COUNT calculates the number of (non-null) data values in a column. The only aggregate function not being applied to columns is COUNT(*). This function returns the number of rows (whether or not particular columns have null values). Aggregate functions, together with statistical aggregates and superaggregates, are described in detail in Chapter 5.

SCALAR FUNCTIONS

In addition to aggregate functions, SQL Server provides several scalar functions that are used in the construction of scalar expressions. (A scalar function operates on a single value or list of values, as opposed to aggregate functions, which operate on the data from multiple rows.) Scalar functions can be categorized as follows:

- Numeric functions
- Date functions
- String functions
- Text/image functions
- System functions

Numeric Functions

Numeric functions within the Transact-SQL language are mathematical functions for modifying numeric values. The following numeric functions are available:

Function	Explanation
ABS(n)	Returns the absolute value (i.e., negative values are returned as positive) of the numeric expression **n**. Example: SELECT ABS(-5.767) = 5.767, SELECT ABS(6.384) = 6.384
ACOS(n)	Calculates arc cosine of **n**. **n**, as well as the resulting value, belongs to the FLOAT data type.
ASIN(n)	Calculates the arc sine of **n**. **n**, as well as the resulting value, belongs to the FLOAT data type.

Function	Explanation
ATAN(n)	Calculates the arc tangent of **n**. **n**, as well as the resulting value, belongs to the FLOAT data type.
ATN2(n,m)	Calculates the arc tangent of **n/m**. **n**, **m**, as well as the resulting value, belongs to the FLOAT data type.
CEILING(n)	Returns the smallest integer value greater or equal to the specified value **n**. Examples: SELECT CEILING(4.88) = 5, SELECT CEILING(-4.88) = -4.
COS(n)	Calculates the cosine of **n**. **n**, as well as the resulting value, belongs to the FLOAT data type.
COT(n)	Calculates the cotangent of **n**. **n**, as well as the resulting value, belongs to the FLOAT data type.
DEGREES(n)	Converts radians to degrees. Examples: SELECT DEGREES(PI()/2) = 90.0, SELECT DEGREES(0.75) = 42.97
EXP(n)	Calculates the value $\mathbf{e}^n$. Examples: SELECT EXP(0.75) = 2.12, SELECT EXP(1) = 2.7183
FLOOR(n)	Calculates the largest integer value less than or equal to the specified value **n**. Example: FLOOR(4.88) = 4.
LOG(n)	Calculates the natural (i.e., base e) logarithm of **n**. Examples: SELECT LOG(4.67) = 1.54, SELECT LOG(0.12) = -2.12
LOG10(n)	Calculates the logarithm (base 10) for **n**. Examples: SELECT LOG_{10}(4.67) = 0.67 , SELECT LOG_{10}(0.12) = -0.92
PI()	Returns the value of the number pi (3.14).
POWER(x,y)	Calculates the value $\mathbf{x}^y$. Examples: SELECT POWER(3.12,5) = 295.65, SELECT POWER(81,0.5) = 9
RADIANS(n)	Converts degrees to radians. Examples: SELECT RADIANS (90.0) = 1.57, SELECT RADIANS(42.97) = 0.75
RAND	Returns a random number between 0 and 1 with a FLOAT data type.

Function	Explanation
ROUND(n,p)	Rounds the value of the number **n** by using the precision **p**. Use positive values of **p** for rounding right of the decimal point, negative values to round on the left side. An optional parameter 1 causes **n** to be truncated. Examples: SELECT ROUND(5.4567,3) = 5.4570, SELECT ROUND(345.4567,-1) = 350.0000, SELECT ROUND(345.4567,-1,1) = 340.0000
ROWCOUNT_BIG	Returns the number of rows that have been affected by the last Transact-SQL statement executed by the system. The return value of this function has the BIGINT data type. (See also the global variable @@ROWCOUNT.)
SIGN(n)	Returns the sign of the value **n** as a number (+1 for positive, -1 for negative value, and 0 for zero). Example: SELECT SIGN(0.88) = 1
SIN(n)	Calculates the sine of **n**. **n**, as well as the resulting value, belongs to the FLOAT data type.
SQRT(n)	Calculates the square root of **n**. Example: SELECT SQRT(9) = 3
TAN(n)	Calculates the tangent of **n**. **n**, as well as the resulting value, belongs to the FLOAT data type.

Date Functions

Date functions calculate the respective date or time portion of an expression or return the value from a time interval. All date functions use the following date or time units:

- yy (year)
- qq (quarter)
- mm (month)
- dy (day of year) for a single day within the year (0 < **n** < 366)
- dd (day) for a day
- dw (day of week) for a weekday

- wk (week)
- hh (hour)
- mi (minute)
- ss (second)
- ms (millisecond)

SQL Server supports the following date functions:

Function	Explanation
GETDATE()	Returns the current system date and time. Example: SELECT GETDATE() = 2000-01-10 13:03:31.390
DATEPART(item,date)	Returns the specified part **item** of a date **date** as an integer. Examples: SELECT DATEPART(month, GETDATE()) = 1, SELECT DATEPART(weekday, GETDATE()) = 2
DATENAME(item, date)	Returns the specified part **item** of the date **date** as a character string (Mon,Tue,...). Example: SELECT DATENAME(weekday,GETDATE()) = Monday
DATEDIFF(item,dat1,dat2)	Calculates the difference between the two date parts **dat1** and **dat2** and returns the result as an integer in units specified by the value **item**. Example: SELECT DATEDIFF(YEAR, BirthDate, GETDATE()) AS Age FROM employees = returns the age of each employee
DATEADD(item,number,date)	Adds the number **number** of units specified by the value **item** to the given date **date**. Example: SELECT DATEADD(DAY,3,HireDate) AS Age FROM employees = adds 3 days to the enterdate of every employee

String Functions

String functions are used for manipulating data values in a column, usually of a string data type. SQL Server supports the following string functions:

Function	Explanation
ASCII(character)	Converts the specified character to the equivalent decimal (ASCII-) Code. Returns an integer. Example: SELECT ASCII("A") = 65
CAST(a AS type [(length)])	Converts an expression **a** into the specified data type **type** (if possible). Example: SELECT CAST(3000000000 AS BIGINT) = 3000000000
CHAR(integer)	Converts the ASCII-Code to the equivalent character. Example: SELECT CHAR(65) = "A"
CONVERT(type[(length)],a)	Equivalent to CAST, but the arguments are specified differently.
CHARINDEX(z1,z2)	Returns the starting position where the partial string **z1** first occurs in the string **z2**. Returns 0 if **z1** does not occur in **z2**. Example: SELECT CHARINDEX("bl","table") = 3
DIFFERENCE(z1,z2)	Returns the difference of SOUNDEX values of two strings **z1** and **z2**. (SOUNDEX returns a number, which specifies the sound of a string. With this method, strings with similar sounds can be determined.) Example: SELECT DIFFERENCE("spelling","telling") = 2 (sounds a little bit similar, 0 = doesn't sound similar)
LOWER(z1)	Converts all uppercase letters of the string **z1** to lowercase letters. Lowercase letters and numbers, and other characters, do not change. Example: SELECT LOWER("BIG") = "big"
LTRIM(z)	Removes leading blanks in the string **z**. Example: SELECT LTRIM(" String") = "String"
NEWID()	Creates a unique ID number that consists of a 16-byte binary string intended to store the UNIQUEIDENTIFIER data type. Example: SELECT NEWID() = e.g. D9792566-ABDD-11D3-9FC6-0050041D4A60
PATINDEX(z1,expr)	Returns the starting point of the partial string **z1** in the expression **expr**. Example: SELECT PATINDEX("%gs%","longstring") = 4

Function	Explanation
REPLICATE(z,i)	Repeats string **z, i** times. Example: SELECT REPLICATE('a',10) = aaaaaaaaaa
REVERSE(z)	Displays the string **z** in the reverse order. Example: SELECT REVERSE ("calculate") = etaluclac
RIGHT(z,length)	Returns the last **length** characters from the string **z**. Example: SELECT RIGHT("Notebook",4) = book
RTRIM(z)	Removes trailing blanks of the string **z**. Example: SELECT RTRIM("Notebook ",4) = "Notebook"
SOUNDEX(a)	Returns a four-character SOUNDEX code to determine the similarity between two strings. Example: SELECT SOUNDEX("spelling") = S145
SPACE(length)	Returns a string with spaces of length specified by **length**. Example: SELECT SPACE(5) = " "
STR(f,[len [,d]])	Converts the specified float expression **f** into a string. **len** is the length of the string including decimal point, sign, digits, and spaces (10 by default), and **d** is the number of digits to the right of the decimal point to be returned. Example: SELECT STR(3.45678,4,2) = "3.46"
STUFF(z1,a,length,z2)	Replaces the partial string **z1** with the partial string **z2** starting at position **a**, replacing **length** characters of **z1**. Examples: SELECT STUFF("Notebook",5,0," in a ") = "Note in a book", SELECT STUFF("Notebook",1,4,"Hand") = "Handbook"
SUBSTRING(z,a,length)	Creates a partial string from string **z** starting at the position **a** with a length of **length**. Example: SELECT SUBSTRING("wardrobe",1,4) = "ward"
UPPER(z)	Converts all lowercase letters of string **z** to uppercase letters. Uppercase letters and numbers do not change. Example: SELECT UPPER("loWer") = "LOWER"

Text/Image Functions

Text/image functions are designed for use with columns of the text/image data types. SQL Server supports the following text/image functions:

Function	Explanation
PATINDEX(%pattern%, expr)	Returns an integer value specifying the position of the string **pattern** in the expression **expr**. If the value 0 is returned, the string was not found. Example: SELECT PATINDEX("%gs%","longstring") = 4, SELECT RIGHT(ContactName,LEN(ContactName)-PATINDEX("% %",ContactName)) AS "First Name" FROM Customers = returns all First Names from the column customers
TEXTPTR(column)	Returns a pointer pointing to the first page in which the TEXT or IMAGE column **column** is stored. The result can be used with the UPDATETEXT, WRITETEXT, or READTEXT statements.
TEXTVALID("table.column", pointer)	Returns 1 if the pointer **pointer** is valid for the TEXT or IMAGE column **column**.

In addition to these functions, the TEXTSIZE option in the SET statement defines the maximum number of bytes that can be returned with a SELECT statement from a TEXT or IMAGE column. The current value is stored in the global variable **@@textsize** (see Chapter 8 for additional information).

System Functions

SQL Server system functions provide extensive information about database objects. Most system functions use an internal numeric identifier (ID), which is assigned to each database object by SQL Server at its creation. System functions can be grouped into functions with and without parameters. The SQL Server system functions with parameters are described here:

Function	Explanation
COALESCE(a_1,a_2,...)	Returns for a given list of expressions $\mathbf{a_1}$, $\mathbf{a_2}$,... the value of the first expression that is not NULL.
COL_LENGTH(obj, col)	Returns the maximum length of the values of column **col** belonging to a database object (table or view) **obj**. Example: SELECT COL_LENGTH("customers","CustomerID") = 10

Function	Explanation
COL_NAME(o_id,s_id)	Returns for the specified object identifier **o_id** the name of the column belonging to this object with the identifier **s_id**. Example: SELECT COL_NAME(OBJECT_ID('products') ,4) = "CategoryID"
DATABASEPROPERTYEX (database, property)	Returns the current setting of the specified database option or property for the specified database. (This system function is described in detail in Chapter 18.)
DATALENGTH(z)	Calculates the length (in bytes) of the result of the expression **z**. Example: SELECT DATALENGTH(ProductName) FROM Products returns the length of each field.
DB_ID([db_name])	Returns the identifier of the database **db_name**. If no name is specified, the identifier of the current database is returned. Example: SELECT DB_ID('Northwind') = 6
DB_NAME([db_id])	Returns the name of the database with the identifier **db_id**. If no identifier is specified, the name of the current database is displayed. Example: SELECT DB_NAME(6) = "Northwind"
GETANSINULL('dbnam')	Returns 1 if the use of null values in the database **dbnam** complies with the ANSI SQL standard. (See also the explanation of null values at the end of this chapter.) Example: SELECT GETANSINULL('Northwind') = 1
HOST_ID([host])	Returns the identifier of the host system. Example: SELECT HOST_ID() = 106
HOST_NAME([h_id])	Returns the name of the host. Example: SELECT HOST_NAME() = ORACLENIX
INDEX_COL(table, i, no)	Returns the name of the indexed column in the table **table,** defined by the index identifier **i** and the position **no** of the column in the index.
ISNULL(expr, value)	Returns the value of **expr** if that value is not null; otherwise, it returns **value** (see Example 5.22).

Function	Explanation
NULLIF($expr_1$,$expr_2$)	Returns the null value if the expressions $\mathbf{expr_1}$ and $\mathbf{expr_2}$ are equal. Example: SELECT NULLIF(project_no, 'p1') FROM projects. (Returns NULL for the project with the project_no='p1')
OBJECT_ID(obj_name)	Returns the identifier for the database object **obj_name**. Example: SELECT OBJECT_ID('products') = 453576654
OBJECT_NAME(obj_id)	Returns the name of the database object with the identifier **obj_id**. Example: SELECT OBJECT_NAME(453576654) = "products"
SUSER_SID([name])	Returns the user's security identification number (SID) from the login name **name**. If no name is specified, the identifier of the current user is retrieved. Example: SELECT SUSER_SID("sa") = 0x01
SUSER_SNAME([sid])	Returns the user's login name from the user's security identification number **sid**. If no identifier is specified, the name of the current user is retrieved. Example: SELECT SUSER_SNAME(0x01) = "sa"
USER_ID([user_name])	Returns the identifier of the user **user_name**. If no name is specified, the identifier of the current user is retrieved. Example: SELECT USER_ID("guest") = 2
USER_NAME([user_id])	Returns the name of the user with the identifier **user_id**. If no name is specified, the name of the current user is retrieved. Example: SELECT USER_NAME(2) = "guest"

The following system functions of SQL Server do not use parameters:

Function	Explanation
CURRENT_TIMESTAMP	Returns the current date and time. Example: SELECT CURRENT_TIMESTAMP = "2000-01-11 17:22:55.670"
CURRENT_USER	Returns the name of the current user. Example: SELECT CURRENT_USER = "dbo"

Function	Explanation
SYSTEM_USER	Returns the login ID of the current user. Example: SELECT SYSTEM_USER = "sa"
USER	Same as CURRENT_USER.

All string functions can be nested in any order, for example, REVERSE(CURRENT_USER).

SCALAR OPERATORS

Scalar operators are used for operations with scalar values. SQL Server supports numeric and Boolean operators as well as concatenation.

There are unary and binary arithmetic operators. Unary operators are + and - (as signs). Binary arithmetic operators are +, -, *, /, and %. (The first four binary operators have their respective mathematical meanings, whereas % is the modulo operator.)

Boolean operators have two different notations in SQL Server depending on whether they are applied to bit strings or to other data types. The operators NOT, AND, and OR are applied to all data types (except BIT). They are described in detail in Chapter 5.

The bitwise operators for manipulating bit strings are listed here, and Example 3.6 shows how they are used:

~ (complement, i.e., NOT)

& (conjunction of bit strings, i.e., AND)

| (disjunction of bit strings, i.e., OR)

^ (exclusive disjunction, i.e., XOR or Exclusive OR)

▼ EXAMPLE 3.6

```
 ~(1001001) = (0110110)
(11001001) | (10101101) = (11101101)
(11001001) & (10101101) = (10001001)
(11001001) ^ (10101101) = (01100100)
```

The concatenation operator + can be used to concatenate two character strings or bit strings.

Global Variables

Global variables are special system variables that can be used as if they were scalar constants. SQL Server supports the following global variables, which have to be preceded by the prefix @@:

Variable	Explanation
@@CONNECTIONS	Returns the number of login attempts since starting SQL Server.
@@CPU_BUSY	Returns the total CPU time (in units of ticks, or 3.33 milliseconds) used since starting SQL Server.
@@DBTS	Returns the current value of the TIMESTAMP column for the current database.
@@ERROR	Returns the information about the return value of the last executed Transact-SQL statement.
@@IDENTITY	Returns the last inserted value for the column with the IDENTITY property (see Example 5.55).
@@IDLE	Returns the time (in units of ticks, or 3.33 milliseconds) that SQL Server has been idle since it was first started.
@@IO_BUSY	Returns the used I/O time (in units of ticks, or 3.33 milliseconds) since starting SQL Server.
@@LANGID	Returns the identifier of the language that is currently used by SQL Server.
@@LANGUAGE	Returns the name of the language that is currently used by SQL Server.
@@MAX_CONNECTIONS	Returns the maximum number of simultaneous connections to SQL Server currently in effect.
@@VERSION	Returns the current version of the SQL Server software.
@@NESTLEVEL	Returns the current nesting level of the stored procedure being executed.
@@PROCID	Returns the identifier for the stored procedure currently being executed.
@@ROWCOUNT	Returns the number of rows that have been affected by the last Transact-SQL statement executed by the system.
@@SERVERNAME	Retrieves the information concerning the local database server. This information contains, among other things, the name of the server and the name of the instance.
@@SPID	Returns the identifier of the server process.
@@TEXTSIZE	Retrieves the current maximum number of bytes for text/image objects, which can be returned as the result of a SELECT statement.

Variable	Explanation
@@TOTAL_READ	Returns the total number of read operations since SQL Server was first started.
@@TOTAL_WRITE	Returns the total number of write operations since SQL Server was first started.

NULL VALUES

A null value is a special value that may be assigned to a column. This value is normally used when information in a column is missing, unknown, or not applicable. For example, in the case of an unknown home telephone number for a company's employee, it is recommended that the null value be assigned to the column **home_telephon_no**.

Any arithmetic expression results in a NULL if any operand of that expression is itself a null value. Therefore, in unary arithmetic expressions (if A is an expression with a null value), both +A and -A return NULL. In binary expressions, if one (or both) of the operands A or B has the null value, A + B, A - B, A * B, A / B, and A%B also result in a NULL. (A and B have to be numerical expressions.)

If an expression contains a relational operation and one (or both) of the operands has (have) the null value, the result of this operation will be NULL. Hence, each of the expressions A = B, A <> B, A < B, and A > B also returns NULL.

In the Boolean AND, OR, and NOT, the behavior of the null values is specified by the following truth tables, where T stands for true, U for unknown (NULL), and F for false. In these tables, follow the row and column represented by the values of the Boolean expressions that the operator works on, and the value where they intersect represents the resulting value.

AND	T	U	F
T	T	U	F
U	U	U	F
F	F	F	F

OR	T	U	F
T	T	T	T
U	T	U	U
F	T	U	F

NOT	
T	F
U	U
F	T

Any null value in the argument of aggregate functions AVG, SUM, MAX, MIN, and COUNT is eliminated before the respective function is calculated (except for the function COUNT(*)). If a column contains only null values, the function returns NULL. The aggregate function COUNT(*) handles all null values the same as non-null values. If the column contains only null values, the result of the function COUNT(DISTINCT column_name) is 0.

A null value has to be different from all other values. For numeric data types, there is a distinction between the value zero and NULL. The same is true for the empty string and NULL for string data types.

A column of a table allows null values if its definition (see Chapter 4) explicitly contains NULL. On the other hand, null values are not permitted if the definition of a column explicitly contains NOT NULL. If the user does not specify NULL or NOT NULL for a column with a data type (except TIMESTAMP), the following values are assigned:

- NULL: If the ANSI_NULL_DFLT_ON option of the SET statement is set to ON or the option 'ANSI null default' of the system procedure **sp_dboption** has the value TRUE.
- NOT NULL: If the ANSI_NULL_DFLT_OFF option of the SET statement is set to ON or the option 'ANSI null default' of the system procedure **sp_dboption** is set to FALSE.

If the SET statement and the system procedure **sp_dboption** are not both activated, a column will contain the value NOT NULL by default. (The columns of TIMESTAMP data type can only be declared as NOT NULL columns.)

▼ EXAMPLE 3.7

```
sp_dboption projects, 'ANSI null default', TRUE
```

After the execution of the system procedure **sp_dboption** in Example 3.7, all columns of the database **projects** will have NULL as a nullability setting (unless NOT NULL is specified when the column is created).

There is also another option of the SET statement—CONCAT_NULL_YIELDS_NULL. This database option influences the concatenation operation with a null value so that anything you concatenate to a null value will yield NULL again. For instance, 'San Francisco' + NULL = NULL.

CONCLUSION

The basic features of SQL Server consist of Transact-SQL data types, predicates, and functions. Data types supported by SQL Server comply with data types of the ANSI SQL92 standard. SQL Server supports a variety of useful system functions.

The next chapter will introduce you to Transact-SQL statements. The data definition language portion of Transact-SQL comprises all of the statements needed for creating, altering, and removing database objects.

EXERCISES

▼ E.3.1

What is a difference between the numeric data types INT, SMALLINT, and TINYINT?

▼ E.3.2

What is a difference between the data types CHAR and VARCHAR? When should you use the latter (instead of the former) and vice versa?

▼ E.3.3

How can you set the format of a column with the DATETIME data type so that its values can be entered in the form "yyyy/mm/dd"?

In the following two exercises, use the SELECT statement in Query Analyzer's window to display the result of all system functions and global variables. (For instance, SELECT host_id() displays the ID number of the current host.)

▼ E.3.4

Using SQL Server system functions, find the ID number of the **test** database (Exercise 2.1).

▼ E.3.5

Using the system variables, display the current version of the SQL Server software and the language that is used by this software.

▼ E.3.6

Using the bitwise operators &, |, and ^, calculate the following operations with the bit strings:

(11100101) & (01010111)
(10011011) | (11001001)
(10110111) ^ (10110001)

▼ E.3.7

What is the result of the following expressions?

A + NULL
NULL = NULL
B OR NULL
B AND NULL
A is a numerical and B a logical expression.

▼ E.3.8

When can you use both single quotes and quotation marks to define string and DATETIME constants?

▼ E.3.9

What is a delimited identifier and when do you need it?

CHAPTER 4

Data Definition Language

This chapter describes all the Transact-SQL statements concerning data definition language (DDL). At the beginning of the chapter all DDL statements are divided into three groups. The first group includes statements that create objects, the second group includes statements that modify objects, and the third group includes statements that remove objects.

CREATING DATABASE OBJECTS

The organization of a database involves many different objects. All objects of a database can be physical or logical. The physical objects are related to the organization of the data on the physical device (disk). Logical objects represent a user's view of a database. Databases, tables, columns, and views (virtual tables) are examples of logical objects.

NOTE: In versions prior to 7.0, SLQ Server supported three groups of physical objects: database devices, dump devices, and segments. With previous versions, users could create, alter, or drop those objects using Transact-SQL statements and/or system procedures. With the release of SQL Server 7, database devices have been replaced by files and file groups (which database administrators can manage). Dump devices still exist, but have been renamed "backup devices." Segments are gone.

The first database object that has to be created is a database itself. SQL Server supports both system and user databases. An authorized user can create user databases, while system databases are generated during the installation of SQL Server. The SQL Server system databases are:

- **master**
- **tempdb**
- **model**
- **msdb**
- **distribution**

This chapter describes the creation, alteration, and removal of user databases, while all system databases will be covered in detail in Chapter 15.

Creation of a Database

Two basic methods are used to create a SQL Server database. The first is to use SQL Server Enterprise Manager (see Chapter 2). The second method is to use the Transact-SQL statement CREATE DATABASE. This statement has the general form:

```
CREATE DATABASE db_name
   [ON [PRIMARY] file_spec1 {, file_spec2} ...]
   [LOG ON file_spec3 {, file_spec4} ...]
```

```
[FOR RESTORE]
        [COLLATE collation_name]
```

NOTE: For the syntax of the Transact-SQL statements, we use conventions described in the section "Syntax Conventions" in Chapter 1. According to the conventions, optional item(s) are written in brackets and braces followed by the "..." indicating that item(s) can be repeated any number of times.

db_name is the name of the database. The maximum size of a database name is 128 characters. (The rules for identifiers described in Chapter 3 apply to database names.) The maximum number of databases managed by a single SQL Server system is 32,767.

All databases in SQL Server are stored in files. These files can be explicitly specified by the system administrator or implicitly provided by the system. If the ON option exists in the CREATE DATABASE statement, all files containing the data of a database are explicitly specified.

NOTE: The syntax of the CREATE DATABASE statement since SQL Server 7 has undergone a lot of changes. It is no longer possible for SQL Server databases to use database devices, as in versions previous to SQL Server 7. Instead of devices, databases now use disk files. Each file contains data of a single database. Files themselves can be organized into file groups. File groups provide the ability to distribute data over different disk drives and to back up and restore subsets of the database (useful for very large databases). Internally, SQL Server still maintains the device construct. Scripts containing database creation to device still function so long as the device is specified ahead of time and is referenced to a file.

file_spec1, file_spec2,... represent file specifications, which include further options such as the logical name of the file, the physical name, and the size (see Example 4.2). The PRIMARY option specifies the first (and most important) file that contains system tables and other important internal information concerning the database. If the PRIMARY option is omitted, the first file listed in the specification is used as the primary file.

The system administrator uses the LOG ON option to define one or more files as the physical destination of the transaction log of the database. If the LOG ON option is not specified, the transaction log of the database will still be created because every database must have at least one transaction log file. (SQL Server keeps a record of each change it makes to the database. SQL Server keeps all those records, in particular before and after values, in one or more files called the transaction log. Each database of the system has its own transaction log.)

NOTE: It is no longer possible to have the transaction log in the same file with the data!

With the COLLATE option, you can specify the default collation for the database. If the COLLATE option is not specified, the database is assigned the default collation of the

model database, which is the same as the default collation of the SQL Server instance. (For more information on collation, see Chapter 14.)

The FOR RESTORE clause is supported for compatibility with older versions of SQL Server but has no effect in SQL Server 2000.

During the creation of a new database, SQL Server uses the **model** database as a template. The properties of a **model** database can be changed to suit the personal conception of the system administrator.

Ideally, only a limited number of users should have the authorization to create a database. After the installation of the system, only the system administrator has this privilege. The system administrator can subsequently grant this privilege to other users via the GRANT CREATE DATABASE statement. The creator of the database is called the database owner and has special privileges concerning the database and its objects. (Granting and revoking database privileges is discussed in detail in Chapter 12.)

Example 4.1 creates a simple database without any further specifications.

▼ EXAMPLE 4.1

```
CREATE DATABASE test_db
```

The output is

```
CREATE DATABASE: allocating 0.63/B Mbytes on disk 'test_db'
CREATE DATABASE: allocating 0.49/B Mbytes on disk 'test_db_log'
```

Example 4.1 creates a database named **test_db** with default specifications. This means the logical name of the data file is **test_db**, and its original size is 3MB. Similarly, the logical name of the transaction log is **test_db_log**, and its original size is 1MB.

Example 4.2 creates a database with explicit specifications for database and transaction log files.

▼ EXAMPLE 4.2

```
CREATE DATABASE projects
 ON (NAME=projects_dat,
   FILENAME = 'C:\MSSQL7\DATA\projects.mdf',
   SIZE = 10,
   MAXSIZE = 100,
   FILEGROWTH = 5)
LOG ON
 (NAME=projects_log,
   FILENAME = 'C:\MSSQL7\DATA\projects.ldf',
   SIZE = 40,
```

```
MAXSIZE = 100,
FILEGROWTH = 10)
```

Example 4.2 creates a database called **projects**. Because the PRIMARY option is omitted, the first file is assumed as the primary file. This file has the logical name **projects_dat** and is stored in the file **projects.mdf**. The original size of this file is 10MB. Additional portions of 5MB of disk storage are allocated by the system, if needed. (The MB, TB, and KB suffixes can be used to specify kilobytes, terabytes or megabytes, respectively—the default is MB. If the MAXSIZE option is not specified or is set to UNLIMITED, the file will grow until the disk is full.)

There is also a single transaction log file with the logical name **projects_log** and the physical name **projects.ldf**. All options of the file specification for the transaction log have the same name and meaning as the corresponding options of the file specification for the data file.

Using the Transact-SQL language, a user can select the current database with the USE statement. (The alternative way is to select the database name in the **Database** pull-down menu in the toolbar of SQL Server Query Analyzer.)

The system administrator can assign a default database to a user by using the system procedures **sp_defaultdb** or **sp_addlogin** (see Chapter 12). In this case, the users do not need to execute the USE statement if they want to use their default database.

CREATE TABLE—A Basic Form

The CREATE TABLE statement creates a new base table with all corresponding columns and their data types. The basic form of the CREATE TABLE statement is

```
CREATE TABLE table_name
   (col_name1 type1 [NOT NULL | NULL]
   [{, col_name2 type2 [NOT NULL | NULL]} ...])
```

NOTE: The notion of the base table specifies the named table, which exists in its own right. Besides base tables, there are also some special kinds of tables such as temporary tables and views (see Chapter 5 and Chapter 9, respectively).

table_name is the name of the created base table. The maximum number of tables per database is limited by the number of objects in the database (there can be over 2 billion objects in a database, including tables, views, stored procedures, triggers, rules, defaults, and constraints). **col_name1, col_name2,...** are the names of the table columns. The maximum number of columns per base table is 1,024. **type1, type2,...** are data types of corresponding columns (see Chapter 3). The maximum total length of all the columns in a table (in bytes) is 8,060.

NOTE: The name of a database object can generally contain four parts in the form:
[server_name.[db_name.[owner_name.]]]object_name
object_name is the name of the database object. **owner_name** is the name of the creator of the object. **server_name** and **db_name** are names of the server and database to which the database object belongs. Table names, combined with the owner name, must be unique within the database. Similarly, column names must be unique in the table.

The first column-level constraint that will be discussed in this book is the existence and nonexistence of null values within a column. If the NOT NULL is specified, the assignment of null values for the column is not allowed. (In that case, the column may not contain nulls, and if there is a null value to be inserted, SQL Server returns an error message.)

The privilege to create a table in a database, immediately after the creation of the database, is implicitly granted to the system administrator and the database owner. After that, the system administrator and the database owner can grant the table privilege to other users by using the GRANT CREATE TABLE statement. (Granting and revoking table privileges is discussed in detail in Chapter 12.)

The creator of a table must not be its owner. This means, if the table is created in the form **owner_name.table_name** and the owner name is not identical to the current user, the table owner will be the user with **owner_name**. Similarly, a table created with the CREATE TABLE statement must not belong to the current database, if some other (existing) database name, together with the owner name, is specified as the prefix of the table name.

Temporary tables are a special kind of base table. They are stored in the **tempdb** database and are automatically dropped at the end of the session. The properties of temporary tables and examples concerning them are given at the end of Chapter 5.

Example 4.3 shows the creation of all tables of the sample database. (The sample database should be the current database.)

▼ EXAMPLE 4.3

```
CREATE TABLE employee  (emp_no INTEGER NOT NULL,
                  emp_fname CHAR(20) NOT NULL,
                  emp_lname CHAR(20) NOT NULL,
                  dept_no CHAR(4) NULL)
CREATE TABLE department(dept_no CHAR(4) NOT NULL,
                  dept_name CHAR(25) NOT NULL,
                  location CHAR(30) NULL)
CREATE TABLE project   (project_no CHAR(4) NOT NULL,
                  project_name CHAR(15) NOT NULL,
                  budget FLOAT NULL)
CREATE TABLE works_on  (emp_no INTEGER NOT NULL,
                  project_no CHAR(4) NOT NULL,
```

```
job CHAR (15) NULL,
enter_date DATETIME NULL)
```

CREATE TABLE—The Enhanced Form

The enhanced form of the CREATE TABLE statement has the following syntax:

```
CREATE TABLE table_name
  col_name1 type1 [DEFAULT {expression1 | NULL }
      [ [IDENTITY [(init_value, incr)]] [NOT NULL | NULL] [column-constraint]
        { [, col_name2 type2 [DEFAULT {expression1 | NULL }
    [ [IDENTITY [(init_value, incr)]] [NOT  NULL | NULL] [column-constraint]] }...
      table-constraints
[COLLATE <collation_name>]
```

The DEFAULT clause specifies the default value of the column—that is, whenever a new row is inserted into the table, the default value for the particular column will be used if there is no value specified for it. A constant value, such as the system functions USER, CURRENT_USER, SESSION_USER, SYSTEM_USER, CURRENT_TIMESTAMP, and NULL, among others, can be used as the default values.

A column with the IDENTITY property allows only integer values, which are usually implicitly assigned by the system. Each value, which should be inserted in the column, is calculated by incrementing the last inserted value of the column. Therefore, the definition of a column with the IDENTITY property contains (implicitly or explicitly) an initial value and an increment. (The default values for the initial value and the increment are both 1.)

NOTE: Because SQL Server generates the values with the IDENTITY property, these values are always different, even when multiple users are adding rows at the same time. This feature is very useful in a multiuser environment, where it is quite difficult for an ordinary program to generate unique numeric values (see Example 5.55).

The following restrictions apply to the IDENTITY property:

- The column must be numeric—that is, of type INTEGER, SMALLINT, TINYINT, NUMERIC, or DECIMAL. (If the column is of the type NUMERIC or DECIMAL, the number of digits to the right of the decimal point must be 0.)
- There can be at most one column in the table with the IDENTITY property.
- The column with this property does not allow null values.

The IDENTITY property can be used with the CREATE TABLE, the ALTER TABLE, and the SELECT statements. The use of this property with the SELECT statement will be discussed in the next chapter.

CREATE TABLE and Declarative Integrity Constraints

One of the most important features that a DBMS must provide is a way of maintaining the integrity of data. The constraints, which are used to check the modification or insertion of data, are called *integrity constraints*. The task of maintaining integrity constraints can be handled by the user in application programs or by the DBMS. The most important benefits of handling integrity constraints by the DBMS are:

- Increased reliability of data
- Reduced programming time
- Simple maintenance

Using the DBMS to define integrity constraints increases the reliability of data because there is no possibility that the integrity constraints can be forgotten by a programmer. (If an integrity constraint is handled by application programs, *all* programs concerning the constraint must include the corresponding code. If the code is omitted in one application program, the consistency of data is compromised.)

An integrity constraint not handled by the DBMS must be defined in every application program that uses the data involved in the constraint. In contrast, the same integrity constraint must be defined only once if it is to be handled by the DBMS. Additionally, application-enforced constraints are usually more complex to code than are database-enforced constraints.

If an integrity constraint is handled by the DBMS, the modification of the structure of the constraint must be handled only once, in the DBMS. The modification of a structure in application programs requires the modification of every program that involves the corresponding code.

There are two groups of integrity constraints handled by a DBMS:

- Declarative integrity constraints
- Procedural integrity constraints that are handled by triggers (for the definition of triggers, see Chapter 13)

The declarative constraints are defined using the DDL statements CREATE TABLE and ALTER TABLE. They can be column-level constraints or table-level constraints. Column-level constraints, together with the data type and other column properties, are placed within the declaration of the column, while table-level constraints are always defined at the end of the CREATE TABLE or ALTER TABLE statement, after the definition of all columns (see Examples 4.5 and 4.6).

> ***NOTE:*** There is only one difference between column-level constraints and table-level constraints: a column-level constraint can be applied only upon one column, while a table-level constraint can cover more than one column of a table (see Example 4.7).

Each declarative constraint has a name. The name of the constraint can be explicitly assigned using the CONSTRAINT option in the CREATE TABLE statement or the ALTER TABLE statement. If the CONSTRAINT option is omitted, SQL Server assigns an implicit name for the constraint.

NOTE: Using explicit constraint names is strongly recommended, although they are optional. The search for an integrity constraint can be greatly enhanced if an explicit name for a constraint is used.

All declarative constraints can be categorized into five groups:

- Default values
- Uniqueness
- Definition of the primary keys
- Definition of the foreign keys and the referential constraints
- CHECK clause

The definition of the default value using the DEFAULT option has been shown earlier in this chapter. All other constraints are described in detail in the following sections.

The UNIQUE Clause

Sometimes more than one column or group of columns of the table have unique values and therefore can be used as the primary key. All columns or groups of columns that qualify to be primary keys are called *candidate keys*. Each candidate key is defined using the UNIQUE clause in the CREATE TABLE or the ALTER TABLE statement.

The UNIQUE clause has the following form:

```
[CONSTRAINT c_name]
   UNIQUE [CLUSTERED | NONCLUSTERED] (col_name1 [{, col_name2} ...])
```

The CONSTRAINT option in the UNIQUE clause assigns an explicit name to the candidate key. The option CLUSTERED or NONCLUSTERED relates to the fact that SQL Server always generates an index for each candidate key of a table. The index can be clustered—that is, the physical order of rows is specified using the indexed order of the column values. If the order is not specified, the index is nonclustered (see also Chapter 10). **col_name1, col_name2**,... are column names that build the candidate key. (The maximum number of columns per candidate key is 16.)

Example 4.4 shows the use of the UNIQUE clause.

▼ EXAMPLE 4.4

```
CREATE TABLE on_sale
   (stor_id INTEGER NULL,
```

```
name CHAR(20) NULL,
CONSTRAINT storid_uniq UNIQUE (stor_id))
```

Each value of the column **stor_id** of the table **on_sale** is unique, including the null value. (Just as with any other value with a UNIQUE constraint, if null values are allowed on a column with a UNIQUE constraint, there can be at most one row with the null value.) If an existing value should be inserted into the column **stor_id**, SQL Server rejects it. The explicit name of the constraint that is defined in Example 4.4 is **storid_uniq**.

The PRIMARY KEY Clause

The *primary key* of a table is a column or group of columns whose values are different in every row. Each primary key is defined using the PRIMARY KEY clause in the CREATE TABLE or the ALTER TABLE statement.

The PRIMARY KEY clause has the following form:

```
[CONSTRAINT c_name]
 PRIMARY KEY [CLUSTERED | NONCLUSTERED] (col_name1 [{,col_name2} ...])
```

All options of the PRIMARY KEY clause have the same meaning as the corresponding options with the same name in the UNIQUE clause. In contrast to UNIQUE, the PRIMARY KEY column must be NOT NULL, and its default value is CLUSTERED.

▼ EXAMPLE 4.5

```
CREATE TABLE employee  (emp_no INTEGER NOT NULL,
           emp_fname CHAR(20) NOT NULL,
           emp_lname CHAR(20) NOT NULL,
           dept_no CHAR(4) NULL,
          CONSTRAINT prim_empl PRIMARY KEY (emp_no))
```

The **employee** table is re-created and its primary key defined in Example 4.5. The primary key of the table is specified using the declarative integrity constraint named **prim_empl**. This integrity constraint is a table-level constraint and is specified after the definition of all columns of the table **employee**.

Example 4.6 is equivalent to Example 4.5 except for the specification of the primary key of the **employee** table as a column-level constraint.

▼ EXAMPLE 4.6

```
CREATE TABLE employee
   (emp_no INTEGER NOT NULL CONSTRAINT prim_empl PRIMARY KEY,
    emp_fname CHAR(20) NOT NULL,
    emp_lname CHAR(20) NOT NULL,
    dept_no CHAR(4) NULL)
```

The FOREIGN KEY Clause

A *foreign key* is a column or group of columns in one table that contain(s) values that match the PRIMARY KEY values in the same or another table. Each foreign key is defined using the FOREIGN KEY clause combined with the REFERENCES clause.

The FOREIGN KEY clause has the following form:

```
[CONSTRAINT c_name]
    [[FOREIGN KEY] (col_name1 [{, col_name2} ...]])
    REFERENCES table_name (col_name3 [{, col_name4} ...])
        [ON DELETE {CASCADE | NO ACTION}]
        [ON UPDATE {CASCADE | NO ACTION}]
```

The FOREIGN KEY clause defines all columns explicitly that belong to the foreign key. The REFERENCES clause specifies the table name with all columns that build the corresponding PRIMARY KEY. The number and the data types of the columns in the FOREIGN KEY clause must match the number and the corresponding data types of columns in the REFERENCES clause (and, of course, both of these must match the number and data types of the columns in the PRIMARY KEY of the referenced table).

The table that contains the foreign key is called the *referencing table*, and the table that contains the corresponding primary key is called the *parent table* or *referenced table*.

▼ EXAMPLE 4.7

```
CREATE TABLE works_on (emp_no INTEGER NOT NULL,
        project_no CHAR(4) NOT NULL,
         job CHAR (15) NULL,
         enter_date DATETIME NULL,
         CONSTRAINT prim_works PRIMARY KEY(emp_no, project_no),
         CONSTRAINT foreign_works FOREIGN KEY(emp_no)
            REFERENCES employee (emp_no))
```

The **works_on** table in Example 4.7 is specified with two declarative integrity constraints: **prim_works** and **foreign_works**. Both constraints are table-level constraints, where the former specifies the primary key and the latter the foreign key of the **works_on** table. Further, the constraint **foreign_works** specifies the **employee** table as the parent table and its **emp_no** column as the corresponding primary key of the column with the same name in the referencing **works_on** table.

The FOREIGN KEY clause can be omitted if the foreign key is defined as a column-level constraint, because the column being constrained is the implicit column "list" of the FOREIGN KEY, and the keyword REFERENCES is sufficient to indicate what kind of constraint this is. The maximum number of FOREIGN KEY constraints in a table is 63.

A definition of the foreign keys in tables of a database imposes the specification of another important integrity constraint: the referential constraint, described next.

Referential Constraints

A *referential constraint* enforces insert and update rules for the tables with the foreign key and the corresponding primary key constraint. Examples 4.6 and 4.7 specify two such constraints: **prim_emp** and **foreign_works**. The REFERENCES clause in Example 4.7 determines the **employee** table as the parent table.

There are four cases in which the modification of the values in the foreign key or in the primary key can cause problems. All these cases will be shown using the sample database. The first two cases affect modifications of the referencing table, while the last two concern modifications of the parent table.

Case 1

Insert a new row into the **works_on** table with the employee number 11111.

The insertion of the new row in the referencing table **works_on** introduces a new employee number for which there is no matching employee in the parent table **employee**. If the referential constraint for both tables is specified as is done in Examples 4.6 and 4.7, SQL Server rejects the insertion of a new row. The corresponding Transact-SQL statement is:

```
INSERT INTO works_on (emp_no, ...)
  VALUES (11111, ...)
```

Case 2

Modify the employee number 10102 in all rows of the **works_on** table. The new number is 11111.

In Case 2, the existing value of the foreign key in the **works_on** table should be replaced using the new value, for which there is no matching value in the parent table **employee**. If the referential constraint for both tables is specified as is done in Examples 4.6 and 4.7, SQL Server rejects the modification of the rows in the **works_on** table. The corresponding Transact-SQL statement is:

```
UPDATE works_on
  SET emp_no = 11111 WHERE emp_no = 10102
```

Case 3

Modify the employee number 10102 in the corresponding row of the **employee** table. The new number is 22222.

In Case 3, the existing value of the primary key in the parent table and the foreign key of the referencing table is modified only in the parent table. The values in the referencing table are unchanged. Therefore, SQL Server rejects the modification of the row with the employee number 10102 in the **employee** table. Referential integrity requires that no rows in the referencing table (the one with the FOREIGN KEY clause) can exist unless a corresponding row in the referenced table (the one with the PRIMARY KEY clause) also exists. Otherwise, the rows in the referenced table would be "orphaned." If the modification described above were permitted, then rows in the **works_on** table having the employee number 10102 would be orphaned; therefore, SQL Server would reject it. The corresponding Transact-SQL statement is:

```
UPDATE employee
  SET emp_no = 22222 WHERE emp_no = 10102
```

Case 4

Delete the row of the **employee** table with the employee number 10102.

Case 4 is similar to Case 3. The deletion would remove the employee for which matching rows exist in the referencing table.

Example 4.8 shows the definition of tables of the sample database with all existing primary key and foreign key constraints.

▼ EXAMPLE 4.8

```
CREATE TABLE department(dept_no CHAR(4) NOT NULL,
              dept_name CHAR(25) NOT NULL,
              location CHAR(30) NULL,
              CONSTRAINT prim_dept PRIMARY KEY (dept_no))
CREATE TABLE employee  (emp_no INTEGER NOT NULL,
         emp_fname CHAR(20) NOT NULL,
         emp_lname CHAR(20) NOT NULL,
         dept_no CHAR(4) NULL,
         CONSTRAINT prim_emp PRIMARY KEY (emp_no),
         CONSTRAINT foreign_emp FOREIGN KEY(dept_no) REFERENCES
department(dept_no))
CREATE TABLE project   (project_no CHAR(4) NOT NULL,
         project_name CHAR(15) NOT NULL,
         budget FLOAT NULL,
        CONSTRAINT prim_proj PRIMARY KEY (project_no))
CREATE TABLE works_on  (emp_no INTEGER NOT NULL,
 project_no CHAR(4) NOT NULL,
 job CHAR (15) NULL,
 enter_date DATETIME NULL,
 CONSTRAINT prim_works PRIMARY KEY(emp_no, project_no),
 CONSTRAINT foreign1_works FOREIGN KEY(emp_no) REFERENCES
employee(emp_no),
 CONSTRAINT foreign2_works FOREIGN KEY(project_no) REFERENCES
project(project_no))
```

The ON DELETE and ON UPDATE Options

SQL Server 2000 can now react differently if the values of the primary key of a table should be modified or deleted. If you try to update values of a foreign key, and these modifications result in inconsistencies in the corresponding primary key (see Case 1 and Case 2 in the previous section), the database system will always reject the modification and will display a message similar to the following:

Server: Msg 547, Level 16, State 1, Line 1

UPDATE statement conflicted with COLUMN FOREIGN KEY constraint 'FKemployee'. The conflict occurred in database 'sample', table 'employee', column 'dept_no'. The statement has been terminated.

But, if you try to modify the values of a primary key, and these modifications result in inconsistencies in the corresponding foreign key (see Case 3 and Case 4 in the previous section), a database system could react very flexibly. Generally, there are four options for how a database system can react:

- NO ACTION (or RESTRICT)
- CASCADE
- SET NULL
- SET DEFAULT

The NO ACTION option allows you to modify (i.e., update or delete) only those values of the parent table that do not have any corresponding values in the foreign key of the referencing table. This is the only option that was supported by previous versions of SQL Server. The CASCADE option allows you to modify (i.e., update or delete) all values of the parent table. If this option is specified, a row is updated (i.e., deleted) from the referencing table if the corresponding value in the primary key has been updated or the whole row with that value has been deleted from the parent table. This is the new option supported by SQL Server 2000.

The SET NULL option allows you again to update or delete all values of the parent table. If you want to update a value of the parent table and this modification would lead to data inconsistencies in the referencing table, the database system sets all corresponding values in the foreign key of the referencing table to NULL. Similarly, if you want to delete the row in the parent table and the deletion of the value in the primary key would lead to data inconsistencies, the database system sets all corresponding values in the foreign key to NULL. That way, all data inconsistencies are omitted. The SET DEFAULT option is analogous to the SET NULL option, with one exception: All corresponding values in the foreign key are set to a default value. (Obviously, the default value must still exist in the primary key of the parent table after modification.)

NOTE: SQL Server 2000 does not support the last two alternatives.

Example 4.9 shows the use of the ON DELETE and ON UPDATE options.

▼ EXAMPLE 4.9

```
CREATE TABLE works_on1
(emp_no INTEGER NOT NULL,
 project_no CHAR(4) NOT NULL,
 job CHAR (15) NULL,
 enter_date DATETIME NULL,
 CONSTRAINT prim_works1 PRIMARY KEY(emp_no, project_no),
 CONSTRAINT foreign1_works1 FOREIGN KEY(emp_no)
    REFERENCES employee(emp_no) ON DELETE CASCADE,
 CONSTRAINT foreign2_works1 FOREIGN KEY(project_no)
    REFERENCES project(project_no) ON UPDATE CASCADE)
```

Example 4.9 shows the creation of the **works_on1** table that uses the ON DELETE CASCADE and ON UPDATE CASCADE options. If you load the **works_on1** table with the content shown in Figure 1-4, each deletion of a row in the **employee** table will cause the deletion of all rows in the **works_on1** table that have the corresponding value in the **emp_no** column. Similarly, each update of a value in the **project_no** column of the **project** table will cause the same modification on all corresponding values in the **project_no** column of the **works_on1** table.

The CHECK Clause

The *check constraint* specifies conditions for the data inserted into a column. Each row inserted into a table or each value updating the value of the column must meet these conditions. The CHECK clause is used to specify check constraints. This clause can be defined in the CREATE TABLE or the ALTER TABLE statement. The syntax of the CHECK clause is:

```
[CONSTRAINT c_name]
   CHECK [NOT FOR REPLICATION] expression
```

The "expression" must evaluate to a Boolean value (TRUE or FALSE) and can reference any columns in the current table (or just the current column if specified as a column-level constraint), but no other tables. The CHECK clause is not enforced during a replication of the data if the option NOT FOR REPLICATION exists. (A database, or a part of it, is said to be replicated if it is stored at more than one site. Replication can be used to enhance the availability of data. Chapter 25 describes data replication.)

▼ EXAMPLE 4.10

```
CREATE TABLE customer
   (cust_no INTEGER NOT NULL,
   cust_group CHAR(3) NULL,
   CHECK (cust_group IN ('c1', 'c2', 'c10')))
```

The **customer** table that is created in Example 4.10 contains the **cust_group** column with the corresponding check constraint. SQL Server returns an error if the **cust_group** column, after a modification of its existing values or after the insertion of a new row, would contain a value different from the values in the set ('c1', 'c2', 'c10').

Creating Other Database Objects

The CREATE DEFAULT statement creates a default value. The created default is then assigned (or "bound") to a column, and if during the insertion of new rows no value is explicitly specified for the column, the column will be assigned the default value rather than NULL. Establishing (or binding) the default value for a particular column must be done using the system procedure **sp_bindefault**. The preferred method of establishing default values for columns is to specify them in the DEFAULT clause of the CREATE DATABASE statement, as discussed previously.

A *rule* is a condition that is defined for the values of a column or for a user-defined data type. Rules are created using the CREATE RULE statement. After its creation, the rule must be bound to a column or a user-defined data type using the system procedure **sp_bindrule**. Both of the statements CREATE DEFAULT and CREATE RULE will be discussed in detail later in the chapter.

The database contains not only base tables that exist in their own right but also *views*, which are virtual tables. The data of a base table exists physically—that is, it is stored on a disk—while a view is derived from one or more base tables. The CREATE VIEW statement creates a new view from one or more existing tables (or views) using a SELECT statement, which is an inseparable part of the CREATE VIEW statement. Since the creation of a view always contains a data manipulation statement, the CREATE VIEW statement belongs to the DML rather than to the DDL. For this reason, the creation and removal of views is discussed in Chapter 10, after the presentation of all Transact-SQL statements for data modification.

The CREATE INDEX statement creates a new *index* on a specified table. The indices are primarily used to allow efficient access to the data stored on a disk. The existence of an index can greatly improve the access to data. Indices, together with the CREATE INDEX statement, are discussed in detail in Chapter 9.

A *stored procedure* is an additional database object that can be created using the corresponding CREATE PROCEDURE statement. (A stored procedure is a special kind of sequence of statements written in Transact-SQL, using the SQL language and SQL extensions. Chapter 8 describes stored procedures in detail.)

A *trigger* is a database object that specifies an action as a result of an operation. This means, when a particular data-modifying action (modification, insertion, or deletion) occurs on a particular table, SQL Server automatically invokes one or more additional action(s). The CREATE TRIGGER statement creates a new trigger. Triggers are described in detail in Chapter 13.

Since the release of SQL Server 6.5, the option of creating a schema using the CREATE SCHEMA statement has been available. A *schema* is a database object that includes statements for creation of tables, views, and user privileges. (You can think of a schema as a construct that collects together several tables, corresponding views, and user privileges.)

NOTE: The notion of *schema* was originally defined in 1986 in the SQL standard. This standard states that all data definition statements concerning a database *must* be defined inside one or more schemas. The SQL89 standard modified this requirement into an option: every single data definition statement can now stand for itself or can be grouped together with some other such statements to build a schema.

▼ EXAMPLE 4.11

```
CREATE SCHEMA AUTHORIZATION pete
CREATE TABLE salesman
   (no INT NOT NULL UNIQUE,
    fname CHAR(20) NOT NULL,
    lname CHAR(20) NOT NULL,
    product_no CHAR(10))
CREATE TABLE product
     (product_no CHAR(10) NOT NULL UNIQUE,
     product_name CHAR(20) NULL,
      price MONEY NULL)
CREATE VIEW product_info
    AS SELECT product_no, product_name
        FROM product
```

Example 4.11 creates a schema that contains two tables, **salesman** and **product,** and one view, **product_info**. The schema is owned by the user **pete**.

NOTE: SQL Server 2000 supports the ANSI/ISO information schema. To understand what the information schema is, you need to understand the notion of a *catalog*. A catalog is a named collection of schemas. Every catalog contains the schema named INFORMATION_SCHEMA, which contains the views of the system tables. (The information schema is discussed in detail together with the SQL Server system tables in Chapter 11.)

Integrity Constraints and Domains

A *domain* is the set of all possible legitimate values that columns of a table may contain. Almost all DBMSs use data types to define the set of possible values for a column. This method of enforcing "domain integrity" is incomplete, as can be seen from the following example.

The **person** table has a column, **zip**, that specifies the ZIP code of the city in which the person lives. This column can be defined using SMALLINT or CHAR(5) data types. The definition with the SMALLINT data type is inaccurate, because the SMALLINT data type contains all positive and negative values between $-2^{15}-1$ and 2^{15}. The definition of a ZIP code using the CHAR(5) is even more inaccurate, because all characters and special signs can also be used in such a case. Therefore, for an accurate definition of ZIP codes, we need to define an interval of positive integers between 00601 and 99950 and assign it to the column **zip**.

CHECK constraints (defined in the CREATE TABLE or ALTER TABLE statement) can enforce more precise domain integrity because their expressions are flexible, and they are always enforced when the column is inserted or modified.

SQL Server provides support for domains with three different mechanisms:

- User-defined data types
- Defaults
- Rules

User-Defined Data Types

A user-defined data type is a special kind of data type that is defined by users using the existing base data types. The system procedure **sp_addtype** is used to create a new user-defined data type. After the execution of the **sp_addtype** procedure, SQL Server inserts a new row into the system table **systypes**.

The system procedure **sp_addtype** has the following syntax:

```
sp_addtype type_name data_type [,null_type]
```

type_name is the name of the new user-defined data type that must be unique in the current database. **data_type** is a Transact-SQL base data type on which the user-defined data type is based. **length** must be specified for all character-based data types. **null_type** specifies how the new user-defined data type handles null values (NULL or NOT NULL).

Example 4.12 shows the first step in the creation of the user-defined data type **zip**.

▼ EXAMPLE 4.12

```
sp_addtype zip, INTEGER, NULL
```

An existing user-defined data type can be used with the CREATE TABLE statement to define one or more columns in a database. The use of the system procedure

sp_addtype is only the first step in the creation of a domain. Using the Transact-SQL statements CREATE DEFAULT and CREATE RULE and the system procedures **sp_bindefault** and **sp_bindrule**, it is possible to further define properties for an existing user-defined data type. All these statements and system procedures are described in the following two sections.

The system procedure **sp_droptype** removes an existing user-defined data type.

Creation of Default Values

SQL Server provides two methods for declaring default values for a column of a table. The first method uses the DEFAULT clause in the CREATE TABLE or ALTER TABLE statement and is described at the beginning of this chapter. The second method uses the CREATE DEFAULT statement and the **sp_bindefault** system procedure.

The Transact-SQL statement declares a general default value, which subsequently can be bound to a column of a table in a current database. The syntax of this statement is:

```
CREATE DEFAULT default_name
   AS expression
```

The system procedure **sp_bindefault** is used to bind the defined default value to specific columns.

> ***NOTE:*** After the creation of a database, only the system administrator and the database owner have the privilege of creating defaults. They can then grant this privilege to other users using the GRANT CREATE DEFAULT statement. (Granting and revoking of privileges is discussed in detail in Chapter 12.)

▼ EXAMPLE 4.13

```
CREATE DEFAULT zip_default AS 94710
GO
sp_bindefault 'zip_default', 'zip'
```

The CREATE DEFAULT statement in Example 4.13 first declares the default value (94710) for a default named **zip_default**. After that, the system procedure **sp_bindefault** is used to bind this default value to the user-defined data type **zip** (which was created in Example 4.12). (**sp_bindefault** also contains the option FUTUREONLY, which leaves existing columns with this user-defined data type unchanged.)

> ***NOTE:*** The CREATE DEFAULT statement is a SQL Server extension to the SQL standard. The SQL standard as well as SQL Server support another integrity constraint clause called DEFAULT, which can be also used to define the default value of a column. You should use the standardized DEFAULT clause instead of the CREATE RULE statement. (The DEFAULT clause is described earlier in this chapter.)

The Transact-SQL statement DROP DEFAULT removes an existing default, while the system procedure **sp_unbindefault** removes the connection between the default and the data type or column.

Rules

In the previous two sections we described two necessary steps to define a new domain and to bind it to one or more columns of the current database. But if we use only those two steps, the new domain will have exactly the same set of possible data values as the underlying base data type (in this case, INTEGER).

Often it is necessary to restrict the values of a user-defined data type to a specific set of values. (For example, ZIP codes in the United States can be between 00601 and 99950.) This can be done using rules. The Transact-SQL statement:

```
CREATE RULE rule AS condition
```

creates a rule that can be bound to a column or a user-defined data type to restrict their values. **condition** can be any expression that is valid in a WHERE clause of a SELECT statement (SELECT statements will be covered in depth in Chapters 5 and 6). Additionally, **condition** contains a variable, which has a prefix @. The variable corresponds to the value that is inserted in the column using the INSERT or the UPDATE statement.

NOTE: The CREATE RULE statement is a SQL Server extension to the SQL standard. The SQL standard as well as SQL Server support another integrity constraint clause called CHECK, which can be also used to define rules. You should use the CHECK clause instead of the CREATE RULE statement, because first, it is standardized and second, SQL Server can use this clause during the optimization of corresponding queries. (The CHECK clause is explained earlier in this chapter.)

After the creation of a database, only the system administrator and the database owner have the privilege of creating rules. They can then grant this privilege to other users using the GRANT CREATE RULE statement.

NOTE: The CREATE RULE statement cannot be combined with other Transact-SQL statements in a single group of statements.

▼ EXAMPLE 4.14

```
CREATE RULE zip_rule
   AS @number > 600 and @number < 99951
```

After its definition, the rule has to be bound to a column or to a user-defined data type. The system procedure **sp_bindrule** provides this binding.

▼ EXAMPLE 4.15

```
sp_bindrule zip_rule, 'zip'
```

The system procedure **sp_bindrule** in Example 4.15 binds the rule **zip_rule** (Example 4.13) to the user-defined data type **zip** (Example 4.12). Hence, the domain of the data type **zip** is restricted with this step to the range between 00601 and 99950. (The system procedure **sp_bindrule** also contains the option FUTUREONLY, which leaves existing bindings between a column and the rule unchanged.)

The Transact-SQL statement DROP RULE removes an existing rule, while the system procedure **sp_unbindrule** unbinds an existing rule from a column or a user-defined data type in the current database.

The user-defined data type can now be used for the definition of one or more columns in the current database; in Example 4.16, it is used in the CREATE TABLE statement.

▼ EXAMPLE 4.16

```
CREATE TABLE address
  (city CHAR(25) NOT NULL,
   zip_code ZIP,
   street CHAR(30) NULL)
```

MODIFYING DATABASE OBJECTS

SQL Server supports changing the structure of the following database objects:

- Database
- Table
- Stored procedure
- View
- Trigger

Changing the database schema and table schema is described here, while the schema modification of the last three database objects is described in Chapters 8, 9, and 13, respectively.

Altering a Database

The ALTER DATABASE statement changes the physical structure of a database. This statement has the following form:

```
ALTER DATABASE db_name
   ADD FILE file_spec1 [TO FILEGROUP group_name1]
   | ADD LOG FILE file_spec2
   | DROP FILE 'file_name'
   | MODIFY FILE (NAME = old_name, NEWNAME = new_name ...)
   | CREATE FILEGROUP group_name2 | DROP FILEGROUP filegroup_name3
   | SET option_specifications  [ WITH terminations]
```

This statement allows the creation and the modification of database files, transaction log files, and/or file groups. The three clauses ADD FILE, MODIFY FILE, and DROP FILE specify the creation of a new file, the modification of an existing file, and the deletion of an existing file, respectively. Additionally, a new file can be assigned to an existing file group using the TO FILEGROUP option.

The CREATE FILEGROUP clause creates a new file group, while DELETE FILEGROUP removes an existing file group from the system. There is also a clause concerning transaction logs. The ADD LOG FILE clause creates a new transaction log and adds it to the existing transaction logs of the database.

file_spec1, file_spec2,... represent file specifications, which include further options such as the logical name and the physical name of the file (see Example 4.17).

▼ EXAMPLE 4.17

```
USE master
GO
ALTER DATABASE projects
ADD FILE (NAME=projects_dat1,
    FILENAME = 'C:\MSSQL7\DATA\projects1.mdf',
    SIZE = 10,
    MAXSIZE = 100,
    FILEGROWTH = 5)
```

The ALTER DATABASE statement in Example 4.17 adds a new file to store the data of the **projects** database.

SQL Server 2000 supports the SET clause in the ALTER DATABASE statement. Using this clause, you can set several different options. All options that you can set are divided into five groups:

- State options
- Cursor options
- Auto options
- SQL options
- Recovery options

The state options control:

- User access to the database (SINGLE_USER, RESTRICTED_USER, or MULTI_USER)
- The status of the database (ONLINE or OFFLINE)
- The read/write modus (READ_ONLY or READ_WRITE)

The cursor options control the way cursors are used. (Cursors allow processing data one row at a time and are used with stored procedures. For more information on stored procedures, see Chapter 8.) The auto options control the art of the database shutdown (the option AUTO_CLOSE) and how index statistics are built (the options AUTO_CREATE_STATISTICS and AUTO_UPDATE_STATISTICS). Index statistics are described in detail in Chapter 9.

The SQL options control the ANSI compliance of the database and its objects. All SQL options can be edited using the DATABASEPROPERTYEX() function and modified using the **sp_dboption** system procedure. The function and the system procedure are described in detail in Chapter 18. The recovery options FULL, BULK-LOGGED, and SIMPLE influence the art of database recovery. (For more information on this topic, see Chapter 20.)

The system procedure **sp_renamedb** modifies the name of an existing database.

Altering a Table—A Basic Form

The ALTER TABLE statement modifies the schema of a table. SQL Server allows addition, removal, and modification of one or more columns from an existing table. The ALTER TABLE statement has the following basic form:

```
ALTER TABLE table_name
   ADD col_name type [NULL | IDENTITY]
   [, col_name type [NULL | IDENTITY] ...]
   DROP COLUMN col_name [{, col_name} ...]
   ALTER COLUMN col_name type {NULL | IDENTITY}
   [{, col_name type NULL | IDENTITY} ...]
```

The owner of a table, the system administrator, and the database owner have the privilege of modifying the schema of the table.

▼ EXAMPLE 4.18

```
ALTER TABLE employee
   ADD telephone_no CHAR(12) NULL
```

The ALTER TABLE statement in Example 4.18 adds the column **telephone_no** to the **employee** table. Note that new columns must either be nullable or must have a default constraint (this becomes obvious when you think about how this new column for existing rows can be populated).

The DROP COLUMN clause provides the ability to drop an existing column of the table.

▼ EXAMPLE 4.19

```
ALTER TABLE employee
   DROP COLUMN telephone_no
```

The ALTER TABLE statement in Example 4.19 removes the **telephone_no** column, which was added to the **employee** table in Example 4.18.

SQL Server also supports an ALTER COLUMN clause. This clause allows for modification of properties of an existing column.

▼ EXAMPLE 4.20

```
ALTER TABLE department
   ALTER COLUMN location CHAR(25) NOT NULL
```

The ALTER TABLE statement in Example 4.20 changes the previous properties of the **location** column (CHAR(30), nullable) of the **department** table.

Altering a Table—Enhanced Form

The enhanced form of the CREATE TABLE statement specifies the creation or modification of integrity constraints. Its syntax is:

```
ALTER TABLE table_name
   [WITH CHECK | NOCHECK]
   ADD col_name type [{NULL | IDENTITY}]
   [{, col_name type NULL | IDENTITY} ...]
   DROP COLUMN col_name [{, col_name} ...]
   ALTER COLUMN col_name type {NULL | IDENTITY}
   [{, col_name type NULL | IDENTITY} ...]
   ADD table_constraint
   DROP table_constraint
```

Hence, there are three enhancements:

- Adding a new integrity constraint
- Dropping an existing integrity constraint
- The CHECK or NOCHECK option

▼ EXAMPLE 4.21

```
CREATE TABLE sales
   (order_no INTEGER NOT NULL PRIMARY KEY,
   order_date DATETIME NOT NULL,
   ship_date DATETIME NOT NULL)
ALTER TABLE sales
   ADD CONSTRAINT order_check CHECK(order_date <= ship_date)
```

The first Transact-SQL statement in Example 4.21 creates the **sales** table with two columns of the data type DATETIME: **order_date** and **ship_date**. The subsequent ALTER TABLE statement defines an integrity constraint named **order_check**, which compares both of the values and displays an error message if the shipping date is earlier than the order date.

Example 4.22 shows the use of the ALTER TABLE statement to define the primary key and the foreign key of a table.

▼ EXAMPLE 4.22

```
ALTER TABLE product
   ADD CONSTRAINT prim_prod PRIMARY KEY(product_no)
ALTER TABLE salesman
     ADD CONSTRAINT prim_sales PRIMARY KEY (no),
     CONSTRAINT foreign_sales FOREIGN KEY(product_no)
     REFERENCES product
```

The first ALTER TABLE statement in Example 4.22 declares the primary key for the **product** table (Example 4.11). The second statement defines the primary and foreign keys of the **salesman** table.

Each declarative integrity constraint can be removed using the DROP clause of the ALTER TABLE statement.

▼ EXAMPLE 4.23

```
ALTER TABLE sales
DROP CONSTRAINT order_check
```

The ALTER TABLE statement in Example 4.23 drops the CHECK constraint **order_check**, defined in Example 4.21.

As previously stated, an integrity constraint always has a name that can be explicitly declared using the CONSTRAINT option or implicitly declared by the system. The name of all the declared constraints for a table can be viewed using the system procedure **sp_helpconstraint**.

Example 4.24 shows the use of the system procedure **sp_helpconstraint**.

▼ EXAMPLE 4.24

```
sp_helpconstraint employee
```

The result is

Object Name	constraint_type	constraint_name	delete_action	update_action	constraint_keys
employee	PRIMARY KEY (clustered)	prim_empl	(N/A)	(N/A)	emp_no

Table is referenced by

projects.dbo.works_on: foreign_works

A constraint that is created with the WITH CHECK option is enforced during future insert and update operations. Additionally, the existing values in the column(s) are checked against the constraint. Otherwise, a constraint that is created with the WITH NOCHECK constraint is disabled in both cases. Both options can be applied only with the CHECK and the FOREIGN KEY constraints.

The system procedure **sp_rename** modifies the name of an existing table (and any other existing database object). Examples 4.25 and 4.26 show the use of this system procedure.

▼ EXAMPLE 4.25

```
sp_rename department, subdivision
```

The object 'department' was renamed to 'subdivision'.

▼ EXAMPLE 4.26

```
sp_rename "sales.order_no" , ordernumber
```

The column was renamed to 'ordernumber'.

Example 4.26 renames the **order_no** column in the **sales** table (Example 4.21). If the object to be renamed is a column in a table, the specification must be in the form **table.column**.

REMOVING DATABASE OBJECTS

All Transact-SQL statements to remove a database object have the general form

```
DROP object object_name
```

The statement

```
DROP DATABASE database1 {, database2 ...}
```

removes one or more databases. This means the database is dropped from system tables in the **master** database, and all of the operating system files that make up the database are deleted. As with any statement that modifies **master**, you should back up **master** immediately after executing the DROP DATABASE statement. Only the database owner or the system administrator can remove a database.

One or more tables can be removed from a database with the following statement:

```
DROP TABLE table_name1 {, table_name2 ...}
```

All data, indices, and triggers belonging to the removed table are also dropped. (In contrast, all views that are defined using the dropped table are not removed.) Only the table owner (or the database owner) can remove a table.

In addition to DATABASE and TABLE, **objects** in the DROP statement can be:

- DEFAULT
- RULE
- PROCEDURE
- INDEX
- VIEW
- TRIGGER
- SCHEMA
- STATISTICS

The statement DROP DEFAULT removes an existing default. Similarly, the statement DROP RULE drops a rule. The rest of the statements are described in different chapters: the DROP PROCEDURE statement in Chapter 8, the DROP VIEW statement in Chapter 10, the DROP INDEX statement in Chapter 9, and the DROP TRIGGER statement in Chapter 13. Finally, DROP STATISTICS corresponds to the UPDATE STATISTICS statement, which is described in Chapter 9.

CONCLUSION

SQL Server supports many data definition statements that create, alter, and remove database objects. The following database objects can be created and removed using the CREATE object and the DROP object statement, respectively:

- Database
- Table
- View
- Trigger
- Stored procedure

- Index
- Rule
- Default

A structure of the first five database objects in the above list can be altered using the ALTER **object** statement.

The Transact-SQL language provides four data manipulation statements: SELECT, INSERT, UPDATE, and DELETE. The next chapter is concerned with the simple form of the SELECT statement.

EXERCISES

▼ E.4.1

Using the CREATE DATABASE statement, create a new database named **test_db** with explicit specifications for database and transaction log files. The database file with the logical name **test_db_dat** is stored in the file C:\tmp\test_db.mdf, the initial size is 5MB, the maximum size is unlimited, and the file growth is 8 percent. The log file called **test_db_log** is stored in the file C:\tmp\test_db_log.ldf, the initial size is 2MB, the maximum size is 10MB, and the file growth is 500KB.

▼ E.4.2

Using the ALTER DATABASE statement, add a new log file to the **test_db** database. The log is stored in the file C:\tmp\emp_log.ldf and the initial size of the file is 2MB, with growth of 2MB and an unlimited maximum size.

▼ E.4.3

Using the ALTER DATABASE statement, change the file size of the created database to 10MB.

▼ E.4.4

In Example 4.3, there are some columns of the four created tables defined with the NOT NULL specification. For which column is this specification required and for which not?

▼ E.4.5

Why are the columns **dept_no** and **project_no** in Example 4.3 defined as CHAR-values (and not as numerical values)?

▼ E.4.6

Create the tables **customers** and **orders** with the following columns. (Do not declare the corresponding primary and foreign keys.)

Table customers:

customerid char(5) not null,
companyName varchar(40) not null,
contactName char(30) null,
address varchar(60) null,
city char(15) null,
phone char(24) null,
fax char(24) null

Table orders:

orderid integer not null,
customerid char(5) not null,
orderdate datetime null,
shippeddate datetime null,
freight money null,
shipname varchar(40) null,
shipaddress varchar(60) null,
quantity integer null

▼ E.4.7

Using the ALTER TABLE statement, add a new column named **shipregion** to the **orders** table. The fields should be nullable and contain integers.

▼ E.4.8

Using the ALTER TABLE statement, change the data type of the column **shipregion** from INTEGER to CHARACTER with length 8. The fields may contain null values.

▼ E.4.9

Delete the formerly created column **shipregion**.

▼ E.4.10

Describe exactly what happens if a table is deleted with the DROP TABLE statement.

▼ E.4.11

Re-create the tables **customers** and **orders**, enhancing their definition with all primary and foreign keys constraints.

▼ E.4.12

Use the Enterprise Manager to create the diagram (i.e., entity-relationship model) for the tables **orders** and **customers**.

▼ E.4.13

Using Enterprise Manager, try to insert a new row into the **orders** table with the following values:

(10, 'ord01', getdate(), getdate(), 100.0, 'Windstar', 'Ocean', 1).

Why is it not possible?

▼ E.4.14

Using the ALTER TABLE statement, add the current system date and time as the default value to the **orderdate** column of the **orders** table.

▼ E.4.15

Using the ALTER TABLE statement, create an integrity constraint that limits the possible values of the **quantity** column in the **orders** table to values between 1 and 30.

▼ E.4.16

With the help of the corresponding system procedures and the Transact-SQL statements CREATE DEFAULT and CREATE RULE, create the user-defined data type "Western Countries". The possible values for the new data type are CA (for California), WA (for Washington), OR (for Oregon), and NM (for New Mexico). The default value is CA. Finally, create a table called **regions** with the columns **city** and **country**, using the new data type for the latter.

▼ E.4.17

Display all integrity constraints for the **orders** table.

▼ E.4.18

Delete the primary key of the **customers** table. Why isn't that working?

▼ E.4.19

Delete the integrity constraint defined in Example 4.15.

▼ E.4.20

Rename the **city** column of the **customers** table. The new name is **town**.

CHAPTER 5

Simple Queries

This chapter and the next describe the most important Transact-SQL statement—SELECT. In this chapter you will learn how to use the SELECT statement to perform simple queries. Every clause in this statement is described, and numerous examples using our sample database are given to demonstrate the practical use of each clause. The second part of this chapter introduces aggregate functions and the UNION operator.

SELECT STATEMENT—A BASIC FORM

The Transact-SQL language has one basic statement for retrieving information from a database: the SELECT statement. With this statement, it is possible to query information from one or more tables of a database (or even from multiple databases). The result of a SELECT statement is another table, which is also known as a *result set*.

The simplest form of the SELECT statement contains both a SELECT and a FROM clause. This form of the SELECT statement has the following syntax:

```
SELECT [ ALL | DISTINCT] column_list
   FROM tab_1 [tab_alias1] [{,tab_2 [tab_alias2]}...]
```

tab_1, tab_2,... are names of tables from which information is retrieved. **tab_alias1, tab_alias2,...** provide aliases for the corresponding tables. An alias is another name for the corresponding table that can be used as a shorthand way of referring to the table or as a way to refer to two logical instances of the same physical table. Don't worry, this will become clearer as examples are presented.

NOTE: This chapter demonstrates the retrieval of information from a single table in a database. The next chapter describes the use of a join operation, and therefore the query of more than one table in a database.

column_list contains one or more of the following specifications:

- The asterisk symbol (*), which specifies all columns of the named tables in the FROM clause (or from a single table when qualified, as in: tab_2.*)
- The explicit specification of column names to be retrieved
- The specification **column_name** [as] **column_heading,** which is a way to replace the name of a column or to assign a new name to an expression
- An expression
- A system or an aggregate function

NOTE: Besides the specifications listed above, there are other options that will be partly presented later in this chapter and in the next chapter.

A SELECT statement can retrieve either certain columns or rows from a table. The first operation is called *projection* (or *SELECT list*) and the second one, *selection* (or *select operation*). The combination of both operations is also possible in a SELECT statement.

▼ EXAMPLE 5.1

Get full details of all departments.

```
SELECT * from department
```

The result is

dept_no	dept_name	location
d1	Research	Dallas
d2	Accounting	Seattle
d3	Marketing	Dallas

The SELECT statement in Example 5.1 retrieves all rows and all columns from the **department** table. The symbol * is shorthand for a list of all column names in the table named in the FROM clause, in the order in which those columns are defined in the CREATE TABLE statement for that table. The column names serve as column headings of the resulting output.

▼ EXAMPLE 5.2

Get full details of all departments.

```
SELECT dept_no, dept_name, location
  FROM department
```

The result is

dept_no	dept_name	location
d1	Research	Dallas
d2	Accounting	Seattle
d3	Marketing	Dallas

The SELECT statement in Example 5.2 is equivalent to the SELECT statement in Example 5.1. The FROM clause contains several options concerning locks. All these options, together with the notion of the transaction, will be explained in detail in Chapter 14.

WHERE CLAUSE

The simplest form of the SELECT statement, described in the previous section, is not very useful for queries. In practice, there are always several more clauses in a SELECT statement than in the statements shown in Examples 5.1 and 5.2. The following is the syntax of the SELECT statement with (almost) all possible clauses:

SELECT *select_list*
[INTO *new_table_*]
FROM *table*
[WHERE *search_condition*]
[GROUP BY *group_by_expression*]
[HAVING *search_condition*]
[ORDER BY *order_expression* [ASC | DESC]]

NOTE: The clauses in the SELECT statement must be written in syntactical order—for example, the GROUP BY clause must come after the WHERE clause and before the HAVING clause.

In this section we will start with the definition of the first clause (after the FROM clause): WHERE. Often, it is necessary to define one or more conditions that limit the selected rows. The WHERE clause specifies a Boolean expression (an expression that returns a value of TRUE or FALSE) that is tested for each row to be returned (potentially). If the expression is true, then the row is returned; if it is false, it is discarded (see Example 5.3).

▼ EXAMPLE 5.3

Get the name and number of all departments located in Dallas.

```
SELECT dept_name, dept_no
  FROM department
  WHERE location = 'Dallas'
```

The result is

dept_name	dept_no
Research	d1
Marketing	d3

In addition to the equal sign, the WHERE clause can contain other comparison operators, including:

<> (or !=)	not equal
<	less than
>	greater than
>=	greater than or equal
<=	less than or equal
!>	not greater than
!<	not less than

Example 5.4 shows the use of a comparison operator in the WHERE clause.

▼ EXAMPLE 5.4

Get the last and first names for all employees with an employee number ≥ 15000.

```
SELECT emp_lname, emp_fname
  FROM employee
  WHERE emp_no >= 15000
```

The result is

emp_lname	emp_fname
Smith	Matthew
Barrimore	John
James	James
Moser	Sybill

An expression can also be a part of the condition in the WHERE clause. Example 5.5 shows this.

▼ EXAMPLE 5.5

Get the project name for all projects with budget > 60000 £. The current rate of exchange is 0.51 £ per $1.

```
SELECT project_name
  FROM project
  WHERE budget*0.51 > 60000
```

The result is

project_name
Apollo
Mercury

Comparisons of strings (that is, values of data types CHAR, VARCHAR, NCHAR, NVARCHAR, TEXT, or NTEXT) are executed in accordance with the collating sequence in effect (this is the "sort order" specified when SQL Server was installed). If two strings are compared using ASCII code (or any other code), each of the corresponding (first, second, third, and so on) characters will be compared. One character is smaller than the other if it appears in the code table before the other one. Two strings of different lengths will be compared, after the shorter one is padded at the right with blanks, so the length of both strings will be equal. Numbers compare algebraically. Values of data type DATETIME compare in chronological order.

NOTE: Columns with TEXT and IMAGE data types cannot be used in the WHERE clause. (The only exceptions are with the LIKE and IS NULL operators.)

Boolean Operators

WHERE clause conditions can either be simple or contain multiple conditions. Multiple conditions can be built using the Boolean operators AND, OR, and NOT (see Example 5.6). The behavior of these operators has been described in Chapter 3 using truth tables.

▼ EXAMPLE 5.6

Get employee and project numbers of all clerks that work on project p2.

```
SELECT emp_no, project_no
  FROM works_on
  WHERE project_no = 'p2'
  AND job = 'Clerk'
```

The result is

emp_no	project_no
25348	p2
28559	p2

If two conditions are connected by the AND operator, rows are retrieved for which both conditions are true.

▼ EXAMPLE 5.7

Get employee numbers for all employees that work either for project p1 or project p2 (or both).

```
SELECT project_no, emp_no
  FROM works_on
  WHERE project_no = 'p1'
  OR project_no = 'p2'
```

The result is

project_no	emp_no
p1	10102
p2	25348
p2	18316
p2	29346
p1	9031
p1	28559
p2	28559
p1	29346

If two conditions are connected by the OR operator, all rows of a table are retrieved in which either the first or the second condition (or both) are true.

The result of Example 5.7 contains some duplicate values of column **emp_nr**. If this redundant information is to be eliminated, the DISTINCT option should be used, as shown here:

```
SELECT DISTINCT emp_no
  FROM works_on
  WHERE project_no = 'p1'
  OR project_no = 'p2'
```

In this case, the result is

emp_no
9031
10102
18316
25348

```
28559
29346
```

NOTE: Columns with TEXT and IMAGE data types cannot be retrieved with the DISTINCT option.

You should note that the DISTINCT clause can be used only once in a SELECT list and it must precede all column names in that list. Therefore, Example 5.8 is *wrong*.

▼ EXAMPLE 5.8 **(EXAMPLE OF AN ILLEGAL STATEMENT)**

```
SELECT emp_fname, DISTINCT emp_no
     FROM works_on
    WHERE project_no = 'p1'
    OR project_no = 'p2'
```

The result is

```
Server: Msg 156, Level 15, State 1, Line 1
Incorrect syntax near the keyword 'DISTINCT'.
```

NOTE: When there is more than one column in the SELECT list, the DISTINCT clause displays all rows where the combination of columns is distinct.

The WHERE clause may include any number of the same or different Boolean operations. You should be aware that the three Boolean operations have different priorities for evaluation: the NOT operation has the highest priority, AND is evaluated next, and the OR operation has the lowest priority. If you do not pay attention to these different priorities for Boolean operations, you will get unexpected results, as Example 5.9 shows.

▼ EXAMPLE 5.9

```
SELECT *
  FROM employee
  WHERE emp_no = 25348 AND emp_lname = 'Smith'
  OR emp_fname = 'Matthew' AND dept_no = 'd1'

SELECT *
FROM employee
```

```
WHERE ((emp_no = 25348 AND emp_lname = 'Smith')
OR emp_fname ='Matthew') AND dept_no = 'd1'
```

The result is

emp_no	emp_fname	emp_lname	dept_no
25348	Matthew	Smith	d3

emp_no	emp_fname	emp_lname	dept_no

As the results of Example 5.9 show, the two SELECT statements display two different results. In the first SELECT statement, the system evaluates both AND operators first (from the left to the right); and then the OR operator is evaluated. In the second SELECT statement, the use of parentheses changes the operation execution, with all expressions within parentheses being executed first, in sequence from left to right. As you can see, the first statement returned one row, while the second one returned zero rows.

The existence of several Boolean operations in a WHERE clause complicates the corresponding SELECT statement and makes it error prone. In such cases, the use of parentheses is highly recommended, even if they are not necessary. The readability of such SELECT statements will be greatly improved and possible errors can be avoided. Here is the first SELECT statement from Example 5.9 (modified using the recommended form):

```
SELECT *
  FROM employee
  WHERE (emp_no = 25348 AND emp_lname = 'Smith')
  OR (emp_fname = 'Matthew' AND dept_no = 'd1')
```

The third Boolean operator, NOT, changes the logical value of the corresponding condition. The truth table for NOT in Chapter 3 shows that the negation of the true value is false and vice versa; the negation of the NULL value is also NULL.

▼ EXAMPLE 5.10

Get employee numbers and first names of all employees who do not belong to the department d2.

```
SELECT emp_no, emp_lname
  FROM employee
  WHERE NOT dept_no = 'd2'
```

The result is

emp_no	emp_lname
25348	Smith
10102	Jones
18316	Barrimore
28559	Moser

In this case, the NOT operator can be replaced by the comparison operator <> (not equal). Example 5.11 is thus equivalent to Example 5.10.

NOTE: In this book we use the operator **<>** (instead of **!=**) to remain consistent with the SQL standard.

▼ EXAMPLE 5.11

```
SELECT emp_no, emp_lname
  FROM employee
  WHERE dept_no <> 'd2'
```

IN and BETWEEN Operators

An IN operator allows the specification of two or more expressions to be used for a query search. The result of the condition returns true if the value of the corresponding column equals one of the expressions specified by the IN predicate.

▼ EXAMPLE 5.12

Get all the columns for employees whose employee numbers equal either 29346 or 28559 or 25348.

```
SELECT *
  FROM employee
  WHERE emp_no IN (29346, 28559, 25348)
```

The result is

emp_no	emp_fname	emp_lname	dept_no
25348	Matthew	Smith	d3
29346	James	James	d2
28559	Sybill	Moser	d1

An IN operator is equivalent to a series of conditions, connected with one or more OR operators. (The number of OR operators is equal to the number of expressions following the IN operator minus one.) Example 5.13 is equivalent to Example 5.12.

▼ EXAMPLE 5.13

```
SELECT *
  FROM employee
  WHERE emp_no = 29346
  OR emp_no = 28559
  OR emp_no = 25348
```

The IN operator can be used together with the Boolean operator NOT (see Example 5.14). In this case, the query retrieves rows that do not include any of the listed values in the corresponding columns.

▼ EXAMPLE 5.14

Get all columns for employees whose employee numbers are neither 10102 nor 9031.

```
SELECT *
  FROM employee
  WHERE emp_no NOT IN (10102, 9031)
```

The result is

emp_no	emp_fname	emp_lname	dept_no
25348	Matthew	Smith	d3
18316	John	Barrimore	d1
29346	James	James	d2
2581	Elke	Hansel	d2
28559	Sybill	Moser	d1

In contrast to the IN operator, which specifies each individual value, the BETWEEN operator specifies a range, which determines the lower and upper bounds of qualifying values.

▼ EXAMPLE 5.15

Get the names and budgets for all projects whose budget is in the range between $95,000 and $120,000 inclusive.

```
SELECT project_name, budget
  FROM project
  WHERE budget BETWEEN 95000 AND 120000
```

The result is

project_name	**budget**
Apollo	120000.0
Gemini	95000.0

The BETWEEN operator searches for all values in the range inclusively; that is, qualifying values can be between *or equal to* the lower and upper boundary values.

The BETWEEN operator is logically equal to two individual comparisons, which are connected with the Boolean operator AND. Example 5.16 is equivalent to Example 5.15.

▼ EXAMPLE 5.16

```
SELECT project_name, budget
  FROM project
  WHERE budget >= 95000 AND budget <= 120000
```

Like the BETWEEN operator, the NOT BETWEEN operator can be used to search for column values that do not fall within the specified range. The BETWEEN operator can also be applied to columns with character and date values (see Example 5.17).

▼ EXAMPLE 5.17

Get employee numbers of all analysts who did not enter their project in 1998.

```
SELECT emp_no
  FROM works_on
  WHERE job = 'Analyst'
  AND enter_date NOT BETWEEN '01.01.1998' AND '12.31.1988'
```

The result is

emp_no
10102
2581

Examples 5.18 and 5.19 show another query that can be written using two different but equivalent ways.

▼ EXAMPLE 5.18

Get the names of all projects with a budget that is less than $100,000 and greater than $150,000.

```
SELECT project_name
  FROM project
   WHERE budget NOT BETWEEN 100000 AND 150000
```

The result is

project_name
Gemini
Mercury

Using comparison operators, the solution will look different than in Example 5.18.

▼ EXAMPLE 5.19

Get the names of all projects with a budget that is less than $100,000 and greater than $150,000.

```
SELECT project_name
  FROM project
   WHERE budget < 100000 OR budget > 150000
```

NOTE: Although the English phrasing suggests the use of the AND operator (see the text in Example 5.19), the logical meaning of the query demands the use of the OR operator, because, if you use AND instead of OR, you will get no results at all. (The reason is that there cannot be a budget that is at the same time less than $100,000 and greater than $150,000.) Therefore, Example 5.19 shows a possible problem, which can appear between English phrasing of an exercise and its logical meaning.

Queries Involving Null Values

A NULL in the CREATE TABLE or ALTER TABLE statement specifies that a special value called NULL (which usually represents unknown values) is allowed in the column. These values differ from all other values in a database. In the SELECT statement, the WHERE clause generally returns rows for which the comparison evaluates to true. Our concern regarding queries is, how will comparisons involving NULL values be evaluated in the WHERE clause?

All comparisons with NULL values will return false (even when preceded by NOT). To retrieve the rows with NULL values in the column, Transact-SQL includes the operator feature IS [NOT] NULL. This specification in a WHERE clause of a SELECT statement has the following general form:

```
column IS [NOT] NULL
```

Example 5.20 shows the use of the operator IS NULL.

▼ EXAMPLE 5.20

Get employee numbers and corresponding project numbers for employees with unknown jobs who work on project p2.

```
SELECT emp_no, project_no
  FROM works_on
  WHERE project_no = 'p2'
  AND job IS NULL
```

The result is

emp_no	project_no
18316	p2
29346	p2

NOTE: There is a difference in syntax between SQL Server 6.5 and SQL Server 2000 concerning the use of NULL with the comparison operators. The syntax column < NULL (column <= NULL) or column > NULL (column >= NULL) was illegal in version 6.5 and is now legal. SQL 2000 provides consistency for all comparison operators and NULL; that is, the use of all comparison operators and NULL is now syntactically correct. (Note also that the use of such conditions is to be avoided, because, as already stated, nothing is considered to be equal to NULL.)

Example 5.21 shows syntactically correct, but logically incorrect, usage of NULL.

▼ EXAMPLE 5.21

```
SELECT project_no, job
  FROM works_on
  WHERE  job <> NULL
```

The result is

project_no	job

NOTE: The result of Example 5.21 is different in version 6.5 (provided that the option ANSI_WARNINGS in the SET statement is not set to ON). Version 6.5 falsely displays eight rows from the **works_on** table.

The condition

column IS NOT NULL

is equivalent to the condition

NOT (column IS NULL)

The system function ISNULL allows a display of the specified value as substitution for NULL (see Example 5.22).

▼ EXAMPLE 5.22

```
SELECT emp_no, ISNULL(job, 'Job unknown') task
  FROM works_on
  WHERE project_no = 'p1'
```

The result is

emp_no	task
10102	Analyst
9031	Manager
28559	Job unknown
29346	Clerk

In Example 5.22, we use a column heading **task** for the **job** column.

LIKE Operator

LIKE is an operator that compares column values with a specified pattern. The data type of the column can be any character or date data type. The general form of the LIKE operator is

column [NOT] LIKE 'pattern'

pattern may be a string or date constant or expression (including columns of tables) and must be compatible with the data type of the corresponding column. For the specified column, the comparison between the value in a row and the pattern evaluates to true if the column value matches the pattern expression.

Certain characters within the pattern—called wildcard characters—have a specific interpretation. Two of them are

% (percent sign)

_ (underscore)

The percent sign specifies any sequence of zero or more characters. The underscore specifies any single character. Example 5.23 shows the use of the percent sign.

▼ EXAMPLE 5.23

Get the names and numbers of all employees whose last names begin with the letter *J*.

```
SELECT emp_fname, emp_lname, emp_no
  FROM employee
  WHERE emp_lname LIKE 'J%'
```

The result is

emp_fname	emp_lname	emp_no
Ann	Jones	10102
James	James	29346

Example 5.24 shows the use of the both wildcard characters % and _.

▼ EXAMPLE 5.24

Get the names and numbers of all employees whose first names contain the letter *a* as the second character.

```
SELECT emp_fname, emp_lname, emp_no
  FROM employee
  WHERE emp_fname LIKE '_a%'
```

The result is

emp_fname	emp_lname	emp_no
Matthew	Smith	25348
James	James	29346

In addition to the percent sign and the underscore, Transact-SQL supports other characters that have a special meaning when used with the LIKE operator. These characters ([,], and ^) are best explained in the next two examples.

▼ EXAMPLE 5.25

Get full details of all departments whose locations begin with a character in the range *C* through *F*.

```
SELECT *
  FROM department
  WHERE location LIKE '[C-F]%'
```

The result is

dept_no	dept_name	location
d1	Research	Dallas
d3	Marketing	Dallas

As shown in Example 5.25, the square brackets, [and], delimit a range or list of characters. The order in which characters appear in a range is defined by the collating sequence, which is determined when SQL Server is installed or later.

The character ^ specifies the negation of a range or a list of characters. This character has this meaning only within a pair of square brackets (see Example 5.26).

▼ EXAMPLE 5.26

Get the numbers and names of all employees whose last names do not begin with the letters *J*, *K*, *L*, *M*, *N*, or *O* and whose first names do not begin with the letters *E* or *Z*.

```
SELECT emp_no, emp_fname, emp_lname
  FROM employee
  WHERE emp_lname LIKE '[^J-O]%'
  AND emp_fname LIKE '[^EZ]%'
```

The result is

emp_no	emp_fname	emp_lname
25348	Matthew	Smith
18316	John	Barrimore

The condition

```
column NOT LIKE 'pattern'
```

is equivalent to the condition

```
NOT (column LIKE 'pattern')
```

Example 5.27 shows the use of the LIKE operator (together with NOT).

▼ EXAMPLE 5.27

Get full details of all employees whose first names do not end with the character *n*.

```
SELECT *
  FROM employee
  WHERE emp_fname NOT LIKE '%n'
```

The result is

emp_no	emp_fname	emp_lname	dept_no
25348	Matthew	Smith	d3
29346	James	James	d2
2581	Elke	Hansel	d2
9031	Elsa	Bertoni	d2
28559	Sybill	Moser	d1

Any of the wildcard characters (%, _, [,], or ^) enclosed in square brackets stand for themselves. An equivalent feature is available through the ESCAPE option. Therefore, both SELECT statements in Example 5.28 have the same meaning.

▼ EXAMPLE 5.28

```
SELECT project_no, project_name
  FROM project
  WHERE project_name LIKE '%[_]%'

SELECT project_no, project_name
  FROM project
  WHERE project_name LIKE '%!_%' ESCAPE '!'
```

The result is

project_no	project_name

project_no	project_name

Both SELECT statements search for the underscore as an actual character in the column **project_name**. In the first SELECT statement, this search is established by enclosing the sign _ in square brackets. The second SELECT statement uses a character (in the example, it is the character **!**) as an escape character. The escape character overrides the meaning of the underscore as the wildcard character and leaves it to be interpreted as an ordinary character. (Our result contains no rows because there are no project names including the underscore character.)

NOTE: The SQL standard only supports the use of %, _, and the ESCAPE operator. For this reason, we recommend using the ESCAPE operator instead of a pair of square brackets if any wildcard character must stand for itself.

SIMPLE SUBQUERIES

All previous examples in this chapter contain comparisons of column values with an expression or constant. Additionally, the Transact-SQL language offers the ability to compare column values with the result of another SELECT statement. Such SELECT statements, which are nested in the WHERE clause of another SELECT statement, are called subqueries. The first SELECT statement in a subquery is often called the *outer query*—in contrast to the *inner query*, which denotes the second SELECT statement. The inner query will always be evaluated first, and the outer query receives the values of the inner query.

NOTE: A subquery can also be nested in an INSERT, UPDATE, or a DELETE statement, which will be discussed in Chapter 7.

There are two types of subqueries:

- Simple
- Correlated

In a simple subquery, the inner query is evaluated exactly once. A correlated subquery differs from a simple one in that its value depends upon a variable from the outer query. Therefore, the inner query of a correlated subquery is evaluated each time the system retrieves a new row from the outer query. The correlated subquery will be discussed in Chapter 6.

A simple subquery can be used with the following operators:

- Comparison operators
- IN operator
- ANY or ALL operator
- EXISTS function

Subqueries and Comparison Operators

Example 5.29 shows the simple subquery that is used with the operator =.

▼ EXAMPLE 5.29

Get the first and last names of employees who work in the research department.

```
SELECT emp_fname, emp_lname
  FROM employee
  WHERE dept_no =
   (SELECT dept_no
     FROM department
    WHERE dept_name = 'Research')
```

The result is

emp_fname	emp_lname
John	Barrimore
Sybill	Moser

SQL Server first evaluates the inner query. That query returns the number of the research department (d1). Thus, after the evaluation of the inner query, the subquery in Example 5.29 can be represented with the following equivalent query:

```
SELECT emp_fname, emp_lname
  FROM employee
  WHERE dept_no = 'd1'
```

A subquery can be used with other comparison operators, too. Example 5.30 shows the use of the operator <.

▼ EXAMPLE 5.30

Get all project numbers of employees whose employee numbers are smaller than the number of the employee named Moser.

```
SELECT DISTINCT project_no
  FROM works_on
  WHERE emp_no <
   (SELECT emp_no
     FROM employee
    WHERE emp_lname = 'Moser')
```

The result is

project_no
p1
p2
p3

Any comparison operator can be used provided the inner query returns exactly one row. This is obvious, because the comparison between particular column values of the outer query and a set of values (as a result of the inner query) is not possible.

Subqueries and IN Operator

The IN operator allows the specification of a set of expressions (or constants) that are subsequently used for the query search. This operator can be applied to a subquery for the same reason—that is, when the result of an inner query contains a set of values.

Example 5.31 shows the use of the IN operator.

▼ EXAMPLE 5.31

Get full details of all employees whose departments are located in Dallas.

```
SELECT *
  FROM employee
  WHERE dept_no IN
  (SELECT dept_no
     FROM department
     WHERE location = 'Dallas')
```

The result is

emp_no	emp_fname	emp_lname	dept_no
25348	Matthew	Smith	d3
10102	Ann	Jones	d3
18316	John	Barrimore	d1
28559	Sybill	Moser	d1

Each inner query may contain further queries. This type of subquery is called a subquery with multiple levels of nesting. The maximum number of inner queries in a subquery depends on the amount of memory SQL Server has for each SELECT statement. In the case of subqueries with multiple levels of nesting, the system first evaluates the innermost query and returns the result to the query on the next nesting level, and so on. Finally, the outermost query evaluates the final outcome.

▼ EXAMPLE 5.32

Get the last names of all employees who work on the project Apollo.

```
SELECT emp_lname
  FROM employee
  WHERE emp_no IN
  (SELECT emp_no
     FROM works_on
```

```
WHERE project_no IN
(SELECT project_no
   FROM project
  WHERE project_name = 'Apollo'))
```

The result is

emp_lname
Jones
James
Bertoni
Moser

The innermost query in Example 5.32 evaluates to the **project_no** value p1. The middle inner query compares this value with all values of the **project_no** column in the **works_on** table. The result of this query is the set of employee numbers: (10102, 29346, 9031, 28559). Finally, the outermost query displays the corresponding last names for the selected employee numbers.

ANY and ALL Operators

The operators ANY and ALL are always used in combination with one of the comparison operators. The general syntax of both operators is

```
column operator [ANY | ALL] query
```

where **operator** stands for a comparison operator.

NOTE: Do not use ANY and ALL operators! Every query using ANY or ALL can be better formulated with the EXISTS function (see Chapter 6). Additionally, the semantic meaning of the ANY operator can be easily confused with the semantic meaning of the ALL operator and vice versa.

The ANY operator evaluates to true if the result of an inner query contains at least one row that satisfies the comparison. Example 5.33 shows the use of the ANY operator.

▼ EXAMPLE 5.33

Get the employee numbers, project numbers, and job names for employees who have not spent the most time on one of the projects.

```
SELECT DISTINCT emp_no, project_no, job
  FROM works_on
```

```
WHERE enter_date > ANY
(SELECT  enter_date
  FROM works_on)
```

The result is

emp_no	project_no	job
2581	p3	Analyst
9031	p1	Manager
9031	p3	Clerk
10102	p3	Manager
18316	p2	NULL
25348	p2	Clerk
28559	p1	NULL
28559	p2	Clerk
29346	p1	Clerk
29346	p2	NULL

Each value of the **enter_date** column in Example 5.33 is compared with all values of this column. For all dates of this column, except the oldest one, the comparison is evaluated to true at least once. The row with the oldest date does not belong to the result because the comparison does not evaluate to true in any case. In other words, the expression "enter_date > ANY (SELECT enter_date FROM works_on)" is true if there are *any* (one or more) rows in the **works_on** table with a value of the **enter_date** column less than the value of **enter_date** for the current row. This will be true for all but the minimum (or earliest) value of **enter_date** in the table.

The keyword SOME is the synonym for ANY.

Example 5.34 shows the use of the ANY operator.

▼ EXAMPLE 5.34

Get the first and last names for all employees who work on project p1.

```
SELECT emp_fname, emp_lname
  FROM employee
  WHERE emp_no = ANY
  (SELECT emp_no
     FROM works_on
    WHERE project_no = 'p1')
```

The result is

emp_fname	emp_lname
Ann	Jones
James	James
Elsa	Bertoni
Sybill	Moser

The ALL operator evaluates to true if the evaluation of the table column in the inner query returns all values of that column. Example 5.35 shows the use of the ALL operator.

▼ EXAMPLE 5.35

Get jobs of the employee with the smallest employee number.

```
SELECT job
  FROM works_on
  WHERE emp_no <= ALL
  (SELECT emp_no
     FROM employee)
```

The result is

job
Analyst

EXISTS Function

The EXISTS function checks the inner query of a subquery and evaluates to true if its result contains at least one row. The syntax of the EXISTS function is

```
[NOT] EXISTS (query)
```

Chapter 6 contains all examples regarding the EXISTS function.

Queries in the FROM Clause

The previous versions of SQL Server only allowed you to place a query in the WHERE clause of the SELECT statement, as shown in earlier examples. Generally, it should be possible to write a query anyplace in a SELECT statement where a table can appear. (The result of a query is always a table or, in a special case, an expression.) SQL Server now allows you to write a query as part of the FROM clause. Example 5.36 shows the use of a query inside the FROM clause.

▼ EXAMPLE 5.36

Get the names of all employees with employee numbers greater than or equal to 10000.

```
SELECT emp_fname, emp_lname
  FROM (SELECT *
             FROM employee
            WHERE emp_no >= 10000 ) AS empno_10000
```

The result is

emp_fname	emp_lname
Matthew	Smith
Ann	Jones
John	Barrimore
James	James
Sybill	Moser

The name **empno_10000** is an alias table name for the result of the SELECT statement in the FROM clause. (The alias for a table must be specified if a query is placed in the FROM clause of a SELECT statement.)

GROUP BY CLAUSE

The GROUP BY clause defines one or more columns as a group such that all rows within any group have the same values for those columns. Example 5.37 shows the use of the GROUP BY clause.

▼ EXAMPLE 5.37

Get all jobs of employees.

```
SELECT job
  FROM works_on
  GROUP BY job
```

The result is

job
NULL
Analyst
Clerk
Manager

In Example 5.37, the GROUP BY clause builds different groups for all possible values (NULL, too!) appearing in the **job** column.

NOTE: There is a restriction regarding the use of columns in the GROUP BY clause. Each column appearing in the SELECT list of the query must also appear in the GROUP BY clause. This does not hold for constants and for columns that are part of an aggregate function (see Example 5.45). This makes sense, because only columns in the GROUP BY clause are guaranteed to have a single value (for each group).

A table can be grouped by any combination of its columns. Example 5.38 shows the grouping of rows of the **works_on** table using two columns.

▼ EXAMPLE 5.38

Group all employees using their project numbers and jobs.

```
SELECT project_no, job
  FROM works_on
  GROUP BY project_no, job
```

The result is

project_no	job
p1	Analyst
p1	Clerk
p1	Manager
p1	NULL
p2	NULL
p2	Clerk
p3	Analyst
p3	Clerk
p3	Manager

NOTE: All versions previous to SQL Server 7 displayed the ordered output every time the GROUP BY clause was used. This behavior is not compatible with the SQL standard, so SQL Server 7 and SQL Server 2000 needs the ORDER BY clause to be specified explicitly to produce the ordered output.

The result of Example 5.38 shows that there are nine groups with different combinations of project numbers and jobs. The only two groups that contain more than one row are

p2	Clerk	25348, 28559
p2	NULL	18316, 29346

The sequence of the column names in the GROUP BY clause need not correspond to the sequence of the names in the SELECT list.

NOTE: Columns of data types TEXT and IMAGE cannot be used in the GROUP BY clause.

AGGREGATE FUNCTIONS

Aggregates are functions that are used to get summary values. All aggregate functions can be divided in three groups:

- Convenient aggregate functions
- Statistical aggregate functions
- Superaggregates

The following sections describe all these groups.

Convenient Aggregates

The Transact-SQL language supports six aggregate functions (an aggregate function is one that acts upon a set of values rather than a single one):

- MIN
- MAX
- SUM
- AVG
- COUNT
- COUNT_BIG

All aggregate functions operate on a single argument that can be a column or an expression. (The only exception is the second form of the COUNT and COUNT_BIG function: COUNT(*) and COUNT_BIG(*).)The result of each aggregate function is a constant value, which is displayed in a separate column of the result.

The aggregate functions appear in the SELECT list, which can include a GROUP BY clause. If there is no GROUP BY clause in the SELECT statement, and the SELECT list includes at least one aggregate function, then no simple columns can be included in the

SELECT list (other than as arguments of an aggregate function). Therefore, Example 5.39 is *wrong*.

▼ EXAMPLE 5.39 (EXAMPLE OF AN ILLEGAL STATEMENT)

```
SELECT emp_lname, MIN (emp_no)
  FROM employee
```

The **emp_lname** column of the **employee** table must not appear in the SELECT list of Example 5.39, because it is not the argument of an aggregate function. On the other hand, all column names that are not arguments of an aggregate function may appear in the SELECT list if they are used for grouping.

The argument of an aggregate function can be preceded by one of two keywords:

- ALL
- DISTINCT

ALL indicates that all values of a column are to be considered. DISTINCT eliminates duplicate values of a column before the aggregate function is applied. (ALL is the default value.)

> ***NOTE:*** Aggregate functions cannot be used in the WHERE clause of the SELECT statement.

Aggregate Functions MIN and MAX

The aggregate functions MIN and MAX compute the smallest and the largest value in the column, respectively. If there is a WHERE clause, the MIN and MAX functions return the smallest or largest of values from selected rows. Example 5.40 shows the use of the aggregate function MIN.

▼ EXAMPLE 5.40

Get the smallest employee number.

```
SELECT MIN(emp_no) min_employee_number
  FROM employee
```

The result is

min_employee_number
2581

Example 5.40 shows that column headings can also be applied to aggregate functions to enhance the readability of the result.

The result of Example 5.40 is not user friendly. For instance, the name of the employee with the smallest number is not known. As already shown in Example 5.39, the explicit specification of the **emp_name** column in the SELECT list is not allowed. To retrieve the name of the employee with the smallest employee number, we use a subquery in Example 5.41, where the inner query contains the SELECT statement of Example 5.40.

▼ EXAMPLE 5.41

Get the number and the last name of the employee with the smallest employee number.

```
SELECT emp_no, emp_lname
  FROM employee
  WHERE emp_no =
  (SELECT MIN(emp_no)
     FROM employee)
```

The result is

emp_no	emp_lname
2581	Hansel

Example 5.42 shows the use of the aggregate function MAX.

▼ EXAMPLE 5.42

Get the employee number of the manager who was entered last in the **works_on** table.

```
SELECT emp_no
  FROM works_on
  WHERE enter_date =
  (SELECT MAX(enter_date)
     FROM works_on
    WHERE job = 'Manager')
```

The result is

emp_no
10102

The argument of the functions MIN and MAX can also be a string value or a date. If the argument has a string value, the comparison between all values will be provided using the actual collating sequence. For all arguments of data type DATETIME, the earliest date specifies the smallest and the latest date the largest value in the column.

The DISTINCT option cannot be used with the aggregate functions MIN and MAX. All null values in the column that is the argument of the aggregate function MIN or MAX are always eliminated before MIN or MAX is applied.

Aggregate Function SUM

The aggregate function SUM calculates the sum of the values in the column. The argument of the function SUM must be numeric. Example 5.43 shows the use of the aggregate function SUM.

▼ EXAMPLE 5.43

Calculate the sum of all budgets of projects.

```
SELECT SUM (budget) sum_of_budgets
  FROM project
```

The result is

sum_of_budgets
401500.0

The use of the DISTINCT option eliminates all duplicate values in the column before the function SUM is applied. Similarly, all null values are always eliminated before SUM is applied.

Aggregate Function AVG

The aggregate function AVG calculates the average of the values in the column. The argument of the function AVG must be numeric (see Example 5.44).

▼ EXAMPLE 5.44

Calculate the average of all budgets with a money amount greater than $100,000.

```
SELECT AVG(budget) avg_budget
  FROM project
  WHERE budget > 100000
```

The result is

avg_budget
153250.0

All null values are eliminated before the function AVG is applied.

Aggregate Functions COUNT and COUNT_BIG

The aggregate function COUNT has two different forms. The syntax of the first form is

```
COUNT ([DISTINCT] col_name)
```

This form of the function COUNT calculates the number of values in the **col_name** column. When the DISTINCT keyword is used, all duplicate values are eliminated before the function COUNT is applied. This form of COUNT does not count rows with null values for the column.

Example 5.45 shows the use of the first form of the aggregate function COUNT.

▼ EXAMPLE 5.45

Count all different jobs in each project.

```
SELECT project_no, COUNT(DISTINCT job) job_count
  FROM works_on
  GROUP BY project_no
```

The result is

project_no	job_count
p1	4
p2	1
p3	3

As can be seen from the result of Example 5.45, all null values are eliminated before the function COUNT(DISTINCT col_name) or COUNT(col_name) is applied. (The sum of all values in the **job_count** column is 8 instead of 11.)

The second form of the function COUNT has the form COUNT(*). This aggregate function counts the number of rows in the table. Or, if there is a WHERE clause in the SELECT statement, it returns the number of rows for which the WHERE condition is true. Example 5.46 shows the use of the second form of the aggregate function COUNT.

▼ EXAMPLE 5.46

How many employees work on each project?

```
SELECT project_no, COUNT(*) emp_count
  FROM works_on
  GROUP BY project_no
```

The result is

project_no	emp_count
p1	4
p2	4
p3	3

In contrast to the first form of the function COUNT, the second form does not eliminate null values (see Example 5.47).

▼ EXAMPLE 5.47

Get the number of each job in all projects.

```
SELECT job, COUNT(*) job_count
  FROM works_on
  GROUP BY job
```

The result is

job	job_count
NULL	3
Analyst	2
Clerk	4
Manager	2

The COUNT_BIG function is analogous to the COUNT function. The only difference between them is their return values: COUNT_BIG always returns a value of the BIGINT data type, while the COUNT function always returns a value of the INTEGER data type.

Statistical Aggregates

The following aggregate functions belong to the group of statistical aggregates:

- VAR
- VARP
- STDEV
- STDEVP

Aggregate Functions VAR and VARP

The aggregate function VAR computes the variance of all the values listed in a column or expression. This aggregate can be computed using the following formula:

$$\text{variance} = \text{SUM}(\text{value}_1^{\ 2} + \text{value}_2^{\ 2} + ...+ \text{value}_n^{\ 2} - (\text{SUM}(\text{value}_1 + ...+ \text{value}_n)^2 / (n*(n-1))$$

(**n** is the number of values listed in a column or expression.) Example 5.48 shows the use of the VAR aggregate function.

▼ EXAMPLE 5.48

```
SELECT VAR(budget) variance_of_budgets
    FROM project
```

The result is

variance_of_budgets
2236583333.3333321

The aggregate function VARP computes the variance for the population of all the values listed in a column or expression.

Aggregate Functions STDEV and STDEVP

The aggregate function STDEV computes the standard deviation of all the values listed in a column of expression. (The standard deviation is computed as the square root of the corresponding variance.) Example 5.49 shows the use of the STDEV function.

▼ EXAMPLE 5.49

```
SELECT STDEV(budget) std_dev_of_budgets
    FROM project
```

The result is

std_dev_of_budgets
47292.529360706983

The aggregate function STDEVP computes the standard deviation for the population of all the values listed in a column or expression.

Superaggregates (Operators CUBE and ROLLUP)

The result of an aggregate function is always one-dimensional—that is, a constant. The Transact-SQL language supports some other functions that yield multidimensional results:

- CUBE
- ROLLUP

The application area of these two functions (including also the function TOP n) is a data warehouse. Therefore, they are described in detail in Chapter 27, which discusses data warehousing.

HAVING CLAUSE

The HAVING clause defines the condition that is then applied to groups of rows. The HAVING clause has the same meaning to groups of rows that the WHERE clause has to each individual row. The syntax of the HAVING clause is

```
HAVING condition
```

where **condition** contains aggregate functions or constants.

Example 5.50 shows the use of the HAVING clause with the aggregate function COUNT(*).

▼ EXAMPLE 5.50

Get project numbers for all projects employing less than four persons.

```
SELECT project_no
  FROM works_on
  GROUP BY project_no
  HAVING COUNT(*) < 4
```

The result is

project_no
p3

In Example 5.50, the system uses the GROUP BY clause to group all rows according to existing values in the **project_no** column. After that, it counts the number of rows in each group and selects those groups with three or fewer rows.

The HAVING clause can also be used without aggregates. Example 5.51 shows this.

▼ EXAMPLE 5.51

Group rows of the **works_on** table by jobs and eliminate those jobs that do not begin with the letter *M*.

```
SELECT job
  FROM works_on
  GROUP BY job
     HAVING job LIKE 'M%'
```

The result is

job
Manager

The HAVING clause can also be used without the GROUP BY clause, although it is uncommon in practice. In such a case, all rows of the entire table belong to a single group.

NOTE: Columns with TEXT or IMAGE data types cannot be used with the HAVING clause.

ORDER BY CLAUSE

The ORDER BY clause defines the particular order of the rows in the result of a query. This clause has the following syntax:

```
ORDER BY {[col_name | col_number [ASC | DESC]]} , ...
```

The **col_name** column defines the order. **col_number** is an alternative specification, which identifies the column by its ordinal position in the sequence of all columns in the SELECT list (1 for the first column, 2 for the second one, and so on). ASC indicates ascending and DESC indicates descending order, with ASC as the default value.

Example 5.52 shows the use of the ORDER BY clause.

▼ EXAMPLE 5.52

Get employee names and employee numbers, in ascending order of employee numbers.

```
SELECT emp_no, emp_fname, emp_lname
  FROM employee
  ORDER BY emp_no
```

The result is

emp_no	emp_fname	emp_lname
2581	Elke	Hansel
9031	Elsa	Bertoni
10102	Ann	Jones
18316	John	Barrimore
25348	Matthew	Smith

28559	Sybill	Moser
29346	James	James

NOTE: Since SQL Server 7, the ORDER BY clause must be specified explicitly to produce the ordered output. (The previous versions of SQL Server displayed the ordered output every time the GROUP BY clause was used.)

NOTE: The columns in the ORDER BY clause need not appear in the SELECT list. However, the ORDER BY columns must appear in the SELECT list if SELECT DISTINCT is specified. Also, this clause may not reference columns from tables that are not listed in the FROM clause.

As the syntax of the ORDER BY clause shows, the order criterion may contain more than one column (see Example 5.53).

▼ EXAMPLE 5.53

Get department numbers and employee names for employees with employee numbers < 20000, in ascending order of last and first names.

```
SELECT emp_fname, emp_lname, dept_no
  FROM employee
  WHERE emp_no < 20000
  ORDER BY emp_lname, emp_fname
```

The result is

emp_fname	emp_lname	dept_no
John	Barrimore	d1
Elsa	Bertoni	d2
Elke	Hansel	d2
Ann	Jones	d3

It is also possible to identify the columns in the ORDER BY clause by the ordinal position of the column in the SELECT list. The ORDER BY clause in Example 5.53 could be written in the following form:

```
ORDER BY 2,1
```

The use of column numbers instead of column names is an alternative solution, if the order criterion contains any aggregate function. (The other way is to use column headings, which then appear in the ORDER BY clause.) However, using column names rather than numbers in the ORDER BY clause is recommended to reduce the difficulty of maintaining the query if any columns need to be added or deleted from the SELECT list. Example 5.54 shows the use of column numbers.

▼ EXAMPLE 5.54

For each project number, get the project number and the number of all employees, in descending order of the employee number.

```
SELECT project_no, COUNT(*) emp_quantity
  FROM works_on
  GROUP BY project_no
  ORDER BY 2 DESC
```

The result is

project_no	emp_quantity
p1	4
p2	4
p3	3

The Transact-SQL language orders null values at the beginning of all values if the order is ascending, and at the end of all values if the order is descending.

NOTE: Columns with TEXT or IMAGE data types cannot be used in the ORDER BY clause.

SELECT STATEMENT AND IDENTITY PROPERTY

As already stated in Chapter 4, columns with numeric data types can have the IDENTITY property. SQL Server generates values of such columns sequentially, starting with an initial value.

Some system functions and global variables are related to the IDENTITY property. The IDENTITYCOL variable can be used instead of the name of the column with the IDENTITY property. Example 5.55 shows the use of the IDENTITY property and the IDENTITYCOL variable.

▼ EXAMPLE 5.55

```
CREATE TABLE product
  (product_no INTEGER IDENTITY(10000,1) NOT NULL,
   product_name CHAR(30) NOT NULL,
   price MONEY)
```

```
SELECT IDENTITYCOL
  FROM product
  WHERE product_name = 'Soap'
```

The result could be

product_no
10005

The **product** table is created first in Example 5.55. This table has the column **product_no** with the IDENTITY property. The values of the **product_no** column are automatically generated by the system, beginning with 10000 and incrementing by 1 for every subsequent value: 10000, 10001, 10002, and so on.

The system variable IDENTITYCOL in the SELECT statement corresponds to the name of the column with the IDENTITY property—that is, with the column **product_no**.

The system functions

- IDENT_SEED
- IDENT_INCR

can be used to find out the beginning value and the increment of the column with the IDENTITY property, respectively.

Normally, the system sets identity values; they are not supplied by the user. If, however, you want to supply your own values for particular rows, then before inserting the explicit value, the IDENTITY_INSERT option must be set to ON using the SET statement:

```
SET IDENTITY_INSERT table_name ON
```

SET OPERATORS

In addition to the operators described in the previous sections, there are three set operators that connect two or more queries:

- UNION
- INTERSECTION
- DIFFERENCE

NOTE: The Transact-SQL language directly supports only the UNION operator.

The result of the union of two sets is the set of all elements appearing in either or both of the sets. Accordingly, the union of two tables is a new table consisting of all rows appearing in either or both of the tables.

The general form of the UNION operator is

select_1 UNION [ALL] select_2 {[UNION [ALL] select_3]}...

select_1, select_2,... are SELECT statements that build the union. If the ALL option is used, all resulting rows, including duplicates, are to be displayed. The ALL option has the same meaning with the UNION operator as in the SELECT list. There is only one difference: the option ALL is the default in the SELECT list, but it must be specified with the UNION operator to display all resulting rows, including duplicates.

The sample database in its original form is not suitable for a demonstration of the UNION operator. For this reason, we introduce a new table, **employee_enh**, which is iden tical to the existing **employee** table, up to the additional **domicile** column. The **domicile** column contains the place of residence of every employee.

The new **employee_enh** table has the following form:

emp_no	emp_fname	emp_lname	dept_no	domicile
25348	Matthew	Smith	d3	San Antonio
10102	Ann	Jones	d3	Houston
18316	John	Barrimore	d1	San Antonio
29346	James	James	d2	Seattle
9031	Elke	Bertoli	d2	Portland
2581	Elisa	Kim	d2	Tacoma
28559	Sybill	Moser	d1	Houston

Creation of the **employee_enh** table provides an opportunity to show the use of the INTO clause of the SELECT statement. SELECT INTO has two different parts: first, it creates the new table with the columns corresponding to the columns listed in the SELECT list. Second, the existing rows of the original table will be inserted in the new table. (The name of the new table appears with the INTO clause, and the name of the original table appears in the FROM clause of the SELECT statement.)

Example 5.56 shows the creation of the **employee_enh** table.

▼ EXAMPLE 5.56

```
USE master
GO
sp_dboption sample, 'SELECT INTO/BULKCOPY', TRUE
USE sample
CHECKPOINT
SELECT *
  INTO employee_enh
  FROM employee
```

```
ALTER TABLE employee_enh
  ADD domicile CHAR(25) NULL
```

Some requirements must be fulfilled if SELECT INTO is to be applied. First, the option **select into/bulk copy** must be set on. This can be done by the database administrator with the system procedure **sp_dboption** only inside the **master** database (the USE statement changes the database context to the specified database) or from Enterprise Manager. Second, the system checkpoint (see Chapter 20) is required after the use of the **sp_dboption** system procedure. After that, SELECT INTO generates the **employee_enh** table and inserts all rows from the initial table into the new one (assuming there was no WHERE clause used with the SELECT INTO statement). Finally, the ALTER TABLE statement appends the **domicile** column to the **employee_enh** table.

After the execution of Example 5.56, the **domicile** column contains no values. The values can be added using SQL Server Enterprise Manager or the UPDATE statement.

Example 5.57 shows the union of the tables **employee_enh** and **department**.

▼ EXAMPLE 5.57

```
SELECT domicile
  FROM employee_enh
UNION
SELECT location
  FROM department
```

The result is

domicile
San Antonio
Houston
Portland
Tacoma
Seattle
Dallas

Two tables can be connected with the UNION operator if they are compatible with each other. This means they have the same number of columns, and the corresponding columns have the compatible data types. (For example, INT and SMALLINT are compatible data types.)

The ordering of the result of the union can be done only if the ORDER BY clause is used with the last SELECT statement (see Example 5.58). The same is valid for the

COMPUTE clause, which is described later in this chapter. The GROUP BY and the HAVING clauses can be used with the particular SELECT statements, but not with the union itself.

▼ EXAMPLE 5.58

Get the employee number for employees who either belong to department d1 or entered their project before 1/1/1998, in ascending order of employee number.

```
SELECT emp_no
  FROM employee
  WHERE dept_no = 'd1'
UNION
SELECT emp_no
  FROM works_on
  WHERE enter_date < '01.01.1998'
ORDER BY 1
```

The result is

emp_no
9031
10102
18316
28559
29346

The OR and UNION operators are similar. Sometimes, the OR operator can be used instead of the UNION operator, as the two equivalent examples, Examples 5.59 and 5.60, show. In this case, the set of the SELECT statement is replaced through one SELECT statement with the set of OR operators.

▼ EXAMPLE 5.59

Get employee numbers and names for employees who either belong to department d1 or d2.

```
SELECT emp_no, emp_fname, emp_lname
  FROM employee
  WHERE dept_no = 'd1'
UNION
SELECT emp_no, emp_fname, emp_lname
  FROM employee
  WHERE dept_no = 'd2'
```

The result is

emp_no	emp_fname	emp_lname
2581	Elke	Hansel
9031	Elsa	Bertoni
29346	James	James
18316	John	Barrimore
28559	Sybill	Moser

▼ EXAMPLE 5.60

```
SELECT emp_no, emp_fname, emp_lname
  FROM employee
  WHERE dept_no ='d1' OR dept_no = 'd2'
```

The UNION operator can be replaced with the OR operator only if the same table is used in all SELECT statements connected by the UNION operator.

Besides UNION, there are two other set operators: INTERSECTION and DIFFERENCE. The intersection of two tables is the set of rows belonging to both tables. The difference of two tables is the set of all rows, where the resulting rows belong to the first table but not to the second one.

The Transact-SQL language does not support these two operators directly. The INTERSECTION operator can be simulated using the EXISTS function (see Example 6.21), and the DIFFERENCE operator using the NOT EXISTS function (see Example 6.22).

CASE EXPRESSIONS

In database application programming, it is sometimes necessary to modify the representation of data. For instance, a person's gender can be coded using the values 1, 2, and 3 (for female, male, and child, respectively). Such a programming technique can reduce the time for the implementation of a program. The CASE expression in the Transact-SQL language makes this type of encoding easy to implement.

NOTE: CASE does not represent a statement (as in most programming languages), but an expression. Therefore, the CASE expression can be used (almost) everywhere where the Transact-SQL language allows the use of an expression.

The CASE expression has two different forms:

- Simple CASE expression
- Searched CASE expression

The syntax of the simple CASE expression is

```
CASE expression_1
  {WHEN expression_2 THEN result_1} ...
  [ELSE result_n]
END
```

A Transact-SQL statement with the simple CASE expression looks for the first expression in the list of all WHEN clauses that matches **expression_1** and evaluates the corresponding THEN clause. If there is no match, the ELSE clause is evaluated.

The syntax of the searched CASE expression is

```
CASE
  {WHEN condition_1 THEN result_1} ...
    [ELSE result_n]
END
```

A Transact-SQL statement with the searched CASE expression looks for the first expression that evaluates to true. If none of the WHEN conditions evaluates to true, the value of the ELSE expression is returned. Example 5.61 shows the use of the searched CASE expression.

▼ EXAMPLE 5.61

```
SELECT project_name,
   CASE
    WHEN budget > 0 AND budget < 100000  THEN 1
    WHEN budget >= 100000 AND budget < 200000  THEN 2
    WHEN budget >= 200000 AND budget < 300000  THEN 3
    ELSE 4
   END budget_weight
  FROM project
```

The result is

project_name	budget_weight
Apollo	2
Gemini	1
Mercury	2

Budgets of all projects are weighted in Example 5.61, and the calculated weights (together with the name of the corresponding project) are displayed.

COMPUTE CLAUSE

The COMPUTE clause uses aggregate functions (MIN, MAX, SUM, AVG, and COUNT) to calculate summary values that appear as additional rows in the result of a query. The aggregate functions used with the COMPUTE clause are referred to as row aggregate functions.

The aggregate functions are usually applied to rows of a table to calculate a scalar value, which then appears in the result query as an additional row (see Example 5.62). The query using this form of aggregate functions has, again, a row as a result.

The result of a COMPUTE clause is not a table: it is a report. Hence, the COMPUTE clause, in contrast to all other described operators and clauses, does not belong to the relational model, which is a basis for SQL Server and all other relational database systems.

The COMPUTE clause has an optional BY portion. BY defines the grouping form of the result. If BY is omitted, the row aggregate function is applied to all rows of a result query. The option BY **column_name** specifies that the values of the **column_name** column are used to build groups. The ORDER BY clause is required if the COMPUTE clause with BY is used.

Examples 5.62 and 5.63 show the use of the COMPUTE clause, with and without the BY portion.

▼ EXAMPLE 5.62

```
SELECT emp_no, project_no, enter_date
  FROM works_on
  WHERE project_no = 'p1' OR project_no = 'p2'
COMPUTE MIN(enter_date)
```

The result is

emp_no	project_no	enter_date
10102	p1	1997-10-01 00:00:00.000
25348	p2	1998-02-15 00:00:00.000
18316	p2	1998-06-01 00:00:00.000
29346	p2	1997-12-15 00:00:00.000
9031	p1	1998-04-15 00:00:00.000
28559	p1	1998-08-01 00:00:00.000
28559	p2	1999-02-01 00:00:00.000
29346	p1	1998-01-04 00:00:00.000

```
min
1997-10-01 00:00:00.000
```

▼ EXAMPLE 5.63

```
SELECT emp_no, project_no, enter_date
  FROM works_on
  WHERE project_no = 'p1' OR project_no = 'p2'
  ORDER BY project_no
COMPUTE MIN(enter_date) BY project_no
```

The result is

emp_no	project_no	enter_date
10102	p1	1997-10-01 00:00:00.000
9031	p1	1998-04-15 00:00:00.000
28559	p1	1998-08-01 00:00:00.000
29346	p1	1998-01-04 00:00:00.000

```
min
1997-10-01 00:00:00.000
```

emp_no	project_no	enter_date
25348	p2	1998-02-15 00:00:00.000
18316	p2	1998-06-01 00:00:00.000
29346	p2	1997-12-15 00:00:00.000
28559	p2	1999-02-01 00:00:00.000

```
min
1997-12-15 00:00:00.000
```

A COMPUTE clause can have multiple uses in a SELECT statement. Hence, Example 5.63 can be written using one SELECT statement and the following COMPUTE statements:

```
COMPUTE MIN(enter_date) BY project_no

COMPUTE MIN(enter_date)
```

Example 5.64 shows the use of multiple aggregate functions in a COMPUTE clause.

▼ EXAMPLE 5.64

```
SELECT project_no, budget
    FROM project
    WHERE budget < 150000
  COMPUTE SUM(budget), AVG(budget)
```

The result is

project_no	budget
p1	120000.0
p2	95000.0

sum	avg
215000.0	107500.0

There are some restrictions concerning the COMPUTE clause:

- SELECT INTO is not allowed (because the result of the COMPUTE clause is *not* a table).
- All columns in the COMPUTE clause must appear in a SELECT list.
- The name of each column in the COMPUTE BY clause must appear in the ORDER BY clause.
- The order of the columns in the COMPUTE BY and the ORDER BY clauses must be identical.

TEMPORARY TABLES

A temporary table is a special kind of a table that differs in two ways from base tables:

- Each temporary table is implicitly dropped by the system.
- Each temporary table is stored in the **tempdb** system database.

Temporary tables can be local or global. Local temporary tables are removed at the end of the current session. They are specified with the prefix #—for example, **#table_name**. Global temporary tables, which are specified with the prefix **##**, are dropped at the end of the session that created this table.

Examples 5.65 and 5.66 show the creation of the local temporary table **project_temp**.

▼ EXAMPLE 5.65

```
CREATE TABLE #project_temp
  (project_no CHAR(4) NOT NULL,
   project_name CHAR(25) NOT NULL)
```

▼ EXAMPLE 5.66

```
SELECT project_no, project_name
  INTO #project_temp
  FROM project
```

Examples 5.65 and 5.66 are equivalent. They use two different Transact-SQL statements to create the local temporary table **#project_temp**. However, Example 5.66 actually populates the temporary table with the data from the **project** table, while Example 5.65 does not.

COMPUTED COLUMNS

A *computed column* is a column of a table that is used to store the result of a computation of a table's data. The most important property of a computed column is that it does not store computed data. Example 5.67 shows the table with two computed columns.

▼ EXAMPLE 5.67

```
CREATE TABLE orders
    (orderid INT NOT NULL,
     price MONEY NOT NULL,
     quantity INT NOT NULL,
     orderdate DATETIME NOT NULL,
     total AS price * quantity,
     shippeddate AS DATEADD (DAY, 7, orderdate))
```

The **orders** table in Example 5.67 has two computed columns: **total** and **shippeddate**. The column **total** is computed using two other columns—**price** and **quantity**—while the other column—**shippeddate**—is computed using the date function DATEADD and the column **orderdate**.

There are several restrictions concerning computed columns:

- Column(s) that build the computed column must belong to the same table.
- The DEFAULT constraint cannot be attached to a computed column.
- The computed column cannot contain a subquery.

Since SQL Server 2000, you can define indexes on a computed column if the following conditions are satisfied:

- The computed column must be deterministic. (Expressions are deterministic if they always return the same result for a given set of inputs.)
- The QUOTED_IDENTIFIER and ANSI_NULL options must be set ON when the CREATE TABLE statement with the computed column is executed.

▲ The result value of the computed column cannot evaluate to the text/image data type.

CONCLUSION

We have now covered all the features of the SELECT statement regarding data retrieval from only one table. Every SELECT statement that retrieves data from a table must contain at least the SELECT and the FROM clauses. The FROM clause specifies the table(s) from which the data is retrieved. The most important optional clause is the WHERE clause, containing one or more conditions that can be combined using the Boolean operators AND, OR, and NOT. Hence, the conditions in the WHERE clause place the restriction on the selected row.

The next chapter completes the handling of the SELECT statement, introducing the different kinds of join operations that allow the retrieval of data from more than one table.

EXERCISES

▼ E.5.1

Get all rows of the **works_on** table.

▼ E.5.2

Get the employee numbers for all clerks.

▼ E.5.3

Get the employee numbers for employees working in project p2, and having an employee number smaller than 10000. Solve this problem with two different but equivalent SELECT statements.

▼ E.5.4

Get the employee numbers for employees who didn't enter their project in 1998.

▼ E.5.5

Get the employee numbers for all employees who have a leading job (i.e., Analyst or Manager) in project p1.

▼ E.5.6

Get the enter dates for all employees in project p2 whose jobs have not been determined yet.

▼ E.5.7

Get the employee numbers and last names of all employees whose first name contains two letters *t*.

▼ E.5.8

Get the employee numbers and first names of all employees whose last names have a letter *o* or *a* as the second character and end with the letters *es*.

▼ E.5.9

Find the employee numbers of all employees whose department is located in Seattle.

▼ E.5.10

Find the last and first names of all employees who entered their projects on 04.01.1998.

▼ E.5.11

Group all departments using their locations.

▼ E.5.12

What is a difference between the DISTINCT and GROUP BY clauses?

▼ E.5.13

How does the GROUP BY clause manage the NULL values? Does it correspond to the general treatment of these values?

▼ E.5.14

What is the difference between COUNT(*) and COUNT(column)?

▼ E.5.15

Find the biggest employee number.

▼ E.5.16

Get the jobs that are done by more than two employees.

▼ E.5.17

Find the employee numbers of all employees who are clerks or work for department d3.

▼ E.5.18

Why is the following statement wrong?

```
SELECT project_name
   FROM project
   WHERE project_no =
      (SELECT project_no FROM works_on WHERE Job = 'Clerk')
```

Write the correct syntax form for the statement.

▼ E.5.19

What is a practical use of temporary tables?

▼ E.5.20

What is a difference between global and local temporary tables?

CHAPTER 6

Complex Queries

This chapter covers the more complex features of the SELECT statement. Queries that use more than one table to retrieve the result will be the focus here. In addition to looking at all forms of the join operator, which is the most important operator for relational DBMSs, the chapter discusses correlated subqueries and the EXISTS function.

JOIN OPERATOR

The previous chapter demonstrated the use of the SELECT statement to query rows from one table of a database. If the Transact-SQL language only supports such simple SELECT statements, the attachment of two or more tables to retrieve data would not be possible. Consequently, all data of a database would have to be stored in one table. Although the storage of all the data of a database inside one table is possible, it has one main disadvantage—the stored data are highly redundant.

Transact-SQL provides the join operator, which allows retrieval of data from more than one table. This operator is probably the most important operator for relational database systems, because it allows data to be spread over many tables and thus achieves a vital property of database systems—nonredundant data.

NOTE: Chapter 5 introduced the UNION operator, which also attaches two or more tables. However, the UNION operator always attaches two or more SELECT statements, while the join operator "joins" two or more tables using just one SELECT. Further, the UNION operator attaches rows of tables, while, as you will see later, the join operator "joins" columns of tables.

The join operator is applied to base tables and views. In this chapter, joins between base tables are discussed, while joins concerning views will be discussed in Chapter 10.

Two tables can be joined together in (at least) five different ways:

- Using equijoin
- Using Cartesian product (i.e., a cross join)
- Using a natural join
- Using a thetajoin
- Using an outer join

Two Syntax Forms to Implement Joins

To join two or more tables you can use two different syntax forms:

- ANSI join syntax
- SQL Server join syntax

The ANSI join syntax is introduced in the SQL92 standard and defines the join operation explicitly—that is, using the corresponding name for each type of join operation. This syntax enhances the readability of queries and therefore its use is recommended. (SQL Server supports this syntax since version 6.5.) Rather than indicating the join relationships implicitly via the WHERE clause, the new join keywords specify them explicitly in the FROM clause. The keywords concerning the explicit definition of join are

- CROSS JOIN
- [INNER] JOIN
- LEFT [OUTER] JOIN
- RIGHT [OUTER] JOIN
- FULL [OUTER] JOIN

CROSS JOIN specifies the Cartesian product of two tables. INNER JOIN defines the natural join of two tables, while LEFT OUTER JOIN and RIGHT OUTER JOIN characterize the join operations of the same names, respectively. Finally, FULL OUTER JOIN specifies the union of the right and left outer joins. (All these different join operations will be explained in the following sections of this chapter.)

The SQL Server join syntax is "old-style" syntax, where each join operation is defined implicitly, using the so-called join columns. Each example in this chapter concerning the join operation is solved using both syntax forms: You will find the solution with the ANSI join syntax first, and after that the equivalent solution with the SQL Server join syntax.

Equijoin

Equijoin is best explained through the use of an example.

▼ EXAMPLE 6.1

Get full details of each employee; that is, besides the employee's number, first and last names, and the corresponding department number, also get the name of his or her department and its location, with duplicate columns displayed.

ANSI join syntax:

```
SELECT employee.*, department.*
    FROM employee INNER JOIN department
    ON employee.dept_no = department.dept_no
```

SQL Server join syntax:

```
SELECT employee.*, department.*
  FROM employee, department
  WHERE employee.dept_no = department.dept_no
```

The result is

emp_no	emp_fname	emp_lname	dept_no	dept_no	dept_name	location
25348	Matthew	Smith	d3	d3	Marketing	Dallas
10102	Ann	Jones	d3	d3	Marketing	Dallas
18316	John	Barrimore	d1	d1	Research	Dallas
29346	James	James	d2	d2	Accounting	Seattle
9031	Elsa	Bertoni	d2	d2	Accounting	Seattle
2581	Elke	Hansel	d2	d2	Accounting	Seattle
28559	Sybill	Moser	d1	d1	Research	Dallas

The SELECT list in Example 6.1 includes all columns of the tables **employee** and **department**. This is a characteristic of an equijoin. Hence, the result of an equijoin always contains one or more pairs of columns that have identical values in every row.

The FROM clause in the SELECT statement specifies the tables, which are joined. The connection between these tables is specified in the WHERE clause using one or more pairs of corresponding columns in both tables. The condition employee.dept_no = department.dept_no in Example 6.1 specifies a *join condition*, and both columns are said to be *join columns*.

Example 6.1 can be used to show how a join operation works. Note that this is one illustration of how you can think about the join process; SQL Server actually has several strategies from which it chooses to implement the join operator. Imagine each row of the **employee** table combined with each row of the **department** table. The result of this combination is a table with 7 columns (4 from the table **employee** and 3 from the table **department**) and 21 rows (see Table 6-1).

In the second step, all rows from Table 6-1 that do not satisfy the join condition employee.dept_no = department.dept_no are removed. These rows are prefixed in Table 6-1 with the * sign. The rest of the rows represent the result of Example 6.1.

The semantics of the corresponding join columns must be identical. This means both columns must have the same logical meaning. It is not required that the corresponding join columns have the same name (or even an identical type), although this will often be the case.

NOTE: It is not possible for a database system to check the logical meaning of a column. Therefore, database systems can only check the data type and the length of string data types. SQL Server requires that the corresponding join columns have compatible data types, such as INT and SMALLINT. (The best way to declare corresponding join columns is by using domains.)

The sample database contains three pairs of columns in which each column of the pair has the same logical meaning (and, as is natural, they have the same names as well). The tables **employee** and **department** can be joined using the columns **employee.dept_no**

emp_no	emp_fname	emp_lname	dept_no	dept_no	dept_name	location
*25348	Matthew	Smith	d3	d1	Research	Dallas
*10102	Ann	Jones	d3	d1	Research	Dallas
18316	John	Barrimore	d1	d1	Research	Dallas
*29346	James	James	d2	d1	Research	Dallas
*9031	Elsa	Bertoni	d2	d1	Research	Dallas
*2581	Elke	Hansel	d2	d1	Research	Dallas
28559	Sybill	Moser	d1	d1	Research	Dallas
*25348	Matthew	Smith	d3	d2	Accounting	Seattle
*10102	Ann	Jones	d3	d2	Accounting	Seattle
*18316	John	Barrimore	d1	d2	Accounting	Seattle
29346	James	James	d2	d2	Accounting	Seattle
9031	Elsa	Bertoni	d2	d2	Accounting	Seattle
2581	Elke	Hansel	d2	d2	Accounting	Seattle
*28559	Sybill	Moser	d1	d2	Accounting	Seattle
25348	Matthew	Smith	d3	d3	Marketing	Dallas
10102	Ann	Jones	d3	d3	Marketing	Dallas
*18316	John	Barrimore	d1	d3	Marketing	Dallas
*29346	James	James	d2	d3	Marketing	Dallas
*9031	Elsa	Bertoni	d2	d3	Marketing	Dallas
*2581	Elke	Hansel	d2	d3	Marketing	Dallas
*28559	Sybill	Moser	d1	d3	Marketing	Dallas

Table 6-1. Result of the Cartesian Product Between the Tables **employee** and **department**

and **department.dept_no**. The join columns of the tables **employee** and **works_on** are the columns **employee.emp_no** and **works_on.emp_no**. Finally, the tables **project** and **works_on** can be joined using the join columns **project.project_no** and **works_on.project_no**.

The names of columns in a SELECT statement can be qualified. "Qualifying" a column name means that, to avoid any possible ambiguity about which table the column belongs to, the column name is preceded by its table name (or the alias of the table), separated by a period: **table_name.column_name**.

In most SELECT statements a column name does not need any qualification, although the use of qualified names is generally recommended for readability. If column names within a SELECT statement are ambiguous (like the columns **employee.dept_no** and **department.dept_no** in Example 6.1), the qualified names for the columns *must* be used.

In a SELECT statement with a join, the WHERE clause can include other conditions in addition to the join condition (see Example 6.2).

▼ EXAMPLE 6.2

Get full details of all employees who work on the project Gemini.
ANSI join syntax:

```
SELECT *
    FROM works_on JOIN project
     ON project.project_no = works_on.project_no
    WHERE project_name = 'Gemini'
```

SQL Server join syntax:

```
SELECT project.*, works_on.*
  FROM works_on, project
  WHERE project.project_no = works_on.project_no
  AND project_name = 'Gemini'
```

The result is

emp_no	project_no	job	enter_date	project_no	project_name	budget
25348	P2	Clerk	1998-02-15	p2	Gemini	95000.0
18316	P2	NULL	1998-06-01	p2	Gemini	95000.0
29346	P2	NULL	1997-12-15	p2	Gemini	95000.0
28559	P2	Clerk	1999-02-01	p2	Gemini	95000.0

NOTE: The qualification of the column **project_name** in Example 6.2 is not necessary, because there is no ambiguity regarding this name.

Cartesian Product

The previous section illustrated a possible method of producing an equijoin. In the first step of this process, each row of the **employee** table is combined with each row of the **department** table. This intermediate result was made by the operation called Cartesian product.

▼ EXAMPLE 6.3

ANSI join syntax:

```
SELECT *
   FROM employee CROSS JOIN department
```

SQL Server join syntax:

```
SELECT *
  FROM employee, department
```

The result of Example 6.3 is shown in Table 6-1. A Cartesian product combines each row of the first table with each row of the second one. In general, the Cartesian product of two tables such that the first table has ***n*** rows and the second table has ***m*** rows will produce a result with ***n*** times ***m*** rows (or ***n*m***). Thus, the resulting set in Example 6.3 is 7*3 = 21 rows.

NOTE: The notation SELECT * FROM table1, table 2 is equivalent to the notation SELECT table1.*, table2.* FROM table1, table2. The * in this case means all columns from all tables in the FROM clause.

If the WHERE clause in a SELECT statement contains something other than the join condition, the result of the SELECT is still a Cartesian product of both tables, reduced to the rows that evaluate to true for the condition (see Example 6.4).

▼ EXAMPLE 6.4

ANSI join syntax:

```
SELECT *
  FROM works_on CROSS JOIN project
  WHERE works_on.project_no = 'p3'
```

SQL Server syntax:

```
SELECT *
  FROM works_on, project
  WHERE works_on.project_no = 'p3'
```

The result is

emp_no	project_no	job	enter_date	project_no	project_name	budget
10102	p3	Manager	1999-01-01	p1	Apollo	120000.0
2581	p3	Analyst	1998-10-15	p1	Apollo	120000.0
9031	p3	Clerk	1997-11-15	p1	Apollo	120000.0
10102	p3	Manager	1999-01-01	p2	Gemini	95000.0
2581	p3	Analyst	1998-10-15	p2	Gemini	95000.0
9031	p3	Clerk	1997-11-15	p2	Gemini	95000.0
10102	p3	Manager	1999-01-01	p3	Mercury	186500.0
2581	p3	Analyst	1998-10-15	p3	Mercury	186500.0
9031	p3	Clerk	1997-11-15	p3	Mercury	186500.0

In practice, the use of a Cartesian product is highly unusual. Sometimes users generate the Cartesian product of two tables when they forget to include the join condition in the WHERE clause of the SELECT statement. In this case, the output does not correspond to the expected result because it contains too many rows. (The existence of many and unexpected rows in the result is a hint that a Cartesian product of two tables, rather than the intended join, has been produced.)

Natural Join

In the equijoin operation, there is always one or more pairs of columns that have identical values in every row. The elimination of one of these join columns from the SELECT list gives a user a simpler and more reasonable result. The operation, which eliminates such columns from the equijoin, is called a natural join.

▼ EXAMPLE 6.5

ANSI join syntax:

```
SELECT employee.*, dept_name, location
    FROM employee JOIN department
    ON employee. dept_no = department.dept_no
```

SQL Server join syntax:

```
SELECT employee.*, dept_name, location
  FROM employee, department
  WHERE employee. dept_no = department.dept_no
```

The result is

emp_no	emp_fname	emp_lname	dept_no	dept_name	location
25348	Matthew	Smith	d3	Marketing	Dallas
10102	Ann	Jones	d3	Marketing	Dallas
18316	John	Barrimore	d1	Research	Dallas
29346	James	James	d2	Accounting	Seattle
9031	Elsa	Bertoni	d2	Accounting	Seattle
2581	Elke	Hansel	d2	Accounting	Seattle
28559	Sybill	Moser	d1	Research	Dallas

The SELECT list in Example 6.5 contains all columns from the tables **employee** and **department** except for the **dept_no** column from the second table, which is a part of the join condition and therefore superfluous in the result.

NOTE: Natural join is the most useful form of all join operations. Therefore, unless otherwise specified, the term *join* always refers to the natural join operation.

The SELECT list of a natural join need not contain all nonidentical columns from both tables (it simply doesn't include the redundant join column). Example 6.6 shows this.

▼ EXAMPLE 6.6

Get the department number for all employees who entered their projects on October 15, 1998.

ANSI join syntax:

```
SELECT dept_no
   FROM employee JOIN works_on
   ON employee.emp_no = works_on.emp_no
  WHERE enter_date = '10.15.1998'
```

SQL Server join syntax:

```
SELECT dept_no
  FROM employee, works_on
  WHERE employee.emp_no = works_on.emp_no
  AND enter_date = '10.15.1998'
```

The result is

dept_no
d2

Thetajoin

Join columns need not be compared using the equality sign. A join operation using a general join condition—that is, using a comparison operator other than equality—is called a thetajoin. In Example 6.7, the **employee_enh** table is used.

▼ EXAMPLE 6.7

Get all the combinations of employee information and department information where the domicile of an employee alphabetically precedes the location of a department.

ANSI join syntax:

```
SELECT employee_enh.*, department.*
  FROM employee_enh JOIN department
  ON domicile < location
```

SQL Server syntax:

```
SELECT employee_enh.*, department.*
  FROM employee_enh, department
  WHERE domicile < location
```

The result is

emp_no	emp_fname	emp_lname	dept_no	domicile	dept_no	dept_name	location
25348	Matthew	Smith	d3	San Antonio	d2	Accounting	Seattle
10102	Ann	Jones	d3	Houston	d2	Accounting	Seattle
18316	John	Barrimore	d1	San Antonio	d2	Accounting	Seattle
9031	Elsa	Bertoni	d2	Portland	d2	Accounting	Seattle
28559	Sybill	Moser	d1	Houston	d2	Accounting	Seattle

In Example 6.7, the corresponding values of columns **domicile** and **location** are compared. In every resulting row, the value of the **domicile** column is ordered alphabetically before the corresponding value of the **location** column.

Joining More Than Two Tables

Theoretically, there is no upper limit on the number of tables that can be joined using a SELECT statement. (One join condition always combines two tables!) However, SQL Server has an implementation restriction: the maximum number of tables that can be joined in a SELECT statement is 64.

NOTE: Usually, a maximum of 8–10 tables are joined in a SELECT statement. If you need to join more than 10 tables in a SELECT statement, your database design is probably not optimal.

▼ EXAMPLE 6.8

Get the first and last names of all analysts whose department is located in Seattle.
ANSI join syntax:

```
SELECT emp_fname, emp_lname
    FROM works_on JOIN employee ON works_on.emp_no=employee.emp_no
                  JOIN department ON employee.dept_no=department.dept_no
    AND location = 'Seattle'
   AND job = 'analyst'
```

SQL Server join syntax:

```
SELECT emp_fname, emp_lname
  FROM works_on, employee, department
  WHERE works_on.emp_no = employee.emp_no
```

```
AND employee.dept_no = department.dept_no
AND job = 'analyst'
AND location = 'Seattle'
```

The result is

emp_fname	emp_lname
Elke	Hansel

The result in Example 6.8 can be obtained only if you join at least three tables: **works_on**, **employee**, and **department**. These tables can be joined using two pairs of join columns:

```
(works_on.emp_no, employee.emp_no)
(employee.dept_no,department.dept_no)
```

Example 6.9 uses all four tables from the sample database.

▼ EXAMPLE 6.9

Get the project names (with redundant duplicates eliminated) being worked on by employees in the Accounting department.

ANSI join syntax:

```
SELECT DISTINCT project_name
    FROM project JOIN works_on
    ON project.project_no = works_on.project_no
          JOIN employee ON works_on.emp_no = employee.emp_no
          JOIN department ON employee.dept_no = department.dept_no
    WHERE dept_name = 'Accounting'
```

SQL Server join syntax:

```
SELECT DISTINCT project_name
  FROM project, works_on, employee, department
  WHERE project.project_no = works_on.project_no
  AND works_on.emp_no = employee.emp_no
  AND employee.dept_no = department.dept_no
  AND dept_name = 'Accounting'
```

The result is

project_name
Apollo
Gemini
Mercury

Notice that when joining three tables, you use two join conditions (linking two tables each) to achieve a natural join. When you join four tables, you use three such join conditions. In general, if you join ***n*** tables, you will need ***n-1*** join conditions to avoid a Cartesian product. Of course, more than ***n-1*** join conditions, as well as other conditions, are certainly permissible to further reduce the result set.

Joining a Table with Itself

In addition to joining two or more different tables, a join operation can also be applied to a single table. In this case, the table is joined with itself, whereby a single column of the table is compared with itself. The comparison of a column with itself means that the table name appears twice in the FROM clause of a SELECT statement. Therefore, you need to be able to reference the name of the same table twice. This can be accomplished using aliases. The same is true for the column names in the join condition of a SELECT statement. In order to distinguish both column names, you use the qualified names. Example 6.10 joins the **department** table with itself.

▼ EXAMPLE 6.10

Get full details of all departments located at the same location as at least one other department.

ANSI join syntax:

```
SELECT t1.dept_no, t1.dept_name, t1.location
   FROM department t1 JOIN department t2
      ON  t1. location = t2.location
   WHERE t1.dept_no <> t2.dept_no
```

SQL Server join syntax:

```
SELECT DISTINCT t1.dept_no, t1.dept_name, t1.location
  FROM department t1, department t2
  WHERE t1. location = t2.location
  AND t1.dept_no <> t2.dept_no
```

The result is

dept_no	dept_name	location
d3	Marketing	Dallas
d1	Research	Dallas

The FROM clause in Example 6.10 contains two aliases for the **department** table: **t1** and **t2**. The first condition in the WHERE clause specifies the join columns, while the second condition eliminates unnecessary duplicates by making certain that each department is compared with *different* departments.

In Example 6.11, the **employee_enh** table is used.

▼ EXAMPLE 6.11

Get the employee number, last name, and domicile of each employee who works for the same department and lives in the same city as at least one other employee.
ANSI join syntax:

```
SELECT t1.emp_no, t1.emp_lname, t1.domicile
   FROM employee_enh t1 JOIN  employee_enh t2
      ON t1.domicile = t2.domicile
   WHERE t1.dept_no = t2.dept_no
   AND t1.emp_no <> t2.emp_no
```

SQL Server join syntax:

```
SELECT DISTINCT t1.emp_no, t1.emp_lname, t1.domicile
  FROM employee_enh t1, employee_enh t2
  WHERE t1.domicile = t2.domicile
  AND t1.dept_no = t2.dept_no
  AND t1.emp_no <> t2.emp_no
```

The result is

emp_no	emp_lname	domicile

In Example 6.11, the join condition includes two pairs of identical columns: **domicile** and **dept_no**. The last condition, **t1.emp_no** <> **t2.emp_no**, prevents comparisons of employees with themselves. (In the sample database, there are no employees working for the same department and living in the same city as any other employees.)

Outer Join

In the previous examples of equijoin, thetajoin, and natural join, the resulting set included only rows from one table that have corresponding rows in the other table. Sometimes it is necessary to retrieve, in addition to the matching rows, the unmatched rows from one or both of the tables. Such an operation is called an *outer join*.

Examples 6.12 and 6.13 show the difference between natural join and the corresponding outer join. (All examples in this section use the **employee_enh** table.)

▼ EXAMPLE 6.12

Get full details of all employees plus locations of their departments such that the living place and the working place of an employee are located in the same city.
ANSI join syntax:

```
SELECT employee_enh.*, department.location
   FROM employee_enh JOIN department
        ON domicile = location
```

SQL Server join syntax:

```
SELECT employee_enh.*, department.location
  FROM employee_enh, department
  WHERE domicile = location
```

The result is

emp_no	emp_fname	emp_lname	dept_no	domicile	location
29346	James	James	d2	Seattle	Seattle

Example 6.12 uses an equijoin to display the resulting set of rows. If you would also like to know all other existing living places of employees, you have to use the left outer join. SQL Server uses the operator *= to specify the left outer join. This is called a *left* outer join because all rows from the table on the *left* side of the *= symbol are returned, whether or not they have a matching row in the table on the right. A *right* outer join is similar, but as you have probably guessed, it returns all rows of the table on the *right* of the symbol (and the symbol is replaced by =*). The asterisk symbol (*) indicates which table gets all of its rows returned.

▼ EXAMPLE 6.13

Get full details for all employees plus locations of their departments, for all cities that are either the living places, or both living and working places, of employees.
ANSI join syntax:

```
SELECT employee_enh.*, department.location
    FROM employee_enh LEFT OUTER JOIN department
        ON domicile = location
```

SQL Server join syntax:

```
SELECT employee_enh.*, department.location
  FROM employee_enh, department
  WHERE domicile *= location
```

The result is

emp_no	emp_fname	emp_lname	dept_no	domicile	location
25348	Matthew	Smith	d3	San Antonio	NULL
10102	Ann	Jones	d3	Houston	NULL
18316	John	Barrimore	d1	San Antonio	NULL
29346	James	James	d2	Seattle	Seattle
9031	Elsa	Bertoni	d2	Portland	NULL

emp_no	emp_fname	emp_lname	dept_no	domicile	location
2581	Elke	Hansel	d2	Tacoma	NULL
28559	Sybill	Moser	d1	Houston	NULL

As you can see, when there is no corresponding row in the other table (**department**, in this case), its columns are populated by null values. Example 6.14 shows the use of the right outer join.

▼ EXAMPLE 6.14

Get full details of all departments, plus living places of their employees, for all cities that are either the locations of departments or the living and working places of an employee. ANSI join syntax:

```
SELECT employee_enh.domicile, department.*
    FROM employee_enh RIGHT OUTER JOIN department
        ON domicile =location
```

SQL Server join syntax:

```
SELECT employee_enh.domicile, department.*
  FROM employee_enh, department
  WHERE domicile =* location
```

The result is

domicile	dept_no	dept_name	location
Seattle	d2	Accounting	Seattle
NULL	d1	Research	Dallas
NULL	d3	Marketing	Dallas

In addition to the left and right outer joins, there is also the full outer join, which is defined as the union of the left and right outer joins. In other words, all rows from both tables are represented in the result set. If there is no corresponding row in one of the tables, its columns are returned with null values. This operation is specified using the FULL OUTER JOIN operator.

Every outer join operation can be simulated using the UNION operator plus the EXISTS function. Example 6.15 is equivalent to Example 6.13.

▼ EXAMPLE 6.15

Get full details for all employees, plus locations of their departments, for all cities that are either the living places, or both living and working places, of employees.

```
SELECT employee_enh.*, department.location
  FROM employee_enh JOIN department
```

```
  ON domicile = location
UNION
SELECT employee_enh.*, 'NULL'
  FROM employee_enh
  WHERE NOT EXISTS
  (SELECT *
     FROM department
    WHERE location = domicile)
```

The first SELECT statement in the union specifies the natural join of the tables **employee_enh** and **department** with the join columns **domicile** and **location**. This SELECT statement retrieves all cities that are at the same time the living places and working places of each employee. The second SELECT statement in the union retrieves, additionally, all rows from the **employee_enh** table that do not match the condition in the natural join.

CORRELATED SUBQUERIES

A subquery is said to be a *correlated subquery* if the inner query depends on the outer query for any of its values. Examples 6.16 and 6.17 show how the same query can be formulated using a simple subquery and a correlated subquery.

▼ EXAMPLE 6.16

Get the last names of all employees who work on the project p3.

```
SELECT emp_lname
  FROM employee
  WHERE emp_no IN
  (SELECT emp_no
     FROM works_on
    WHERE project_no = 'p3')
```

The result is

emp_lname
Jones
Bertoni
Hansel

In the simple subquery of Example 6.16, the inner query is evaluated once, and the result set is passed to the outer query. The outer subquery then evaluates the final result.

▼ EXAMPLE 6.17

Get the last names of all employees who work on project p3.

```
SELECT emp_lname
  FROM employee
  WHERE 'p3' IN
  (SELECT project_no
     FROM works_on
    WHERE works_on.emp_no = employee.emp_no)
```

The inner query in Example 6.17 must be evaluated many times because it contains the **emp_no** column, which belongs to the **employee** table in the outer query, and the value of the **emp_no** column changes every time SQL Server examines a different row of the **employee** table in the outer query.

Let's walk through how SQL Server might process the query in Example 6.17. First, the system retrieves the first row of the **employee** table (for the outer query) and compares the employee number of that column (25348) with values of the **works_on.emp_no** column in the inner query. Since the only **project_no** for this employee is p2, the inner query returns the value p2. The single value in the set is not equal to the constant value p3 in the outer query, so the outer query's condition (WHERE 'p3' IN …) is not met and no rows are returned by the outer query for this employee. Then, the system retrieves the next row of the **employee** table and repeats the comparison of employee numbers in both tables. The second employee has two rows in the **works_on** table with **project_no** values of p1 and p3, so the result set of the inner query is (p1,p3). One of the elements in the resulting set is equal to the constant value p3, so the condition is evaluated to true and the corresponding value of the **emp_lname** column in the second row (Jones) is displayed. The same process will be applied to all rows of the **employee** table, and the final resulting set with three rows is retrieved.

Example 6.18 shows the correlated subquery using the **department** table in both inner and outer queries. This example is equivalent to Example 6.10.

▼ EXAMPLE 6.18

Get full details of all departments at the same location.

```
SELECT t1.*
  FROM department t1
  WHERE t1.location IN
  (SELECT t2.location
     FROM department t2
    WHERE t1.dept_no <> t2.dept_no)
```

The result is

dept_no	dept_name	location
d1	Research	Dallas
d3	Marketing	Dallas

More examples of correlated subqueries are shown in the next section.

EXISTS Function and Subqueries

The EXISTS function takes a subquery as an argument and returns true if the subquery returns one or more rows, and returns false if it returns zero rows. This function will be explained using examples.

▼ EXAMPLE 6.19

Get the last names of all employees who work on project p1.

```
SELECT emp_lname
  FROM employee
  WHERE EXISTS
  (SELECT *
     FROM works_on
    WHERE employee.emp_no = works_on.emp_no
   AND project_no = 'p1')
```

The result is

emp_lname
Jones
James
Bertoni
Moser

The subquery of the EXISTS function almost always depends on a variable from an outer query. Therefore, the EXISTS function usually specifies a correlated subquery.

Let's walk through how SQL Server might process the query in Example 6.19. First, the outer query considers the first row of the **employee** table (Smith). Next, the EXISTS subquery is evaluated to determine whether there are any rows in the **works_on** table whose employee number matches the one from the current row in the outer query, and whose **project_no** is p1. Because Mr. Smith does not work on the project p1, the result of the inner query is an empty set and the EXISTS function is evaluated to false. Therefore, the employee named Smith does not belong to the final resulting set. Using this process, all rows of the **employee** table are tested, and the resulting set is displayed.

Example 6.20 shows the use of the NOT EXISTS function.

▼ EXAMPLE 6.20

Get the last name of all employees who work for a department not located in Seattle.

```
SELECT emp_lname
  FROM employee
  WHERE NOT EXISTS
  (SELECT *
```

```
FROM department
WHERE employee.dept_no = department.dept_no
AND location = 'Seattle')
```

The result is

emp_lname
Smith
Jones
Barrimore
Moser

The SELECT list of an outer query involving the EXISTS function is not required to be of the form "SELECT *," as in the previous examples. The form "SELECT column_list," where **column_list** is one or more columns of the table, is an alternate form. Both forms are equivalent, because the EXISTS function tests only the existence (i.e., nonexistence) of rows in the resulting set. The first form (SELECT *) is recommended.

As already stated in Chapter 5, the EXISTS function can be used to represent both set operations: the intersection and the difference. Examples 6.21 and 6.22 use the EXISTS function and the NOT EXISTS function to represent the intersection and the difference of two tables, respectively.

▼ EXAMPLE 6.21

Get all the cities that are locations of a department as well as living places of employees.

```
SELECT DISTINCT domicile
  FROM employee_enh
  WHERE EXISTS
  (SELECT *
    FROM department
   WHERE domicile = location)
```

The result is

domicile
Seattle

▼ EXAMPLE 6.22

Get all the living places of employees that are not the locations of any department.

```
SELECT DISTINCT domicile
  FROM employee_enh
  WHERE NOT EXISTS
```

```
    (SELECT *
       FROM department
      WHERE domicile=location)
```

The result is

domicile
Houston
Portland
San Antonio
Tacoma

The EXISTS function can also be used to represent the ANY and ALL operators. Example 6.23 uses EXISTS to represent the ANY operator.

▼ EXAMPLE 6.23

Get the first and last names of all employees who work on project p1.

```
SELECT emp_fname, emp_lname
  FROM employee
  WHERE EXISTS
  (SELECT *
     FROM works_on
    WHERE project_no = 'p1'
    AND employee.emp_no = works_on.emp_no)
```

The result is

emp_fname	emp_lname
Ann	Jones
James	James
Elsa	Bertoni
Sybill	Moser

Example 6.24 uses NOT EXISTS to represent the ALL operator.

▼ EXAMPLE 6.24

Get the job of the employee with the smallest employee number.

```
SELECT DISTINCT job
  FROM works_on
```

```
WHERE NOT EXISTS
(SELECT *
   FROM employee
  WHERE  works_on.emp_no > employee.emp_no)
```

The result is

job
Analyst

SHOULD YOU USE JOIN OR SUBQUERIES?

Almost all SELECT statements that join tables and use the join operator can be rewritten as subqueries and vice versa. Writing the SELECT in the form of a join is often easier for SQL programmers to read and understand, and can also help SQL Server find a more efficient strategy for retrieving the appropriate data. However, there are few problems that can be easier solved using subqueries, and also some others that can be easier solved using joins.

Subquery Advantages

Subqueries are advantageous over joins when you have to calculate an aggregate value on the fly and use it in the outer query for comparison. Example 6.25 shows this.

▼ EXAMPLE 6.25

Get the employee numbers and enter dates of all employees with enter dates equal to the earliest date.

```
SELECT emp_no, enter_date
   FROM works_on
   WHERE enter_date = (SELECT min(enter_date)
                          FROM works_on)
```

This problem cannot be solved with a join, because you would have to write the aggregate function in the WHERE clause and it is not allowed. (You can solve the problem using two separate queries in relation to the **works_on** table.)

Join Advantages

Joins are advantageous over subqueries if the SELECT list in a query contains columns from more than one table. Example 6.26 shows this.

▼ **EXAMPLE 6.26**

Get the employee numbers, last names, and jobs for all employees that entered their projects on October 15, 1998.

```
SELECT employee.emp_no, emp_lname, job
   FROM employee, works_on
  WHERE employee.emp_no = works_on.emp_no
  AND enter_date = '10.15.1998'
```

The SELECT list of the query in Example 6.26 contains columns **emp_no** and **emp_lname** from the **employee** table and the **job** column from the **works_on** table. For this reason, the following (and equivalent) solution in Example 6.27 with the subquery displays an error, because subqueries can display information only from the outer table.

▼ **EXAMPLE 6.27** **(DISPLAYS AN ERROR!!)**

```
SELECT emp_no, emp_lname, job
  FROM employee
  WHERE emp_no = (SELECT emp_no FROM works_on
                          WHERE enter_date = '10.15.1998')
```

CONCLUSION

This chapter and Chapter 5 have shown the use of the SELECT statement. Three other important DML statements—INSERT, DELETE, and UPDATE—will be described in the next chapter.

EXERCISES

Write all solutions concerning the exercises that use a join operation with the SQL92 style as well as with the conventional (SQL Server) style.

▼ **E.6.1**

Create:

a. Equijoin
b. Natural join
c. Cartesian product

for the **project** and **works_on** tables.

▼ **E.6.2**

If you intend to join several tables in a query (say **N**), how many join conditions are needed?

▼ E.6.3
Get the employee numbers and jobs of all employees working in project Gemini.

▼ E.6.4
Get the first and last names of all employees that work for departments Research or Accounting.

▼ E.6.5
Get the enter dates of all clerks that belong to the department d1.

▼ E.6.6
Get the names of projects on which two or more clerks are working.

▼ E.6.7
Get the first and last names of the employees that are managers and work on project Mercury.

▼ E.6.8
Get the first and last names of all employees who entered the project at the same time as at least one other employee.

▼ E.6.9
Get the employee numbers of the employees living in the same location and belonging to the same department. (Hint: Use the extended sample database.)

▼ E.6.10
Get the employee numbers of all employees belonging to the Marketing department. Find two equivalent solutions using:

a. The join operator
b. The correlated subquery

CHAPTER 7

Modification of a Table's Contents

In addition to the SELECT statement, which was introduced in Chapters 5 and 6, there are three other DML statements: INSERT, UPDATE, and DELETE. Like the SELECT statement, these three modification statements operate either on tables or on views. This chapter discusses each statement and gives examples of their use.

INSERT STATEMENT

The INSERT statement inserts rows (or parts of them) into a table. It has two different forms:

1. INSERT INTO tab_name | view_name [(col_list)]
   { DEFAULT VALUES | VALUES ({DEFAULT | expression_1}...) }
2. INSERT INTO tab_name | view_name [(col_list)]
   {select_statement | execute_statement}

Using the first form, exactly one row (or parts of it) is inserted into the **tab_name** table or into the underlying table of the **view_name** view. The second form of the INSERT statement inserts the resulting set of rows from the SELECT statement or from the stored procedure, which is executed using the EXECUTE statement. (The stored procedure must return data, which is then inserted into the table.) (The SELECT statement can select values from a different table or the same table as the target of the INSERT statement, as long as the types of the columns are compatible.)

With both forms, every inserted value must have the compatible data type as the corresponding column of the table. To do so, all character-based values and date/time data must be enclosed in apostrophes (or quotation marks), while all numeric values need no such enclosing.

Inserting a Single Row

In the first and second forms of the INSERT statement, the explicit specification of the column list is optional. This means omitting the list of columns is equivalent to specifying a list of all columns in the table.

The option DEFAULT VALUES inserts default values for all the columns. If a column is of the data type TIMESTAMP or has the IDENTITY property, the value, which is automatically incremented by the system, will be inserted. For other data types, the column is set to the appropriate non-null default value, if a default exists, or NULL if it doesn't. If the column is not nullable, and has no DEFAULT value, then the INSERT statement fails and an error will be indicated.

Examples 7.1–7.4 insert rows into the four tables of the sample database. This action shows the use of the INSERT statement to load a small amount of data into a database.

▼ EXAMPLE 7.1

Load data into the **employee** table.

```
INSERT INTO employee VALUES (25348, 'Matthew', 'Smith','d3')
INSERT INTO employee VALUES (10102, 'Ann', 'Jones','d3')
INSERT INTO employee VALUES (18316, 'John', 'Barrimore', 'd1')
INSERT INTO employee VALUES (29346, 'James', 'James', 'd2')
INSERT INTO employee VALUES (9031, 'Elsa', 'Bertoni', 'd2')
INSERT INTO employee VALUES (2581, 'Elke', 'Hansel', 'd2')
INSERT INTO employee VALUES (28559, 'Sybill', 'Moser', 'd1')
```

▼ EXAMPLE 7.2

Load data into the **department** table.

```
INSERT INTO department VALUES ('d1', 'Research', 'Dallas')
INSERT INTO department VALUES ('d2', 'Accounting', 'Seattle')
INSERT INTO department VALUES ('d3', 'Marketing', 'Dallas')
```

▼ EXAMPLE 7.3

Load data into the **project** table.

```
INSERT INTO project VALUES ('p1', 'Apollo', 120000.00)
INSERT INTO project VALUES ('p2', 'Gemini', 95000.00)
INSERT INTO project VALUES ('p3', 'Mercury', 186500.00)
```

▼ EXAMPLE 7.4

Load data into the **works_on** table.

```
INSERT INTO works_on VALUES (10102,'p1', 'Analyst', '1997.10.1')
INSERT INTO works_on VALUES (10102, 'p3', 'Manager', '1999.1.1')
INSERT INTO works_on VALUES (25348, 'p2', 'Clerk', '1998.2.15')
INSERT INTO works_on VALUES (18316, 'p2', NULL, '1998.6.1')
INSERT INTO works_on VALUES (29346, 'p2', NULL, '1997.12.15')
INSERT INTO works_on VALUES (2581, 'p3', 'Analyst', '1998.10.15')
INSERT INTO works_on VALUES (9031, 'p1', 'Manager', '1998.4.15')
INSERT INTO works_on VALUES (28559, 'p1', 'NULL', '1998.8.1')
INSERT INTO works_on VALUES (28559, 'p2', 'Clerk', '1999.2.1')
INSERT INTO works_on VALUES (9031, 'p3', 'Clerk', '1997.11.15')
INSERT INTO works_on VALUES (29346, 'p1','Clerk'', '1998.1.4')
```

There are a few different ways to insert values into a new row. Examples 7.5 through 7.7 show these possibilities.

▼ EXAMPLE 7.5

```
INSERT INTO employee VALUES (15201, 'Dave', 'Davis', NULL)
```

The INSERT statement in Example 7.5 corresponds to the INSERT statements in Examples 7.1–7.4. The explicit use of the keyword NULL inserts the null value into the corresponding column.

The insertion of values into some (but not all) of a table's columns usually requires the explicit specification of the corresponding columns. The omitted columns must be either nullable or have a DEFAULT value.

▼ EXAMPLE 7.6

```
INSERT INTO employee (emp_no, emp_fname, emp_lname)
        VALUES (15201, 'Dave', 'Davis')
```

Examples 7.5 and 7.6 are equivalent. The **department_nr** column is the only nullable column in the **employee** table because we declared all other columns in the **employee** table with the NOT NULL clause in the CREATE TABLE statement.

The order of column names in the VALUE clause of the INSERT statement can be different from the original order of those columns, which is determined in the CREATE TABLE statement. In this case, it is absolutely necessary to list the columns in the new order.

▼ EXAMPLE 7.7

```
INSERT INTO employee (emp_lname, emp_fname, dept_no, emp_no)
        VALUES ('Davis', 'Dave', 'd1', 15201)
```

Inserting Multiple Rows

The second form of the INSERT statement inserts one or more rows selected with a subquery.

▼ EXAMPLE 7.8

Get all the numbers and names for departments located in Dallas, and load the selected data into a new table.

```
CREATE TABLE dallas_dept
      (dept_no CHAR(4) NOT NULL,
       dept_name CHAR(20) NOT NULL)
```

```
INSERT INTO dallas_dept (dept_no, dept_name)
  SELECT dept_no, dept_name
     FROM department
    WHERE location = 'Dallas'
```

The new table, **dallas_dept**, created in Example 7.8, has the same columns as the **department** table except for the **location** column. The subquery in the INSERT statement selects all rows with the value 'Dallas' in the **location** column. The selected rows will be subsequently inserted in the new table.

The content of the **dallas_dept** table can be selected with the following SELECT statement:

```
SELECT * FROM dallas_dept
```

The result is

dept_no	dept_name
d1	Research
d3	Marketing

▼ EXAMPLE 7.9

Get all employee numbers, project numbers, and project enter dates for all clerks who work in project p2, and load the selected data into a new table.

```
CREATE TABLE clerk_t
   (emp_no INT NOT NULL,
    project_no CHAR(4),
    enter_date DATETIME)

INSERT INTO clerk_t (emp_no, project_no, enter_date)
  SELECT emp_no, project_no, enter_date
    FROM works_on
    WHERE job = 'Clerk'
    AND project_no = 'p2'
```

The new table, **clerk_t**, contains the following rows:

emp_no	project_no	enter_date
25348	p2	1998-02-15 00:00:00.000
28559	p2	1999-02-01 00:00:00.000

The tables **dallas_dept** and **clerk_t** (Examples 7.8 and 7.9) were empty before the INSERT statement inserted the rows. If, however, the table already exists and there are rows in it, the new rows will be appended.

Inserting rows within a view has certain limitations. The INSERT statement and views will be discussed in detail in Chapter 10.

UPDATE STATEMENT

The UPDATE statement modifies values of table rows. This statement has the general form:

```
UPDATE tab_name | view_name
   SET column_1 = expression [{column_2 = expression}...]
   [FROM tab_name1 | view_name1 [{tab_name2 | view_name2} ...]]
   [WHERE condition]
```

Rows in the **tab_name** table (or rows in the table that are associated with the **view_name** view) are modified in accordance with the WHERE clause. For each row to be modified, the UPDATE statement changes the values of the columns in the SET clause, assigning a constant (or generally an expression) to the associated column. If the WHERE clause is omitted, the UPDATE statement modifies all rows of the table. (The FROM clause will be discussed in relation to Example 7.13 later in this chapter.)

NOTE: An UPDATE statement can only modify data of a single table.

There are certain limitations to modifying rows using a view. The UPDATE statement and views will be discussed in detail in Chapter 10.

▼ EXAMPLE 7.10

Set the task of employee number 18316, who works on project p2, to be 'Manager'.

```
UPDATE works_on
  SET job = 'Manager'
  WHERE emp_no = 18316
  AND project_no = 'p2'
```

The UPDATE statement in Example 7.10 modifies exactly one row of the **works_on** table, because the combination of the columns **emp_no** and **project_no** builds the primary key of that table (and is therefore unique). This example modifies the task of the employee, which was previously unknown or set to NULL.

Example 7.11 modifies rows of a table with an expression.

▼ EXAMPLE 7.11

Change the budgets of all projects to be represented in English pounds. The current rate of exchange is 0.56£ for $1.

```
UPDATE project
   SET budget = budget*0.56
```

In the example, all rows of the **project** table will be modified because of the omitted WHERE clause. The modified rows of the **project** table can be displayed with the following Transact-SQL statement:

```
SELECT * FROM project
```

The result is

project_no	project_name	budget
p1	Apollo	67200.0
p2	Gemini	53200.000000000007
p3	Mercury	104440.00000000001

▼ EXAMPLE 7.12

Due to her illness, set all tasks on all projects for Mrs. Jones to NULL.

```
UPDATE works_on
    SET job = NULL
    WHERE emp_no IN
    (SELECT emp_no
       FROM employee
      WHERE emp_lname = 'Jones')
```

Example 7.12 uses a subquery in the WHERE clause of the UPDATE statement. Because of the use of the IN operator, more than one row can result from the subquery.

Example 7.12 can also be solved using the FROM clause of the UPDATE statement. The FROM clause contains the names of tables that are involved in the UPDATE statement. All these tables must be subsequently joined. Example 7.13 shows the use of the FROM clause. This example is identical to the previous one.

NOTE: The FROM clause is a Transact-SQL extension to the ANSI SQL standard.

▼ EXAMPLE 7.13

```
UPDATE works_on
 SET job = NULL
  FROM works_on, employee
  WHERE emp_lname = 'Jones'
  AND works_on.emp_no = employee.emp_no
```

Example 7.14 illustrates the use of CASE in the UPDATE statement. (For a detailed discussion of this expression, refer to Chapter 5.) The budget of each project will be increased by a percentage (20, 10, or 5) depending on its previous amount of money. Those projects with a lower budget will be increased by the higher percentages.

▼ EXAMPLE 7.14

```
UPDATE project
 SET budget = CASE
      WHEN budget >0 and budget < 100000  THEN budget*1.2
      WHEN budget >= 100000 and budget < 200000  THEN budget*1.1
      ELSE budget*1.05
      END
```

DELETE STATEMENT

The DELETE statement deletes rows from a table. This statement has two different forms:

1. DELETE table_name | view_name
   [FROM table_name1 | view_name1 [{,table_name2 | view_name2}...]]
   [WHERE predicate]
2. DELETE table_name | view_name
   [WHERE condition]

All rows that satisfy the condition in the WHERE clause will be deleted. Explicitly naming columns within the DELETE statement is not necessary (or allowed), because all columns of the appropriate rows will be deleted (see Example 7.15).

▼ EXAMPLE 7.15

Delete all managers in the **works_on** table.

```
DELETE FROM works_on
  WHERE job = 'Manager'
```

The WHERE clause in the DELETE statement can contain a subquery.

▼ EXAMPLE 7.16

Mrs. Moser is on leave. Delete all rows in the database concerning her.

```
DELETE FROM works_on
   WHERE emp_no IN
   (SELECT emp_no
      FROM employee
     WHERE emp_lname = 'Moser')

DELETE FROM employee
   WHERE emp_lname = 'Moser'
```

Example 7.16 can also be performed using the FROM clause. This clause has the same semantics as the FROM clause in the UPDATE statement. Example 7.17 is identical to the previous one.

▼ EXAMPLE 7.17

```
DELETE works_on
   FROM works_on, employee
   WHERE works_on.emp_no = employee.emp_no
   AND emp_lname = 'Moser'

DELETE FROM employee
   WHERE emp_lname = 'Moser'
```

The use of the WHERE clause in the DELETE statement is optional. If the WHERE clause is omitted, all rows of a table will be deleted (see Example 7.18).

▼ EXAMPLE 7.18

```
DELETE FROM works_on
```

There are certain limitations to deleting rows using a view. The DELETE statement and views will be discussed in detail in Chapter 10.

NOTE: There is a significant difference between the DELETE and the DROP TABLE statements. The DELETE statement deletes (partially or totally) the contents of a table. On the other hand, the DROP TABLE statement deletes both the contents and the schema of a table. Thus, after a DELETE statement, the table still exists in the database (although possibly with zero rows), but after a DROP TABLE statement, the table no longer exists.

Transact-SQL language also supports the TRUNCATE TABLE statement. This statement normally provides a "faster executing" version of the DELETE statement without the WHERE clause. The TRUNCATE TABLE statement deletes all rows from a table more quickly than does the DELETE statement because it drops the contents of the table page by page, while DELETE drops the contents row by row. Additionally, the TRUNCATE TABLE statement does not place the modifications of a table into the transaction log.

NOTE: The TRUNCATE TABLE statement is a Transact-SQL extension to the SQL standard.

The TRUNCATE TABLE statement has the form:

TRUNCATE TABLE table_name

CONCLUSION

Generally, there are only three SQL statements that can be used to modify a table: INSERT, UPDATE, and DELETE. (The Transact-SQL language supports one additional nonstandard statement: TRUNCATE TABLE.) They are generic in that for all types of row insertion, you use only one statement: INSERT. The same is true for the modification or deletion of rows with the UPDATE statement or DELETE statement.

Chapters 4 through 7 have introduced all SQL statements that belong to DDL and DML. Most of these statements can be grouped together to build a sequence of Transact-SQL statements. Such a sequence is the basis for *stored procedures*, which will be covered in the next chapter.

EXERCISES

▼ E.7.1

Insert the data of a new employee called Julia Long, whose employee number is 11111. Her department number is not known yet.

▼ E.7.2

Create a new table called **emp_d1_d2** with all employees who work for department d1 or d2, and load the corresponding rows from the **employee** table. Find two different, but equivalent, solutions.

▼ E.7.3

Create a new table of all employees who entered their projects in 1998 and load it with the corresponding rows from the **employee** table.

▼ E.7.4

Modify the job of all employees in project p1 who are managers. They have to work as clerks from now on.

▼ E.7.5

The budgets of all projects are no longer determined. Assign all budgets the NULL value.

▼ E.7.6

Modify the jobs of the employee with the employee number 28559. From now on she will be the manager in all her projects.

▼ E.7.7

Increase the budget of the project where the manager has the employee number 10102. The increase is 10 percent.

▼ E.7.8

Change the name of the department for which the employee named James works. The new department name is Sales.

▼ E.7.9

Change the enter date for the projects for those employees who work in project p1 and belong to department Sales. The new date is 12.12.1998.

▼ E.7.10

Delete all departments that are located in Seattle.

▼ E.7.11

The project p3 has been finished. Delete all information concerning this project in the sample database.

▼ E.7.12

Delete the information in the **works_on** table for all employees who work for the departments located in Dallas.

CHAPTER 8

SQL Extensions and Stored Procedures

This chapter introduces additional Transact-SQL statements, referred to as "SQL extensions." These extensions can be used to create powerful scripts and stored procedures (scripts that are stored on the server and can be reused). Some stored procedures are written by users, and others are provided by Microsoft and are referred to as system stored procedures. These will be touched on in this chapter but covered in more detail later in the book. The last section of the chapter covers the use of text and image data.

SQL EXTENSIONS

The preceding four chapters introduced Transact-SQL statements that belong to the data definition language and the data manipulation language. Most of these statements can be grouped together to build a batch. A *batch* is a sequence of SQL statements and SQL extensions that are sent to SQL Server for execution together. The number of statements in a batch is limited by the size of the compiled batch object.

There are a number of restrictions concerning the appearance of different SQL statements inside a batch. The most important is that the data definition statements CREATE VIEW, CREATE PROCEDURE, CREATE RULE, CREATE TRIGGER, and CREATE DEFAULT must each be the only statement in a batch.

NOTE: In contrast to other dialects of the SQL language, Transact-SQL allows the use of SQL extensions in a batch. This means other SQL dialects cannot use flow-control statements inside a SQL statement group.

The following sections describe each SQL extension of the Transact-SQL language separately.

Block of Statements

A block allows the building of units with one or more SQL statements. Every block begins with the BEGIN statement and terminates with the END statement:

```
BEGIN
statement_1
statement_2
...
END
```

A block can be used inside the IF statement to allow the execution of more than one statement, depending on a certain condition (see Example 8.1).

IF Statement

The Transact-SQL statement IF corresponds to the statement with the same name that is supported by almost all programming languages. This statement executes one SQL statement (or more, enclosed in a block) *if* a Boolean expression, which follows the keyword IF, evaluates to true. If the IF statement contains an ELSE statement, a second group of SQL statements can be executed if the condition in the IF part evaluates to false.

▼ EXAMPLE 8.1

```
IF (SELECT COUNT(*)
        FROM works_on
        WHERE project_no = 'p1'
        GROUP BY project_no ) > 3
    PRINT 'The number of employees in the project p1 is 4 or more'
    ELSE BEGIN
        PRINT 'The following employees work for the project p1'
        SELECT emp_fname, emp_lname
        FROM employee, works_on
        WHERE employee.emp_no = works_on.emp_no
        AND project_no = 'p1'
    END
```

Example 8.1 shows the use of a block inside the IF statement. The Boolean condition:

```
(SELECT COUNT(*)
        FROM works_on
        WHERE project_no = 'p1'
        GROUP BY project_no) > 3
```

is evaluated to true for the sample database. Therefore, the single PRINT statement in the IF part is executed. Notice that this example uses a subquery to return the number of rows (using the aggregate function COUNT(*)) that satisfy the WHERE condition (project_no='p1'). The result of the example above is:

```
The number of employees in the project p1 is 4 or more
```

NOTE: The ELSE part of the IF statement in Example 8.1 contains two SQL statements: PRINT and SELECT. Therefore, the block with the BEGIN and END statements is required to enclose the two statements. (The PRINT statement is another SQL extension. It returns a user-defined message.)

WHILE Statement

The WHILE statement repeatedly executes one SQL statement (or more, enclosed in a block) *while* the Boolean expression evaluates to true. In other words, if the expression is true, the statement (or block) is executed, and then the expression is evaluated again to determine if the statement(s) should be executed again. This process repeats until the expression evaluates to false.

A block within the WHILE statement can optionally contain one of two statements used to control the execution of the statements within the block: BREAK or CONTINUE. The BREAK statement stops the execution of the statements inside the block and starts the execution of the statement immediately following this block. The CONTINUE statement stops only the current execution of the statements in the block and starts the execution of the block from its beginning.

▼ EXAMPLE 8.2

```
WHILE (SELECT SUM(budget)
          FROM project) < 500000
      BEGIN
        UPDATE project SET budget = budget*1.1
        IF (SELECT MAX(budget)
             FROM project) > 240000
         BREAK
      ELSE CONTINUE
     END
```

In Example 8.2, the budget of all projects will be increased by 10 percent until the sum of budgets is greater than $500,000. However, the repeated execution will be stopped if the budget of one of the projects is greater than $240,000. The execution of Example 8.2 gives the following output:

```
(3 rows affected)

(3 rows affected)

(3 rows affected)
```

Local Variables

Local variables are an important extension to the Transact-SQL language. They are used to store values (of any type) within a batch. They are "local" because they can only be referenced within the same batch in which they were declared. SQL Server also supports global variables, which are described in Chapter 3.

Every local variable must be defined using the DECLARE statement. (For the syntax of the DECLARE statement, see Example 8.3.) The definition of each variable contains its name and the corresponding data type. Variables are always referenced in a batch using the prefix @. The assignment of a value to a local variable is done using the following:

- The special form of the SELECT statement
- The SET statement

The usage of both statements for a value assignment is demonstrated in Example 8.3.

▼ EXAMPLE 8.3

```
DECLARE @avg_budget MONEY, @extra_budget MONEY
        SET @extra_budget = 15000
        SELECT @avg_budget = AVG(budget) FROM project
        IF (SELECT budget
                FROM project
                WHERE project_no='p1') < @avg_budget
        BEGIN
          UPDATE project
              SET budget = budget + @extra_budget
               WHERE project_no ='p1'
          PRINT 'Budget for p1 increased by @extra_budget'
        END
        ELSE PRINT 'Budget for p1 unchanged'
```

The result is

```
Budget for p1 increased by @extra_budget
```

The batch in Example 8.3 calculates the average of all project budgets and compares this value with the budget of project p1. If the latter value is smaller than the calculated value, the budget of project p1 will be increased by the value of the local variable **@extra_budget**.

Miscellaneous Procedural Statements

The procedural extensions of the Transact-SQL language also contain the following statements:

- RETURN
- GOTO
- RAISEERROR
- WAITFOR

The RETURN statement has the same functionality inside a batch as the BREAK statement inside WHILE. This means that the RETURN statement causes the execution of the batch to terminate and the first statement following the end of the batch to begin executing.

The GOTO statement branches to a label, which stands in front of a Transact-SQL statement within a batch. The RAISEERROR statement generates a user-defined error message and sets a system error flag. A user-defined error message must be greater than 50000. (All error numbers <= 50000 are system defined and are reserved by SQL Server.) The error values are stored in the global variable @@ERROR (see Chapter 3). Example 23.1 shows the use of the RAISEERROR statement.

The WAITFOR statement defines either the time interval (if the DELAY option is used) or a specified time (if the TIME option is used) that the system has to wait before executing the next statement in the batch. The syntax of this statement is

```
WAITFOR {DELAY 'time' | TIME 'time'}
```

DELAY tells SQL Server to wait until the specified amount of time has passed. TIME specifies a time in one of the acceptable formats for date/time data. Example 14.4 shows the use of the WAITFOR statement.

STORED PROCEDURES

A stored procedure is a special kind of batch written in Transact-SQL, using the SQL language and SQL extensions. It is saved on the database server to improve the performance and consistency of repetitive tasks. SQL Server supports stored procedures and system procedures. Stored procedures are created in the same way as all other database objects—that is, by using the data definition language. System procedures are provided with the product by Microsoft and can be used to access and modify the information in the system tables. This section describes the stored procedures, while the section later in this chapter is dedicated to the system procedures.

When a stored procedure is created, an optional list of parameters can be defined. The procedure accepts the corresponding arguments each time it is invoked. Stored procedures can optionally return a value, which displays the user-defined information or, in the case of an error, the corresponding error message.

A stored procedure is precompiled before it is stored as an object in the database. Therefore, the execution plan of a procedure is stored in the database and used whenever the stored procedure is executed. This property of stored procedures offers an important benefit: the repeated compilation of a procedure is (almost always) eliminated, and the execution performance is therefore increased.

The above property of stored procedures offers another benefit concerning the volume of data that must be sent to and from SQL Server. It might take less than 50 bytes to call a stored procedure containing several thousand bytes of statements. The accumulated effect of this savings when multiple users are performing repetitive tasks can be quite significant.

Stored procedures can also be used for the following purposes:

- To control access authorization
- To create an audit trail of activities in database tables
- To separate data definition and data manipulation statements concerning a database and all corresponding applications

The use of stored procedures provides security control above and beyond the use of the GRANT and the REVOKE statements (see Chapter 12), which define different access privileges for a user. This is because the authorization to execute a stored procedure is independent of the authorization to modify the objects that the stored procedure contains, as will be seen in the next section.

Stored procedures that audit write and/or read operations concerning a table are an additional security feature of the database. With the use of such procedures, the database administrator can track modifications made by users or application programs.

Creation and Execution of Stored Procedures

Stored procedures are created with the CREATE PROCEDURE statement, which has the following syntax:

```
CREATE PROC[EDURE] [owner.]proc_name [;number]
[({@param1 } type1 [ VARYING] [= default1] [OUTPUT])]

        {[({@param2 } type2 [ VARYING] [= default2] [OUTPUT])]}...
[WITH {RECOMPILE | ENCRYPTION | RECOMPILE, ENCRYPTION}]
[FOR REPLICATION]
AS batch
```

owner is the name of the user to whom the ownership of the created stored procedure is assigned. **proc_name** is the name of the new stored procedure. The optional specification **number** allows the owner of the stored procedure to group procedures with the same name. This means all stored procedures with the same name but with different numbers create a group. The benefit of such procedures is that all grouped procedures can be dropped using a single DROP statement.

NOTE: Members of a procedure group cannot be dropped individually.

@param1, **@param2**,... are parameters, and **type1**, **type2**,... specify their data types, respectively. The parameter in a stored procedure has the same logical meaning as the local variable for the batch. Parameters are values passed from the caller of the stored procedure and are used within the stored procedure. **default1** specifies the optional default value of the corresponding parameter. (Default can also be NULL.)

The OUTPUT option indicates that the parameter is a return parameter and can be returned to the calling procedure or to the system (see Example 8.7).

As stated previously, the execution plan for a stored procedure is generated once and can be executed many times. The WITH RECOMPILE option ignores the existing execution plan and generates a new one each time the procedure is executed.

NOTE: The use of the WITH RECOMPILE option destroys one of the most important benefits of the stored procedures: the performance advantage gained by a single precompilation. For this reason, the WITH RECOMPILE option should only be used when database objects used by the stored procedure are modified frequently or when the parameters used by the stored procedure are volatile.

The Transact-SQL statements CREATE DEFAULT, CREATE RULE, CREATE PROCEDURE, CREATE VIEW, and CREATE TRIGGER must each be defined as a single statement inside a batch.

By default, only the members of the **sysadmin** fixed server role, and the **db_owner** and **db_ddladmin** fixed database roles, can use the CREATE PROCEDURE statement. However, the members of these roles may assign this privilege to other users using the GRANT CREATE PROCEDURE statement.

▼ EXAMPLE 8.4

```
CREATE PROCEDURE increase_budget (@percent INT=5)
        AS UPDATE project
              SET budget = budget + budget*@percent/100
```

The stored procedure **increase_budget** increases the budgets of all projects for a certain percentage value that is defined using the parameter **@percent**. The procedure also defines the default value (5), which is used if there is no argument at the execution time of the procedure.

NOTE: It is possible to create stored procedures that reference nonexistent tables. This feature allows you to debug procedure code without creating the underlying tables first, or even connecting to the target server.

In contrast to "base" stored procedures that are placed in the current database, it is possible to create temporary stored procedures that are always placed in the temporary **tempdb** database. You might create a temporary stored procedure to avoid executing a particular batch of statements repeatedly within a connection. You can create *local* or *global* temporary procedures by preceding the **procedure_name** with a single pound sign (**#procedure_name**) for local temporary procedures and a double pound sign (**##procedure_name**) for global temporary procedures. A local temporary stored procedure can only be executed by the user who created it, and only during the same connection. A global temporary procedure can be executed by all users, but only until the last connection executing it (usually the creator's) ends.

SQL Server supports the creation of stored procedures using the Create Stored Procedure Wizard. To create a stored procedure using the wizard, click the **Run a Wizard** button in the toolbar of SQL Server Enterprise Manager and double-click the corresponding wizard (from the **Database** portion of the **Wizard** tree).

Using the Create Stored Procedure Wizard, you can do the following:

- Select a database that stores the new stored procedure
- Select a table of the database and the corresponding modification operation (INSERT, UPDATE, and DELETE)
- Edit and modify the generated procedure properties and the Transact-SQL statement(s) that make up the batch of the stored procedure

The EXECUTE statement executes an existing procedure. The execution of a stored procedure is allowed for each user who is either the owner or has the EXECUTE privilege for the procedure (see Chapter 12). The EXECUTE statement has the following syntax:

```
[[EXEC[UTE]] [@return_status =]procedure_name [;number]
     {[[@parameter1 =] value | [@parameter1=] @variable [OUTPUT]]}..
     [WITH RECOMPILE]
```

All options in the EXECUTE statement, other than the **return_status**, have the equivalent logical meaning as the options with the same names in the CREATE PROCEDURE statement. **return_status** is an optional integer variable that stores the return status of a procedure. The value of a parameter can be assigned using either a value (**value**) or a local variable (**@variable**). The order of parameter values is not relevant if they are named, but if they are not named, parameter values must be supplied in the order defined in the CREATE PROCEDURE statement.

NOTE: When an EXECUTE statement is the first statement in a batch, the word "EXECUTE" can be omitted from the statement. In spite of it, it would be safer if you include this word in every batch you write.

▼ EXAMPLE 8.5

```
EXECUTE increase_budget 10
```

The EXECUTE statement in Example 8.5 executes the stored procedure **increase_budget** (Example 8.4) and increases the budgets of all projects by 10 percent each.

▼ EXAMPLE 8.6

```
CREATE PROCEDURE modify_empno (@old_no INTEGER, @new_no INTEGER)
        AS UPDATE employee
              SET emp_no = @new_no
              WHERE emp_no = @old_no
         UPDATE works_on
              SET emp_no = @new_no
             WHERE emp_no = @old_no
```

The procedure **modify_empno** in Example 8.6 demonstrates using stored procedures as part of the maintenance of the referential constraint (in this case, between the tables **employee** and **works_on**). Such a stored procedure can be used inside the definition of a trigger, which actually maintains the referential constraint (see Example 13.3).

▼ EXAMPLE 8.7

```
CREATE PROCEDURE delete_emp @employee_no INT, @counter INT OUTPUT
        AS SELECT @counter = COUNT(*)
             FROM works_on
              WHERE emp_no = @employee_no
       DELETE FROM employee
             WHERE emp_no = @employee_no
        DELETE FROM works_on
            WHERE emp_no = @employee_no
```

This stored procedure can be executed using the following statements:

```
DECLARE @quantity INT
       EXECUTE delete_emp @employee_no=28559, @counter=@quantity OUTPUT
```

The batch in Example 8.7 contains the creation of the stored procedure **delete_emp** as well as its execution. The stored procedure **delete_emp** calculates the number of projects on which the employee (with the employee number **@employee_no**) works. The calculated value is then assigned to the parameter **@counter**. After the deletion of all rows with the assigned employee number from the tables **employee** and **works_on**, the calculated value will be assigned to the local variable **@quantity**.

NOTE: The value of the parameter will be returned to the calling procedure if the OUTPUT option is used. In Example 8.7, the stored procedure **delete_emp** passes the parameter **@counter** to the calling statement, so the procedure returns the value to the system. Therefore, the parameter **@counter** must be declared with the OUTPUT option in the procedure as well as in the EXECUTE statement.

Since Version 7, SQL Server supports a Transact-SQL statement, ALTER PROCEDURE, that modifies the structure of a stored procedure. The ALTER PROCEDURE statement is usually used to modify Transact-SQL statements in the batch of a stored procedure. All options of the ALTER PROCEDURE statement correspond to the options with the same name in the CREATE PROCEDURE statement. The main purpose of this statement is to avoid reassignment of existing privileges for the stored procedure.

A stored procedure (or a group of stored procedures with the same name) is removed using the DROP PROCEDURE statement. Only the owner of the stored procedure and the members of the **db_owner** and **sysadmin** fixed roles can remove the procedure (see Chapter 12).

The SQL Server system catalog contains two system tables related to stored procedures: **sysobjects** and **syscomments**. There are also two system procedures that provide relevant information about stored procedures: **sp_helptext** and **sp_depend**. For the definition of these system tables and system procedures, see Chapter 11.

System Stored Procedures

System stored procedures are special types of stored procedures that are automatically generated during installation and are therefore an integral part of the SQL Server system. Names of all system stored procedures begin with the prefix "sp_". System stored procedures are used for the following purposes:

- To directly access (with read and write operations) the system tables
- To retrieve and modify access privileges of a database
- To control and manage the memory used by each database

NOTE: The above list is neither complete nor exclusive. For example, some system stored procedures belong to the first and the second groups in the list.

We will discuss system procedures in different chapters, depending on their purpose. Most of them are described in Chapter 11 along with the SQL Server system tables.

USER-DEFINED FUNCTIONS

In programming languages there are generally two types of routines:

- Procedures
- Functions

Procedures are made up of several statements that have zero or more input parameters, but do not return any output parameters. In contrast to it, functions generally return one or more parameters.

NOTE: As you will see below, SQL Server functions do not support output parameters, but return a single data value.

Creation and Execution of User-Defined Functions

User-defined functions are created with the CREATE FUNCTION statement, which has the following syntax:

```
CREATE FUNCTION [owner.]function_name
    [({@param1 } type1 [= default1])] {[({@param2 } type2 [= default2] )]}...
    RETURNS {scalar_type | [@variable] TABLE}
    [WITH {ENCRYPTION | SCHEMABINDING}
    [AS] {block | RETURN (select_statement)}
```

owner is the name of the user to whom the ownership of the created user-defined function is assigned. **function_name** is the name of the new function. **@param1**, **@param2**,... are input parameters, and **type1**, **type2**,... specify their data types, respectively. Parameters are values passed from the caller of the user-defined function and are used within the function. **default1**, **default2** specify the optional default value of the corresponding parameter. (Default can also be NULL.)

The RETURNS clause defines a data type of the value returned by the user-defined function. This data type can be any of the standard data types supported by SQL Server, including the TABLE data type. (The only standard data types that you cannot use are the TIMESTAMP data type and **text/image** data.)

User-defined functions are either scalar-valued or table-valued. In the RETURNS clause of a scalar-valued function, you specify one of the standard data types. Functions are table-valued if the RETURNS clause contains the reserved word TABLE. Depending on how the body of the function is defined, table-valued functions can be classified as inline or multistatement functions. If the RETURNS clause specifies TABLE with no accompanying list of columns, the function is an inline function. Inline functions return the result set of a SELECT statement as a variable of the TABLE data type. A multistatement table-valued function includes a name followed by TABLE. (The name defines an internal variable of the type TABLE.) You can use this variable to insert rows into it and then return the variable as the return value of the function.

The WITH ENCRYPTION option encrypts the system table columns that contain the text of the CREATE FUNCTION statement. In that case, you cannot use the **sp_helptext** system procedure (or Enterprise Manager) to view the text used to create the function. (Use this option to enhance the security of the SQL Server system.)

The alternative clause, WITH SCHEMABINDING, binds the user-defined function to the database objects that it references. Any attempt to modify the structure of the database object that the function references fails. (The binding of the function to the database object(s) it references is removed only when the function is altered so that the SCHEMABINDING option is not specified any more.)

Database objects that are referenced by a function must fulfill certain conditions, if you want to use the SCHEMABINDING clause during the creation of that function. These are as follows:

- All views and user-defined functions referenced by the function must be schema-bound.
- All objects (tables, views, or user-defined functions) must be in the same database as the function.

block is the BEGIN-END block that contains the implementation of the function. The final statement of the block must be a RETURN statement with an argument. (The value of the argument is the value returned by the function.) In the body of a BEGIN-END block, only the following statements are allowed:

- Assignment statements such as SET
- Control-of-flow statements such as WHILE and IF
- DECLARE statements defining local data variables
- SELECT statements containing SELECT lists with expressions that assign to variables that are local to the function
- INSERT, UPDATE, and DELETE statements modifying variables of the TABLE data type that are local to the function

By default, only the members of the **sysadmin** fixed server role, and the **db_owner** and **db_ddladmin** fixed database roles, can use the CREATE FUNCTION statement. However, the members of these roles may assign this privilege to other users using the GRANT CREATE FUNCTION statement (see Chapter 12).

Example 8.8 shows the creation of the function called **compute_costs**.

▼ EXAMPLE 8.8

```
-- This function computes additional total costs that arise
-- if budgets of projects increase
CREATE FUNCTION compute_costs (@percent INT =10)
    RETURNS DECIMAL(16,2)
  BEGIN
   DECLARE @additional_costs DEC (14,2), @sum_budget dec(16,2)
  SELECT @sum_budget = SUM (budget) FROM project
  SET @additional_costs = @sum_budget * @percent/100
  RETURN @additional_costs
 END
```

The function **compute_costs** computes additional costs that arise when all budgets of projects increase. The only input variable, **@percent**, specifies the percentage of increase of budgets. In the BEGIN-END block, we first declare two local variables: **@sum_budget** and **@additional_costs**. The function assigns to the former the sum of all budgets, using the special form of the SELECT statement. After that, the function computes total additional costs and returns this value using the RETURN statement.

Each user-defined function can be invoked in Transact-SQL statements, such as SELECT, INSERT, UPDATE, or DELETE. To invoke a function, specify the name of it, followed by parentheses. Within the parentheses, you can specify one or more arguments. Arguments are values or expressions that are passed to the input parameters that are defined immediately after the function name. When you invoke a function, and all parameters have no default values, you must supply argument values for all of the parameters and you must specify the argument values in the same sequence in which the parameters are defined in the CREATE FUNCTION statement.

Example 8.9 shows the use of the function **compute_costs** (Example 8.8) in a SELECT statement.

▼ EXAMPLE 8.9

```
SELECT project_no, project_name
   FROM project
  WHERE budget < dbo.compute_costs(25)
```

The result is

project_no	project_name
p2	Gemini

The SELECT statement in Example 8.9 displays names and numbers of all projects where the budget is lower than the total additional costs of all projects for a given percentage.

NOTE: Each function used in a Transact-SQL statement must be specified using its two-part name—that is, **owner_name.function_name**.

Example 8.10 shows a function that returns a variable of the type TABLE.

▼ EXAMPLE 8.10

```
CREATE FUNCTION employees_in_project (@pr_number CHAR(4))
   RETURNS TABLE
AS RETURN (SELECT emp_fname, emp_lname
                 FROM works_on, employee
                WHERE employee.emp_no = works_on.emp_no
               AND project_no = @pr_number)
```

The **employees_in_project** function is used to display names of all employees that belong to a particular project. The input parameter **@pr_number** specifies a project number. While the function generally returns many rows, the RETURNS clause contains the TABLE data type. (Note that the BEGIN-END block in Example 8.10 must be omitted, while the RETURN clause contains a SELECT statement.)

Example 8.11 shows the use of the function **employees_in_project**.

▼ EXAMPLE 8.11

```
SELECT *
   FROM employees_in_project('p3')
```

The result is

emp_fname	emp_lname
Ann	Jones
Elsa	Bertoni
Elke	Hansel

SQL Server 2000 also supports the Transact-SQL statement ALTER FUNCTION that modifies the structure of a user-defined function. The ALTER FUNCTION statement is usually used to remove the schema binding. All options of the ALTER FUNCTION statement correspond to the options with the same name in the CREATE FUNCTION statement.

A user-defined function is removed using the DROP FUNCTION statement. Only the owner of the function (or the members of the **db_owner** and **sysadmin** fixed database roles) can remove the function (see also Chapter 12).

The system table **sysobjects** is enhanced in SQL Server 2000 so that you can display the information about existing user-defined functions. The system procedure **sp_helptext** also provides relevant information about user-defined functions. For the definition of the system table **sysobjects**, see Chapter 11.

USING TEXT AND IMAGE DATA

SQL Server supports three data types concerning large objects (LOBs): TEXT, NTEXT (for Unicode data), and IMAGE. A column of the TEXT or NTEXT data type contains values with textual data, while a column of the IMAGE data type represents bit strings. Columns of the TEXT or NTEXT data type are usually used to store documents whose lengths could exceed 8,000 bytes, while the IMAGE data type can represent any data with a large amount of information (for example, audio, video, and photographs.)

For the purpose of representing text/image data, a new column, **pers_file**, will be added to the **employee** table, creating a new table, **emp_text** (see Example 8.12). This column contains a personal file of each employee. (Columns of the data types TEXT, NTEXT, and IMAGE are defined in the same way as columns of other data types.)

▼ EXAMPLE 8.12

```
CREATE TABLE emp_text
        (emp_no INT NOT NULL,
         emp_fname CHAR(20) NOT NULL,
         emp_lname CHAR(20) NOT NULL,
         dept_no CHAR(4) NULL,
         pers_file TEXT NULL)
```

Text/image data are stored separately from all other values of a database. Every column of a text/image data type is stored in the corresponding table as a pointer of type VARBINARY(16). For each table that contains more than one column of text/image data, all values of the columns are stored together.

All text/image data are initialized during the process of insertion or modification of values. (The only exception is the insertion of NULL values.) During the initialization phase, the corresponding pointer is created and at least one data page is allocated for the value. Example 8.13 shows the initialization of the **pers_file** column of the **emp_text** table for the employee with the employee number 11111.

▼ EXAMPLE 8.13

```
INSERT INTO emp_text
        VALUES (11111, 'Miles', 'Ann', 'd1',
                'Mrs. Miles has worked in department d1 since 2/1/1998. ')
```

NOTE: All columns with TEXT, NTEXT, or IMAGE data types should accept NULL values. Inserting a NULL value into such a column does not start the initialization process, so the system does not have to assign memory to it.

Retrieval of Text and Image Data

The SELECT statement is used to retrieve text/image data. The number of displayed bytes depends on the global variable @@TEXTSIZE. (A value is assigned to this variable using the SET statement.) The READTEXT statement can be used instead of the SELECT statement to retrieve text/image data. This statement has the following form:

```
READTEXT table_name.col_name
        pointer_name offset size
        [HOLDLOCK]
```

pointer_name defines the pointer that is used in the **table_name** table to point to text/image data. The built-in function TEXTPTR() is used to return the value of the pointer (see Example 8.14). **offset** specifies the number of bytes that will be skipped before starting to read data. **size** defines the total number of bytes of data to be read.

▼ EXAMPLE 8.14

```
DECLARE @pointer_1 VARBINARY(16)
      SELECT @pointer_1 = TEXTPTR(pers_file)
           FROM emp_text
           WHERE emp_no = 11111
      READTEXT emp_text.pers_file @pointer_1 0 50
```

In Example 8.14, the pointer **pointer_1** is declared and the value of the **pers_file** column for employee number 11111 is assigned. The READTEXT statement retrieves the first 50 characters of the value.

Modification of Text and Image Data

Text/image data can be modified using the following statements:

- UPDATE
- WRITETEXT
- UPDATETEXT

The use of the UPDATE statement limits the amount of modified data to 128K. (The WRITETEXT statement does not have such a limitation.) The syntax of UPDATE with respect to text/image columns is the same as with other columns. The syntax of the WRITETEXT statement is

```
WRITETEXT table_name.col_name
      pointer_name [WITH LOG] data
```

The only new option is WITH LOG. The use of the WITH LOG option causes data to be logged in the transaction log. (By default, all changes to text/image data are not logged.)

> ***NOTE:*** The logging of text/image data has both benefits and disadvantages. The logging of such data increases the security of the database, because in the case of an error, text/image data can be restored along with other data. On the other hand, very large amounts of data must be logged, causing an enormous increase of transaction log size and affecting performance.

In contrast to the WRITETEXT statement, which modifies the whole text/image data, the UPDATETEXT statement updates text/image data only in part. The UPDATETEXT statement has similar features to the WRITETEXT statement and can also copy the content of another TEXT, NTEXT, or IMAGE data type. The second pointer specifies the beginning of the content of the value of another column, which is to be copied.

NOTE: Use WRITETEXT when you want to replace the entire text value, and use UPDATETEXT when you only want to replace part of it.

CONCLUSION

A stored procedure is a special kind of batch, written in the Transact-SQL language. Stored procedures are used for the following purposes:

- To control access authorization
- To create an audit trail of activities in database tables
- To enforce consistency and business rules with respect to data modification
- To improve the performance of repetitive tasks

In contrast to most other SQL dialects, Transact-SQL allows the use of SQL statements and procedural extensions inside a batch rather than restricting their use to within a stored procedure. The next chapter discusses another database object: indices.

EXERCISES

▼ E.8.1

Create a batch that inserts 3,000 rows in the **employee** table. The values of the **emp_no** column should be unique and between 1 and 3,000. All values of the columns **emp_lname, emp_fname**, and **dept_no** should be set to 'Jane', 'Smith', and 'd1', respectively.

▼ E.8.2

Modify the batch E.8.1 so that the values of the **emp_no** column should be generated randomly using the RAND function. (Hint: Use also the datetime system functions DATEPART and GETDATE to generate the random values.)

CHAPTER 9

Indices and Query Optimization

This chapter describes indices and their role in optimizing response time of queries. All Transact-SQL statements pertaining to indices are listed and explained. Additionally, general recommendations are given in cases where indices are appropriate. In the second part of the chapter, examples and comparisons of query optimizations show the performance benefits that can be achieved if the appropriate SELECT statement is used. The final discussion highlights the role of SQL Server's query optimizer.

INDICES

SQL Server uses indices to provide fast access to data. An index is in many ways analogous to a book index. When you are looking for a topic in a book, you use its index to find the page(s) where this topic is described. Similarly, when you search for a row of a table, SQL Server uses an index to find its physical location.

However, there are two main differences between a book index and a SQL Server index. First, you (as a book reader) can decide whether or not to use the book index. This possibility generally does not exist if you use SQL Server: The database system itself decides whether to use an existing index or not. Second, a particular book index is edited together with the book and does not change at all. This means, you can find a topic exactly on the page where it is determined in the index. In contrast to it, a SQL Server index changes each time when the corresponding data is changed. (Targeted retrieval of data using an index is called *index access*.)

In contrast to index access, SQL Server (and all other database systems) supports sequential access. *Sequential access* means that each row is retrieved and examined in sequence (from first to last) and returned in the result set if the search condition in the WHERE clause evaluates to true. Therefore, all rows are fetched according to their physical memory location. (Sequential access is also called a *table scan*.)

Indices in SQL Server are constructed using the b-tree data structure. As its name suggests, a b-tree has a treelike structure in which all of the bottommost nodes (leaf nodes) are the same number of levels away from the top (root) of the tree. This property is maintained even when new data is added or deleted from the indexed column.

Figure 9-1 illustrates the structure of the b-tree and the direct access to the row of the **employee** table with the value 25348 in its **emp_no** column. (It is assumed that the **employee** table has an index on the **emp_no** column.) You can also see that each b-tree consists of a root node, leaf nodes, and zero or more intermediate nodes.

Searching for the data value 25348 can be executed as follows: Starting from the root of the b-tree, a search proceeds for a value greater than or equal to the value to be retrieved. Therefore, the value 29348 is retrieved from the root node; then the value 28559 is fetched from the intermediate level, and the searched value, 25348, is retrieved at the leaf level. With the help of the respective pointers, the appropriate row is retrieved. (An alternative, but equivalent, search method would be to search for smaller or equal values.)

Index access is the preferred and obviously advantageous method for accessing tables with many rows. With index access, SQL Server generally takes only a few I/O opera-

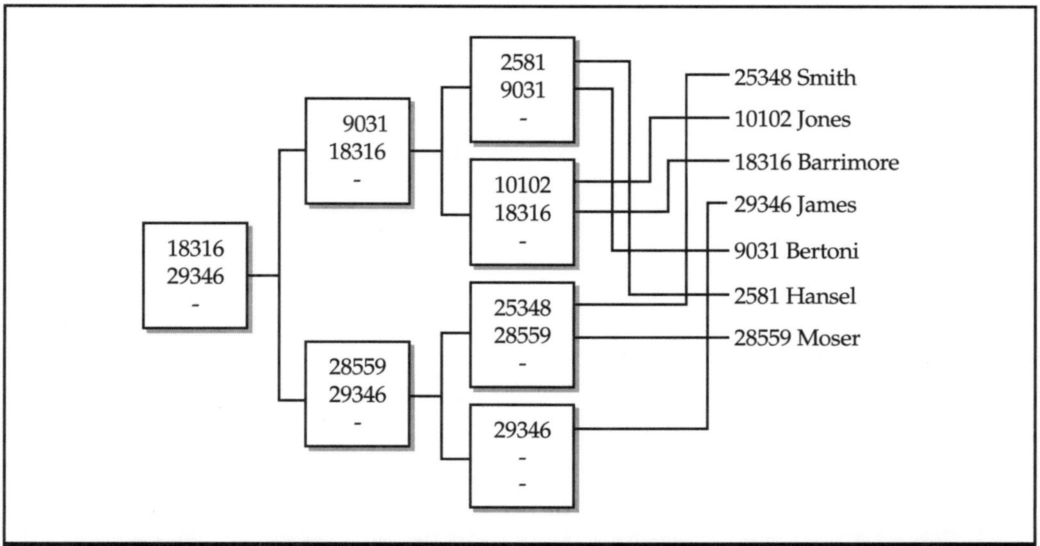

Figure 9-1. B-tree for the **employee** table

tions to find any row of a table in a very short time, whereas sequential access requires much more time to find a row physically stored at the end of the table.

The system table that stores information about indices is **sysindexes**. **sysindexes** contains, among other things, a row for each index of the current database. There is also a system procedure, **sp_helpindex**, which lists indices of a table. (The system table and system stored procedure will be described in detail later in this chapter.)

Before we start to discuss the creation of an index, we will describe the two existing index types.

Clustered and Nonclustered Indices

A clustered index determines the physical order of the data in a table. SQL Server allows the creation of a single clustered index per table, because the rows of the table cannot be physically ordered more than one way.

Clustered indices can be recognized in the system table **sysindexes** through the value 1 in the **indid** column. There is another column of the same table—**root**—that points to the top of the clustered index. SQL Server navigates down from the root of the b-tree structure to the leaf nodes that are linked together in a doubly linked list. The property of a clustered index is that its leaf nodes contain data pages. Figure 9-2 shows the b-tree structure of a clustered index.

A clustered index is implicitly built for each table, where you define the primary key using the primary key constraint. Also, each clustered index in SQL Server is per default

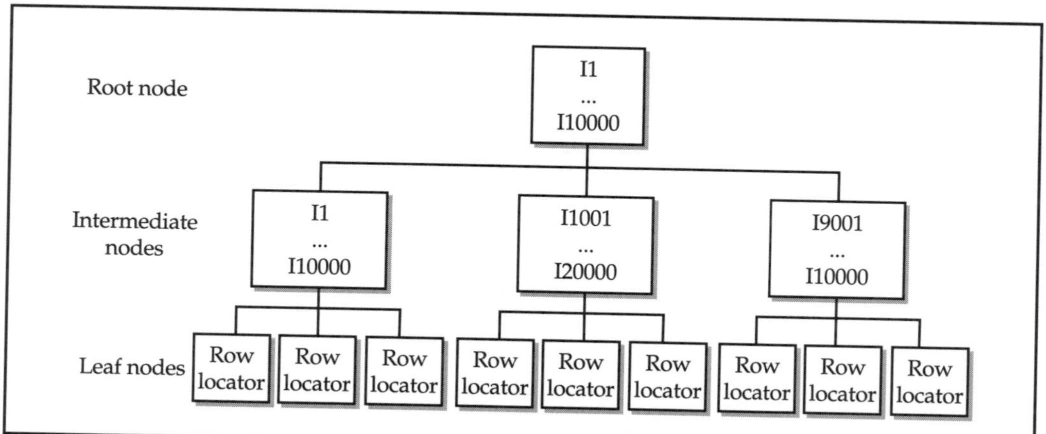

Figure 9-2. Structure of a clustered index

unique—that is, each data value can appear only once in a column for which the clustered index is defined. If a clustered index is built on a nonunique column, the database system will force uniqueness by adding a 4-byte identifier to the rows that have duplicate values.

A nonclustered index has the same index structure as clustered index, with two important differences:

- Nonclustered indices do not change the physical order of the rows in the table.
- The leaf level of a nonclustered index consists of an index key plus a bookmark.

The physical order of rows in a table will not be changed if one or more nonclustered indices are defined for that table. For each (nonclustered) index, SQL Server creates an additional index structure that is stored in index pages.

A bookmark of a nonclustered index shows where to find the row corresponding to the index key. A bookmark part of the index key can have two forms, depending on the form of the table—that is, is the table a clustered table or a heap. (A heap is a table without a clustered index, while each clustered table is so called because it contains a clustered index.) If a clustered index exists, the bookmark of the nonclustered index shows to the b-tree structure of the table's clustered index. If the table has no clustered index, the bookmark is identical to the row identifier (RID).

As you can see from the discussion above, searching for data using a nonclustered index could be twofold: If you have a heap—that is, a table without clustered index—the traversing of the (nonclustered) index structure will be followed by the retrieval of the row using the row identifier. On the other hand, if you have a clustered table, the traversing operation of the index structure will be followed by the traversal of the corresponding clustered index. In both cases, the number of I/O operations is quite high, so you should design a nonclustered index with care and only when you are sure that there will be significant performance gains using it.

Figure 9-3 shows the b-tree structure of a nonclustered index.

Indices and the Corresponding Transact-SQL Statements

The Transact-SQL language supports two DDL statements concerning indices: CREATE INDEX and DROP INDEX. The CREATE INDEX statement creates an index for the particular table. The general format of this statement is:

```
CREATE [UNIQUE] [CLUSTERED | NONCLUSTERED] INDEX index_name
    ON {table_name | view_name}(column1 [ASC | DESC] [{,column2[ASC | DESC]} ...])
       [WITH
       [FILLFACTOR=n]
       [[,] IGNORE_DUP_KEY]
        [[,] PAD_INDEX]
       [[,] DROP_EXISTING]
       [[,] STATISTICS_NORECOMPUTE]]
       [ON file_group]
```

index_name identifies the name of the created index. An index can be established for one or more columns of a single table called **table_name**. **column1**, **column2**,... are names of the columns for which the index is created. As you can see from the syntax of the CREATE INDEX statement, SQL Server 2000 supports indices on views. (Views are described in detail in the next chapter.)

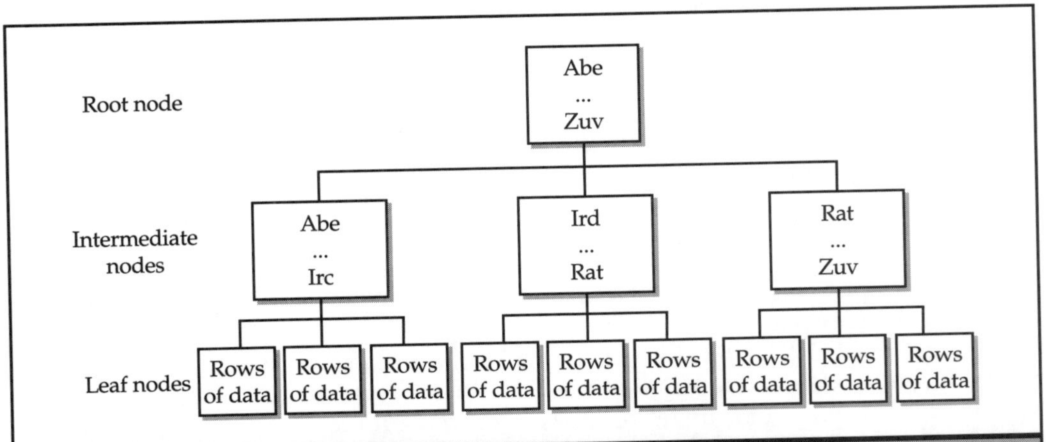

Figure 9-3. Structure of a non-clustered index

NOTE: Each column of a table or view, except those with text/images, can be indexed. That is, the columns with new data types BIGINT and SQL_VARIANT as well as BIT columns can be indexed, too.

An index can be either single or composite. In contrast to a single index, which has one column, a composite index is built on more than one column. Each composite index has certain restrictions concerning its length and the number of pertinent columns. The maximum size of an index is 900 bytes, while it can contain up to 16 columns.

The UNIQUE option specifies that each data value can appear only once in an indexed column(s). For a unique composite index, the combination of data values of all columns in each row must be unique. If UNIQUE is not specified, duplicate values are allowed.

The CLUSTERED option specifies a clustered index. The NONCLUSTERED option (the default) specifies that the index does not change the order of the rows in the table. SQL Server allows a maximum of 249 nonclustered indices per table.

FILLFACTOR=n defines the storage percentage for each index page at the time the index is created. You can set the value of the FILLFACTOR from 1 to 100. If the value of **n** is set to 100, each index page will be 100 percent filled—that is, the existing index pages will have no space for the insertion of new rows. Therefore, this value is recommended only for static tables. (The default value 0 also indicates that the leaf index pages are filled and the intermediate nonleaf pages contain one free entry each.) Setting FILLFACTOR to a value between 1 and 99 causes a creation of the new index structure with leaf pages that are not completely full. The bigger the value of the FILLFACTOR option, the smaller the space that is left free on an index page. For instance, setting FILLFACTOR to 60 means that 40 percent of each leaf index page is left free for future UPDATE and INSERT statements. (The value 60 could be a reasonable value for tables with rather frequent data modification.) For all values of the FILLFACTOR option between 1 and 99, the intermediate nonleaf pages contain one free entry each.

NOTE: The FILLFACTOR value is not maintained—that is, it specifies only how much storage space is reserved with the existing data at the time the storage percentage is defined. If you want to reestablish the original value of the FILLFACTOR option, you need to use the DBCC DBREINDEX statement. (This statement is described at the end of this chapter.)

The PAD_INDEX option is tightly connected to the FILLFACTOR option. The FILLFACTOR option mainly specifies the percentage of space that is left free on leaf index pages. In spite of it, the PAD_INDEX option specifies the place to leave open on each intermediate index page of the b-tree.

Besides the DBCC DBREINDEX statement, you can use the system procedure **sp_configure** to change the value of the FILLFACTOR option. The system procedure **sp_configure** displays or changes several server configuration options. One of these options is FILLFACTOR.

NOTE: The FILLFACTOR option of the system procedure **sp_configure** is an advanced option. If you use the **sp_configure** system stored procedure to change the value of index page fullness, you can change this option only when **show advanced options** is set to 1. The setting takes effect after stopping and restarting the server.

The IGNORE_DUP_KEY option causes the system to ignore the attempt to insert duplicate values in the indexed column(s). This option should be used only to avoid the termination of a long transaction in cases when the INSERT statement inserts duplicate data in the indexed column(s). If this option is on and an INSERT statement attempts to insert rows that would violate the uniqueness of the index, SQL Server returns a warning rather than causing the entire statement to fail. SQL Server does *not* insert the rows that would add duplicate key values; it merely ignores those rows and adds the rest.

The DROP_EXISTING option allows you to enhance performance when re-creating a clustered index on a table that also has a nonclustered index. It specifies that the existing clustered or nonclustered index should be dropped and the specified index rebuilt. As you already know, each nonclustered index in a clustered table contains in its leaf nodes the corresponding values of the table's clustered index. For this reason, all nonclustered indices must be rebuilt when a table's clustered index is dropped. Using the DROP_EXISTING option, you can prevent the nonclustered indices to be rebuilt twice.

The STATISTICS_NORECOMPUTE option specifies that statistics of the specified index should not be automatically recomputed. The ON **file_group** option creates the specified index on the given file group.

SQL Server 2000 has been enhanced to support indices with descending order on column values. The ASC option after the column name specifies that the index is created on the ascending order of the column's values, while DESC specifies the descending order. This gives you more flexibility for using an index. (An index defined on ascending order of column values is generally useless if you search values in reverse order.)

You can also create a new index using Enterprise Manager. In that case, select **Tables** in the **Database** folder, right-click the corresponding table in the details pane, select **All Tasks**, and click **Indexes**. In the **Manage Indexes** dialog box, click **New**. The **Create New Index** dialog box appears. This box contains all options discussed above.

Example 9.1 shows the creation of a nonclustered index.

▼ EXAMPLE 9.1

Create an index for the column **emp_no** of the table **employee**.

```
CREATE INDEX i_empno   ON employee (emp_no)
```

Example 9.2 shows the creation of a unique index.

▼ EXAMPLE 9.2

Create a composite index **i_empno_prno** for the columns **emp_no** and **project_no** on the **works_on** table. The compound values in both columns must be unique. Eighty percent of each index leaf page should be filled.

```
CREATE UNIQUE INDEX i_empno_prno
ON works_on (emp_no, project_no)
WITH FILLFACTOR= 80
```

The creation of a unique index for a column is not possible if the column already contains duplicate values. The creation of such an index is possible if each existing data value (including the NULL value) occurs only once. Also, any attempt to insert or modify an existing data value into a column with an existing unique index will be rejected by the system.

Example 9.3 demonstrates how duplicate data can be located and deleted within a column to allow the creation of a unique index for the column.

▼ EXAMPLE 9.3

For each employee, delete the rows of the **works_on** table that do not contain the most recent entry date for a project.

```
USE master
      GO
      sp_dboption projects, "SELECT INTO/BULKCOPY", TRUE
      USE sample
      GO
      SELECT emp_no, MAX(enter_date) max_date
          INTO #works_on
          FROM works_on
          GROUP BY emp_no
          HAVING COUNT(*) > 1
      DELETE works_on
          FROM works_on, #works_on
          WHERE works_on.emp_no = #works_on.emp_no
          AND works_on.enter_date < #works_on.max_date
```

The temporary **#works_on** table, created in Example 9.3, contains the rows of the **works_on** table that fulfill the two conditions: duplicate values of the **emp_no** column and its latest date.

The DELETE statement retrieves all rows from the temporary table with the duplicate values in the **emp_no** column. The WHERE clause restricts the retrieval to only those rows that do not contain the latest date in the **enter_date** column. Hence, the DELETE statement deletes all rows from the **works_on** table that do not fulfill these two conditions.

After the execution of the Transact-SQL statements in Example 9.3, the **works_on** table contains the following rows:

emp_no	project_no	job	enter_date
10102	p3	Manager	1999-01-01 00:00:00.000
25348	p2	Clerk	1998-02-15 00:00:00.000
18316	p2	NULL	1998-06-01 00:00:00.000
29346	p2	NULL	1997-12-15 00:00:00.000
2581	p3	Analyst	1998-10-15 00:00:00.000
9031	p1	NULL	1998-04-15 00:00:00.000
28559	p2	Clerk	1999-02-01 00:00:00.000
22334	p2	NULL	1998-01-15 00:00:00.000

As illustrated above, each data value in the **emp_no** column occurs only once. Therefore, it is now possible to create a unique index for the **works_on** table.

SQL Server supports the creation of indices using the Create Index Wizard. To create an index using the wizard, click the **Run a Wizard** button in the toolbar of SQL Server Enterprise Manager and double-click the wizard (from the **Database** section). (The wizard will be explained in detail in Chapter 24.)

The DROP INDEX statement removes one or more existing indices from the current database (see Example 9.4).

▼ EXAMPLE 9.4

Remove the index created in Example 9.1.

```
DROP INDEX employee.i_empno
```

The DROP INDEX statement requires the specification of the qualified index name—that is, the index name must be written in the following form: tablename.indexname.

NOTE: The DROP INDEX statement cannot be used to remove indices that are implicitly generated by SQL Server for integrity constraints, such as PRIMARY KEY or UNIQUE. To remove such indices, you must first drop the constraint.

Editing Index Information

To edit information about an existing index you can use the following features of SQL Server:

- System table **sysindexes**
- System procedure **sp_helpindex**
- Enterprise Manager

The system table **sysindexes** appears in the **master** database and in every user-defined database. It contains a row for each index and a row for each table without a clustered index. (It also contains a row for each table including **text/image** data.) Table 9-1 shows the most important columns of **sysindexes**.

Column	Description
name	The name of an index (for indid > 0 and indid >= 250) or a table.
id	The object ID (from **sysobjects**) of a table (for indid > 0 and indid >= 250). For indid 0 or 255, the ID of a table on which the index is created.
indid	The identification number of an index: indid=0 specifies a table, indid=1 specifies a clustered index, indid>1 and <=250 specifies a nonclustered index, and indid=255 specifies an entry for a table that contains **text/image** data.
dpages	Displays the number of used index leaf pages, if the entry in this system table specifies a nonclustered index—(i.e., if 1 <indid <= 250. If indid=0 or indid=1, **dpages** is the count of used data pages).
reserved	The total number of pages reserved for all indices and table data (if indid = 0 or 1). If 1 <indid <= 250 the number of pages reserved for the index.
used	The total number of pages used for all index and table data (if indid = 0 or 1). If 1 < indid <= 250, the number of pages used for the index.
firstIAM	The pointer to the first IAM page that is used to track index pages.
first	Pointer to the first or root page.

Table 9-1. The Selected Columns of the system table **sysindexes**

System stored procedure **sp_helpindex** displays all indices on a table as well as columns statistics. The syntax of this procedure is:

sp_helpindex [@db_object =] 'name',
where **db_object** the name of a table is.

To edit information about an existing index (or to create a new one) using Enterprise Manager, choose the database in the **Databases** folder and select **Tables**. Right-click the table for which you want to get information, select **All Tasks**, and choose **Manage Indexes**. In the **Manage Indexes** dialog box, you can do the following:

- View existing indices of the selected table
- Create new indices
- Delete existing ones

Indices and Keys

Just as indices are part of the Transact-SQL language, so are keys (as integrity constraints). Before considering the relationship between indices and keys, several key types must be explained. The following keys exist in the relational data model:

- Candidate key
- Primary key
- Foreign key

The primary key of a table is a column or group of columns whose values are different in every row. Sometimes more than one column or group of columns of the table have unique values. In that case, all columns or groups of columns that qualify to be primary keys are called candidate keys. A foreign key is a column or group of columns in one table that contain values that match the primary key values in the same or another table.

A unique index for each primary key and each candidate key of a table should exist. Also, each column representing a primary or a candidate key should contain the NOT NULL constraint. This requirement has its origins in the relational model: each primary or candidate key is viewed as a mathematical function that defines each element uniquely.

NOTE: You do not have to create a unique index for each primary key because SQL Server automatically generates an index for each primary key to enforce the uniqueness.

For each foreign key, the creation of a nonunique index is recommended. (The join column in the referenced table represents a foreign key.) The creation of an index for a foreign key significantly reduces the execution time needed for the corresponding join operation. (The specification of UNIQUE in this case would be wrong, because a foreign key allows duplicate data values.)

Example 9.5 creates a nonunique index for each foreign key in the sample database.

▼ EXAMPLE 9.5

```
CREATE INDEX i_emp_deptno ON employee(dept_no)
CREATE INDEX i_works_empno ON works_on(emp_no)
CREATE INDEX i_works_prno ON works_on(project_no)
```

Guidelines for Creating Indices

Although SQL Server does not have any practical limitations concerning the number of indices, it is advisable to limit them for a couple of reasons. First, each index uses a certain amount of disk space, so it is possible for the number of index pages to exceed the number of data pages within a database. Second, in contrast to the benefits of using an index for retrievals, the insertion of rows into a table with the indexed column causes a loss of performance because the index tree must be modified. (The same is true for the deletion of rows.)

The following sections give general recommendations for the creation of an index.

WHERE Clause

If the WHERE clause in a SELECT statement contains a search condition with a single column, an index on this column should be created. The use of an index is especially recommended if the selectivity of the condition is high (i.e., the ration is small). (The *selectivity* of a condition is defined as the ratio of the number of rows satisfying the condition to the total number of rows in the table.) The most successful processing of a retrieval with the indexed column will be achieved if the selectivity of a condition is 5 percent or less.

The column should not be indexed if the selectivity of the condition is constantly 80 percent or more. In such a case, additional I/O operations will be needed for the existing index pages, which would eliminate any time savings gained by direct access. In this particular case, a table scan would be faster (and SQL Server query optimizer will usually choose to use a table scan, rendering the index useless).

AND Operator

If a search condition in an often-used WHERE clause contains one or more AND operators, it is best to create a composite index that includes all the columns of the table specified in the FROM clause of the SELECT statement. Example 9.6 shows the creation of a composite index that includes all the columns specified in the WHERE clause of the SELECT statement.

▼ EXAMPLE 9.6

```
CREATE INDEX i_works ON works_on(emp_no, enter_date)
SELECT *
   FROM works_on
   WHERE emp_no = 29346 AND enter_date='12.15.1997'
```

The AND operator in the SELECT statement in Example 9.6 contains two conditions. As such, both of the columns appearing in each condition should be indexed using a composite index.

Join Operator

In the case of a join operation, it is recommended that each join column be indexed. Join columns often represent the primary key of one table and the corresponding foreign key of the other or the same table. Both columns should be indexed according to the discussion in the previous sections.

▼ EXAMPLE 9.7

```
SELECT emp_lname, emp_fname
   FROM employee, works_on
   WHERE employee.emp_no = works_on.emp_no
   AND enter_date = '10.15.1998'
```

For Example 9.7, the creation of two separate indices for the **emp_no** column in both the **employee** and **works_on** tables is recommended. Also, an additional index should be created for the **enter_date** column.

These recommendations are general rules of thumb. They ultimately depend on how your database will be used in production and which columns are used most frequently. An index on a column that is never used will be counterproductive.

> ***NOTE:*** A great new feature included in SQL Server since version 7 is the Index Tuning Wizard. This wizard will analyze a sample of your actual workload (supplied via either a script file from you or a captured trace file from SQL Profiler) and recommend indices for you to add or delete based on that workload. Use of the Index Tuning Wizard is highly recommended. For more information on the Index Tuning Wizard, see Chapter 24.

GENERAL CRITERIA TO IMPROVE EFFICIENCY

Earlier sections have illustrated the efficiency of a database application and the possible improvements that can be made in response time using indices. This part of the chapter demonstrates how programming style can influence the efficiency of your database applications.

A component of SQL Server called the query optimizer provides solutions to the problem of how each query should be executed (for example, what indices should be used, in what order tables should be accessed, how joins should be implemented). These solutions are called query execution plans, and the main task of the optimizer is to select the optimal plan. (The SQL Server query optimizer is described in detail later in this chapter.) Sometimes the information available to the optimizer is not sufficient for it to determine the optimal plan. Therefore, it is very important to know how programmers can improve the efficiency of their applications. In the following sections, some of these issues are discussed.

Join vs. Correlated Subquery

Each query can usually be expressed with one of the many different, but equivalent, SELECT statements. For example, each join operation can be expressed using the equivalent correlated subquery and vice versa. These methods differ in that a join operation is considerably more efficient than the corresponding correlated subquery. Example 9.8 shows the difference.

▼ EXAMPLE 9.8

Get last names of all employees working on project p3.

Solution A:

```
SELECT emp_lname
   FROM employee, works_on
   WHERE employee.emp_no = works_on.emp_no
   AND project_no = 'p3'
```

Solution B:

```
SELECT emp_lname
   FROM employee
WHERE 'p3' IN (SELECT project_no
        FROM works_on
        WHERE employee.emp_no=works_on.emp_no)
```

The performance of solution A is better than the performance of solution B. The inner query in solution B of Example 9.8 must be evaluated several times because it contains the **emp_no** column, which belongs to the **employee** table in the outer query. Thus, the value of the **emp_no** column changes each time SQL Server examines a different row of the **employee** table in the outer query. The join in solution A works faster because it evaluates all values of the **project_no** column of the **works_on** table only once.

Incomplete Statements

In practice, it is possible for a programmer to specify an incomplete SQL statement. Such a statement is not only erroneous but strongly influences the efficiency of the whole application. A typical example is the Cartesian product of two tables.

The Cartesian product is described in detail in Chapter 6. The result of a Cartesian product contains each combination of rows of two tables. For example, if one table contains 10,000 and the other 100 rows, the result of the Cartesian product of both tables will be a table with 1 million rows.

The use of a Cartesian product in practice is highly unusual. Sometimes users accidentally generate the Cartesian product of two tables when they forget to include the join condition in the WHERE clause of the SELECT statement. In this case, users have an incomplete SELECT statement where the join condition is omitted. In general, if your query is accessing **n** different tables, you should have at least **n-1** join conditions relating all of the tables to avoid a Cartesian product.

NOTE: SQL Server supports the ROWCOUNT option in the SET statement, which restricts the display of selected rows to a certain amount. As such, the use of this option limits the number of rows that can be created by an unintentional Cartesian product. (ROWCOUNT is described in detail at the end of this chapter.)

LIKE Operator

LIKE compares the values of a column with a specified pattern. If this column is associated with an index, the search for the character string is performed with the existing index. A condition based on a wildcard in the initial position forces SQL Server to examine each value in the column—that is, the existing index is of no use. The reason is that indices work by quickly determining whether the requested value is greater than or less than the values at various nodes of the b-tree. If the initial character(s) of the desired values are not specified, then these comparisons cannot be done.

▼ EXAMPLE 9.9

Get employee numbers of all employees whose last names end with *es*.

```
SELECT emp_no
   FROM employee
   WHERE emp_lname LIKE '%es'
```

It is not possible to process the query in Example 9.9, even if the index for the **emp_lname** column exists. The reason is that the characters at the beginning of the data values are not known within the search condition in the WHERE clause.

Transact-SQL Statements and Query Performance

SQL Server supports two statements that enable the optimization of queries:

- UPDATE STATISTICS
- SET

The statistics in the system tables are not constantly updated. The UPDATE STATISTICS statement updates information about the distribution of key values in the specified indices. The modification of information using the UPDATE STATISTICS statement should be processed by the user in the following cases:

- After the initial load of data
- After the execution of a DML statement (INSERT, UPDATE, or DELETE) that affects a large number of rows

On the other hand, the UPDATE STATISTICS statement is automatically run when you create or re-create an index on a table that already contains data. Also, the UPDATE STATISTICS statement is executed by SQL Server periodically as the data in the tables change. The frequency at which the statistical information is updated is determined by the volume of data in the index and the amount of changing data.

The second statement, SET, has several options. Some of these options are used for query optimization and some for other purposes. The following options are used for query optimization:

- SHOWPLAN_TEXT
- SHOWPLAN_ALL
- NOEXEC
- FORCEPLAN
- ROWCOUNT
- STATISTICS IO
- STATISTICS TIME

Generally, ON activates an option, whereas OFF turns it off.

Users running a query can display the textual execution plan for that query by activating either SHOWPLAN_TEXT or SHOWPLAN_ALL before they enter the corresponding SELECT statement. The SHOWPLAN_ALL option displays the same detailed information about the selected execution plan for the query as SHOWPLAN_TEXT with the addition of an estimate of the resource requirements for that statement. (Either one of these two options causes the SQL Server system not to execute the query.)

Example 9.10 shows the use of the SET SHOWPLAN_TEXT option.

▼ EXAMPLE 9.10

```
SET SHOWPLAN_TEXT ON
GO
SELECT employee.dept_no
   FROM employee, works_on
   WHERE employee.emp_no = works_on.emp_no
   AND works_on.project_no = 'p1'
```

NOTE: SQL Server will display the output shown below only if both tables, **employee** and **works_on**, have a significant number of rows. To achieve this, use Examples 9.12 and 9.13 to insert 3,000 and 12,000 rows in the **employee** and **works_on** tables, respectively.

The result is:

```
StmtText
---------------------
SET SHOWPLAN_TEXT ON
StmtText
--------------------------------------------------------------------------------
SELECT employee.dept_no
   FROM employee, works_on
   WHERE employee.emp_no = works_on.emp_no
   AND works_on.project_no = 'p1'
StmtText
--------------------------------------------------------------------------------------
  |—Bookmark Lookup(BOOKMARK:([Bmk1000]), OBJECT:([sample1].[dbo].[employee]))
      |—Nested Loops(Inner Join, OUTER REFERENCES:([works_on].[emp_no]))
       |—Table Scan(OBJECT:([sample1].[dbo].[works_on]), WHERE:([works_on].[project_no]= 'p1'))
          |—Index Seek(OBJECT:([sample1].[dbo].[employee].[i_empno]),
SEEK:([employee].[emp_no]=[works_on].[emp_no]) ORDERED FORWARD)
```

The result of Example 9.10 shows the selected execution plan for the specified SELECT statement. The join columns in the **employee** and **works_on** tables are indexed, so the query optimizer chooses in this case the nested-loop method to execute the join operation. (The nested-loop join method will be explained in detail later in this chapter.)

The NOEXEC option compiles all the statements but does not execute them. The NOEXEC option is set on until the statement SET NOEXEC OFF is executed. The option FORCEPLAN makes it possible for you to directly influence a query optimization. Using this option causes SQL Server to access the tables in the same order as they are listed in the FROM clause of the SELECT statement.

The option ROWCOUNT causes the system to stop processing a DML statement after the specified number of rows are returned. The activation of such an option can be very useful if the result of a query (for example, a semantic error) returns too many rows. The option ROWCOUNT is turned off with the statement SET ROWCOUNT 0.

The option STATISTICS IO causes the system to display statistical information concerning the amount of disk activity generated by the query—for example, the number of read and write I/O operations processed with the query. The option STATISTICS TIME causes the system to display the processing, optimization, and execution time of the query.

QUERY OPTIMIZER

A query can usually be performed in several different, but equivalent, ways. The query optimizer generates several query execution plans or specific steps to perform a query. After that, it assigns a cost to each plan and selects the plan with the lowest cost. (This is also called *systematic query optimization*.)

Besides using cost estimates to select the best solution, the query optimizer of SQL Server (and all other DBMSs) uses heuristic rules to improve the performance of the execution of a query. The existence of heuristic rules is based upon the fact that every query can be generated using several solutions. The main heuristic rule is to apply unary operations (selection and projection) *before* binary operations (mainly the join operation).

Optimizer Statistics

The existence of indices on columns in a query affects the choice of a particular execution plan and, therefore, the performance of the query. This is especially true for indices on filter columns—that is, columns that appear in conditions of the WHERE clause (see Example 9.11). The decision whether an existing index will be used by the optimizer depends on its selectivity and its index type. If the selectivity of an index is high—that is, only a few rows are identified by the index key value—the index is usually used. The question is: How does the SQL Server optimizer determine the selectivity of an index?

The optimizer uses special statistics kept for an index to determine the selectivity. These statistics are called distribution statistics, and they describe the selectivity and distribution of the key values in an index. The following statistics kept for a table and its indices (among others) are used by the optimizer:

- Number of rows in the table
- Number of pages used to store the data
- Number of distribution steps
- Number of rows sampled for statistics

Example 9.11 shows how decisions of the SQL Server optimizer are influenced by the different selectivity of columns in the WHERE clause.

▼ EXAMPLE 9.11

```
select * from works_on
    where enter_date = '01/01/1998'
   and job = 'Analyst'
```

Assuming that the **works_on** table has an index on each of the columns **enter_date** and **job**, which index should be first used? For instance, say both indices have the following statistics:

Number of rows: 100,000
Estimated row count(for **works_on.enter_date**) = 100
Estimated row count(for **works_on.job**) = 40,000

Using these statistics, the optimizer estimates that the selectivity of the **enter_date** column is 0.1 percent (100/100,000) and the selectivity of the **job** column is 40 percent. From this calculation, the optimizer would usually choose the execution plan based on the index for the **enter_date** column, because the selectivity of that column is significantly higher than that of the **job** column.

NOTE: The example shown above simplifies the work of the optimizer. Generally, there are several other statistics that the optimizer takes into account when it chooses the appropriate execution plan.

The statistics that the optimizer needs to find the optimal execution plan are stored in the **statblob** column of the **sysindexes** system table. This column has the IMAGE data type and therefore the information is stored as a bit string. To interpret the information, you have to use the DBCC SHOW_STATISTICS statement, which has the following syntax:

```
dbcc show_statistics (table_name, index_name)
```

table_name and **index_name** are the names of the table and corresponding index—that is, for which you want to display the statistics information.

Implementing the Join Operation

The join operation is the most time-consuming operation in query processing. For this reason, SQL Server supports three different processing techniques for join:

- Nested-loop join
- Merge join
- Hash join

Nested-Loop Join

The nested-loop join is the only processing technique supported in the versions previous to SQL Server 7. The nested-loop join works by "brute force." In other words, for each row of the outer table, each row from the inner table is retrieved and compared.

The pseudocode in Algorithm 9.1 demonstrates the nested-loop processing technique for two tables.

▼ ALGORITHM 9.1

(A and B are two temporary tables.)

```
for each row in the outer table do:
   read the row into A
   for each row in the inner table do:
     read the row into B
      if A.join_column = B.join_column then
         accept the row and add it to the resulting set
      end if
   end for
end for
```

The nested-loop join is very slow if there is no index for one of the join columns. Without indices, SQL Server would have to scan the outer table once and the inner table **n** times, where **n** is the number of rows of the outer table. Therefore, the query optimizer chooses this method only if the join column of the *inner* table is indexed, so the inner table does not have to be scanned for each row in the outer table.

Merge Join

The merge join provides a cost-effective alternative to constructing an index for a nested-loop join. The rows of the joined tables must be physically sorted using the values of the join column. Both tables are then scanned in order of the join columns, matching the rows with the same value for the join columns.

No index is required when the query optimizer performs a merge join.

The pseudocode in Algorithm 9.2 demonstrates the merge join processing technique for two tables.

▼ ALGORITHM 9.2

a. Sort the outer table in ascending order using the join column

b. Sort the inner table in ascending order using the join column

```
for each row in the outer table do:
   read the row into A
   for each row from the inner table with a value less than or equal to the join
column do:
      read the row into B
```

```
        if A.join_column = B.join_column then
           accept the row and add it to the resulting set
        end if
     end for
  end for
```

The merge join processing technique has a high overhead if the rows from both tables are unsorted. However, this method is preferable when the values of at least one of the join columns are sorted.

Hash Join

A hash join is used when there is no ordered input. The rows of both tables are hashed to the same hash file, using the same hashing function on the join columns as hash keys. The hash join method requires no index. Therefore, this method is highly applicable for ad hoc queries (where indices cannot be expected).

Optimizer Hints

Optimizer hints are optional parts in a SELECT statement that instruct different components of SQL Server to execute one specific behavior. In other words, using optimizer hints, you do not allow the query optimizer to search and find the way to execute a query because you tell it exactly what to do. For this reason, optimizer hints should be used when you think that the SQL Server optimizer does not choose the best execution plan to perform a query. Before using them, you have to understand some general issues as to how the optimizer makes its decisions.

The optimizer uses the following general guidelines to create an optimal execution plan for a query:

- An existing nonclustered index is not used when the large portion of a table is read. For instance, if the following query for the **works_on** table is executed:

```
select * from works_on
        where job = 'Analyst'
```

and the nonclustered index for the **job** column exists, the SQL Server optimizer will choose the table scan instead of index access, assuming that 40 percent of all employees have such a job. In that case, it is more efficient to read the data pages sequentially than to first traverse the b-tree structure and then read each row one after the other.

- A restrictive condition in the WHERE clause of a SELECT statement that filters rows will be performed first (or very early) in the execution plan of the optimizer. For instance, if the following query is executed:

```
 select job
from employee, works_on
where employee.emp_no = works_on.emp_no
and emp_fname = 'John'
```

the optimizer will first filter all details of employees that have the specified first name and then perform the join condition, because filtering rows in the **employee** table will reduce the number of input rows for the join operation, and this can then be executed more effectively.

- When the optimizer chooses between several indices to access a table, it will usually use the index for an expression that has the highest selectivity. For instance, if the following query is executed:

```
select emp_no
   from works_on
   where datepart(month,enter_date) = '12'
   and project_no = 'p1'
```

and two nonclustered indices for the **enter_date** and **project_no** columns exist, the optimizer will usually choose the index for the **enter_date** column, assuming that this column has significantly higher selectivity (see also Example 9.11).

- When neither column in the join condition has an index, the optimizer usually chooses the hash join method.
- When the cardinality of one table is small and the other table has an index on the join column, the optimizer usually chooses the nested-loop method.

SQL Server provides, among others, the following two types of optimizer hints:

- Index hints
- Join hints

Before introducing these hints, in the following sections you will find a discussion about the reasons to use them and the requirements for their demonstration.

Why to Use Optimizer Hints

In most cases, the SQL Server optimizer chooses the fastest execution plan. However, there are some special situations where the optimizer, for some particular reasons, cannot find the optimal solution. In such cases, you should use optimizer hints to force it to use a particular execution plan, which could perform better.

There are two reasons why the optimizer does not choose the fastest execution plan:

- It is not perfect.
- The system does not provide the optimizer with the appropriate information.

NOTE: Query hints can help you only if the execution plan chosen by the optimizer is not optimal. In the second case, you have to create or modify distribution using the UPDATE STATISTICS statement.

As you already know, the UPDATE STATISTICS statement updates information concerning distribution of key values for a table. Although SQL Server updates statistics information automatically each time the optimizer determines that the information is out-of-date, you should execute this statement for a table any time the data in the table changes significantly. That way, you ensure that the optimizer generates the best execution plan based on the newest statistical information.

NOTE: In most cases, you should use optimizer hints only temporarily and for testing. In other words, avoid using them as a permanent part of a query. There are two reasons for this statement. First, if you force the optimizer to use a particular index and later define an index that results in better performance of the query, the query and the application to which it belongs cannot benefit from the new index. Second, Microsoft continuously makes efforts to make the optimizer better. If you bind a query to a specific execution plan, the query cannot benefit from new and improved features in the subsequent versions of SQL Server.

Requirements for a Demonstration of Query Hints

The sample database, as defined in the first chapter of this book, is not suitable for a practical demonstration of query hints because all four tables contain just a few rows. Generally, if a table contains a few rows (not more than 200), there is no reason to define indices for such a table because in such a case a sequential scan always outperforms the corresponding index access. For this reason, you need all tables in the sample database with significantly more rows. Examples 9.12 and 9.13 show two batches that insert 3,000 and 12,000 rows in the **employee** and **works_on** tables, respectively.

▼ EXAMPLE 9.12

```
-- This procedure inserts 3000 row in the table employee
declare @i integer, @emp_no integer
declare @emp_lname char(20), @emp_fname char(20)
declare @dept_no char(4)
set @i = 1
set @emp_lname = 'Smith'
set @emp_fname = 'Jane'
set @dept_no = 'd1'
while @i < 3001
begin
insert into employee
  values (@i, @emp_fname, @emp_lname, @dept_no)
set @i = @i+1
end
```

▼ **EXAMPLE 9.13**

```
-- This procedure inserts 12000 row in the table works_on
declare @i integer, @j integer
declare @job char(20), @enter_date datetime
declare @project_no char(4)
declare @dept_no  char(4)
set @i = 1
set @j = 1
set @job = 'Analyst'
set @enter_date = GETDATE()
set @dept_no = 'd1'
while @i < 3000
begin
  while @j < 5
    begin
      if (@j = 1) set @dept_no = 'd1'
      else if (@j = 2) set @dept_no = 'd2'
       else if (@j = 3) set @dept_no = 'd3'
       else set @dept_no = 'd4'
   insert into works_on
       values (@i, @dept_no, @job, @enter_date)
   set @j = @j+1
  end
set @i = @i+1
set @j = 1
end
```

Index Hints

SQL Server supports two index hints:

- INDEX
- FASTFIRSTROW

NOTE: The FASTFIRSTROW index hint causes the optimizer to use the nonclustered index if one matches a column in the ORDER BY clause. This option is a deprecated feature and can be replaced by the FAST hint.

The INDEX query hint is used to specify one or more indices that are then used in a query. This hint must be specified in the FROM clause of the query. You can use this hint to force index access if the optimizer for some reason chooses to perform a table scan for a given query.

NOTE: The following examples demonstrate the general use of query hints, but don't give you any recommendations as to using them in any particular queries. (In most cases shown below, the use of query hints would be counterproductive.)

Example 9.14 shows the use of the INDEX hint.

▼ EXAMPLE 9.14

```
SET SHOWPLAN_TEXT ON
GO
select *
   from works_on (INDEX(i_job, i_enterdate))
   where job  = 'Analyst'
   and enter_date='12/01/1998'
```

The INDEX query hint in Example 9.14 (see Figure 9-4) forces the use of both the **i_job** and **i_enterdate** indices. (If both indices do not exist, you have to create them on the columns **job** and **enter_date** of the **works_on** table, respectively.)

The other form of the INDEX query hint—INDEX(0)—forces the optimizer not to use any of the existing indices. Example 9.15 shows the use of this hint.

```
StmtText
-----------------------
SET SHOWPLAN_TEXT ON
StmtText
--------------------------------------------------------------------------------
select *
   from works_on (INDEX(i_job, i_enterdate))
   where job  = 'Analyst'
   and enter_date='12/01/1998'
StmtText
--------------------------------------------------------------------------------------------------------------
  |--Bookmark Lookup(BOOKMARK:([Bmk1000]), OBJECT:([sample1].[dbo].[works_on]))
      |--Hash Match(Inner Join, HASH:([Bmk1000])=([Bmk1000]),
RESIDUAL:([Bmk1000]=[Bmk1000]))
         |--Index Seek(OBJECT:([sample1].[dbo].[works_on].[i_job]),
SEEK:([works_on].[job]='Analyst') ORDERED FORWARD)
         |--Index Seek(OBJECT:([sample1].[dbo].[works_on].[i_enterdate]),
SEEK:([works_on].[enter_date]='Dec  1 1998 12:00AM') ORDERED FORWARD)
```

Figure 9-4. The textual output of the execution plan for the query in Example 9.14

▼ **EXAMPLE 9.15**

```
select * from works_on (index(0))
   where emp_no = 10102
```

The textual form of the execution plan for the query in Example 9.15 (see Figure 9-5) shows that the optimizer does not use the existing index for the **emp_no** column of the **works_on** table, because the query hint forces the optimizer to perform a table scan for the given SELECT statement.

NOTE: You cannot specify INDEX(0) together with INDEX(index_name).

Join Hints

Join hints influence the SQL Server optimizer by performing the join operation in a query. They force the optimizer either to join tables in the order that the SELECT statement lists the tables or to use the join method explicitly specified in the statement. There are five join hints:

- FORCE ORDER
- LOOP
- HASH
- MERGE
- REMOTE

The FORCE ORDER hint forces the optimizer to join tables in the order they are specified in a query. Examples 9.16 and 9.17 show the use of this join hint.

```
StmtText
-----------------------
SET SHOWPLAN_TEXT ON
StmtText
---------------------------------------------------------------
select * from works_on (index(0))
   where emp_no = 10102
StmtText
-------------------------------------------------------------------------------------
  |--Table Scan(OBJECT:([sample1].[dbo].[works_on]),
WHERE:([works_on].[emp_no]=10102))
```

Figure 9-5. The textual form of the execution plan for the query in Example 9.15

▼ EXAMPLE 9.16

```
SET SHOWPLAN_TEXT ON
GO
select emp_lname, emp_fname
        from works_on JOIN employee
       ON employee.emp_no = works_on.emp_no
       WHERE works_on.job = 'Analyst'
```

The textual form of the execution plan (see Figure 9-6) shows that the optimizer first performs index access on the **works_on** table and after that a table scan on the **employee** table.

▼ EXAMPLE 9.17

```
SET SHOWPLAN_TEXT ON
GO
select emp_lname, emp_fname
        from works_on JOIN employee
       ON employee.emp_no = works_on.emp_no
       WHERE works_on.job = 'Analyst'
       option (force order)
```

```
StmtText
----------------------
SET SHOWPLAN_TEXT ON
StmtText
----------------------------------------------------------------------------------------------------
select emp_lname, emp_fname
        from works_on JOIN employee
       ON employee.emp_no = works_on.emp_no
       WHERE works_on.job = 'Analyst'
StmtText
---------------------------------------------------------------------------------------
  |--Merge Join(Inner Join, MERGE:([employee].[emp_no])=([works_on].[emp_no]),
RESIDUAL:([employee].[emp_no]=[works_on].[emp_no]))
      |--Sort(ORDER BY:([employee].[emp_no] ASC))
      |    |--Table Scan(OBJECT:([sample1].[dbo].[employee]))
      |--Filter(WHERE:([works_on].[job]='Analyst'))
           |--Bookmark Lookup(BOOKMARK:([Bmk1000]),
OBJECT:([sample1].[dbo].[works_on]))
                |--Index Scan(OBJECT:([sample1].[dbo].[works_on].[i_empno1]), ORDERED
FORWARD)
```

Figure 9-6. The textual form of the execution plan for the query in Example 9.16

Figure 9-7 shows the textual form of the execution plan for the query in Example 9.17.

As you can see from Example 9.17 and Figure 9-7, the optimizer performs the join operation in the order in which the **employee** and **works_on** tables appear in the query (from right to left). (Note that this does not necessarily mean that the new execution plan performs better than that chosen by the optimizer.)

The query hints LOOP JOIN, MERGE JOIN, and HASH JOIN force the optimizer to use the loop join, merge join, and hash join, respectively. These three join hints can be used only when the join operation conforms to the SQL92 standard—that is, when a join relationship is explicitly indicated with the JOIN and other keywords in the FROM clause instead of implicitly indicating it via the WHERE clause.

Examples 9.18 and 9.19 show a query that uses the loop join method and the modification of the method after the MERGE JOIN hint is explicitly defined (in the same way you can apply the HASH JOIN hint).

▼ EXAMPLE 9.18

```
SET SHOWPLAN_TEXT ON
GO
select emp_lname, emp_fname
        from works_on JOIN employee
       ON employee.emp_no = works_on.emp_no
```

```
StmtText
----------------------
SET SHOWPLAN_TEXT ON
StmtText
------------------------------------------------------------------------------------------
select emp_lname, emp_fname
        from works_on JOIN employee
       ON employee.emp_no = works_on.emp_no
       WHERE works_on.job = 'Analyst'
       option (force order)
StmtText
------------------------------------------------------------------------------------------
  |--Bookmark Lookup(BOOKMARK:([Bmk1002]), OBJECT:([sample1].[dbo].[employee]))
     |--Nested Loops(Inner Join, OUTER REFERENCES:([works_on].[emp_no]) WITH
PREFETCH)
        |--Table Scan(OBJECT:([sample1].[dbo].[works_on]),
WHERE:([works_on].[job]='Analyst'))
        |--Index Seek(OBJECT:([sample1].[dbo].[employee].[i_empno]),
SEEK:([employee].[emp_no]=[works_on].[emp_no]) ORDERED FORWARD)
```

Figure 9-7. The textual form of the execution plan for the query in Example 9.17

As you can see from Figure 9-8, the optimizer chooses the nested-loop method, because the larger table (**works_on**) is indexed on the join column.

▼ EXAMPLE 9.19

```
SET SHOWPLAN_TEXT ON
GO
select emp_lname, emp_fname
        from works_on JOIN employee
        ON employee.emp_no = works_on.emp_no
  option (merge join)
```

Figure 9-9 shows the textual form of the execution plan for the query in Example 9.19. The SQL Server optimizer uses the merge join method, because the specification in the FROM clause contains such a join hint.

> ***NOTE:*** The specific join hint can be written either in the FROM clause of a query or using the OPTION clause at the end of it. (The use of the OPTION clause is recommended if you want to write several hints together.)

```
StmtText
----------------------------
update statistics works_on
StmtText
----------------------
SET SHOWPLAN_TEXT ON
StmtText
------------------------------------------------------------------------------------------
select emp_lname, emp_fname
        from works_on JOIN employee
        ON employee.emp_no = works_on.emp_no
StmtText
----------------------------------------------------------------------------------------------------
  |--Nested Loops(Inner Join, OUTER REFERENCES:([employee].[emp_no]) WITH
PREFETCH)
      |--Table Scan(OBJECT:([sample1].[dbo].[employee]))
      |--Clustered Index Seek(OBJECT:([sample1].[dbo].[works_on].[c_empno]),
SEEK:([works_on].[emp_no]=[employee].[emp_no]) ORDERED FORWARD)
```

Figure 9-8. The textual form of the execution plan of the query in Example 9.18

```
StmtText
-----------------------
SET SHOWPLAN_TEXT ON
StmtText
------------------------------------------------------------------------------------------
select emp_lname, emp_fname
         from works_on JOIN employee
        ON employee.emp_no = works_on.emp_no
  option (merge join)
StmtText
--------------------------------------------------------------------------------------------------------------
  |--Merge Join(Inner Join, MANY-TO-MANY
MERGE:([works_on].[emp_no])=([employee].[emp_no]),
RESIDUAL:([employee].[emp_no]=[works_on].[emp_no]))
      |--Clustered Index Scan(OBJECT:([sample1].[dbo].[works_on].[c_empno]), ORDERED
FORWARD)
      |--Sort(ORDER BY:([employee].[emp_no] ASC))
         |--Table Scan(OBJECT:([sample1].[dbo].[employee]))
```

Figure 9-9. The textual form of the execution plan for the query in Example 9.19

THE DBCC COMMAND AND INDICES

DBCC specifies a group of statements that are used to check the physical and logical consistency of a database. (Some of them can also fix a database problem.) There are two DBCC statements concerning indices:

- DBCC DBREINDEX
- DBCC UPDATEUSAGE

The DBCC DBREINDEX statement rebuilds an index for a table or all indices defined for a table. By allowing an index to be rebuilt dynamically, you don't have to drop and re-create it. This is especially advantageous if an index is created implicitly using the PRIMARY KEY or UNIQUE integrity constraint. In such a case, you don't have to drop and re-create the defined constraint.

The DBCC UPDATEUSAGE statement corrects the **rows**, **used**, **reserved**, and **dpages** columns of the **sysindexes** table for tables and clustered indices. Size information is not maintained for nonclustered indices. If there are no inaccuracies in **sysindexes**, DBCC UPDATEUSAGE returns no data. If inaccuracies are found and corrected and the WITH NO_INFOMSGS option is not used, UPDATEUSAGE returns the rows and columns being updated in **sysindexes**.

CONCLUSION

Indices are used to access data more efficiently. They can affect not only SELECT statements but also performance on INSERT, UPDATE, and DELETE statements. An index can be clustered or nonclustered, unique or nonunique, and single or composite. The clustered index physically sorts the rows of the table in the order of the specified column(s). A unique index specifies that each value can appear only once in that column of the table. A composite index is composed of more than one column.

The query optimizer is the part of SQL Server that decides how to best perform a query. It generates several query execution plans for the given query and selects the plan with the lowest cost.

The next chapter will discuss the system catalog of the SQL Server system, showing the structure of its most important system tables.

EXERCISES

▼ E.9.1

Create a nonclustered index for the **enter_date** column of the **works_on** table. Sixty percent of each index leaf page should be filled.

▼ E.9.2

Create a unique composite index for the **l_name** and **f_name** columns of the **employee** table. Is there any difference if you change the order of the columns in the composite index?

▼ E.9.3

How can you drop the index that is implicitly created for the primary key of a table?

▼ E.9.4

Discuss the benefits and disadvantages of an index.

> ***NOTE:*** In the following exercises, create indices that will improve performance of the queries. (We assume that all tables of the sample database that are used in the following exercises have a very large number of rows.)

▼ E.9.5

```
SELECT emp_no, emp_fname, emp_lname
       FROM employee
       WHERE emp_lname = 'Smith'
```

▼ E.9.6

```
SELECT emp_no, emp_fname, emp_lname
       FROM employee
       WHERE emp_lname = 'Hansel'
       AND emp_fname = 'Elke'
```

▼ E.9.7

```
SELECT job
   FROM works_on, employee
  WHERE employee.emp_no = works_on.emp_no
```

▼ E.9.8

```
SELECT emp_lname, emp_fname
       FROM employee, department
       WHERE employee.dept_no = department.dept_no
       AND dept_name = 'Research'
```

CHAPTER 10

Views

Chapter 10 is dedicated exclusively to the database object called a *view*. The structure of this chapter corresponds to the structure of Chapters 4–7, in which the DDL and DML statements for base tables were described. The first section of this chapter covers the DDL statements concerning views: CREATE VIEW, ALTER VIEW, and DROP VIEW. The second part of the chapter describes the DML statements SELECT, INSERT, UPDATE, and DELETE with views. The SELECT statement will be looked at separately from the other three statements. SQL Server 2000 supports the new form of a view called an *indexed view*. This new feature is also described in a section of this chapter.

In contrast to base tables, views cannot be used for modification operations without certain limitations. These limitations are described at the end of each corresponding section.

DDL STATEMENTS AND VIEWS

In the previous chapters, base tables were used to describe DDL and DML statements. A base table contains data stored on the disk. By contrast, views, by default, do not exist physically—that is, their content is not stored on the disk. (This is not true for so-called indexed views, which will be discussed later in this chapter.) Views are database objects that are always derived from one or more base tables using information stored in the system catalog. This information (including the name of the view and the way the rows from the base tables are to be retrieved) is the only information concerning views that is physically stored. Thus, views are called virtual tables.

sysobjects is the most important system table concerning views. (This system table contains a row for every database object of the current database.) The **type** column of this system table describes the type of the object, whereby the character *V* stands for view. (Similarly, *S* denotes a system table and *U* a user table.) The other two important columns of **sysobjects** are **name** and **id**. These specify the object name and the object identifier, respectively, and are unique within the entire database. (For more information on the system table **sysobjects**, see Chapter 11.)

The second system table concerned with views is **syscomments**. The **text** column is the most important column of this table. It contains the SELECT statement, which describes the way rows will be retrieved from one or more base tables.

There are also two system procedures concerning views. **sp_helptext** displays the SELECT statement belonging to a particular view, and **sp_rename** renames, if necessary, the name of a view (or any other database object).

Creation of a View

A view is created using the CREATE VIEW statement. The general form of this statement is

```
CREATE VIEW view_name [(column_list)]
   [WITH {ENCRYPTION | SCHEMABINDING}]
   AS select
   [WITH CHECK OPTION]
```

NOTE: The CREATE VIEW statement must be the only statement in a batch.

view_name is the name of the defined view. **select** specifies the SELECT statement that retrieves rows and columns from one or more tables. **column_list** declares column names from the underlying tables. If this optional specification is omitted, column names of the underlying base tables are used (or they can be specified in the SELECT statement). The WITH ENCRYPTION option encrypts the SELECT statement in the system table **syscomments**. Therefore, this option can be used to enhance the security of the SQL Server system.

The SCHEMABINDING clause binds the view to the schema (i.e., structure) of the underlying table. When SCHEMABINDING is specified, tables, views and user-defined functions referenced in the SELECT statement must include the two-part names in the form **owner.db_object**, where **db_object** may be a table, a view, or a user-defined function.

Any attempt to modify the structure of views or tables that participate in a view created with this clause fails. (You have to drop the view or change it so that it no longer has the SCHEMABINDING clause if you want to apply the ALTER or DROP statement to the referenced objects.)

NOTE: The SELECT statement in a view cannot include the ORDER BY, INTO, or COMPUTE clauses. Additionally, a temporary table cannot be referenced in the query.

Views can be used for different purposes:

- To restrict the use of particular columns and/or rows of tables. Therefore, views can be used for controlling access to a particular part of one or more tables. (Chapter 12 describes in detail the use of views for security purposes.)
- To hide the details of complicated queries. If database applications need queries that involve complicated join operations, the creation of corresponding views can simplify the use of such queries.
- To restrict inserted and updated values to certain ranges (see the description of the option WITH CHECK OPTION later in the chapter).

A limited number of users have the authorization to create a view. After the installation of the system and the creation of the database, only the system administrator and the database owner have this privilege. They can then grant this privilege to other users using the GRANT CREATE VIEW statement. Additionally, the creator of a view must have read access for each column that is contained within the view query. (Granting and revoking database privileges is discussed in detail in Chapter 12.)

▼ EXAMPLE 10.1

```
CREATE VIEW v_Clerk
  AS SELECT emp_no, project_no, enter_date
    FROM works_on
   WHERE job = 'Clerk'
```

The query in Example 10.1 retrieves the rows of the **employee** table, for which the condition job = 'Clerk' evaluates to true. **v_clerk** is defined as the rows and columns returned by this query. Table 10-1 shows the **works_on** table with the rows that belong to the **v_clerk** view bolded.

A view is used exactly like any base table of a database. You can think about selecting from a view as if the statement were transformed into an equivalent operation on the underlying base table(s). Hence, the following query:

```
SELECT emp_no
  FROM v_clerk
  WHERE project_no = 'p2'
```

is converted into the equivalent SELECT statement that uses the base table **works_on**:

```
SELECT emp_no
  FROM works_on
  WHERE job = 'clerk'
    AND project_no = 'p2'
```

emp_no	project_no	job	enter_date
10102	p1	Analyst	1997.10.1 00:00:00
10102	p3	Manager	1999.1.1 00:00:00
25348	**p2**	**Clerk**	**1998.2.15 00:00:00**
18316	p2	NULL	1998.6.1 00:00:00
29346	p2	NULL	1997.12.15 00:00:00
2581	p3	Analyst	1998.10.15 00:00:00
9031	p1	Manager	1998.4.15 00:00:00
28559	p1	NULL	1998.8.1. 00:00:00
28559	**p2**	**Clerk**	**1999.2.1 00:00:00**
9031	**p3**	**Clerk**	**1997.11.15 00:00:00**
29346	**p1**	**Clerk**	**1998.1.4 00:00:00**

Table 10-1. The Base Table **works_on**

All modification operations are treated in a manner similar to queries. This means that an update of a view actually updates the table that it depends on. (The same is true for an insert or a delete operation.) The modification operations have some restrictions, which are described later in corresponding sections of this chapter.

Example 10.1 specifies the selection of rows—that is, it creates a horizontal subset from the base table **works_on**. It is also possible to create a view that limits the columns as well as the rows to be included in the view. Example 10.2 shows the creation of such a view.

▼ EXAMPLE 10.2

```
CREATE VIEW v_without_budget
  AS SELECT project_no, project_name
       FROM project
```

The **v_without_budget** view in Example 10.2 contains all columns of the **project** table, but not the **budget** column.

As we already stated, specifying column names with a view in the general format of the CREATE VIEW statement is optional. On the other hand, there are also two cases in which the explicit specification of column names is required:

- If a column of the view is derived from an expression or an aggregate function
- If two or more columns of the view have the same name in the underlying tables

▼ EXAMPLE 10.3

```
CREATE VIEW v_count(project_no, count_project)
  AS SELECT project_no, COUNT(*)
       FROM works_on
      GROUP BY project_no
```

The column names of the **v_count** view in Example 10.3 must be explicitly specified because the SELECT statement contains the aggregate function COUNT(*), and all columns in a view must be named.

▼ EXAMPLE 10.4

```
CREATE VIEW v_seattle (emp_no,f_name,l_name, dept_no, no, dept_name,
location)
  AS SELECT employee.*, department.*
    FROM employee, department
    WHERE employee.dept_no = department.dept_no
    AND location = 'Seattle'
```

The SELECT list in Example 10.4 contains two columns with the same name—**dept_no**—so the explicit specification of the column list is required in the CREATE VIEW statement. (The alternative would be to list the columns in the SELECT statement and exclude the redundant **department.dept_no** column from the view.)

> ***NOTE:*** The explicit specification of the column list in the CREATE VIEW statement can be avoided if you use column headers (see Example 10.5).

▼ EXAMPLE 10.5

```
CREATE VIEW v_count
  AS SELECT project_no, COUNT(*) count_project
       FROM works_on
      GROUP BY project_no
```

A view can be derived from another existing view.

▼ EXAMPLE 10.6

```
CREATE VIEW v_project_p2
  AS SELECT emp_no
       FROM v_clerk
      WHERE project_no ='p2'
```

The **v_project_p2** view in Example 10.6 is derived from the **v_clerk** view (Example 10.1). Every query using the **v_project_p2** view is converted into the equivalent query on the underlying base table **works_on**.

SQL Server supports the creation of views using the Create View Wizard. To create a view using the wizard, click the **Run a Wizard** button in the toolbar of SQL Server Enterprise Manager, expand the **Database** section, and then open the Create View Wizard. Using the wizard, you can:

- Select the database that stores the new view
- Select underlying tables and columns from these tables for the view
- Name the view and define conditions in the WHERE clause of the view query

Altering and Removing Views

Since the release of version 7, SQL Server supports the ALTER VIEW statement that modifies the structure of a view. The ALTER VIEW statement is usually used to modify the definition of the view query. The syntax of ALTER VIEW is virtually identical to that of the CREATE VIEW statement.

You can use the ALTER VIEW statement to avoid reassigning existing privileges for the view. Also, altering an existing view using this statement does not affect the stored procedures that depend upon the view. Otherwise, if you use the DROP VIEW and CREATE VIEW statements to remove and re-create a view, any stored procedure (or any other application) that uses the view will not work properly, at least in the time period between removing and re-creating the view.

▼ EXAMPLE 10.7

```
ALTER VIEW v_without_budget
  AS SELECT project_no, project_name
        FROM project
       WHERE project_no >= 'p3'
```

The ALTER VIEW statement in Example 10.7 extends the SELECT statement of the **v_without_budget** view (Example 10.2) with the new condition in the WHERE clause.

NOTE: With SQL Server 2000, the ALTER VIEW statement can also be applied to indexed views. This statement removes all indices that exist for such a view. (Indexed views are explained in detail at the end of this chapter.)

The DROP VIEW statement removes the definition of the specified view from the system tables. Only the creator of the view, the system administrator, or the database owner can remove a view.

▼ EXAMPLE 10.8

```
DROP VIEW v_count
```

The DROP VIEW statement in Example 10.8 removes the **v_count** view (Example 10.3). If the DROP VIEW statement removes a view, all other views derived from it will be dropped, too.

▼ EXAMPLE 10.9

```
DROP VIEW v_clerk
```

The DROP VIEW statement in Example 10.9 also implicitly removes the **v_project_p2** view (Example 10.6).

NOTE: A view is not automatically dropped if the underlying table is removed. This means that any view from the removed table must be exclusively removed using the DROP VIEW statement. On the other hand, if a table with the same logical structure as the removed one is subsequently created, the view can be used again.

DML STATEMENTS AND VIEWS

Views are retrieved and modified with the same Transact-SQL statements that are used to retrieve and modify base tables.

View Retrieval

A query (SELECT statement) on a view is always transformed into the equivalent query on the base table(s) that it depends on.

▼ EXAMPLE 10.10

```
CREATE VIEW v_d2
  AS SELECT emp_no, emp_lname
       FROM employee
      WHERE dept_no ='d2'
GO

SELECT emp_lname
    FROM v_d2
    WHERE emp_lname LIKE 'J%'
```

The result is

emp_lname
James

> ***NOTE:*** Both Transact-SQL statements in Example 10.10 have to be executed in separate batches because the CREATE VIEW statement must be the only statement in a batch. The GO statement can be used to indicate the end of a batch.

The SELECT statement in Example 10.10 is transformed into the following equivalent form, using the underlying table of the **v_d2** view:

```
SELECT emp_lname
   FROM employee
   WHERE emp_lname LIKE 'J%'
   AND dept_no ='d2'
```

The next three sections describe the use of views with the three other DML statements: INSERT, UPDATE, and DELETE. Data modification with these statements is treated in a manner similar to a retrieval. The only difference is that there are some restrictions on a view used for insertion, modification, and deletion of data from the table that it depends on.

INSERT Statement and a View

A view can be used with the INSERT statement as if it were a base table. When a view is used to insert rows, the rows are actually inserted into the underlying base table.

▼ EXAMPLE 10.11

```
CREATE VIEW v_dept
  AS SELECT dept_no, dept_name
       FROM department
GO

INSERT INTO v_dept
   VALUES ('d4', 'Development')
```

The **v_dept** view, which is created in Example 10.11, contains the first two columns of the **department** table. The subsequent INSERT statement inserts the row into the underlying table using the values 'd4' and 'Development'. The **location** column, which is not referenced by the **v_dept** view, is assigned a NULL value.

Using a view, it is generally possible to insert a row that does not satisfy the conditions of the view query's WHERE clause. The option WITH CHECK OPTION is used to restrict the insertion of only such rows that satisfy the conditions of the query. If this option is used, SQL Server tests every inserted row to ensure that the conditions in the WHERE clause are evaluated to true. If this option is omitted, there is no check of conditions in the WHERE clause, and therefore every row is inserted into the underlying table. This could lead to the confusing situation of a row being inserted into a view but subsequently not being returned by a SELECT statement against that view, because the WHERE clause is enforced for the SELECT. WITH CHECK OPTION is also applied to the UPDATE statement.

▼ EXAMPLE 10.12

```
CREATE VIEW v_1997_check
  AS SELECT emp_no, project_no, enter_date
       FROM works_on
       WHERE enter_date BETWEEN '01.01.1997' AND '12.31.1997'
       WITH CHECK OPTION
GO

INSERT INTO v_1997_check
   VALUES (22334, 'p2', '1.15.1998')
```

Example 10.12 shows the use of WITH CHECK OPTION. SQL Server tests whether the inserted value of the **enter_date** column evaluates to true for the condition in the WHERE clause of the SELECT statement. The attempted insert fails because the condition is not met.

▼ EXAMPLE 10.13

```
CREATE VIEW v_1997_nocheck
  AS SELECT emp_no, project_no, enter_date
        FROM works_on
       WHERE enter_date BETWEEN '01.01.1997' AND '12.31.1997'
GO

INSERT INTO v_1997_nocheck
   VALUES (22334, 'p2', '1.15.1998')

SELECT *
   FROM v_1997_nocheck
```

The result is

emp_no	project_no	enter_date
10102	p1	1997-10-01 00:00:00.000
29346	p2	1997-12-15 00:00:00.000
9031	p3	1997-11-15 00:00:00.000

In Example 10.13, there is no WITH CHECK OPTION. Therefore, the INSERT statement is executed and the row is inserted into the underlying **works_on** table. Notice that the subsequent SELECT statement does not display the inserted row because it cannot be retrieved using the **v_1997_nocheck** view.

The insertion of rows into the underlying tables is *not* possible if the corresponding view contains any of the following features:

- If the FROM clause in the view definition involves two or more tables and the column list includes columns from more than one table
- If a column of the view is derived from an aggregate function
- If the SELECT statement in the view contains the GROUP BY clause or the DISTINCT option
- If a column of the view is derived from a constant or an expression

▼ **EXAMPLE 10.14**

```
CREATE VIEW v_sum(sum_of_budget)
  AS SELECT SUM(budget)
       FROM project
GO

SELECT *
  FROM v_sum
```

Example 10.14 creates the **v_sum** view that contains an aggregate function in its SELECT statement. Since the view in Example 10.14 represents the result of an aggregation of many rows (and not a single row of the **project** table), it does not make sense to try to insert a row into the underlying table using the **v_sum** view.

UPDATE Statement and a View

A view can be used with the UPDATE statement as if it were a base table. When a view is used to modify rows, the content of the underlying base tables is actually modified.

▼ **EXAMPLE 10.15**

```
CREATE VIEW v_p1
  AS SELECT emp_no, job
       FROM works_on
      WHERE project_no = 'p1'
GO

UPDATE v_p1
   SET job = NULL
  WHERE job = 'Manager'
```

You can think about updating the view in Example 10.15 as if the UPDATE statement were transformed into the following equivalent statement:

```
UPDATE works_on
  SET job = NULL
  WHERE job = 'Manager'
  AND project_no = 'p1'
```

WITH CHECK OPTION has the same logical meaning for the UPDATE statement as for the INSERT statement (see the previous section).

▼ EXAMPLE 10.16

```
CREATE VIEW v_100000
  AS SELECT project_no, budget
       FROM project
      WHERE budget > 100000
      WITH CHECK OPTION
GO

UPDATE v_100000
  SET budget = 93000
  WHERE project_no = 'p3'
```

Example 10.16 shows the use of WITH CHECK OPTION with the UPDATE statement. SQL Server tests whether the modified value of the **budget** column evaluates to true for the condition in the WHERE clause of the SELECT statement. The attempted modification fails because the condition is not met—that is, the value 93000 is not greater than the value 100000.

The modification of columns in the underlying tables is *not* possible if the corresponding view contains the following features:

- If the FROM clause in the view definition involves two or more tables and the column list includes columns from more than one table
- If a column of the view is derived from an aggregate function
- If the SELECT statement in the view contains the GROUP BY clause or the DISTINCT option
- If a column of the view is derived from a constant or an expression

▼ EXAMPLE 10.17

```
CREATE VIEW v_uk_pound (project_number, budget_in_pounds)
  AS SELECT project_no, budget*0.65
       FROM project
      WHERE budget > 100000
GO

SELECT *
  FROM v_uk_pound
```

The result is

project_number	budget_in_pounds
p1	78000.0
p3	121225.0

The **v_uk_pound** view in Example 10.17 cannot be used with an UPDATE statement (nor with an INSERT statement) because the **budget_in_pounds** column is calculated using an arithmetic expression.

DELETE Statement and a View

A view can be used to delete rows of a table that it depends on.

▼ EXAMPLE 10.18

```
CREATE VIEW v_project_p1
  AS SELECT emp_no, job
        FROM works_on
       WHERE project_no = 'p1'
GO

DELETE FROM v_project_p1
  WHERE job = 'Clerk'
```

Example 10.18 creates a view that is then used to delete several rows from the **works_on** table.

The deletion of rows in the underlying tables is *not* possible if the corresponding view contains the following features:

- If the FROM clause in the view definition involves two or more tables and the column list includes columns from more than one table
- If a column of the view is derived from an aggregate function
- If the SELECT statement in the view contains the GROUP BY clause or the DISTINCT option

In contrast to the INSERT and the UPDATE statements, the DELETE statement allows the existence of a constant or an expression in a column of the view that is used to delete rows from the underlying table. Example 10.19 shows the use of such a view.

▼ EXAMPLE 10.19

```
CREATE VIEW v_budget (budget_reduction)
  AS SELECT budget*0.9
         FROM project
GO

DELETE FROM v_budget
```

The DELETE statement in Example 10.19 deletes all rows of the **project** table, which is referenced by the **v_budget** view.

PARTITIONED VIEWS

A partitioned view allows the data in a large table to be split into several parts (subtables) based on ranges of values in one of the table's columns. The data ranges for each part are defined in a CHECK constraint specified on the selected column. Using the UNION ALL clause, you can define a view to combine all parts into a single result set.

> ***NOTE:*** The advantage of partitioned views is that the query optimizer examines the CHECK constraint to determine which parts contain the rows referenced by a particular SELECT statement. That way, the search of a result set can be limited to a few parts.

Example 10.20 shows the use of a partitioned view. (We assume that the **works_on** table used in this example has many more rows than in the sample database, because partitioning a table is useful only if the table is very large.)

▼ EXAMPLE 10.20

```
CREATE TABLE enter_date_1997
   (emp_no INTEGER NOT NULL,
    project_no CHAR(4) NOT NULL,
    job CHAR (15) NULL,
    enter_date DATETIME NULL CHECK (DATEPART(yy, enter_date) = 1997))

CREATE TABLE enter_date_1998
   (emp_no INTEGER NOT NULL,
    project_no CHAR(4) NOT NULL,
    job CHAR (15) NULL,
    enter_date DATETIME NULL CHECK (DATEPART(yy, enter_date) = 1998))

CREATE TABLE enter_date_1999
   (emp_no INTEGER NOT NULL,
    project_no CHAR(4) NOT NULL,
    job CHAR (15) NULL,
    enter_date DATETIME NULL CHECK (DATEPART(yy, enter_date) = 1999))
GO

CREATE VIEW all_years
  AS SELECT * FROM enter_date_1997
    UNION ALL
    SELECT * FROM enter_date_1998
    UNION ALL
    SELECT * FROM enter_date_1999
```

Example 10.20 first creates three tables based on the starting date of an employee in the corresponding project. A view is then defined that uses UNION ALL to select the data from all three parts as a single result set. Suppose now that the following SELECT statement on the **all_years** view is executed:

```
SELECT *
  FROM all_years
  WHERE job = 'Clerk'
  AND enter_date BETWEEN '06/01/1998' AND '02/01/1999'
```

The SQL Server query optimizer recognizes that the search condition in this query references only rows in two tables, and therefore limits its search only to those tables. That way, you can achieve significant performance gains.

INDEXED VIEWS

As you already know, a view always contains a query that acts as a filter. SQL Server builds dynamically the result set from each query that references a view. ("Dynamically" means that if you modify the content of a table, the corresponding view will always show the new information.) Also, if the view contains computations based on one or more columns of the table, the computations are performed each time you access the view. Therefore, SQL Server cannot use an index on a column that is a part of an expression that represents the computation.

Building dynamically the result set of a query can decrease performance, if the view with its SELECT statement processes many rows from one or more tables. If such a view is frequently used in queries, you could significantly increase performance by creating an index on the view.

SQL Server 2000 allows you to create indices on views. Such views are called indexed or materialized views. When a unique clustered index is created on a view, the view is executed and the result set is stored in the database in the same way a table with a clustered index is stored. (Clustered indices are described in detail in Chapter 9.)

NOTE: Indexed views are implemented through syntax extensions to the CREATE INDEX and CREATE VIEW statements. In the CREATE INDEX statement, you can now specify the name of a view instead of a table name. The syntax of the CREATE VIEW statement is extended with the SCHEMABINDING clause. For more information on extensions to both statements, see their descriptions in this chapter.

Creating an Indexed View

An indexed view is created using the CREATE VIEW statement with the WITH SCHEMABIDNIG clause. Example 10.21 shows a typical view that can be indexed to gain performance.

▼ EXAMPLE 10.21

```
CREATE VIEW v_enter_month
 WITH SCHEMABINDING
 AS SELECT emp_no, DATEPART(MONTH, enter_date)  AS enter_month
    FROM dbo.works_on
```

The **employee** table in the sample database contains the **enter_date** column, which represents the starting date of an employee in the corresponding project. If you want to retrieve all employees that entered their projects in a specified month, you can use the view in Example 10.21. To retrieve such a result set using index access, SQL Server cannot use a table index, because an index on the **enter_date** column would locate the values of that column by the date, and not by the month. In such a case, SQL Server 2000 indexed views can help.

To make a view indexed, you have to first create a unique clustered index on the column(s) of the view. (As we already stated, a clustered index is the only index type that contains the data values in its leafs.) After you create that index, SQL Server allocates storage for the view, and then you can create any number of nonclustered indices because the view is treated as a (base) table.

An indexed view can be created only if the following options of the SET statement are set to ON. (The reason is that the view must always display the same result set.)

- ARITHABORT
- CONCAT_NULL_YIELDS_NULL
- QUOTED_IDENTIFIER
- ANSI_NULLS
- ANSI_PADDING
- ANSI_WARNINGS

Also, the NUMERIC_ROUNDABORT option must be set to OFF.

NOTE: All SQL Server 2000 client tools set all above options (except ARITHABORT) to the correct values. You can set the value of the ARITHABORT option using the **sp_configure** system procedure.

To create an indexed view, the view definition has to meet the following requirements:

- All referenced (system and user-defined) functions used by the view have to be deterministic—that is, they must always return the same result for the same arguments.
- The view must reference only base tables.
- The view and the referenced base table(s) must have the same owner and belong to the same database.

- The referenced user-defined functions must be created with the SCHEMABINDING option.
- The view result set columns referenced in the CREATE INDEX statement cannot be of the **text/image** data type.
- The SELECT statement in the view cannot contain the following clauses and options: DISTINCT, UNION, COMPUTE, TOP, MIN, MAX, COUNT, SUM (on a nullable expression), TOP, subqueries, and OUTER.

SQL Server allows you to verify all the above requirements with the **isindexable** parameter of the **objectproperty** function. If the value of the function is 1, all requirements are met and you can create the clustered index. Example 10.22 shows the execution of the **objectproperty** function and Example 10.23 the creation of a unique clustered index on the columns **enter_month** and **emp_no** of the **v_enter_month** view.

▼ EXAMPLE 10.22

```
SELECT objectproperty(object_id('v_enter_month'), 'isindexable')
```

▼ EXAMPLE 10.23

```
CREATE  UNIQUE CLUSTERED INDEX
      c_workson_deptno ON v_enter_month (enter_month, emp_no)
```

After creation of the unique clustered index, you can create any number of nonclustered indices for that view.

The **sp_spaceused** system procedure allows you to check whether the view is materialized—that is, does it use the storage space or not. The result of Example 10.24 shows that the **v_enter_month** view uses storage space for the data as well as for the defined index.

▼ EXAMPLE 10.24

```
sp_spaceused 'v_enter_month'
```

The result is

name	rows	reserved	data	index_size	unused
v_enter_month	11	24KB	8KB	16KB	0KB

Modifying an Indexed View

If you drop the unique clustered index on an indexed view, all nonclustered indices on the view are dropped, too. (Nonclustered indices can be dropped one by one.) After dropping its clustered index, the view is treated by the system as a standard view.

NOTE: If you drop an indexed view, all indices on that view are dropped.

If you want to change a standard view to an indexed one, you have to create a unique clustered index on it. To do it, you must first specify the SCHEMABINDING option for that view. You can either drop the view and re-create it specifying the SCHEMABINDING clause in the CREATE SCHEMA statement, or you can create another view that has the same text as the existing view but a different name.

NOTE: If you create a new view with a different name, you must ensure that the new view meets all of the requirements for an indexed view that are described above.

Benefits of Indexed Views

Besides possible performance gains for complex views that are frequently referenced in queries, the use of indexed views has two other advantages:

- All modifications to data are reflected in the corresponding indexed view.
- Index of a view can be used even if the view is not explicitly referenced in the FROM clause.

When you create an indexed view, the result set of the view (at the time the index is created) is stored on the disk. Therefore, all data that is modified in the base table(s) will also be modified in the corresponding result set of the indexed view.

A use of the index of an indexed view is possible even if the view name does not appear in the FROM clause of a query.

Besides all the benefits that you can gain using indexed views, there is also a (possible) disadvantage: Indices for indexed views are usually more complex to maintain than indices on base tables. The maintenance of indices on indexed views is generally higher than the maintenance of indices on base tables, because the structure of a unique clustered index on an indexed view is more complex than a structure of the corresponding index on a base table. For this reason, there are additional requirements when indices should be created for a view. (See also "Guidelines for Creating Indices" in Chapter 9.)

There are several types of queries that can achieve significant performance benefits if a view that is referenced by it is indexed. These are as follows:

- Queries that process many rows and contain join operations or aggregate functions
- Join operations and aggregate functions that are frequently performed by one or several queries

If a query references a (standard) view and the database system has to process many rows using join, the SQL Server optimizer will usually use the hash join method. However, if you define a clustered index on that view, the performance of the query could be significantly enhanced, because the optimizer can use the nested loop join instead of the hash join. (The same is true for aggregate functions.)

If a query that references a standard view does not process many rows, the use of an indexed view could be still beneficial if the query is used very frequently. (The same is true for groups of queries that join the same tables or use the same type of aggregates.)

If the restrictions on the types of views that can be indexed may prevent you from using an indexed view in a particular query, you may try to create partial solutions—each with the corresponding indexed view—and after that, union all partial solutions to an entire one. For instance, you cannot design an indexed view to process the aggregation of data in tables from different databases and with the subsequent join of their results, because an indexed view cannot reference tables from several databases. You can, however, create an indexed view in each database that does the aggregation of data. If the optimizer can match the indexed view against all partial queries, at least the aggregation processing will be speeded up. While the join processing is not faster, the overall query is faster because it uses the aggregations stored in the indexed view.

Using Indexed Views

Probably the most important property of indexed views is that a query does not have to explicitly reference a view to use the index on that view. In other words, if the query contains references to columns in the base table(s), which exist also in the indexed views, and the optimizer estimates that using the indexed view is the best choice, it chooses the view indices (in the same way it chooses table indices when they are not directly referenced in a query).

We will now show how different query plans are created by the query optimizer. Example 10.25 shows the query that uses the indexed view defined in Example 10.21, where the query optimizer chooses to access rows using a table scan. Figure 10-1 represents the textual output of the query execution.

▼ EXAMPLE 10.25

```
select * from v_enter_month
        where enter_month = 67
```

Optimizer Hints Concerning Indexed Views

As you already know from Chapter 9, optimizer hints are optional parts of a SELECT statement that instruct different components of SQL Server (usually the query optimizer) to execute one specific behavior. SQL Server 2000 supports two optimizer hints concerning indexed views:

- EXPAND VIEW
- NOEXPAND

```
StmtText
----------------------
SET SHOWPLAN_TEXT ON

StmtText
------------------------------------------------------------------
select * from v_enter_month
          where enter_month = 6

(1 row(s) affected)

StmtText
-----------------------------------------------------------------------------------------------------------
  |--Compute Scalar(DEFINE:([Expr1002]=datepart(month, [works_on].[enter_date])))
       |--Table Scan(OBJECT:([sample].[dbo].[works_on]), WHERE:(datepart(month,
works_on].[enter_date])=[@1]))
```

Figure 10-1. The textual execution plan of the query in Example 10.25

With the EXPAND VIEW hint, you do not allow the query optimizer to create an execution plan using the existing view indices. Therefore, if you specify this hint in the SELECT statement, the SQL Server query optimizer ignores all indices on a view when estimating the best execution plan for covering columns referenced in the query—that is, it treats the indexed view as a standard one.

You can use the other hint—NOEXPAND—to force the optimizer to consider the use of any indices defined on the view. The NOEXPAND hint specified with the INDEX() optimizer hint forces the optimizer to use the specified indices. (The NOEXPAND hint cannot be specified for a standard view.) Example 10.26 shows a query that uses the indexed view defined in Example 10.21, where the query optimizer chooses to access rows using the existing clustered index. Figure 10-2 represents the textual output of the query execution.

```
StmtText
------------------------
SET SHOWPLAN_TEXT ON

StmtText
---------------------------------------------------------------------------
select * from v_enter_month with (noexpand)
  where enter_month = 6

StmtText
---------------------------------------------------------------------------------------------------------------------------------
--------------------------------
  |--Clustered Index Seek(OBJECT:([sample].[dbo].[v_enter_month].[c_workson_deptno]),
EEK:([v_enter_month].[enter_month]=6) ORDERED FORWARD)
```

Figure 10-2. The textual execution plan of the query in Example 10.26

▼ EXAMPLE 10.26

```
select * from v_enter_month with(noexpand)
  where enter_month = 6
```

NOTE: Use optimizer hints only temporarily and for testing. This is also valid for the EXPAND VIEW and NOEXPAND hints.

CONCLUSION

Views can be used for different purposes:

- To restrict the use of particular columns and/or rows of tables—that is, to control access to a particular part of one or more tables
- To hide the details of complicated queries
- To restrict inserted and updated values to certain ranges

Views are created, retrieved, and modified with the same Transact-SQL statements that are used to create, retrieve, and modify base tables. The query on a view is always transformed into the equivalent query on an underlying base table. Update operations are treated in a manner similar to a retrieval. The only difference is that there are some restrictions on a view used for insertion, modification, and deletion of data from a table that it depends on. Even so, SQL Server handles the modification of rows and columns in a more systematic way than other relational DBMSs.

The next chapter will introduce the system catalog of the SQL Server system, showing the structure of its most important system tables.

EXERCISES

▼ E.10.1

Create a view that comprises the data of all employees that work for the department d1.

▼ E.10.2

For the **project** table, create a view that can be used by employees who are allowed to view all data of this table except the **budget** column.

▼ E.10.3

Create a view that comprises the first and last names of all employees who entered their projects in the second half of the year 1988.

▼ E.10.4

Solve the previous exercise so that the original columns **f_name** and **l_name** have new names in the view: **first** and **last**, respectively.

▼ E.10.5

Use the view in E.10.1 to display full details of all employees whose last names begin with the letter *M*.

▼ E.10.6

Create a view that comprises full details of all projects on which the employee named Smith works.

▼ E.10.7

Using the ALTER VIEW statement, modify the condition in the view in E.10.1. The modified view should comprise the data of all employees that work either for the department d1 or d2, or both.

▼ E.10.8

Delete the view created in E.10.3. What happens with the view created in E.10.4?

▼ E.10.9

Using the view from E.10.2, insert the details of the new project with the project number p2 and the name Moon.

▼ E.10.10

Create a view (with the WITH CHECK OPTION clause) that comprises the first and last names of all employees whose employee number is less than 10,000. After that, use the view to insert data for a new employee named Kohn with the employee number 22123, who works for the department d3.

▼ E.10.11

Solve the exercise E.10.10 without the WITH CHECK OPTION clause and find the differences in relation to the insertion of the data.

▼ E.10.12

Create a view (with the WITH CHECK OPTION clause) with full details from the **works_on** table for all employees that entered their projects during the years 1998 and 1999. After that, modify the entering date of the employee with the employee number 29346. The new date is 06/01/1997.

▼ E.10.13

Solve the exercise E.10.12 without the WITH CHECK OPTION clause and find the differences in relation to the modification of the data.

CHAPTER 11

System Catalog

This chapter will discuss SQL Server's system catalog. The introduction is followed by a description of the structure of several system tables, each of which is part of the system catalog. The retrieval of information from system tables using the SELECT statement is also covered in this chapter. Four alternate ways of retrieving information from system tables are provided by the use of system procedures, system and property functions, as well as information schema, which are described at the end of the chapter.

SYSTEM TABLES

The system catalog consists of system tables describing the structure of objects such as databases, base tables, views, and indices in the SQL Server system. SQL Server frequently accesses the system catalog for information that is essential for the system to function properly.

NOTE: SQL Server distinguishes the system tables of the **master** database from those of a particular user-defined database. The former is called a *system catalog*, the latter a *database catalog*. Therefore, system tables occur only once in the entire system (if they belong exclusively to the system catalog), while others occur once in each database, including the **master** database.

In SQL Server and other relational database systems, all the system tables have the same logical structure as base tables. As a result, the same Transact-SQL statements used to retrieve and modify information in the base tables can also be used to retrieve and modify information in the system tables.

NOTE: Modifying system information using the DDL statements INSERT, UPDATE, and DELETE can be very dangerous for the entire system. Microsoft also discourages the direct querying of system tables in scripts or user-defined procedures. In both cases, you should use system procedures instead.

The following sections describe the structure of the most important system tables.

Sysobjects

The main system table of SQL Server, **sysobjects**, appears in every database. **sysobjects** contains a row for each database object. Table 11-1 shows the most important columns of this system table.

Syscolumns

The system table **syscolumns** appears in the **master** database and in every user-defined database. It contains a row for every column of a base table or a view and a row for each parameter in a stored procedure. Table 11-2 shows the most important columns of **syscolumns**.

Column	Description
id	The unique identification number of a database object
name	The name of a database object
uid	The identification number of the object owner
type	The type of a database object. Can be one of the following strings: C = check constraint; D = default; F = foreign key constraint; L = transaction log; P = stored procedure; K = primary key or unique constraint; R = rule; RF = replication stored procedure; S = system table; TR = trigger; U = user table; V = view; X = extended stored procedure
crdate	The creation date of a database object

Table 11-1. Selected Columns of the System Table **sysobjects**

Sysindexes

The system table **sysindexes** appears in the **master** database and in every user-defined database. It contains a row for each index and a row for each table without a clustered index. (It also contains a row for each table including **text/image** data.) This system table is described in detail in Chapter 9.

Sysusers

The system table **sysusers** appears in the **master** database and in every user-defined database. It contains a row for each Windows NT user, Windows NT group, SQL Server user, or SQL Server role in the entire database. (For the definition of users, groups, and roles, see Chapter 12.) Table 11-3 shows the most important columns of **sysusers**.

Column	Description
id	The identification number of the table to which this column belongs or the identification number of the stored procedure to which the parameter belongs
colid	The identification number of a column or parameter
name	Name of a column or a procedure parameter

Table 11-2. Selected Columns of the System Table **syscolumns**

Column	Description
uid	The identification number of a user, unique in the entire database
sid	The system ID of the corresponding database creator
name	The user name or the group name, unique in the entire database

Table 11-3. Selected Columns of the System Table **sysusers**

Sysdatabases

The system table **sysdatabases** contains a row for every system and user-defined database on the SQL Server system. It appears only in the **master** database. Table 11-4 shows the most important columns of **sysdatabases**.

Sysdepends

The system table **sysdepends** contains a row for every dependency relationship between tables, views, and stored procedures. It appears in the **master** database and in every user-defined database. Table 11-5 shows the most important columns of **sysdepends**.

Column	Description
dbid	The unique identification number of the database
name	The unique name of the database
sid	The system ID of the database creator
crdate	The creation date
filename	The operating system path and the name of the primary file of the database

Table 11-4. Selected Columns of the System Table **sysdatabases**

Column	Description
id	The identification number of the table, view, or stored procedure
number	The number of the stored procedure (otherwise NULL)
depid	The identification number of the dependent object

Table 11-5. Selected Columns of the System Table **sysdepends**

Sysconstraints

The system table **sysconstraints** contains one row for every integrity constraint that is defined for a database object using the CREATE TABLE or ALTER TABLE statement. It appears in the **master** database and in every user-defined database. Table 11-6 shows the most important columns of **sysconstraints**.

QUERYING SYSTEM TABLES

As already stated in this chapter, all SQL Server system tables have the same structure as base tables. Therefore, each system table, like base tables, can be queried by using the SELECT statement. Examples 11.1, 11.2, and 11.3 show queries using the system tables for our sample database.

Column	Description
constid	The identification number of the integrity constraint
id	The identification number of the table with the integrity constraint
colid	The identification number of the column on which the integrity constraint is defined; 0 specifies that the constraint is defined as a table constraint
status	The type of the integrity constraint: 1 = PRIMARY KEY constraint; 2 = UNIQUE KEY constraint; 3 = FOREIGN KEY constraint; 4 = CHECK constraint; 5 = DEFAULT constraint; 16 = column-level constraint; 32 = table-level constraint

Table 11-6. Selected Columns of the System Table **sysconstraints**

NOTE: During the execution of all SELECT statements in this section, the current database must be the sample database. Using the Transact-SQL language, a user can select the current database with the USE statement. (The alternative is to select the database name in the **Database** pull-down menu in the toolbar of SQL Server Query Analyzer.)

▼ EXAMPLE 11.1

Get the table ID, the user ID, and the table type of the **employee** table.

```
SELECT id table_id, uid user_id, type table_type
   FROM sysobjects
  WHERE name = 'employee'
```

The result is:

table_id	user_id	table_type
530100929	1	U

▼ EXAMPLE 11.2

Get the names of all tables of the sample database that contain the **project_no** column.

```
SELECT sysobjects.name
   FROM sysobjects, syscolumns
   WHERE sysobjects.id = syscolumns.id
   AND syscolumns.name = 'project_no'
   AND sysobjects.type = 'U'
```

The result is:

Name
project
works_on

▼ EXAMPLE 11.3

Who is the owner of the **employee** table?

```
SELECT sysusers.name
   FROM sysusers, sysobjects
   WHERE sysusers.uid = sysobjects.uid
   AND sysobjects.name = 'employee'
   AND sysobjects.type = 'U'
```

The result is:

name
dbo

By default, SQL Server system tables cannot be modified using the Transact-SQL statements INSERT, UPDATE, and DELETE. The only way to do this is to change the corresponding configuration variable using the RECONFIGURE WITH OVERRIDE statement and to set its option ALLOW UPDATE to 1. (Only the system administrator can execute the RECONFIGURE statement.) After that, only authorized users are allowed to modify system tables.

NOTE: Do not modify the value of ALLOW UPDATE in the RECONFIGURE statement! Updating system information using the DDL statements INSERT, UPDATE, and DELETE can be very dangerous for the entire system. For example, should any information about a base table in the system catalog be dropped, any further use of that table (and of the database to which it belongs) will not be possible. To modify system information, use only system procedures, which are described in the next section.

ACCESSING SYSTEM TABLES INDIRECTLY

The previous section describes the use of the SELECT statement for accessing system tables. The retrieval of system information directly has several disadvantages:

- It requires the knowledge of Transact-SQL (i.e., SELECT statement).
- Microsoft changes the structure of system tables often.

To access the system tables directly, you have to use the Transact-SQL language. In the SQL Server user community, there are a lot of end users who do not want to learn the language and therefore need some other ways to retrieve system information.

Structure of system tables can change frequently. Microsoft introduces significant changes to SQL Server system catalog with each new version. Therefore, any database application that contains code that accesses system tables directly can get erroneous with a new upgrade of SQL Server. For this reason, Microsoft strongly discourages retrieval of system information using system tables.

You can retrieve system information using one the following four mechanisms:

- System stored procedures
- System functions
- Property functions
- Information schema

The following sections describe these mechanisms.

System Procedures

System procedures are used to provide many administrative and end-user tasks, such as renaming database objects, identifying users, and monitoring authorization and resources. Almost all existing system procedures access system tables to retrieve and modify system information.

NOTE: In contrast to the direct modification of system tables, system procedures can be used for easy and reliable modification of system tables.

Some procedures are described and explained in this chapter. Depending on the subject matter of the chapters, certain system procedures were discussed in previous chapters, and additional procedures will be discussed in later chapters of the book.

sp_help

The system procedure **sp_help** displays information about one or more database objects. The name of any database object or data type can be used as a parameter of this procedure. If **sp_help** is executed without any parameter, information on all database objects of the current database will be displayed. Example 11.4 displays all information for the **sales** table of the sample database.

▼ EXAMPLE 11.4

```
use sample
sp_help sales
```

The result is:

name	owner	type	treated_datetime
sales	dbo	User table	1998-06-11 09:30:36.807

column_name	type	computed	Length	prec	scale	nullable
order_no	int	no	4	10	0	no
order_date	datetime	no	8	0	0	no
ship_date	datetime	no	8	0	0	no

identity	seed	increment	not for replication
No identity column defined	NULL	NULL	NULL

index_name	index_description	index_keys
PK__sales__0EA330E9	clustered, unique, primary key located on default	order_no

constraint_type	constraint_name	status_enabled	status_for_replication	constraint_keys
CHECK Table Level	order_check	Enabled	Is_For_Replication	([order_date] <= [ship_date])
PRIMARY KEY (clustered)	PK__sales__ 0EA330E9	(n/a)	(n/a)	order_no

No foreign keys reference this table.

sp_depends

The system procedure **sp_depends** displays the dependency information among tables, views, triggers, and stored procedures.

Example 11.5 displays the dependency information for the **v_clerk** view (Example 9.1).

▼ EXAMPLE 11.5

```
use sample
sp_depends v_clerk
```

The result is:

In the current database the specified object references the following:

name	type	Updated	selected	column
dbo.works_on	user table	No	No	emp_no
dbo.works_on	user table	No	No	project_no
dbo.works_on	user table	No	No	job
dbo.works_on	user table	No	No	enter_date

In the current database, the specified object is referenced by the following:

Name	type
dbo.v_project_p2	view

The system procedure **sp_depends** in Example 11.5 displays the dependency information of the **v_clerk** view (Example 9.1). This information contains the name of the underlying table (**works_on**) and the name of the view (**v_project_p2**), which is created using the **v_clerk** view.

sp_helptext

The system procedure **sp_helptext** displays the contents of a stored procedure, a trigger, or a view.

Example 11.6 displays the contents of the stored procedure **increase_budget** (Example 8.4).

▼ EXAMPLE 11.6

```
sp_helptext increase_budget
```

The result is:

Text

```
CREATE PROCEDURE increase_budget (@percent INT=5) AS UPDATE project
SET budget = budget + budget*@percent/100
```

System Functions

All system functions are described in Chapter 3. Some of them access system tables and can therefore be used to retrieve system information. Example 11.7 shows two SELECT statements that query the same information from the **sysobjects** system table.

▼ EXAMPLE 11.7

```
SELECT id
  FROM sysobjects
  WHERE name = 'employee'

SELECT object_id('employee')
```

The second SELECT statement in Example 11.7 uses the system function OBJECT_ID to retrieve the ID of the **employee** table. (This information can be stored in a variable and used when calling a command (or system procedure) with the object's ID as parameter.)

The following system functions, among others, access system tables:

- OBJECT_ID (object_name)
- OBJECT_NAME (object_id)
- USER_ID ([user_name])
- USER_NAME ([user_id])
- DB_ID ([db_name])
- DB_NAME ([db_id])
- INDEX_COL (table, index_id, col_id)

Using Example 11.8, you will see that the INDEX_COL system function is much easier to use than retrieving the same information using system tables. (The INDEX_COL function displays the name of the column that an index key is based on.)

▼ EXAMPLE 11.8

```
select index_col ('employee', 1,1)
```

The result is:

```
c_empno
```

Example 11.8 retrieves the clustered index (index_id = 1) of the first column (col_id = 1) of the **employee** table. (To display the same information using system tables directly, you have to join three system tables: **sysobjects**, **syscolumns**, and **sysindexes**.)

Property Functions

Property functions return properties of database objects, data types, or files. Generally, property functions can return more information than system functions, because they support dozens of properties (as parameters), which you can explicitly specify.

Almost all property functions are threefold (i.e., return one of the following three values): 0, 1, or NULL. If the value is 0, the object does not have the specified property. If the value is 1, the object has the specified property. Similarly, the value NULL specifies that the existence of the specified property for the object is unknown to the system.

SQL Server 2000 supports, among others, the following property functions:

- OBJECTPROPERTY (id, property)
- COLUMNPROPERTY (id, column, property)
- FILEPROPERTY (filename, property)
- TYPEPROPERTY (type, property)

The OBJECTPROPERTY function returns information about objects in the current database. The COLUMNPROPERTY function returns information about a column or procedure parameter. The FILEPROPERTY function returns the specified file name property value for a given file name and property name. The TYPEPROPERTY function returns information about a data type. (The description of existing properties for each property function is beyond the scope of this book.)

Information Schema

The information schema consists of read-only views that provide information about all tables, views, and columns of SQL Server to which you have access. In contrast to the system catalog that manages the metadata applied to the system as a whole, the information schema primarily manages the environment of a database.

NOTE: The information schema was originally introduced in the SQL92 standard. SQL Server provides the information schema views so applications developed on other database systems can obtain the SQL Server system catalog without having to use it directly. These standard views use different terminology from SQL Server, so when you interpret the column names, be aware that catalog = database, schema = owner, and domain = user-defined data type.

The following sections provide a description of the three most important information schema views.

Information_schema.tables

The **Information_schema.tables** view contains one row for each table in the current database to which the user has access. The view retrieves the information from the system table **sysobjects**. Table 11-7 shows the four columns of this view.

Information_schema.views

The **Information_schema.views** view contains one row for each view in the current database accessible by the user. The view retrieves information from the system tables **sysobjects** and **syscomments**. Table 11-8 shows the five columns of this view.

Information_schema.columns

The view **Information_schema.columns** contains one row for each column in the current database accessible by the user. The view retrieves the information from the system tables **sysobjects**, **systypes**, **syscolumns**, and **syscomments**. Table 11-9 shows the six selected columns of this view.

Column	Description
table_catalog	The name of the catalog (database) to which the view belongs
table_schema	The name of schema (owner) to which the view belongs
table_name	The table name
table_type	The type of the table (can be "BASE TABLE" or "VIEW")

Table 11-7. The View **Information_schema.tables**

Column	Description
table_catalog	The name of the catalog (database) to which the view belongs
table_schema	The name of schema (owner) to which the view belongs
table_name	The name of the underlying table
view_definition	The text of the view definition
check_option	Specifies whether the check option is set to ON; if so, "CASCADE" is returned; otherwise, "NONE" is returned

Table 11-8. The View **Information_schema.views**

Information_schema.referential_constraints

The **information_schema.referentail_constraints** view is a modified view in SQL Server 2000 that contains one row for each referential constraint owned by the current user and defined in the current database. The view retrieves the information from the system tables **sysreferences, sysindexes,** and **sysobjects**. Table 11-10 shows the most important columns of this view.

Column	Description
table_catalog	The name of the catalog (database) to which the column belongs
table_schema	The name of schema (owner) to which the column belongs
table_name	The name of the table to which the column belongs
column_name	The column name
ordinal_position	The column identification number
data_type	The data type of the column

Table 11-9. The View **Information_schema.columns**

Column	Description
constraint_catalog	The name of the catalog (database) to which the referential constraint belongs
constraint_schema	The name of schema (owner) to which the referential constraint belongs
constraint_name	The constraint name
delete_rule	The action that is taken if a DELETE statement violates referential integrity defined by this constraint (could be NO ACTION or CASCADE)
update_rule	The action that is taken if an UPDATE statement violates referential integrity defined by this constraint (could be NO ACTION or CASCADE)

Table 11-10. The View **Information_schema.referential_constraints**

Information_schema.routines

The **information_schema.routines** view is a new view in SQL Server 2000 that contains one row for each function or stored procedure accessible by the current user and defined in the current database. The view retrieves the information from the system tables **syscolumns** and **sysobjects**. Table 11-11 shows the most important columns of this view.

Column	Description
routine_catalog	The name of the catalog (database) to which the routine (function of stored procedure) belongs
routine_schema	The name of schema (owner) to which the routine belongs
routine_name	The name of the function or stored procedure
routine_type	The type of the routine. Returns PROCEDURE for a stored procedure and FUNCTION for user-defined function
routine_definition	Definition text of the function or stored procedure if the function or stored procedure is not encrypted. Otherwise, NULL
routine_body	Returns always SQL (for a user-defined function implemented using SQL). Will be modified in future releases

Table 11-11. The View **Information_schema.routines**

CONCLUSION

The SQL Server catalog contains a single system catalog and several database catalogs. The system catalog is a collection of system tables belonging to the **master** database. Each database catalog contains system tables of the user-defined database.

System tables of the system or database catalog can be queried using the SELECT statement or the system procedures provided by SQL Server. The benefit of using system procedures is that they provide easy and reliable access to system tables. They are also beneficial because the columns of system tables are subject to change (as they did between versions 6.5 and 7.0), and embedding queries of system tables within user-defined stored procedures, triggers, or scripts can cause problems when upgrading to a new version. It is also strongly recommended to exclusively use system procedures for modification of system tables.

The information schema is a collection of views defined on system tables that provide unified access to the SQL Server system catalog for all database applications developed on other database systems. Microsoft encourages the use of the information schema, because these views will not change when the system is upgraded, while the names of system tables may.

The next chapter introduces you to database security and the two existing authentication modes: Windows NT security mode and Mixed mode.

EXERCISES

▼ E.11.1

Using system tables, find the operating system path and the name of the file of the **sample** database.

▼ E.11.2

Using system tables, find the name of the clustered index (if it exists) that is defined for the **employee** table of the sample database.

▼ E.11.3

Using system tables, find how many integrity constraints are defined for the **employee** table of the sample database.

▼ E.11.4

Using system tables, find out if there is any integrity constraint defined for the **dept_no** column of the **employee** table.

▼ E.11.5

Which system table is used by the system procedure **sp_depends** to display the dependency information among tables and other database objects?

▼ E.11.6

Find the name of the column that has the user-defined data type **western_countries** (E.4.16). Hint: Use the system tables **systypes** and **syscolumns**. These two tables have to be joined together using three columns: **xtype**, **type**, and **usertype**.

▼ E.11.7

Using the information schema, display all user tables that belong to the **Northwind** database.

▼ E.11.8

Using the information schema, find all columns of the **employee** table with their ordinal positions and the corresponding data types.

CHAPTER 12

SQL Server Security

SQL Server security protects data in the database against unauthorized access. This important feature of every database system (see Chapter 1) requires the evaluation of two primary questions:

- Which user has been granted legitimate access to the SQL Server system? (Authentication)
- Which access privileges are valid for a particular user? (Permissions)

The following sections discuss these two issues and describe the Transact-SQL statements that grant and limit access to users. Later in the chapter, views and stored procedures are shown, which can also be used to protect data in databases and restrict the access to data by unauthorized users.

ACCESS TO SQL SERVER

Granting appropriate access to the SQL Server system is known as *authentication*. SQL Server performs authentication using logins (also known as login accounts). Logins are known internally to SQL Server by unique security identification numbers (SIDs).

SQL Server has two kinds of login accounts:

- Windows
- SQL Server

A Windows login is an account that exists at the operating system level. A SQL Server login is created within SQL Server and is associated with a password. (Some SQL Server login names are identical to the existing Windows account names.)

NOTE: In addition to Windows and SQL Server logins, there are also Windows groups and SQL Server roles. A Windows group is a collection of Windows user accounts. Assigning a user account membership to a group gives the user all the permissions granted to the group. Similarly, a SQL Server role is a collection of SQL Server users. (Roles are discussed in detail later in this chapter.)

SQL Server security includes two different security subsystems:

- Windows
- SQL Server

Windows security specifies security at the operating system level—that is, the method by which users connect to Windows using their Windows *user accounts*. SQL Server security specifies the additional security necessary at the SQL Server system level—that is, how users who have already logged onto the operating system can subsequently connect to SQL Server.

Based on these two security subsystems, SQL Server can operate in one of these two security modes:

- Windows
- Mixed

NOTE: In Microsoft vocabulary, security mode is also called authentication mode.

Windows security mode exclusively uses Windows user accounts to log into the SQL Server system. SQL Server accepts the user account, assuming it has already been validated at the operating system level. This kind of connection to a database system is called a *trusted connection*, because SQL Server trusts that the operating system already validated the account name and the corresponding password.

Mixed mode allows users to connect to SQL Server using the Windows security or the SQL Server security. This means some login accounts can be set up to use Windows authentication, while others can use SQL Server authentication.

Windows security and Mixed mode security can be set up using SQL Server Enterprise Manager. SQL Server security can be set up using either Transact-SQL system procedures or SQL Server Enterprise Manager. (For setting Windows and/or SQL Server security using SQL Server Enterprise Manager, see Chapter 19.) The following system procedures are used to set up SQL Server security:

- sp_addlogin
- sp_droplogin
- sp_password

There are also three system procedures concerning Windows users and groups: **sp_grantlogin**, **sp_revokelogin**, and **sp_denylogin**. The system procedure **sp_grantlogin** allows a Windows user or group to connect to SQL Server or resets previous **sp_denylogin** restrictions for users within the group. The system procedure **sp_revokelogin** removes the login entries for a Windows user or group from SQL Server. The system procedure **sp_denylogin** prevents a Windows user or group from connecting to SQL Server (even if a group that contains this user or group is granted access). Only the system or security administrators can execute these three system procedures.

sp_addlogin

The **sp_addlogin** system procedure creates a new SQL Server login, which can subsequently be used by the user to log into the SQL Server system. It has the following syntax:

```
sp_addlogin 'login_name' [,'passwd' [,'database' [,'language']]]
```

login_name is the new login name, and **passwd** is the corresponding password. The optional specification **database** specifies the name of the default database that the login is connected to immediately after the login process. Only the system or security administrator can execute this system procedure.

sp_addlogin adds a record to the **sysxlogins** table of the **master** database using the **syslogins** view. Example 12.1 shows the use of the **sp_addlogin** system procedure.

▼ **EXAMPLE 12.1**

```
sp_addlogin 'peter', 'xxyyzz', 'sample'
GO
sp_addlogin 'mary', 'zzyyxx', 'sample'
GO
sp_addlogin 'paul', 'xyz123', 'sample'
```

The **sp_addlogin** system procedure in Example 12.1 creates three new SQL Server logins: **peter, paul,** and **mary**. The default database for all three logins is **sample**.

sp_droplogin

The **sp_droplogin** system procedure drops an existing SQL Server login name. **sp_droplogin** removes a login name by deleting the corresponding row from the system table **sysxlogins**. It is not possible to remove a SQL Server login name that still has access to any database of the SQL Server system. The user must first be removed using the system procedure **sp_revokedbaccess** (discussed a bit later in the chapter).

sp_password

The **sp_password** system procedure adds a new password to a SQL Server login name or replaces the existing one. Users can change their own password at any time by using this system procedure. The system administrator can change any password by using **sp_password** and specifying NULL as the parameter for the old password.

DATABASE SECURITY PERMISSIONS

A Windows user account or a SQL Server login name allows a user to log into the SQL Server system. A user who subsequently wants to access a particular database of the system needs a *database user account* to work in the database. Therefore, users must have a database user account for each database they want to use. If there is no such account, the user may be allowed to work in the database under the **guest** account, if one exists (see below).

The database user account can be mapped from the existing Windows user accounts, Windows groups (of which the user is a member), SQL Server login names, or roles.

Default User Accounts

Each database within the SQL Server system has two default user accounts:

- guest
- dbo

The SQL Server system allows users without user accounts to access a database using the **guest** user account. (In this case, the database must contain a **guest** user account.) You can apply permissions to the guest in the same way as to any other user account. Also, you can drop and add the **guest** user account from any database except the **master** and **tempdb** system databases. (The **dbo** user account will be described in detail later in this chapter.)

Setting User Accounts

Database security permissions can be set up using either Transact-SQL system procedures or SQL Server Enterprise Manager. (To set database security permissions using SQL Server Enterprise Manager, see Chapter 19.) The following system procedures are used to establish database security permissions:

- sp_grantdbaccess
- sp_revokedbaccess
- sp_helpuser
- sp_changedbowner

sp_grantdbaccess

The **sp_grantdbaccess** system procedure adds a new database user name to the current database and associates it with an existing security account (login). The login can be a Windows user, Windows group, or SQL Server login. The syntax of this system procedure is:

```
sp_grantdbaccess 'login_name' [,'new_name']
```

login_name is the name of an existing login account. The optional specification **new_name** declares the new name (also known as 'user name') for **login_name** in the current database. (If **new_name** is omitted, **login_name** will be the database user name in the current database.)

> ***NOTE:*** Each database of the SQL Server system has its own specific users. Therefore, the **sp_grantdbaccess** system procedure must be executed once for each database where a user account should exist for a database login name.

Example 12.2 shows the use of the **sp_grantdbaccess** system procedure.

▼ EXAMPLE 12.2

```
sp_grantdbaccess 'peter', 'peter'
GO
sp_grantdbaccess 'mary', 'mary'
GO
sp_grantdbaccess 'paul', 'paul'
```

In Example 12.2, the **sp_grantdbaccess** system procedure creates the database user names, which are identical to the corresponding logins created in Example 12.1.

> ***NOTE:*** The system procedure **sp_grantdbaccess** replaces the system procedure **sp_adduser**, which was used in versions previous to SQL Server 7 for the same purpose. The **sp_adduser** system procedure is supported in SQL Server 2000 for backward compatibility.

sp_revokedbaccess

The **sp_revokedbaccess** system procedure removes an existing database user name from the current database. (The database user name can be the name of a Windows user, Windows group, or Microsoft SQL Server user.) **sp_revokedbaccess** removes a user name by deleting the corresponding row from the **sysusers** system table.

> ***NOTE:*** The system procedure **sp_revokedbaccess** replaces the system procedure **sp_dropuser**, which was used in versions previous to SQL Server 7 for the same purpose. The **sp_dropuser** system procedure is supported in SQL Server 2000 for backward compatibility.

sp_helpuser

The **sp_helpuser** system procedure displays information about one or more database user names in the current database. If the user name is omitted, **sp_helpuser** displays the information about all existing database users and roles in the current database.

sp_changedbowner

The **sp_changedbowner** system procedure changes the owner of the current database. After the execution of the procedure, the specified login is the new database owner (**dbo**) of the current database. For more information concerning **dbo**, see the corresponding section later in this chapter.

All members of the **sysadmin** fixed server role and the owner of the current database can execute this system procedure.

ROLES

When several users need to perform activities in a particular database (and there is no corresponding Windows group), the database owner can add a *role* in this database. A database role specifies a group of database user names that can access the same objects of the database.

Members of a database role can be any of the following:

- Windows groups and user accounts
- SQL Server user names
- Other roles

NOTE: SQL Server groups, which were supported by the earlier versions of SQL Server, are replaced in SQL Server 7 by roles. The reason for this name modification is that the new SQL standard (SQL99) introduces this feature with that name.

The security architecture in SQL Server includes several roles that have special implicit permissions. There are two types of predefined roles in addition to roles that can be created by the database owner. These roles are classified as follows:

- Fixed server
- Fixed database
- User-defined

Fixed Server Roles

Fixed server roles are defined at the server level and therefore exist outside of databases belonging to the database server. Table 12-1 lists all existing fixed server roles.

Fixed Server Role	Description
sysadmin	Performs any activity in SQL Server
serveradmin	Configures server settings
setupadmin	Installs replication and manages extended procedures
securityadmin	Manages logins and CREATE DATABASE permissions, and reads audits
processadmin	Manages SQL Server processes
dbcreator	Creates and modifies databases
diskadmin	Manages disk files

Table 12-1. Fixed Server Roles

The following two system procedures are used to add or delete members to a fixed server role:

- sp_addsrvrolemember
- sp_dropsrvrolemember

NOTE: You cannot add, modify, or remove fixed server roles. Additionally, only the members of fixed server roles can execute both system procedures to add or remove login accounts to/from the role.

The sa Login

The **sa** login is the login of the system administrator. In previous versions, where roles did not exist, the **sa** login was granted all possible permissions concerning system administration tasks. In SQL Server 2000, the **sa** login is included for backward compatibility. (It still has all the permissions it had in releases before version 7.) The **sa** login is always a member of the **sysadmin** fixed server role and cannot be dropped from the role.

Concerning databases, the **sa** login is mapped to the database owner **(dbo)** inside all databases. This mapping cannot be changed.

Fixed Server Roles and Their Permissions

Each fixed server role has its implicit permissions within a SQL Server system. You can view the permissions for each fixed server role using the **sp_srvrolepermission** system procedure. The syntax of this procedure is:

```
sp_srvrolepermission [[@srvrolename =] 'role']
```

If you do not specify the value for **role**, the permissions for all fixed server roles are displayed. In the following sections, permissions of each fixed server role are discussed.

sysadmin

Members of the **sysadmin** fixed server role are granted all possible permissions for the SQL Server system. For example, only someone with this role (or a user who has been granted the CREATE DATABASE permission from a member of this role) can create databases.

This fixed server role has special relationships with the **sa** login and the **dbo** user. The **sa** login is always a member of this role and cannot be dropped from the role. Also, any member of the **sysadmin** fixed server role is mapped to the database owner (**dbo**) inside each database. For more information on these relationships, see the corresponding sections later in this chapter.

serveradmin

Members of the **serveradmin** fixed server role can perform the following activities:

- Add other logins to this server role
- Run the DBCC PINTABLE command (to pin a table in the main memory)
- Run the **sp_configure** system procedure (to display or change system options)
- Run the RECONFIGURE option (to update all modifications made with the **sp_configure** system procedure)
- Shut down SQL Server using the SHUTDOWN command
- Run the **sp_tableoption** system procedure to set option values for a user-defined table

setupadmin

Members of the **setupadmin** fixed server role can perform the following activities:

- Add other logins to this server role
- Add, drop, or configure linked servers
- Mark a stored procedure at startup

securityadmin

Members of the **securityadmin** fixed server role perform all activities in relation to server access and its security. They may perform the following system activities:

- Add other logins to this server role
- Read the SQL Server error log
- Grant, revoke, or deny the CREATE DATABASE permission
- Run the following system procedures: **sp_addlinkedsrvlogin**, **sp_addlogin**, **sp_defaultdb**, **sp_defaultlanguage**, **sp_denylogin**, **sp_droplinkedsrvlogin**, **sp_droplogin**, **sp_grantlogin**, **sp_helplogins**, **sp_remoteoption**, and **sp_revokelogin**. (All these system procedures are related to the system security.)

processadmin

Members of the **processadmin** fixed server role manage SQL Server processes, such as aborting user's runaway queries. They can perform the following activities:

- Add other logins to this server role
- Execute the KILL command (to kill user processes)

dbcreator

Members of the **dbcreator** fixed server role manage all activities concerning the creation and modification of a database. They can perform the following activities:

- Add other logins to this server role
- Run the CREATE DATABASE and ALTER DATABASE statements
- Modify the name of a database using the **sp_renamedb** system procedure

diskadmin

Members of the **diskadmin** fixed server role can perform the following activities concerning files and file groups that are used to store database objects:

- Add other logins to this server role
- Run the following system procedures: **sp_addumpdevice**, **sp_diskdefault**, and **sp_dropdevice**
- Run the DISK INIT statement

Fixed Database Roles

Fixed database roles are defined at the database level and therefore exist in each database belonging to the database server. Table 12-2 lists all of the fixed database roles.

Fixed Database Role	Description
db_owner	Users who can perform almost all activities in the database
db_accessadmin	Users who can add or remove users
db_datareader	Users who can see data from all user tables in the database
db_datawriter	Users who can add, modify, or delete data in all user tables in the database
db_ddladmin	Users who can perform all DDL operations in the database
db_securityadmin	Users who can manage all activities concerning security permissions in the database
db_backupoperator	Users who can back up the database (and issue DBCC and CHECKPOINT statements, which are often performed before a backup)
db_denydatareader	Users who cannot see any data in the database
db_denydatawriter	Users who cannot change any data in the database

Table 12-2. Fixed Database Roles

Besides the fixed database roles listed in Table 2-2, there are two special fixed database roles: **dbo** and **public**, which will be explained first.

The Database Owner (dbo)

dbo is a special user that has relationships with two other roles: the **sysadmin** fixed server role and the **db_owner** fixed database role. First, the logins of the system administrator (**sa**) and any member of the **sysadmin** fixed server role are mapped to **dbo** inside all databases. Therefore, any database object created by any member of the **sysadmin** fixed server role belongs implicitly to **dbo**. Second, **dbo** has the same rights as members of the **db_owner** fixed database role. (This user is the only one who can add members to the **db_owner** role.)

There is a significant difference between **dbo** and **db_owner**: the **db_owner** fixed database role can have any number of members, while there is always only one **dbo** for each database. Also, if a member of the **db_owner** role creates an object, his or her user name will be the owner's name of that object. (In the case of the database owner, **dbo** is the owner of that object.)

A login is considered to be the database owner in the following cases:

- The login that created a database
- A member of the **sysadmin** fixed server role
- A user, who is assigned as the database owner (using the **sp_changedbowner** system procedure)

> ***NOTE:*** The **dbo** user cannot be dropped.

public Role

The **public** role is a special fixed database role to which every legitimate user of a database belongs. This provides a mechanism for giving all users without appropriate permissions a set of (usually limited) permissions. The **public** role maintains all default permissions for users in a database and cannot be dropped. (Example 12.12 shows the use of the **public** role.)

By default, the **public** role allows users to do the following:

- Access any database with a **guest** account
- View system tables and display information from the **master** database using certain system procedures
- Execute statements that do not require permissions—for example, PRINT

Fixed Database Roles and Their Permissions

Each fixed database role has its specific permissions within a database. This means that permissions of a member of a fixed database role are limited to a specific database. You can view the permissions for each fixed database role using the **sp_dbfixedrolepermission** system procedure. The syntax of this procedure is:

```
sp_dbfixedrolepermission [[@rolename =] 'role']
```

If you do not specify the value for **role**, the permissions for all fixed database roles are displayed. In the following sections, permissions of each database role are discussed.

db_owner

Members of the **db_owner** fixed database role may perform the following activities in the specific database:

- Add members to or remove members from any other fixed database role
- Run all data definition language statements
- Run BACKUP DATABASE and BACKUP LOG statements
- Explicitly start the checkpoint process using the CHECKPOINT statement
- Run the following DBCC commands: DBCC CHECKALLOC, DBCC CHECKCATALOG, DBCC CHECKDB, DBCC TEXTALL, DBCC TEXTALLOC, DBCC UPDATEUSAGE
- Grant, revoke, or deny the following permissions on every database object: SELECT, INSERT, UPDATE, DELETE, and REFERENCES
- Add users or roles to a database with the following system procedures: **sp_addapprol**, **sp_addrole**, **sp_addrolemember**, **sp_approlepassword**, **sp_changeobjectowner**, **sp_dropapprole**, **sp_droprole**, **sp_droprolemember**, **sp_dropuser**, **sp_grantdbaccess**
- Rename any database object using the **sp_rename** system procedure

db_accessadmin

Members of the **db_accessadmin** fixed database role perform all activities in relation to database access. They may perform the following activities in the specific database:

- Run the following system procedures: **sp_addalias**, **sp_dropalias**, **sp_dropuser**, **sp_grantdbaccess**, **sp_revokedbaccess**

db_datareader

Members of the **db_datareader** fixed database role have SELECT permissions on any database object (table or view) in a database. However, they cannot grant this permission to any other user or role. (The same is true for the REVOKE statement.)

db_datawriter

Members of the **db_datawriter** fixed database role have INSERT, UPDATE, and DELETE permissions on any database object (table or view) in a database. However, they cannot grant the permission to any other user or role. (The same is true for the REVOKE statement.)

db_ddladmin

Members of the **db_ddladmin** fixed database role can perform the following activities:

- Run all data definition language statements
- Grant the REFERENCES permission on any table
- Modify the structure of any stored procedures with the **sp_procoption** and **sp_recompile** system procedures
- Rename any database object using the **sp_rename** system procedure
- Modify table options and the owner of any database object using the system procedures **sp_tableoption** and **sp_changeobjectowner**, respectively

db_securityadmin

Members of the **db_securityadmin** fixed database role manage security in the database. They can perform the following activities:

- Run all Transact-SQL statements concerning security (GRANT, DENY, and REVOKE)
- Run the following system procedures: **sp_addapprole**, **sp_addrole**, **sp_addrolemember**, **sp_approlepassword**, **sp_changeobjectowner**, **sp_dropapprole**, **sp_droprole**, **sp_droprolemember**

db_backupoperator

Members of the **db_backupoperator** fixed database role manage the process of backing up a database. They can perform the following activities:

- Run BACKUP DATABASE and BACKUP LOG statements
- Explicitly start the checkpoint process using the CHECKPOINT statement
- Run the following DBCC commands: DBCC CHECKALLOC, DBCC CHECKCATALOG, DBCC CHECKDB, DBCC TEXTALL, DBCC TEXTALLOC, DBCC UPDATEUSAGE

db_denydatareader

As the name states, members of the **db_denydatareader** fixed database role do not have the SELECT permission on any database object (table or view) in the database. You should use this role if your database contains sensitive data that should not be read by some users.

db_denydatawriter

Members of the **db_denydatawriter** fixed database role do not have the INSERT, UPDATE, and DELETE permissions on any database object (table or view) in the database.

Application Roles

Application roles allow you to enforce security for a particular application. In other words, they allow the application itself to accept the responsibility of user authentication, instead of SQL Server. For instance, if clerks in your firm may change an employee's data only using the existing application (and not Transact-SQL statements or any other tool), you can create an application role for it.

Application roles differ significantly from all other role types. First, application roles have no members, because they use the application only and therefore do not need to grant any permissions directly to users. Second, you need a password to activate an application role.

When an application role is activated for a session by the application, the session loses all permissions applied to the login, user account, or roles in all databases for the duration of the session. Because these roles are applicable only to the database in which they exist, the session can gain access to another database only by virtue of permissions granted to the **guest** user account in the other database. For this reason, if there is no **guest** user account in a database, the session cannot gain access to that database.

Creating Application Roles

Using the **sp_addapprole** system procedure, you can create application roles and assign permissions to them. This procedure has the following syntax:

sp_addapprole [@rolename =] '*role*', [@passwd_name =] '*password*'

role specifies the name of the application role, while **password** is the corresponding password. (The value for **password** is required to activate the role.)

Only members of the **db_owner**, **db_securityadmin**, and **sysadmin** fixed roles can execute the **sp_addapprole** system procedure.

NOTE: Permissions for an application role are managed in the same way as permissions for any other roles—that is, using Enterprise Manager or the Transact-SQL statements GRANT, REVOKE, and DENY.

Activating Application Roles

After a connection is started, it must execute the **sp_setapprole** system procedure to activate the permissions that are associated with an application role. This procedure has the following syntax:

```
sp_setapprole [@rolename =] 'role' , [@password =] 'password'
              [,[@encrypt =] 'encrypt_style']
```

role is the name of the application role defined in the current database. **password** specifies the corresponding password, while **encrypt_style** defines the encryption style specified for the password.

When you activate an application role using the **sp_setapprole** system procedure, you have to know the following:

- After the activation of an application role, you cannot deactivate it in the current database until the session is disconnected from SQL Server.
- An application role is always database bound—that is, its scope is the current database. If you change the current database within a session, you are allowed to perform (other) activities based on the permissions in that database.

NOTE: Any user can execute the **sp_setapprole** system procedure by providing the correct password for the application role.

User-Defined Database Roles

Generally, user-defined database roles are applied when a group of database users need to perform a common set of activities within a database and no applicable Windows group exists. These roles are managed using the Transact-SQL statements or SQL Server Enterprise Manager. The management of roles using Transact-SQL is described later in this chapter, while the use of SQL Server Enterprise Manager for the same activity is explained in Chapter 19.

The following system procedures are used to set up and display the user-defined database roles:

- sp_addrole
- sp_addrolemember
- sp_droprolemember
- sp_droprole
- sp_helprole

NOTE: The system procedures **sp_addgroup**, **sp_dropgroup**, and **sp__helpgroup**, which were supported by earlier versions of SQL Server, map to the system procedures **sp_addrole**, **sp_droprole**, and **sp_helprole**, respectively.

sp_addrole

The **sp_addrole** system procedure creates a new role in the current database. Only members of the **db_securityadmin** or **db_owner** database roles can execute this system procedure. The syntax of **sp_addrole** is:

```
sp_addrole 'role' [,'owner']
```

role is the name of the new role, and **owner** is the owner of the role. If **owner** is omitted, the database owner (**dbo**) is the owner of the new role.

sp_addrolemember

After adding a role to the current database with the system procedure **sp_addrole**, you can use the system procedure **sp_addrolemember** to add members of the role. The member of the role can be any valid SQL Server user, Windows group or user, or another SQL Server role. Only members of the **db_owner** database role can execute this system procedure. Additionally, role owners can execute **sp_addrolemember** to add a member to any role that they own.

sp_droprolemember

The **sp_droprolemember** system procedure removes an existing member from the role. **sp_droprolemember** removes a role member by deleting a row from the **sysmembers** system table. (It is not possible to use this system procedure to remove an existing Windows user from a Windows group.) Only members of the **db_owner** or **db_securityadmin** database roles can execute this system procedure.

sp_droprole

After removing all members from the role using the system procedure **sp_droprolemember**, you can use the **sp_droprole** system procedure to remove a role from the current database. (A role with existing members cannot be dropped.) **sp_droprole** removes the corresponding row from the **sysusers** system table in the current database. Only members of the **db_owner** or **db_securityadmin** database roles can execute this system procedure.

sp_helprole

The **sp_helprole** system procedure displays information (role name and role ID number) about a particular role or all roles in the current database if no role name is provided. Only the members of the **db_owner** or **db_securityadmin** roles can execute this system procedure.

TRANSACT-SQL STATEMENTS CONCERNING SECURITY

Only authorized users are able to execute statements or perform operations on an object. Otherwise, the execution of the Transact-SQL statement or the operation on the database object will be rejected.

Two groups of permissions control the actions of a user:

- Statement permissions
- Object permissions

Statement Permissions and GRANT Statement

Statement permissions allow a user to perform certain Transact-SQL statements. Statement permissions apply to these statements:

- CREATE DATABASE
- CREATE DEFAULT
- CREATE PROCEDURE
- CREATE FUNCTION
- CREATE RULE
- CREATE TABLE
- CREATE VIEW
- BACKUP DATABASE
- BACKUP LOG

The GRANT statement grants permissions to users of SQL Server. The syntax of the GRANT statement for statement permissions is:

```
GRANT {ALL | statement_list}
  TO account_list
```

statement_list specifies one or more statements (separated by commas) for which the permissions are granted. **account_list** lists all accounts (separated by commas) to which permissions are granted. The components of **account_list** can be a Windows user account or group, a database user name, or a role. ALL specifies that all existing statement permissions are granted.

▼ EXAMPLE 12.3

```
USE sample
    GRANT CREATE TABLE, CREATE PROCEDURE
      TO peter, paul, mary
```

In Example 12.3, the users **peter**, **paul**, and **mary** can execute the Transact-SQL statements CREATE TABLE and CREATE PROCEDURE.

SQL Server 2000 extends the syntax of the GRANT statement so that it can be used to give a user CREATE FUNCTION permission, which is needed to create, alter, or drop a user-defined function (see also Chapter 8). Example 12.4 allows the user **mary** to create user-defined functions in the sample database.

▼ EXAMPLE 12.4

```
USE sample
   GRANT CREATE FUNCTION
      TO mary
```

▼ EXAMPLE 12.5

```
USE sample
   GRANT ALL
     TO mary
```

In Example 12.5, the user **mary** can use all allowed Transact-SQL statements in the sample database.

Only the system administrator and the database owner can execute the GRANT statement for statement permissions. (The GRANT CREATE DATABASE can be used only by the system administrator.)

Object Permissions and GRANT Statement

Object permissions apply to specific operations on database objects (tables, views, and stored procedures). The syntax of the GRANT statement for object permissions is:

```
GRANT {ALL | permission_list}
  ON {table_name [columns_list] | procedure_name}
  TO account_list
  [WITH GRANT OPTION]
  [AS {group_name | role_name}]
```

ALL and **account_list** have the same logical meaning as the options with the same name in the first form of the GRANT statement. **table_name** can be the name of a table or a view. AS specifies the name of the account that has the permissions necessary to execute the GRANT statement. (AS is required when the user executing the GRANT statement belongs to multiple groups or roles.)

permission_list is the list of operation permissions. Table 12-3 lists all operation permissions. (The first five permissions in Table 12-3 are related to base tables or views, while the last one is related to stored procedures.)

Permission	Description
SELECT	Provides the ability to select (read) rows. You can restrict this permission to one or more columns by listing them. (If the list is omitted, all columns of the table can be selected.)
INSERT	Provides the ability to insert rows.
UPDATE	Provides the ability to modify column values. You can restrict this permission to one or more columns by listing them. (If the list is omitted, all columns of the table can be modified.)
DELETE	Provides the ability to delete rows.
REFERENCES	Provides the ability to reference columns of the foreign key in the referenced table when the user has no SELECT permission for the referenced table. (SQL Server 2000 extends the use of the REFERENCES permission to views and user-defined functions.)
EXECUTE	Provides the ability to execute the specified stored procedure or user-defined functions.

Table 12-3. Object Permissions

NOTE: When an object permission is granted to a Windows user account or a database user account, this account is the only account affected by the permission. On the other hand, if a permission is granted to a group or role, the permission affects all users belonging to the group (role).

By default, if user A grants a permission to user B, then user B can only use the permission to execute the Transact-SQL statement listed in the GRANT statement. The WITH GRANT OPTION gives user B the additional capability of granting the privilege to other users (see Example 12.10).

▼ EXAMPLE 12.6

```
GRANT SELECT ON employee
  TO peter, mary
```

In Example 12.6, the users **peter** and **mary** can read rows from the **employee** table.

▼ EXAMPLE 12.7

```
GRANT UPDATE ON works_on (emp_no, enter_date)
  TO paul
```

In Example 12.7, the user **paul** can modify two columns of the **works_on** table: **emp_no** and **enter_date**.

▼ EXAMPLE 12.8

```
GRANT EXEC ON increase_budget
  TO mary
```

In Example 12.8, the user **mary** can execute the stored procedure **increase_budget** (Example 8.4).

▼ EXAMPLE 12.9

```
GRANT ALL ON project
  TO peter
```

In Example 12.9, the user **peter** can perform all operations on the **project** table (including the execution of all stored procedures defined on this table).

▼ EXAMPLE 12.10

```
GRANT SELECT ON works_on
  TO mary
  WITH GRANT OPTION
```

In Example 12.10, the user **mary** can use the SELECT statement to retrieve rows from the **works_on** table and also may grant this privilege to other users of the current database.

DENY Statement

The DENY statement prevents users from performing actions. This means it removes existing permissions from user accounts or prevents users from gaining permissions through their group/role membership that might be granted in the future. This statement can be used for statement and object permissions and therefore has two syntax forms.

1. Statement permissions:

```
DENY {ALL | statement_list}
  TO account_list
```

2. Object permissions:

```
DENY {ALL | permission_list}
  {[column_list] ON table_name | ON {table_name [column_list] | procedure_name}}
  TO account_list
        [CASCADE]
```

All options of the DENY statement have the same logical meaning as the options with the same name in the GRANT statement. The CASCADE option specifies that permissions will be denied user A and any other users to whom user A passed this permission. (If the CASCADE option is not specified in the DENY statement and the corresponding object permission was granted with the WITH GRANT OPTION, an error is returned.)

The DENY statement can be applied to a particular user, a Windows group, or a SQL Server role. This statement prevents the user, group, or role from gaining access to the permission granted through their group or role membership. This means that if a user belongs to a group (or role) and the granted permission for the group is denied to him or her, this user will be the only one of the group who cannot use this permission. On the other hand, if a permission is denied for a whole group, all members of the group will be denied the permission.

> ***NOTE:*** You can think of the GRANT statement as a "positive" and the DENY statement as a "negative" user authorization. Usually, the DENY statement is used to deny already existing permissions for groups (roles) to a few members of the group.

▼ EXAMPLE 12.11

```
DENY CREATE TABLE, CREATE PROCEDURE
  TO peter, paul
```

The DENY statement in Example 12.11 denies two already granted statement permissions (Example 12.3) to the users **peter** and **paul**.

▼ EXAMPLE 12.12

```
GRANT SELECT ON project
  TO PUBLIC

DENY SELECT ON project
  TO peter, mary
```

Example 12.12 shows the negative authorization of some users of the current database. First, the retrieval of all rows of the **project** table is granted to all users of the sample database. After that, this permission is denied to two users: **peter** and **mary**.

REVOKE Statement

The REVOKE statement removes one or more already granted (or denied) permissions. This statement can be used for statement and object permissions and therefore has two syntax forms.

1. Statement permissions:

```
REVOKE {ALL | statement_list}
  FROM account_list
```

2. Object permissions:

```
REVOKE [GRANT OPTION FOR]
  {ALL [PRIVILEGES] | permission_list}
  ON table_name [column_list]
  {TO | FROM} account_list
  [CASCADE]
  [AS {group | role}]
```

The only new option in the REVOKE statement is GRANT OPTION FOR. (All other options have the same logical meaning as the options with the same names in the GRANT or DENY statement.) GRANT OPTION FOR is used to remove the effects of the WITH GRANT OPTION in the corresponding GRANT statement. This means the user will still have the previously granted object permissions, but will no longer be able to grant the permission to other users.

NOTE: The REVOKE statement revokes "positive" permissions specified with the GRANT statement as well as "negative" permissions generated by the DENY statement. Therefore its function is to neutralize the specified (positive or negative) permissions.

▼ EXAMPLE 12.13

```
REVOKE SELECT ON project
  FROM PUBLIC
```

The REVOKE statement in Example 12.12 revokes the granted permission for the **public** role. At the same time, the existing "negative" permissions for the users **peter** and **mary** are not revoked (Example 12.11), because the explicitly granted or denied permissions are not affected by revoking roles or groups.

VIEWS AND DATA ACCESS

As already stated in Chapter 10, views can be used for the following purposes:

- To restrict the use of particular columns and/or rows of tables
- To hide the details of complicated queries
- To restrict inserted and updated values to certain ranges

Restricting the use of particular columns and/or rows means that the view mechanism of SQL Server provides itself with the control of data access. For example, if the table with employee data also contains the salaries of each employee, then access to these salaries can be restricted using a view, which accesses all columns of the table except the **salary** column. Subsequently, retrieval of data from the table can be granted to all users of the database using the view, while only a small number of (privileged) users will have the same permission for all data of the table.

Examples 12.14, 12.15, and 12.16 show the use of views to restrict the access to data.

▼ EXAMPLE 12.14

```
CREATE VIEW v_without_budget
  AS SELECT project_no, project_name
         FROM project
```

Using the **v_without_budget** view, it is possible to divide users into two groups: first, the group of privileged users who can read (write) the budget of all projects and, second, the group of common users who can read all rows from the **projects** table, but not the data from the **budget** column.

▼ EXAMPLE 12.15

```
ALTER TABLE employee
  ADD user_name CHAR(60) DEFAULT SYSTEM_USER
GO

CREATE VIEW v_my_rows
  AS SELECT emp_no, emp_fname, emp_lname, dept_no
     FROM employee
     WHERE user_name = SYSTEM_USER
```

> ***NOTE:*** The Transact-SQL statements in Example 12.15 must be separately executed, because the CREATE VIEW statement must be the first statement in the batch. That is why the GO statement is used (to mark the end of the first batch).

The schema of the **employee** table is modified in Example 12.15 by adding the new column **user_name**. Every time a new row is inserted into the **employee** table, the system login name is inserted into the **user_name** column. After the creation of corresponding views, every user can retrieve only the rows that they inserted into the table. (The same is true for the UPDATE statement.)

▼ EXAMPLE 12.16

```
CREATE VIEW v_analyst
  AS SELECT employee.emp_no, emp_fname, emp_lname
         FROM employee, works_on
         WHERE employee.emp_no = works_on.emp_no
         AND job = 'Analyst'
```

The **v_analyst** view represents a horizontal and a vertical subset (in other words, it limits the rows and columns that can be accessed) of the **employee** table.

STORED PROCEDURES AND DATA ACCESS

Stored procedures can also be used to restrict data access. The restriction of data access using stored procedures is based upon the property that the permission to execute a stored procedure is independent of any permissions for database objects that are referenced by the stored procedure. More precisely, granting permission to execute a stored procedure suffices if the owner of the stored procedure is also the owner of all the referenced database objects.

▼ EXAMPLE 12.17

```
CREATE PROCEDURE analyst_data
AS SELECT employee.emp_no, emp_fname, emp_lname
       FROM employee, works_on
       WHERE employee.emp_no = works_on.emp_no
       AND job = 'Analyst'
```

In Example 12.17, users of the **analyst_data** stored procedure see a horizontal and a vertical subset of the **employee** table. Neither the SELECT permission for the **employee** table nor the same permission for the **works_on** table is needed to use this procedure. (The user must have only the EXEC permission for the **analyst_data** procedure.)

CONCLUSION

SQL Server can operate in one of two security modes:

- Windows
- Mixed

Windows security mode exclusively uses Windows user accounts to log into the SQL Server system. Mixed mode allows users to connect to SQL Server using the Windows security system or the SQL Server security system. Additionally, SQL Server provides three security facilities for controlling access to database objects:

- Transact-SQL statements GRANT, DENY, and REVOKE
- Views
- Stored procedures

Of these three facilities, the use of Transact-SQL to control object and statement permissions is most extensive because it allows the *selective* use of read and write operations to restrict data access. (Views and stored procedures provide only the general restriction of data access.)

SQL Server provides a mechanism called a *trigger* that enforces general integrity constraints. This mechanism is discussed in detail in the next chapter.

EXERCISES

▼ E.12.1

What is a difference between Windows security mode and Mixed mode?

▼ E.12.2

What is a difference between a login and account name?

▼ E.12.3

Using system procedures, create three new SQL Server logins called **ann**, **burt**, and **chuck**. The corresponding passwords are **abc**, **def**, and **fgh**, respectively. The default database is the sample database. After creating the logins, check their existence using SQL Server system tables.

▼ E.12.4

Using system procedures, create three new database names for the logins in E.12.3. The new names are **s_ann**, **s_burt**, and **s_chuck**.

▼ E.12.5

Create a new user-defined database role called **managers** and add three members (see E.12.4) to the role. After that, display the information concerning this role and its members.

▼ E.12.6

Using the GRANT statement, allow the user **s_peter** to create tables and the user **s_mary** to create stored procedures in the sample database.

▼ E.12.7

Using the GRANT statement, allow the user **s_paul** to update the columns **lname** and **fname** of the **employee** table.

▼ E.12.8

Using the GRANT statement, allow the users **s_peter** and **s_mary** to read the values from the columns **emp_lname** and **emp_fname** of the **employee** table. (Hint: create the corresponding view first.)

▼ E.12.9

Using the GRANT statement, allow the user-defined role **managers** to insert new rows in the **projects** table.

▼ E.12.10

Revoke the SELECT rights from the user **s_peter**.

▼ E.12.11

Using Transact-SQL, do not allow the user **s_mary** to insert the new rows in the **projects** table either directly or indirectly (using roles).

▼ E.12.12

Discuss the difference between the use of views and Transact-SQL statements in relation to SQL Server security.

▼ E.12.13

Display the existing information about the user **s_mary** in relation to the sample database. (Hint: use the system procedure **sp_helpuser**.)

CHAPTER 13

Triggers

SQL Server provides a mechanism called a *trigger* for enforcing procedural integrity constraints. The introductory notes are followed by a description of triggers, which can be used to implement general constraints. Several examples show the main application areas for triggers.

INTRODUCTION

As previously stated in Chapter 4, a DBMS handles two types of integrity constraints:

- Declarative integrity constraints, defined by using the CREATE TABLE and ALTER TABLE statements
- Procedural integrity constraints (handled by triggers)

The use of the CREATE TABLE or ALTER TABLE statement in relation to triggers has several benefits, with simplicity as the most important one. This means, to implement a constraint using declarative constraints, only a few lines of code are necessary. On the other hand, to implement the same constraint using a trigger, some dozen (or more) lines of code are required (see Examples 4.7 and 13.4).

Another advantage of declarative integrity constraints occurs when a trigger is created after data is loaded into the table. In this case, the trigger checks only the subsequent violations of the specified integrity constraint. (The equivalent declarative constraint checks per default also if the existing data in the table violates the constraint.) Otherwise, triggers are more flexible than the declarative constraints, because *every* integrity constraint can be implemented using triggers. (The same is not true for declarative constraints.)

HOW TRIGGERS WORK

A trigger is a mechanism that is invoked when a particular action occurs on a particular table. Each trigger has three general parts:

- A name
- The action
- The execution

The action of a trigger can either be an INSERT, an UPDATE, or a DELETE statement. The execution part of a trigger usually contains a stored procedure or a batch.

A trigger is created using the CREATE TRIGGER statement, which has the following form:

```
CREATE TRIGGER trigger_name
  ON table_name | view_name
  {FOR | AFTER | INSTEAD OF} { [INSERT] [,] [UPDATE] [,] [DELETE]}
  [WITH ENCRYPTION]
  AS {batch | IF UPDATE(column) [{AND|OR} UPDATE(column)] batch}
```

trigger_name is the name of the trigger. **table_name** is the name of the table for which the trigger is specified. Since SQL Server 2000, you can also define triggers for views.

NOTE: A trigger must be the first statement in the batch and can apply to only one table or view.

The AFTER and INSTEAD OF are two additional options, which you can define for a trigger since SQL Server 2000. (The FOR clause is the synonym for AFTER.) AFTER triggers fire after the triggering event occurs. INSTEAD OF triggers are executed instead of the corresponding triggering event. AFTER triggers can be created only on tables, while INSTEAD OF triggers can be created on both tables and views. For more information using these two trigger types, see the corresponding sections later in this chapter.

The options INSERT, UPDATE, and DELETE specify the trigger action. (The trigger action is the type of Transact-SQL statement that activates the trigger.) These three statements can be written in any possible combination. (The DELETE statement is not allowed if the IF UPDATE is used.)

As can be seen from the syntax of the CREATE TRIGGER statement, AS can be followed either by a batch or by one or more IF UPDATE clauses with their specific group of Transact-SQL statements. The IF UPDATE clause is used as an additional trigger condition if an insert or update trigger is specified for a particular column or columns of the table. In the CREATE TRIGGER statement there can be more than one IF UPDATE clause, and they are combined using the Boolean conditions AND and OR. (The use of the IF UPDATE clause is therefore equivalent to the definition of a column-level constraint.)

NOTE: SQL Server allows multiple triggers to be created for each table and for each modification action (INSERT, UPDATE, and DELETE). In earlier versions, only one trigger per table was allowed for each type of modification statement. By default, there is no defined order in which multiple triggers for a given modification action are executed. (See also the Section "First and Last Triggers" at the end of this chapter.)

After the creation of the database, only the database owner, data definition language administrators, and the table owner on which the trigger is defined have the authority to create a trigger for the current database. (In contrast to the permissions for other CREATE **object** statements, this permission is not transferable.)

When creating a triggered action, you usually must indicate whether you are referring to the value of a column before or after the effect of the triggering statement. For this reason, two virtual tables with special names are used to test the effect of the triggering statement:

- **deleted**
- **inserted**

The structure of these tables is equivalent to the structure of the table for which the trigger is specified. The **deleted** table contains copies of rows that are deleted from the triggered table. Similarly, the **inserted** table contains copies of rows that are inserted into the triggered table. If the trigger operates on an UPDATE statement, then the **deleted** table represents the data *before* modification, and the **inserted** table represents the data *after* modification.

The **deleted** table is used if the DELETE or UPDATE clause is specified in the CREATE TRIGGER statement. The **inserted** table is used if the INSERT or UPDATE clause is specified in the CREATE TRIGGER statement. This means, for each DELETE statement executed in the triggered action, the **deleted** table is created. Similarly, for each INSERT statement executed in the triggered action, the **inserted** table is created.

An UPDATE statement is treated as a DELETE, followed by an INSERT. Therefore, for each UPDATE statement executed in the triggered action, the **deleted** and the **inserted** tables are created (in this sequence).

Application Areas for AFTER Triggers

As you already know, AFTER triggers fire after the triggering event has been processed. You can specify an AFTER trigger either by using the AFTER or FOR reserved keyword. AFTER triggers can be created only on base tables.

> ***NOTE:*** Previous versions of SQL Server supported only AFTER triggers using the FOR keyword.

AFTER triggers can be used to perform the following actions, among others:

- Create an audit trail of activities in one or more tables of the database (see Example 13.1)
- Implement a (business) rule (see Example 13.2)
- Enforce referential integrity (see Examples 13.3 and 13.4)

▼ EXAMPLE 13.1

```
/* The table audit_budget is used as an audit trail of activities
   in the table project */

CREATE TABLE audit_budget
 (project_no CHAR(4) NULL,
  user_name CHAR(16) NULL,
  time DATETIME NULL,
  budget_old FLOAT NULL,
  budget_new FLOAT NULL)
GO

CREATE TRIGGER modify_budget
  ON project AFTER UPDATE
  AS IF UPDATE(budget)
  BEGIN
  DECLARE @budget_old FLOAT
  DECLARE @budget_new FLOAT
  DECLARE @project_number CHAR(4)
  SELECT @budget_old = (SELECT budget FROM deleted)
  SELECT @budget_new = (SELECT budget FROM inserted)
  SELECT @project_number = (SELECT project_no FROM deleted)
  INSERT INTO audit_budget VALUES
  (@project_number,USER_NAME(),GETDATE(),@budget_old, @budget_new)
  END
```

Example 13.1 shows how triggers can be used to implement an audit trail of the activity within a table. This example creates the **audit_budget** table, which stores all modifications of the **budget** column of the **project** table. Recording all the modifications of this column will be executed using the **modify_budget** trigger.

Every modification of the **budget** column using the UPDATE statement activates the trigger. In doing so, the values of the rows of the virtual tables **deleted** and **inserted** are assigned to the corresponding variables **@budget_old**, **@budget_new**, and **@project_number**. The assigned values, together with the user name and the current time, will be subsequently inserted into the **audit_budget** table.

NOTE: Example 13.1 assumes that only one row will be updated at a time. Therefore, it is a simplification of a general case in which a trigger handles multirow updates. The implementation of such a general (and complicated) trigger is beyond the introductory level of this book.

If the following Transact-SQL statement:

```
UPDATE project
  SET budget = 200000
  WHERE project_no = 'p2'
```

is executed, the content of the **audit_budget** table is as follows:

project_no	user_name	getdate	budget_old	budget_new
p2	dbo	1997-06-06 11:51	95000.00	200000.00

▼ EXAMPLE 13.2

```
-- The trigger total_budget is an example of using a trigger to implement a business
rule

CREATE TRIGGER total_budget
  ON project AFTER UPDATE
  AS IF UPDATE (budget)
   BEGIN
   DECLARE @sum_old FLOAT
   DECLARE @sum_new FLOAT
   SELECT @sum_old = (SELECT SUM(budget) FROM deleted)
   SELECT @sum_new = (SELECT SUM(budget) FROM inserted)
   IF @sum_new < @sum_old*1.5
     BEGIN
     PRINT 'The modification of budgets executed'
     END
   ELSE
     BEGIN
     PRINT 'No modification of budgets'
     ROLLBACK TRANSACTION
     END
   END
```

Example 13.2 creates the rule controlling the modification of the budget for the projects. The **total_budget** trigger tests every modification of the budgets and executes only such UPDATE statements where the modification does not increase the sum of all budgets by more than 50 percent. Otherwise, the UPDATE statement is rolled back using the ROLLBACK TRANSACTION statement. (This statement is described in Chapter 14.)

▼ EXAMPLE 13.3

```
CREATE TRIGGER workson_integrity
  ON works_on AFTER INSERT, UPDATE
  AS IF UPDATE(emp_no)
   BEGIN
   IF (SELECT employee.emp_no
      FROM employee, inserted
      WHERE employee.emp_no = inserted.emp_no) IS NULL
```

```
    BEGIN
    ROLLBACK TRANSACTION
    PRINT 'No insertion/modification of the row'
    END
  ELSE PRINT 'The row inserted/modified'
  END
```

The **workson_integrity** trigger in Example 13.3 checks the referential integrity for the **employee** and **works_on** tables. This means that every modification of the **emp_no** column in the referenced **works_on** table is checked, and any violation of the constraint is rejected. (The same is true for the insertion of new values into the **emp_no** column.) The ROLLBACK TRANSACTION in the second BEGIN block rolls back the INSERT or UPDATE statement after a violation of the referential constraint.

The trigger in Example 13.3 checks case 1 and case 2 for referential integrity between the **employee** and **works_on** tables. Example 13.4 introduces the trigger that checks for the violation of integrity constraints between the same tables in case 3 and case 4.

▼ EXAMPLE 13.4

```
CREATE TRIGGER refint_workson2
  ON employee AFTER DELETE, UPDATE
  AS IF UPDATE (emp_no)
  BEGIN
   IF (SELECT COUNT(*)
     FROM WORKS_ON, deleted
     WHERE works_on.emp_no = deleted.emp_no) > 0
    BEGIN
    ROLLBACK TRANSACTION
    PRINT 'No modification/deletion of the row'
    END
   ELSE PRINT 'The row is deleted/modified'
  END
```

Application Areas for INSTEAD OF Triggers

INSTEAD OF triggers fire instead of the triggering event. They are executed after the corresponding **inserted** and **deleted** tables are created, but before any integrity constraint or any other action is preformed.

INSTEAD OF triggers can be created on tables as well as on views. When a Transact-SQL statement references a view that has an INSTEAD OF trigger, SQL Server executes the trigger instead of taking any action against any table. The trigger always uses the information in the **inserted** and **deleted** tables built for the view to create any statements needed to build the requested event.

There are certain requirements on column values that are supplied by an INSTEAD OF trigger combined with an INSERT or UPDATE statement:

- Values cannot be specified for computed columns.
- Values cannot be specified for columns with the TIMESTAMP data type.
- Values cannot be specified for columns with an IDENTITY property, unless the IDENTITY_INSERT option is set to ON.

These requirements are valid only for INSERT and DELETE statements that reference a base table. An INSERT statement that references a view that has an INSTEAD OF trigger must supply values for all non-nullable columns of that view. (The same is true for an UPDATE statement: An UPDATE statement that references a view that has an INSTEAD OF trigger must supply values for each view column that does not allow nulls and that is referenced in the SET clause.)

Example 13.5 shows the different behavior during insertion of values for computed columns using a table and its corresponding view.

▼ EXAMPLE 13.5

```
CREATE TABLE orders
   (orderid INT NOT NULL,
    price MONEY NOT NULL,
    quantity INT NOT NULL,
    orderdate DATETIME NOT NULL,
    total AS price * quantity,
    shippeddate AS DATEADD (DAY, 7, orderdate))
GO

CREATE VIEW all_orders
   AS SELECT orderid, price, quantity, orderdate, total, shippeddate
    FROM orders
GO

CREATE TRIGGER tr_orders
   ON all_orders INSTEAD OF INSERT
   AS BEGIN
     INSERT INTO orders
      SELECT  orderid, price, quantity, orderdate
        FROM inserted
      END
```

An INSERT statement must specify a value for a view column that maps to a computed column in a base table. This can be avoided if you use an INSTEAD OF trigger (as in Example 13.5), because it can ignore this value by using an INSERT statement that inserts the values into the base table. (An INSERT statement that refers directly to the base table cannot supply a value for a computed column.)

First and Last Triggers

SQL Server allows multiple triggers to be created for each table or view and for each modification action (INSERT, UPDATE, and DELETE) on them. Additionally, SQL Server 2000 allows you to define the order of multiple triggers defined for a given event. Using the system stored procedure **sp_settriggerorder**, you can specify that one of the AFTER triggers associated with a table be either the first AFTER trigger or the last AFTER trigger executed for each triggering action. This system procedure has a parameter called **@order** that can contain three values:

- **first**
- **last**
- **none**

The parameter **@first** specifies that the trigger is the first AFTER trigger fired for a modification action. **@last** specifies that the trigger is the last AFTER trigger fired for a triggering action. The option **@none** specifies that there is no specific order in which the trigger should be fired. (This option is generally used to reset a trigger from being either first or last.)

Example 13.6 shows the use of the system stored procedure **sp_settriggerorder**.

▼ EXAMPLE 13.6

```
sp_settriggerorder @triggername = 'audit_budget', @order = 'first', @stmttype='update'
```

NOTE: There can be only one first and one last AFTER trigger on a table. The sequence in which all AFTER triggers, other than the first and last triggers, fire is undefined.

To display the order of a trigger you can use the following:

- **sp_helptrigger**
- OBJECTPROPERTY function

The system procedure **sp_helptrigger** contains the **order** column, which displays the order of the specified trigger. Using the OBJECTPROPERTY function, you can specify one of the two following properties: **ExecIsFirstTrigger** and **ExecIsLastTrigger** as the second parameter of this function. (The first parameter is always the identification number of the database object.)

NOTE: Because an INSTEAD OF trigger is fired before data modifications are made to the underlying table, INSTEAD OF triggers cannot be specified as first or last triggers.

Modifying Trigger's Structure

SQL Server supports also the Transact-SQL statement ALTER TRIGGER that modifies the structure of a trigger. The ALTER TRIGGER statement is usually used to modify the body of the trigger. All clauses and options of the ALTER TRIGGER statement correspond to the clauses and options with the same name in the CREATE TRIGGER statement.

If you use the ALTER TRIGGER statement to alter an ordered trigger, the order of the (first or last) trigger is dropped. Use the **sp_settriggerorder** system procedure to specify the order of the trigger again.

The ALTER TRIGGER permissions default to members of the **db_owner** and **db_ddladmin** fixed database roles, and to the table owner. In contrast to the permissions of the CREATE object statements, these permissions are not transferable.

The DROP TRIGGER statement removes one or more existing triggers from the current database.

CONCLUSION

A Transact-SQL trigger is a mechanism that resides in the database server and offers an alternative to the CREATE TABLE and ALTER TABLE statements for the implementation of integrity constraints. It specifies that when a modification of the table using an INSERT, an UPDATE, or a DELETE statement is executed, the database server should automatically perform one or more additional actions. (A trigger cannot be used with the SELECT statement.)

The next chapter discusses the features concerning SQL Server as a multiuser software system and describes the notions of transaction and locking.

EXERCISES

▼ E.13.1

Using triggers, define the referential integrity for the primary key of the **department (dept_no)** table and the column with the same name, which is the foreign key of the **works_on** table.

▼ E.13.2

With the help of triggers, define the referential integrity for the primary key of the **project (project_no)** table and the column with the same name, which is the foreign key of the **works_on** table.

CHAPTER 14

Transactions

This chapter describes two related concepts: concurrency control and transactions. The chapter begins by explaining what a transaction is and defining the Transact-SQL statements related to it. Locking, as a method to solve the problem of concurrency control, is discussed, along with the notions of isolation levels and deadlocks, which arise from the use of locking.

INTRODUCTION

If your SQL Server system is a single-user system, your database application programs can retrieve and modify data in the database without any restrictions. A single-user system is a special case of a DBMS, because usually many users and programs retrieve and modify data from a particular database. The situation in which several user application programs read and write the same data at the same time is called *concurrency*. Thus, each DBMS must have some kind of control mechanism to solve concurrency problems.

To demonstrate the possible concurrency problems, let's revisit the scenario from Chapter 1, which shows a problem that can arise if a DBMS does not contain such control mechanisms:

1. The owners of bank account 4711 at bank X have an account balance of $2,000.
2. The two joint owners of this bank account, Mrs. A and Mr. B, go to two different bank tellers, and each withdraws $1,000 *at the same time.*
3. After these transactions, the amount of money in bank account 4711 should be $0 and not $1,000.

Another general problem that can arise for a database system is different software and hardware errors. Every DBMS has a *recovery subsystem*, which is responsible for recovery from all kinds of software and hardware errors. This means the recovery subsystem must return data in the database to a consistent state.

Both of these problems, concurrency and data recovery, are solved using transactions. (The recovery of data will be discussed in detail in Chapter 20.) A transaction specifies a sequence of Transact-SQL statements that build a logical unit. The following example will explain what a transaction is. In the sample database, the employee Ann Jones should be assigned a new employee number. The employee number must be modified in two different tables at the same time. The row in the **employee** table and all corresponding rows in the **works_on** table must be modified at the same time. (If only one of these tables is modified, data in the sample database would be inconsistent because the values of the primary key in the **employee** table and the corresponding values of the foreign key in the **works_on** table for Mrs. Jones would not match.)

▼ **EXAMPLE 14.1**

```
BEGIN TRANSACTION /* The beginning of the transaction */
UPDATE employee
   SET emp_no = 39831
   WHERE emp_no = 10102
   IF (@@error <> 0)
      ROLLBACK TRANSACTION /* Rollback of the transaction */
UPDATE works_on
   SET emp_no = 39831
   WHERE emp_no = 10102
   IF (@@error <> 0)
      ROLLBACK TRANSACTION
COMMIT TRANSACTION /*The end of the transaction */
```

The consistent state of data in Example 14.1 can be obtained only if both UPDATE statements or neither of them are executed. The global variable **@@error** is used to test the execution of each Transact-SQL statement. If an error occurs, **@@error** is set to a negative value and the execution of all statements is rolled back. (Definitions of the Transact-SQL statements BEGIN TRANSACTION, COMMIT TRANSACTION, and ROLLBACK TRANSACTION are given in the next section.)

TRANSACT-SQL STATEMENTS AND TRANSACTIONS

There are six Transact-SQL statements regarding transactions:

- BEGIN TRANSACTION
- BEGIN DISTRIBUTED TRANSACTION
- COMMIT TRANSACTION
- ROLLBACK TRANSACTION
- SAVE TRANSACTION
- SET IMPLICIT_TRANSACTION

The BEGIN TRANSACTION statement starts the transaction. It has the following syntax:

```
BEGIN TRANSACTION [transaction_name]
   [WITH MARK ['description']]
```

transaction_name is the name assigned to the transaction, which can be used only on the outermost pair of nested BEGIN...COMMIT or BEGIN...ROLLBACK statements. The WITH MARK option specifies that the transaction is to be marked in the log. **description** is a string that describes the mark. If WITH MARK is used, a transaction name must be specified. (For more information on transaction log marking for recovery, see Chapter 20.)

The BEGIN DISTRIBUTED TRANSACTION statement specifies the start of a distributed transaction managed by the Microsoft Distributed Transaction Coordinator (MS DTC). A *distributed* transaction is one that involves databases on more than one server. The server executing this statement is the transaction coordinator and therefore controls the completion of the distributed transaction.

The COMMIT TRANSACTION statement successfully ends the transaction started with the BEGIN TRANSACTION statement. This means all modifications made by the transaction are stored on the disk.

NOTE: SQL Server also supports the COMMIT WORK statement, which is functionally equivalent to COMMIT TRANSACTION, with the exception that COMMIT TRANSACTION accepts a user-defined transaction name. The COMMIT WORK statement is supported in the SQL92 standard.

In contrast to the COMMIT TRANSACTION statement, the ROLLBACK TRANSACTION statement reports an unsuccessful end of the transaction. Programmers use this statement if they assume that the database might be in an inconsistent state. In this case, all executed modification operations within the transaction are rolled back.

NOTE: SQL Server also supports the ROLLBACK WORK statement, which is functionally equivalent to ROLLBACK TRANSACTION, with the exception that ROLLBACK TRANSACTION accepts a user-defined transaction name. The ROLLBACK WORK statement is supported in the SQL92 standard.

The SAVE TRANSACTION statement sets a savepoint within a transaction. A *savepoint* marks a specified point within the transaction so that all updates that follow can be canceled without canceling the entire transaction. (To cancel an entire transaction, use the ROLLBACK TRANSACTION statement.)

NOTE: The SAVE TRANSACTION statement actually does not commit any modification operation; it only creates a target for the subsequent ROLLBACK statement with the label with the same name as the SAVE statement.

Example 14.2 shows the use of the SAVE TRANSACTION statement.

▼ EXAMPLE 14.2

```
BEGIN TRANSACTION
INSERT INTO department (dept_no, dept_name)
    VALUES ('d4', 'Sales')
SAVE TRANSACTION a
INSERT INTO department (dept_no, dept_name)
    VALUES ('d5', 'Research')
SAVE TRANSACTION b
INSERT INTO department (dept_no, dept_name)
   VALUES ('d6', 'Management')
ROLLBACK TRANSACTION b
INSERT INTO department (dept_no, dept_name)
  VALUES ('d7', 'Support')
ROLLBACK TRANSACTION a
COMMIT TRANSACTION
```

The only statement in Example 14.2 that is executed is the first INSERT statement. The third INSERT statement in the example is rolled back by the ROLLBACK TRANSACTION **b**, and the other two INSERT statements are rolled back by the ROLLBACK TRANSACTION **a** statement.

NOTE: The SAVE TRANSACTION statement, in combination with the IF or WHILE statement, is a useful transaction feature for the execution of parts of an entire transaction. On the other hand, the use of this statement is contrary to the principle of operational databases that a transaction should be as short as possible, because long transactions generally reduce data availability.

Each Transact-SQL statement always belongs implicitly or explicitly to a transaction. An explicit transaction is specified with the pair of statements BEGIN TRANSACTION and COMMIT TRANSACTION (or ROLLBACK TRANSACTION). If BEGIN and COMMIT are not used, every DML statement builds its own transaction implicitly.

SQL Server provides implicit transactions for compliance with SQL standard. When a session operates in implicit transaction mode, selected statements implicitly issue the BEGIN TRANSACTION statement. This means that you do nothing to start such a transaction. However, the end of each implicit transaction must be explicitly committed or rolled back using the COMMIT (i.e. ROLLBACK) statement. (If you do not explicitly commit the transaction, the transaction and all the data changes it contains are rolled back when the user disconnects.)

To enable an implicit transaction, you have to issue the SET IMPLICIT_TRANSACTIONS ON statement. This statement sets implicit transaction mode for the current session. When a connection is in implicit transaction mode and the connection is not currently in a transaction, executing any of the following statements starts a transaction:

ALTER TABLE	FETCH	REVOKE
CREATE	GRANT	SELECT
DELETE	INSERT	TRUNCATE TABLE
DROP	OPEN	UPDATE

In other words, if you have a sequence of statements from the list above, each statement will represent a single transaction.

Explicit transactions can be nested. In this case, each pair of statements BEGIN/COMMIT or BEGIN/ROLLBACK is used inside one or more such pairs. (The nested transactions are usually used in stored procedures, which themselves contain transactions and are invoked inside another transaction.) The global variable **@@trancount** contains the number of active transactions for the current user.

BEGIN, COMMIT, and ROLLBACK can be specified using a name assigned to the transaction. (The named ROLLBACK TRANSACTION statement corresponds either to a named transaction or to the SAVE TRANSACTION statement with the same name.) You can use a named transaction only in the outermost statement pair of nested BEGIN/COMMIT or BEGIN/ROLLBACK statements.

Transaction Logging

SQL Server keeps a record of each change it makes to the database during a transaction. This is necessary in case an error occurs during the execution of the transaction. In this situation, all previously executed statements within the transaction have to be rolled back. As soon as SQL Server detects the error, it uses the stored records to return the database to the consistent state that existed before the transaction was started.

SQL Server keeps all those records, in particular the before and after values, in one or more files called the *transaction log*. Each database of the SQL Server system has its own transaction log. Thus, if it is necessary to roll back one or more modification operations executed on the tables of the current database, SQL Server uses the entries in the transaction log to restore the values of columns that the database had before the transaction was started.

The transaction log is used to roll back or restore a transaction. If an error occurs and the transaction does not completely execute, SQL Server uses all existing "before" values from the transaction log (called *before images*) to roll back all modifications since the start of the transaction. For further details concerning transaction logs, see Chapter 20.

NOTE: Versions prior to 7.0 of SQL Server used the **syslogs** system table as the transaction log of the database.

LOCKING

Concurrency can lead to several negative effects, such as the reading of nonexistent data or loss of modified data. Consider this real-world example illustrating one of these negative effects, called *dirty read*: The user U_1 in the personnel department gets an address change for the employee Jim Smith. U_1 does the address change, but when controlling the bank account of Mr. Smith in the consecutive dialog step, he realizes that he modified the address of the wrong person. (The enterprise employs two persons with the name Jim Smith.) Fortunately, the application allows the user to cancel this change by pressing a button. User U_1 presses the button knowing that he has committed no error.

At the same time, the user U_2 in the technical department retrieves the data of the latter Mr. Smith to send the newest technical document to his home, because the employee seldom comes to the office. As the employee's address was wrongly changed just before the user U_2 retrieved the address, he prints out the wrong label address and sends the document to the wrong person.

To prevent errors like these, every DBMS must have mechanisms that control the access of data by all users at the same time. SQL Server, like almost all relational DBMSs, uses locks to guarantee the consistency of the database in case of multiuser access. SQL Server gives an application program the ability to lock the data it needs, guaranteeing that no other program can modify the same data. When another application program requests the modification of the locked data, SQL Server either stops the program with an error or makes a program wait.

Lock Granularity

You can apply locks to the following database objects:

- Row
- Page
- Index
- Extent
- Table
- Database itself

A row is the smallest database object that can be locked. The support of row-level locking includes both data rows and index entries. Previous releases of SQL Server were able to lock at the row level only with the INSERT statement, but since version 7 SQL Server has the capability to lock single rows for all types of DML statements.

SQL Server can also lock the page on which the row that has to be locked is stored. A user can determine which database object will be locked using the PAGLOCK, TABLOCK, and ROWLOCK hints in the SELECT statement. (The size of the object that is being locked is called *lock granularity*.) SQL Server automatically chooses the appropriate lock granularity.

Locking is also done on disk units, called *extents*, that are 64K in size (see Chapter 15). Extent locks are set automatically when a table (or index) grows and the additional disk space is needed.

Lock granularity affects concurrency. In general, the larger the lock granularity used, the more concurrency is reduced. This means that row-level locking maximizes concurrency because it leaves all but one row on the page unlocked. On the other hand, system overhead is increased because each locked row requires one lock. Page-level locking (and table-level locking) restricts the availability of data but decreases the system overhead. Thus, if SQL Server did not support row-level locking, the new page size of 8KB would result in the general reduction of concurrency in relation to the previous versions, because 8KB pages can hold approximately four times as many rows as 2KB pages.

If many page locks are held during a transaction, SQL Server upgrades the lock into a table lock. This process of converting many page-level locks into one table lock (or many row-level locks into one page lock) is called *lock escalation*. The escalation threshold is the boundary at which SQL Server applies the lock escalation. Escalation thresholds are determined dynamically by SQL Server and require no configuration.

Concerning locks, a user can explicitly affect only the behavior of transactions that acquire a lock that conflicts with the existing lock for the same object. The SET LOCK_TIMEOUT statement can be used to specify the number of milliseconds a transaction will wait for a lock to be released. The value of –1 (the default value) indicates no time-out.

Kinds of Locks

SQL Server uses different kinds of locks depending on the database object that needs to be locked. At the row level and page level, there are three different types of locks:

- Shared (S)
- Exclusive (X)
- Update (U)

A shared lock reserves a database object (page or row) for reading only. Other processes cannot modify the locked object while the lock remains. On the other hand, several processes can hold a shared lock for an object at the same time—that is, there can be several shared locks for an object.

An exclusive lock reserves a page or row for the exclusive use of a single transaction. It is used for DML statements that modify the object (INSERT, UPDATE, and DELETE). An exclusive lock cannot be set if some other process holds a shared or exclusive lock on the object—that is, there can be only one exclusive lock for an object. Once an exclusive object is set for the page (or row), no other lock can be placed on the same object.

An update lock can be placed only if no other update or exclusive lock exists. On the other hand, it can be placed on objects that already have shared locks. (In this case, the update lock acquires another shared lock on the same object.) If a transaction that modifies the object is committed, the update lock is changed to an exclusive lock if there are no other (shared or exclusive) locks on the object. There can be only one update lock for an object.

Page-level locking also allows an intent lock, described shortly.

NOTE: Update locks prevent certain common types of deadlocks. (Deadlocks are described at the end of this chapter.)

Table 14-1 shows the compatibility matrix for shared, exclusive, and update locks. The matrix is interpreted as follows: Suppose transaction T_1 holds a lock as specified in the first column of the matrix, and suppose some other transaction T_2 requests a lock as specified in the corresponding column heading. In this case, "yes" indicates that a lock of the transaction T_2 is possible, whereas "no" indicates a conflict with the existing lock.

NOTE: SQL Server supports other lock types in addition to those already discussed. Because of their complexity, these locks will not be covered in this introductory book.

At the table level, there are five different types of locks:

- Shared (S)
- Exclusive (X)
- Intent share (IS)
- Intent exclusive (IX)
- Share with intent exclusive (SIX)

The first two locks correspond to the row-level (or page-level) lock with the same name, respectively. Generally, an *intent* lock shows an intention to lock the next-lower object in the hierarchy of the database objects. Therefore, intent locks are placed at a level in the hierarchy above that which the process intends to lock. This is an efficient way to

	Shared	**Update**	**eXclusive**
Shared	Yes	Yes	No
Update	Yes	No	No
eXclusive	No	No	No

Table 14-1. Compatibility Matrix for Row-Level and Page-Level Locks

tell whether such locks will be possible, and it prevents other processes from locking the higher level before the desired locks can be attained.

Table 14-2 shows the compatibility matrix for all kinds of table locks. The matrix is interpreted exactly as the matrix in Table 14-1.

SQL Server supports a configuration option called LOCKS that specifies the number of locks for your system. The default value 0 means that SQL Server assigns 2 percent of the memory it uses to locks. To change this advanced configuration option, use the **sp_configure** system procedure.

The most important system procedure concerning locks is **sp_lock**. This procedure displays information about the processes that hold locks. The syntax of **sp_lock** is

```
sp_lock [spid_list]
```

where **spid_list** is the list of the ID numbers (maximum two) of SQL Server processes. If the list is omitted, SQL Server displays information about all active SQL Server processes.

▼ EXAMPLE 14.3

```
SET SHOWPLAN_TEXT ON
GO
BEGIN TRANSACTION
UPDATE employee SET emp_lname = 'Robinson'
  WHERE emp_no = 28559
```

If there is a clustered index on the **emp_no** column of the **employee** table and the batch in Example 14.3 is executed, the **sp_lock** system procedure displays the following result:

spid	dbid	objId	type	resource	mode	status
6	8	0	DB		S	GRANT
6	8	0	DB		S	GRANT
6	8	117575457	PAG	1:291	IX	GRANT
6	8	117575457	TAB		IX	GRANT

spid and **dbid** specify the process and database ID, respectively. The **type** column defines the lock type (DB = database, PAG = page, and TAB = base table). The most important column concerning locks is **mode.** In Example 14.3, it specifies that there is a shared lock for the entire (sample) database, an intent exclusive lock for the page numbered 1:291, and the same type of lock for the entire **employee** table.

	S	X	IS	SIX	IX
S	Yes	No	Yes	No	No
X	No	No	No	No	No
IS	Yes	No	Yes	Yes	Yes
SIX	No	No	Yes	No	No
IX	No	No	Yes	No	Yes

Table 14-2. Compatibility Matrix for Table Locks

The SELECT Statement and Locking

The FROM clause of the DML statements contains, among others, the following options concerning locking:

- UPDLOCK
- TABLOCK
- TABLOCKX
- ROWLOCK
- PAGLOCK

NOTE: There are some other options concerning isolation levels. These options are described in the next section.

UPDLOCK places update locks for each row of the table during the read operation. All update locks are held until the end of the transaction. TABLOCK (TABLOCKX) places a shared (exclusive) table lock on the table. All locks are held until the end of the transaction. ROWLOCK replaces the existing shared table lock with shared row locks for each qualifying row of the table. Similarly, PAGLOCK replaces a shared table lock with shared page locks for each page containing qualifying rows.

NOTE: All the above options can be combined in any order if the combination makes sense. (For example, the combination between TABLOCK and PAGLOCK is senseless, because both options are applied to different database objects.)

ISOLATION LEVELS

Generally, a SELECT statement causes a shared lock to be placed on a row or page. This lock can be acquired only if no other transaction already holds an exclusive lock for that object. The availability of data in this case is rather low, because each read operation has to wait for a while. (In this case, the SET LOCK_TIMEOUT statement is set to –1, and there is no time-out for the transaction.)

If data availability is an important issue, the isolation of read operations from the concurrent actions of other transactions can be loosened using isolation levels. An *isolation level* specifies the degree to which read operations of a program are isolated from the concurrent actions of other transactions. (Therefore, isolation levels are related to shared locks.)

SQL Server supports all four standardized isolation levels:

- READ UNCOMMITTED
- READ COMMITTED
- REPEATABLE READ
- SERIALIZABLE

READ UNCOMMITTED is the simplest isolation level, because it does not isolate the read operations from other transactions at all. When a transaction retrieves a row at this isolation level, it acquires no locks and respects none of the existing locks. The data that is read by such a transaction may be inconsistent. In this case, a transaction reads data that is updated from some other active transaction. If the latter transaction rolls back later, the former reads data that never really existed.

NOTE: The isolation level READ UNCOMMITTED is usually very undesirable and should only be used when the accuracy of read data is not important or the data is seldom modified.

A transaction that reads a row and uses the isolation level READ COMMITTED tests only whether an exclusive lock is placed on the row. If no such lock exists, it fetches the row. (This action prevents reading data that is not committed and that can be subsequently rolled back.) After reading the data values, data can then be changed by some other transaction.

Using the isolation level REPEATABLE READ, shared locks are placed on all data that is read, preventing other transactions from updating the data. This isolation level does not prevent another transaction from inserting new rows, which are included in subsequent reads, so the same SELECT statement can display different results at different times.

The isolation level SERIALIZABLE acquires a range lock on all data that is read by the corresponding transaction. Therefore, this isolation level also prevents the insertion of new rows by another transaction until the former transaction is committed or rolled back.

NOTE: The isolation level SERIALIZABLE is implemented by SQL Server 7 using a key-range locking method. This method locks individual rows and the ranges between them. A *key-range* lock acquires locks for index entries rather than locks for the particular pages or the entire table. In this case, any modification operation of another transaction cannot be executed, because the necessary changes of index entries are not possible.

Each isolation level in the preceding description reduces the concurrency more than the previous one. Thus, the isolation level READ UNCOMMITTED reduces concurrency the least. On the other hand, it also has the smallest isolation from concurrent transactions. SQL Server's default isolation level is READ COMMITTED.

An isolation level can be set using the following:

- The SET TRANSACTION ISOLATION LEVEL statement
- Several options in the FROM clause of the SELECT statement

The SET TRANSACTION ISOLATION LEVEL statement has four options with the same names and meanings as the standard isolation levels just described. The FROM clause in the SELECT statement supports six options concerning isolation levels:

- READUNCOMMITTED
- READCOMMITTED
- REPEATABLEREAD
- SERIALIZABLE
- NOLOCK
- HOLDLOCK

The first four options correspond to the isolation levels with the same name. NOLOCK and HOLDLOCK are synonyms for READUNCOMMITTED and REPEATABLEREAD, respectively. The specification of isolation levels in the FROM clause of the SELECT statement overrides the current value set by the SET TRANSACTION ISOLATION LEVEL statement.

The DBCC USEROPTIONS statement returns, among other things, the current isolation level of the SQL Server process. (For a description of the DBCC statement, see Chapter 23.)

DEADLOCK

A *deadlock* is a special situation in which two transactions block the progress of each other. The first transaction has a lock on some database object that the other transaction wants to access and vice versa. (In general, there can be several transactions, causing a deadlock by building a circle of dependencies.) Example 14.4 shows the deadlock situation between two transactions.

NOTE: The parallelism of processes cannot be achieved naturally using our small sample database because every transaction in it is executed very quickly. Therefore, Example 14.4 uses the WAITFOR statement to pause both transactions for ten seconds and to simulate the deadlock.

▼ EXAMPLE 14.4

```
BEGIN TRANSACTION
UPDATE works_on
  SET job = 'Manager'
  WHERE emp_no = 18316
  AND project_no = 'p2'

WAITFOR DELAY '00:00:10'

UPDATE employee
  SET emp_lname = 'Green'
  WHERE emp_no = 9031
COMMIT TRANSACTION
```

```
BEGIN TRANSACTION
UPDATE employee
  SET dept_no = 'd2'
  WHERE emp_no = 9031

  WAITFOR DELAY '00:00:10'

DELETE FROM works_on
  WHERE emp_no = 18316
  AND project_no = 'p2'
COMMIT TRANSACTION
```

If both transactions in Example 14.4 are executed at the same time, the deadlock appears and the system returns the following output:

```
Server: Msg 1205, Level 13, State 40001

Your server command (process id #6) was deadlocked with another process and
has been chosen as deadlock victim. Re-run your command.
```

As can be seen from the output of Example 14.4, SQL Server handles a deadlock by choosing one of the transactions as a "victim" (actually, the one that closed the loop in lock requests) and rolling it back. (The other transaction is executed after that.) A programmer can handle a deadlock by implementing the conditional statement, which tests for the returned error number (-1205) and then executes the rolled back transaction again.

Users can affect the determined behavior of the SQL Server system concerning the choice of the "victim" by using the SET DEADLOCK_PRIORITY statement. If you use the LOW option of this statement for your process, it will be chosen for the victim, even if it did not close the loop in lock requests. (The default option is NORMAL.)

CONCLUSION

Concurrency in multiuser systems such as SQL Server has a decided effect on performance. When access to the data is handled such that only one program at a time can use the data, processing slows dramatically. SQL Server, like all other DBMSs, solves this problem by using transactions. A transaction is a sequence of Transact-SQL statements that logically belong together. All statements inside a transaction build an atomic unit. This means that either all statements are executed or, in the case of failure, all statements are canceled.

Concurrency can lead to several negative effects that SQL Server prevents using locks. The effect of the lock is to prevent other transactions from changing the locked object. The decision as to which database object should be locked is called lock granularity. Lock granularity affects concurrency because the narrower lock (row lock, for example) maximizes concurrency.

The next chapter concludes the second part of the book. It describes the overall environment of the SQL Server system.

EXERCISES

▼ E.14.1

What is a purpose of transactions?

▼ E.14.2

What is the difference between a local and a distributed transaction?

▼ E.14.3

What is the difference between implicit and explicit transaction mode?

▼ E.14.4

What kind of locks are compatible with an exclusive lock?

▼ E.14.5

How can you test the successful execution of each T-SQL statement?

▼ E.14.6

When will you use the SAVE TRANSACTION statement?

▼ E.14.7

Discuss the difference between row-level and page-level locking.

▼ E.14.8

Does a user have the possibility of explicitly influencing the locking behavior of the system?

▼ E.14.9

What is a difference between two basic locks (i.e., S lock and X lock) and an intent lock?

▼ E.14.10

What does lock escalation mean?

▼ E.14.11

Discuss the difference between the READ UNCOMMITTED and SERIALIZABLE isolation levels.

▼ E.14.12

What is deadlock?

▼ E.14.13

Which process is used as a victim in a deadlock situation? Can a user influence the decision of the SQL Server system?

CHAPTER 15

SQL Server System Environment

This chapter describes several different SQL Server features that belong to the system environment. First of all, there is a detailed description of the SQL Server disk storage elements, system databases, and utilities. After that, the notion of Unicode and national language support are explained. The new feature of SQL Server 2000—multiple instance support—is also discussed in this chapter. Finally, the architecture of the SQL Server system is discussed and illustrated.

DISK STORAGE

The storage architecture of SQL Server contains two units for storing database objects:

- Page
- Extent

The main unit of data storage in SQL Server is the page. The size of pages in SQL Server is 8K. Each page has a 96-byte header used to store the system information. Data rows are placed on the page immediately after the header. In SQL Server, a row cannot span two or more pages. Therefore, the maximum size of a single row (excluding text/image data) is 8,060 bytes.

SQL Server has six distinct types of pages:

- Data pages
- Index pages
- Text/image pages
- Global allocation map (GAM) pages
- Page free space (PFS) pages
- Index allocation map (IAM) pages

NOTE: Data and index pages are actually physical parts of a database where the corresponding tables and indexes are stored. The content of a database is stored in one or more files and each file is divided in page units. Therefore, each table or index page (as a database physical unit) can be uniquely identified using a database ID, database file ID, and a page number.

When you create a table or index, SQL Server allocates a fixed amount of space to contain the data belonging to the table or index. When the space fills, SQL Server must allocate space for additional storage. The physical unit of storage in which space is allocated to a table (index) is called an *extent*. An extent comprises eight contiguous pages, or 64K. SQL Server has two types of extents:

- Uniform extents
- Mixed extents

Uniform extents are owned by a single table or index, while mixed extents are shared by up to eight tables or indices. A new table or index is always allocated pages from mixed extents first. After that, if the size of the table (index) is greater than eight pages, it is switched to uniform extents.

The following sections describe the first three types of existing pages. The discussion of GAM, PFS, and IAM pages is beyond the scope of this book.

Data Pages

Data pages are used to store data of a table. (The only data types that are not directly stored in data pages are values of columns of text/image data type.) Each data page has the following three parts:

- Page header
- Space for data
- Row offset table

NOTE: Transaction log files do not contain data pages. Instead of pages, they contain a series of log records.

Page Header

Each page has a 96-byte page header used to store the system information, such as page ID, the ID of the database object to which the page belongs, and previous and next page in a page chain. As you already guessed, the page header is stored at the beginning of each page. Table 15-1 shows the information stored in the page header.

Space Reserved for Data

The part of the page reserved for data has a variable length that depends upon a number and length of rows stored on the page. For each row stored on the page, there is an entry in the space reserved for data and an entry in the row offset table at the end of the page. (A data row cannot span two or more pages, except for values of text/image columns that are stored in their own specific pages.) Each row is stored subsequently after already stored rows, until the page is filled. If there is not enough space for a new row of the same table, it will be stored on the next page in the chain of pages.

For all tables that have only fixed-length columns, the same number of rows is stored at each page. If a table has at least one variable-length column (a VARCHAR column, for instance), the number of rows per page may differ and SQL Server then stores as many rows per page as will fit on it.

Row Offset Table

The last part of a page is tightly connected to a space reserved for data, because each row stored on a page has a corresponding entry in the row offset table. The row offset table con-

Page Header Information	Description
pageId	Database file number plus number of the page.
level	For index pages, the level of the page. (Leaf level is level 0, the first intermediate level is level 1 and so on.)
flagBits	Additional information concerning the page.
nextPage	Database file number plus page number of the next page in the chain (if a table has a clustered index).
prevPage	Database file number plus page number of the previous page in the chain (if a table has a clustered index).
objId	ID of the database object to which the page belongs.
lsn	Log sequence number.
slotCnt	Total number of slots used on this page.
indexId	Index ID of the page (0, if the page is data page).
freeData	Byte offset of the first available free space on the page.
pminlen	Number of bytes in fixed-length part of rows.
freeCnt	Number of free bytes on page.
reservedCnt	Number of bytes reserved by all transactions.
xactReserved	Number of bytes reserved by the most recently started transaction.
xactId	ID of the most recently started transaction.
tornBits	One bit per sector for detecting torn page write.

Table 15-1. Information Contained in the Page Header

tains two byte entries consisting of the row number and the offset byte address of the row on the page. (The entries in the row offset table are in reverse order from the sequence of the rows on the page.) Suppose that each row of a table is fixed-length, 36 bytes in length. The first table row is stored at byte offset 96 of a page (because of page header). The corresponding entry in the row offset table is written in the last two bytes of a page indicating in the first byte the row number (in this case 0) and in the second byte the row offset (96). The next row is stored subsequently in the next 36 bytes of the page. Therefore, the corresponding entry in the row offset table is stored in the third and fourth but last bytes of the page, indicating again the row number (1) and the row offset (132) (see Figure 15-1).

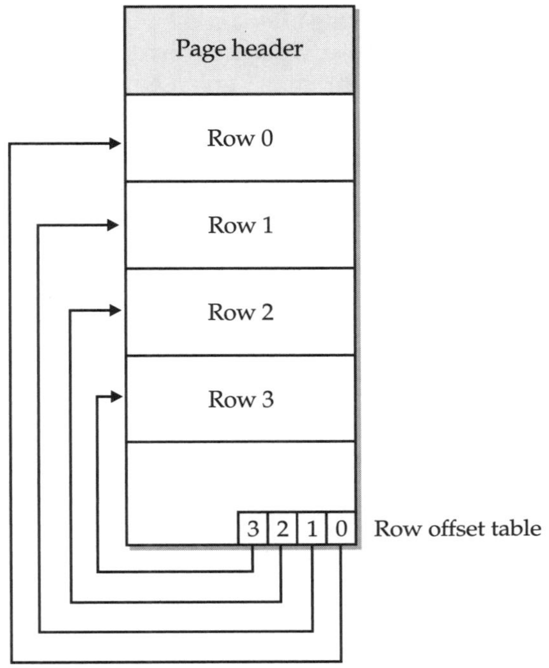

Figure 15-1. The structure of a data page

Text and Image Data

SQL Server supports three data types concerning large objects: TEXT, NTEXT, and IMAGE. (We call these data types generally text/image data.) A column of the TEXT or NTEXT data type contains values with textual data, and therefore is used to store documents whose lengths exceed 8,000 bytes. The IMAGE data type can represent any data with a large amount of information, because it represents bit strings.

If a table contains one or more columns of the data type TEXT, NTEXT, or IMAGE, the data of these columns are not stored together with the data of other columns of the table. Only a pointer, which contains the physical address of the page where the text/image data is actually located, is stored with the data of other columns. All pages with the text/image data of a table are managed as a single unit and are therefore stored in one collection of pages. This means that one such page can hold data from different columns of a table if these columns contain text/image data.

A value of a column of the TEXT, NTEXT, or IMAGE data type is stored in a collection of 8K pages that must not be located one after another. Since SQL Server 7, all pages are organized logically in a b-tree structure, while in previous versions they were linked together in a page chain. The benefit of the new implementation is that operations (such as the UPDATETEXT statement, for instance) starting in the middle of the string perform better, because they can quickly move through the tree instead of making the scan through the page chain.

Index Pages

Index pages are used to store index values. An index page is identical to a data page except that it has only two parts: the row offset table does not appear at the end of an index page. The description of different forms of index pages is beyond the scope of this book.

SYSTEM DATABASES

During the installation of SQL Server, four system databases are generated:

- master
- model
- tempdb
- msdb

The **master** database is the most important database of the SQL Server system. It comprises all system tables that are necessary to work with the database system. For example, the **master** database contains information about all other databases managed by SQL Server, system connections to clients, and user authorizations.

The **model** database is used as a template when user-defined databases are created. It contains the subset of all system tables of the **master** database, which every user-defined database needs. The system administrator can change the properties of the **model** database to adapt it to the specific needs of his or her system.

The **tempdb** database provides the storage space for temporary tables and other temporary objects needed. For example, SQL Server stores intermediate results of the calculation of each complex expression in the **tempdb** database. The **tempdb** database is used by all the databases belonging to the entire system. Its content is destroyed every time the user process finishes or the system stops.

The information that allows SQL Server Agent to function is stored in the **msdb** database. This means the **msdb** database is used for storing alerts, jobs, and recording operators. (For a detailed description of the **msdb** database in relation to the SQL Server Agent, see Chapter 22.)

NOTE: There is another system database, called the **distribution** database, that is installed on the distribution server in case data is replicated. (For more information on the distribution server and data replication, see Chapter 25.)

UTILITIES

Utilities are components of SQL Server that provide different features such as data reliability, data definition, and statistics maintenance functions. All SQL Server utilities have two main properties:

- They are invoked using an operating system command.
- Each utility has several optional parameters.

This section describes the following SQL Server utilities:

- bcp
- osql
- isql
- console

bcp Utility

The **bcp** (Bulk CoPy) utility copies the contents of a table or view into an operating system file. It can also be used to load data from an operating system file into a table. Additionally, different formats for loading or unloading the file can be specified. This utility is described in detail in Chapter 21, because the loading and unloading of data is usually the system administrator's task.

osql Utility

The **osql** utility is an interactive Transact-SQL interface for SQL Server. It uses ODBC to communicate with the server. The general form of this utility is

```
osql {option [parameter]} ...
```

where **option** is the specific option of the utility, while **parameter** specifies the value of the defined option. The **osql** utility has a lot of options. The most important of these are described in Table 15-2.

▼ EXAMPLE 15.1

```
osql –S NTB11900 –U sa –i ms0510.sql –o ms0510.rpt
```

Option	Description
-S server_name	Specifies the name of SQL Server to which the connection is made. If this option is omitted, the connection is made to the database server set with the environment variable SQLSERVER. If this environment variable is not set, SQL Server tries to connect to the local machine.
-U login_id	Specifies the SQL Server login. The login must be created using the system procedure **sp_addlogin**. If this option is omitted, the value of the environment variable ISQLUSER is used.
-P password	Specifies a password corresponding to the SQL Server login. If this option is omitted, the value of the environment variable ISQLPASSWORD is used. If the variable is not set, the utility prompts for a password.
-c command_end	Specifies the command terminator. (The default value is "go".) This option can be used to set the command terminator to ";", which is the default terminator for almost all other database systems.
-i input_file	Specifies the name of the file, which contains a batch or a stored procedure. The file must contain (at least one) command terminator. The sign "<"can be used instead of "-i".
-o output_file	Specifies the name of the file, which receives the result from the utility. The sign ">" can be used instead of "-o".
-E	Uses a trusted connection (see Chapter 12) instead of requesting a password.
-e	Echoes each statement that runs as input.
-D option | datasource	Uses this option to connect to an ODBC data source. The option is either defined using the ODBC driver (**options**) or the connection uses the options defined in the data source (**datasource**).
-L	This option shows a list of all SQL Server instances found on the network.
-t seconds	This option specifies the number of seconds. The time interval defines how long the utility should wait before it considers the connection to the server to be a failure.

Table 15-2. Useful Options of the osql Utility

Option	Description
-?	Standard request for all options of the **osql** utility.
-p	Prints out the performance statistics for your queries.
-n	Removes numbering and the prompt symbol (>) from input lines.
-d dbname	Specifies which database should be a current database when **osql** is started.

Table 15-2. Useful Options of the osql Utility *(continued)*

In Example 15.1, the system administrator of the SQL Server system named "NTB11900" executes the batch stored in the file "ms0510.sql" and stores the result in the output file "ms0510.rpt". The system prompts for the password of the system administrator because the option –P is omitted.

odbcping Utility

The **odbcping** utility tests the ability of the client to connect to a server. It also tests the integrity of an ODBC data source. The general form of this utility is

odbcping [?] | [{ **-S** *server* | **-D** *datasource* } [**-U** *login*] [**-P** *password*]]

The options _-S, -U and –P have the same meaning as the options with the same names for the **osql** utility. The option –D specifies the name of a data source.

NOTE: Since SQL Server 2000, the **odbcping** utility is no longer installed by the Setup program. If you need to run the utility, you can run it from the *x*:\x86\binn directory on the SQL Server compact disc, or manually copy it to your computer.

isql Utility

The **isql** utility is another interactive Transact-SQL interface for SQL Server, similar to **osql**. The only difference is that the **isql** utility uses the DB-Library to communicate with the server. The **isql** utility's options are the same as those of the **osql** utility.

console Utility

The **console** utility displays all messages related to the process of backing up and restoring a database. It must be running before the BACKUP or RESTORE statement is executed. (For definitions of the BACKUP and RESTORE statements, see Chapter 20.) The system administrator and dump operators can use this utility. The syntax is

console [/S server_name] [/P pipe_name]

where **server_name** specifies the server computer on the network. (This option is required when the **console** command is executed from a remote computer.) **pipe_name** is the pipe that is used to start the server. (The **console** utility uses Named Pipes.)

NOTE: The **console** utility is now stored in the directory *x*:\Program Files\Microsoft SQL Server\Mssql\Binn. You have to add this directory to the system path if the execution of the **console** utility from the command prompt is not possible.

INSTANCES OF SQL SERVER

SQL Server 2000 supports for the first time multiple instances of the database engine. An instance is a database server that does not share its system and user databases with other servers running on the same computer.

NOTE: Multiple instances of SQL Server 2000 correspond in previous versions to several SQL Server systems running on different machines.

SQL Server 2000 supports two instance types:

- Default
- Named

The *default instance* of the database server operates the same way as the database servers in earlier versions of SQL Server. The computer name on which the instance is running specifies solely the name of the default instance. Any installation of SQL Server version 7.0 or 6.5 operates under SQL Server 2000 as a default instance.

Any instance of the database server other than the default instance is called a *named instance*. To identify a named instance, you have to specify its name as well as the name of the computer on which the instance is running: for example, NTB11901\INSTANCE1. On one computer, there can be any number of named instances of SQL Server 2000 (in addition to the default instance). Additionally, you can configure named instances on a computer that does not have the default instance.

Although all instances running on a computer do not share most system resources (SQL Server and SQL Server Agent services, system and user databases, as well as registry keys), there are some components that are shared among them:

- SQL Server program group
- Analysis Services server
- Development libraries

The existence of only one SQL Server program group on a computer also means that only one copy of each utility exists, which is represented by an icon in the program group. (This includes SQL Server Books Online, too.) Therefore, each utility works with all instances configured on a computer.

You should consider using multiple instances if:

- You have different type of database on your computer.
- Your computer is powerful enough to manage multiple instances.

The main purpose of multiple instances is to divide databases that exist in your organization into different groups. For instance, if SQL Server manages databases that are used by different users (production databases, test databases, sample databases), you should divide them to run under different instances. That way you can encapsulate your production databases from databases that are used by casual or inexperienced users. A single-processor machine will not be the right hardware platform to run multiple instances of SQL Server, because of limited resources. For this reason, you should consider the use of multiple instances only with multiprocessor or clustered computers.

UNICODE

Since SQL Server is used around the world, it has to be able to process the specific data of any language (or country). This means users outside the United States can use characters of their own writing system. These users expect SQL Server not only to support the same basic set of features as the native language edition of the system, but also to achieve the same level of quality. This entire process of supporting national languages is called the *internalization* of the software.

Generally, the internalization of SQL Server affects the following components of the system:

- Selection of the character set
- Selection of the collating sequence
- Installation of country-specific error messages
- Specification of date and money formats

Character Encoding

A mix of standards governs how characters can be encoded. Some standards are 7-bit, called single-byte character sets; others are 8-bit, called multibyte character sets. Previous versions of SQL Server used the code pages, while SQL Server 2000 uses Unicode.

Code Page Model

The Microsoft operating systems previously supported mainly English and a few Western European languages. All code pages at that time were composed of 256 characters. Each character was represented by a 1-byte numeric value. Twenty-six letters of the English alphabet (both uppercase and lowercase forms), punctuation marks, Greek letters, line drawing characters, and ligatures were available. (A *ligature* is a combination of two or more characters used to represent a single typographical character.)

Every code page consists of two parts. The ASCII (American Standard Code for Information Interchange) characters range with a code from 0 through 127, and the extended characters in a specific code range from 128 to any number. (The latter is called High-ASCII code range.) The High-ASCII code range comprises accented characters and various symbols in a Western character set and ideographs in a Far Eastern code page. (An *ideograph* is a character of Chinese origin representing a word or a syllable that is generally used in more than one Asian language.) Each country is assigned one code page that includes its native characters in the extended character range.

Character Encoding Using Unicode

Unicode is a 16-bit character encoding method adopted by Microsoft Windows NT. This character encoding was developed, maintained, and promoted by the Unicode Consortium. Unicode comprises almost all characters used in computers today. This includes most of the world's written scripts, publishing characters, and mathematical and technical symbols. Some 35,000 code points have already been assigned characters. In addition to modern languages, Unicode covers languages such as classical Greek and Hebrew. A private-use zone of 6,500 code points is available to applications for user-defined characters.

In contrast to the first code pages, which were not designed with expansion in mind, Unicode is a uniform character encoding method. This means that with Unicode it is possible to process characters of different writing systems in one document. Therefore, Unicode eliminates the need for code that handles multiple code pages.

The Unicode standard directly addresses only encoding and interpreting text, and not any other actions performed on the text. This means the Unicode standard does not describe how the identified code value will be rendered on screen or paper. (The software or hardware-rendering engine of a computer is responsible for the appearance of the character on the screen or paper.)

Unicode Data Types and Functions

SQL Server supports three Unicode data types:

- NCHAR
- NVARCHAR
- NTEXT

The NCHAR data type stores fixed-length Unicode characters. It should be used for the definition of alphanumeric columns, where all data values are approximately of the same length. The NVARCHAR data type stores Unicode characters of varying length. It should be used for the definition of alphanumeric columns, where the length of data values oscillates dramatically. The NTEXT data type stores large character data (with more than 4,000 characters).

There are also two functions related to Unicode:

- UNICODE ('char_expression')
- NCHAR (int_expression)

The function UNICODE returns the integer value for the first character of the Unicode character string **char_expression**. NCHAR returns the Unicode character for the integer value **int_expression**.

Example 15.2 returns the Unicode character *L* together with its integer value.

▼ EXAMPLE 15.2

```
DECLARE @var1 NVARCHAR(40)
SET @var1 = N'Latin character'
SELECT UNICODE(@var1) 'Integer value',NCHAR(UNICODE(@var1)) 'Unicode
character'
```

The result is:

Integer value	Unicode character
73	L

SQL SERVER ARCHITECTURE

SQL Server 2000 is a highly scalable database system. This means the same database engine can be installed and used in the same way on any computer, from a mobile laptop computer running Windows 9x to an SMP computer (symmetric multiprocessor) running Windows NT/2000 Server Enterprise Edition. The low memory footprint of SQL Server 2000 allows it to be used with laptop computers and the Windows operating system. On the other hand, the use of SQL Server with SMP computers takes advantage of its multithreaded architecture.

Before explaining the architecture of SQL Server, let's take a look at the existing multiprocessor hardware architectures.

Multiprocessor Hardware Architectures

There are three approaches to the architecture of multiprocessor computers:

- Symmetric multiprocessing (SMP)
- Clusters
- Massively parallel processors (MPP)

Symmetric multiprocessing specifies a system in which several processors share the main memory and disks. (Such systems are also called shared-disk systems, because they share a single operating system instance that manages one or more disks.) SMP systems usually have a high-speed interconnect that connects all processors. The benefits of SMP systems are as follows:

- Easy administration
- Little reprogramming of the DBMS

An SMP system is easy to administer because it looks like one computer with one instance of the operating system. On the other hand, if SMP systems are scaled to many CPUs, they become more difficult to administer.

Generally, the DBMS need not be reprogrammed at all to be used with an SMP system if different processes are simply assigned to different CPUs. However, the DBMS is reprogrammed to support the multithreaded architecture, where the processes are divided into threads that help the DBMS take better advantage of SMP systems. (For a definition of a thread, see the next section.)

The disadvantage of an SMP system is its restricted scalability. This means the number of processors that can be synchronized together is limited by the amount of main memory, which provides this task.

A *cluster* usually specifies a group of SMP computers that are connected through a network. The benefits of clusters are better scalability and reliability (i.e., clusters can tolerate failures of single computers because the remaining computers in the cluster can take over the processing).

MPP systems offer the most scalability. As with clusters, an MPP system specifies many computers that are connected using a network. Those systems are also called *shared-nothing* systems, because each processor has its own main memory, its own operating system, and its own DBMS. Although MPP systems offer outstanding scalability, they are difficult to administer. (The next release of SQL Server, code-named Yukon, will support shared-nothing systems.)

NOTE: At this time, SQL Server supports SMP systems and clusters. In spite of this, SQL Server with SMP hardware suits databases of almost all sizes, because SMP implementations are improving steadily. This means the number of processors and the power of each of them is growing. Also, memory speed is increasing, and bus management is improving. Because of these factors, SQL Server can manage the largest databases that exist.

Multithreading Architecture of SQL Server

SQL Server supports SMP systems using two special architectural features:

- N:1-architecture
- Native multithreaded processing

N:1-architecture defines the architecture of a DBMS, where **N** user application programs are executed using a single process (see Figure 15-2). In addition to N:1-architecture, there is also 1:1-architecture, where each user application starts one process. The disadvantage of the latter is that if the number of users increases, the performance of the system degrades, because at some point the main memory cannot manage all existing processes. (N:1-architecture is also called single-process architecture.)

SQL Server supports SMP systems using threads rather than processes. A *thread* is a part of a process that can be executed on its own. Therefore, threads are sometimes called *lightweight* processes. With threads, it is possible for a DBMS to work efficiently on several database applications using just a few processors. The reason is that a switch from one thread to a thread of another process can be executed significantly faster than a switch from one process to another.

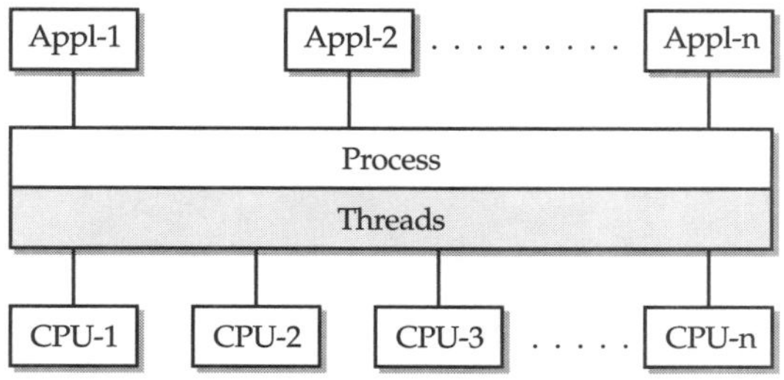

Figure 15-2. The multithreaded, single-process architecture of SQL Server

NOTE: Native multithreaded processing means that SQL Server supports multiprocessing using Windows NT threads. By using operating system threads, task scheduling within SQL Server is preemptive, and it allows dynamic load balancing across multiple CPUs.

SMP computers, together with SQL Server multithreaded architecture, are used to execute different database tasks in parallel. The following tasks, among others, can be parallelized using SQL Server 2000:

- Data load
- Backup and recovery
- Query execution

SQL Server allows data to be loaded in parallel using the **bcp** utility. The table into which the data is loaded must not have any indices, and the load operation must not be logged. (For further discussion of the **bcp** utility, see Chapter 20.)

NOTE: Only applications using the ODBC or SQLOLEDB-based APIs can perform parallel data loads into a single table.

SQL Server can back up databases or transaction logs to multiple devices (tape or disk) using parallel striped backup. In this case, database pages are read by multiple threads one extent at a time.

SQL Server provides parallel queries to enhance the query execution. With this feature, the independent parts of a SELECT statement can be executed using several native threads on an SMP computer. Each query that is planned for the parallel execution contains an exchange operator in its query execution plan. (An *exchange operator* is an operator in a query execution plan that provides process management, data redistribution, and flow control.) For such a query, SQL Server generates a parallel query execution plan. Parallel queries significantly improve the performance of the SELECT statements that process very large amounts of data.

CONCLUSION

SQL Server is an advanced relational DBMS that is superior to other DBMSs in two areas:

- Internalization of the database software
- Architecture of the database system

SQL Server is one of the first database systems to use Unicode as the future standard for the internalization of the software. Using Unicode, it is possible to process characters of different writing systems in one document, eliminating the need for code that handles multiple code pages. SQL Server also has a modern technology for using multiprocessor systems such as SMP computers. This technology is based upon the single-process architecture and native multithreaded processing.

This chapter closes the second part of the book. The next part is dedicated to system administration tasks of SQL Server. Chapter 16 introduces you to the general tasks of the system administrator and the SQL Server administration tools.

EXERCISES

▼ E.15.1

What is a difference between a data and index page?

▼ E.15.2

What is a difference between the **isql** and **osql** utility? Which tool should you prefer?

▼ E.15.3

If you create a temporary database, where will its data be stored?

▼ E.15.4

Discuss the benefits and disadvantages of multiple instances.

▼ E.15.5

What does the notion of multithreading mean?

▼ E.15.6

Which database management tasks can be parallelized using SQL Server?

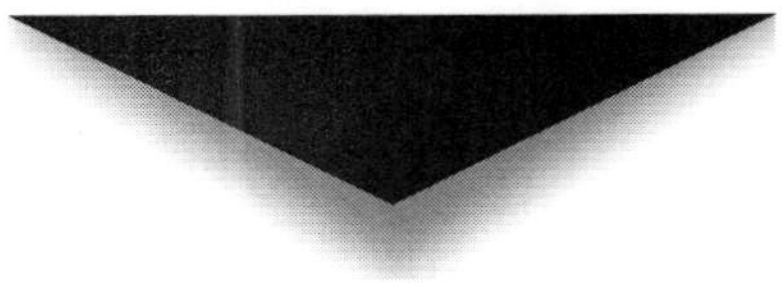

PART III

SQL Server: System Administration

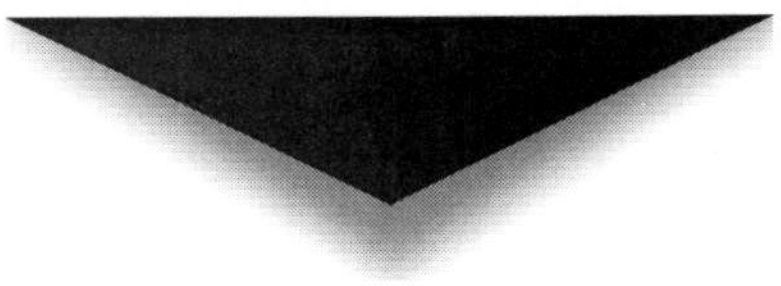

CHAPTER 16

Overview of System Administration

This chapter describes general issues concerning system administration and introduces you to the tools in the SQL Server program group and tasks of the SQL Server administrator.

ADMINISTRATION TOOLS

SQL Server is a high-performance DBMS that is scalable from laptops to SMP clusters. Additionally, SQL Server meets high-end requirements of distributed client/server computing and supports both OLTP and OLAP database applications. SQL Server achieves all these goals by means of the following properties:

- Close integration with Windows NT/2000 and Windows 9*x*
- Dynamic self-management and multisite management
- Job scheduling and alerting

As stated in the previous chapter, SQL Server supports multiprocessing using Windows NT/2000 threads. By using operating system threads, task scheduling within SQL Server is preemptive, and it allows dynamic load balancing across multiple CPUs. In addition, SQL Server uses several other Windows NT/2000 components, such as Performance Monitor and event viewer.

The system administrator's job in SQL Server 2000 has been significantly eased by the support of dynamic memory management and dynamic disk space management. The multisite management is supported through a Windows-based interface with visual drag-and-drop control that allows the creation and modification of server groups.

Using job scheduling and alerting, the system administrator can create different tasks (replication of data, command execution) and schedule them for execution at specified times. The execution of a task can be subsequently followed by e-mail and/or pager notification to one or more operators.

SQL Server also provides SQL Distributed Management Objects (SQL-DMO) to support enterprise-wide system administration. SQL-DMO (see Figure 16-1) is a collection of administration objects based on COM. With SQL-DMO, you can implement functions or scripts for the centralized administration of database servers and creation of jobs.

SQL Server Program Group

SQL Server offers a lot of easy-to-use graphical interfaces that can be used by the system administrator to achieve administrative goals. These tools belong to the SQL Server program group (see Figure16-2). Table 16-1 describes all the administration tools, which are covered in detail in other chapters as noted.

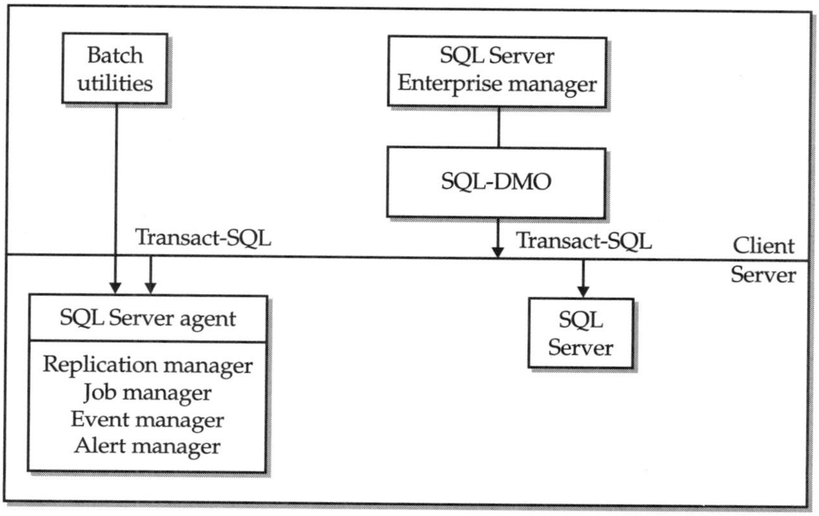

Figure 16-1. Components of SQL-DMO

Figure 16-2. SQL Server program group

Tool	Description
Analysis Services	Used to define multidimensional cubes and analyze data in data warehousing systems (see Chapter 27).
Client Network Utility	Used to configure client-side connections to the server. The default network protocol is Named Pipes. (This and all other protocols are described in the next chapter.)
Configure SQLXML Support in IIS	You can configure your SQL Server as XML server, if IIS is installed (see Chapter 29).
SQL Server Enterprise Manager	Used by both administrators and end users whose tasks are, among other things, to administer multiple servers, develop databases, and replicate data. (For more information on using SQL Server Enterprise Manager, see Chapter 2.)
Import and Export Data	Allow the use of Data Transformation Services (DTS). This topic is discussed in detail in Chapter 21.
SQL Server Profiler	Used by the system administrator to monitor server and user activities. This tool is discussed in Chapter 24.
SQL Server Query Analyzer	Used by end users to generate and execute Transact-SQL statements and to analyze query execution plans for retrieval statements. (For more information on using SQL Server Query Analyzer, see Chapter 2.)
Server Network Utility	Allows you to enable or disable existing protocols that are used for client/server communication.
SQL Service Manager	Used to start, stop, and pause SQL Server, SQL Server Agent, and Microsoft Distributed Transaction Coordinator. (SQL Service Manager is described in the next chapter.)

Table 16-1. SQL Server 7 Program Group

SYSTEM ADMINISTRATOR

The system administrator's job consists of all tasks that are generally necessary to allow other users to work with the SQL Server system. These tasks are as follows:

- Planning the installation and installing SQL Server
- Starting and stopping the system
- Managing databases and transaction logs
- Backing up and restoring databases and transaction logs
- Troubleshooting SQL Server
- Tuning SQL Server
- Setting up and using data replication

These tasks are described in the following chapters of this part of the book. The next chapter explains the first two tasks: planning the installation, and installing and starting the system. Managing databases and transaction logs is discussed in Chapter 18, while all aspects of system security (managing user accounts and assigning user permissions) are explained in Chapter 19. Chapter 20 discusses backing up and restoring databases and transaction logs, while Chapter 21 describes import, export, and distribution of data. Job automation is explained in Chapter 22. SQL Server error messages and their resolution are described in Chapter 23, and Chapter 24 discusses further performance issues (also covered in Chapter 10). Chapter 25 explains all issues concerning data replication.

It can be difficult to separate system administration tasks from database administration tasks. For example, the deficit on disk storage space for a user-defined database can be either the task of the system administrator (if a new file has to be created for the database) or of the database administrator (if the ALTER DATABASE statement must be applied). Therefore, in this part of the book we shall make no distinction between system administration tasks and general database administration tasks.

CONCLUSION

The system administrator is primarily responsible for allowing all other database users the continuous use of SQL Server. On the other hand, SQL Server offers a lot of easy-to-use graphical utilities that can be used by the system administrator to achieve his or her goals.

The next chapter begins the discussion of singular administrative tasks. Before the installation of the system, the system administrator must plan this task very carefully. After that, the installation of the system must be done. The next chapter describes both of these tasks.

CHAPTER 17

Planning the Installation and Installing SQL Server

This chapter describes all tasks involved in the installation of SQL Server. First, the necessary steps in planning the installation are covered, followed by actual installation of the database server and clients. A separate section is dedicated to the process of upgrading SQL Server. The last part of the chapter discusses several postinstallation steps and lists the different alternatives for starting, stopping, and pausing the system.

PLANNING THE INSTALLATION

The specification of an installation plan should always precede the actual installation of the SQL Server system. Careful planning is absolutely necessary because several decisions have to be made before the installation of the system is started. The system administrator should have clear answers to the following questions before beginning the installation process:

- What is the purpose of the SQL Server system?
- What are the hardware and software requirements?
- How many users will be active at the same time?

Purpose of SQL Server

The purpose of the SQL Server system can be manifold. For example, you may use your system exclusively for education, or it may be a production system. In the case of production systems, you will need to make decisions concerning the number of users and amount of stored data, because these systems differ widely. Another decision concerning modern database systems is whether the system is used for operational or analytical tasks.

NOTE: SQL Server 2000 supports multiple instances of the database server. That way you can use several instances for different purposes (production, education, testing).

If yours is a large database with a few hundred users, or if your system carries a heavy transaction load, performance of database operations will be an issue. In both cases, the use of symmetric multiprocessor (SMP) or cluster computers will be a general requirement to guarantee scalability and good response times of the relational DBMS. If you have a huge database, the purchase of enough disk storage could be the issue. In this case, SQL Server will usually perform better if you use several smaller disks instead of one or two large disks.

You must differentiate between systems used for operational goals (i.e., systems that require fast access and short transactions) and systems used for analytical goals (i.e., systems that use complex retrieval operations on huge databases), because both tasks cannot be optimally achieved using one database server. For this reason, SQL Server 2000 is bundled with the MS Analysis Services. SQL Server is used for operational goals, whereas the

Analysis Services are used for analytical purposes. (For more information on SQL Analysis Services, see Part IV of the book.)

Hardware and Software Requirements

The fact that SQL Server only runs on Microsoft operating systems simplifies decisions concerning hardware and system software requirements. The system administrator only has to meet the requirements concerning hardware and a network.

Hardware Requirements

Windows NT/2000 and Windows 9*x* are supported only on the Intel and compatible systems hardware platforms. (Hardware platforms with DEC Alpha AXP and compatible systems do not support Microsoft operating systems any more.)

Officially, the minimum main memory is 32MB, and the necessary disk space for installation of SQL Server ranges between 60MB (for minimum installation) and 180MB (for full installation). However, almost everybody recognizes that such a minimal configuration will not perform very well, and as a general guideline, main memory of your computer should be at least 64MB. (The Enterprise Edition requires 64MB as the minimum main memory.)

Network Requirements

As a client/server database system, SQL Server allows clients to use different network protocols to communicate with the server and vice versa. During connectivity installation, the system administrator must decide which network protocols (as libraries) should be available to give clients access to the system. The following network protocols can be selected on the server side:

- Named Pipes
- TCP/IP
- Multiprotocol Net-Library
- NWLink IPX/SPX
- AppleTalk ADSP
- Banyan Vines

NOTE: SQL Server listens simultaneously on multiple network protocols. This means that clients with different network protocols can access SQL Server at the same time if all available protocols are selected during the installation phase.

Named Pipes is the default network protocol for SQL Server on the Windows NT/2000 platform. After the installation process, you can drop the support for Named Pipes and use another network protocol for communication between the server and clients.

The Transmission Control Protocol/Internet Protocol (TCP/IP) network protocol allows SQL Server to communicate using standard Windows Sockets as the Internet protocol communication (IPC) method across the TCP/IP protocol. (Windows 9*x* uses this network protocol by default.) If your SQL Server system uses TCP/IP, you have to enter the TCP/IP port number in the **Port Number** box during the installation process.

Multiprotocol provides the ability to communicate simultaneously over one or more IPC mechanisms supported by Windows NT/2000. This Net-Library supports the use of Windows security over all protocols that remote procedure call (RPC) supports. (This is the only network protocol supported by SQL Server that does not require any configuration parameters.)

The NWLink Internet Packet eXchange/Sequenced Packet eXchange (IPX/SPX) network protocol is the standard protocol for Novell SPX and Windows NT/2000. If you set up SQL Server to communicate using this protocol, you can type the **Novell Bindery service name** during the installation process. (The default service name is the computer name of the server computer.)

The AppleTalk ADSP protocol allows Apple Macintosh clients to connect to SQL Server using the AppleTalk network protocol. If you select AppleTalk, you will be prompted for the **AppleTalk service object name** during the setup process.

SQL Server supports Banyan Vines, a network protocol that is often used for communication by personal computers. If you set up SQL Server to communicate using Banyan Vines, you will be prompted for the **Street Talk service name** that must first be created using the MSERVICE program.

The decision about network protocols affects the selection of the security type of SQL Server. Two security types are supported: SQL Server authentication and Windows authentication (see Chapter 12). You can use the SQL Server security with all network protocols described above, whereas the Windows security is allowed only with Named Pipes and Multiprotocol.

NOTE: Concerning performance, the Named Pipes network protocol is the fastest of all protocols listed above. Using TCP/IP or NWLink IPX/SPX is faster than using Multiprotocol, which is the union of all three protocols (TCP/IP, NWLink IPX/SPX, and Named Pipes).

Installation Recommendations

During the installation process, a lot of specifications must be made. As a general guideline, it is better to familiarize yourself with their effects before running the Setup program. The following questions should be answered before the installation process is started:

- Where will the root directory be stored?
- Which security type will be used?
- Which user accounts will be assigned to the SQL Server Agent service and SQL Server service? (This applies only to Windows NT/2000.)
- Where will Books Online be stored?

The root directory is where the Setup program stores all program files and those files that do not change as you use SQL Server. By default, SQL Server stores all program files in the directory MSSQL, although you can change this setting during the installation process. Using the default name is recommended because it uniquely determines the version of the SQL Server system.

After the installation process is completed, you select between the Windows and Mixed security modes. Windows security mode specifies security exclusively at the operating system level—that is, the way users connect to Windows NT/2000 using their user accounts and group memberships. Mixed security mode allows users to connect to SQL Server using Windows security or SQL Server security. Mixed security mode is recommended because it allows users to choose between two alternatives.

Create a Windows user account to assign to the SQLServerAgent service and another user account to assign to the MSSQLServer service. (Both services can use the same account.) These accounts are necessary in the last step of your installation process.

NOTE: Both user accounts should be created before starting the installation process. If necessary, you can always change the logon accounts of these services later.

Books Online can be installed on the disk or installed and run from CD. Installing it to run from the CD requires about 2MB of disk space, while installing it on a hard disk requires about 15MB. Installing Books Online on the hard disk gives you faster performance.

INSTALLING SQL SERVER

If you have done an installation of a complex software product before, you will probably recognize the uncertain feeling when starting the installation for the first time. This feeling comes from the complexity of the product to be installed and the diversity of questions to be answered during the installation process. Because you may not completely understand the product, you (or the person who installs the software) may be less than confident about giving valid answers for the things that have to be done. This section will help you to find a way through your installation by giving you answers to most of the questions beforehand.

Beginning the Installation

To begin the installation, insert the SQL Server 2000 CD. After that the system shows to you the SQL Server Automenu (see Figure 17-1). If the Automenu is not shown automatically, you have to run the Setup program, located by default on the SQL Server 2000 CD, to start the installation.

The SQL Server Automenu

As you can see from Figure 17-1, there are several different options that you can start on the SQL Server Automenu. Your best choice for the first pick will be to start with the Release Notes. The benefit of Release Notes is that they contain the newest information, which is not provided in the Books Online. Read this information carefully to get a picture of features that are modified shortly before the delivery of the final release. (Release Notes also contain the list of bugs; it can be useful for you to know the existence of some of them.)

Microsoft's Web site could be an additional source for further information. Similarly to Release Notes, you can find a lot of interesting documents (especially important are White Papers that Microsoft provides during the implementation of each new SQL Server version). You can search for documents that are of interest for you and download them.

The following sections describe the rest of the options shown in the initial menu.

Prerequisites

The prerequisites can be divided into hardware and software prerequisites. The hardware prerequisites are already described at the beginning of this chapter. The software prerequisites depend on the operating system on which you are installing your database system. For both Windows NT/2000 and Windows 9*x*, MS Internet Explorer Version 5 is

Figure 17-1. The SQL Server 2000 Automenu

required. This tool is required for all client and server installations of SQL Server 2000. A minimal installation of Internet Explorer is sufficient, and this browser does not need to be your default browser.

For Windows NT/2000 computers, you must have version 4.0, with Service Pack 6 (or later). (For the network and client prerequisites, see the corresponding sections in this chapter.)

Install SQL Server 2000 Components

After you have installed all prerequisites, you can start with the installation of the SQL Server components by selecting the option in the SQL Server Automenu with the same name. The menu with all SQL Server 2000 components appears (see Figure 17-2).

Before we discuss all components, you have to know which kind of SQL Server 2000 exists. Microsoft has six editions for SQL Server:

- Standard Edition
- Enterprise Edition
- Personal Edition
- Desktop Edition
- Windows CE Edition
- Developer Edition

Figure 17-2. The Install SQL Server 2000 Components menu

The Standard Edition is the "default" version of SQL Server 2000. This edition comprises the full functionality of the database server and can be run only on Windows NT/2000. If needed, you can upgrade the Standard Edition to the Enterprise Edition on an enterprise computer.

The Enterprise Edition is the special form of the SQL Server system, which is intended for use with time-critical applications with a huge number of users. In contrast to the Standard Edition, this edition contains additional features that can be useful for very high-end installations with symmetrical multiprocessors or clusters. The most important additional features of the Enterprise Edition are as follows:

- Log shipping (see Chapter 20)
- Failover clustering
- Creating partitions as storage containers for the data and aggregations of a cube (see Chapter 28)

The Personal Edition of SQL Server 2000 is used for mobile laptop applications or systems with a small number of users. (The number of users is limited to 50, but you should use it only if the number is significantly smaller.) The Small Business Edition is used with Windows NT/2000 or MS BackOffice Small Business Server.

The Desktop Edition is usually used as a remote database server that supports a central server and allows development of database applications. This edition is used with Windows NT/2000 or Windows 9*x*. The Windows CE Editon is used as the data store on Windows CE devices.

The Developer Edition is used by programmers that develop SQL Server 2000 database applications. In contrast to other editions, this edition is licensed for use only as a development system and not as a production system.

Now we can turn back to the installation of SQL Server 2000 components. As you can see from Figure 17-2, you can install either SQL Server 2000 (Standard or Desktop Edition) or Analysis Services or English Query. We will describe the installation of the Standard Edition. (The installation of Analysis Services is described in Chapter 27, while English Query is beyond the scope of this book.)

NOTE: The installation process of the Desktop Edition is very similar to the installation of the Standard Edition. In contrast to it, the installation process of the Enterprise Edition has many additional steps, especially when the clustering is involved. For this reason, we will not describe the installation process of the Enterprise Edition.

To start the installation process of the Standard Edition, click the option with the same name. In the following menu (see Figure 17-3), enter the name of the computer on which you want to create a new installation. You can install the database system on your local computer or on any remote computer that belongs to the network. The available options are the same for both a local and a remote installation. (If you select a remote installation, the installation process prompts you for information about the remote computer.) However, to perform a remote installation, certain requirements must be met:

- Both the local and remote computer must be running Microsoft Windows NT/2000.
- You must be logged on to the local computer with a user account that is an administrator on the remote computer.

We will discuss the local installation, so select **Local Computer**. After that, the installation process searches the files on your computer to determine whether SQL Server was previously installed. If the installation process does not find SQL Server files, it shows the new menu (see Figure 17-4) where you can choose one of the installation options concerning a new or upgrade installation. When you select **Create a new instance of SQL Server**, the installation process shows you the Software License Agreement (see Figure 17-5). You should read this agreement carefully and decide whether you want to accept it or not. In the latter case, the installation process will be stopped.

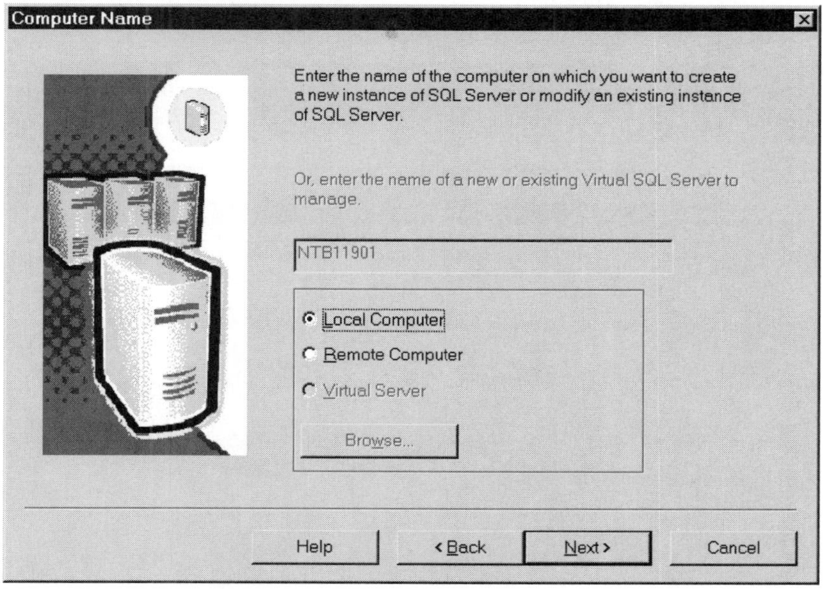

Figure 17-3. The Computer Name menu

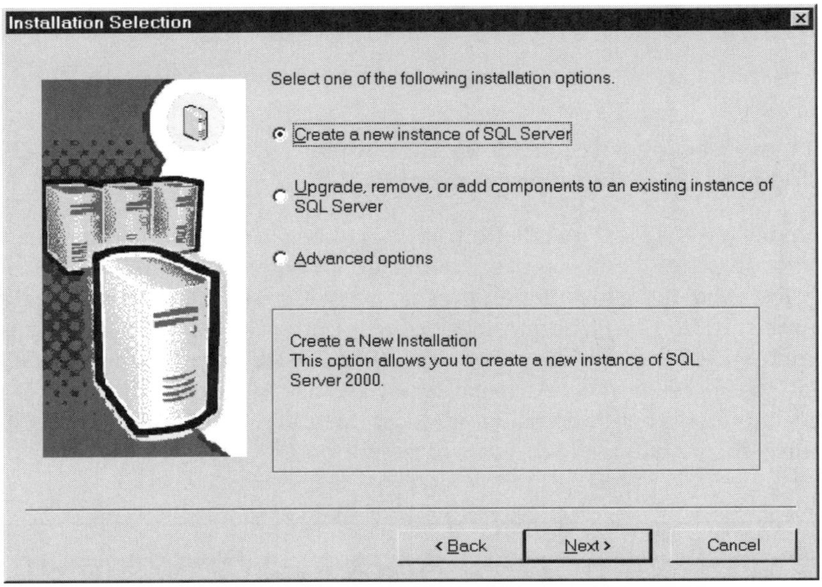

Figure 17-4. The Installation Selection menu

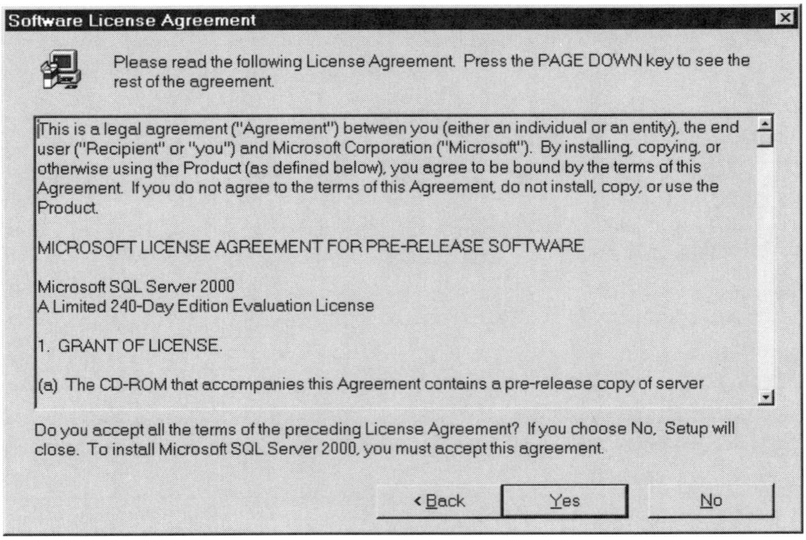

Figure 17-5. The Software License Agreement menu

The next menu allows you to select which part of client/server software you want to install on your computer (see Figure 17-6). If you want to make the full product installation select the option **Server and Client Tools**. (The installation process of client tools is described later in this chapter.)

The next step of the installation process allows you to install a default or named instance of the database server (see Figure 17-7). As you already know, SQL Server 2000 supports multiple instances, and each instance of the database server has its own set of database objects (system and user databases) that are not shared between different instances. Accept the installing of the default instance and continue further the installation process with the selection of one of the installation types (see Figure 17-8).

To install the database server, you can use three different installation types:

- Typical installation
- Minimum installation
- Custom installation

These options differ in the number of SQL Server tools available after installation. The typical installation uses the default installation options and is best for most users. It includes SQL Server, the client management tools, and SQL Server online documentation. The minimum installation installs the minimum configuration necessary to run and use

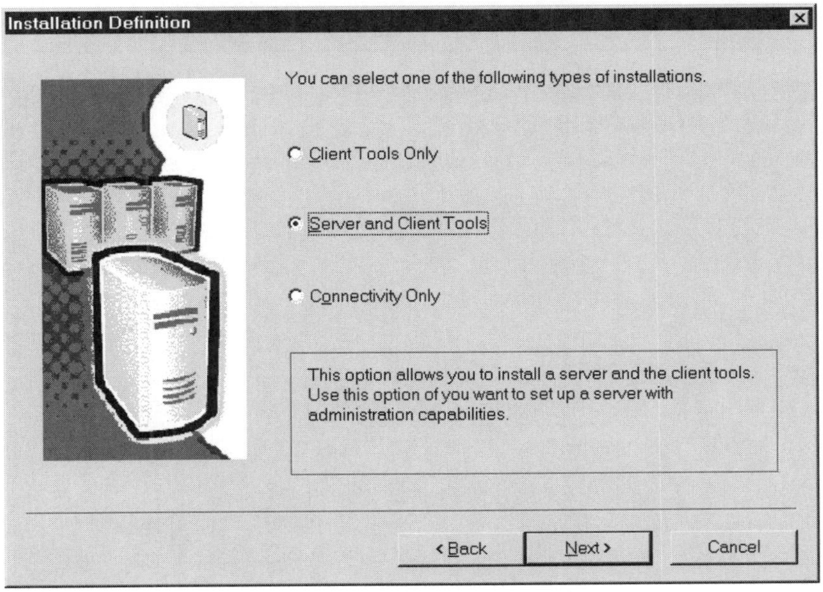

Figure 17-6. The Installation Definition menu

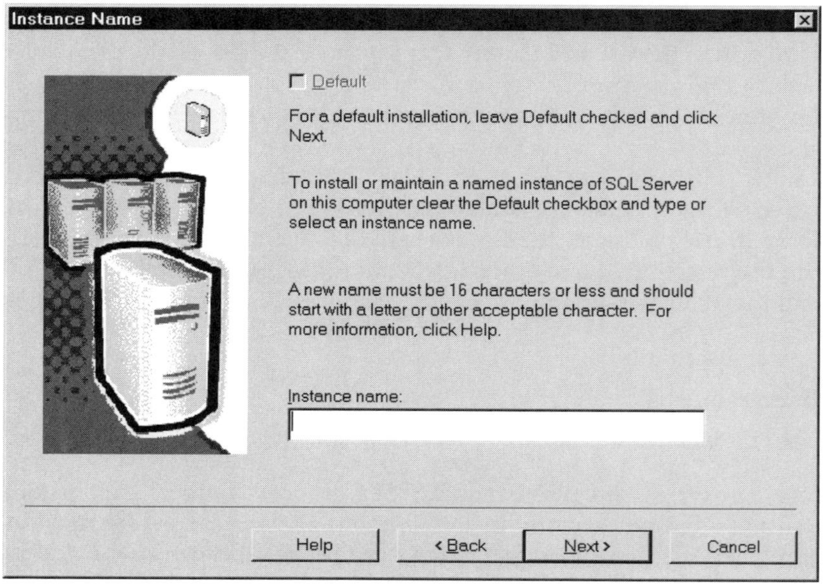

Figure 17-7. The Instance Name menu

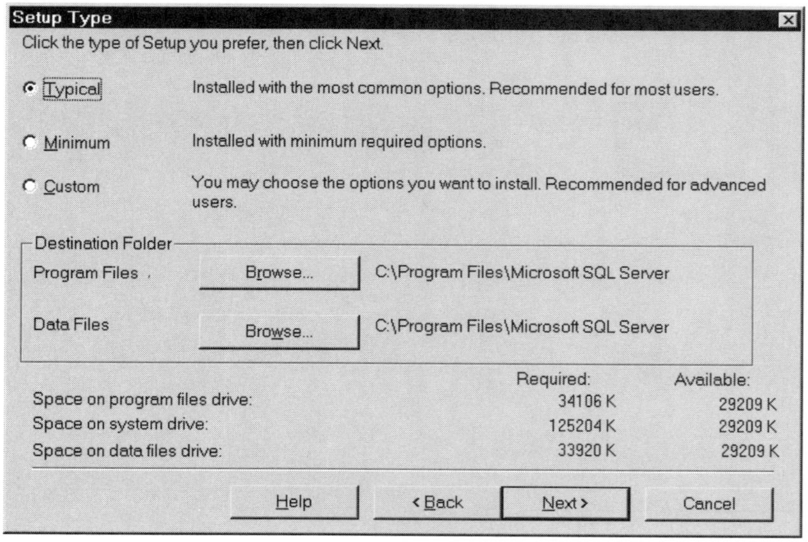

Figure 17-8. The Setup Type menu

SQL Server. (This type of installation should be used when disk space on your computer is extremely limited.) Using the custom installation, you can add, modify, or remove various installation options. Custom installation is best suited for expert users, who know exactly which SQL Server components they want to install or remove.

Any installation type (typical, minimum, and custom) requires general information in the beginning steps. The questions concern user information, such as personal name, organization name, and product ID. This information should be entered in the following menus and is used as licensing information. In addition to these questions, certain installation steps are done either automatically (typical installation) or manually (custom installation), which can have far-reaching consequences for later use of the system. The different outcomes are discussed below, in the context of the consecutive installation steps offered within the typical installation.

The last step in the custom installation is to assign a Windows user account to SQL Server and the SQL Server Agent (see Figure 17-9). Both components can use either a local account or a domain account. By default, a domain user account is used, which allows the system to interact with different servers across a network and to perform such operations as data replication, which involves several computers. (System Accounts for SQL Server and the SQL Server Agent are required in a typical installation as well as in a custom installation.)

In the same step, you may choose the **Auto Start** option, which allows changing the running mode for the MSSQLServer and SQLServerAgent processes. By default, both processes must be manually started and stopped.

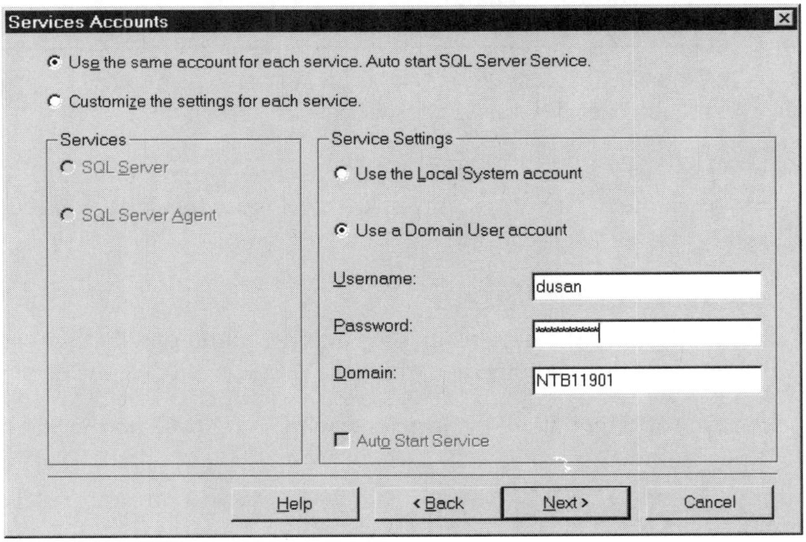

Figure 17-9. The Services Accounts menu

NOTE: Systems Management Server (SMS) version can be used to install SQL Server on multiple Windows NT/2000 computers. The SQL Server CD contains several SMS files that allow the creation of packages in SMS and the execution of the installation process.

Installing Client Tools

If you have computers that only need client access to the SQL Server system located on a different computer within the network, the best choice is to install only the client software on these machines. This software can be installed on computers running Windows NT/2000 or Windows 9*x*. The installation process can be executed directly from the SQL Server CD, or the client software can be copied to a hard disk first and installed afterward. The installation of client software on a computer with the Windows 9*x* operating system requires the existence of an autoexec.bat file.

Installing SQL Server's client management tools requires running the Setup program located on the SQL Server CD or clicking the setup.exe file, if the appropriate software is copied to the disk. Follow the same steps that you used for the full product installation and choose the **Client Tools Only** option in the Installation Definition menu (see Figure 17-6). After that, select the client management tools you want to install. (Clear the check boxes next to the client management tools you do not want installed.)

Upgrading SQL Server

Generally, upgrading an existing SQL Server system is more complex than installing a new one. Before you begin the upgrade process, back up existing SQL Server databases so that you can completely restore them if necessary.

NOTE: SQL Server 2000 supports only updates of SQL Server Version 6.*x* and 7. Upgrades of SQL Server 4.2 are not supported. Version 4.2 must be upgraded to 6.*x*.

The upgrade process is managed with the SQL Server Upgrade Wizard. Before you use the wizard, you have to perform some tasks that ensure the correct execution of the wizard.

Before Using the Upgrade Wizard

The tasks you should perform before using the wizard depend on whether you upgrade from Version 6.*x* or 7. There are some general tasks that you should perform:

- Run the appropriate database consistency checks (DBCC) on the SQL Server databases to make sure they are in a consistent state.
- Back up all system and user-defined databases, so you can completely restore them if necessary.

You should perform the following tasks if you are upgrading from SQL Server Version 6.*x*:

- Set the **tempdb** system database to 25MB.
- Ensure that all database users have logins in the **master** database.
- Make sure that your 6.*x* server has a server name (using SELECT @@servername). If it is NULL, you must assign it one (using the system procedure **sp_addserver**).
- Disable any startup stored procedures. (Stored procedures processed at startup may cause the upgrade process to hang.)
- Quit all SQL Server services and user applications.

Upgrading from Version 6.5 Using SQL Server Upgrade Wizard

You can convert data from SQL Server Version 6.5 to the formats for SQL Server 2000 using the SQL Server Upgrade Wizard. The wizard upgrades any or all of your databases, transferring all catalog data, objects, and user data. It also transfers replication settings, SQL Executive settings, and most of the SQL Server 6.5 configuration options. (The wizard does not support consolidation of databases from multiple SQL Server 6.5 installations.)

The upgrade process does not remove the SQL Server 6.5 system from your computer. Also, the version 6.5 data set exists in parallel to the SQL Server 2000 data set. (You should take this fact into account because of additional disk space that is necessary for the version 6.5 system as well as 6.5 data.)

NOTE: Named and default instances in SQL Server 2000 enhanced ways to work with earlier versions that are already installed on your computer. For instance, you can run version 6.5 and a named instance of SQL Server 2000 at the same time, or you can have version 6.5 in a version switch configuration with SQL Server 2000. The same is true for version 7. (For the definition of default and named instances, see Chapter 15.)

You can perform Version 6.*x* upgrade using the following:

- Named Pipe
- Tape

The Named Pipe transfer method is the most reliable and provides the best performance. On the other hand, the tape transfer method is recommended if you are low on disk space, because the SQL Server Upgrade Wizard allows you to delete all of the SQL Server 6.5 devices, if you wish. That way you can free disk space before SQL Server 2000 data set is created. To start the wizard, in the Start menu of SQL Server click **SQL Server Upgrade Wizard** after pointing to **Programs** and **MS SQL Server Switch**. In the first upgrade step, you choose the data transfer method. (The default value is Named Pipe.) The upgrade process can be done on the same or a different machine. The next step allows you to specify the name of the local or remote computer on which SQL Server will reside.

Also in this step, you have to enter the **sa** (system administrator) password for SQL Server 6.*x*. After that, click **Yes** in the message box if you are ready to continue the upgrade process. The system then shuts down SQK Server 6.*x* and starts SQL Server 2000. In the **Code Page Selection** screen, accept or change the default settings, and then click **Next.**

In the next step, include all databases that should be upgraded, and separately specify all databases that should not be upgraded in the **Exclude** list. Further, examine and make changes to the proposed disk configuration within the **Layout** utility.

In the **System objects to transfer** step, select the object types to transfer. You have the following three options:

- Server configuration, which manages the transfer of logins and server configuration options. (For a discussion of logins, see Chapter 12.)
- Replication settings, which transfers all objects concerning data replication. (For more information on data replication, see Chapter 25.)
- SQL Executive settings, which transfers all tasks of this SQL Server 6.*x* utility to the corresponding SQL Server Agent utility in SQL Server 2000.

In the last two steps of the installation process, the behavior of NULL values and the use of quoted identifiers must be set. To decide how to handle these two steps, see the description of both terms in Chapter 2.

Upgrading from Version 7

You upgrade from version 7 using the SQL Server 2000 CD. First, select **Install SQL Server 2000 Components**, select the edition of SQL Server you want to install, and then click **Next** at the Welcome screen of the SQL Server Installation Wizard.

NOTE: Upgrades of version 7 must be done within the same SQL Server edition.

The next step allows you to specify the name of the local or remote computer on which SQL Server will reside. In the **Installation Options** dialog box, click **Upgrade,** and in the **Instance Name** dialog box, click **Next**. After that, in the **Upgrade** dialog box, click **Yes, upgrade my programs** to start the upgrade process. (All further steps are identical to the corresponding steps described already in the full installation of the program.)

CONFIGURING SQL SERVER AFTER INSTALLATION

After SQL Server is installed, you need to perform several configuration tasks before you begin to use it. Generally, the following tasks are performed using SQL Server Enterprise Manager:

- Create server groups and register the server
- Set server options

Create Server Groups and Register the Server

SQL Server can contain one or more server groups. A *server group* is a set of SQL Server systems that can be put together to specify the organizational structure of your company. At the beginning, there is always one default group named SQL Server Group. Groups are created using Enterprise Manager. From the **Action** menu, choose **New SQL Server Group**. (The alternative way is to right-click **Microsoft SQL Server** and select **New SQL Server Group**.) The **Server Groups** dialog box appears (see Figure 17-10). Group names must be unique.

When you run Enterprise Manager for the first time, it automatically registers the local SQL Server. (Registering any SQL Server allows it to be administered from Enterprise Manager.) Subsequently, additional servers can be registered using the Register SQL Server Wizard.

When you register a server, you must specify the following:

- The server name
- The security type (if you use SQL Server security, you must provide the SQL Server login ID and password of the server you are registering)
- The name of the group where you want the server to be listed after it is registered

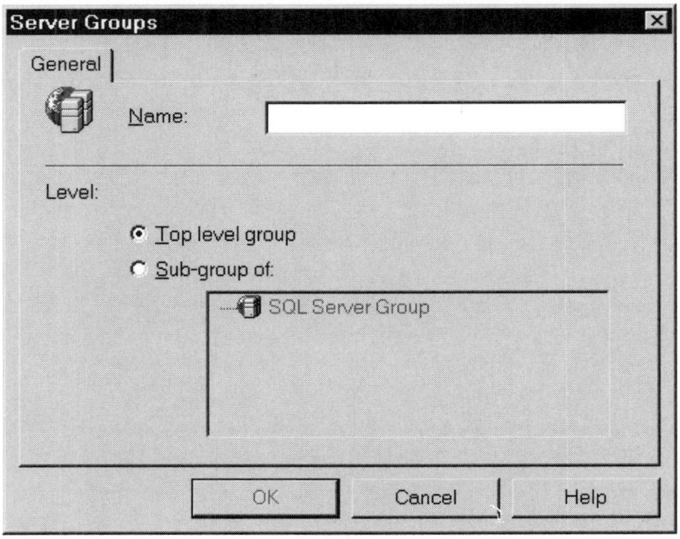

Figure 17-10. Server Groups dialog box

Set Server Options

One of the most important features of SQL Server 2000 is that it performs several standard system administration operations for you. Many server configuration options have been simplified and streamlined so that, in most cases, you do not have to set server options. However, if any of the default values are not appropriate for your situation, right-click the server and choose **Properties**. The **SQL Server Properties** dialog box appears (Figure 17-11). On the **General** tab, you can select only the autostart options for SQL Server, SQL Server Agent, and MS Distributed Transaction Coordinator.

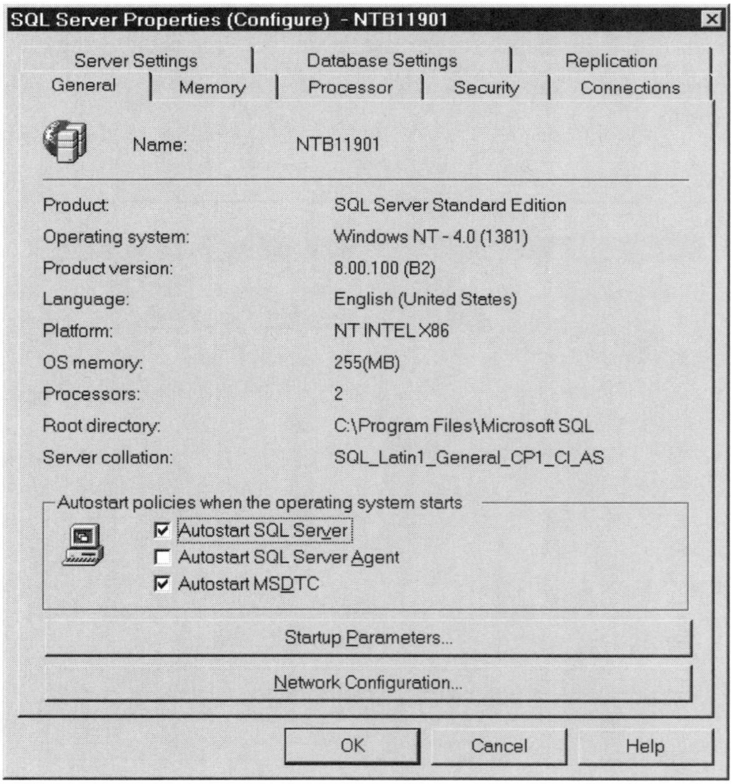

Figure 17-11. SQL Server Properties dialog box

STARTING, PAUSING, AND STOPPING SQL SERVER

The most convenient way to start a SQL Server system is automatically with the boot process of the computer. However, certain circumstances might require different handling of the system. Therefore, SQL Server offers several options for starting the system.

If you choose the autostart options in the **SQL Server Properties** dialog box (see Figure 17-11), the database server will be started together with the Windows NT/2000 or Windows 9*x* operating system. SQL Server 2000 can also be started, stopped, or paused using different methods. (Pausing SQL Server prevents new connections only. Users who are already connected to the system are not affected.) These methods are as follows:

- Service Manager
- SQL Server Enterprise Manager
- Services application in Control Panel
- The **sqlservr** application
- The **net** command

NOTE: All methods listed above can also be used to start and stop the SQL Server Agent. (For more information on SQL Server Agent, see Chapter 22.)

To open Service Manager, first click the **Start** menu and then **Service Manager** in the Microsoft SQL Server program group (see Figure 17-12). To stop SQL Server, double-click the red light. To pause SQL Server, double-click the yellow light.

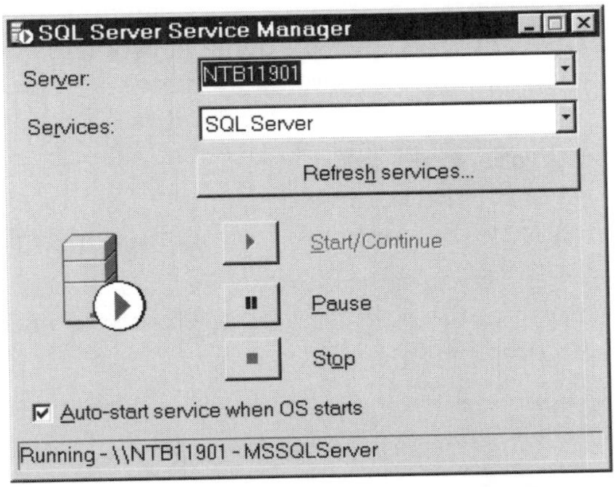

Figure 17-12. SQL Service Manager

To start, stop, or pause SQL Server using SQL Server Enterprise Manager, click the **Action** menu and select the appropriate function. You can also start, stop, or pause SQL Server from the **Windows NT Services** dialog box, which is located in the Control Panel. (To reach the Control Panel, click the **Start** menu and then the **Settings** menu.) Additionally, the **Service** dialog box allows you to start SQL Server.

The **sqlservr** application can only be used to start SQL Server. This application is invoked using the following command:

```
sqlservr option_list
```

option_list contains all options that can be invoked using the application. Table 17-1 describes the most important options.

The **net start**, **net stop**, and **net pause** commands start, stop, and pause the SQL Server, respectively. The **net** command in Example 17.1 starts SQL Server.

▼ EXAMPLE 17.1

```
net start mssqlserver
```

Option	Description
-c	Indicates that SQL Server is started independently of the Windows NT/2000 Service Control Manager. In this case, SQL Server will be stopped if you log off the operating system or use the **shutdown** statement.
-m	Indicates that SQL Server is started in the single user mode. This option is used if you have problems with SQL Server and want to perform maintenance on it (this option must be used to restore the **master** database).
-s registry_key	Indicates that you want to start SQL Server using an alternate set of startup parameters stored in the Windows NT/2000 Registry. This option is usually used to select from multiple startup configurations.
-d master_file	Indicates the path for the file where the **master** database is stored.

Table 17-1. Useful Options of the **sqlservr** Application

CONCLUSION

The installation of SQL Server requires some work in the preinstallation and postinstallation phases. In the preinstallation phase, the system administrator determines software and hardware requirements and prepares different specifications for the installation process. The installation or upgrade phase immediately follows the preinstallation phase. The postinstallation phase contains the following steps:

- Create server groups and register the server
- Set server options

The next chapter describes the management of all system resources.

CHAPTER 18

Managing Databases and Database Files

This chapter describes how SQL Server stores data and how the system administrator manages it. The following tasks are part of data management:

- Managing file groups
- Managing databases
- Managing transaction logs

MANAGING FILE GROUPS

As stated in Chapter 15, SQL Server uses 8K contiguous blocks of disk space to store data. Such a block is called a *page*. When you create a table or index, SQL Server uses eight contiguous pages called an *extent* to store the data belonging to that table or index. (An extent can be used by more than one table or index.)

All databases have one primary file that is implicitly specified by the suffix .mdf. Optionally, there can be one or more secondary data files, specified by the suffix .ndf. Similarly, each database has one or more transaction logs, specified by the suffix .ldf. (All three suffixes are recommended extensions, but they can be modified if necessary.)

All files that are used to store databases and transaction logs have a physical name—the operating system file name—and a logical name that is used by SQL Server components. A collection of files belonging to a single disk can be grouped to build file groups. With file groups, you can locate different tables or indices on a specific file (or set of files). SQL Server supports three different types of file groups:

- Primary
- User-defined
- Default

The primary file group is implicitly created by the system during the creation of the database to which it belongs. All system tables are always in the primary file group, while user-defined tables can belong either to the primary file group or any user-defined file group. This means all user-defined tables, together with the corresponding indices, are placed in the primary file group if they are not explicitly assigned to another file group.

A user-defined file group must be explicitly created by the system administrator and subsequently attached to the corresponding database using the CREATE DATABASE or ALTER DATABASE statement (see Chapter 4).

NOTE: No file can belong to more than one file group.

The default file group contains all database objects that are not in a specific file group. If no default file group is explicitly specified, the primary file group is the default file group. (You can use the ALTER DATABASE statement if you want to change the default file group.)

NOTE: It is very important to choose the appropriate size for the primary file group, because if it runs out of space no new metadata (i.e., system information) can be added to the catalog. (If a user-defined file group runs out of space, only the user data stored in the files of the file group is affected.)

Viewing File Groups

All file groups belonging to a database can be viewed using the following:

- SQL Server Enterprise Manager
- System procedure **sp_helpfilegroup**

To display all file groups with the corresponding files, right-click the database and choose **Properties**. In the **Database Properties** dialog box, all existing file groups of the current database are listed under the tab **Filegroups** (see Figure 18-1).

The system procedure **sp_helpfilegroup** displays the specified file group with all its properties (file names and their sizes). If no file group name is specified, it displays the properties of all file groups in the current database.

MANAGING DATABASES

Managing databases consists of the following tasks:

- Creating databases
- Viewing and modifying database options
- Modifying and removing databases

Creating Databases

In addition to the CREATE DATABASE statement and the Create Database Wizard (see Chapter 4), a database can be created using Enterprise Manager. Right-click the **Data-**

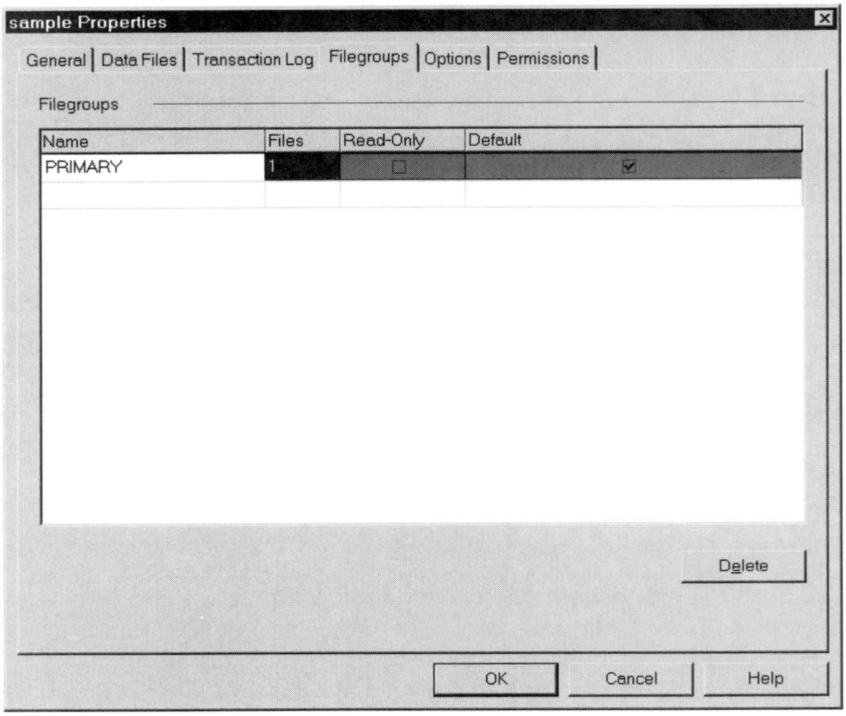

Figure 18-1. The Database Properties dialog box—The Filegroups tab

bases folder of your SQL Server system in the console tree and choose **New Database**. The **Database Properties** dialog box (see Figure 18-2) appears.

The name of the database must be specified in this dialog box. (All other specifications are optional.) After you select the **Data Files** tab, the corresponding dialog box appears (see Figure 18-3). The **Automatically grow file** check box must be checked in this dialog box if the growth of the file(s) of the database should be managed dynamically by SQL Server. Otherwise, only the disk space assigned to the file can be used to store data of the database.

The additional portions of disk storage are assigned by checking the radio button **In megabytes** and specifying the amount of storage. Two other radio buttons, **Unrestricted file growth** and **Restrict file growth**, specify whether the data file can grow without restrictions. (The specification **Unrestricted file growth** corresponds to the value "UNLIMITED" of the option FILEGROWTH in the CREATE DATABASE statement.)

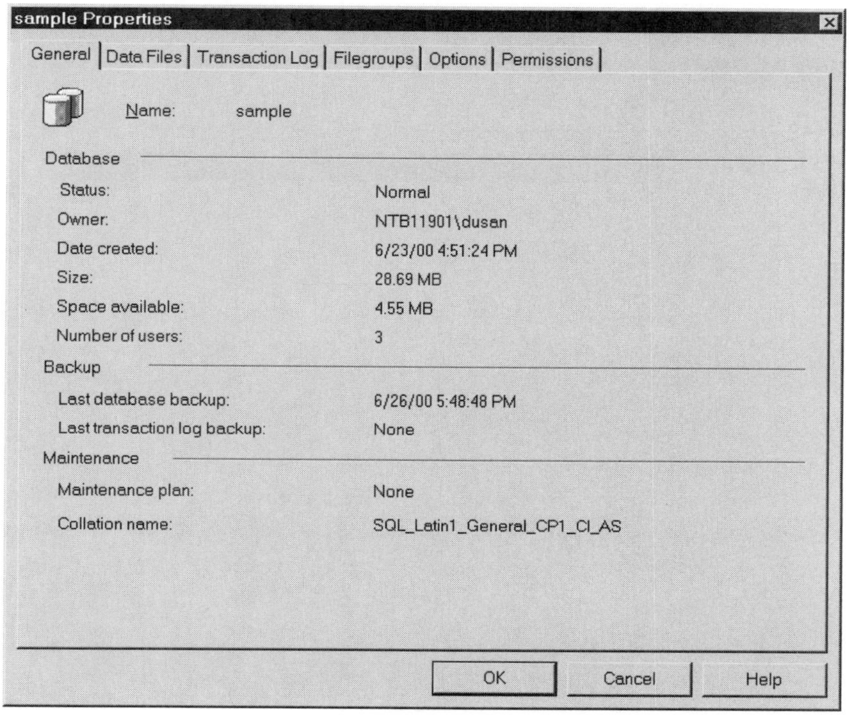

Figure 18-2. The Database Properties dialog box for the sample database

NOTE: The master database should be backed up each time you create, modify, or drop a database.

Viewing and Modifying Database Options

After the creation of a database, all database options are set by default (see Figure 18-4). Database options can be viewed and modified using the following:

- SQL Server Enterprise Manager
- System procedure **sp_dboption**
- ALTER DATABASE statement

Also, you can use the DATABASEPROPERTYEX function to view all options.

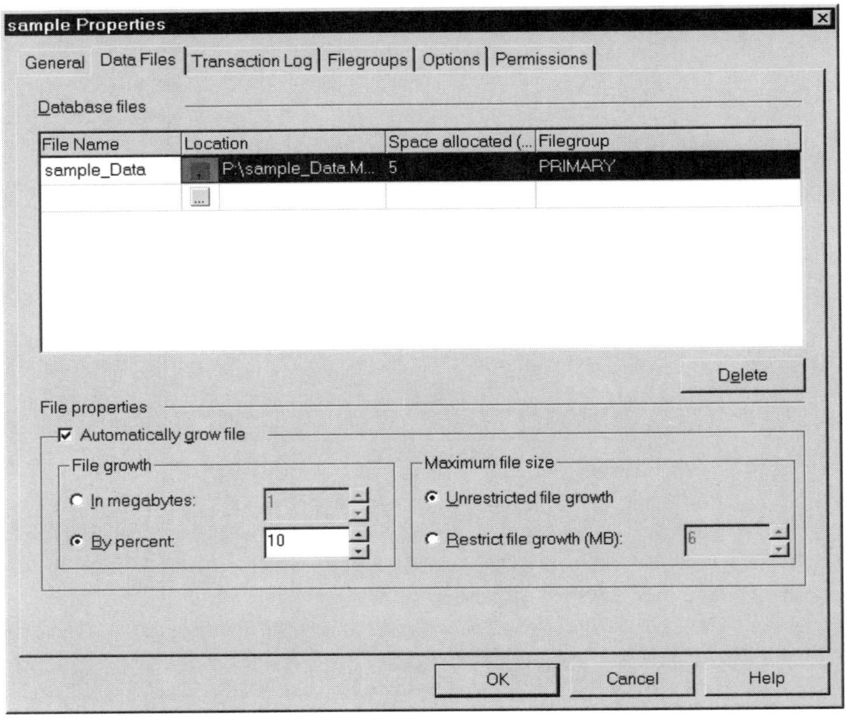

Figure 18-3. The Database Properties dialog box—The Data Files tab

NOTE: Enterprise Manager allows the setting of only certain options, but with **sp_dboption** you can modify all options.

To display or modify the database options of a database, right-click the name of the database and choose **Properties**. In the **Properties** dialog box, click the **Options** tab. Table 18-1 lists some of the database options.

NOTE: The only option you can set for the **master** database is **Truncate log on checkpoint**.

To display the list of all available options, use the system procedure **sp_dboption** without parameters. The general form of this procedure is:

```
EXECUTE sp_dboption [db_name, option, {TRUE | FALSE}]
```

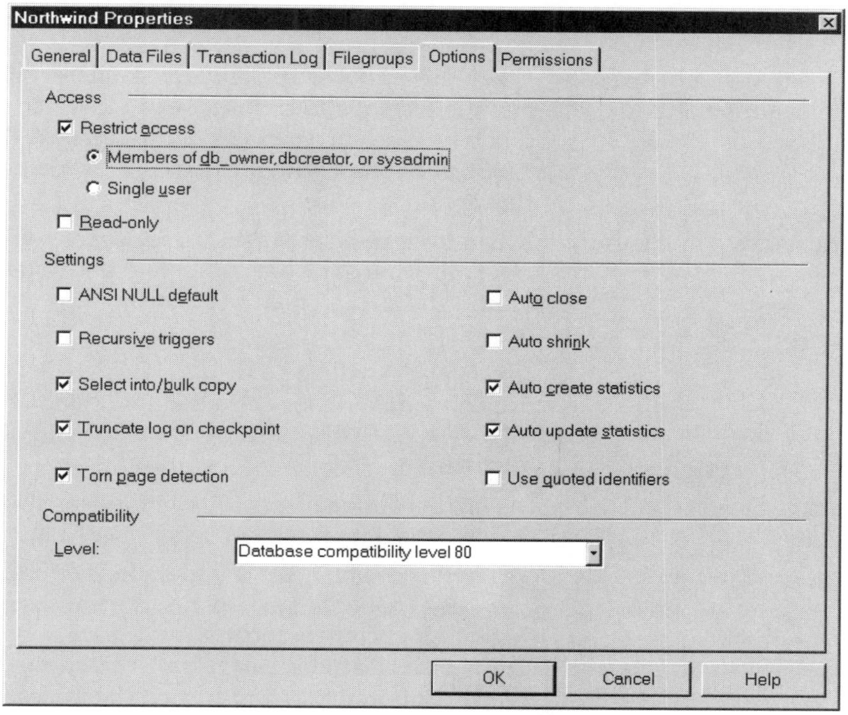

Figure 18-4. Database Options dialog box

db_name is the name of the database for which the options should be modified. **option** specifies one of options listed in Table 18-1.

▼ EXAMPLE 18.1

execute sp_dboption sample, 'read only', TRUE

In Example 18.1, the sample database is defined as read-only. (Because SQL Server understands any unique string that is part of the option name, you can write, for example, 'read' instead of 'read only'.)

NOTE: The system procedure **sp_dboption** is a deprecated feature in SQL Server 2000 and is supported only for backward compatibility.

Option	Description
Restrict access (members of db_owner or sysadmin)	When this option is set, only the database owner and the system administrator can access the database. The current users of the database can continue to work with the database. By default, this option is not set.
Restrict access (single user)	When this option is set, only one user at a time (including the database owner and the system administrator) can use the database.
ANSI NULL default	This option specifies whether a table column of the database will be defined as NULL or NOT NULL by default. (See also the discussion of the ANSI_NULL_DFLT_ON option at the end of Chapter 3.)
Recursive triggers	When this option is set, you can implement triggers that invoke other triggers (see Chapter 13).
Select into/bulk copy	When this option is set, all operations on the database are not logged; that is, the transaction log does not contain records, which are necessary in the case of database recovery. Therefore, do not set this option for the production databases. (Additionally, the SELECT INTO statement and "fast bcp" can be performed only when this option is set.)
Read only	When this option is set, only read operations can be performed on the database.
Truncate log on checkpoint	When this option is set, the transaction log is automatically truncated after a checkpoint. (For more information on checkpoints, see Chapter 20.)
Auto shrink	When this option is set, the size of database files could shrink periodically.

Table 18-1. Database Options

The DATABASEPROPERTYEX function

This function displays the current value of the specified database option or property. The syntax of this function is:

```
DATABASEPROPERTYEX (db_name, property)
```

property specifies the name of the option or property, for which a value should be returned. In most cases, the returned value can be either 1 (true) or 0 (false) or NULL (invalid input). Table 18-2 shows the list of selected properties with their descriptions.

Property	Description
IsAnsiNullDefault	Returns 1 if the use of NULL values in the database complies with the ANSI SQL standard. (See also the explanation of NULL values at the end of Chapter 3.)
IsAnsiNullEnabled	Returns 1 if all comparisons to a NULL evaluate according to the ANSI SQL standard (i.e., to unknown).
IsAutoShrink	All files that belong to the database will be checked for automatic periodic shrinking.
IsAutoCreateStatistics	Existing statistics are implicitly updated by the system when they are out of date.
IsAutoUpdatedStatistics	Autoupdated statistics database option is enabled.
IsNullConcat	This database option influences the concatenation operation with a NULL value. The value 1 means that anything you concatenate to a NULL value will yield again NULL.
IsQuotedIdentifiersEnabled	Double quotation marks are used on identifiers.
IsInStandby	The database modus is read-only, with restore log allowed.
Status	Displays the status of the database. The values are ONLINE, OFFLINE, RESTORING, RECOVERING, and SUSPECT.
Updateability	Has two values: READ_ONLY (data can be read but not written) and READ_WRITE (data can be read and modified)
Collation	Default collation name for the database (see Chapter 16).

Table 18-2. Database Options and Properties

Modifying Databases

The administrative tasks concerning the modification of a database in SQL Server 2000 are easy to perform. The only task you can do manually to modify a database is to expand or shrink its size by changing the size of the corresponding database files.

The task of expanding the database files can also be done automatically using Enterprise Manager or the ALTER DATABASE statement. In the first case, check the **Automatically grow file** check box in the **Database Properties** dialog box (see Figure 18-3). Using this method, the administrative tasks concerning a database can be significantly reduced. (The alternative way is to set the FILEGROWTH option of the MODIFY FILE clause option in the ALTER DATABASE statement.)

If you do not set an existing database file to grow automatically, you can still expand the database size by either increasing the size of the file or adding new (secondary) file(s) to the database. The easiest way to increase the size of the existing file is to change the value in the **Space allocated** field for that file. A new file can be added to the database by using the ALTER DATABASE statement or by specifying a new database file in the **Database Properties** dialog box. In both cases, the physical name, the logical name, and the size of the file must be specified.

You can shrink the database size by shrinking the size of the entire database or by shrinking the size of the corresponding files. You can shrink a database automatically using Enterprise Manager or the system procedure **sp_dboption**. In the former case, right-click the database you want to shrink, choose the **Task** function, click **Shrink Database,** and choose the percentage for **Maximum free space in files after shrinking**. In the latter case, set the **Autoshrink** option of the system procedure **sp_dboption** to true.

NOTE: Automatic shrinking of a database occurs periodically, whenever a certain amount of free disk space is available in the database.

When the database should shrink immediately, use the DBCC SHRINKDATABASE command. After executing this command, the system tries to shrink all data files belonging to the database for the specific percentage. The used pages that are stored at the end of these disk files will be moved to the space on the disk that is below the percentage threshold. For instance, if your database is stored in 10MB and you shrink it to 70 percent, all database rows that are located in the last 3MB are moved to the 7MB disk space that is below the threshold, and the 3MB disk space at the end of the file will be released.

If your database needs more storage space than is specified with the DBCC SHRINKDATABASE command, the reallocation process will be performed, but only the existing part of free disk space will be released.

NOTE: You cannot shrink your database smaller than the model database is.

Example 18.2 uses the specified value (20 percent) as a target for free space that remains after shrinking the sample database.

▼ EXAMPLE 18.2

```
DBCC SHRINKDATABASE (sample, 20)
```

The DBCC command with the SHRINKFILE option is used to shrink the size of a specific file of a database.

You can remove a database using the DROP DATABASE statement (see Chapter 4) or Enterprise Manager. Removing a database deletes all database objects within the database and removes all files used by the database. Additionally, all system tables in the **master** database concerning the database are modified to remove references to the database.

To remove a database using Enterprise Manager, open the **Database** folder, right-click the database, and choose **Delete**. In contrast to the DROP DATABASE statement, with Enterprise Manager you can remove only one database at a time.

MANAGING TRANSACTION LOGS

SQL Server records the changes that INSERT, UPDATE, or DELETE statements make during a transaction in one or more files called the transaction log. Each SQL Server database uses its own transaction log to record modifications to the data.

In the case of error, SQL Server starts the process called automatic recovery. During this process, SQL Server uses the records stored in the transaction log to roll back all incomplete transactions. Also, for all committed transactions, the changes are rolled forward so that all of the changes of the transaction are applied to the database. (For more information on transaction logs, see Chapter 14.)

Transaction log files are created at the same time database files are created. You can use Enterprise Manager or the CREATE DATABASE statement to create file(s) for the transaction log. (See the description of the database creation at the beginning of this chapter.)

Using the ALTER DATABASE statement, or Enterprise Manager, you can modify transaction log files. (For the description of the ALTER DATABASE statement, see Chapter 4.) To modify (or view) transaction log files using Enterprise Manager, right-click the database, choose **Properties**, and select the **Transaction Log** tab in the **Database Properties** dialog box (see Figure 18-5).

The modification of existing files and the creation of new transaction log files can be done in the same way as the database files are modified or created.

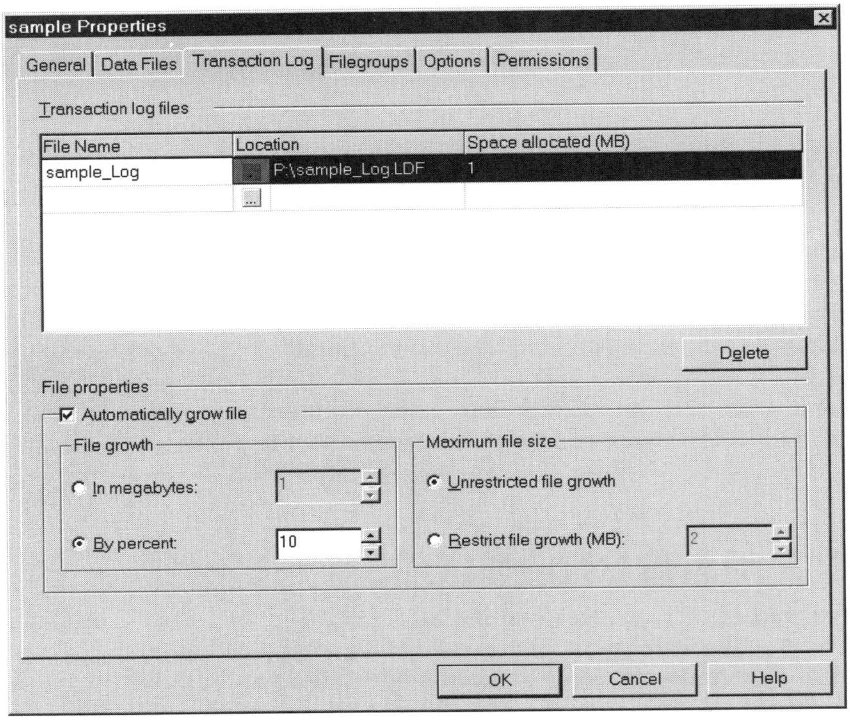

Figure 18-5. Database Properties dialog box—Transaction Log tab

NOTE: The size of the transaction log must be carefully planned, and its growth must be monitored, because there are some operations (such as loading the data into a table with existing indices) that fill the transaction log very quickly. For this reason, create an alert (see Chapter 22) to notify you when the transaction log threshold is reached.

CONCLUSION

The most significant property of SQL Server is its easy-to-manage features that are part of the database engine. The amount of time and effort that goes into managing databases and files since version 7 is negligible compared with the previous versions of SQL Server.

All tasks concerning management of databases and their files can be done using either SQL Server Enterprise Manager or the Transact-SQL statements CREATE

DATABASE and ALTER DATABASE. For displaying database and file properties, some system procedures can also be used.

The next chapter discusses the SQL Server security system and how security issues can be managed.

EXERCISES

▼ E.18.1

When is the primary file group of a database identical to its default file?

▼ E.18.2

Discuss the differences in using the **sp_dboption** system stored procedure and the DATABASEPROPERTYEX function.

▼ E.18.3

Which SQL Server utility would you prefer to use to modify database options?

▼ E.18.4

How can you know whether SQL Server implicitly shrinks the size of database files?

▼ E.18.5

Can data of a database and its transaction log use the same file?

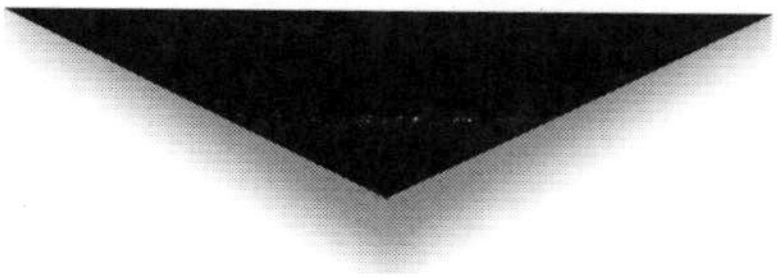

CHAPTER 19

Managing Security

This chapter discusses security issues in SQL Server from the point of view of the system administrator. After a few introductory notes, the features of SQL Server Enterprise Manager that allow users to access the SQL Server system and databases within it are described.

INTRODUCTION

SQL Server security is based on Windows authorization and optionally uses the SQL Server security subsystem. Therefore, SQL Server can operate in two different modes:

- Windows security mode
- Mixed mode

When a user connects to SQL Server in Windows security mode, the SQL Server client starts a *trusted connection*, which means SQL Server searches for the Window user account (or group account) in the list of SQL Server login accounts. If the account exists, the user's SQL Server login account is the operating system's user or group account. In this case, SQL Server does not verify a corresponding password because it "trusts" that Windows NT/2000 has verified it already.

Mixed mode allows users to connect to SQL Server using the Windows security or SQL Server security. This means a user logs into Windows NT/2000 using his or her account or logs into the SQL Server system using his or her login name. In the latter case, SQL Server verifies that a login exists in the list of SQL Server login accounts and that the specified password matches the stored password for the same account.

Both modes have their specific benefits. Windows mode offers advanced security features, which are not implemented for the SQL Server security system. The most important features are the auditing and account lockout after the specification of an invalid password. Additionally, maintenance tasks are reduced, because you only have to maintain a Windows user account (or group account) and the corresponding password. On the other hand, using SQL Server authorization in a Mixed mode allows you to use two-level security and therefore to enhance the security of the overall system.

For more information on all features concerning SQL Server security issues, see the section "Access to SQL Server" in Chapter 12.

> ***NOTE:*** For all production database systems, I strongly recommend using Mixed mode with the SQL Server authorization, because the addition of another layer of security makes the database more secure against misuse.

Implementing a Security Mode

SQL Server Enterprise Manager can be used to select the security mode. To set up Windows security mode, right-click a server and click **Properties**. In the **SQL Server Prop-**

erties dialog box, choose the **Security** tab and click **Windows NT/2000 only** (see Figure 19-1). Mixed mode can be selected similarly; the only difference is that you have to click **SQL Server** and **Windows NT/2000** in the **SQL Server Properties** dialog box.

NOTE: Windows authentication mode is not available when SQL Server is running on Windows 9*x*.

After successful connection to SQL Server, the access to database objects is independent of whether Windows or SQL Server authorization is used.

Managing SQL Server Logins

For Windows users and groups, SQL Server provides the system procedure **sp_grantlogin,** which allows them to connect to the database system using the Windows authorization mode. Alternatively, a SQL Server login can be created using the system procedure **sp_addlogin** (see Chapter 12) or Enterprise Manager.

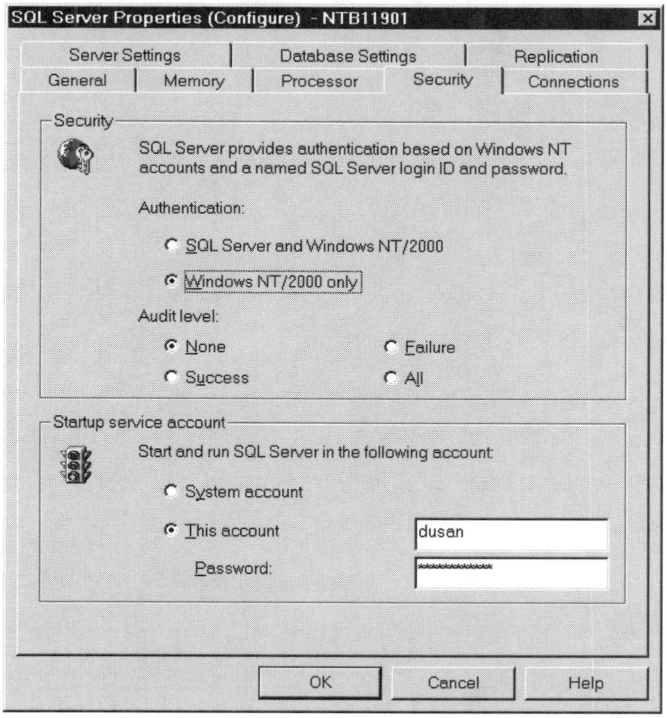

Figure 19-1. SQL Server Properties dialog box

To create a new login using Enterprise Manager, expand a server, expand **Security**, right-click **Logins**, and click **New Login**. The **SQL Server Login Properties** dialog box (see Figure 19-2) appears. Specify the new login name and the authentication mode. Optionally, the default database and language can also be specified for the new login. (The default database is the database the user is automatically connected to immediately after logging into SQL Server.) After that, the user can log into SQL Server under the new account.

DATABASE SECURITY PERMISSIONS

To grant SQL Server login access to a database using Enterprise Manager, expand a server and the folder **Databases**. Then expand the database, right-click **Users**, and click **New Database User**. In the **Database User Properties** dialog box (see Figure 19-3), select a login name and enter a user name. Optionally, you can select database role memberships (in addition to the PUBLIC role). An alternative method is to use the system procedure **sp_grantdbaccess** (see the section "Setting User Accounts" in Chapter 12).

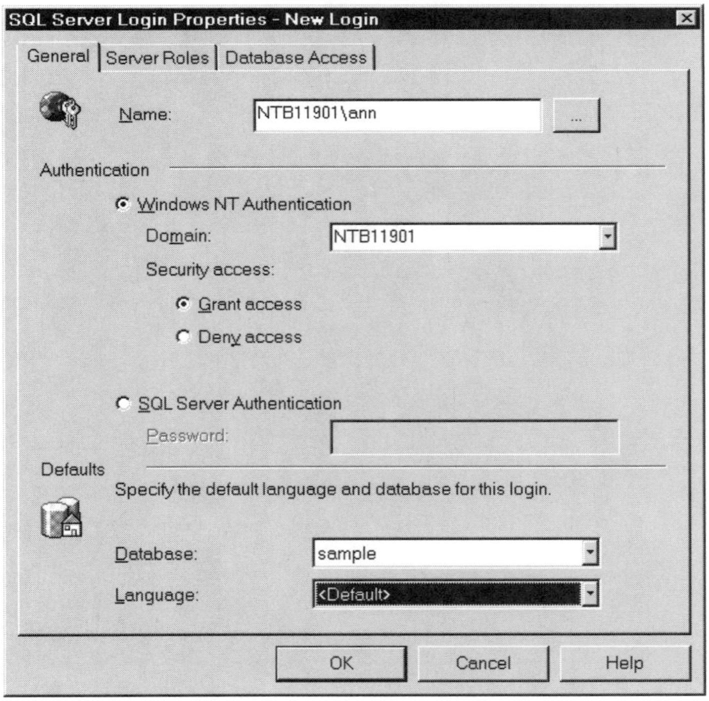

Figure 19-2. SQL Server Login Properties dialog box

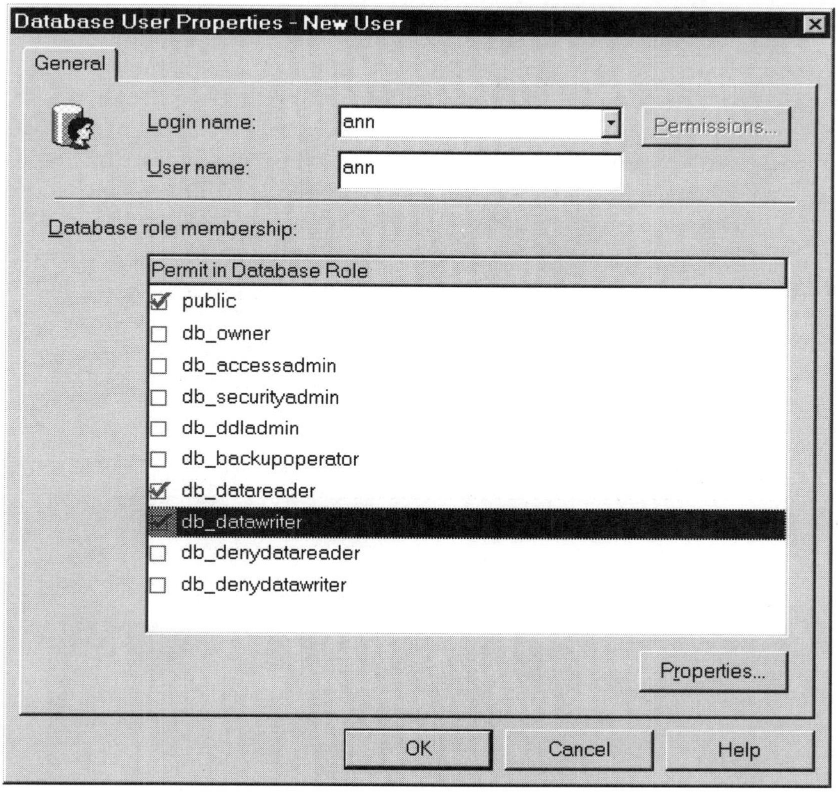

Figure 19-3. Database User Properties dialog box

Roles

A role groups database users into a single unit, providing the same permissions to all of them. The purpose of roles is to assign a name to each functional area in an organization. As employees rotate into certain positions, you simply add them as members of the role. This way, you do not have to assign new permissions to them and revoke the old ones.

There are four types of roles:

- Fixed server roles
- Fixed database roles
- User-defined roles
- Application roles

The management of these roles will be described in the following sections.

Assigning a Login Account to a Fixed Role

To assign a login account to a fixed server role using Enterprise Manager, expand a server, expand **Security**, and click **Server Roles**. In the details pane, right-click the role and then click **Properties**. On the **General** tab of the **Server Role Properties** dialog box, click **Add**. Click the login you want to add. (The alternative way is to use the system procedure **sp_addsrvrolemember**—see the section "Fixed Server Roles" in Chapter 12.)

To assign a user to a fixed database role using Enterprise Manager, expand the server and expand **Databases**. After expanding the database, click **Roles**. In the details pane, right-click the role and then click **Properties**. In the **Database Role Properties** dialog box (see Figure 19-4), click **Add** and select the user(s) to add. (An alternative method is to use the system procedure **sp_addrolemember**—see the section "Fixed Database Roles" in Chapter 12.)

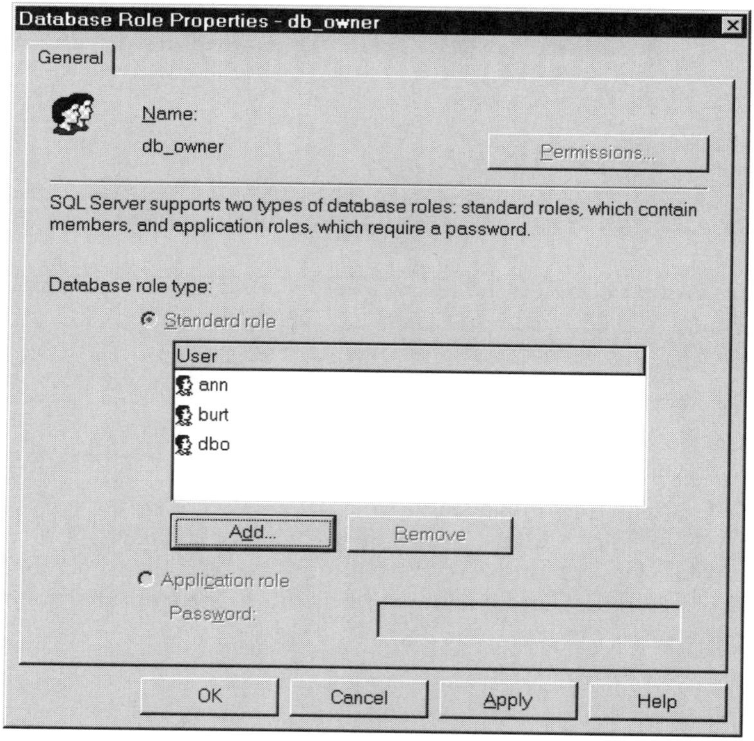

Figure 19-4. Database Role Properties dialog box

Managing User-Defined Roles

To create a user-defined role using Enterprise Manager, expand the server and expand **Databases**. After expanding the database, right-click **Roles**, then click **New Database Role**. In the **Database Role Properties – New Role** dialog box (see Figure 19-5), enter the name of the new role. Click **Add** to add members to the new role. (An alternative method is to use the system procedure **sp_addrole**—see the section "User-Defined Database Roles" in Chapter 12.)

After adding new user-defined roles, you can add users or roles to it using Enterprise Manager or the system procedure **sp_addrolemember.** To add the user or role using Enterprise Manager, expand the server and expand **Databases**. After expanding the database, click **Roles**. In the details pane, right-click the user-defined role and then click **Properties**. In the **Database Role Properties** dialog box (see Figure 19-4), under **User**, click **Add**, and click the user(s) to add.

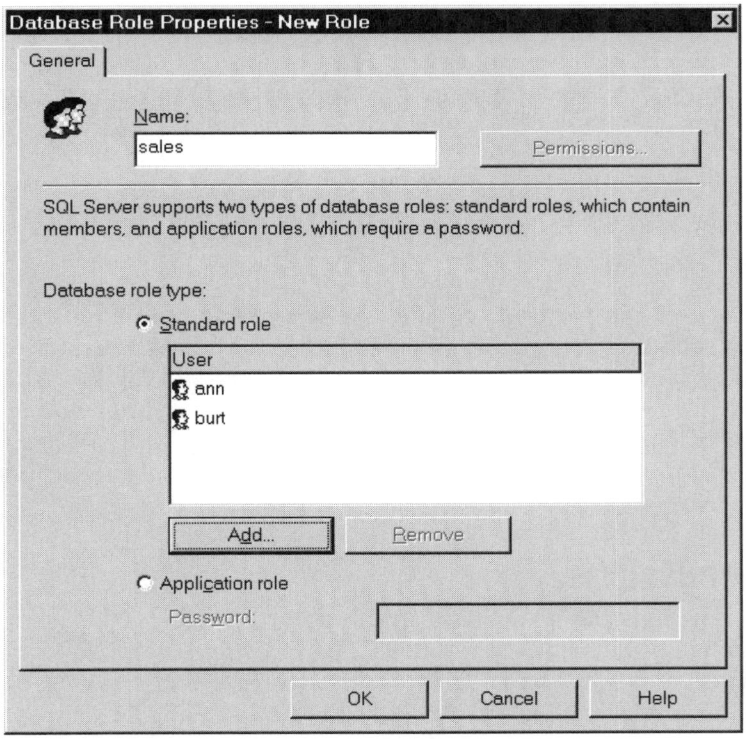

Figure 19-5. Database Role Properties – New Role dialog box

Managing Application Roles

To assign a user to an application role using Enterprise Manager, expand the server and expand **Databases**. After expanding the database, right-click **Roles**, then click **New Database Role**. In the **Database Role Properties – New Role** dialog box (see Figure 19-5), enter the name of the new role. Click **Application role** and enter the password for the new role. (An alternative method is to use the system procedure **sp_addapprole**—see the section "Application Roles" in Chapter 12.)

MANAGING PERMISSIONS

After you have created database user accounts for specific databases, you have to assign specific permissions to the security of the particular database. Depending on the application type, permissions can be grouped in either of the following:

- Statement permissions
- Object permissions

Activities concerning the creation of database objects are called *statement permissions*. On the other hand, *object permissions* apply to specific operations on database objects.

There are three permission state types:

- Granted (or positive)
- Denied (or negative)
- None

A database user can perform activities that are granted to him or her. In this case, there is a corresponding entry in the system table **sysprotects** of the database. The negative entry in the same table prevents users from performing activities. This entry overrides a permission, which was granted to a user explicitly or implicitly using a role to which the user belongs. Therefore, the user cannot perform this activity in any case. In the last case (none), the user has no explicit privileges but can perform an activity if a role to which he or she belongs has the appropriate permission.

Statement Permissions

Statement permissions can be managed using either Enterprise Manager or the Transact-SQL statements GRANT, DENY, and REVOKE. Using Enterprise Manager, expand the server and expand **Databases**. Right-click the database, and then click **Properties**. After clicking the **Permissions** tab, the **Database Properties** dialog box appears (see Figure 19-6). Check the permission for the statement you want to grant. (A "✓" specifies a granted permission, an "X" a denied permission, and blank no permission.)

The management of statement permissions using the Transact-SQL statements GRANT, DENY, and REVOKE is described in detail in Chapter 12.

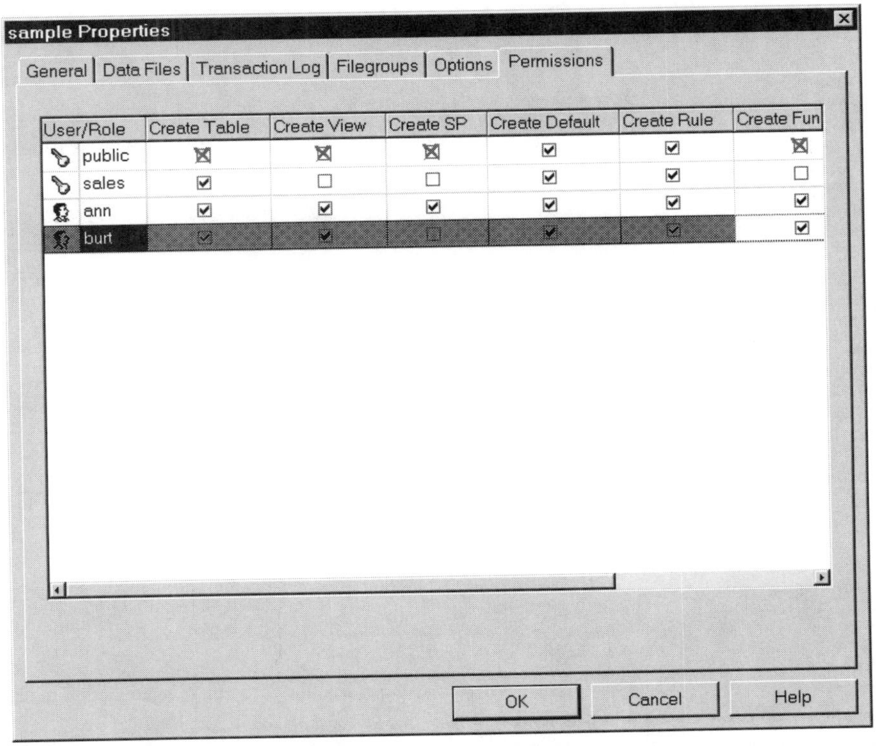

Figure 19-6. Database Properties dialog box—Permissions tab

Object Permissions

Object permissions can be managed for a single database object, or permissions on multiple objects can be managed for a single user, group, or role. This can be done using either Enterprise Manager or the Transact-SQL statements GRANT, DENY, and REVOKE.

To manage object permissions using Enterprise Manager, expand the server and expand **Databases**. Then expand the database and click **Tables**, **Views**, or **Stored Procedures**, depending on the database object for which you want to manage permissions. In the details pane, right-click the object, point to **All Tasks**, and then click **Manage Permissions**. The **Object Properties** dialog box for that object appears (see Figure 19-7). Check the option **List all users/user-defined database roles/public**, and check the permissions you want to grant.

To manage permissions on multiple objects for a single user, group, or role, expand the server and expand **Databases**. Then expand the database to which the account (user,

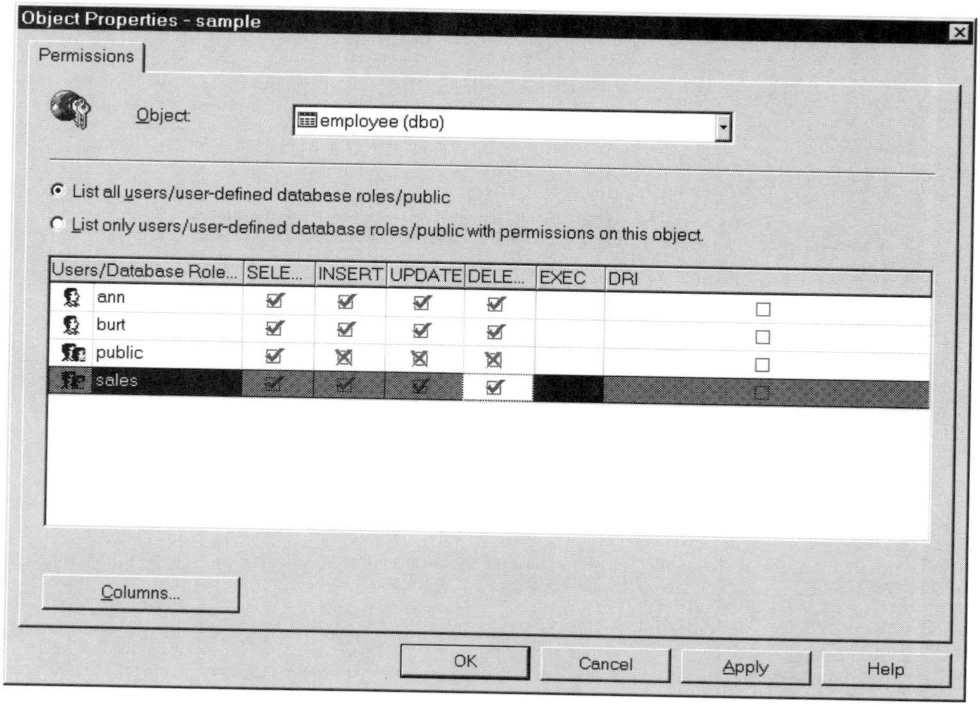

Figure 19-7. Object Properties dialog box

group, or role) belongs. Click **Users** or **Roles**, depending on the type of account you chose. In the details pane, right-click the account and then click **Properties**. After clicking **Permissions**, the **Database User/Role Properties** dialog box (see Figure 19-8) appears. (Only permissions applicable to the corresponding object are listed.) Check the permissions you want to grant for each database object. (As before, a "✓" specifies a granted permission, an "X" a denied permission, and blank no permission.)

CONCLUSION

All tasks concerning the management of SQL Server security can be done using either SQL Server Enterprise Manager or system procedures. Additionally, the Transact-SQL statements GRANT, DENY, and REVOKE allow you to manage statement and object permissions. Generally, Transact-SQL statements plus system procedures offer more possibilities for managing the security issues than Enterprise Manager.

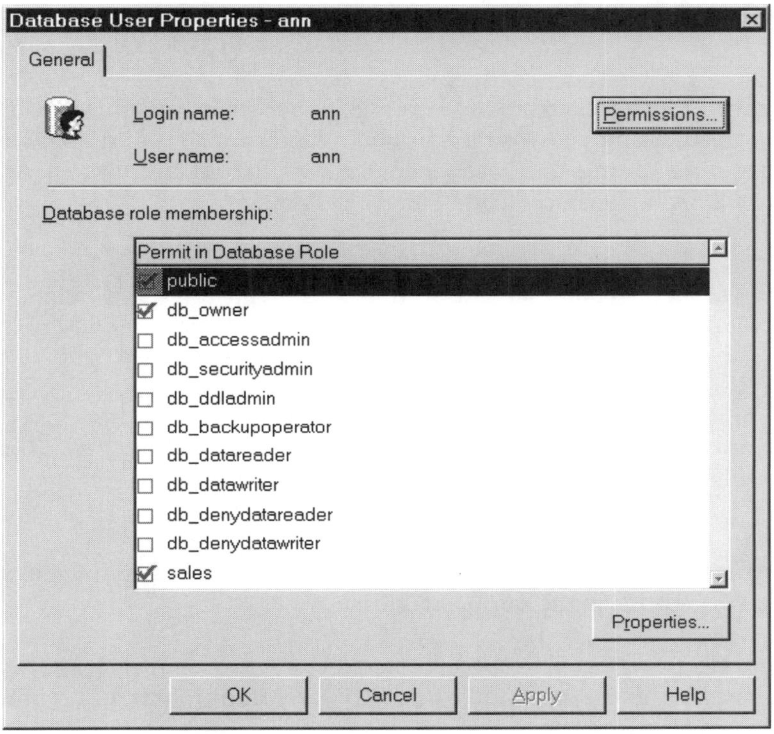

Figure 19-8. Database User Properties dialog box

Concerning security, you can use SQL Server Enterprise Manager to do the following tasks:

- Implement a security mode
- Manage SQL Server logins
- Manage statement and object permissions

Windows mode and Mixed mode authentication are implemented similarly. While Enterprise Manager manages all statement permissions for all users of a database at once, it manages object permissions either for a single database object and multiple users or vice versa.

The next chapter introduces you to how SQL Server and the system administrator can prevent the loss of data.

EXERCISES

▼ E.19.1

Using Enterprise Manager, create three new SQL Server logins called peter, paul, and mary. The corresponding passwords are "abc", "def", and "fgh", respectively. The default database is the sample database where the user should have access. After creating the logins, check their existence inside Enterprise Manager.

▼ E.19.2

Using Enterprise Manager and the sample database, create three new database names for the logins in Exercise 19.1. The new names are 's_peter', 's_paul', and 's_mary'.

▼ E.19.3

Using Enterprise Manager, create a new user-defined database role called 'managers' and add the users from Exercise 19.2 to the role. After that, display the information concerning this role and its members.

▼ E.19.4

Using Enterprise Manager, allow the user s_peter to create tables and the user s_mary to create stored procedures in the sample database.

▼ E.19.5

Is it possible to allow the user s_paul to update the columns **lname** and **fname** of the **employee** table using the Enterprise Manager?

▼ E.19.6

Using the Enterprise Manager, allow the user-defined-role 'managers' to insert new rows into the **projects** table.

CHAPTER 20

Backup and Recovery

This chapter covers two of the most important tasks concerning system administration: backup and recovery. The introduction describes the different reasons for software and hardware failures and explains the transaction log—a vital part of the backup and recovery processes. Then the various forms of backups are discussed, followed by procedures for restoring databases (including system databases).

INTRODUCTION

Backup determines how a copy of the database(s) and/or transaction logs is made and which media are used for this process. All these precautions have to be taken to prevent data loss. You can lose data as a result of different hardware or software errors, which are discussed next. Knowing something about the transaction log will help you understand how SQL Server (and all other DBMSs) keep information that is needed to recover data from failures.

Software and Hardware Failures

The reasons for data loss can be divided into five main groups:

- Program errors
- Administrator (human) errors
- Computer failures (system crash)
- Disk failures
- Catastrophes (fire, earthquake) or theft

During execution of a program, conditions may arise that abnormally terminate the program. Such program errors concern only the database application and usually have no impact on the entire database system. As these errors are based on faulty program logic, the database system cannot recover in such situations. The recovery should therefore be done by the programmer, who has to handle such exceptions using the COMMIT and ROLLBACK statements. (Both of these Transact-SQL statements are described in Chapter 14.)

Another source of data loss is human error. Users with sufficient permissions, or the database administrator, may accidentally lose or corrupt data (people have been known to drop the wrong table, update or delete data incorrectly, etc.). Of course, we would prefer that this never happen, and we can establish practices that make it unlikely that production data is compromised in this way, but we have to recognize that people make mistakes, and data can be affected. The best we can do is try to avoid it, and be prepared to recover when it happens.

A computer failure specifies different hardware or software errors. A hardware crash is an example of a system failure. In this case, the contents of the computer's main memory may be lost. A disk failure occurs either when a read/write head of the disk crashes or when the I/O system discovers corrupted disk blocks during I/O operations.

In the case of catastrophes or theft, the system must keep enough information to recover from the failure. This is normally done by means of media that offer the needed recovery information on a piece of hardware that has not been damaged by the failure.

Transaction Log

SQL Server keeps an image of the old contents of the record of each row that has been changed during a transaction. (A transaction specifies a sequence of Transact-SQL statements that build a logical unit; see also Chapter 14.) This is necessary in case an error occurs later during the execution of the transaction and all executed statements inside the transaction have to be rolled back. As soon as SQL Server detects such a situation, it uses the stored records to bring the database back to the consistent state it was in before the transaction was started.

SQL Server keeps all those records in one or more system files, called the transaction log. In particular, this log contains the "before" and "after" values of each changed column during transactions. The transaction log can then be used to perform automatic recovery or a restore process. (The notion of automatic recovery is described later in this chapter.) After a failure, SQL Server uses stored values from the transaction log (called *before images*) to restore all pages on the disk to their previous consistent state. In the case of a restore, the transaction log is always used together with a database backup copy to recover the database. The transaction log is generally needed to prevent a loss of all changes that have been executed since the last database backup. (The use of transaction logs, together with database backups, is explained further in "Transaction Log Backup" later in this chapter.)

BACKUP

SQL Server provides static as well as dynamic backup. (Dynamic backup means that a database backup can be performed while users are working on data.) In contrast to some other DBMSs, which back up all databases together, SQL Server does the backup of each database separately. This method increases security when it comes time to restore each database, because a restoration of each database separately is more secure than restoring all databases at once.

SQL Server provides four different backup methods:

- Full database backup
- Differential database backup
- Transaction log backup
- Database file (or file group) backup

Full Database Backup

A full database backup captures the state of the database at the time the backup is started. During the full database backup, the system copies the data as well as the schema of all tables of the database and the corresponding file structures. If the full database backup is executed dynamically, SQL Server records any activity that took place during the backup. Therefore, even all uncommitted transactions in the transaction log are written to the backup media.

Differential Backup

A differential backup is a new feature since SQL Server 7. Using this feature, only the parts of the database that have changed since the last full database backup are read and then written to the copy. (As in the full database backup, any activity that took place during the differential backup is backed up, too.) The advantage of a differential backup is speed. It minimizes the time required to back up a database, because the amount of data to be backed up is considerably smaller than in the case of the full backup. (Remember that a full database backup includes a copy of all database pages.)

Transaction Log Backup

A transaction log backup considers only the changes recorded in the log. This form of backup is therefore not based on physical parts (pages) of the database, but on logical operations—that is, changes executed using the DML statements INSERT, UPDATE, and DELETE. Again, because the amount of data is smaller, this process can be performed significantly quicker than the full database backup and quicker than a differential backup.

NOTE: It does not make sense to back up a transaction log unless a full database backup is performed at least once!

There are two main reasons to perform the transaction log backup: first, to store the data that has changed since the last transaction log backup or database backup on a secure medium; second (and more importantly), to properly close the transaction log up to the beginning of the active portion of it. (The active portion of the transaction log contains all uncommitted transactions.)

Using the full database backup and the valid chain of all closed transaction logs, it is possible to propagate a database copy on a different computer. This database copy can then be used to replace the original database in case of a failure. (The same scenario can be established using a full database backup and the last differential backup.)

SQL Server does not allow you to store the transaction log in the same file in which the database is stored. One reason for this is that if the file is damaged, the use of the transaction log to restore all changes since the last backup will not be possible.

Using a transaction log to record changes in the database is a common feature used by nearly all existing relational DBMSs. Nevertheless, situations may arise when it becomes helpful to switch this feature off. For example, the execution of a heavy load can last for hours. Such a program runs much faster when the logging is switched off. On the other hand, switching off the logging process is dangerous, as it destroys the valid chain of transaction logs. To ensure the database recovery, it is strongly recommended that you perform full database backup after the successful end of the load.

One of the most common system failures occurs because the transaction log is filled up. Be aware that the use of a transaction log in itself may cause a complete standstill of the system. If the storage used for the transaction log fills up to 100 percent, SQL Server must stop all running transactions until the transaction log storage is freed again. This problem can only be avoided by making frequent backups of the transaction log: each time you close a portion of the actual transaction log and store it to a different storage media, this portion of the log becomes reusable, and SQL Server thus regains disk space.

NOTE: A differential backup and a transaction log backup both minimize the time required to back up the database. But there is one significant difference between them: the transaction log backup contains all changes of a row that has been modified several times since the last backup, while a differential backup contains only the last modification of that row.

Some differences between transaction log backups and differential backups are worth noting. The benefit of differential backups is that you save time in the restore process, because to recover a database completely, you need a full database backup and only the *latest* differential backup. If you use transaction logs for the same scenario, you have to apply the full database backup and *all* existing transaction logs to bring the database to a consistent state. A disadvantage of differential backups is that you cannot use them to recover data to a specific point in time because they do not store intermediate changes to the database. (See the description of the STOPAT option of the RESTORE LOG statement later in this chapter.)

NOTE: The time of finishing is significant for backup. This means that the process of backing a database is consistent with the end of the backup.

Database File Backup

Database file backup allows you to back up specific database files (or file groups) instead of the entire database. In this case, SQL Server backs up only files you specify. Individual files (or file groups) can be restored from database backup, allowing recovery from a failure that affects only a small subset of the database files. Individual files or file groups can be restored from either a database backup or a file group backup. This means that you can use database and transaction log backups as your backup procedure, and still be able to restore individual files (or file groups) from the database backup.

NOTE: The database file backup is recommended only when a database that should be backed up is very large and there is not enough time to perform a full database backup.

PERFORMING BACKUP

You can perform backup operations using the following:

- SQL Server Enterprise Manager
- Create Backup Wizard
- Transact-SQL statements

Each of these backup methods is described in the following sections.

Backup Using Enterprise Manager

Before a database or transaction log backup can be done, it is necessary to specify (or create) backup devices. Enterprise Manager allows you to create disk devices and tape devices in a similar manner. In both cases, expand the server, click **Management**, right-click **Backup**, and choose **New Backup Device**. In the **Backup Device Properties** dialog box (see Figure 20-1), either enter the name of the disk device (if you clicked **File name**) or the name of the tape device (if you clicked **Tape drive name**). In the former case, you can click the button with the **...** on the right side of the field to display existing backup device locations. In the latter case, if no tape devices are listed, then no tape devices exist on the local computer.

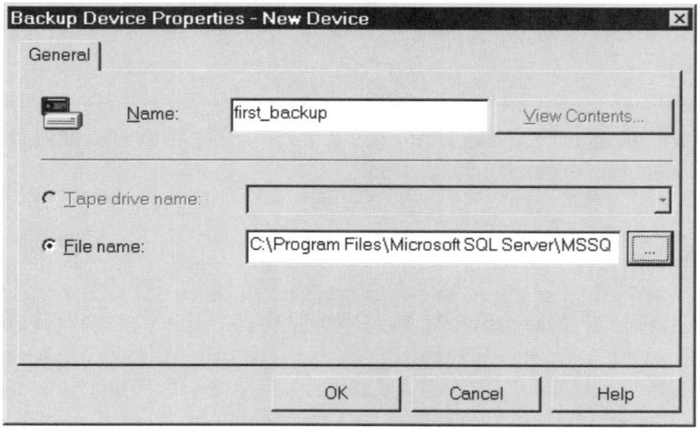

Figure 20-1. Backup Device Properties – New Device dialog box

After you specify backup devices, a database backup can be done. Expand the server, choose **Databases**, and right-click the database. After pointing to **All Tasks**, choose **Backup Database**. The **SQL Server Backup** dialog box appears (see Figure 20-2). On the **General** tab of the dialog box, enter the backup set name in the **Name** field and, in the **Description** field, a description of this set. For the full database backup, click **Database – complete**.

In the **Destination** frame, select an existing device by clicking on the **Add** button. (The **Remove** button allows you to remove one or more backup devices from the list of devices to be used.) To append to an existing backup on the selected device, check the **Append to media** check box under the **Destination** frame. The **Overwrite existing media** check box in the same frame overwrites any existing backups on the selected backup device. In the **Schedule** frame, you can optionally determine at what time the backup operation will be done for later or periodic execution. (For a description of creating a schedule, see the following section.)

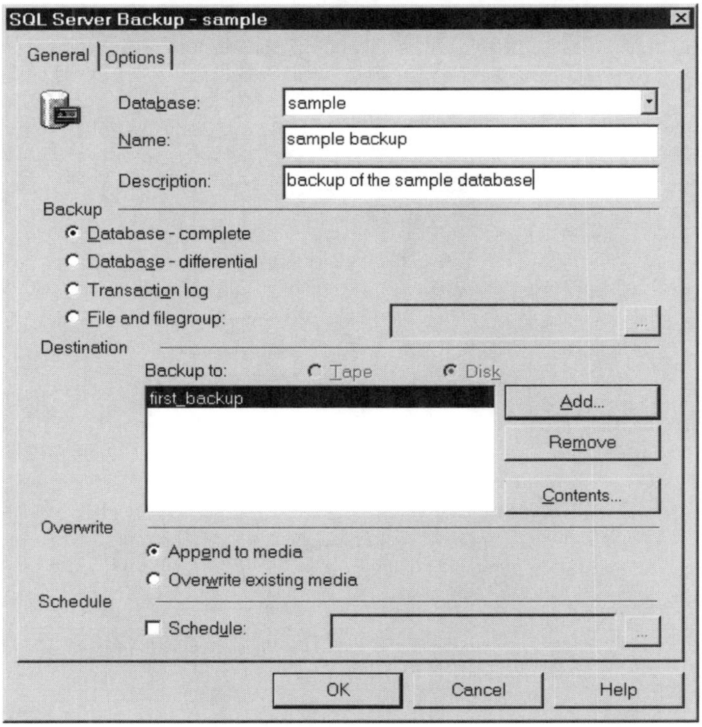

Figure 20-2. SQL Server Backup dialog box—General tab

For verification of the database backup, choose the **Options** tab of the **SQL Server Backup** dialog box (see Figure 20-3) and then click **Verify backup upon completion**. On the **Options** tab, you can also initialize backup media by clicking **Initialize and label media** and then entering the media set name and description.

Follow the same steps for creation and verification of a differential database backup or transaction log backup except that **Database – differential or Transaction log** must be clicked (on the **General** tab).

After all options have been selected, click the **OK** button. The database or the transaction log is then backed up. The name, physical location, and the type of the backup devices can be shown by selecting the server and clicking the **Backup** folder.

Scheduling Backups with Enterprise Manager

A well-planned timetable for the scheduling of backup operations will help you avoid system shortages when users are working. For example, dynamic backup is not recommended unless there are no times when users are not using the database system. Enter-

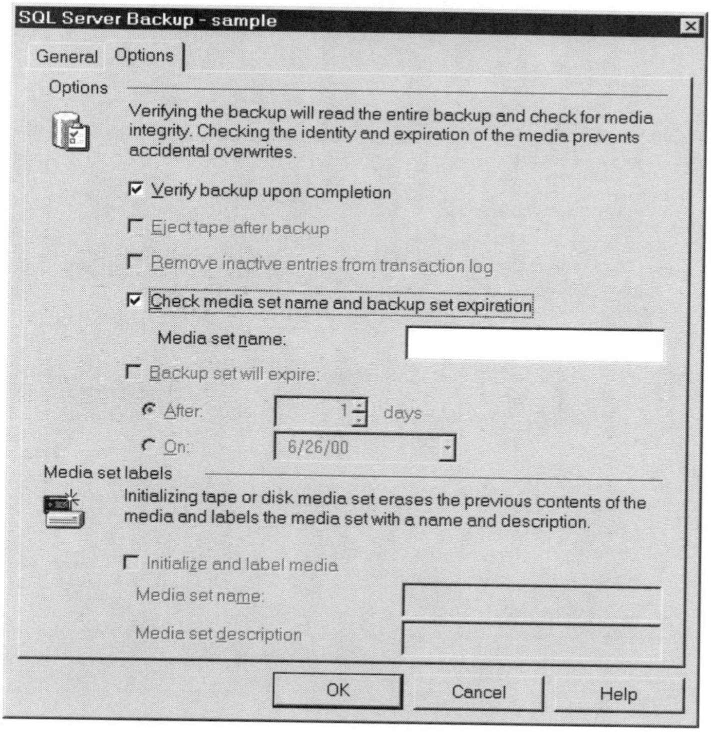

Figure 20-3. SQL Server Backup dialog box—Options tab

prise Manager supports this planning by offering an easy-to-use graphical interface for scheduling backups.

The backup operation can be executed at once or planned for later periodic execution. If the **Schedule** check box in the **SQL Server Backup** dialog box is checked, the schedule of the backup operation will be specified. SQL Server offers the default period for the database or transaction log backup (once weekly on Sunday 0:00), but this default value can be overwritten by clicking **...** on the right side of the field. In this case, the **Edit Schedule** dialog box (see Figure 20-4) appears.

First, you have to choose the schedule name. Always choose a descriptive name for the scheduled job. Using a descriptive name allows you to recognize the job easily later in the event log of Windows NT/2000 or error log of SQL Server (see Chapter 23).

NOTE: To schedule backups, the SQL Server Agent service must be started. This service can be started manually or automatically (see Chapter 16).

In the **Schedule type** frame, you have four options for when a backup should occur:

- Start automatically when SQL Server Agent starts
- Start whenever the CPU(s) become idle
- One time
- Recurring

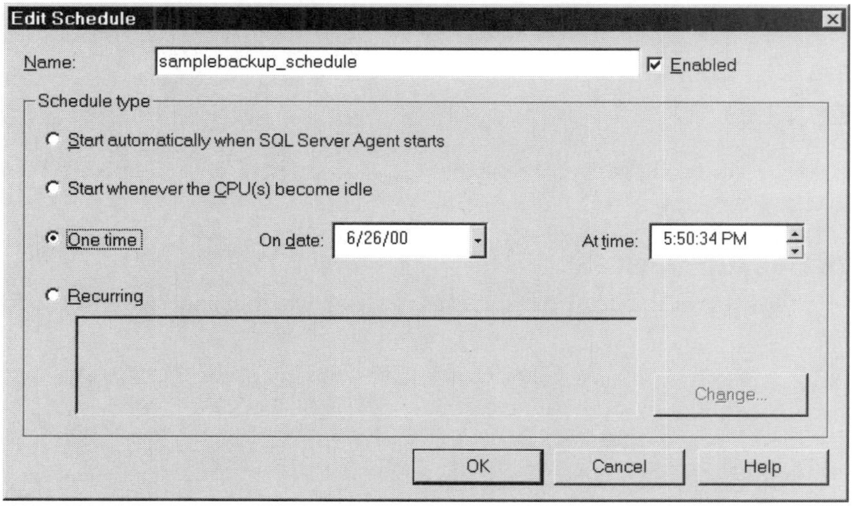

Figure 20-4. Edit Schedule dialog box

In the first two cases, SQL Server starts the backups at irregular time intervals. ("Whenever CPU(s) become idle" means that the database activity is low. In this case, only a few database operations interfere with the backup process.)

For the task to occur one time, check the **One time** check box and then set the date and time the backup process should be executed. (The default value is the current date and time.) The **Recurring** check box (see Figure 20-5) allows you to schedule the backup process periodically (daily, weekly, monthly, etc.). For more information on periodic execution of the backup process, see Chapter 22.

Create Backup Wizard

The Create Backup Wizard offers you an easy way to perform the database and transaction log backup. Before you start the wizard, expand the server for the database you want to back up. On the **Tools** menu of Enterprise Manager, click **Wizards,** choose **Management**, and double-click **Backup Wizard**. With the wizard, you can perform the following steps:

1. Specify what type of backup to perform.
2. Specify what backup devices (tape, disk, Named Pipes) to use when backing up the database or the transaction log.
3. Choose to append or overwrite the backup media.
4. Verify the backup.

Backup Using Transact-SQL Statements

All types of backup operations can be executed using two Transact-SQL statements:

- BACKUP DATABASE
- BACKUP LOG

Before we describe these two Transact-SQL statements, we will specify the existing types of backup devices.

Types of Backup Devices

SQL Server allows you to back up databases, transaction logs, and files to the following backup devices:

- Disk
- Tape
- Named Pipe

Disk files are the most common media used for storing backups. Disk backup devices can be located on a server's local hard disk or on a remote disk on a shared network re-

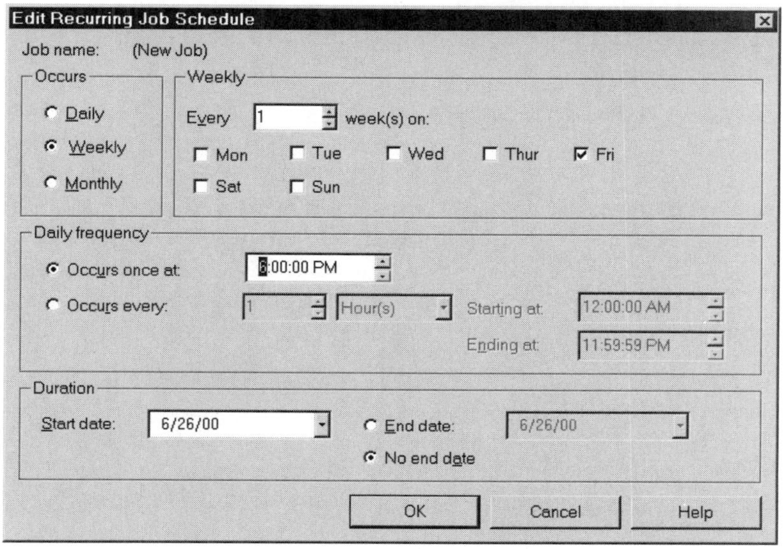

Figure 20-5. Edit Recurring Job Schedule dialog box

source. SQL Server allows you to append a new backup to a file that already contains backups from the same or different databases. By appending a new backup set to existing media, the previous contents of the media remain intact, and the new backup is written after the end of the last backup on the media. By default, SQL Server always appends new backups to disk files.

NOTE: Do not back up to a file on the same physical disk where the database or its transaction log is stored! If the disk with the database crashes, the backup that is stored on the same disk will be also damaged.

Tape backup devices are generally used in the same way as disk devices. However, when you back up to a tape, the tape drive must be attached locally to SQL Server. The advantage of tape devices in relation to disk devices is their simple administration and operation.

SQL Server provides also the ability to backup to a Named Pipe in order to allow users to take advantage of the backup and restore features of third-party software packages. To use a Named Pipe backup device, you specify the name of the Named Pipe that will be used by a client application.

BACKUP DATABASE Statement

The BACKUP DATABASE statement is used to perform a full database backup or a differential database backup. This statement has the following syntax:

```
BACKUP DATABASE {db_name | @variable} TO device_list
  [WITH option_list]
```

db_name is the name of the database that should be backed up. (The name of the database can also be supplied using a variable **@variable**.) **device_list** specifies one or more device names, where the database backup will be stored. **device_list** can be a list of names of disk files, tapes, or Named Pipe. **option_list** comprises several options that can be specified for the different backup forms. The most important options are the following:

- SKIP/NOSKIP
- INIT/NOINIT
- FORMAT
- DIFFERENTIAL
- UNLOAD/NOUNLOAD

The SKIP option disables the backup set expiration and name checking, which is usually performed by the BACKUP statement to prevent overwrites of backup sets. The NOSKIP option, which is a default, instructs the BACKUP statement to check the expiration date and name of all backup sets before allowing them to be overwritten.

The INIT option is used to overwrite any existing data on the backup media. This option does not overwrite the media header, if one exists. If there is a backup that has not yet expired, the backup operation fails. In this case, use the combination of SKIP and INIT options to overwrite the backup device. The NOINIT option, which is a default, appends a backup to existing backups on the media.

The FORMAT option is used to write a header on all of the files (or tape volumes) that are used for a backup. Therefore, use this option to initialize a backup medium. When you use the FORMAT option to back up to a tape device, the INIT option and the SKIP option are implied. Similarly, the INIT option is implied if the FORMAT option is specified for a file device. The DIFFERENTIAL option specifies a differential database backup. If this option is omitted, a full database backup will be performed.

The UNLOAD and NOUNLOAD options are performed only if the backup medium is a tape device. The UNLOAD option, which is the default, specifies that the tape is automatically rewound and unloaded from the tape device after the backup is completed. Use the NOUNLOAD option if SQL Server should not rewind (and unload) the tape from the tape device automatically.

BACKUP LOG Statement

The BACKUP LOG statement is used to perform a backup of the transaction log. This statement has the following syntax:

```
BACKUP LOG {db_name | @variable}
  [WITH {NO_LOG | TRUNCATE_ONLY}]
  TO device_list
  [WITH option_list]
```

db_name, **@variable**, and **device_list** have the same meanings as the parameters with the same names in the BACKUP DATABASE statement. **option_list** has the same options as the BACKUP DATABASE statement and also supports the additional option NO_TRUNCATE. Therefore, the only difference between these two statements is in the existence of three additional options with the BACKUP LOG statement that specify the different methods of backing up a transaction:

- NO_TRUNCATE
- NO_LOG
- TRUNCATE_ONLY

You should use the NO_TRUNCATE option if you want to back up the transaction log without truncating it—that is, this option does not clear the committed transactions in the log. After the execution of this option, SQL Server writes all recent database activities in the transaction log. Therefore, the NO_TRUNCATE option allows you to recover data right up to the point of the database failure.

NOTE: Use the NO_TRUNCATE option if the database files are corrupted or lost. In that case, restore the database backup first and restore the transaction log backup as the last backup in the recovery process.

In contrast to the NO_TRUNCATE option, the other two options remove the inactive part of the log without making a backup copy of it. Therefore, using the options TRUNCATE_ONLY and NO_LOG, you do not have to specify the list of devices because the transaction log backup is not saved.

The TRUNCATE_ONLY option removes the inactive part of the transaction log without making a backup copy of it. TRUNCATE_ONLY is used to save space in the transaction log file(s) (usually because the files or the disk containing the transaction log is full). It clears information from the log that would be crucial for full recovery, so it should be immediately followed by a full database backup. Truncating logging is itself a logged operation and is, in the case of the TRUNCATE_ONLY option, always recorded in the log.

The NO_LOG option removes the inactive part of the transaction log exactly as the TRUNCATE_ONLY option does. In contrast to the TRUNCATE_ONLY option, the NO_LOG option does not record the process of truncating logging in the log.

NOTE: Perform the full database backup immediately after the use of the TRUNCATE_ONLY or NO_LOG option, because you cannot recover the changes that have been truncated by these two options.

Each of these three options has a different effect on the recovery process of a database. It is important for you to understand when each of these three options should be used in the backup process.

After the last full database backup of your database, you will usually make several transaction log backups. These backups build a logical chain, which can be used to restore the database to the last consistent state it was in before the last transaction log was created. This is only possible if there are no "gaps" produced by the administrator's activities. The gaps arise if you use the TRUNCATE_ONLY or NO_LOG options. Therefore, the valid chain of transaction logs can only spring up if you use the NO_TRUNCATE option.

Nevertheless, situations may arise in which it is not possible to maintain the valid chain of transaction logs for a recovery. This will happen, for example, when your database crashes, leaving the original database in an invalid state. In this case, use the TRUNCATE_ONLY or NO_LOG option. One of these invalid states results from the transaction log being full. In such a case, you can use only the NO_LOG option because it does not write any records in the transaction log. (In this case, even the process of truncating logging is not recorded in the log.)

In addition to the three options in the BACKUP LOG statement, SQL Server offers another feature to truncate the inactive portion of the transaction log. Set the **trunc. log on ckpt** database option of the system procedure **sp_dboption** to true if you want to truncate the transaction log automatically when a checkpoint occurs. In this case, SQL Server does not save the changes that are made to the database in the transaction log. Therefore, you cannot use the transaction log as part of the recovery process.

Which Databases to Back Up?

The following databases should be backed up regularly:

- The **master** database
- All production databases
- The **msdb** database

Back Up master Database

The **master** database is the most important database of the SQL Server system because it contains information about all the databases in the system. Therefore, the **master** database should be backed up on a regular basis. Additionally, you should back up the **master** database anytime certain statements and stored procedures are executed, because SQL Server modifies the **master** database automatically.

NOTE: You can perform full database backups of the **master** database only. (SQL Server does not support differential, transaction log, and file backups for the **master** database.)

Many activities cause the modification of the **master** database. Some of them are listed below:

- The creation, alteration, and removal of a database
- The alteration of the transaction log
- The addition or removal of servers using the **sp_addserver** and **sp_dropserver** system procedures

NOTE: Without a backup of the **master** database, you must completely rebuild all system databases, because if the **master** database is damaged, all references to the existing user-defined databases are lost. In this case invoke the **rebuildm** utility, which rebuilds all system databases as a unit.

Back Up Production Databases

Each production database should be backed up on a regular basis. Additionally, you should back up any production database when the following activities are executed:

- After creating it
- After creating indices
- After clearing the transaction log
- After performing nonlogged operations

Always make a full database backup after it has been created in case a failure occurs between the creation of the database and the first regular database backup. Remember that backups of the transaction log cannot be applied without a full database backup.

Backing up the database after creation of one or more indices saves time during the restore process, because the index structures are backed up together with the data. Backing up the transaction log after creation of indices does not save time during the restore process at all, because the transaction log only records the fact that an index was created (and does not record the modified index structure).

Backing up the database after clearing the transaction log is necessary because the transaction log no longer contains a record of database activity, which is used to recover the database. (See the description of the NO_LOG and TRUNCATE_ONLY options at the beginning of this chapter.)

All operations that are not recorded to the transaction log are called nonlogged operations. Therefore, all changes made by these operations cannot be restored during the recovery process. The following Transact-SQL statements and utilities do not record changes in the transaction log:

- The WRITETEXT and UPDATETEXT statements without WITH LOG (see Chapter 8)
- The SELECT INTO statement
- The bulk copy program (see the description of the **bcp** utility in Chapter 21)

NOTE: Since SQL Server 2000, some physical file operations, such as adding and deleting files from file groups, are logged and can be recovered. Therefore, it is no longer necessary to perform a backup of a database after such operations.

Back Up msdb Database

The **msdb** database is used for storing alerts, jobs, and recording operators that are subsequently used by the SQL Server Agent service. Therefore, any modification of these operators changes the **msdb** database. Back up the **msdb** database after each modification of it. (If you do not have a current backup of the **msdb** database when a failure occurs, you can rebuild all of the system databases using the **rebuildm** utility and subsequently re-create each job, alert, and operator.)

NOTE: Another way to create the new (and empty) **msdb** database is by executing the instmsdb.sql script from the \INSTALL directory.

Minimizing System Downtime

You can use various strategies to avoid data loss and downtime due to disk failures. Two general strategies supported by SQL Server are discussed here:

- Standby server
- RAID technology

NOTE: Versions prior to SQL Server 7 supported a third strategy for preventing data loss: SQL Server mirroring. SQL Server mirroring is not supported any more, because the mirroring feature of Windows NT/2000 can be used instead. (The operating system mirroring corresponds to RAID 1 technology; see the discussion of RAID a bit later in this chapter.)

Using a Standby Server

A standby server is just what its name implies—another server that is standing by in case something happens to the production server (also called the primary server). The standby server also runs and contains files, databases (system and user-defined), and user accounts identical to those on the production server.

A standby server is implemented by initially restoring a full database backup of the database and applying transaction log backups to keep the database on the standby server synchronized with the production server. To set up a standby server, set the **read only** database option to true. This option prevents users from performing any write operations in the database.

The general steps to use a copy of a production database are as follows:

- Restore the production database using the RESTORE DATABASE statement with the STANDBY clause.
- Apply each transaction log to the standby server using the RESTORE LOG statement with the STANDBY clause.
- When applying the final transaction log backup, use the RESTORE LOG statement with the RECOVERY clause. (This final statement recovers the database without creating a file with before images, making the database available for write operations, too.)

After the restoration of the database and transaction logs, users can work with an exact copy of the production database. Only the noncommitted transactions at the time of failure will be permanently lost.

NOTE: In the event of failure of the production server, user processes are not automatically brought to the standby server. Additionally, all user processes need to restart any tasks with the uncommitted transactions due to the failure of the production server.

Log Shipping

Log shipping is a new feature of SQL Server 2000 that allows the transaction logs from one database to be constantly sent and used by another database. This allows you to have a warm standby server and also provides a way to offload data from the source machine to read-only destination computers.

NOTE: Log shipping is available only with the Enterprise Edition of SQL Server.

You can use the Database Maintenance Plan Wizard to set up log shipping. The first step is to select databases on the destination servers. If the databases do not exist, the wizard allows you to create them. In the second step—initialization of the destination databases—you specify whether the full database backup or the most recent backup file is used. Finally, you set a load delay (in minutes) that defines how old a log must be before it is loaded. That way, you can prevent the immediate shipping of possible corrupted log of the source database.

NOTE: The user setting up log shipping must be a member of the **sysadmin** server role, in order to have permission to modify the database to log ship.

RAID

RAID (redundant array of inexpensive disks) is a special disk configuration in which multiple disk drives build a single logical striped drive. Striping the drives allows files to span multiple disk devices. RAID technology provides improved reliability at the cost of performance decrease. Generally, there are six RAID levels: 0 through 5.

RAID can be hardware- or software-based. Hardware-based RAID is more costly (because you have to buy additional disk controllers), but usually performs better. Software-based RAID can be supported either by the operating system or by the database system itself. SQL Server does not support software-based RAID. (Versions previous to SQL Server 7 supported RAID 1.) Windows NT/2000 provides RAID levels 0, 1, and 5. The RAID technology has impacts on the following features:

- Fault tolerance
- Performance

The benefits and disadvantages of each RAID level in relation to these two features will be explained below.

Windows NT-Based RAID RAID provides protection from hard disk failure and accompanying data loss with three methods: disk striping, mirroring, and parity. These three methods correspond to RAID levels 0, 1, and 5, respectively. RAID 0 specifies disk striping without parity. Using RAID 0, the data is written across several disk drives in order to allow data access more readily and all read and write operations can be speeded up. For this reason, RAID 0 is the fastest RAID configuration. The disadvantage of disk striping is that it does not offer fault tolerance at all. This means if one disk fails, all the data on that array become inaccessible.

Mirroring is the special form of disk striping, which uses the space on a disk drive to maintain a duplicate copy of some files. Therefore RAID 1, which specifies disk mirroring, protects data against media failure by maintaining a copy of the database (or a part of it) on another disk. If there is a drive loss with mirroring in place, the files for the lost drive can be rebuilt by replacing the failed drive and rebuilding the damaged files. The hardware configurations of mirroring are more expensive, but provide additional speed. The advantage of the Windows NT/2000 solution for mirroring is that it can be configured to mirror disk partitions, while the hardware solutions are usually implemented on the entire disk.

In contrast to RAID 0, RAID 1 is much slower, but the reliability is higher. Also, RAID 1 costs much more than RAID 0, since each mirrored disk drive must be doubled. It can sustain at least one failed drive and may be able to survive failure of up to half of the drives in the set of the mirrored disks without forcing the system administrator to shut down the server and recover from file backup. (RAID 1 is the best-performing RAID option when fault tolerance is required.)

Mirroring also has performance impacts in relation to read and write operations. When mirroring is used, write operations decrease performance, because each such operation costs two disk I/O operations, once to the original and once to the mirrored disk drive. On the other hand, mirroring increases performance of read operations, because

SQL Server will be able to read from either disk drive, depending on which one is least busy at the time.

Parity (i.e., RAID level 5) is implemented by calculating recovery information about data written to disk and writing this parity information on the other drives that form the RAID array. If a drive fails, a new drive is inserted into the RAID array and the data on that failed drive is recovered by taking the recovery information (parity) written on the other drives and using this information to regenerate the data from the failed drive.

The advantage of parity is that you need one additional disk drive to protect any number of existing disk drives. The disadvantages of parity concern performance and fault tolerance. Due to the additional costs associated with calculating and writing parity, additional disk I/O operations are required. (Read I/O operation costs are the same for mirroring and parity.) Also, using parity, you can sustain only one failed drive before the array must be taken offline and recovery from backup media must be performed. Because disk striping with parity requires additional costs associated with calculating and writing parity, RAID 5 requires four disk I/O operations, where RAID 0 requires only one operation and RAID 1 two. (Read I/O operations costs are the same for RAID 1 and RAID 5.)

RECOVERY

Whenever a transaction is submitted for execution, SQL Server is responsible either for executing the transaction completely and recording its changes permanently in the database or for guaranteeing that the transaction has no effect at all on the database. This approach ensures that the database is consistent in case of a failure, because failures do not damage the database itself, but instead affect transactions that are in progress at the time of the failure. SQL Server supports both automatic and manual recovery.

Automatic Recovery

Automatic recovery is a fault-tolerant feature that SQL Server executes every time it is restarted after a failure or shutdown. The automatic recovery process checks to see if the restoration of databases is necessary. If it is, each database is returned to its last consistent state using the transaction log.

SQL Server examines the transaction log from the last checkpoint to the point at which the system failed or was shut down. (A *checkpoint* is the most recent point at which all data changes are written permanently to the database from memory. Therefore, a checkpoint ensures the physical consistency of the data.) The transaction log contains committed transactions (transactions that are successfully executed, but their changes have not yet been written to the database) and uncommitted transactions (transactions that are not successfully executed before a shutdown or failure occurred). SQL Server rolls forward all committed transactions, thus making permanent changes to the database, and undoes the part of the uncommitted transactions that occurred before the checkpoint.

SQL Server first performs the automatic recovery of the **master** database, followed by the recovery of all other system databases. Then, all user-defined databases are recovered.

Manual Recovery

A manual recovery of a database specifies the application of the backup of your database and subsequent application of all transaction logs in the sequence of their creation. After this, the database is in the same (consistent) state as it was at the point when the transaction log was backed up for the last time.

When you recover a database using a full database backup, SQL Server first re-creates all database files and places them in the corresponding physical locations. After that, the system re-creates all database objects.

In contrast to the backup process, which can be executed dynamically, the recovery of a database is a static process. This means only a single member of the **sysadmin** or **db_owner** role can restore backups of the database.

Is My Backup Set Ready for Recovery?

After executing the BACKUP statement, the selected device (tape, disk, or Named Pipes) contains all data of the object you chose to back up. The stored data is called a *backup set*. Before you start a recovery process, you should be sure that

- The backup set contains the data you want to restore.
- The backup set is usable.

SQL Server supports four Transact-SQL statements that allow you to get the answers to the two questions formulated above. These are:

- RESTORE LABELONLY
- RESTORE HEADERONLY
- RESTORE FILELISTONLY
- RESTORE VERIFYONLY

RESTORE LABELONLY This statement is used to display the header information of the media (tape) used for a backup process. The output of the RESTORE LABELONLY statement is a single row that contains the summary of the header information (name of the media, the description of the backup process, and the date of a backup process). The syntax of this statement is:

```
RESTORE LABELONLY
    FROM device_name
    [WITH {UNLOAD | NOUNLOAD}]
```

device_name is the name of either a specific backup device or a variable that is used as the placeholder for the backup device. The UNLOAD option specifies that the tape device is automatically rewound and unloaded at the end of the recovery process. The other option—NOUNLOAD—leaves the tape device unwound after the recovery process.

NOTE: The RESTORE LABELONLY reads just the header file, so use this statement if you want to get a quick look what your backup media contains.

RESTORE HEADERONLY The former statement—RESTORE LABELONLY—gives you the concise information concerning the header file of your backup device. If you want to get the information concerning backups that are stored on a backup device, you should use the RESTORE HEADERONLY statement. This statement displays a one-line summary for each backup on a backup device. In contrast to the RESTORE LABELONLY statement, the RESTORE HEADERONLY statement can be time-consuming if the device contains several backups.

NOTE: This statement has the same options as the RESTORE LABELONLY statement.

RESTORE FILELISTONLY The RESTORE FILELISTONLY statement returns a result set with a list of the database and log files contained in the backup set. You can display the information concerning only one backup set at a time. For this reason, if the specified backup device contains several backups, you have to specify the position of the backup set to be processed. The syntax of this statement is:

```
RESTORE FILELISTONLY
    FROM device_name
    [WITH [FILE = number] [,{UNLOAD | NOUNLOAD}]]
```

The only additional option (in contrast to the previous statements) is the FILE option. It specifies the position of the backup set on the device. The default value is 1, meaning that is the result set of the first backup on the device.

You should use the RESTORE FILELISTONLY statement if you don't know exactly either which backup sets exist or if you don't know where the files of a particular backup set are stored. In both cases, you can check all or part of the devices to make a global picture of existing backups.

RESTORE VERIFYONLY After you have found your backup, you can do the next step: Verify the backup without using it for the restore process. The verification can be done with the RESTORE VERIFYONLY statement. This statement checks the existence of all backup devices (tapes or files) and whether the information can be read. The syntax of this statement is:

```
RESTORE VERIFYONLY
    FROM device_name
    [WITH [FILE = number] [,{UNLOAD | NOUNLOAD}]
    [, LOADHISTORY]]
```

As you can see from the syntax, the options of the RESTORE VERIFYONLY correspond to the options of the RESTORE FILELISTONLY statement. There is only one additional option—LOADHISTORY—that causes the backup information to be added to the backup history tables.

Restoring Databases and Logs Using Enterprise Manager

To restore a database from a full database backup, expand the server, choose **Databases**, and right-click the database. After pointing to **All Tasks**, choose **Restore Database**. The **Restore database** dialog box appears (see Figure 20-6). On the **General** tab in the **Restore** frame, click **Database**. Select the database backup you want to restore in the **Restore as database** list.

NOTE: Do not forget the sequence of restoring different types of backups! First restore the full database backup. After that, restore all corresponding transaction logs in the sequence of their creation.

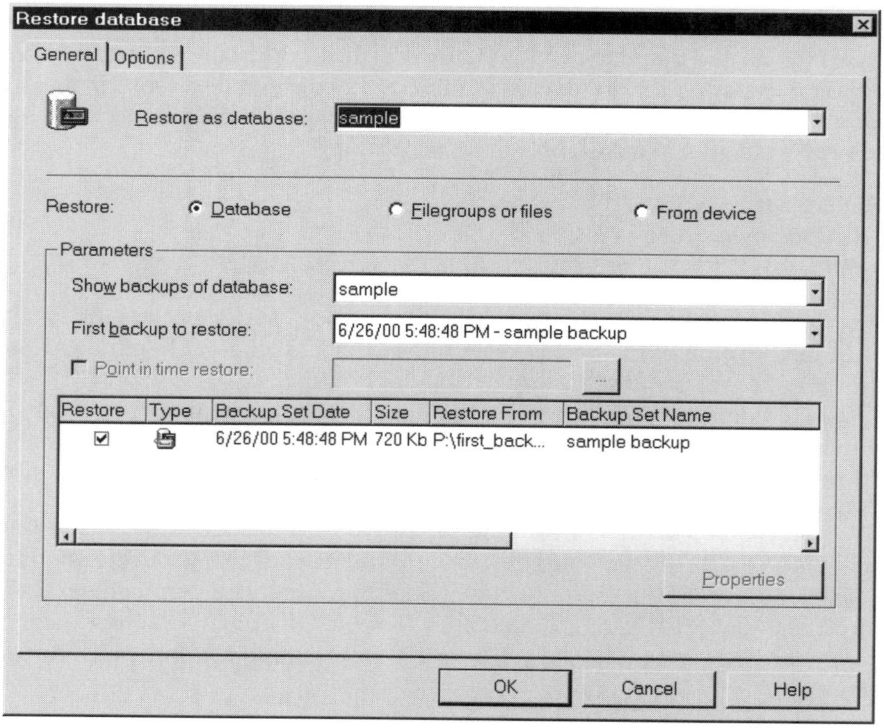

Figure 20-6. Restore Database dialog box—General tab

To select the appropriate restore options, choose the **Options** tab (see Figure 20-7) of the **Restore database** dialog box. In the **Recovery completion state** frame, you can choose one of the three existing options. The first option (**Leave database operational. No additional transaction logs can be restored**) instructs SQL Server to roll forward any committed transaction and to roll back any uncommitted transaction. After applying this option, the database is in a consistent state and is ready for use. This option is equivalent to the RECOVERY option of the RESTORE DATABASE statement. (The RESTORE DATABASE statement is described in the next section.)

NOTE: Use this option only with the last transaction log to be restored or with a full database restore when no subsequent transaction logs need to be applied.

If you click the second option (**Leave database nonoperational but able to restore additional transaction logs**), SQL Server does not roll back uncommitted transactions be-

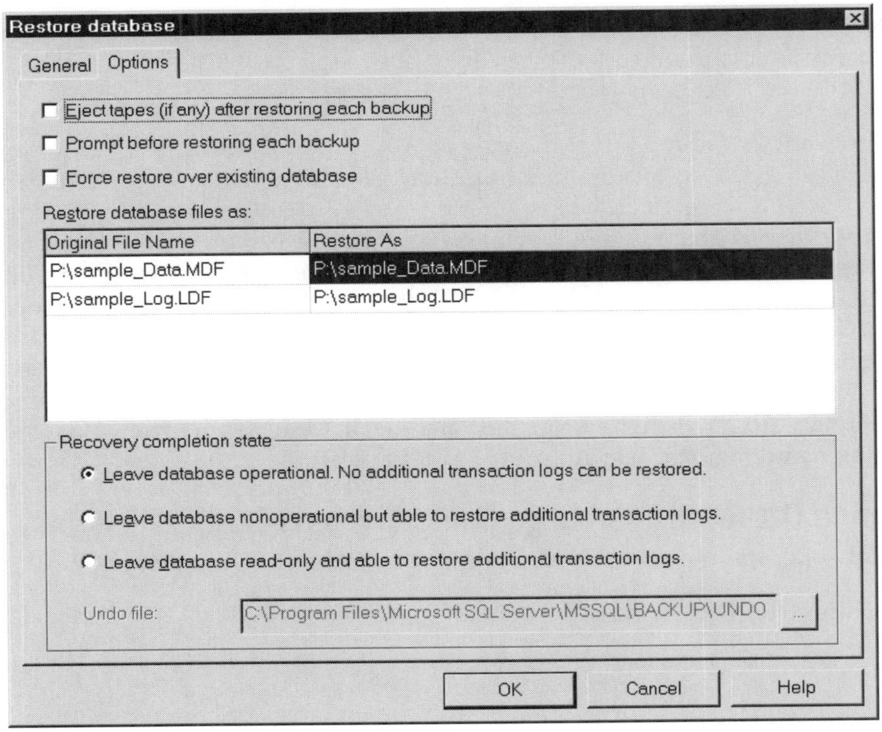

Figure 20-7. Restore Database dialog box—Options tab

cause you will be applying further backups. After this option is applied, the database is unavailable for use. This option is equivalent to the NORECOVERY option of the RESTORE DATABASE statement.

NOTE: Use this option with all but the last transaction log to be restored or with a differential database restore.

The third option (**Leave database read-only and able to restore additional transaction logs**) specifies the file (in the **Undo file** dialog box) that is subsequently used to roll back the recovery effects. (See also the STANDBY option in the RESTORE DATABASE statement.)

The process of a database restoration from a differential database backup is equivalent to the process of a restoration from a full database backup. The only difference is that only the first option in the **Options** tab (**Leave database operational. No additional transaction logs can be restored**) can be applied to the restoration from a differential database backup.

NOTE: If you restore from a differential backup, first restore the full database backup before you restore a differential one. In contrast to transaction log backups, only the latest differential backup is applied because it includes all changes since the full backup!

If you want to restore a transaction log backup, follow the same steps as for the restoration of a full database backup. In the **Options** tab, only the first two options can be applied.

To restore a database with a new name, expand the server, choose **Databases**, and right-click the database. After pointing to **All Tasks**, choose **Restore Database**. In the **Restore database** dialog box (see Figure 20-6), choose **Database** if you want to restore from a database backup. After that, on the **General** tab, click **From device** and enter the name of the database you want to create in **Restore as database**. Click **Select devices**. In the **Choose Restore Devices** dialog box (see Figure 20-8), click **Add** and enter the name of the backup device from which to restore the database. In **Only restore from media with the following name**, click the backup set you want to restore.

Restoring Databases and Logs Using Transact-SQL Statements

All restore operations can be executed using two Transact-SQL statements:

- RESTORE DATABASE
- RESTORE LOG

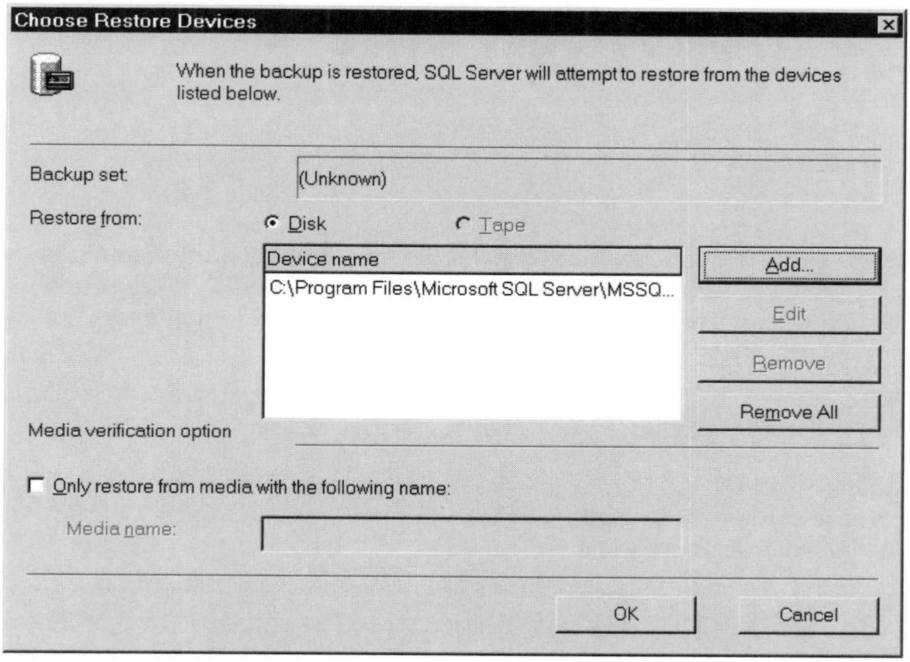

Figure 20-8. Choose Restore Devices dialog box

The RESTORE DATABASE statement is used to perform the restore process for a database. This statement has the following syntax:

```
RESTORE DATABASE {db_name | @variable}
    [FROM device_list]
    [WITH option_list]
```

db_name is the name of the database that will be restored. (The name of the database can be supplied using a variable **@variable**.) **device_list** in the FROM clause specifies one or more device names, where the database backup is stored. (If the FROM clause is not specified, the restore of a backup does not take place, but only recovery takes place, and you must specify either the RECOVERY, NORECOVERY, or STANDBY option. This action can take place if you want to switch over to a standby server.) **device_list** can be a list of names of disk files, tapes, or Named Pipe. **option_list** comprises several options that can be specified for the different backup forms. The most important options are:

- RECOVERY/NORECOVERY
- STANDBY
- REPLACE
- PARTIAL

The RECOVERY option instructs SQL Server to roll forward any committed transaction and to roll back any uncommitted transaction. After the RECOVERY option is applied, the database is in a consistent state and is ready for use. This option is the default.

NOTE: Use the RECOVERY option only with the last transaction log to be restored or with a full database restore with no subsequent transaction log backups to restore.

With the NORECOVERY option, SQL Server does not roll back uncommitted transactions because you will be applying further backups. After the NORECOVERY option is applied, the database is unavailable for use.

NOTE: Use the NORECOVERY option either with all but the last transaction log to be restored or with a differential database restore.

The STANDBY option is an alternative to the RECOVERY/NORECOVERY options and is used with the standby SQL Server. In order to access data stored on the standby server, you usually recover the database after a transaction log is restored. On the other hand, if you recover the database on the standby server, you cannot apply additional logs from the production server for the restore process. In that case, you use the STANDBY option to allow users read access to a standby server. Additionally, you allow the system the restoration of additional transaction logs. The STANDBY option implies the existence of the undo file that is used to roll back changes when additional logs are restored.

The REPLACE option replaces an existing database with data from a backup of a different database. In this case, the existing database is first destroyed, and the differences regarding the names of the files in the database and the database name are ignored. (If you do not use the REPLACE option, SQL Server performs a safety check that guarantees an existing database is not replaced if the names of files in the database or the database name itself differs from the corresponding names in the backup set.)

The PARTIAL option specifies a partial restore operation. Because application or user errors can affect an isolated portion of the database, there is often a necessity to restore only a database object such as a table. (See also the description of partial restore later in this chapter.)

The RESTORE DATABASE statement is also used to restore a database from a differential backup. The syntax and the options for restoring a differential backup are the same as for restoring from a full database backup. During a restoration from a differential backup, SQL Server restores only that part of the database that has changed since the last full database backup. Therefore, restore the full database backup *before* you restore a differential backup!

The RESTORE LOG statement is used to perform a restore process for a transaction log. This statement has the following syntax:

```
RESTORE LOG {db_name | @variable}
  FROM backup_device_list
  [WITH option_list]
```

db_name, **@variable**, and **device_list** have the same meanings as the parameters with the same names in the RESTORE DATABASE statement. **option_list** has the same options as the BACKUP DATABASE statement and includes three additional options: STOPAT, STOPATMARK, and STOPBEFOREMARK.

The STOPAT option allows you to restore a database to the state it was in at the exact moment before a failure occurred by specifying a point in time. SQL Server restores all committed transactions that were recorded in the transaction log before the specified point in time. If you want to restore a database by specifying a point in time, execute the RESTORE DATABASE statement using the NORECOVERY clause. After that, execute the RESTORE LOG statement to apply each transaction log backup, specifying the name of the database, the backup device from where the transaction log backup will be restored, and the STOPAT clause. (If the backup of a log does not contain the requested time, the database will not be recovered.)

NOTE: SQL Server 7 allowed you to use the STOPAT clause together with the NORECOVERY option in the RESTORE LOG statement. Since SQL Server 2000, STOPAT may be used with the STANDBY and NORECOVERY options, too.

The STOPATMARK and STOPBEFOREMARK clauses specify recovering to a mark. This topic is described at the end of this chapter.

Partial Recovery

SQL Server allows you the recovery of database parts. The ability to perform partial recovery is especially useful if a table is erroneously dropped and you want to restore it. Using log or differential backups, you can bring the table to a point prior to when the table was removed and store it to another location. Then the content of the table could be extracted and reloaded into the original database.

NOTE: To recover a part of a database, use the PARTIAL clause of the RESTORE DATABASE statement.

Restoring master Database

The corruption of the **master** database can be devastating for the whole system, because it comprises all system tables that are necessary to work with the database system. (This makes a file with the **master** database a good candidate for mirroring using RAID 1.) The restore process of the **master** database is quite different from the same process concerning user-defined databases, as you will see.

A damaged **master** database makes itself known through different failures. Some of these failures are:

- Inability to start SQL Server
- An input/output error
- The execution of the DBCC utility points to such a failure

There are two different ways you have to go to recover the **master** database. The easier way is when you can start your database system. In that case, you just restore the **master** database from the full database backup.

To restore your **master** database, start SQL Server in single-user mode. As you already know from Chapter 17, there are several ways to do it. My favorite way is to use the command window and execute the **sqlservr** application with the option **–m**. In the second step, you restore the **master** database together with all other databases using the last full database backup.

NOTE: If there have been any changes to the **master** database since the last full database backup, you will need to re-create those changes manually.

If the **master** database is damaged and you cannot start SQL Server, rebuild all system databases using the **rebuildm** utility. (You can find it in the \mssql\binn directory.) After that, restart SQL Server and restore backups of the **master** database. If any user-defined databases have been created after the **master** database was backed up, you must reattach these databases using the **sp_attach_db** system procedure.

Restoring Other System Databases

The restore process for all system databases other than **master** is similar. Therefore, we will explain this process using the **msdb** database. The **msdb** database needs to be restored from a backup when either the **master** database has been rebuilt or the **msdb** database itself has been damaged. If the **msdb** database is damaged, restore it using the existing backups. If there have been any changes after the **msdb** database backup was created, re-create those changes manually.

NOTE: You cannot restore a database that is being accessed by users. Therefore, when restoring the **msdb** database, the SQL Server Agent service should be stopped. (The SQL Server Agent service accesses the **msdb** database.)

Recovery Models

Microsoft introduced in SQL Server 2000 the new feature called database recovery model, which allows you to control to what extent you are ready to risk losing committed transactions if a database is damaged. Additionally, the choice of a recovery model has an impact on the size of the transaction log and therefore on the time period needed to back up the log. SQL Server supports three recovery models:

- Full
- Bulk-logged
- Simple

The following sections describe the three recovery models.

Full Recovery

During full recovery, all operations are written to the transaction log. Therefore, this model provides complete protection against media failure. This means that you can restore your database up to the last committed transaction that is stored in the log file. Additionally, data can be recovered to any point in time (prior to the point of failure). To guarantee this, such operations as SELECT INTO and the execution of the **bcp** utility are fully logged, too.

Besides point-in-time recovery the full recovery model allows you also to recover to a log mark. Log marks correspond to a specific transaction and are inserted only if the transaction commits. (For more information on log marks, see the corresponding section later in this chapter.)

The full recovery model also logs all operations concerning the CREATE INDEX statement, implying that the process of data recovery now includes the restoration of index creations. That way, the re-creation of the indexes is faster, because you do not have to rebuild them separately.

The disadvantage of this recovery model is that the corresponding transaction log may be very voluminous and the files on the disk containing the log will be filled up very quickly. Also, for such a voluminous log you will need significantly more time for backup.

NOTE: If you use the full recovery model, the transaction log must be protected from media failure. For this reason it is strongly recommended to use RAID 1 to protect transaction logs.

Bulk-Logged Recovery

Bulk-logged recovery supports log backups by using minimal space in the transaction log for certain large-scale or bulk operations. The logging of the following operations is minimal and cannot be controlled on an operation-by-operation basis:

- SELECT INTO
- CREATE INDEX (including indexed views)
- bcp utility
- WRITETEXT and UPDATETEXT

Although bulk operations are not fully logged, you do not have to perform a full database backup after the completion of such an operation. During bulk-logged recovery, transaction log backups contain both the log as well as the results of a bulk operation. This simplifies the transition between full and bulk-logged recovery models.

The bulk-logged recovery model allows you to recover a database to the end of a transaction log backup (i.e., up to the last committed transaction). In contrast to the full recovery model, bulk-logged recovery does not support generally point-in-time recovery. (You can use bulk-logged recovery for the point-in-time recovery if no bulk operations have been performed.)

The advantage of the bulk-logged recovery model is that bulk operations are performed much faster than under the full recovery model, because they are not fully logged. On the other hand, the backup process for the transaction log may need a significant amount of time because the log can be several times larger than in the case of full recovery.

Simple Recovery

In the simple recovery model, the transaction log is not used to protect your database against any media failure. Therefore, you can recover a damaged database only using full database or differential backup. Backup strategy for this model is very simple: Restore the database using existing database backups and, if differential backups exist, apply the most recent one.

The advantages of the simple recovery model are that the performance of all bulk operations is very high and requirements for the log space very small. On the other hand, this model requires the most manual work because all changes since the most recent database (or differential) backup must be redone.

Recovery Models and Backward Compatibility

The default recovery model of a database is identical to the recovery model defined for the **model** database, which can be twofold: For the Standard and Enterprise Editions, the default mode of the model database is full recovery, while the Personal and Desktop Editions have simple recovery model as the default mode.

You can change the recovery model using the RECOVERY option of the ALTER DATABASE statement. The part of the syntax of the ALTER DATABASE statement concerning recovery models is:

```
ALTER DATABASE db_name
          SET RECOVERY [FULL | BULK_LOGGED | SIMPLE]
          ..........................................
```

If you want to display the current model of your database, use the RECOVERY clause of the DATABASEPROPERTYEX function. Example 20.1 shows the SELECT statement that displays the recovery model for the sample database.

▼ EXAMPLE 20.1

```
SELECT databasepropertyex('sample', 'recovery')
```

The functionality of the new recovery models should replace the similar functionality of two existing database options:

- trunc. log on chkpt
- select into/bulk copy

The simple recovery model corresponds to the case where the **trunc. log on chkpt** option is set to true. (The setting of the other option is irrelevant.) If the **trunc.log on chkpt** option is set to false and the **select into/bulk copy** option to true, the recovery model of the database is bulk-logged. The last combination (both database options false) maps to the full recovery model.

NOTE: The **trunc. log on chkpt** and **select into/bulk copy** database options are deprecated features. However, for SQL Server 2000, these database options are as important as new recovery models. This means that changing either of these two options also changes the recovery model (according to the description above) and vice versa.

Recovery to a Mark

With SQL Server 2000, you can use the transaction log to recover to a specific mark. Log marks correspond to a specific transaction, and are inserted only if the transaction commits. This allows the marks to be tied to specific work and provides the ability to recover to a point that includes or excludes this work.

NOTE: If a marked transaction spans multiple databases on the same database server, the marks are recorded in the logs of all the affected databases.

The BEGIN TRANSACTION statement is enhanced to support transaction log marking. Use the WITH MARK clause (see Chapter 14) to insert marks into the logs. Because the name of the mark is the same as its transaction, a transaction name is required. (The **description** option specifies a textual description of the mark.)

The transaction log records the mark name, description, database, user, date and time information, and the log sequence number (LSN). To allow their reuse, the transaction names are not required to be unique. The date and time information is used along with the name to uniquely identify the mark.

You can use the RESTORE LOG statement (either with the STOPATMARK clause or the STOPBEFOREMARK clause) to specify recovering to a mark. The STOPATMARK clause causes the recover process to roll forward to the mark and include the transaction that contains the mark. If you specify the STOPBEFOREMARK clause, the recover process excludes the transaction that contains the mark.

Both clauses described above support an optional AFTER **datetime** clause. If this clause is omitted, recovery stops at the first mark with the specified name. If the clause is specified, recovery stops at the first mark with the specified name exactly at or after **datetime**.

CONCLUSION

The system administrator or database owner should periodically make a backup copy of the database and its transaction log to allow for recovery in the event of system errors, media failures, or a combination of other reasons (fire, theft). SQL Server provides two kinds of backup copies of the database: full and differential. A full backup captures the state of the database at the time the statement is issued and copies it to the backup media (file, tape device, or Named Pipe). A differential backup copies the parts of the database that have changed since the last full database backup. The benefit of the differential backup is that it completes more rapidly than the full database backup for the same database.

SQL Server performs automatic recovery each time a system failure occurs that does not cause any media failure. (The automatic recovery is also performed when the system is started after each shutdown of the system.) During automatic recovery, any committed transaction found in the transaction log is written to the database, and any uncommitted transaction is rolled back. After any media failure, it may be necessary to recover the database from the archived copy of it and its transaction logs. To recover a database, a full database backup and only the latest differential backup must be used. If you use transaction logs to restore a database, use the full database backup first, and after that, apply all existing transaction logs in the sequence of their creation to bring the database to the consistent state that it was in before the last transaction log backup was created.

The next chapter describes all SQL Server tools and features that you can use for data transfer and data transformation.

EXERCISES

▼ E.20.1
Discuss the differences between the differential and transaction log backup.

▼ E.20.2
When you should back up your production database?

▼ E.20.3
How can you make a differential backup of the master database?

▼ E.20.4
Discuss the use of different RAID technologies concerning fault tolerance of a database and its transaction log.

▼ E.20.5
What are the main differences between manual and automatic recovery?

▼ E.20.6
Which statement should you use to verify your backup, without using it for the restore process?

▼ E.20.7
Discuss the use of the three recovery models.

CHAPTER 21

Data Transfer

This chapter describes several different ways in which data can be transferred from/to SQL Server. After some introductory notes, a list of tools that SQL Server provides to transfer data is given. Then, the most important tool—Data Transformation Services (DTS) and all its components—is described. At the end of the chapter, the **bcp** utility is mentioned, and some general recommendations concerning data transfer are given.

INTRODUCTION

There are cases when an enterprise needs to replace a database system such as Microsoft Access (or even programs with simple sequential files) with a more powerful relational database system. In particular, this means that SQL Server will often be used to replace the existing Access database system with all its databases. In other cases, data may arrive from an affiliate that is using a different relational DBMS, and that data must be taken into account for strategic decisions. Either example implies the need for one or more tools that transfer data from one data source to another.

Data transfer includes importing and exporting data from one data store to another. In the case of SQL Server, transferring data means importing data from a source data store to SQL Server and/or exporting data from SQL Server to a target data store. Between these two processes, data can be transformed to satisfy simple or complex issues that must be resolved before the data is imported to the target data store.

Data transfer can involve the following tasks:

- Loading data into a database
- Archiving (loading a database backup)
- Migrating data

Loading data into a database is simply the process of importing data to a database. In this case, the source is usually a file that contains the data to be loaded.

Archiving data is a special form of data export in which a copy of the database and/or transaction log is made (see Chapter 20). The reverse process—data restore—is a form of data import. (Neither data archiving nor data restoration generally includes any form of data transformation.)

The process of migrating (copying) data from a source to a target data store is more complex than loading data, because it contains several steps. They include identifying the data source, exporting the data (usually to a file), specifying the target data store, and importing the data. Additionally, migrating data between different data stores usually requires the intermediate process of data transformation. Transforming data can include the following tasks:

- Changing data representation
- Restructuring data

Changing data representation can include modification of the different forms of data, such as the internal specification of data types. For example, if data stored on a computer with EBCDIC code has to be made available on a computer using ASCII code, the data representation must be changed.

A common procedure known from the world of data warehouse systems is the *restructuring of data* that originates on different data sources on several computers. To satisfy requirements in the data warehousing world, it is often necessary to do complex aggregations and calculations on masses of rows of the input data stream. These operations may compress many thousands of input rows of the original data store into a relatively small number of rows in an intermediate data file, which eventually will be loaded in the target database. To get more information about the world of data warehousing systems and the processes to model them, see Chapter 26.

Now that you know something about the different purposes and aims of a data transfer process, let's take a look at the methods SQL Server offers to support this task. The following SQL Server tools, statements, and utilities provide data transfer:

- Transact-SQL statements INSERT and SELECT INTO
- Tools and statements for archiving data
- Data Transformation Services (DTS)
- **bcp** utility and the BULK INSERT statement

The INSERT statement inserts one or more rows into a table. The SELECT INTO statement creates a new table and inserts rows selected by the query. Both statements have restricted functionality and should be used to insert (copy) a small number of rows (see also Chapters 7 and 5, respectively). Tools and statements for archiving data are described in Chapter 20.

This chapter covers Data Transformation Services and the **bcp** utility.

DATA TRANSFORMATION SERVICES (DTS)

The purpose of DTS is to import, export, and transform data between multiple data stores. This tool supports homogenous and heterogeneous data stores. *Homogenous* data stores are those in which both the source data store and target data store are SQL Server systems. In the case of homogenous data stores, DTS provides the Copy SQL Server Objects Task. *Heterogeneous* data stores are those in which the data is transferred between SQL Server and some other Microsoft product or some other DBMS. In this case, the Microsoft OLE DB architecture must be used.

First, let's look at what DTS does:

- Copies database schema and data between homogenous or heterogeneous DBMSs
- Creates custom transformation objects
- Provides extracting and transforming services

DTS moves database schema and data between heterogeneous DBMSs. Additionally, in the case of homogenous systems using the Copy SQL Server Objects Task, all other database objects, such as stored procedures, triggers, constraints, and rules, are also copied.

Custom transformation objects are defined using DTS packages. A DTS package allows you to define complex data transformations that will be executed in several steps (see the next section).

Data extracting and data transformation belong to the consolidation phase, which is an early phase in the process of building data warehouses and data marts. To build up a valid data warehousing system, the existence of transformation rules is only one important requirement. Before doing any transformation, data must be extracted in an appropriate way (possibly from heterogeneous platforms), and after the transformation process, the resulting data must be loaded. DTS offers mechanisms that accompany the data warehousing designer on his or her entire journey from data source to target SQL Server Analysis system. Using DTS, it is now possible to export data from defined data sources and pump them through the tubes of a transformation network that leads them directly into the target pool. And as this procedure will occur again and again (to keep the data warehouse up-to-date), you will be happy to know that DTS does this step automatically. (For the description of SQL Server Analysis server, see also Chapter 27.)

DTS Package

The DTS package is a complete description of all work to be performed as part of the data transfer and/or transformation process. It defines one or more steps that perform different types of operations, and these steps are executed consecutively. To create a DTS package, SQL Server need not be either a source data store or a target data store. The DTS package simply describes the processing rules used to transfer and transform data between any data stores that use OLE DB. Therefore, using DTS, you can access all data stores (either as a source or as a target) that support OLE DB.

The communication between data stores is provided by Data Pump (see Figure 21-1), an OLE DB service provider that supports data transfer and data transformation between source data store(s) and a target data store by moving OLE DB rowsets between the stores.

NOTE: DTS Data Pump is implemented as an independent COM server, which can be used separately from SQL Server.

Creation of DTS Packages

The DTS package can be created either manually or by using DTS wizards. To create the DTS package manually, a language that supports OLE automation, such as C++ or Visual

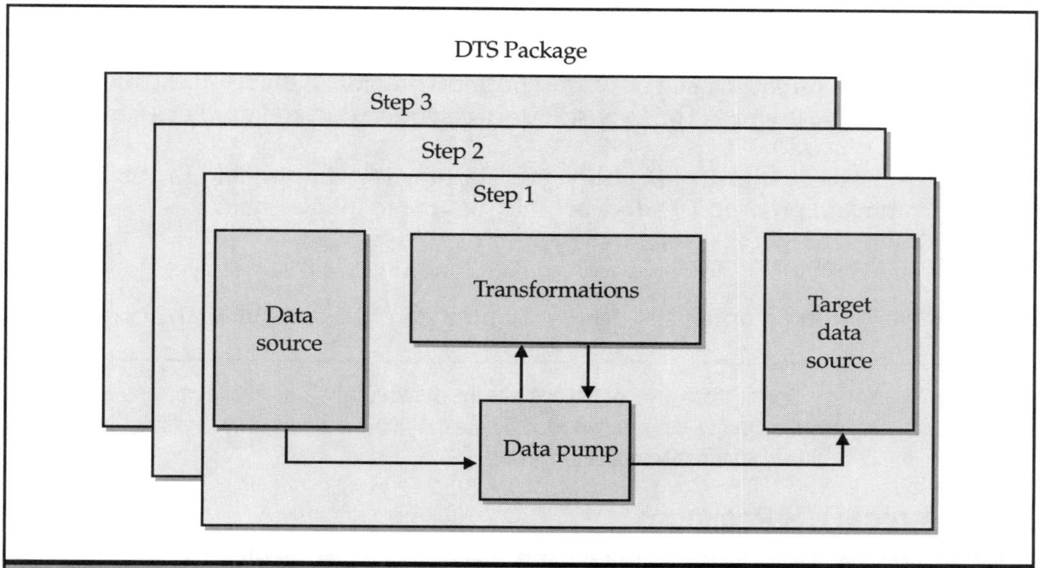

Figure 21-1. DTS package with Data Pump

Basic, must be used. A more convenient way to create DTS packages is through the use of the DTS Import and Export Wizards. They offer the ability to:

- Copy data between homogenous or heterogeneous data stores
- Copy an entire table or the result of a local or distributed query
- Determine transformation rules that specify how data is copied between columns with different properties
- Save the DTS package into the **msdb** system database, the MS Repository, or a COM-structured storage file (see Chapter 27), to conserve them for later reuse or documentation purposes

There are two ways to start DTS Import and Export Wizards:

- Using SQL Server Enterprise Manager
- Using the **dtswiz** utility

To start the DTS Import Wizard using Enterprise Manager, expand the server, expand **Databases**, and right-click the database you wish to import data into. Point to **All Tasks** and choose **Import Data**. The wizard prompts you for all the required information concerning the data import. (The Export Wizard can be started and used in a similar way as the Import Wizard.)

When you execute the **dtswiz** utility, you start the DTS Import and Export Wizards from the command prompt. The **dtswiz** utility has the following syntax:

```
dtswiz {/option parameter}...
```

The most important options of the **dtswiz** utility are listed in Table 21-1.

NOTE: You can specify zero or more options with the **dtswiz** utility. The DTS Import and Export Wizards request any required values not specified. Therefore, the command **dtswiz** without any options starts the DTS wizard interface from the beginning.

Execution of DTS Packages

After the DTS package has been created and saved, it can be executed using:

- SQL Server Enterprise Manager
- DTS Package Designer
- The **dtsrun** utility

To execute a DTS package using Enterprise Manager, right-click the package in the console tree and then click **Execute Package**. To execute a DTS package from DTS Designer, click **Execute** on the toolbar.

Option	Description
/f filename	Saves the created DTS package to the COM-structured storage file filename
/i	Specifies an import to SQL Server
/x	Specifies an export from SQL Server
/r provider	Specifies the provider name used to connect to the source data store when importing, or the target data store when exporting

Table 21-1. Options of the dtswiz Utility

The **dtsrun** utility can additionally retrieve, display, overwrite, or delete a DTS package. The most important options of the **dtsrun** utility are listed in Table 21-2.

Other DTS Tools

Besides Import and Export Wizards, DTS contains other tools (i.e., tasks):

- DTS Package Designer
- Copy SQL Server Objects Task

DTS Package Designer

The DTS Package Designer provides a graphical user interface for designing a DTS package. This tool includes a tool palette and a toolbar you can use to quickly specify the properties of the data transferring and transforming tasks. To invoke the DTS Package Designer, expand the server using Enterprise Manager, right-click **Data Transformation Services**, and choose **New Package**. The DTS Package Designer work surface appears (see Figure 21-2). You can represent the following graphical objects on the work surface:

- A data store icon, which represents either a source or a target
- A solid arrow, which represents the flow of data
- A task object, which represents a DTS custom transformation task
- A label, which is used to describe an element on the work surface
- A dashed arrow, which indicates the order in which tasks are executed

Option	Description
/n package_name	Specifies the name of a DTS package
~	Specifies that the parameter to follow is the encrypted value of the same
/f file_name	Specifies the name of a COM-structured file that contains the DTS package
/!x	Retrieves the DTS package from SQL Server and overwrites the contents of the file specified with the option /**f**, without executing the package
/!d	Deletes the DTS package from SQL Server
/!y	Displays the encrypted command used to execute the DTS package, without executing the package

Table 21-2. Options of the dtsrun Utility

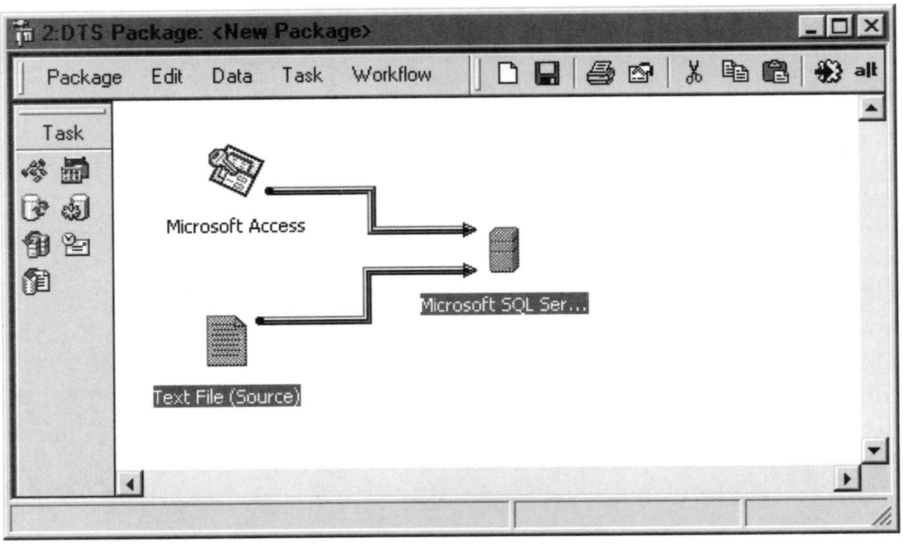

Figure 21-2. DTS Package Designer work surface

Copy SQL Server Objects

The Copy SQL Server Objects Task is used to transfer both database objects and data either from one database to another on the same server or from one SQL Server system to another.

> ***NOTE:*** This task imports and exports all database objects, including tables, views, triggers, stored procedures, constraints, and rules, between SQL Server databases or SQL Server systems. All of the objects in a database can be transferred, or only a subset that you explicitly select. Other DTS components transfer only table structures and data.

Using the Copy SQL Server Objects Task, you can:

- Import data into a Windows NT/2000 or Windows 9x SQL Server
- Import and export database objects and data from one architecture to a different architecture

BCP UTILITY

bcp (Bulk Copy Program) is a useful utility that copies SQL Server data to/from a data file. Therefore, **bcp** is often used to transfer a large amount of data into a SQL Server database from another relational DBMS or vice versa. The syntax of the **bcp** utility is

```
bcp [[db_name.]user_name.]table_name {IN | OUT| FORMAT} file_name
   [{-option parameter} ...]
```

db_name is the name of the database, to which the **table_name** table belongs. IN or OUT specifies the direction of data transfer. The IN option copies from the **file_name** file into the **table_name** table, and the OUT option copies from the **table_name** table to the **file_name** file. The FORMAT option creates a format file based on the options specified. If this option is used, the option **–f** must also be used.

> ***NOTE:*** The IN option appends the content of the file to the content of the database table, whereas the OUT option overwrites the content of the file.

Data to be copied can be either SQL Server specific or ASCII text. The former is also called native mode and the latter the character mode. The parameter **–n** specifies the native mode, and the parameter **–c**, the character mode. The native mode is used to export and import data from one SQL Server system to another, and the character mode is commonly used to transfer data between SQL Server and other systems.

Example 21.1 shows the use of the **bcp** utility.

▼ EXAMPLE 21.1

```
bcp projects..employee out empout.txt –c –t" | " –r"\n" –S INF_DB –U dusan
```

The **bcp** command in Example 21.1 exports the data from the **employee** table of the sample database in the output file **empout.txt**. The option **–c** specifies the character mode; thus, the data is stored in the ASCII file. The option **–t** specifies the field terminator and the option **–r**, the row terminator. (**-n** specifies new line and is the default for the row terminator.) The option **–S** specifies the server running the SQL Server system to connect to. (The default is the local server.) The option **–U** specifies the login ID used to connect to SQL Server. If the option **–P** (for password) is omitted, SQL Server prompts you to give the password for the specified login ID. Figure 21-3 shows the content of the file **empout.txt**.

To import data from a file to a database table, you must have INSERT and SELECT permissions on the table. To export data from a table to a file, you must have SELECT permission on the table. (For the description of INSERT and SELECT permissions, see Chapter 12.)

```
25348|Matthew        |Smith        |d3
10102|Ann            |Jones        |d3
18316|John           |Barrimore    |d1
29346|James          |James        |d2
9031|Elsa           |Bertoni      |d2
2581|Elke           |Hansel       |d2
28559|Sybill         |Moser        |d1
```

Figure 21-3. Content of the file empout.txt

NOTE: The **bcp** utility is an executable program that can be run from a command prompt. Neither SQL Server Query Analyzer nor Enterprise Manager can be used to start this utility.

Be aware that the new BULK INSERT Transact-SQL statement is an alternative to **bcp**. It supports all of the **bcp** options (although the syntax is a bit different) and offers much greater performance!

GENERAL RECOMMENDATIONS

Of all the SQL Server data transferring tools and features, DTS should be your service of choice. It contains several components that take care of all forms of data transfer and data transformation. Use DTS Import and Export Wizards to execute simple data transfers. For more sophisticated data transfers and transformation of data, use DTS Package Designer. The Copy SQL Server Objects Tasks should be used exclusively to transfer data from one SQL Server system to another.

bcp must be executed at a command prompt and is not user friendly. Since DTS components comprise all the functionality of the **bcp** utility, use **bcp** only for backward compatibility.

CONCLUSION

Transferring data means importing and/or exporting data from one data store to another. Optionally, between import and export, data can be transformed in different ways to satisfy the requirements of the target data store. SQL Server supports the following tools and features to transfer data:

- Transact-SQL statements INSERT and SELECT INTO
- Backup and restore (archiving)
- DTS (Data Transformation Services)
- **bcp** utility and the BULK INSERT statement

The next chapter introduces you to the automation of SQL Server's administrative tasks.

EXERCISES

▼ E.21.1

Which tool (i.e., command) can you use as an alternative to the **bcp** utility to copy SQL Server data to the output file?

▼ E.21.2

If you have to make data transformation during a migration of data, which SQL Server tool you should use?

▼ E.21.3

Use the **bcp** utility to copy all rows from the **customers** table of the Northwind database.

CHAPTER 22

Automating System Administration Tasks

The system administrator has many different tasks to perform: surveying one or more databases, tuning and optimizing them, and tailoring database layouts and database tables to fulfill actual and future needs. Generally, a database environment that works optimally during all working hours is the system administrator's goal. To achieve this, he or she has to organize all tasks very efficiently. The service tools provided by SQL Server, and especially SQL Server Agent, help the system administrator reach this goal.

This chapter describes, first, how SQL Server Agent can be used to automate the daily work of the system administrator. In the second part of the chapter, the creation of jobs and the definition of alerts, which are used to respond to system- or user-defined errors, are discussed. The last section of the chapter covers administrative tasks within a multiserver environment.

INTRODUCTION

The most important advantages of the SQL Server system in relation to other relational DBMSs are as follows:

- The graphical user interfaces adapted and integrated into the well-known MS Windows standard interface make it easy for the system administrator to build and manage databases and all database objects.
- The ability to automate administrative tasks and hence to reduce costs.

Here are some important administrative tasks that are performed frequently and therefore could be automated:

- Backing up the database and transaction log
- Transferring data
- Dropping and re-creating indices
- Checking data integrity

You can automate all these tasks so they occur on a regular schedule. For example, you can set the database backup task to occur every Friday at 8:00 P.M. and the transaction log backup task to occur daily at 12:00 P.M.

SQL Server components used in automation include the following:

- SQL Server Service
- Windows NT/2000 event log
- SQL Server Agent

Why does SQL Server need these three components to automate processes? First, the SQL Server Service is needed to write events to the Windows NT/2000 event log. Some events are written automatically, and some must be raised by the system administrator (see the detailed explanation later in this chapter).

The Windows NT/2000 event log is where all operating system messages of Windows NT/2000 and messages of its components are written. (For example, SQL Server errors with severity levels between 19 and 25 are always stored in the Windows NT/2000 event log.) The role of the event log in the automation process is to notify SQL Server Agent about existing events. (For more information on the Windows NT/2000 event log and the severity levels of SQL Server errors, see Chapter 23.)

SQL Server Agent is another service that connects to the Windows NT/2000 event log and the SQL Server Service. The role of SQL Server Agent in the automation process is to take an action after a notification through Windows NT/2000 event log. The action can be performed in connection with SQL Server Service or some other application. Figure 22-1 shows how these three components work together.

SQL SERVER AGENT

SQL Server Agent executes jobs and fires alerts. As you will see in the upcoming sections, jobs and alerts are defined separately and can be executed independently. Nevertheless, jobs and alerts may also be complementary processes, because a job can invoke an alert and vice versa.

Consider an example: A job is executed to inform the system administrator about an unexpected filling of the transaction log that exceeds a tolerable limit. When this event occurs, the associated alert is invoked and, as a reaction, the system administrator may be notified by e-mail or pager.

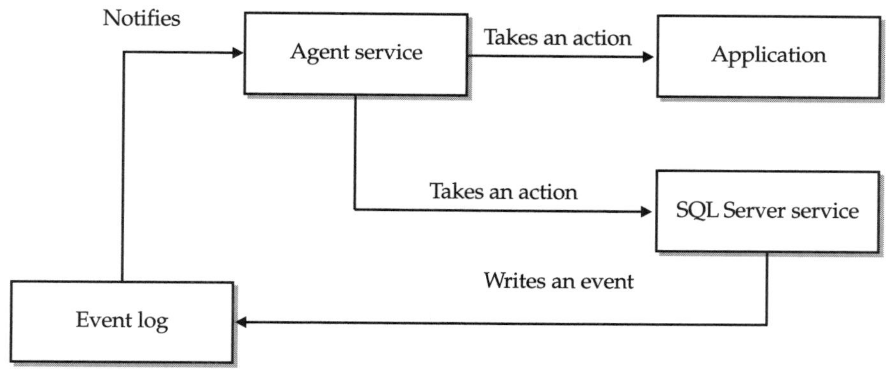

Figure 22-1. SQL Server automation components

Another critical event is a failure in backing up the transaction log. When this happens, the associated alert may invoke a job that truncates the transaction log (see also Chapter 20). This reaction will be appropriate if the reason for the backup failure is an overflow (filling up) of the transaction log. In other cases (for example, the target device for the backup copy is full), such a truncation will have no effect. This example shows the close connection that may exist between events that have similar symptoms.

Running and Configuring SQL Server Agent

SQL Server Agent allows you to automate different administrative tasks. Before you can do this, of course, it must be started. SQL Server Agent can be started in the same way as the SQL Server Service, using any of the following:

- SQL Service Manager
- SQL Server Enterprise Manager
- The Services application in the Control Panel
- The **net** command

For more information on these alternatives, see Chapter 17.

> ***NOTE:*** If you checked the autostart policies for SQL Server Agent, it will be started together with the Windows NT/2000 or Windows 9*x* operating system. It is strongly recommended that you set up this service to start whenever the operating system is started. This way, you will automate one further process.

The configuration of SQL Server Agent consists of the verification of the service login account (see Chapter 19) and the configuration of Mail Profile. During the installation process, a login account is specified for SQL Server Agent (and for the SQL Server Service, too). You can use either a local or a domain user login account for SQL Server Agent.

> ***NOTE:*** A domain user account for SQL Server Agent has some benefits over a local one. While the local user account only allows access to the local computer, the domain user account allows, among other things, the execution of multiserver administrative jobs and communication with other e-mail systems to send or receive e-mail.

As already stated, the invocation of an alert can also include the notification of the operator by e-mail. The Microsoft NT/2000 operating system includes an e-mail application called Windows NT/2000 Mail that communicates with other Windows NT/2000 computers and exchanges information with them. SQL Server uses a mail session called SQL Mail to send text strings, files, or query results to other computers. SQL Mail is a MAPI-enabled (Messaging Application Programming Interface) post office that can send and receive messages to and from other computers using Windows NT/2000 Mail or any other MAPI provider.

Before SQL Server can send and receive messages, the system has to be configured as a mail client. This configuration includes the configuration of a profile name for SQL

Server Agent. The profile name is required by the service to start a mail session and to send a notification by e-mail. A SQL Server Mail session is started every time SQL Server Agent is started.

CREATING JOBS AND OPERATORS

The first step in automating a task is the creation of a corresponding job. A job can be created using the following:

- Create Job Wizard
- SQL Server Enterprise Manager

The easiest way to set up the creation of a job is to use the Create Job Wizard. Generally, there are three steps to follow if you want to create a job:

- Create a job and its steps
- Create a schedule of the job execution if the job is not to be executed by the user on demand
- Notify operators about the status of the job

The following sections explain these steps using an example job created in Enterprise Manager.

Job Steps

A job may contain one or more steps. There are different ways in which a job step can be defined:

- Using Transact-SQL statements
- Executing a utility
- Invoking a program

Many job steps contain Transact-SQL statements. For example, if you want to automate database or transaction log backups, you will use the BACKUP DATABASE statement or BACKUP LOG statement, respectively. Some other jobs may require the execution of a SQL Server utility, which usually will be started with the corresponding command. For example, if you want to automate the data transfer from SQL Server to a data file, or vice versa, you will use the **bcp** command.

As a third alternative, it may be necessary to execute a program that has been developed using Visual Basic or some other programming language. In this case, you should always include the path drive letter in the **Command** text box when you start such a program. This is necessary because SQL Server Agent has to find the executable file.

NOTE: Before a job is created, you should decide if the job will be executed on a local server or on multiple servers. This decision affects the design of any job to be created. (For more information on creating jobs in a multiserver environment, see the last section of this chapter.)

If the job contains several steps, it is important to determine what actions should be taken in case of a failure. Generally, SQL Server will start the next job step if the previous one was successfully executed. However, if a job step fails, any job steps that follow will not be executed. Therefore, you should always specify how often each step should be retried in the case of failure. And, of course, it will be necessary to eliminate the reason for the abnormal termination of the job step (obviously, a repeated job execution will always lead to the same error if the error is not repaired).

NOTE: The number of attempts depends on the type and content of the executed job step (batch, command, or application program).

Creating a Job Using Enterprise Manager

This section illustrates the creation of a job using Enterprise Manager. The job backs up a sample database. To create this job, select the database and click the **New Job** button on the toolbar in Enterprise Manager. The **New Job Properties** dialog box appears (see Figure 22-2). On the **General** tab, enter a name for the job (as you can see in Figure 22-2, the name of the job for backing up the sample database is **backup_sample**). Check the **Enabled** check box to enable the job.

NOTE: All jobs are enabled by default. SQL Server Agent disables jobs if the job schedule is defined either at a specific time that has passed or on a recurring basis with an end date that has also passed. In both cases you must reenable the job manually.

In the **Source** frame, choose whether the job will be executed on a local server only (**Target local server**) or on multiple servers (**Target multiple servers**). If the job will be executed in a multiserver environment, click **Change** and select the servers that belong to the multiple server environment. (Because the backup of the sample database is a local job, **Target local server** is chosen for the example.)

In the **Category** list, choose the category to which the job belongs, and in the **Owner** list, click the owner responsible for performing the job. In the example in Figure 22-2, the job **backup_sample** is not categorized, and the owner is the user who creates the job. You can add a description of the job in the **Description** box, if you wish.

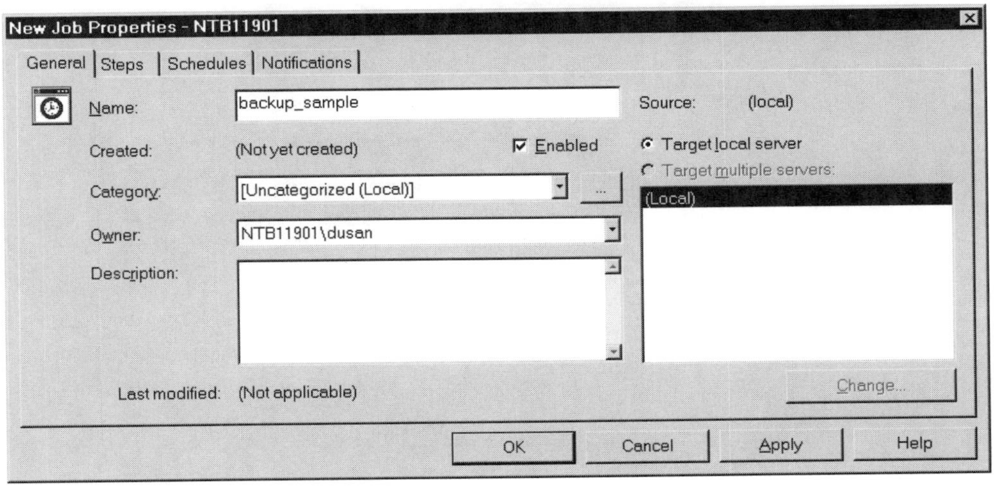

Figure 22-2. New Job Properties dialog box

NOTE: If you have to manage several jobs, categorizing them is recommended. This is especially useful if your jobs are executed in a multiserver environment.

Each job must have one or more steps. Therefore, in addition to the definition of job properties, at least one step must be created before the job can be saved.

To define one or more steps, click the **Steps** tab in the **New Job Properties** dialog box and choose **New**. The **New Job Step** dialog box appears (see Figure 22-3). Enter a name for the job step. (It is called **backup** in the example.) In the **Type** list, click Transact-SQL script, because the backup of the sample database will be executed using the Transact-SQL statement BACKUP DATABASE. In the **Database** list, choose the **master** database.

The Transact-SQL statement can either be directly entered in the **Command** box or invoked from a file. In the latter case, click **Open** and select the file. (The syntax of the statement(s) can be checked by clicking **Parse**.)

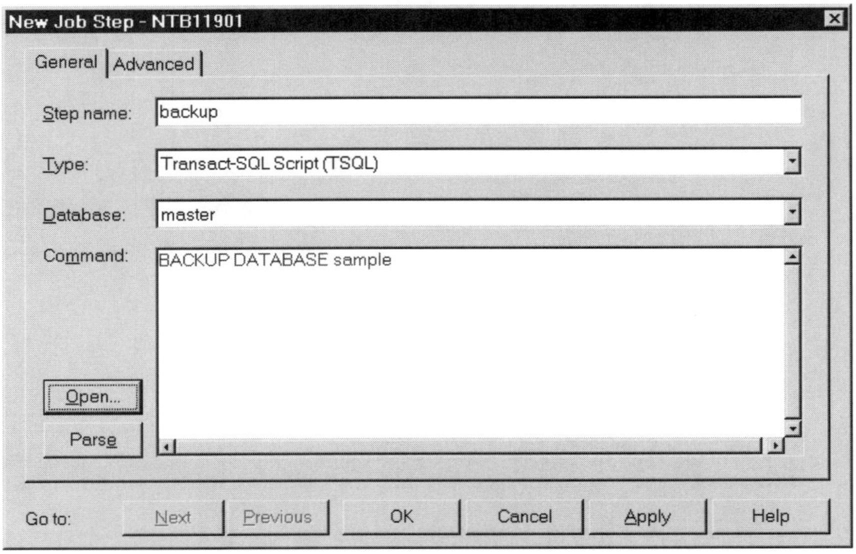

Figure 22-3. New Job Step dialog box

Creating Job Schedules

Each created job can be executed on demand (i.e., manually by the user) or by using one or more schedules. A scheduled job can occur at a specific time or on a recurring schedule.

NOTE: Each job can have multiple schedules. For example, the backup of the transaction log of a production database can be executed with two different schedules, depending on time of day. This means that during peak business hours, you can execute the backup more frequently than during nonpeak hours.

To create a schedule for an existing job using Enterprise Manager, click **SQL Server Agent** (in the **Management** folder) and click **Jobs**. After that, right-click the job in the details pane and click **Properties**. In the **Job Properties** dialog box (see Figure 22-2), click the **Schedules** tab, and then click **New Schedule**. The **New Job Schedule** dialog box appears.

For the sample database, let's set the schedule for the backup to be executed every Friday at 8:00 P.M. To do this, click **Recurring** and then **Change**. In the **Edit Recurring Job Schedule** dialog box (see Figure 22-4), click **Weekly** in the **Occurs** frame, and check

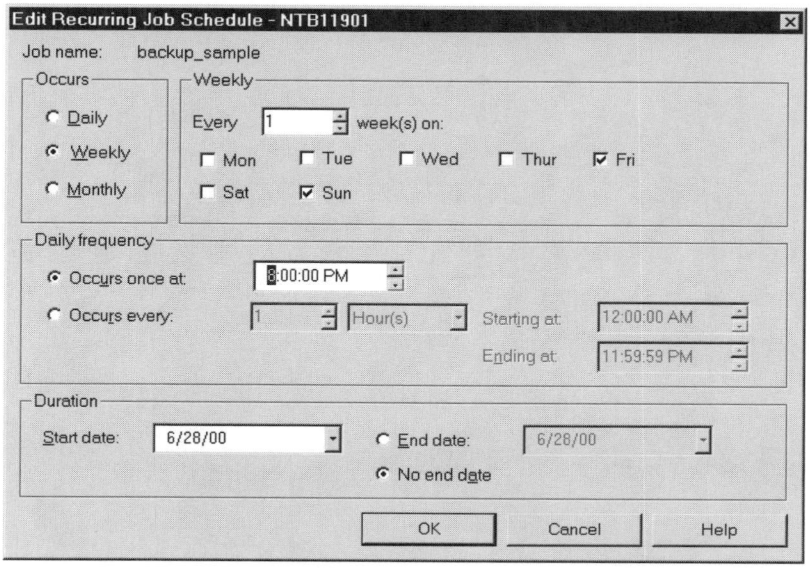

Figure 22-4. Edit Recurring Job Schedule dialog box

Fri(day) in the **Weekly** frame. In the **Daily frequency** frame, check **Occurs once at**, and enter the time (20:00). In the **Duration** frame, enter the **start** and **end** dates. (If the job should be scheduled without the end date, check **No end date**.)

Creating Operators for Notification

When a job completes, several methods of notification are possible. For example, you can instruct the system to write a corresponding message to the Windows NT/2000 event log, hoping that the system administrator reads this log from time to time. A better choice is to explicitly notify one or more operators using e-mail, pager, and/or the **net send** command.

Before an operator can be assigned to a job, you have to create an entry for it. To create an operator using Enterprise Manager, select **SQL Server Agent** (in the **Management** folder), right-click **Operators**, and then click **New Operator**. The **New Operator Properties** dialog box appears (see Figure 22-5). On the **General** tab, enter the name of the operator in the **Name** box. Specify one or more methods of notifying the operator (via e-mail, pager, or the **net send** address). In the **Pager on duty schedule** frame, enter the working hours of the operator if the pager notification is activated. (Using the **Test** button, you can test the e-mail name, pager name, or **net send** address that was entered.)

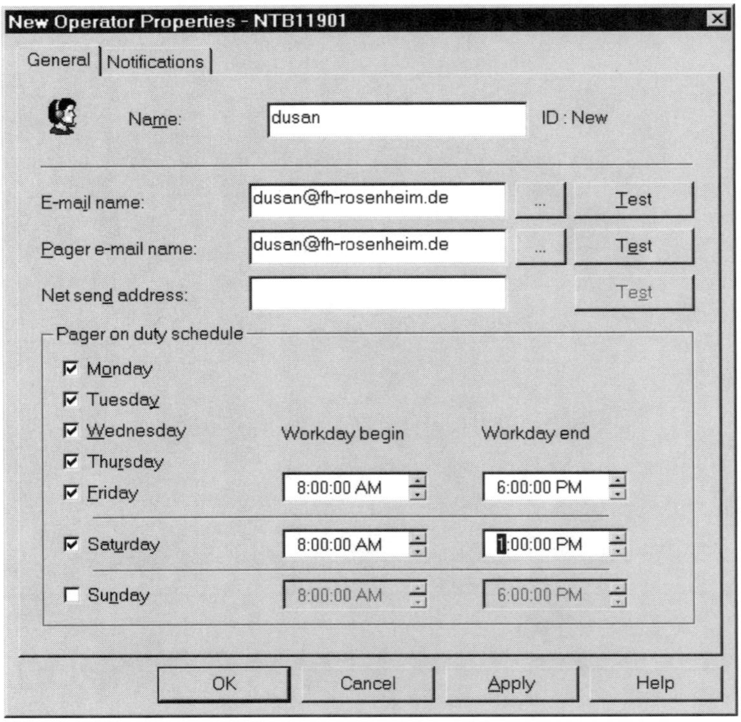

Figure 22-5. New Operator Properties dialog box

To notify one or more operators after the job finishes (successfully or unsuccessfully), click the **Notifications** tab in the **New Operator Properties** dialog box (see Figure 22-6), and check the corresponding boxes. (Besides e-mail, pager, or the **net send** command notification, in this dialog box you also have the option of writing the message to the Windows event log and/or deleting the job.)

Viewing the Job History Log

The SQL Server system stores the information concerning all job activities in the **sysjobhistory** system table of the **msdb** system database. Therefore, this table represents the job history log of your system. You can view the information in this table using Enterprise Manager. To do this, right-click the job and click **View Job History**. (If you want to view the history of a multiserver job, click **Job Status**.)

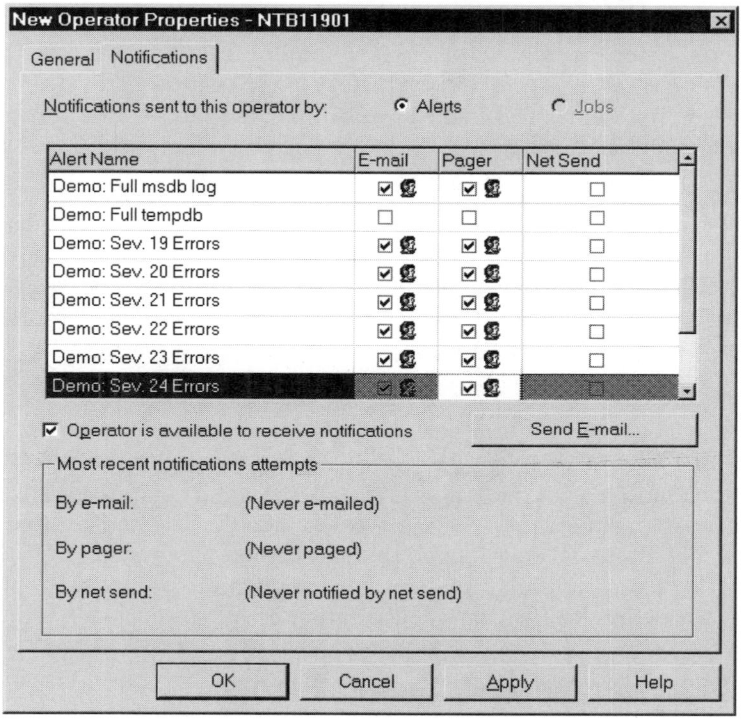

Figure 22-6. New Job Properties dialog box—Notifications tab

Each row of the job history log is displayed in the details pane of Enterprise Manager, and it contains the following information:

- Date and time when the job step occurred
- Whether the job step completed successfully or unsuccessfully
- Operators who were notified
- Duration of the job
- Errors or messages concerning the job step

By default, the maximum size of the job history log is 1,000, while the number of rows for a job is limited to 100. (The job history log is automatically cleared when the maximum size of rows is reached.) If you want to store the information about each job and there are several jobs for your system, increase the size of the job history log and/or the amount of rows per job. Using Enterprise Manager, right-click **SQL Server Agent** (in the **Management** folder) and click **Properties**. On the **Job System** tab of the **SQL Server Agent Properties** dialog box, enter the new values for the total number of rows and/or number of rows per job. If you want the size of the job history log to be unlimited, clear the **Limit size of job history log** check box. (The **Clear Log** button in the same frame allows you to clear the content of the job history log.)

> ***NOTE:*** Though you may be tempted, do not clear the **Limit size of job history log** check box! Depending on activities at your server, the size of the **sysjobhistory** system table can grow rapidly and thus completely fill the **msdb** system database (or your disk drive if the **msdb** database is configured for unlimited growth). In that case, you must restore the **msdb** database using the existing copy. (If you do not have a copy of this database, you will not be able to read the job history log.)

ALERTS

The information about execution of jobs and SQL Server error messages is stored in the Windows NT/2000 event log. SQL Server Agent reads this log and compares the stored messages with the alerts defined for the system. If there is a match, SQL Server Agent fires the alert. Therefore, the alerts can be used to respond to potential problems (such as filling up the transaction log), different SQL Server errors, or user-defined errors.

Defining Alerts to Handle SQL Server Errors

An alert can be defined to raise a response to a particular error number or to the group of errors that belong to a specific severity code (see Chapter 23). Furthermore, the definition of an alert for a particular error is different for system errors and user-defined errors. (The creation of alerts on user-defined errors is described later in this chapter.)

Alerts can be defined using Enterprise Manager or the Create Alert Wizard. The creation of alerts using the wizard is straightforward and hence will not be shown in this book.

Creating Alerts on SQL Server Error Numbers

Example 14.4, where one transaction was deadlocked by another transaction, will be used to show how to create an alert on a SQL Server error number using Enterprise Manager. If a transaction was deadlocked by another transaction, the victim must be executed again. This can be done, among other ways, by using an alert.

To create the deadlock (or any other) alert, right-click **Alerts** and click **New Alert**. In the **New Alert Properties** dialog box (see Figure 22-7), enter the name of the alert in the **Name** box. Click **Error number**, and enter **1205**. (This error number indicates that SQL Server found a deadlock and the process was selected as the "victim.") The system

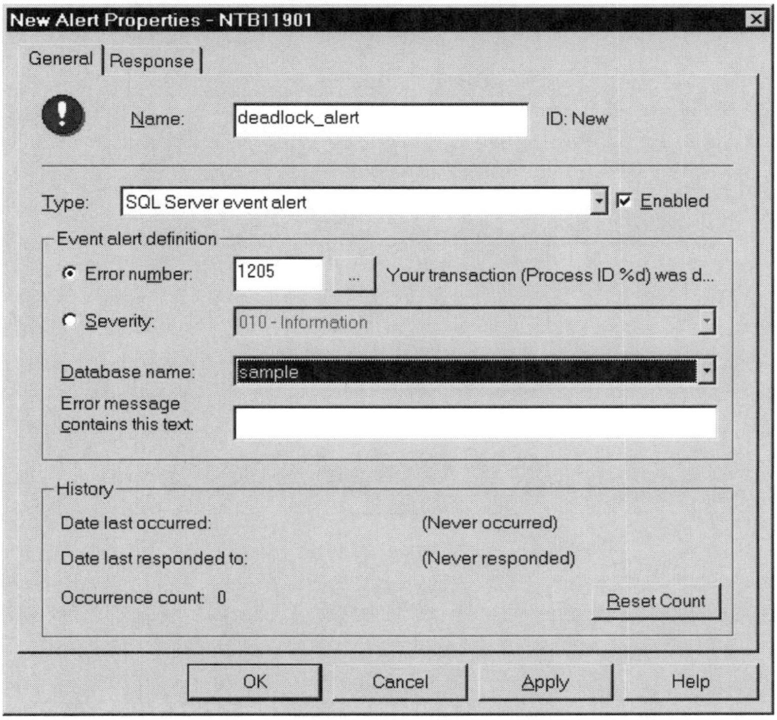

Figure 22-7. New Alert Properties dialog box

automatically displays the message text of the error number to the right side of the number. In the **Database name** list, choose **sample**.

The second step defines the response for the alert. Click the **Response** tab (see Figure 22-8). First select **Execute Job**, and then click a job to execute when the alert occurs. (In the example here, you should define a new job that restarts the victim transaction. This can be done by clicking the three dots (...) on the right side of the box.) In the **Operators to notify** frame, you can select operators and the methods of their notifications.

NOTE: In the example it is assumed that the victim transaction will be terminated. Actually, after receiving the deadlock error 1105, the program resubmits the failed transaction on its own.

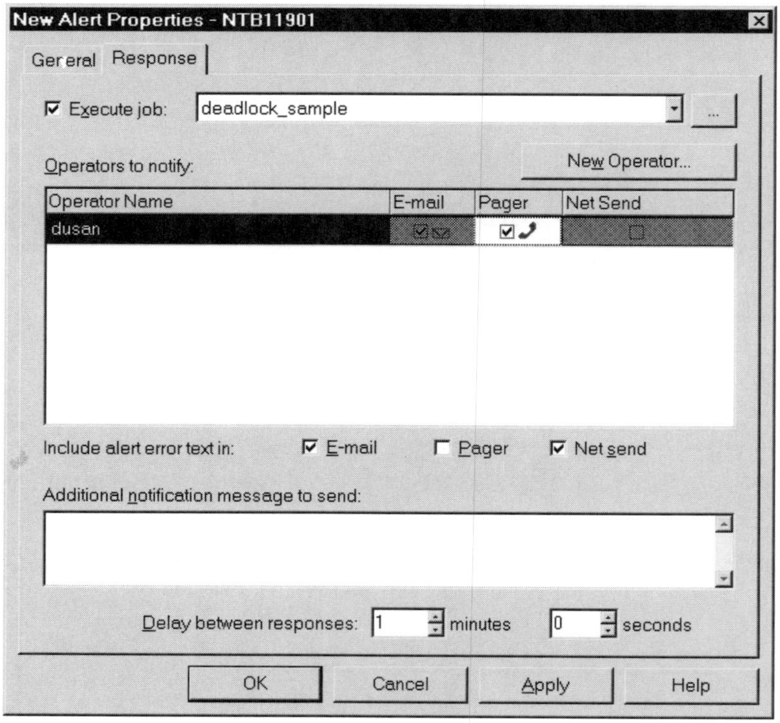

Figure 22-8. New Alert Properties dialog box—Response tab

NOTE: The creation of an alert on a SQL Server error number requires that the error number must be written to the Windows NT/2000 event log. By default, the error number 1205 is not written to the event log because of its low severity level. After the creation of the alert, the system prompts you to confirm that this message should be written to the event log.

Creating Alerts on SQL Server Severity Level

You can also define an alert that will raise a response on error severity levels. Each SQL Server error has a corresponding severity level that is a number between 0 and 25. The higher the severity level is, the more serious the error. SQL Server errors with severity levels 20 through 25 are fatal errors. SQL Server errors with severity levels 19 through 25 are written to the Windows NT/2000 event log.

NOTE: Always define an operator to be notified when a fatal error occurs.

SQL Server provides predefined alerts for all severity levels 19 through 25 (see Figure 22-9). These alerts are demo alerts and should be modified to satisfy specific needs of your database(s). Using the demo alert for severity level 24, let's see how the particular alert can be modified and extended.

Right-click **Demo: Sev. 24 Errors** and click **Properties**. The **Demo: Sev. 24 Error Properties** dialog box appears. On the **General** tab (see Figure 22-10), optionally give a new name to the alert, and enter the name of the database for which this alert should be valid. (You can create an alert to be raised when an error occurs on all databases or on a particular database.)

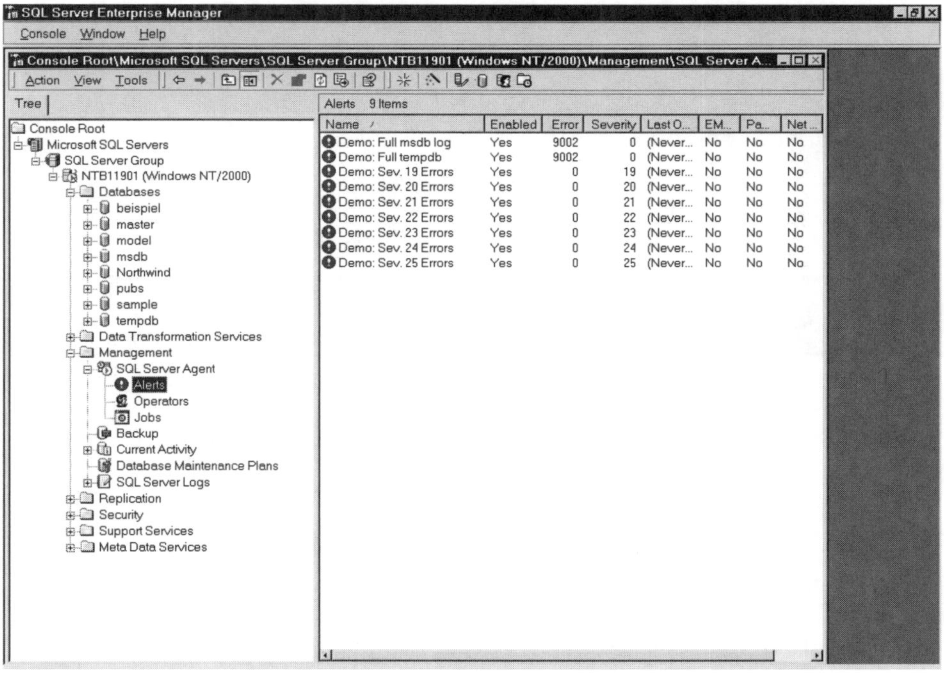

Figure 22-9. Predefined alerts for severity levels 19 through 25

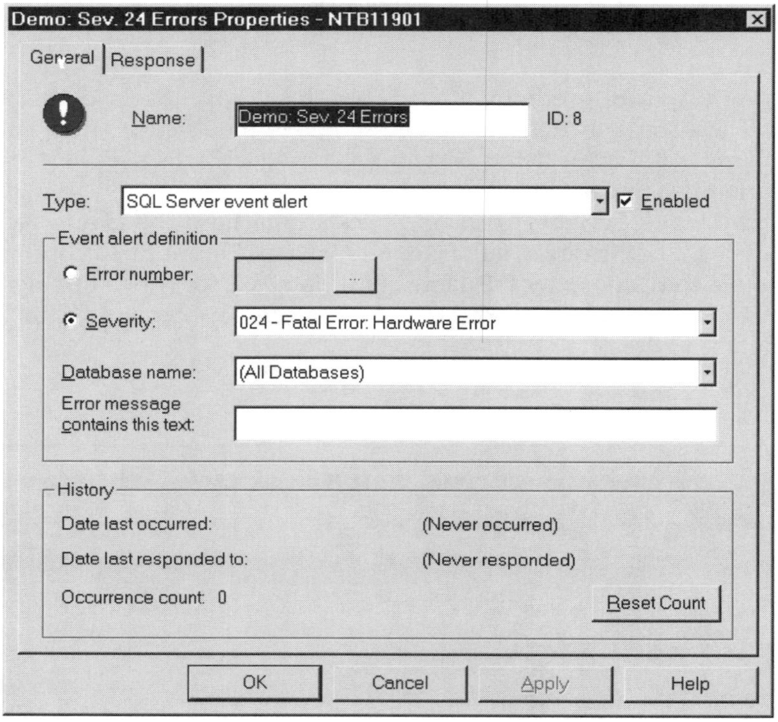

Figure 22-10. Sev. 24 Error Properties dialog box—General tab

On the **Response** tab, we enter one or more operators to be notified via e-mail and pager when an error of severity level 24 occurs.

Defining Alerts to Handle User-Defined Errors

In addition to creating alerts on SQL Server errors, you can create alerts on customized error messages for individual database applications. Using such messages (and alerts), you can define solutions to problems that can occur in an application.

The following steps are necessary if you want to create an alert on a user-defined message:

1. Create the error message.
2. Raise the error from a database application.
3. Define an alert on the error message.

An example is the best way to illustrate the creation of such an alert: the alert is fired if the shipping date of a product is earlier than the order date. (For the definition of the table **sales**, which contains those two columns, see Example 4.21.)

Creating the Error Message

To create user-defined errors, you can use Enterprise Manager or the **sp_addmessage** stored procedure. Example 22.1 creates the error message for the example using the **sp_addmessage** stored procedure.

▼ EXAMPLE 22.1

```
sp_addmessage 50010, 16, 'The shipping date of a product is earlier than the order
date', 'us_english', 'true'
```

The **sp_addmessage** stored procedure in Example 22.1 creates a user-defined error message with error number 50010 and severity level 16. All user-defined error messages are stored in the **sysmessages** system table of the **master** database. The error number in Example 22.1 is 50010 because all user-defined errors must be greater than 50000. (All error numbers less than 50000 are reserved for the SQL Server system.)

For each user-defined error message, you can optionally specify the language in which the message is displayed. The specification can be necessary if multiple languages are installed on your computer. (When language is omitted, the session language is the default language.)

By default, user-defined messages are not written to the Windows NT/2000 event log. On the other hand, you must write the message to the event log if you want to raise an alert on it. Therefore, the corresponding parameter of the **sp_addmessage** system procedure in Example 22.1 must be set to true.

Raising the Error from a Database Application

To raise an error from a database application, you invoke the RAISERROR statement. This statement returns a user-defined error message and sets a system flag in the **@@error** global variable.

Example 22.2 creates the trigger **t_date_comp** that returns a user-defined error 50010 if the shipping date of a product is earlier than the order date.

▼ EXAMPLE 22.2

```
CREATE TRIGGER t_date_comp
  ON sales
  FOR INSERT AS
  DECLARE @order_date DATETIME
  DECLARE @ship_date DATETIME
SELECT @order_date=order_date, @ship_date=ship_date FROM INSERTED
   IF @order_date > @ship_date
        RAISERROR (50010, 16, -1)
```

Defining an Alert on the Error Message

An alert on the user-defined message is defined in the same way as the alert on a SQL Server error message. This means, in the **New Alert Properties** dialog box (see Figure 22-7), enter the name of the alert in the **Name** box. Click **Error number**, and enter user-defined error. For the example, you need to enter the number 50010 in the **Error number** field of the **New Alert Properties** dialog box.

AUTOMATING JOBS IN A MULTISERVER ENVIRONMENT

If several SQL Server systems form a logical unit, it is recommended that you group them together. The benefit of grouping is that all systems can be administered from a central location more easily. In that case, a SQL Server group consists of a master server and one or more target servers. A master server manages all the servers belonging to the same group. Use the Make Master Server Wizard to define a master server and the Make Target Server Wizard to define each target server.

NOTE: To set up a multiserver environment, you must register all servers.

The benefit of a multiserver environment for the automation process is that a job is created once (on the master server) and can then be used many times on each of the target servers. Each target server frequently connects to the master server to check on whether any job is scheduled for execution. (The jobs for target servers are stored in the **sysddownloadlist** system table of the **master** database of the master server.) If a job exists, it is downloaded to the target server and executed on a schedule. The target server sends the information of the job execution to the master server.

CONCLUSION

SQL Server allows you to automate and streamline administrator tasks, such as database backup, data transfer, and maintenance of indices. For the execution of such tasks, SQL Server Agent must be running. The easiest way to create tasks is to use the Create Job Wizard, which automatically defines one or more job steps, creates an execution schedule, and optionally notifies operators by e-mail or pager.

Alerts are defined separately and can also be executed independently of jobs. An alert can handle individual SQL Server errors, user-defined errors, or groups of errors belonging to one of 25 severity levels in the SQL Server system.

The next chapter discusses SQL Server error messages and the system features that can be used to resolve them.

EXERCISES

▼ E.22.1

Name several administrative tasks which could be automated.

▼ E.22.2

You want to back up the transaction log of your database every hour during peak business hours and every four hours during nonpeak hours. What should you do?

▼ E.22.3

You want to test performance of your production database in relation to locks and want to know whether the lock wait time is over 30 seconds. How could you be notified automatically when this event occurs?

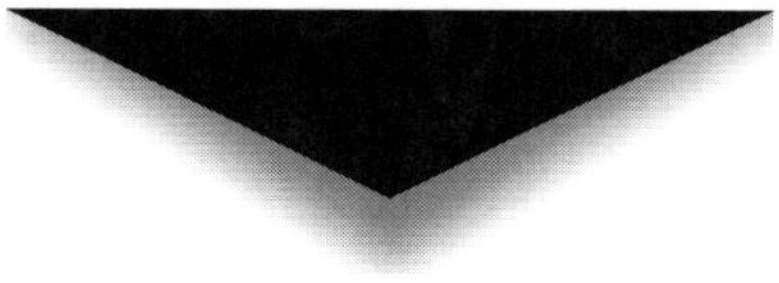

CHAPTER 23

Troubleshooting SQL Server

This chapter discusses SQL Server program and system errors and how to resolve them. The first section describes the general format of SQL Server error messages. It explains the SQL Server error log and the Windows NT/2000 event log, which are used to capture all system messages (and thus most of the errors). The second section of this chapter covers the possible resolutions provided by the SQL Server system.

ERROR MESSAGES

As explained at the beginning of Chapter 20, there are four different groups of errors that might occur in a SQL Server system. SQL Server provides extensive information about each error. The information is structured and includes the following:

- A unique error message number
- An additional number between 0 and 25, which represents the error's severity level
- A line number, which identifies the line where the error occurred
- The error text

> ***NOTE:*** The error text not only describes the detected error but also may recommend how to resolve the problem, which can be very helpful to the user.

Example 23.1 queries a nonexistent table in the sample database.

▼ EXAMPLE 23.1

```
USE sample
    SELECT * FROM authors
```

The result is

```
Server: Msg 208, Level 16, State 1
Invalid object name 'authors'.
```

All error messages are stored in the system table **sysmessages** of the **master** database. The three most important columns of this system table are **error**, **severity**, and **description**, which are described below.

Each unique error number has a corresponding error message. (The error message is stored in the **description** column, and the corresponding error number is stored in the **error** column of the system table **sysmessages**.) In Example 23.1, the message concerning the nonexistent or incorrectly spelled database object corresponds to error number 208.

The severity level of an error (the **severity** column of the system table **sysmessages**) is represented in the form of a number between 0 and 25. The levels between 0 and 10 are simply informational messages, where nothing needs to be fixed. All levels from 11 through 16 indicate different program errors and can be resolved by the user. The values 17 and 18 indicate software and hardware errors that generally do not terminate the running process. All errors with a severity level of 19 and greater are fatal system errors. The connection of the program generating such an error is closed, and its process will then be removed.

The messages relating to program errors (that is, the levels between 11 and 16) are shown on the screen only. All system errors (errors with a severity level of 19 or greater) will also be written to the error log file.

In order to resolve an error, you usually need to read the detailed description of the corresponding error. You can also find detailed error descriptions in the SQL Server online documentation.

SQL Server error messages are written to the SQL Server error log and to the Windows NT/2000 event log.

SQL Server Error Log

Each SQL Server system has an error log in the form of several text files. In addition to system errors, the error log records system activities such as starting, archiving, recovering, and stopping the system. SQL Server always maintains seven files, which are all part of the error log. When viewed in Enterprise Manager, the current error log file name is **Current**, and the other file names are **Archive #1** (the most recent file) up to **Archive #6** (the oldest file). When viewed directly in the SQL Server Log directory, the current error log file is named **Errorlog**; the other log files are named **Errorlog.1** through **Errorlog.6** in ascending order of their age.

The error log is an important source of information for the system administrator. With it, he or she can trace the progress of the system and determine which corrective actions to take. To view the SQL Server error logs from Enterprise Manager, expand the server and the **Management** folder and then expand **SQL Server Logs**. Click on one of the seven error logs to view the desired log. The log details appear in the details pane. Figure 23-1 shows the details of a SQL Server error log.

Windows NT/2000 Event Log

SQL Server also writes system messages to the Windows NT/2000 event log. The event log is the location of all operating system messages for the Windows NT/2000 system, and it is where all application messages are stored. You can view the event log using the Windows NT/2000 Event Viewer.

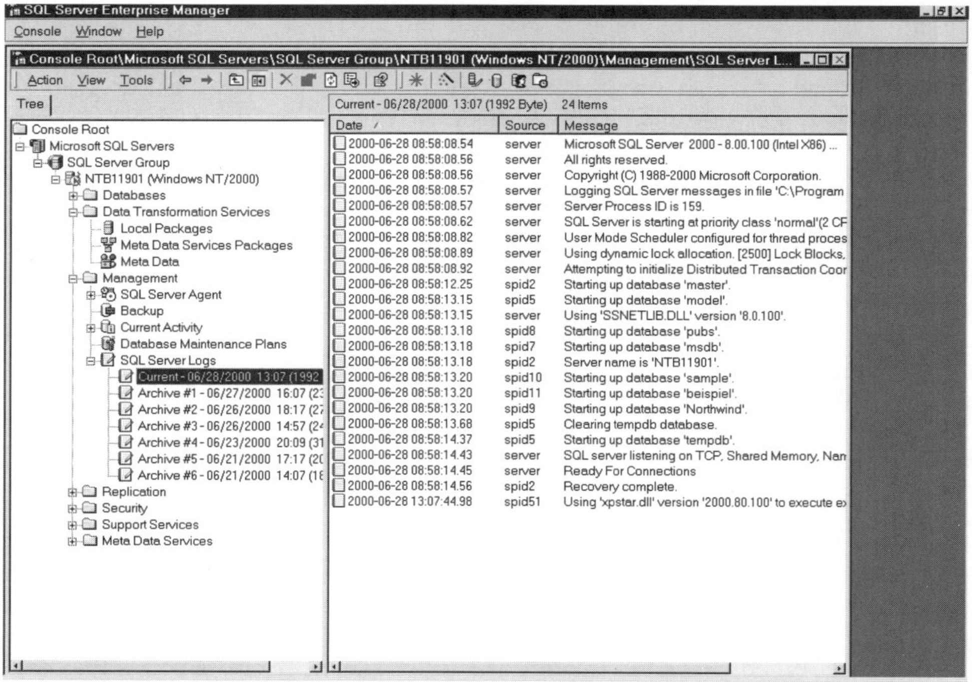

Figure 23-1. SQL Server error log

NOTE: The information in this section only applies to the Windows NT/2000 operating system and not to Windows 9x.

Using the event log for viewing errors has some advantages compared to the error log. First of all, the event log marks all errors with a red stop sign at the beginning of the line. Thus, the system administrator can recognize them immediately. Second, the event log provides an additional component for the search for desired strings.

To view information stored in the Windows NT/2000 event log, click **Start**, select **Programs**, choose **Administrative Tools**, and then select **Event Viewer**. (An alternative is to start Windows NT 2000 help and click the **Index** tab. Type **event logs** and click **Display**. Finally, click **Using Event Viewer to monitor Windows NT events**, and click **Display**.) Figure 23-2 shows the detail of an event log.

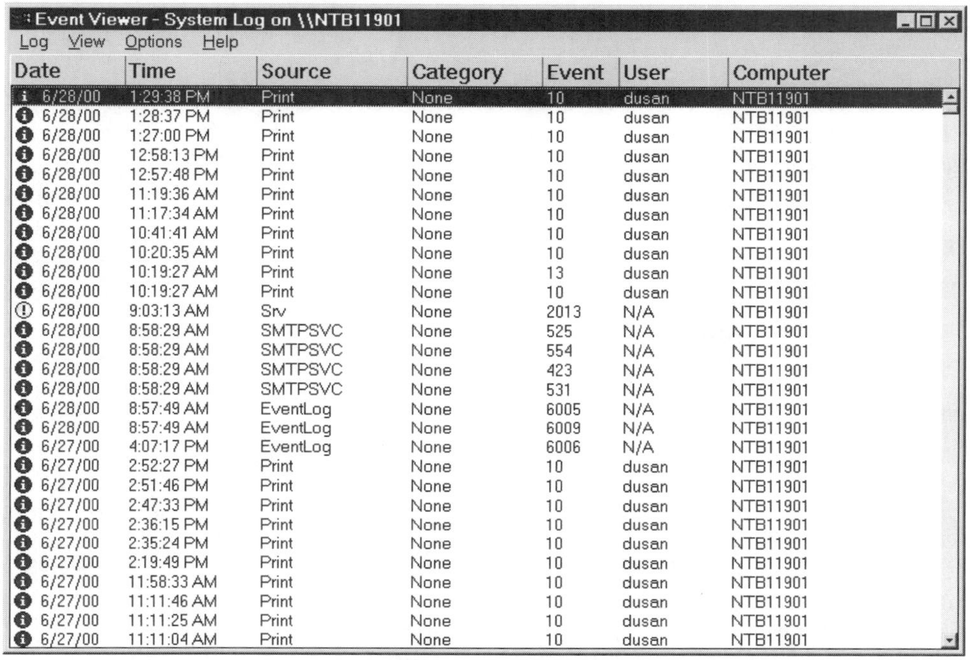

Event Viewer - System Log on \\NTB11901

Log View Options Help

Date	Time	Source	Category	Event	User	Computer
6/28/00	1:29:38 PM	Print	None	10	dusan	NTB11901
6/28/00	1:28:37 PM	Print	None	10	dusan	NTB11901
6/28/00	1:27:00 PM	Print	None	10	dusan	NTB11901
6/28/00	12:58:13 PM	Print	None	10	dusan	NTB11901
6/28/00	12:57:48 PM	Print	None	10	dusan	NTB11901
6/28/00	11:19:36 AM	Print	None	10	dusan	NTB11901
6/28/00	11:17:34 AM	Print	None	10	dusan	NTB11901
6/28/00	10:41:41 AM	Print	None	10	dusan	NTB11901
6/28/00	10:20:35 AM	Print	None	10	dusan	NTB11901
6/28/00	10:19:27 AM	Print	None	13	dusan	NTB11901
6/28/00	10:19:27 AM	Print	None	10	dusan	NTB11901
6/28/00	9:03:13 AM	Srv	None	2013	N/A	NTB11901
6/28/00	8:58:29 AM	SMTPSVC	None	525	N/A	NTB11901
6/28/00	8:58:29 AM	SMTPSVC	None	554	N/A	NTB11901
6/28/00	8:58:29 AM	SMTPSVC	None	423	N/A	NTB11901
6/28/00	8:58:29 AM	SMTPSVC	None	531	N/A	NTB11901
6/28/00	8:57:49 AM	EventLog	None	6005	N/A	NTB11901
6/28/00	8:57:49 AM	EventLog	None	6009	N/A	NTB11901
6/27/00	4:07:17 PM	EventLog	None	6006	N/A	NTB11901
6/27/00	2:52:27 PM	Print	None	10	dusan	NTB11901
6/27/00	2:51:46 PM	Print	None	10	dusan	NTB11901
6/27/00	2:47:33 PM	Print	None	10	dusan	NTB11901
6/27/00	2:36:15 PM	Print	None	10	dusan	NTB11901
6/27/00	2:35:24 PM	Print	None	10	dusan	NTB11901
6/27/00	2:19:49 PM	Print	None	10	dusan	NTB11901
6/27/00	11:58:33 AM	Print	None	10	dusan	NTB11901
6/27/00	11:11:46 AM	Print	None	10	dusan	NTB11901
6/27/00	11:11:25 AM	Print	None	10	dusan	NTB11901
6/27/00	11:11:04 AM	Print	None	10	dusan	NTB11901

Figure 23-2. Windows NT event log

RESOLVING ERRORS

Two of the tools that a system administrator can use to resolve an error are

- The KILL statement
- The DBCC statement

KILL Statement

By using the KILL statement, you can remove a process from the system. The syntax of this command is

```
KILL {spid} [WITH {ABORT | COMMIT}]
```

spid is the unique identification number of the user process within the system (*System Process ID*). ABORT and COMMIT are used exclusively with distributed transactions (transactions involving multiple servers). They specify the different modes of ending these transactions. The information about the existing processes and their corresponding identification numbers can be issued using the system procedure **sp_who**.

DBCC Statement

The DBCC statement verifies and, when necessary, repairs inconsistent logical database objects and the physical data structures of a SQL Server system. This command allows you to verify the objects using several options. The most important options are as follows:

- CHECKTABLE
- CHECKDB
- SHRINKDATABASE
- CHECKALLOC
- CHECKCATALOG
- CHECKFILEGROUP

The CHECKTABLE specification verifies the consistency of the data and index pages, the consistency of the pointers, and the correct sequence of the indices for the specified table. The most important options of this specification are three forms of the REPAIR option: REPAIR_FAST, REPAIR_REBUILD, and REPAIR_ALLOW_DATA_LOS. Using them, you can instruct the system to repair the errors you have found.

The second specification—CHECKDB—is identical to the CHECKTABLE specification except that it verifies all tables of the specified or current database. (The most important options of this specification are, again, REPAIR_FAST, REPAIR_REBUILD, and REPAIR_ALLOW_DATA_LOS.)

You can use the SHRINKDATABASE option as an alternative to free any unused disk space in the database tables. (For more information on this option, see Chapter 18 and Example 18.2.) Use the CHECKALLOC option to check the allocation of data pages and index pages for each table within its extents.

The CHECKCATALOG option verifies the consistency of each system table of the specified database as well as the consistency of the existing links between different system tables. When no database name is specified, the system tables of the current database will be verified.

The CHECKFILEGROUP option checks the structural integrity of all tables and indices that belong to the current database and are stored in the specified file group. During the structural integrity check, SQL Server verifies the existing links between data pages and index pages and also checks the consistency of pointers. If the file group is not specified, SQL Server checks all tables stored in the PRIMARY file group.

CONCLUSION

SQL Server offers several tools and commands for troubleshooting. You should become familiar with how to decode SQL Server error messages and how to use the error log of SQL Server and the event log of Windows NT/2000. Both logs will help you to investigate program errors and system failures. Once you locate the error, you can then use the DBCC command to try and resolve the error.

The next chapter is the logical continuation of this one. It explains how to monitor the SQL Server system.

EXERCISES

▼ E.23.1

Specify all parts of a SQL Server error message.

▼ E.23.2

Discuss the use of Windows NT/2000 Event Viewer and SQL Server error log. Which tool would you prefer to use to view SQL Server error messages?

▼ E.23.3

Which are the most important columns of the system table **sysmessages** concerning errors?

CHAPTER 24

Performance and Tuning

This chapter discusses performance issues and the tools for tuning SQL Server that are relevant to daily administration of the system. After introductory notes concerning the measurements of performance, the factors that affect performance are described. In the last part of the chapter, tools for monitoring SQL Server will be presented, with the focal point on SQL Server Query Analyzer and its ability to support users in tuning database applications. Some tips on how to choose the right tool for the job are given at the end of the chapter.

INTRODUCTION

Improving the performance of the SQL Server system requires many decisions, such as where to store data and how to access the data. This task is different from other administrative tasks because it comprises several different steps that concern all aspects of software and hardware. If the SQL Server system is not performing optimally, the system administrator has to check many factors and possibly tune software (operating system, database system, database applications) as well as hardware.

The performance of SQL Server (and any other relational DBMS that is used as an OLTP system) is measured by two criteria:

- Response time
- Throughput

Response time measures the performance of an individual transaction or program. Response time is treated as the length of time from the moment a user enters a command or statement until the time the system indicates that the command (statement) has completed. To achieve optimum response time of an overall system, almost all existing commands and statements (80 percent to 90 percent of them) must not cross the specified response time limit.

Throughput measures the overall performance of the system by counting the number of transactions that can be handled by SQL Server during the given time period. (The throughput is typically measured in transactions per second.) Therefore, there is a direct relation between response time of the system and its throughput: when the response time of a system degrades (for example, because a lot of users concurrently use the system), the throughput of the system degrades, too.

FACTORS THAT AFFECT PERFORMANCE

Factors affecting performance fall into three general categories:

- Database applications
- SQL Server
- System resources

They in turn can be affected by several factors, which are discussed in the following sections.

Database Applications and Performance

The following factors can affect the performance of the database application:

- Application-code efficiency
- Physical design

Application-Code Efficiency

Applications introduce their own load on the system software and on SQL Server. For this reason, they can contribute to performance problems if you make poor use of system resources. Most performance problems in application programs are caused by the improper choice of Transact-SQL statements and their sequence in an application program.

The following list gives some of the ways you can improve overall performance by modifying code in an application:

- Use clustered indices (examples will be given in the discussion of monitoring tools later in the chapter).
- Reformulate a query by *query flattening* (query flattening means that the optimizer attempts to change each correlated subquery into a "semijoin". The advantage of query flattening is that the subquery is changed to a join and therefore all join algorithms are possible).
- Do not use the NOT IN predicate.
- Use the Parallel Query option to distribute execution of complex and long-lasting queries over several processors, if possible (see also the description of parallel queries in Chapter 15).

NOTE: More hints on how code modification can improve overall performance are given in Chapter 10.

Physical Design

During physical database design, you choose the specific storage structures and access paths for the database files. In this design step, it is sometimes recommended that you denormalize some of the tables in the database to achieve good performance for various database applications. Denormalizing tables means that two or more normalized tables are coupled together, resulting in some redundant data.

Let us take an example to demonstrate the process of denormalization. Figure 24-1 shows two tables from the sample database: **department** and **employee**. These two tables are normalized. (For more information on data normalization, see Chapter 1.) Data in

emp_no	emp_fname	emp_lname	dept_no
25348	Matthew	Smith	d3
10102	Ann	Jones	d3
18316	John	Barrimore	d1
29346	James	James	d2
9031	Elke	Hansel	d2
28559	Sybill	Moser	d1

dept_no	dept_name	location
d1	Research	Dallas
d2	Accounting	Seattle
d3	Marketing	Dallas

Figure 24-1. The Tables **department** and **employee**

those two tables can be specified using just one table: **dept_emp** (see Figure 24-2). The table **dept_emp** shows the denormalized form of data stored in the tables **department** and **employee**. In contrast to the tables **department** and **employee**, which do not contain any data redundancies, the **dept_emp** table contains a lot of redundancies, because several columns of this table (**dept_name**, **location**) are dependent on the **dept_no** column.

emp_no	emp_fname	emp_lname	dept_no	dept_name	Location
25348	Matthew	Smith	d3	Marketing	Dallas
10102	Ann	Jones	d3	Marketing	Dallas
18316	John	Barrimore	d1	Research	Dallas
29346	James	James	d2	Accounting	Seattle
9031	Elke	Hansel	d2	Accounting	Seattle
28559	Sybill	Moser	d1	Research	Dallas

Figure 24-2. The **dept_emp** table

Data denormalization has two benefits and one disadvantage. First, if you have a column that is dependent on another column of the table (such as the **dept_name** column in the **dept_emp** table, which is dependent on the **dept_no** column) for data often required by queries, you can avoid the use of the join operation, which would affect the performance of applications. Second, denormalized data requires fewer tables than normalized data.

On the other hand, a denormalized table requires additional amounts of disk space and data modification is difficult because of data redundancy.

Another option in the physical database design that contributes to good performance is the creation of indices. Chapter 10 gives several guidelines for the creation of indices, and examples are given in the section "SQL Server Query Analyzer" later in this chapter.

SQL Server and Performance

SQL Server can substantially affect the performance of an entire system. The two most important SQL Server components that affect performance are

- Optimizer
- Locks

Optimizer

The optimizer formulates several query execution plans for fetching the data rows that are required to process a query and then decides which plan should be used. The decision concerning the selection of the most appropriate execution plan includes which indices should be used, how to access tables, and the order of joining tables. All these decisions can significantly affect the performance of database applications. The optimizer is discussed in detail in Chapter 10. A discussion of how users can affect the work of the optimizer is explained in the section "SQL Server Query Analyzer" in this chapter.

Locks

The database system uses locks as the mechanism for protecting one user's work from another's. Therefore, locks are used to control the access of data by all users at the same time and to prevent possible errors that can arise from the concurrent access of the same data.

Locking affects the performance of the system through its granularity—that is, the size of the object that is being locked and the isolation level. Row-level locking provides the best system performance, because it leaves all but one row on the page unlocked and hence allows more concurrency than page-level or table-level locking.

Isolation levels affect the duration of the lock for SELECT statements. Using the lower isolation levels, such as READ UNCOMMITTED and READ COMMITTED, the data availability and hence the concurrency of the data can be improved. (Locking and isolation levels are explained in detail in Chapter 14.)

System Resources and Performance

SQL Server runs on the Windows NT and Windows 2000 operating systems, which in itself uses underlying system resources. These resources have a significant impact to the performance of the operating system as well as the database system. Performance of any database system depends on four main system resources:

- CPU
- Memory
- Disk I/O
- Network

The CPU of your computer executes user processes and interacts with other resources of your system. Performance problems in relation to the CPU can occur when the operating system and user programs are making too many requests on it. There are many ways you can increase the performance of your system concerning the CPU, which will be discussed later in this chapter. Generally, the more CPU power available for your computer, the better the overall system is likely to perform.

SQL Server dynamically acquires and frees memory as needed. Performance problems concerning memory can occur only if there is not enough of it to do the required work. When this occurs, many memory pages are written to a pagefile. (The notion of a *pagefile* is explained in detail later in this chapter.) If the process of writing to a pagefile happens very often, the performance of the system can degrade. Therefore, similarly to the CPU rule, the more memory available for your computer, the better the system is likely to perform.

There are two issues concerning disk I/O: disk speed and disk transfer rate. The disk speed determines how fast read and write operations to disk are executed. The disk transfer rate specifies how much data can be written to disk during a time unit (usually measured in seconds). Obviously, the faster the disk, the larger the amount of data is being processed. Also, more disks are generally better than a single disk when many users are using the database system concurrently. (In this case, access to data is usually spread across many disks, thus improving the overall performance of the system.) Note that disk controllers can reduce the performance of the system if they control access to multiple disks.

For a client/server configuration, a SQL Server system sometimes performs poorly if there is a large number of client connections. In that case, the amount of data that needs to be transferred across the network possibly exceeds the network capacity. Another performance issue concerning networks can be the choice of network libraries that enable SQL Server to communicate with its clients.

All these four system resources are dependent on each other. This means that performance problems in one resource can cause performance problems in the other resources. Similarly, an improvement concerning one resource can significantly increase performance of some other (or even all) resources. For example:

- If you increase the number of CPUs, each CPU can share the load evenly and therefore can remedy the disk I/O bottleneck. On the other hand, the inefficient use of the CPU is often the result of a preexisting heavy load on disk I/O and/or memory.
- Also, if more memory is available, there is more chance of finding a page needed by the application (rather than reading the page from disk), which results in a performance gain. In contrast to it, reading from the disk drive, instead of drawing from the immensely faster memory, slows the system down considerably, especially if there are many concurrent processes.

CPU

The CPU (central processing unit), together with memory, is the key component for marking the speed of a computer. It is also the key to the performance of a system, because it manages other resources of the system and executes all applications. SQL Server can run on single-processor systems (i.e., a system with one CPU) or on a special class of multiprocessor systems called symmetric multiprocessing (SMP) systems. Recently, SQL Server uses Microsoft Cluster Server (MSCS) as one of the hardware platforms. MSCS provides cluster technology.

Symmetric multiprocessing specifies a system in which several processors share the main memory and disks. (Such systems are also called shared-disk systems, because they share a single operating system instance that manages one or more disks.) SMP systems usually have a high-speed interconnect that connects all processors. The benefits of SMP systems are easy administration and the need to reprogram the DBMS only slightly.

SQL Server was reprogrammed to be used with an SMP system because different processes had to be assigned parallel to more than one CPU. SQL Server supports the multithreaded architecture, where the processes are divided into threads that help the database system take better advantage of SMP systems. (SQL Server simply starts each thread and Windows NT assigns to each of them a specific CPU.)

The disadvantage of an SMP system is its restricted scalability. This means the number of processors that can be synchronized together is limited by the amount of main memory, which provides this task. For this reason, a new hardware architecture called a *cluster* was introduced.

A cluster specifies a group of computers that are connected through a network. In contrast to SMP systems, all processors within the cluster share a disk subsystem. The benefits of clusters are better scalability and reliability (i.e., clusters can tolerate failures of single computers because the remaining computers in the cluster can take over the processing).

NOTE: There is also a third hardware architecture called MPP (massively parallel processing). This hardware architecture offers the most scalability, because they do not share anything. For this reason those systems are also called *shared-nothing* systems, because each processor has its own main memory, its own disk subsystem, its own operating system, and its own DBMS. Although MPP systems offer outstanding scalability, they are difficult to administer.

Disk I/O

A purpose of a database is to store, retrieve, and modify data. Therefore, SQL Server, like any other database system, must perform a lot of disk activity. In contrast to other system resources, a disk subsystem has two moving parts: the disk itself and the disk head. The rotation of the disk and the movement of the disk head need relatively a lot of time, and therefore disk reads and writes are two of the highest-cost operations that a database system performs. (For instance, access to a disk is usually slower than memory access by a factor of two.)

The data in a SQL Server system is stored in 8K pages. The buffer cache of the RAM is also divided into 8K pages. SQL Server reads data in units of pages. Reads occur not only for data retrieval, but also for any modification operations such as UPDATE and DELETE, because the database system must read the data before it can be modified.

If the needed page is in the buffer cache, it will be read from memory. This I/O operation is called logical I/O or logical read. If it is not in memory, the page is read from disk and put in the buffer cache. This I/O operation is called physical I/O or physical read. Since the buffer cache is shared (because SQL Server uses the architecture with only one memory address space), many users can access the same page. A logical write occurs when data is modified in the buffer cache. Similarly, a physical write occurs when the page is written from the buffer cache to disk. Therefore, more logical write operations can be made on one page before it is written to disk.

SQL Server has several components that have great impact on performance, because they significantly consume the I/O resources. These components are as follows:

- Read ahead
- Lazy writer
- Checkpoint

The first two components will be described in the following sections, while the last one is explained in detail in Chapter 20.

Read Ahead The optimal behavior of a SQL Server system would be to read data and never have to wait for a disk read request. The best way to perform this task for a database system is to know the next several pages that the user will need and to read them from the disk into the buffer pool *before* they are requested by the user process. This mechanism is called *read ahead*, and it allows the system to optimize performance by processing large amounts of data effectively.

The component of SQL Server called Read Ahead Manager manages the read-ahead processes completely internally, so a user has no way to influence this process. (The previous versions of SQL Server supported several server configuration options, which were used by a user to modify the behavior of the database system concerning read-ahead operations.)

Instead of using the usual 8K pages, SQL Server uses 64K blocks of data as the unit for read-ahead reads. That way, the throughput for I/O requests is significantly increased. The read-ahead mechanism is used by a database system to perform large table scans and index range scans. Table scans in SQL Server are performed using the information that is stored in IAM pages to build a serial list of the disk addresses that must be read. This allows the database system to optimize its I/O as large sequential reads in disk order. Read Ahead Manager reads up to 2MB of data at a time. Each extent is read with a single operation.

NOTE: SQL Server provides multiple serial read-ahead operations at once for each file involved in the table scan. This feature can take advantage of striped disk sets.

For index ranges, SQL Server uses the information in the intermediate level of index pages immediately above the leaf level to determine which pages to read. SQL Server scans all these pages and builds a list of the leaf pages that must be read. During this operation, the contiguous pages are recognized and read in one operation. When there are many pages to be retrieved, SQL Server schedules a block of reads at a time. The number of reads scheduled is approximately 40.

The read-ahead mechanism can also have negative impacts on performance if too many pages for a process are read and the buffer cache is unnecessarily filled up. The only thing you can do in this case is create the indexes you will actually need.

The read-ahead activity of the system can be monitored using the following:

- Buffer Manager – Readahead Pages
- dbcc perfmon (iostats)

The **Buffer Manager – Readahead Pages** counter specifies a number of requests per second to read ahead 64K blocks before they are actually encountered. This counter gives you a general idea how busy read-ahead reads are in terms of actual physical I/O. The **dbcc perfmon (iostats)** is SQL Server's deprecated feature that displays the number of read-ahead blocks found in the buffer cache and the number of blocks placed in cache. (Each block that is already hashed by the system is found in the buffer cache.)

Lazy Writer Lazy writer is a system process that is responsible for writing pages from the buffer pool to disk. Therefore, the task of this process is to produce free buffers. To understand why the lazy writer process is necessary, just imagine what would happen without it.

When a page is overwritten in memory, it is marked as dirty, meaning its contents have been changed. Suppose the buffer cache is filled with dirty pages. Any process that reads a page from the disk cannot do it immediately because of the full buffer cache. Before reading the new page, the system has to write a dirty page from the buffer cache to disk to free a place for a new page. This process includes at least two I/O operations (one to the corresponding transaction log and the other to the database) and therefore would cause performance problems.

The start of the lazy writer process is initiated if the number of free buffers falls below the specified minimum size. (The series of free buffers is called the *free buffer list*.) The minimum size of the free list is computed as a percentage of the overall buffer pool size and is set to 3 percent for SQL Server 2000.

Generally the lazy writer process can function in two modes:

- Least recently used (LRU) list
- Clock algorithm

The LRU list contains two queues: a clear queue and a dirty queue. Pages (buffers) in the dirty queue must be written to disk before they can be used by any other user process. When a database server needs to read a page from disk, it finds a page from the least recently used end of the clean queue. After that, this buffer will be put on the most recently used end of the dirty queue.

SQL Server uses the clock algorithm to free pages from the buffer pool. The lazy writer process moves from one page to another and checks whether it has been referenced since the last visit. (The number of references is specified by a counter.) If the reference count of a page is zero, the page is written to disk and is moved to the free list of pages. If the reference count of a page is not zero, the page stays in the buffer pool, but the lazy writer process decrements its reference count.

NOTE: The increment of the page does not happen uniformly. The data and index pages are incremented by one each time the page is referenced, but the pages that are expensive to create (such as pages of an execution plan of a stored procedure) get a higher increment count. On the other hand, the lazy writer process decrements the count of used pages during each visit by dividing the count by 4. That way all frequently referenced pages and pages with high priority stay longer in the buffer pool than all other pages.

SQL Server automatically manages the level of the free list. There are several Performance Monitor counters that display the information concerning the lazy writer process:

- SQL Server: Buffer Manager – Free Buffers
- SQL Server: Buffer Manager – Lazy Writes/sec

The **Buffer Manager – Free Buffers** counter displays the number of free buffers. The constant value for this counter means that the free list keeps up with the user demands for free pages. If the value of the counter drops to zero, you will probably need additional disk drives to provide more disk I/O processing power. The **Buffer Manager – Lazy Writes/sec** counter indicates the number of pages that are written to disk by the lazy writer process and therefore gives you a hint concerning the percentage of dirty pages in the buffer pool.

The only one server option that influences the lazy writer process is the **max async I/O** option. The **max async io** option is an advanced system configuration option that sets the maximum number of asynchronous disk I/O operations that can be issued against a file. The default value (32) is adequate for almost all systems with ordinary disk subsystems. If you have high-performance servers with databases spanning several physical drives, you can increase the value of the **max async io** option and test if there are any performance improvements. (These improvements will appear during intensive I/O operations.) Decreasing the value of this option influences disk queuing.

Memory

Memory is a crucial resource component not only for the running applications but also for the operating system. When an application is executed, it is loaded into memory and a certain amount of memory is allocated to the application. (In Windows NT/2000 terminology, the total amount of memory available for an application is called its *address space*.)

Windows NT/2000 supports virtual memory. This means that the total amount of memory available to applications is the amount of physical memory (or RAM) in the computer plus the size of the specific file on the disk drive called pagefile. (The logical name of the pagefile on Windows NT/2000 is PAGEFILE.SYS.) Once data is moved out of its location in the RAM, it resides in the pagefile. If the system is asked to retrieve data that is not in the proper RAM location, it will load the data from the location where it is stored and additionally produce a so-called page fault.

NOTE: PAGEFILE.SYS should be placed on a different drive than the files used by SQL Server, because the paging process can have an impact on disk I/O activities.

For an entire application, only a portion of it resides in the RAM of the computer. (Recently referenced pages can usually be found in the RAM.) When the information the application needs is not in the RAM, the operating system must page (i.e., read the page from the pagefile into the RAM). This process is called demand paging. The more the system has to page, the worse the performance is.

NOTE: When a page in the RAM is required, the oldest page of the address space for an application is moved to the pagefile to make room for the new page. The replacement of pages is always limited to the address space of the current application. Therefore, there is no chance that pages in the address space of other running applications will be replaced.

As you already know, a page fault occurs if the application makes a request for information and the data page that contains that information is not in the proper RAM location of the computer. The information may either have been paged out to the pagefile or be located somewhere else in the RAM. Therefore, there are two types of page fault: a hard page fault and a soft page fault. A hard page fault means that the page had been paged out (to the pagefile) and has to be brought into the RAM from the disk drive. The soft page fault occurs when the page is found in another location in RAM. Soft page faults consume only CPU resources. Therefore, they are better for performance than hard page faults, which cause disk reads and writes to occur.

NOTE: Page faults are normal in a Windows NT/2000 environment, because the operating system requires pages from the running applications to satisfy the need for memory of the starting ones. However, excessive paging (especially with hard page faults) is a serious performance problem, because it can cause disk bottlenecks and start to consume the additional power of the processor.

Network

For client/server configuration, a SQL Server system sometimes performs poorly if there is a large number of client connections. To avoid such a performance bottleneck, the following general recommendations should be taken into account:

- If a database server sends any rows to an application, only the rows needed by the application should be sent. (In addition, use the ROWCOUNT option in the SET statement to restrict the display of selected rows to a certain amount.)
- If a long-lasting user application executes strictly on a client side, move it to a server side (by executing it as a stored procedure, for example).

SQL SERVER MONITORING TOOLS

All the factors that affect performance can be monitored using different SQL Server and Windows NT tools. These tools can be grouped in three categories:

- Application performance tools
- SQL Server–specific monitoring
- System resource tools

The following sections describe the tools for dealing with performance factors discussed in the first part of the chapter.

Application Performance Tools

As already stated, most performance problems in applications are caused by the improper choice of Transact-SQL statements and/or the inappropriate use of indices. Therefore, you will gain a thorough understanding of the performance of an application by examining each query executed in it. SQL Server Query Analyzer is the most suitable tool for this task.

SQL Server Query Analyzer

As you know by now, Query Analyzer is a tool used to generate, execute, and store Transact-SQL statements. Besides these features, which are described in detail in Chapter 2, you can use Query Analyzer to show the execution plan of a query, either in the form of text or graphics. This allows you to examine the plan and to make corrections concerning indices of the query if the performance of the query is inefficient. The SQL Server optimizer provides several different solutions (called query execution plans) for executing a query of an application program. After that, the optimizer chooses the best plan and executes the query.

When you run the query, you can display the textual execution plan for the query by activating the SHOWPLAN_TEXT or SHOWPLAN_ALL option of the SET statement. Both options display detailed information about the selected execution for the query. (The SQL Server optimizer, the SHOWPLAN_TEXT, and SHOWPLAN_ALL options are described in detail in Chapter 9.)

Using an example, you will see how the performance of a query can be improved by modifying the index of the query. This modification will be shown by the textual and graphical features of SQL Server Query Analyzer.

SQL Server uses two different data organization forms to store data of a table on the disk: heaps and clustered tables. A *heap* is a form of data organization in which table data are not stored in any particular order and there is no particular order to the sequence of the data pages. Tables that have no clustered index are stored in heaps. (For this reason, such a table is sometimes called a heap in SQL Server terminology.)

The data rows of a *clustered table* are stored in order based on the clustered index, and the data pages are linked using the linked list. Which physical data structure SQL Server chooses depends on the form of the CREATE INDEX statement. (Tables without any index as well as tables with only nonclustered indices are stored using heaps.)

Example 24.1 shows two tables that are used to demonstrate the way to improve performance of a query by using clustered indices.

▼ EXAMPLE 24.1

```
CREATE TABLE orders
  (orderid INTEGER NOT NULL,
   orderdate DATETIME,
   shippeddate DATETIME,
   freight money)

CREATE TABLE order_details
  (productid INTEGER NOT NULL,
   orderid INTEGER NOT NULL,
   unitprice money,
   quantity INTEGER)
```

Suppose the **orders** table contains 3,000 rows, and the **order_details** table contains 10 rows per row of the **orders** table on average. (There is a 1:N relationship between the **orders** table and the **order_details** table; that is, for each row of the former table, there is zero, one, or more rows in the latter table.) The following two examples show the batches that can be used to load data into those two tables.

▼ EXAMPLE 24.2

```
declare @i int , @order_id integer
        declare @orderdate datetime
        declare @shipped_date datetime
        declare @freight money
        set @i = 1
        set @orderdate = getdate()
        set @shipped_date = getdate()
        set @freight = 100.00
       while @i < 3001
        begin
        insert into orders (orderid, orderdate, shippeddate, freight)
          values( @i, @orderdate, @shipped_date, @freight)
        set @i = @i+1
        end
```

▼ EXAMPLE 24.3

```
-- This procedure inserts 30000 rows in the table order_details

        declare @i int, @j int
        set @i = 3000
        set @j = 10
        while @j > 0
        begin
        if @i > 0
           begin
           insert into order_details (productid, orderid, quantity)
                 values (@i, @j, 5)
          set @i = @i –1
          end
        else begin
            set @j = @j - 1
            set @i = 3000
           end
        end
        update order_details set quantity = 3
             where orderid in (1511, 2678)
```

Example 24.4 shows the query used to demonstrate the possible performance issues.

▼ EXAMPLE 24.4

```
SELECT orders.orderid, orders.orderdate, order_details.unitprice
     FROM orders, order_details
    WHERE orders.orderid = order_details.ordered
    AND order_details.quantity = 3
```

By creating the indices shown in Example 24.5, both tables are stored in heaps.

▼ EXAMPLE 24.5

```
CREATE UNIQUE INDEX i_order_orderid ON orders(orderid)
CREATE INDEX i_details_prodid ON order_details(productid)
CREATE INDEX i_details_orderid ON order_details(orderid)
```

Figures 24-3 and 24-4 show the textual and graphical forms of the query execution plan for the query in Example 24.4. (To display the textual execution plan of a query, you have to activate the SHOWPLAN_TEXT or SHOWPLAN_ALL option of the SET statement. To display the graphical execution of a query, you have to click **Execute Mode** in the toolbar of Query Analyzer and select **Show Execution Plan**.)

The query execution plan of Figure 24-3 is read from the *bottom up*. Therefore, the SQL Server optimizer first uses index **i_order_orderid** for the index search on the **orderid** column in the **orders** tables and a sequential scan on the **quantity** column. After that, the nested-loop method for the join operation in Example 24.4 is applied.

As the next operator, the bookmark lookup is executed. Bookmark Lookup represents the RID (row identifier) that is used to look up the row that corresponds to the selected index value. Therefore, a bookmark specifies a value that is used to identify the corresponding row.

The physical structure of the tables **orders** and **order_details** can be modified if clustered indices are created (instead of nonclustered ones). Example 24.6 creates two clus-

```
StmtText
-----------------------------------------------------------------------------------------------------
  |--Bookmark Lookup(BOOKMARK:([Bmk1000]), OBJECT:([sample1].[dbo].[orders]))
     |--Nested Loops(Inner Join, OUTER REFERENCES:([order_details].[orderid]))
         |--Table Scan(OBJECT:([sample1].[dbo].[order_details]), WHERE:([order_details].[quantity]=3))
         |--Index Seek(OBJECT:([sample1].[dbo].[orders].[i_order_orderid]),
SEEK:([orders].[orderid]=[order_details].[orderid]) ORDERED FORWARD)
```

Figure 24-3. Textual form of the execution plan with nonclustered indices

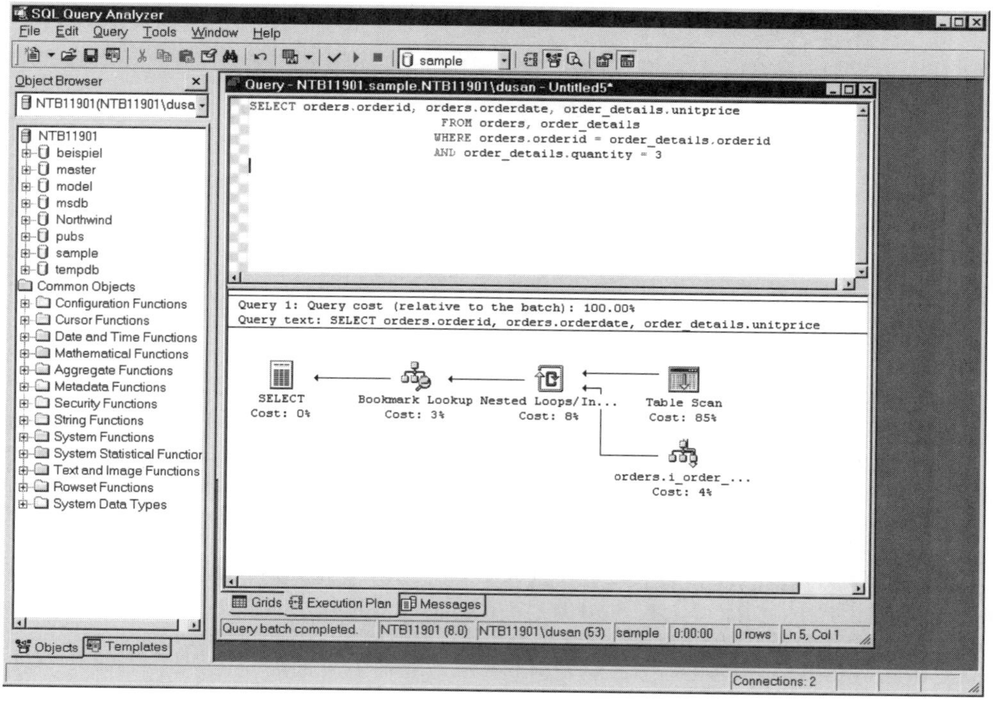

Figure 24-4. Graphical form of the execution plan with nonclustered indices

tered indices for these tables. (The existing indices for the **orderid** column in both tables, **orders** and **order_details**, must be dropped before you create the new indices.)

▼ EXAMPLE 24.6

```
DROP INDEX orders.i_order_orderid
DROP INDEX order_details.i_details_prodid
DROP INDEX oder_details.i_details_orderid
CREATE UNIQUE CLUSTERED INDEX ci_order_orderid ON orders(orderid)
CREATE  CLUSTERED INDEX ci_details_orderid ON order_details(orderid)
```

The creation of clustered indices in Example 24.6 stores both tables as clustered tables; that is, the rows of each table are stored in order based on the clustered index, and the data pages are linked using the linked list.

Figures 24-5 and 24-6 show the textual and graphical forms of the execution plan of the query in Example 24.4.

```
StmtText
--------------------------------------------------------------------------------
  |--Nested Loops(Inner Join, OUTER REFERENCES:([order_details].[orderid]))
       |--Clustered Index Scan(OBJECT:([sample1].[dbo].[order_details].[ci_details_orderid]),
WHERE:([order_details].[quantity]=3))
       |--Clustered Index Seek(OBJECT:([sample1].[dbo].[orders].[ci_order_orderid]),
SEEK:([orders].[orderid]=[order_details].[orderid]) ORDERED FORWARD)
```

Figure 24-5. Textual form of the execution plan with clustered indices

If clustered indices are used, the number of operations is reduced from five to three. This change will result in significant improvements of the execution time for the query in Example 24.4.

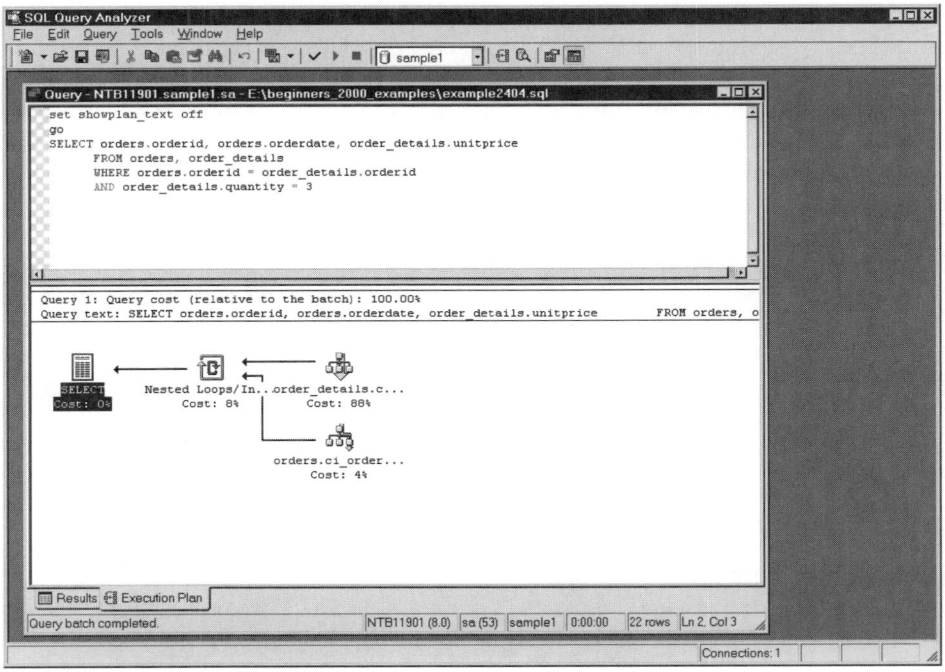

Figure 24-6. Graphical form of the execution plan with clustered indices

SQL Server–Specific Monitoring

In addition to locking, which has already been described, the number of user connections and logging activities is a performance factor specific to SQL Server. You can monitor this performance factor using SQL Server Profiler, several system procedures, Transact-SQL statements, and the DBCC statement. In this section, we will describe all procedures and statements except SQL Server Profiler. This tool is described at the end of this chapter, together with the Index Tuning Wizard.

Using System Procedures to Monitor SQL Server Activities

The following system procedures can be used to monitor SQL Server activities:

- sp_lock
- sp_helpindex
- sp_monitor
- sp_who
- sp_spaceused

The system procedures **sp_lock** and **sp_helpindex** display the overall information about locks and indices, respectively. The former procedure is covered in more detail in Chapter 10.

The system procedure **sp_monitor** displays SQL Server statistics—for example, the number of seconds the CPU has been doing SQL Server activities, the number of seconds SQL Server has been idle, the number of read/write operations by SQL Server, and the number of logins (or attempted logins) to SQL Server.

The system procedure **sp_who** displays information about current SQL Server users, such as the system process ID, the process status, the SQL Server command, and the database used by the process. **sp_spaceused** displays the amount of disk space used for data and indices and the disk space used by a table in the current database.

Using Transact-SQL Statements to Monitor SQL Server Activities

Two Transact-SQL statements can be used to show statistics of a SQL Server system:

- SET STATISTICS_TIME
- SET STATISTICS I/O

Using the DBCC Command for Monitoring

The DBCC command has two general application areas:

- To verify and repair inconsistent logical database objects and their physical data structures
- To check the performance and activities of the overall system

The options of the DBCC command that apply to the first application area are described in Chapter 23. The following options concern system performance:

- SHOW_STATISTICS
- MEMUSAGE
- PERFMON

The SHOW_STATISTICS option computes the current distribution statistics for an index (or a column) of a table. It displays the number of rows, the number of rows sampled for statistics information, the selectivity of the index, and the number of histogram values in the current distribution statistics.

The MEMUSAGE option returns information about memory usage. It displays a snapshot of memory used by logical objects in the buffer and/or procedure cache. With the additional PROCEDURE specification, DBCC MEMUSAGE returns the overall information about memory that is used by the 12 largest logical objects in the procedure cache.

The PERFMON option displays all types of performance statistics: disk I/O (with the IOSTATS specification), memory and cache usage (with the LRUSTATS specification), and network activity (with the NETSTATS specification).

Tools for Monitoring System Resources

System resources such as memory and disk I/O can be examined using the following:

- Windows NT/2000 Event Viewer
- SQL Server Performance Monitor

Windows NT/2000 Event Viewer is used to view the Windows NT event log. (The event log is where all operating system messages of a Windows NT system and all application messages are stored.) For more information on Event Viewer and the event log, see Chapter 23.

SQL Server Performance Monitor

SQL Server Performance Monitor is the Windows NT/2000 component that provides the ability to monitor Windows NT/2000 as well as SQL Server system activities. The benefit of this tool is that it is tightly integrated with Windows NT and therefore displays reliable values concerning different performance issues.

To start SQL Server Performance Monitor, click **Start | Programs | Administrative Tools**, and finally, **Performance Monitor**. The **Performance Monitor** dialog box appears (Figure 24-7).

NOTE: As you can see from Figure 24-7, the use of Performance Monitor is obvious, so there is no need for any explanation.

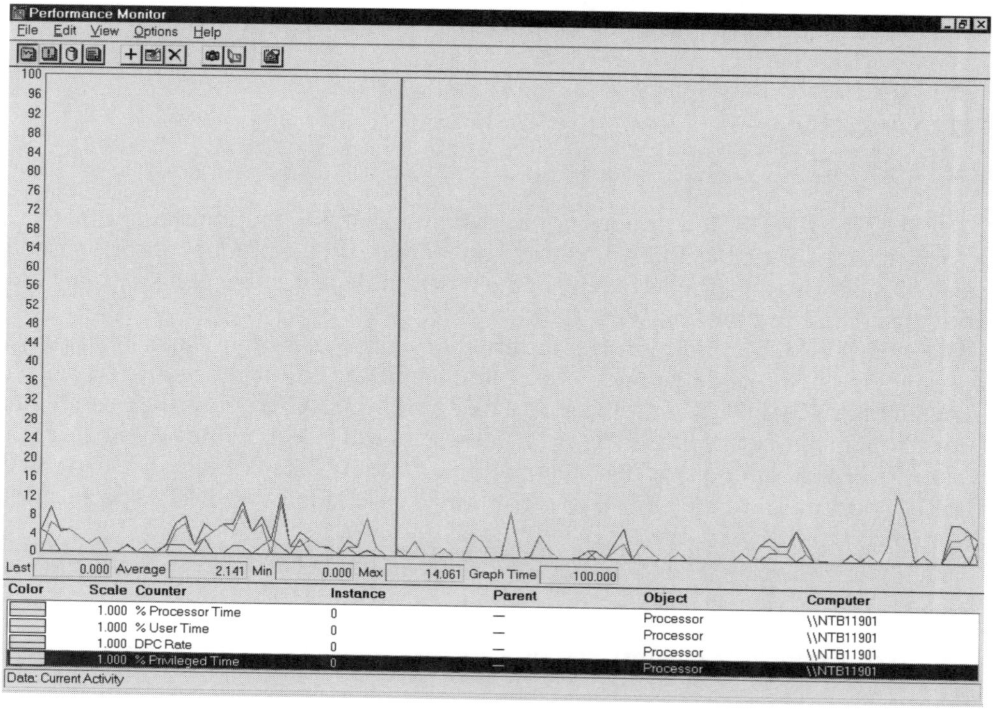

Figure 24-7. Performance Monitor dialog box

CHOOSE THE RIGHT TOOL

The choice of an appropriate tool depends on the performance factors to be monitored and the type of monitoring. The type of monitoring can be

- Real time
- Delayed (by saving information in the file, for example)

Real-time monitoring means that performance issues are investigated as they are happening. If you want to display the actual values of one or a few performance factors, such as number of users or number of attempted logins, use the DBCC command or the corresponding system procedures, because of their simplicity. In fact, the DBCC command as well as system procedures can only be used for real-time monitoring. Therefore, if you want to trace performance activities during a specific time period, you have to use a tool such as SQL Server Profiler.

Probably the best all-around tool for monitoring is SQL Server Performance Monitor, because of its many options. First, you can choose the performance activities you want to track and display them simultaneously. Second, Performance Monitor allows you to set thresholds on specific counters (performance factors) to generate alerts that notify operators. This way, you can react promptly to any performance bottlenecks. Third, you can report performance activities and investigate the resulting chart log files later.

In this section, I'll describe the following tools that are relevant to performance issues:

- SQL Server Profiler
- Index Tuning Wizard

SQL Server Profiler

SQL Server Profiler is a graphical tool that lets system administrators monitor and record database and server activities, such as login, user, and application information. Profiler can display information about several server activities in real time, or it can create filters to focus on particular events of a user, types of commands, or types of Transact-SQL statements. Among others, you can monitor the following events using SQL Server Profiler:

- Login connections, attempts, failures, and disconnections
- CPU use of a statement
- Deadlock problems
- All DML statements (SELECT, INSERT, UPDATE, and DELETE)
- The start or end of a stored procedure

The most useful feature of this tool is the possibility of capturing activities in relation to Transact-SQLS statements, such as SELECT. These activities can be used as input for the Index Tuning Wizard that allows you to select indices for one or more queries. For more information on the Index Tuning Wizard, see the next section.

Index Tuning Wizard

In this section, you will find a discussion about the Index Tuning Wizard that is part of SQL Server and that allows you to automate the index selection problem. The Index Tuning Wizard is tightly connected to another SQL Server tool called SQL Server Profiler. As you already know, SQL Server Profiler can display information about several server activities in real time, or it can create filters to focus on particular events of a user, types of commands, or Transact-SQL statements.

The specific feature of SQL Server Profiler that is used by the Index Tuning Wizard is to watch and record batches executed by users and to provide performance information such as CPU use of a batch and corresponding I/O statistics.

Providing Information for Index Tuning Wizard

The Index Tuning Wizard is usually used together with SQL Server Profiler to automate index selection. You use SQL Server Profiler to record information about the workload being examined into a file with the suffix ".trc". (As an alternative to a workload file, you can use any file that contains a set of Transact-SQL statements. In this case, you do not need Profiler.) The file can be read by the Index Tuning Wizard, and the wizard recommends indexes that should be created for the given workload.

First you have to set up SQL Server Profiler by clicking Profiler in the **Enterprise Manager Tools** menu. On the **File** menu, select **New** and then click **Trace**. In the **Trace Properties** dialog box, type a name for the trace and select an output .trc file for the Profiler information (in the **Capture to file** field). Click OK to start the capture and use Query Analyzer to execute the query in Example 24.7. Finally, stop SQL Server Profiler by clicking **Stop Traces** on the **File** menu and select the corresponding trace.

Let us use an example to see how the Index Tuning Wizard evaluates the file created by SQL Server Profiler. I'll use the tables **orders** and **order_details** (see Example 24.1) to demonstrate the recommendation of indexes by the Index Tuning Wizard. Suppose the **orders** table contains 5,000 rows, and the **order_details** table contains 11 rows per row of the **order_details** table on average. The query in Example 24.7 will be used as an input file for SQL Server Profiler. (We suppose that no indices for the columns that appear in the SELECT statement are created.)

▼ EXAMPLE 24.7

```
SELECT orders.orderid, orders.shippeddate
    FROM orders
  WHERE orders.orderid between 806 and 1600
  and not exists (SELECT order_details.orderid
                    FROM order_details
                    WHERE order_details.orderid = orders.orderid)
```

Working with the Index Tuning Wizard

All these steps were preliminary. The real work with the Index Tuning Wizard begins now. To use the wizard, click the Wizard icon in the toolbar of Enterprise Manager, select **Management**, and choose **Index Tuning Wizard** (see Figure 24-8). (The alternative way is to start SQL Server Profiler in the **SQL Server** menu and select the wizard on the **Tools** tab of the **Profiler** menu.) In the next step, using the **Select Server** and **Database** dialog box (see Figure 24-9), you have to select the server and the corresponding database. In

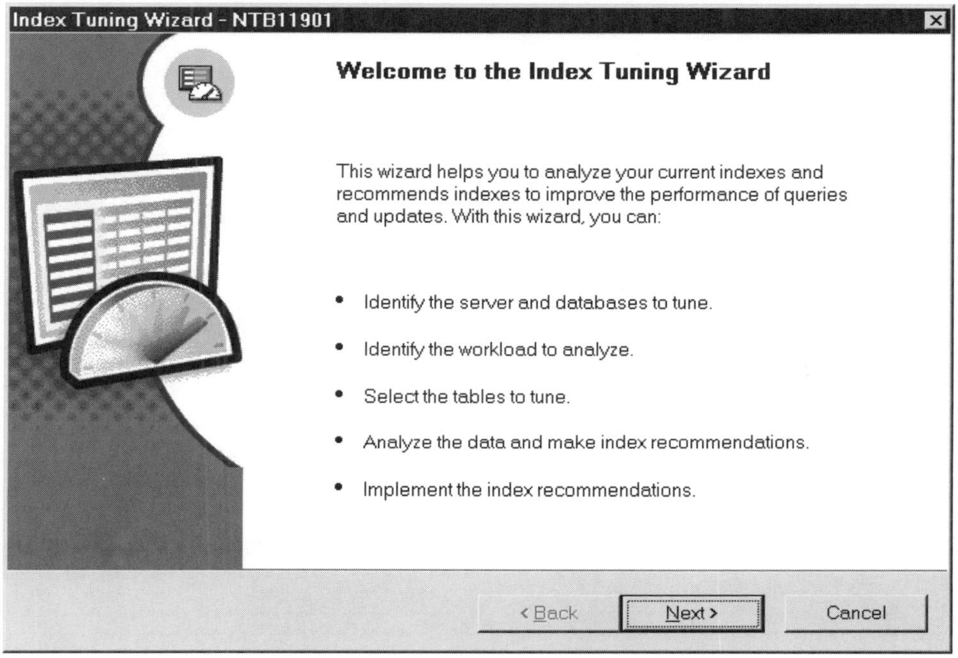

Figure 24-8. Index Tuning Wizard – The Initial Window

this step, you can additionally activate (or deactivate) three check boxes to customize index selection options:

- Keep all existing indexes
- Perform thorough analysis
- Add indexed views

The first option allows you to choose between keeping and dropping existing indexes. If you decide to keep all existing indexes, you can change your index design incrementally (in several steps). Also, you can start from scratch and allow the wizard to decide which indexes are appropriate for the given batch.

For large databases, index selection usually requires a significant amount of time and resources. Instead of starting an exhaustive search for possible indexes, the Index Tuning Wizard offers (by default) the restrictive use of time and resources. This operation mode still gives very accurate results, although the resources and time are significantly lessened.

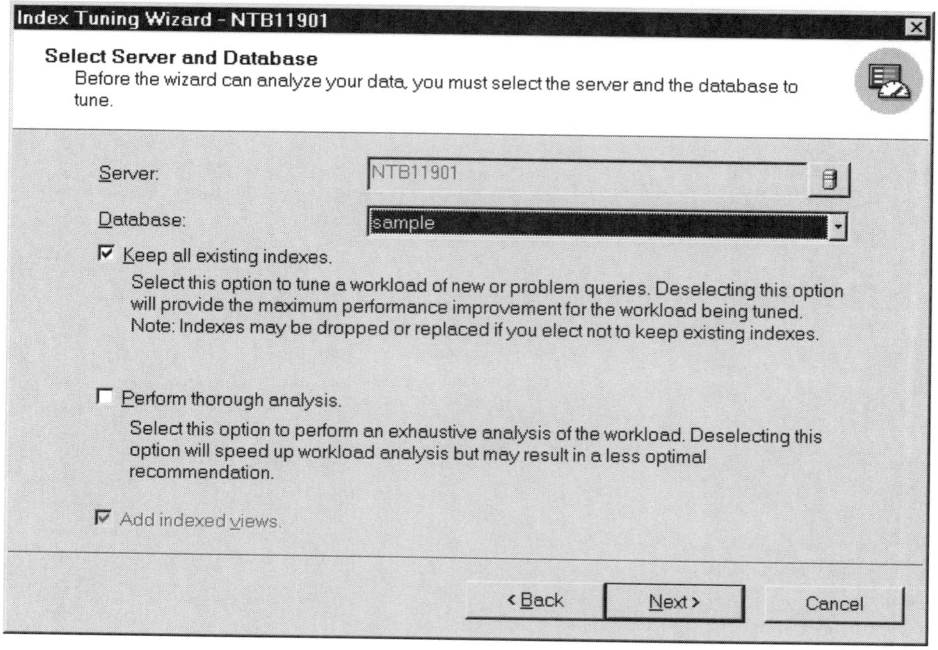

Figure 24-9. The Select Server and Database dialog box

After selection of the server and the corresponding database, choose **My workload file** to make sure that a workload file from SQL Server Profiler will be used for index recommendation. In the next step, you select the workload file, which you created with SQL Server Profiler and which you saved after stopping Profiler. During the specification of the workload file, you can define additional customization options by clicking the **Advanced Options** button (see Figure 24-10). The **Advanced Options** dialog box has two parts: a fixed part and the part with the default values that can be modified. The fixed part informs you about the current data and index size as well as about the space that is available for (index and data) growth.

The first parameter—**Maximum queries to sample**—determines how many queries will be examined from the beginning of the workload. By reducing the value of this parameter, the size of the workload will be reduced, so you can speed up the execution of the wizard. The second index tuning parameter allows you to modify the disk space for the recommended indexes. This parameter depends on your previous decision to drop or keep existing indexes. In the latter case, the disk space includes also the storage for existing indexes.

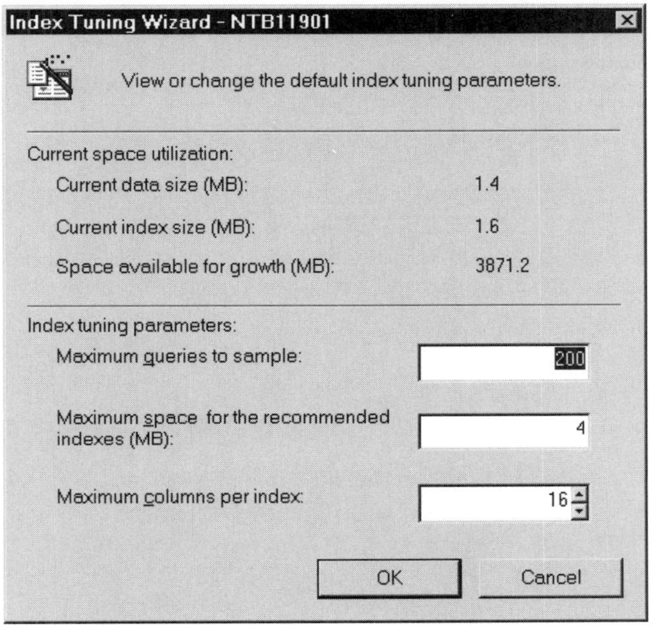

Figure 24-10. The Advanced Option dialog box

Of all index tuning parameters, the most interesting is the parameter to determine the maximum number of columns per index. A single-column index or a composite index built on two columns can be used several times for a workload with many queries and requires less storage space than a composite index built on four or more columns. (This is in the case where you use a workload file on your own instead of using Profiler's trace for the specific workload.) On the other hand, the latter index may be used as a covering index to enable index-only access for some of the queries in the workload.

In the next step, you use the **Select Tables to Tune** dialog box to select tables. This step allows you to narrow the index selection to only the tables that appear in the workload without modifying existing indexes for the other tables in the database. (Choose the tables **orders** and **order_details** and go on.) Finally, during the evaluation step, the Index Tuning Wizard examines the use of different indexes by iteration. In the first iteration, only single-column indexes are considered. The following iterations search for possible indexes built on two columns, three columns, and so on.

The most important step during the index selection is the process of index recommendations through the wizard. In the **Index Recommendations** dialog box (Figure 24-11), there is information about existing and recommended indexes. For each of these indexes,

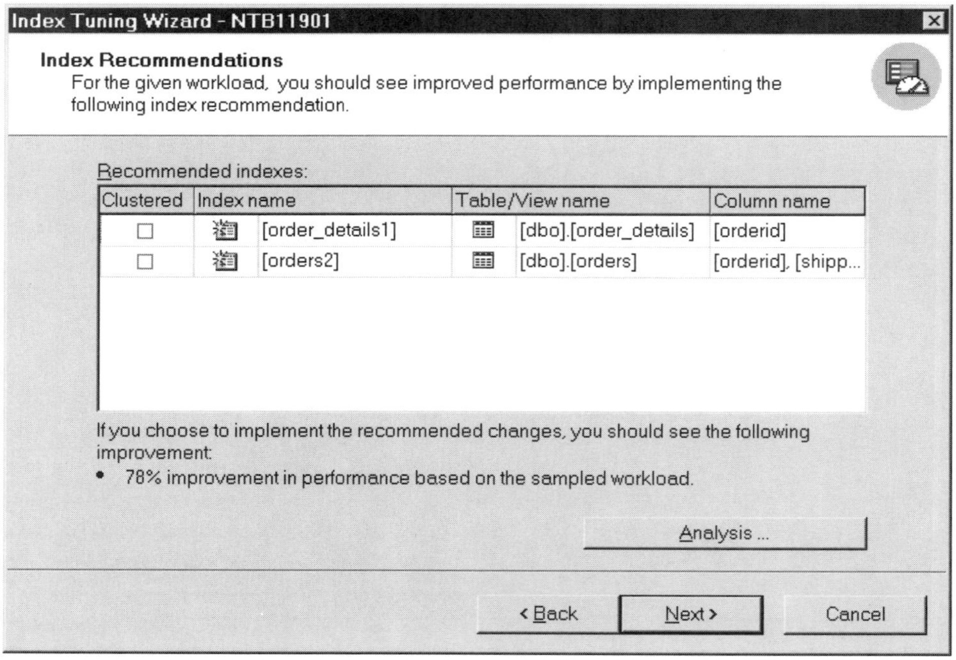

Figure 24-11. The Index Recommendations dialog box

you can see the name of the index, the order of the columns (for composite indexes), and whether the particular index is clustered or nonclustered. For the query in Example 24.7, the Index Tuning Wizard recommends the creation of two indexes: a nonclustered index called **order_details1** for the **orderid** column in the **order_details** table and also a composite nonclustered index called **orders2** for the columns **orderid** and **shippeddate** in the **orders** table.

The Index Tuning Wizard recommendations concerning indexes are expanded by a series of reports that provide information about very interesting options, which let you see how Index Tuning Wizard evaluated the workload. These reports can be seen by clicking the **Analyze** check box in the **Index Recommendations** dialog box.

Index Usage Report (Recommended Configuration) displays information concerning the expected usage of the recommended indexes and their estimated sizes. In contrast to it, **Index Usage Report (Current Configuration)** presents the same information for the current configuration. **Table Analysis Report** displays information about the costs of all queries in the workload (using tables in the database).

Workload Analysis Report provides information about the relative frequencies of all data modification statements. (Costs are calculated relative to the most expensive statement with the current index configuration.) Of all options, the most interesting is **Tuning Summary Report**, which gives you a summary information concerning the use of the Index Tuning Wizard. This report displays, among other things, the total number of queries that were examined and suggestions in relation to removing existing indexes.

In the next step, the recommendation of the Index Tuning Wizard can be accepted or rejected. If you want to accept the recommendation, click **Apply changes** in the **Schedule Index Update Job** dialog box (see Figure 24-12). In this case, the wizard generates the recommended indexes immediately, or you can specify the schedule for the index generation (at a specific day and time). Also, a Transact-SQL script to perform the index generation can be created by activating **Save Script File** in the same dialog box and entering a file name. This feature is useful if you generate this script with one (test) system and intend to use the index recommendation with another (production) system or as an alternative for the already mentioned schedule.

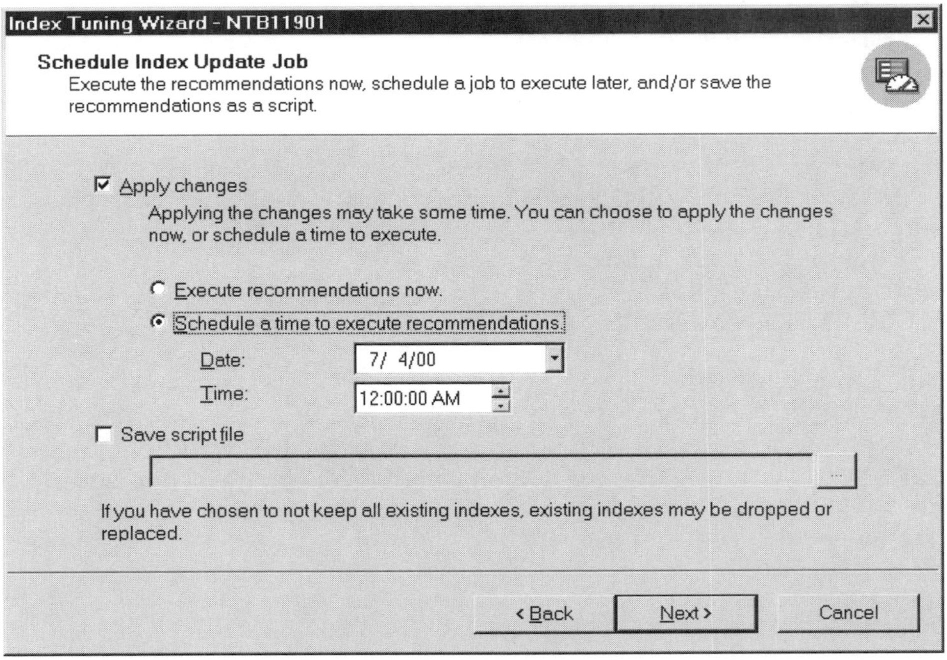

Figure 24-12. The Schedule Index Update Job dialog box

The script in Example 24.8 generates automatically all indexes that are recommended by the Index Tuning Wizard for the traced query.

▼ EXAMPLE 24.8

```
/* Created by: Index Tuning Wizard   */
/* Date: 5/16/00 ...*/
/* Time: 3:34:25 PM ...*/
/* Server Name: NTB11901 ...*/
/* Database Name: sample1 ...*/
/* Workload File Name: C:\TEMP\chapter24_trace.trc */
USE [sample1]
go
SET QUOTED_IDENTIFIER ON
SET ARITHABORT ON
SET CONCAT_NULL_YIELDS_NULL ON
SET ANSI_NULLS ON
SET ANSI_PADDING ON
SET ANSI_WARNINGS ON
SET NUMERIC_ROUNDABORT OFF
go
DECLARE @bErrors as bit
BEGIN TRANSACTION
SET @bErrors = 0
CREATE NONCLUSTERED INDEX [order_details1] ON [dbo].[order_details]
([orderid] )
IF( @@error <> 0 ) SET @bErrors = 1
IF( @bErrors = 0 )
  COMMIT TRANSACTION
ELSE
  ROLLBACK TRANSACTION
BEGIN TRANSACTION
SET @bErrors = 0
CREATE NONCLUSTERED INDEX [orders2] ON [dbo].[orders] ([orderid],
[shippeddate] )
IF( @@error <> 0 ) SET @bErrors = 1
IF( @bErrors = 0 )
  COMMIT TRANSACTION
ELSE
  ROLLBACK TRANSACTION
```

CONCLUSION

Performance issues can be divided into proactive and reactive response areas. Proactive issues concern all activities that affect performance of the overall system and that will affect future systems of an organization. Proper database design and proper choice of the form of Transact-SQL statements in application programs belong to the proactive response area. Reactive performance issues concern activities that are undertaken after the performance bottleneck occurs. SQL Server offers a variety of tools (graphical components, Transact-SQL statements, and stored procedures) that can be used to view and trace performance problems of a SQL Server system.

Of all SQL Server components, SQL Server Performance Monitor is the best tool for monitoring the SQL Server system, because you can use it to track, display, report, and trace any performance bottlenecks.

The next chapter discusses the capability of the SQL Server system to copy data from one database to one or more target databases using data replication.

CHAPTER 25

Data Replication

Besides distributed transactions, data replication is the way to achieve a distributed data environment. A general discussion of these two methods is given in the introductory part of this chapter. After that, SQL Server replication elements are introduced, and the existing replication types are shown. The last part of the chapter covers various aspects of managing replication.

DISTRIBUTED DATA

Today, market forces require most companies to set up their computers (and the applications running on them) so they focus either on business and/or on customers. As a result, data used by these applications must be available ad hoc on different locations and at different times. Such a data environment is provided by several distributed databases that include multiple copies of the same information.

The traveling salesperson provides a good example of the use of a distributed data environment. During the day, the salesperson usually uses a laptop to query all necessary information from the database (prices and availability of products, for example) in order to inform customers on the spot. Afterwards, in the hotel room, he or she again uses the laptop—this time to transmit data (about the sold products) to headquarters.

From this scenario, you can see that a distributed data environment has several benefits compared to centralized computing:

- It is directly available to the people who need it, when they need it.
- It allows local users to operate autonomously.
- It reduces network traffic.
- It makes nonstop processing cheaper.

On the other hand, a distributed data environment is much more complex than the corresponding centralized model and therefore requires much more planning and administration.

Methods for Distributing Data

There are two general methods for distributing data on multiple database servers:

- Distributed transactions
- Data replication

Distributed transactions guarantee that all copies of the data have the same values at the *same time*. This means that all updates to all locations (where the distributed data is stored) are gathered together and executed synchronously. Distributed DBMSs use a method called *two-phase commit* to implement distributed transactions.

Each database involved in a distributed transaction has its own recovery technique, which is used in case of error. (Remember that all statements inside a transaction are executed in their entirety or all canceled.) A global recovery manager (called a coordinator) coordinates the two phases of distributed processing.

In the first phase of this process, the coordinator checks whether all participating sites are ready to execute their part of the distributed transaction. The second phase consists of the actual execution of the transaction at all participating sites. During this process, any error at any site causes the coordinator to stop the transaction. In this case, it sends a message to each local recovery manager to undo the part of the transaction that is already executed at that site.

> ***NOTE:*** The Microsoft Distributed Transaction Coordinator (DTC) supports distributed transactions using two-phase commit.

During the data replication process, copies of the data are distributed from a source database to one or more target databases located on separate computers. Because of this, data replication differs from distributed transactions in two ways: timing and delay in time.

In contrast to the distributed transaction method, in which all data is the same on all participating sites at the same time, data replication allows sites to have different data at the same time. Additionally, data replication is an asynchronous process. This means there is a certain delay during which all copies of data are matched on all participating sites. (This delay can last from a couple of seconds to several days or weeks.)

Data replication is, in most cases, a better solution than distributed transactions because it is more reliable and cheaper. Experience with two-phase commit has shown that administration becomes very difficult if the number of participating sites increases. Also, the increased number of participating sites decreases the reliability, because the probability that a local part of a distributed transaction will fail increases with the increased number of nodes.

Another reason to use data replication instead of centralized data is performance: clients at the site where the data is replicated experience improved performance because they can access data locally rather than using a network to connect to a central database server.

SQL SERVER REPLICATION—AN OVERVIEW

Generally, replication is based on two different concepts:

- Using transaction logs
- Using triggers

As already stated in Chapter 20, SQL Server keeps all values of modified rows ("before" as well as "after" values) in system files called transaction logs. If selected rows need to be replicated, the system starts a new process that reads the data from the transaction log and sends it to one or more target databases.

The other method is based upon triggers. The modification of a table that contains data to be replicated fires the corresponding trigger, which in turn creates a new table with the data and starts a replication process.

Both concepts have their benefits and disadvantages. The log-based replication is characterized by improved performance, because the process that reads data from the transaction log runs asynchronously and has little effect on the performance of the overall system. On the other hand, the implementation of log-based replication is very complex for database companies, because the database system not only has to manage additional processes and buffers but also has to solve the concurrency problems between system and replication processes that access the transaction log.

NOTE: SQL Server uses both concepts: the transaction log method for transactional replication processing and triggers for merge replication processing. (Transactional and merge replication processing are described in detail later in this chapter.)

Publishers, Distributors, and Subscribers

SQL Server replication is based on the so-called publisher–subscriber metaphor. This metaphor describes the different roles servers can play in a replication process. One or more servers publish data that other servers can subscribe to. In between there exists a distributor that stores the changes and forwards them further (to the subscribers). Hence, a node can have three roles in a replication scenario:

- Publisher
- Distributor
- Subscriber

A publisher (or publishing server) maintains its source databases, makes data available for replication, and sends the modified data to the distributor. A distributor (or distribution server) receives all changes to the replicated data from the publisher and stores and forwards them to the appropriate subscribers. A subscriber (or subscribing server) receives and maintains published data.

A SQL Server system can play many roles in a replication process. For example, a server can act as the publisher and the distributor at the same time. This scenario is appropriate for a process with few replications and few subscribers. If there are a lot of subscribers for the publishing information, the distributor can be located on its own server. Figure 25-1 shows a complex scenario in which there are multiple publishers and multiple subscribers. (See also the section "Replication Models" later in this chapter.)

NOTE: You can replicate only user-defined databases.

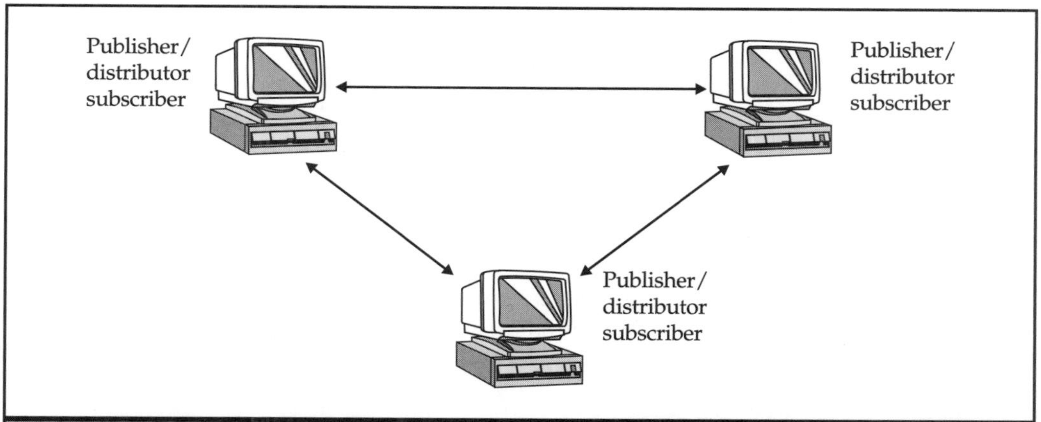

Figure 25-1. SQL Server systems can act as multiple publishers and multiple subscribers

Publications and Articles

The unit of a data to be published is called a publication. An article contains data from a table and/or one or more stored procedures. A table article can be a single table or a subset of data in a table. A stored procedure article can contain one or more stored procedures that exist at the publication time in the database.

A publication contains one or more articles. Each publication can contain data only from one database.

NOTE: A publication is the basis of a subscription. This means you cannot subscribe directly to an article, because an article is always part of a publication.

A *filter* is the process that restricts information, producing a subset. Therefore, a publication contains one or more of the following items that specify types of table articles:

- Table
- Vertical filter
- Horizontal filter
- A combination of vertical and horizontal filters

NOTE: There are certain restrictions on filtering data regarding merge replication.

A vertical filter contains a subset of the columns in a table. A horizontal filter contains a subset of rows in a table.

A subscription can be initiated in two different ways:

- Using a push subscription
- Using a pull subscription

With a *push subscription*, all the administration of setting up subscriptions is performed on the publisher during the definition of a publication. Push subscriptions simplify and centralize administration, because the usual replication scenario contains one publisher and many subscribers. The benefit of a push subscription is higher security, because the initialization process is managed at one place. On the other hand, the performance of the distributor can suffer because the overall distribution of subscriptions runs at once.

With a *pull subscription*, the subscriber initiates the subscription. The pull subscription is more selective than the push subscription, because the subscriber can select publications to subscribe to. In contrast to the push subscription, the pull subscription should be used for publications with low security and a high number of subscribers.

NOTE: The downloading of data from the Internet is a typical form of pull subscription.

Replication Types

SQL Server provides three types of data replication:

- Transactional
- Snapshot
- Merge

All three types of replication can be used within a database, because each publication can have a different type of replication.

Transactional Replication

In transactional replication, the SQL Server transaction log is used to replicate data. All transactions that contain the data to be replicated are marked for replication. A SQL Server component called the Log Reader Agent searches for marked transactions and copies them from the transaction log on the publisher to the **distribution** database (see below). Another component—the Distribution Agent—moves transactions to subscribers, where they are applied to the target tables in the subscription databases.

NOTE: All tables published using transactional replication must explicitly contain a primary key. The primary key is required to uniquely identify the rows of the published table.

Transactional replication can replicate tables (or parts of tables) and one or more stored procedures. The use of stored procedures by transactional replication increases performance, because the amount of data to be sent over a network is usually significantly smaller. Instead of replicated data, only the stored procedure is sent to the subscribers, where it is executed. You can configure the delay of synchronization time between the publisher on one side and subscribers on the other during a transactional replication. (All these changes are propagated by the Log Reader Agent and Distribution Agent.)

The **distribution** database is a system database that is installed on the distributor when the replication process is initiated. This database holds all replicated transactions from publications and publishers that need to be forwarded to the subscribers. It is heavily used only by transactional replications.

NOTE: Before transactional replications can begin, a copy of the entire database must be transferred to each subscriber, which is performed by executing a snapshot.

Snapshot Replication

The simplest type of replication, snapshot replication, copies the data to be published from the publisher to all subscribers. (The difference between snapshot replication and transactional replication is that the former sends all the published data and the latter only the changes of data to the subscribers.)

Snapshot replication is executed using the **bcp** utility. A SQL Server component called Snapshot Agent generates the schema and data of the published tables and stores them in files. The table schema is stored in the file with the suffix .sch, while the data is stored in the file with the suffix .bcp. The .sch and .bcp files build the synchronization set that represents the snapshot of a table at a particular time.

NOTE: Transactional and snapshot replication are one-way replications, which means the only changes to the replicated data are made at the publishing server. Therefore, the data at all subscription servers is read-only, except for the changes made by replication processes.

In contrast to transactional replication, snapshot replication requires no primary key for tables. The reason is obvious: the unit of transfer in snapshot replication is the entire database and not rows of a table. Another difference between these two replication types concerns a delay in time: the snapshot replication will be replicated periodically, which means the delay is significant because all data (changed and unchanged) is transferred from the publisher to the subscribers.

NOTE: Snapshot replication does not use the **distribution** database directly. However, the distribution database contains status information and other details that are used by snapshot replication.

Merge Replication

In transactional and snapshot replication, the publisher sends the data, and a subscriber receives it. (There is no possibility that a subscriber sends replicated data to the publisher.) Merge replication allows the publisher as well as subscribers to update data to be replicated. Because of that, conflicts can arise during a replication process.

After the creation of a publication at the publication server, the SLQ Server component called Snapshot Agent prepares files containing table schema and data and stores them in the distribution working folder at the distributor site. (During the merge replication, the **distribution** database contains only the status of the replication process.) The synchronization job is then used by another component—the Merge Agent—that sends all changed data to the other sites. (Remember that the Merge Agent can send replicated data to the subscribers as well as to the publisher.) Before the send process is started, the Merge Agent also stores the appropriate information that is used to track updated conflicts.

When you use the merge replication scenario, SQL Server makes three important changes to the schema of the publication database:

- It identifies a unique column for each replicated row.
- It adds several system tables.
- It creates triggers for tables in which data is replicated.

SQL Server creates or identifies a unique column in the table with the replicated data. If the base table already contains a column with the UNIQUEIDENTIFIER data type and ROWGUIDCOL property, SQL Server uses that column to identify each replicated row. If there is no such column in the table, SQL Server adds the column **rowguid** of the UNIQUEIDENTIFIER data type with the ROWGUIDCOL property.

NOTE: UNIQUEIDENTIFIER columns may contain multiple occurrences of a value. The ROWGUIDCOL property indicates that the values of the column of the UNIQUEIDENTIFIER data type uniquely identify rows in the table. Therefore, a column of the data type UNIQUEIDENTIFIER with the ROWGUIDCOL property contains unique values for each row across all networked computers in the world and thus guarantees the uniqueness of replicated rows across multiple copies of the table on the publisher and subscribers.

The addition of new system tables provides the way to detect and resolve any update conflict. SQL Server stores all changes concerning the replicated data in the merge system tables **msmerge_contents** and **msmerge_tombstone** and joins them (using the **rowguid** column of the existing column with the UNIQUEIDENTIFIER data type) with the table that contains replicated data to resolve the conflict.

SQL Server creates triggers on tables that contain replicated data on all sites to track changes to the data in each replicated row. These triggers determine the changes made to the table, and they record them in the system tables **msmerge_contents** and **msmerge_tombstone**.

A conflict detection is done by the Merge Agent using the column lineage of the **msmerge_contents** system table when a conflict is detected. The resolution of it can be either priority based or custom based.

Priority-based resolution means that any conflict between new and old values in the replicated row is resolved automatically based on assigned priorities. (The special case of the priority-based method specifies the "first wins" method, where the timely first change of the replicated row is the winner.) The priority-based method is the default. The *custom-based* method uses customized triggers based on business rules defined by the user to resolve conflicts.

Replication Models

The previous section introduced different replication types that SQL Server uses to distribute data between different nodes. The replication types (transactional, snapshot, and merge) provide the functionality for maintaining replicated data. *Replication models*, on the other hand, are used by a company to design its own data replication. Both replication type and replication model are usually determined at the same time.

Depending on requirements, several replication models can be used. Three of the basic ones are as follows:

- Central publisher with distributor
- Central subscriber with multiple publishers
- Multiple publishers and multiple subscribers

Central Publisher with Distributor

In the central publisher with distributor model, there is one publisher and usually one distributor. The publisher creates publications that are distributed by the distributor to several subscribers. (This model is the SQL Server default.)

If the amount of publishing data is not very large, the publisher and distributor can reside on one server. Otherwise, using two separate servers is recommended because of performance issues. (If there is a heavy load of data to be published, the distributor is usually the bottleneck.) Figure 25-2 shows the replication model with the central publisher and the separate distributor.

The publications designed by this model and received at a subscriber are usually read-only. Therefore, in most cases, the transactional replication is the preferred replication type for this model, although the snapshot replication can also be used.

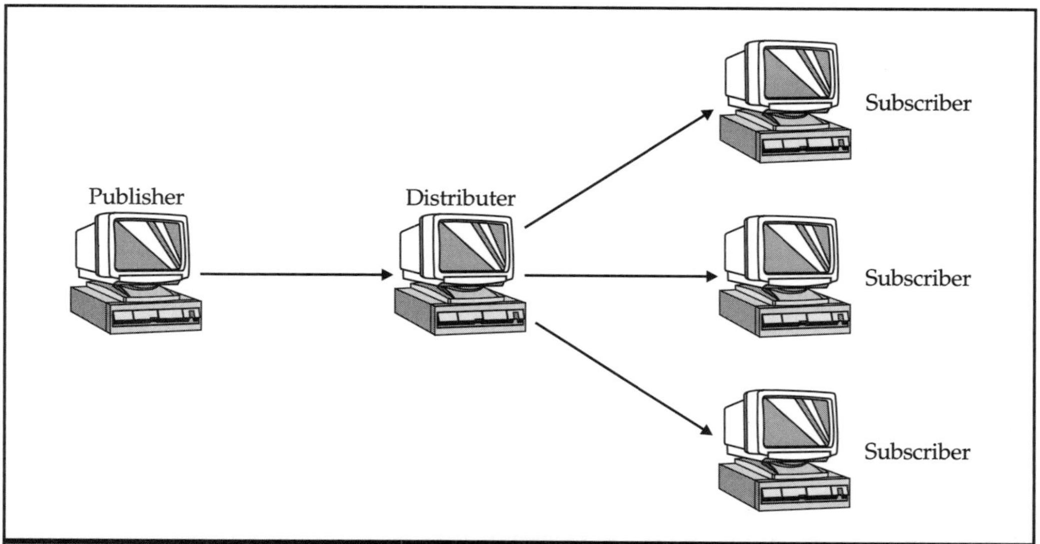

Figure 25-2. Central publisher with separate distributor

Central Subscriber with Multiple Publishers

The scenario described at the beginning of this chapter of the traveling salesperson who transmits data to headquarters is a typical example of the central subscriber with multiple publishers. The data is gathered at a centralized subscriber, and several publishers are sending their data.

For this model, you can use either the transactional or the merge replication type, depending on the use of replicated data. If publishers publish (and therefore update) the same data to the subscriber, merge replication should be used. If each publisher has its own data to publish, transactional replication can be used. (In this case, published tables will be filtered horizontally, and each publisher will be the exclusive owner of a particular table fragment.)

Multiple Publishers with Multiple Subscribers

The replication model in which some or all of the servers participating in data replication play the role of the publisher as well as the subscriber is known as multiple publishers with multiple subscribers. In most cases, this model includes several distributors that are usually placed at each publisher (see Figure 25-1).

This model can be implemented using merge replication only, because publications are modified at each publishing server. (The only other way to implement this model is to use the distributed transactions with two-phase commit.)

MANAGING REPLICATION

All servers that participate in a replication must be registered in SQL Server Enterprise Manager. After registering servers, the distributor, publisher(s), and subscribers must be set up.

Setting Up Distribution and Publishing Servers

The distribution server must be installed, and the **distribution** database must be configured before publishing databases are installed. A distribution server can be set up using the following:

- Configure Publishing and Distribution Wizard
- System procedures

Configure Publishing and Distribution Wizard

The Configure Publishing and Distribution Wizard allows you to configure the distributor, the distribution database, and optionally, the subscriber(s). You can:

- Specify the local or another server as a distributor
- Configure the properties of the server as a distributor
- Configure the properties of the server as a publisher

After the specification of the distributor, you can configure the server for replication using default or customized settings. In the latter case, the information of the **distribution** database must be provided, and publishers and publication databases must be enabled (see Figure 25-3).

NOTE: The distribution working folder must be available at the distributor site if you use merge replication. This is because replication agents use it to store data. The default directory of the replication working folder is /mssql/repldata. (This directory is also required for snapshot replication.)

Configure a Distributor and Publisher Using System Procedures

A distributor (together with the **distribution** database and publishers) can be set up using the following three system procedures:

- sp_adddistributor
- sp_adddistributiondb
- sp_adddistpublisher

The system procedure **sp_adddistributor** sets up the distribution server by creating a new row in the **sysservers** system table. The only required parameter for the procedure is

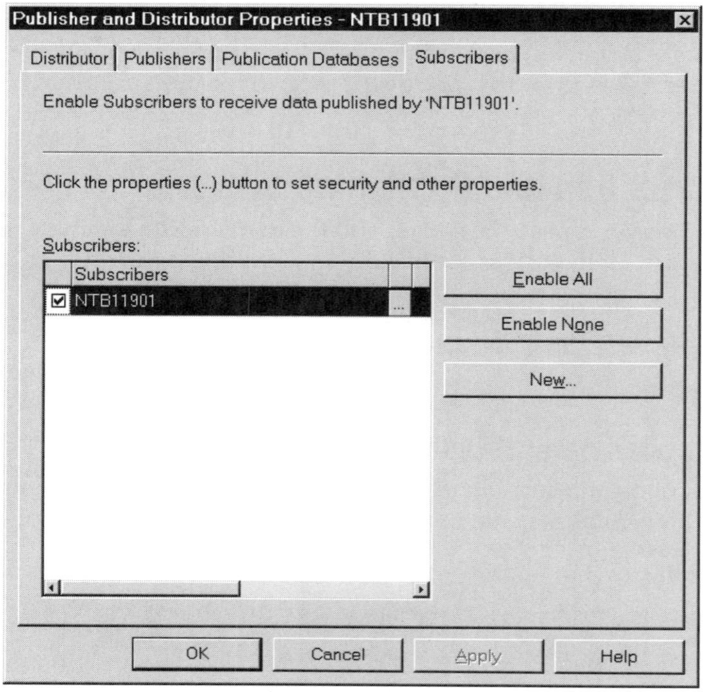

Figure 25-3. Publisher and Distributor Properties

the distributor server name. The system procedure **sp_adddistributiondb** creates a new distribution database and installs the distribution schema. The only required parameter for the procedure is the name of the database. The system procedure **sp_adddistpublisher** creates a remote publisher that uses the distributor created using the **sp_adddistributor** system procedure.

NOTE: The system procedures **sp_adddistributor**, **sp_adddistributiondb**, and **sp_adddistpublisher** must be used in that sequence to set up the distributor, the **distribution** database, and the publisher(s).

There are three other system procedures concerning the publisher: **sp_changedistpublisher**, **sp_dropdistpublisher**, and **sp_helpdistpublisher**. The first one updates properties of the particular publisher, the second one drops a publisher that serves as its own distributor, and the last one returns properties of the publisher.

Setting Up Subscription Servers

A task that concerns subscribers and must be performed at the publisher is enabling the publisher to subscribe. You can use Enterprise Manager to enable a subscriber at the publisher. First click the publishing server, and in the **Tools** menu point to **Replication**. Then click **Configure Publishing, Subscribers and Distribution**. Click the **Subscribers** tab. The list of all existing subscribers appears (see Figure 25-4). Create new subscribers by clicking **New Subscribers** (if necessary) and enable the subscribers.

At the subscriber you:

- Select the publisher(s) that will replicate to the subscriber
- Create and/or select the destination databases for replication
- Create and/or verify the account that is used to access the distributor

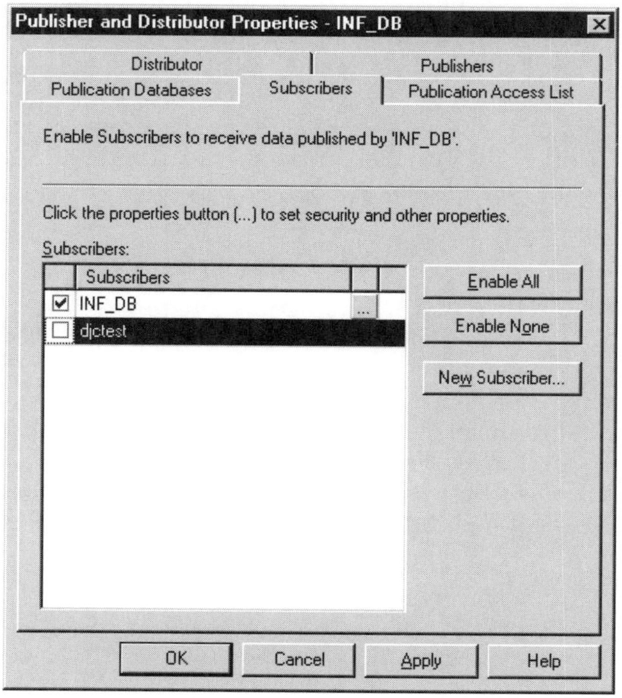

Figure 25-4. Publisher and Distributor dialog box—Subscribers tab

Publishing

Before publishing can start, you must define one or more publications. A publication contains one or more articles, which in turn contain data from a table. You can create one or more publications from databases on a publisher, but one publication can contain data only from one database. (Don't forget that system databases cannot be used for creation of a publication.)

The easiest way to create publications is by using the Create Publication Wizard. Click on **Run a Wizard** in the toolbar of Enterprise Manager, and select **Create Publication Wizard** (under **Replication**). Using the wizard, you can:

- Create a publication
- Filter the data in the publication
- Set the properties of a publication
- Set the replication type (snapshot, transactional, or merge)

Subscribing

Before a publication can be sent to a subscriber, the data in the publishing and subscribing databases must be synchronized. The synchronization of the data is called the initial snapshot that is initiated by the publisher and executed using the Snapshot Agent.

After the initial snapshot, you have to choose between the push and pull subscriptions. A push subscription is always defined at the publisher, while a pull subscription is defined at each subscriber. The Push Subscription Wizard and Pull Subscription Wizard can be used to define the type of subscription.

CONCLUSION

Data replication is the preferred method for distribution of data, because it is cheaper than using distributed transactions. SQL Server 2000 allows you to choose one of three possible replication types, depending on the physical model you use. Theoretically, any replication model can use any of the replication types, although each (basic) model has a corresponding type that is used in most cases.

A publication is the smallest unit of replication. A single database can have many publications with different replication types. (Otherwise, each publication corresponds to only one database.)

The next chapter starts the second to the last part of the book: data warehousing. It introduces you to general terms and concepts you have to know about this important topic of SQL Server.

EXERCISES

▼ E.25.1

Why do you need a primary key for data replication? Which replication type requires a primary key?

▼ E.25.2

How can you limit network traffic and/or database size?

▼ E.25.3

Update conflicts are not recommended. How can you minimize them?

▼ E.25.4

When does SQL Server use Log Reader Agent, Merge Agent, and Snapshot Agent?

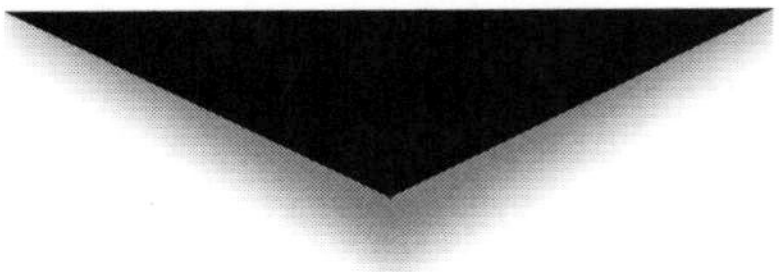

PART IV

Microsoft Analysis Services

CHAPTER 26

Data Warehousing—An Introduction

The goal of this chapter is to introduce you to a new (and very important) area of database technology: data warehousing. The first part of the chapter explains the difference between the online transaction processing world on one side and the data warehousing world on the other side. A *data store* for a data warehousing process can be either a data warehouse or a data mart. Both types of data store are discussed, and their differences are listed in the second part of the chapter. The data warehouse design, data mining, and the need for creation of aggregate tables is explained at the end of the chapter.

ONLINE TRANSACTION PROCESSING VS. DATA WAREHOUSING

From the beginning, relational database systems were used almost exclusively to capture primary business data such as orders and invoices using processing based on transactions. This focus on business data has its benefits and its disadvantages. One benefit is that the poor performance of early database systems improved dramatically, so today many database systems are capable of executing thousands of transactions per second (using appropriate hardware). On the other hand, the focus on transaction processing prevented people in the database business from seeing another natural application of database systems: using them to filter and analyze needed information out of all the existing data in an enterprise or department.

Online Transaction Processing

As already stated, performance is one of the main issues for systems that are based upon transaction processing. These systems are called online transaction processing (OLTP) systems. Based on performance, OLTP systems have some important properties:

- Short transactions—that is, high throughput of data
- Many (possibly hundreds or thousands of) users
- Continuous read and write operations based on a small number of rows
- Data of medium size that is stored in a database

The performance of a database system will increase if transactions in the database application programs are short. The reason is that transactions use locks (see Chapter 14) to prevent possible negative effects of concurrency issues. If transactions are long lasting, the number of locks and their duration increases, decreasing the data availability and thus performance.

Large OLTP systems usually have many users working on the system simultaneously. A typical example is a reservation system for an airline company, which must process thousands of requests for travel arrangements in a single country, or all over the world, almost immediately. In this type of system, most users expect that their response-time requirements will be fulfilled by the system and the system will be available at working hours (or nonstop).

Users of an OLTP system execute their DML statements continuously—that is, they use both read and write operations at the same time and steadily. (Because data is continuously modified, we say that data of an OLTP system is highly dynamic.) All operations (or results of them) on a database usually include only a small amount of data, although it is possible that the database system must access many rows from one or more tables stored in the database.

In recent years, the amount of data stored in an *operational* database (i.e., a database managed by an OLTP system) has increased steadily. Today, there are a lot of databases that store several (or even dozens of) gigabytes of data. As you will see, this amount of data is still relatively small in relation to data warehouses.

Data Warehouse Systems

Data warehousing is the process of integrating enterprise-wide data into a single data store from which end users can run ad hoc queries and reports to analyze the existing data. In other words, the goal of data warehousing is to keep data that can be accessed by users who make their business decisions on the basis of the analysis. These systems are often called *informative* systems, because by accessing data, users get the necessary information for making better business decisions.

The goals of data warehousing systems are different from the goals of OLTP systems. Therefore, a data warehousing system has very different properties from those listed above for an OLTP system. The most important properties of a data warehousing system are as follows:

- Periodic write operations (load) with queries based on a huge number of rows
- Small number of users
- Large size of data stored in a database

Besides data load that is executed at regular intervals (usually daily), data warehouse systems are mostly read-only systems. (Therefore, the nature of the data in such a system is static.) As will be explained in detail later in this chapter, data is gathered from different sources, cleaned (made consistent), and loaded into a database called a data warehouse (or data mart). The cleaned data is not modified at all—that is, users query data using SELECT statements to obtain the necessary information.

Because data warehousing systems are used to gain information, the number of users that simultaneously use such a system is relatively small (at most, several dozen). Users of a data warehousing system usually generate reports that display different factors concerning the finances of an enterprise (or department), or they execute complex queries to compare data.

NOTE: Another difference between OLTP and data warehousing systems (that actually affects the user's behavior) is the daily schedule—that is, how those systems are used during a day. An OLTP system can be used nonstop (if it is designed for such a use), while a data warehouse system can be used as soon as data is made consistent and is loaded into the database.

In contrast to databases in OLTP systems that store only current data, data warehousing systems must also track historical data. (Remember that data warehousing systems make comparisons between data gathered in different time periods.) For this reason, the amount of data stored in a data warehouse is very large.

DATA WAREHOUSES AND DATA MARTS

A *data warehouse* can be defined as a database that includes all corporate data and that can be uniformly accessed by users. After this concise definition, let's try to explain the notion of a data warehouse more accurately. An enterprise usually has a large amount of data stored at different times and in different databases (or data files) that are managed by distinct DBMSs. These DBMSs need not be relational: some enterprises still have databases managed by hierarchical or network database systems. A special team of software specialists examines old source databases (and data files) and converts them into a target store: the data warehouse. Additionally, the converted data in a data warehouse must be consolidated because it holds the information that is the key to the corporation's operational processes. (*Consolidation* of data means that all equivalent queries executed upon a data warehouse at different times provide the same result.) The data consolidation in a data warehouse is provided in several steps:

- Data assembly from different sources (also called extraction)
- Data cleaning (i.e., transformation process)
- Quality assurance of data

Data must be carefully assembled from different sources. In this process, data is extracted from the different sources, converted to an intermediate schema, and moved to a temporary work area. For data extraction, you need tools that extract exactly the data that must be stored in the data warehouse.

Data cleaning ensures the integrity of data that has to be stored in the target database. For example, data cleaning must be done on incorrect entries in data fields, such as addresses, or incompatible data types used to define the same date fields in different sources. For this process, the data cleaning team needs special software.

An example will help explain the process of data cleaning more clearly. Suppose there are two data sources that store personal data concerning employees and that both databases have the attribute **Gender**. In the first database, this attribute is defined as CHAR(6), and the data values are "female" and "male." The same attribute in the second database is declared as CHAR(1) with the values "f" and "m." The values of both data sources are correct, but for the target data source you must clean the data—that is, represent the values of the attribute in a uniform way.

The last part of data consolidation—quality assurance of data—involves a data validation process that specifies the data as the end user should view and access it. Because of this, end users should be closely involved in this process.

By their nature (as a store for the overall data of an enterprise), data warehouses contain huge amounts of data. (Some data warehouses contain as much as 500GB or more of data.) Also, because they must encompass the enterprise, implementation usually takes two to three years. Because of these disadvantages, many companies start with a smaller solution called a data mart.

Data marts are data stores that include all data at the department level and therefore allow users to access data concerning only a single part of their organization. For example, the marketing department stores all data relevant to marketing in its own data mart, the research department puts the experimental data in the research data mart, and so on. Because of this, a data mart has several advantages over a data warehouse:

- Narrower application area
- Shorter development time and lower cost
- Easier data maintenance
- Bottom-up development

As already stated, a data mart includes only the information needed by one part of an organization, usually a department. Therefore, the data that is intended for use by such a small organizational unit can be more easily prepared for the end user's needs.

The development time for a data warehouse averages two years and costs $5 million in total. On the other hand, costs for a data mart average $200,000, and such a project takes about three to five months. For these reasons, development of a data mart is preferred, especially if it is the first data warehousing project in your organization.

The fact that a data mart contains significantly smaller amounts of data than a data warehouse helps you to reduce and simplify all tasks, such as data extraction, data cleaning, and quality assurance of data. It is also easier to design a solution for a department than for the entire organization. (For more information on data warehousing design and a dimensional model, see the next section of this chapter.)

If you design and develop several data marts in your organization, it is possible to unite them all in one big data warehouse. This bottom-up process has several advantages over designing a data warehouse at once: First, each data mart may contain identical target tables that can be unified in a corresponding data warehouse. Second, some tasks are logically enterprise-wide, such as the gathering of financial information by the accounting department. If the existing data marts will be linked together to build a data warehouse for an enterprise, a global repository (i.e., the data catalog that contains information about all data stored in sources as well as in the target database) is required.

NOTE: Be aware that building a data warehouse by linking data marts can be very troublesome because of possible significant differences in the structure and design of existing data marts. Different parts of an enterprise may use different data models and have different instructions for data representation.

DATA WAREHOUSE DESIGN

Only a well-planned and well-designed database will allow you to achieve good performance. Relational databases and data warehouses have a lot of differences that require different design methods. Relational databases are designed using the well-known entity-relationship (ER) model, while the dimensional model is used for the design of data warehouses and data marts. The following section describes the dimensional model, while the ER model was already explained in detail in Chapter 1.

Dimensional Model

Using relational databases, data redundancy is removed using normal forms (see Chapter 1). The normalization process divides each table of a database that includes redundant data into two separate tables. The process of normalization should be finished when all tables of a database contain only nonredundant data.

The highly normalized tables are advantageous for online transaction processing, because in this case all transactions can be made as simple and short as possible. On the other hand, data warehousing processes are based on queries that operate on a huge amount of data and are neither simple nor short. Therefore, the highly normalized tables do not suit the design of data warehouses, because the goal of data warehouse systems is significantly different: there are few concurrent transactions, and each transaction accesses a very large number of records. (Imagine the huge amount of data belonging to a data warehouse that is stored in hundreds of tables. Most queries will join dozens of large tables to retrieve data. Such queries cannot be performed well, even if you use hardware with parallel processors and a database system with the best performance.)

Data warehouses cannot use the ER model because this model is used to design databases with nonredundant data. The logical model used to design data warehouses is called a *dimensional model*.

NOTE: There is another important reason why the ER model is not suited to the design of data warehouses: the use of data in a data warehouse is unstructured. This means the queries are executed ad hoc, allowing a user to analyze data in totally different ways. (On the other hand, OLTP systems usually have database applications that are hard-coded and therefore contain queries that are not modified often.)

In dimensional modeling, every model is composed of one table that stores measures and several other tables that describe dimensions. The former is called the *fact table*, and the latter are called *dimension tables*. Examples of data that are stored in a fact table include inventory sales and expenditures. Dimensional tables usually include time, account, product, and employee data. Figure 26-1 shows an example of a dimensional model.

Each dimension table usually has a single-part primary key and several other attributes that describe this dimension closely. On the other hand, the primary key of the fact table is the combination of the primary keys of all dimension tables (see Figure 26-1). For this reason, the primary key of the fact table is made up of several foreign keys. (The number of dimensions also specifies the number of foreign keys in the fact table.) As you can see in Figure 26-1, the tables in a dimensional model build a star-like structure. Therefore, this model is often called a *star join* or a *star schema*.

Another difference in the nature of data in a fact table and the corresponding dimension tables is that most columns in a fact table are numeric and additive, because such data can be used to execute necessary calculations. (Remember that a typical query on a data warehouse fetches thousands or even millions of rows at a time, and the only useful operation upon such a huge amount of rows is to apply an aggregate function (sum, maximum, average)). For example, columns like **Units_of_product_sold** or **Dollars_cost** are typical columns in the fact table. (Numerical columns of the fact table that does not build the primary key of the table are called *measures*.)

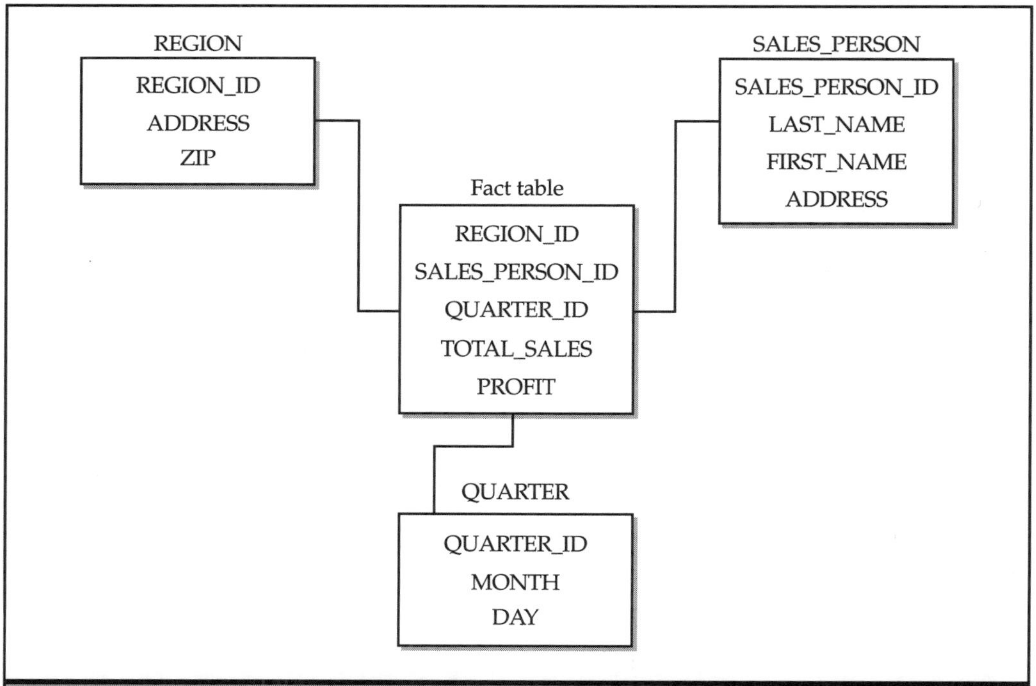

Figure 26-1. Example of the dimensional model

On the other hand, columns of dimension tables are strings that contain textual descriptions of the dimension. For instance, columns such as **Address**, **Location**, and **Name** often appear in dimension tables. (These columns are usually used as headers in reports.) Another consequence of the textual nature of data and their use in queries is that each dimension table contains many more indices than the corresponding fact table. (A fact table usually has only one unique index composed from all columns belonging to the primary key of that table.) Table 26-1 summarizes the differences between fact and dimension tables.

Columns of dimension tables are usually highly *denormalized*, which means that a lot of columns depend on each other. The denormalized structure of dimension tables has one important purpose: all columns of such a table are used as column headers in reports. If the denormalization of data in a dimension table is not desirable (to save disk storage or to improve performance, for example), a dimension table can be decomposed into several subtables. This is usually necessary when columns of a dimension table build hierarchies. (For example, the **Product** dimension could have columns such as **Product_id, Category_id**, and **Subcategory_id** that build three hierarchies, with the primary key, **Product_id**, as the root.) This structure, in which each level of a base entity is represented by its own table, is called a *snowflake schema*. Figure 26-2 shows the snowflake schema of the **Product** dimension.

The extension of a star schema into a corresponding snowflake schema has some benefits (reduction of used disk space, for example) and one main disadvantage: the snowflake schema does not allow you to use columns of snowflaked tables as headers—that is, it prevents you from browsing using all columns that are located outside the dimension table.

Fact Table	Dimension Table
One in a dimensional model.	Many (max. 12–15).
Contains most rows of a data warehousing system.	Contains relatively small amount of data.
Composite primary key (contains all primary keys of dimension tables).	Usually one column of a table builds the primary key of the table.
Columns are numeric and additive.	Columns are descriptive and therefore textual.

Table 26-1. Properties of Fact and Dimension Tables

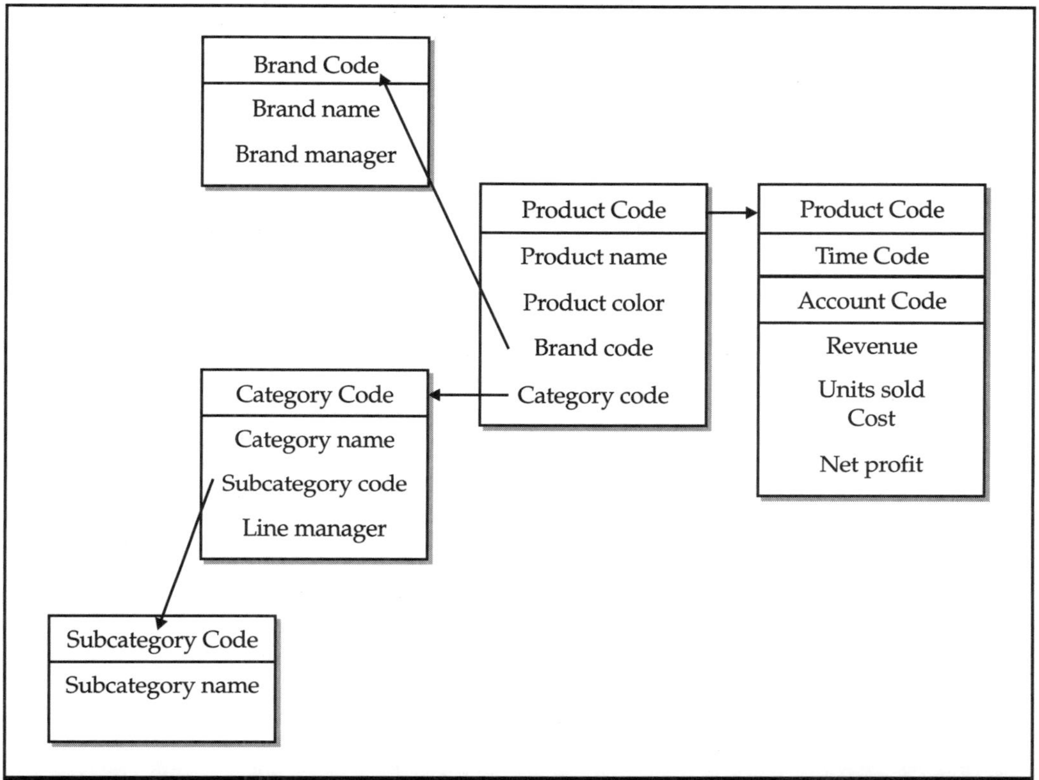

Figure 26-2. Snowflake schema of the **Product** dimension

CUBES AND STORAGE MODES

Data warehousing systems support different types of data storage. Some of these data storage types are based upon a multidimensional database that is also called a cube. A *cube* is a subset of data from the data warehouse that can be organized into multidimensional structures. To define a cube, you first select a fact table from the dimensional schema and identify numerical columns of interest within it. Then you select dimension tables that provide descriptions for the set of data to be analyzed. To demonstrate this, let us show how the cube for car sales analysis might be defined. For example, the fact table may include the columns **Cars_sold**, **Total_sales**, and **Costs**; while the tables **Models**, **Quarter**, and **Region** specify dimension tables. First you can build one dimension of the cube using measures of the fact table. The cube in Figure 26-3 is formed when two dimension tables, **Models** and **Quarter**, are used to build two other dimensions of the cube. Figure 26-4 also shows the third dimension, **Region**.

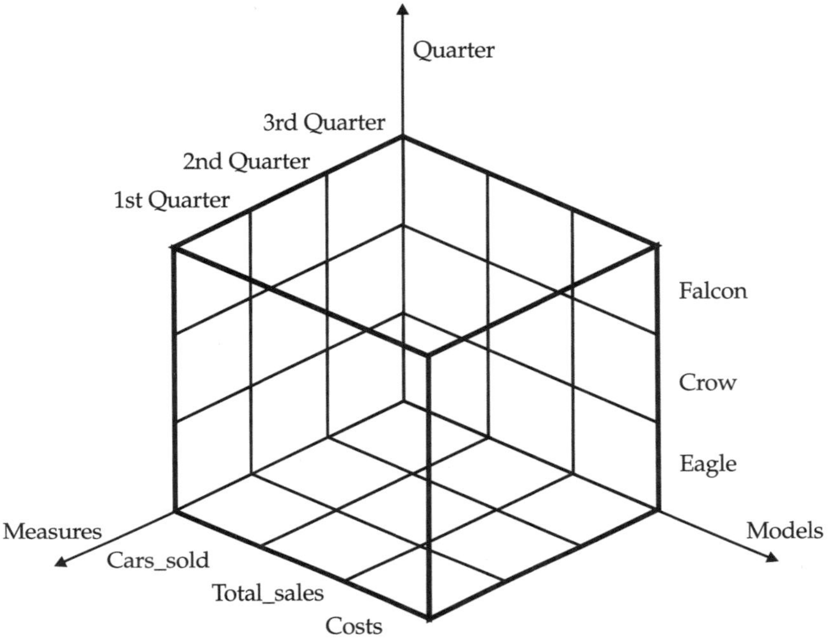

Figure 26-3. Cube for the car sales analysis with dimensions **Model** and **Quarter**

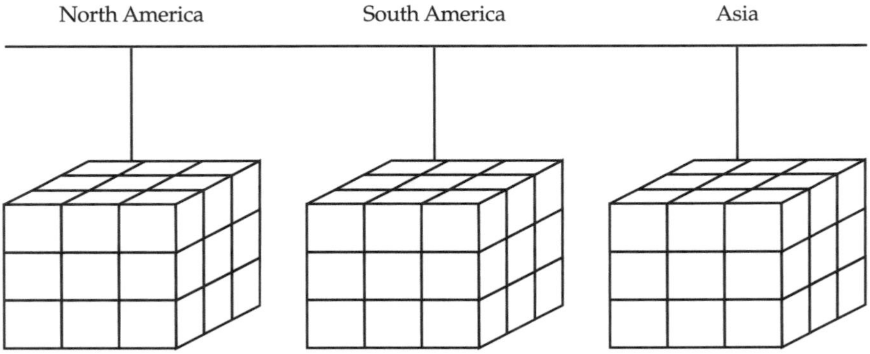

Figure 26-4. Cubes for the car sales analysis with the additional dimension **Region**

In each dimension there are discrete values that are called members. For instance, the **Region** dimension may contain the following members: ALL, North America, South America and Europe. (The ALL member specifies the total of all members in a dimension.)

Additionally, each cube dimension can have a hierarchy of levels that allow users to ask questions at a more detailed level. For example, the **Region** dimension can include the following level hierarchies: **Country**, **Province**, and **City**. Similarly, the **Quarter** dimension can include Month, Week, and Day as level hierarchies.

MOLAP, ROLAP, and HOLAP

MOLAP (multidimensional OLAP) is a type of storage in which the base data and their aggregations are stored using a multidimensional cube. On the other hand, ROLAP (relational OLAP) uses the well-known relational databases to store data in a data warehouse. Although the content of these two storage types is identical for the same data warehouse, there are some significant differences between them. The advantages of ROLAP storage type are as follows:

- Data must not be duplicated.
- Materialized (i.e., indexed) views can be used for summaries.

If the data should also be stored in a multidimensional database, a certain amount of data must be duplicated. Therefore, the ROLAP storage type does not need additional storage to copy the base data. Also, the calculation of summaries (see the next section) can be executed very quickly with ROLAP if the corresponding summary tables are generated using the views.

On the other hand, MOLAP also has several advantages in relation to ROLAP:

- Aggregates are stored in a multidimensional form.
- Query response is generally faster.

Using MOLAP, many aggregates are precalculated and stored in a multidimensional cube. That way the system does not have to calculate the result of such an aggregate each time it is needed. In the case of MOLAP, the database engine and the database itself are usually optimized to work together, so the query response can be faster than in ROLAP.

HOLAP (hybrid OLAP) storage is a combination of the MOLAP and ROLAP storage types. Aggregation data is stored in MOLAP, while the base data is left in the relational database. (Therefore, for queries using summaries, HOLAP is identical to MOLAP.) The advantage of HOLAP storage is that the base data is not duplicated.

AGGREGATION

Data is stored in the fact table in its most detailed form so that corresponding reports can make use of it. On the other hand (as stated earlier), a typical query on a fact table fetches thousands or even millions of rows at a time, and the only useful operation upon such a huge amount of rows is to apply an aggregate function (sum, maximum, average). This different use of data can reduce performance of ad hoc queries if they are executed on low-level (atomic) data, because time- and resource-intensive calculations will be necessary to perform each aggregate function.

For this reason, low-level data from the fact table should be summarized in advance and stored in intermediate tables. Because of their "aggregated" information, such intermediate tables are called *aggregate tables*, and the whole process is called *aggregation*.

> ***NOTE:*** An aggregate row from the fact table is always associated with one or more aggregate dimension table rows. For example, the dimensional model in Figure 26-1 could contain the following aggregate rows: monthly sales aggregates by salespersons by region; region-level aggregates by salespersons by day.

An example will show why low-level data should be aggregated. An end user may want to start an ad hoc query that displays the total sales of the organization for the last month. This would cause the server to sum all sales for each day in the last month. If there are an average of 500 sales transactions per day in each of 500 stores of the organization, and data is stored at the transaction level, this query would have to read 7,500,000 (500 × 500 × 30 days) rows, and build the sum to return the result. Now, let's examine what happens if the data is aggregated in a table that is created using monthly sales by store. In this case, the table will only have 500 rows (the monthly total for each of 500 stores), and the performance gain will be dramatic.

How Much to Aggregate?

Concerning aggregation, there are two extreme solutions: no aggregation at all and exhaustive aggregation for every possible combination of queries that users will need. From the discussion above, it should be clear that no aggregation at all is out of the question because of performance issues. (The data warehouse without any aggregation table probably cannot be used at all as a production data store.) The opposite solution is also not acceptable for several reasons:

- Enormous amount of disk space that is needed to store additional data
- Overwhelming maintenance of aggregate tables
- Initial data load too long

Storing additional data that is aggregated at every possible level consumes an additional amount of disk space that increases the initial disk space by a factor of six or more (depending on the amount of the initial disk space and the number of queries that users will need). The creation of tables to hold the aggregates for all existing combinations is an overwhelming task for the system administrator. Finally, building aggregates at initial data load can have devastating results if this load already lasts for a long time and the additional time is not available.

From this discussion you can see that aggregate tables should be carefully planned and created. During the planning phase, keep these two main considerations in mind when determining what aggregates to create:

- Where is the data concentrated?
- Which aggregates would most improve performance?

The planning and creation of aggregate tables is dependent on the concentration of data in the columns of the base fact table. In a data warehouse, where there is no activity on a given day, the corresponding row is not stored at all. So, if the system loads a large number of rows, as compared to the number of all rows that can be loaded, aggregating by that column of the base fact table improves performance enormously. In contrast, if the system loads few rows, as compared to the number of all rows that can be loaded, aggregating by that column is not efficient.

Here is another example to demonstrate the discussion above. For products in the grocery store, only a few of them (say, 15 percent) are actually sold on a given day. If we have a dimensional model with three dimensions **Products**, **Store**, and **Time**, only 15 percent of the combination of the three corresponding primary keys for the particular day and for the particular store will be occupied. The daily product sales data will thus be *sparse*. In contrast, if all or many products in the grocery store are sold on a given day (because of a special promotion, for example), the daily product sales data will be *dense*.

To find out which dimensions are sparse and which are dense, you have to build rows from all possible combinations of tables and evaluate them. Usually the **Time** dimension is dense, because there are always entries for each day. Given the dimensions **Products**, **Store**, and **Time**, the combination of the **Store** and **Time** dimensions is dense, because for each day there will certainly be data concerning selling in each store. On the other hand, the combination of the **Store** and **Product** dimensions is sparse. In this case, we can say that the dimension **Product** is generally sparse, because its appearance in combination with other dimensions is sparse.

The choice of aggregates that would most improve performance depends on end users. Therefore, at the beginning of a data warehousing project you should interview end users to collect information on how data will be queried, how many rows will be retrieved by these queries, and other criteria.

DATA MINING

Data in a data warehouse can be accessed with two different techniques:

- On-line analytic processing (OLAP)
- Data mining

On-line analytic processing is used for *reporting* on data, while data mining focuses on *finding patterns* in data. (The following text describes data mining, while OLAP is discussed in detail in Chapter 28.)

Data mining is used to explore and analyze large quantities of data in order to discover significant patterns. This discovery is not the only task of data mining: Using this technique you must be able to turn the existing data into information and the information into action. In other words, it is not enough to analyze data: You have to apply the results of data mining meaningfully and to take action upon the given results.

Data Mining Tasks

To achieve the goals previously described, you can use, among others, several different tasks:

- Classification
- Prediction
- Clustering

The following sections describe these tasks.

Classification

Classification is a process that is constantly used by all human beings to better understand the world around them. During this process, we either classify similar objects into classes of objects or examine the features of a specific object to assign it to one of known sets of classes.

In data mining, the classification process is characterized by a definition of all existing classes and a predefined set that comprises all preclassified data. (There are always a limited number of classes.) The goal of classification is to build a model that can be used to classify new, not yet classified data.

Prediction

Prediction is similar to classification, except that it groups data according to some predicted behavior. Using existing (historical) data, you build a model that explains the current behavior. This behavior is then used to predict future behavior. (For instance, in a grocery store, this task is used to discover which items are likely to be purchased together.)

Clustering

Clustering is a process that partitions heterogeneous data into several, more homogenous, subgroups (such subgroups are called *clusters*). Although at first site, the clustering process seems identical to classification, there is a significant difference: Clustering does not use any predefined classes. This means, the existing data are grouped on the basis of self-similarity (i.e., it is your task to determine the meaning of resulting subgroups).

Data Mining Techniques

The tasks already described are the foundation for different techniques that are used in a data mining process. You can apply some of these tasks in a top-down manner, if you use past behavior to verify (or disprove) postulated ideas. (This approach is called *hypothesis testing*.) Other tasks are useful in a bottom-up manner, when there are no prior assumptions and the data itself gives you a hint how to get information. (This approach is called *knowledge discovery*.)

The following techniques, among others can be used in a data mining process:

- Cluster detection
- Decision trees
- Market basket analysis
- Neural networks

NOTE: SQL Server 2000 supports only the first two techniques. Therefore only cluster detection and decision trees will be explained in the following sections.

Automatic Cluster Detection

The starting point for the most data mining techniques is a preclassified set that is used to develop a model for new items. This is not true for the automatic cluster detection technique: Instead of preclassified data, this technique searches for groups of items that are similar to each other, hoping that similar items will behave in similar ways.

NOTE: The automatic cluster technique is almost always used together with other data techniques, because finding clusters does not mean the end of the data mining process.

Automatic cluster detection has several benefits:

- It is easy to apply.
- It can be used with numeric and textual data.

Because automatic cluster detection does not require a preclassified model, it is easier to apply than other data mining techniques. You can also apply this technique for almost all real-life problems, because you can use it with any kind of data (except nonrelational data, such as images and audio).

Decision Trees

Decision trees are a powerful technique that divide items in the preclassifed set into disjointed groups. Each group is described using a rule. Therefore, a decision tree represents a series of questions where the answer to each question determines which path will be followed (i.e., which question is asked next).

The benefits of the decision tree technique are as follows:

- Decision trees are the best technique for classification.
- Rules generated by decision trees are easy to understand and translate.

Decision trees are suited best for classification, because they divide items into disjointed subsets. Additionally, you can perform classification easily with this technique, because it does not require much computation.

Rules in decision trees are easy to generate. That way you can easily translate them into SQL. (The explanation for any rule in a decision tree is usually straightforward.)

CONCLUSION

At the beginning of a data warehouse project, the main question is what to build: a data warehouse or a data mart. Probably the best answer is to start with one or more data marts that can later be united in a data warehouse. Most of the existing tools in the data warehousing market support this alternative.

In contrast to operational databases that use ER models for their design, the design of data warehouses is best done using a dimensional model. These two models show significant differences: if you are already acquainted with the ER model, the best way to learn and use the dimensional model is to forget everything about the ER model and start modeling from scratch.

After this introductory discussion of general considerations about the data warehousing process, the next chapter discusses the server part of MS Analysis Services.

EXERCISES

▼ E.26.1

Discuss the differences between OLTP and data warehousing systems.

▼ E.26.2

Discuss the differences between the ER and dimensional models.

▼ E.26.3

At the beginning of a project with a data warehouse, there is the so called ETL process (E, extracting; T, transforming; L, loading). Explain these three subprocesses.

▼ E.26.4

Discuss the differences between a fact table and corresponding dimension tables.

▼ E.26.5

Discuss the benefits of each of the three storage types (MOLAP, ROLAP, and HOLAP).

▼ E.26.6

Why it is necessary to aggregate data stored in a fact table?

CHAPTER 27

Microsoft Analysis Services

Microsoft Analysis Services is a set of services that are used to manage data stored in a data warehouse or data mart. Analysis Services organizes data from a data warehouse into multidimensional cubes (see Chapter 26) with aggregates to allow the execution of sophisticated reports and complex queries. The key features of MS Analysis Services are:

- Ease of use
- Flexible data model
- Several supported APIs

Analysis Services offers wizards for almost every task that is executed during the design and implementation of a data warehouse. For example, Cube Wizard is used to create a multidimensional cube where aggregate data is stored, while Dimension Wizard allows you to create shared or private dimension tables.

Ease of use is guaranteed by Analysis Manager—an end-user and system administrator tool that is used to create databases and other data warehousing objects. This is based upon the same console application as Enterprise Manager of SQL Server, giving SQL Server users a well-known interface for their analytical tasks. (Analysis Manager is described in detail later in this chapter.)

In contrast to most other data warehousing servers, MS Analysis Services allows you to use the storage mode that is most appropriate for a specific data warehouse system. You can choose between the following storage structures:

- MOLAP
- ROLAP
- HOLAP

In a MOLAP storage structure, data as well as aggregates are stored in a multidimensional cube. The most important benefit of this structure is that it offers the best performance for data analysis, because Analysis Services uses the specialized indexing technique (called bitmap indexing) to improve query performance. On the other hand, data in the cube is duplicated. Therefore, this storage structure consumes the most disk space.

ROLAP (relational OLAP) stores the base data and all aggregates in tables of a relational database. (The base data as well as aggregates are stored in the same database as the source data warehouse database.) The benefits of ROLAP are that it does not require extra storage space and a user can use Transact-SQL for data analysis. The disadvantage of this storage structure is its performance: the queries do not execute as fast as with MOLAP. For this reason, you should use ROLAP for queries that are executed infrequently.

If the base data and all aggregations are separated so that the former is stored in tables of a relational database and the latter in the multidimensional cube, the storage type is called HOLAP (hybrid OLAP). The benefits of storing the base data and aggregations in a HOLAP storage structure are that it consumes less disk space than MOLAP and provides fast response for queries on aggregate data.

MS Analysis Services support the OLE DB for OLAP interface, thus allowing different third-party software to be used as clients. The support of the data transport standard based on OLE DB is called Universal Data Access and is a part of Data Warehouse Framework—an overall specification between different components used in the process of designing, implementing, and managing data warehouses. Using DTS (Data Transformation Services), you can extract data from different data sources (Access, Oracle, and/or SQL Server databases and text files), transform it, and load it into a data warehouse.

ARCHITECTURE OF MS ANALYSIS SERVICES

MS Analysis Services includes several different components, which can be separated into:

- Server components
- Client components

Figure 27-1 shows the client/server architecture of MS Analysis Services.

Server Components

MS Analysis Services contain two server components (see Figure 27-1):

- Analysis Server
- Decision Support Objects (DSO)

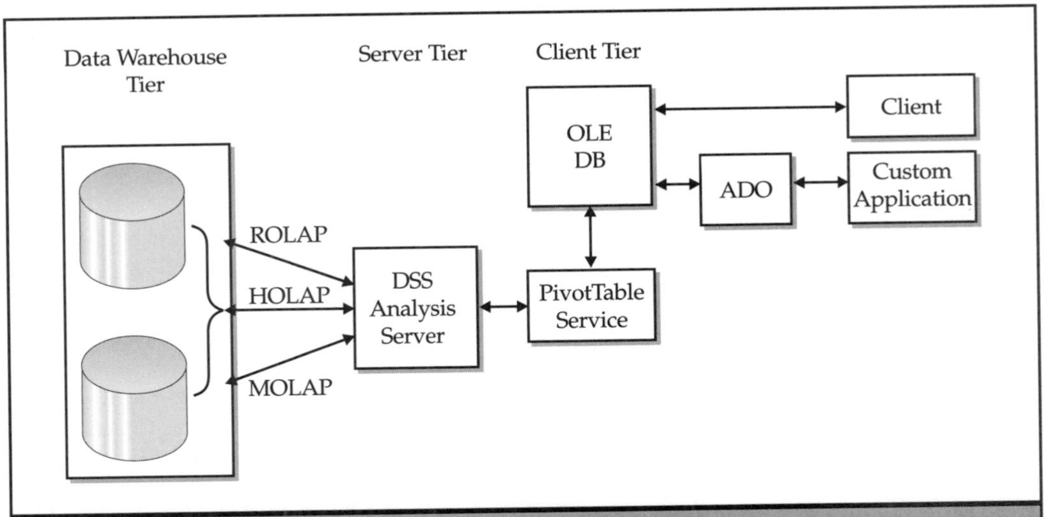

Figure 27-1. Client/server architecture of MS Analysis Services

Analysis Server

Analysis Server is the main component of the Analysis Services. It processes multidimensional cubes and communicates with clients to send query results to them. Also, it manages storage space, allowing the system to store data in tables of a relational database or in cubes.

Each Analysis Server must be registered if it is to be administered by the system. This functionality is provided by Analysis Manager. A server can be registered during the first execution of Analysis Manager or later. If you want to register a server later, start Analysis Manager: click **Start**, point to **Programs**, point to **Microsoft SQL Server**, select **Analysis Services**, and choose **Analysis Manager**. Then you can do any of the following: right-click **Analysis Servers** and select **Register Server**, or click the **Action** button in the toolbar and select **Register Server** from the pull-down menu.

Also, each Analysis Server must be running if you want to analyze data using client software. To verify it, open **Services** in the **Control Panel** and look for **MSSQLServerOLAPService**. If this service is not running, start it.

Decision Support Objects (DSO)

A Decision Support Object is the application programming interface (API) for Analysis Server. It specifies also an object model that consists of interfaces, objects, and methods. You can use it to write custom applications, the task of which is to create data cubes or manage authorization. DSO custom applications can be implemented in any language that supports the Component Object Model (Visual Basic, for instance).

As Figure 27-1 shows, this API is also used by Analysis Manager to communicate with the Analysis Server. (Analysis Manager is described later in this chapter.)

The object model of DSO arranges all elements in groups that are hierarchically structured. The tree in Figure 27-2 shows the hierarchy of objects.

- Analysis Server
- Database
  - Cube
    - Partition
      - Aggregation
  - Virtual Cube
    - Cube
      - Partition
        - Aggregation

Figure 27-2. The hierarchy of the Decision Support Objects (DSO)

The hierarchy in Figure 27-2 can be interpreted in the following way: The server object contains groups of objects that define databases. Each database instance can contain groups of objects that define cubes and/or virtual cubes. A cube contains partitions that themselves contain aggregations. (A virtual cube is a special type of a cube that combines parts from other cubes.)

As can be seen from Figure 27-2, each of the objects contains collections of other objects. A special collection, called MDStore, contains all objects of the hierarchy above that, are stored beneath the Analysis Server. A specific property of MDStore is that it provides methods (i.e., functions) such as Add, Find, and Remove that can be used on all objects in the hierarchy beneath it.

Client Components

MS Analysis Services contain two client components (see Figure 27-1):

- Client interfaces
- PivotTable Service

Client Interfaces

Each client interface allows you to:

- Connect to an Analysis Server
- Browse multidimensional schema
- Select data from a cube using a query
- Retrieve the results

To query a cube, you can use either ADO MD or OLE DB for OLAP. OLE DB for OLAP is the extension to OLE DB that includes objects specific to multidimensional data. You can write client applications by using any COM-compliant language (such as Visual Basic) to communicate with the PivotTable Service.

As you can see from Figure 27-1, ADO MD (multidimensional) allows client applications to access PivotTable Service through OLE DB. ADO MD is an extension to ADO that includes data access interfaces that are optimized for multidimensional applications. This interface is object oriented and language independent. To use ADO MD objects, you can write client applications by using any COM-compliant language.

PivotTable Service

Client applications connect to the Analysis Server through the PivotTable Service. PivotTable Service is a client component that provides both interfaces to data and functionality to manipulate data. In other words, PivotTable Service connects to the Analysis Server as a client and allows you to access multidimensional cubes that are managed by the Analysis Server.

PivotTable Service has several important properties:

- Stores data locally on the client, thus enabling client applications to create and use a local multidimensional database.
- Functions as a service provider for relational data sources that implements multidimensional cubes and exposes the OLE DB interfaces with MDX extensions. (Multidimensional expressions (MDX) are sets of statements that allow users to query multidimensional data. For example, the statements CREATE CUBE and DROP CUBE belong to the MDX extensions.)
- Specifies a local multidimensional data server. This means that client applications connect to Analysis Services for overall data analysis as well as to PivotTable Service for local (stand-alone) analysis services. For the latter reason, you can use PivotTable Service to query (local) data, even if Analysis Services is offline.

Because PivotTable Service is a local data multidimensional server, it has some restrictions concerning performance and system administration. For example, it can work only with a single data cube partition. (On the other hand, you can use MDX to define new data cubes and populate them with data.) Typical system administration activities such as defining users and permissions are not supported by PivotTable Service.

COMPONENTS OF ANALYSIS SERVICES

MS Analysis Services has several components that are used for different purposes:

- Analysis Manager
- Data Transformation Services (DTS)

The following sections describe each of these components.

Analysis Manager

MS Analysis Services include Analysis Manager, a tool that provides an interactive interface for accessing Analysis Server and the MS Repository. Analysis Manager is integrated with the MS Management Console (MMC), which is the standard user interface for all Microsoft administration tools. To start Analysis Manager, click **Start**, point to **Programs**, point to **Microsoft SQL Server,** select **Analysis Services**, and choose **Analysis Manager**. Figure 27-3 shows the Analysis Manager tree structure.

Analogous to the server groups node in Enterprise Manager of SQL Server, Analysis Manager has the Analysis Servers node that contains a node for each Analysis Server on your system. Each Analysis Server contains one or more databases that are represented through subnodes of the server node.

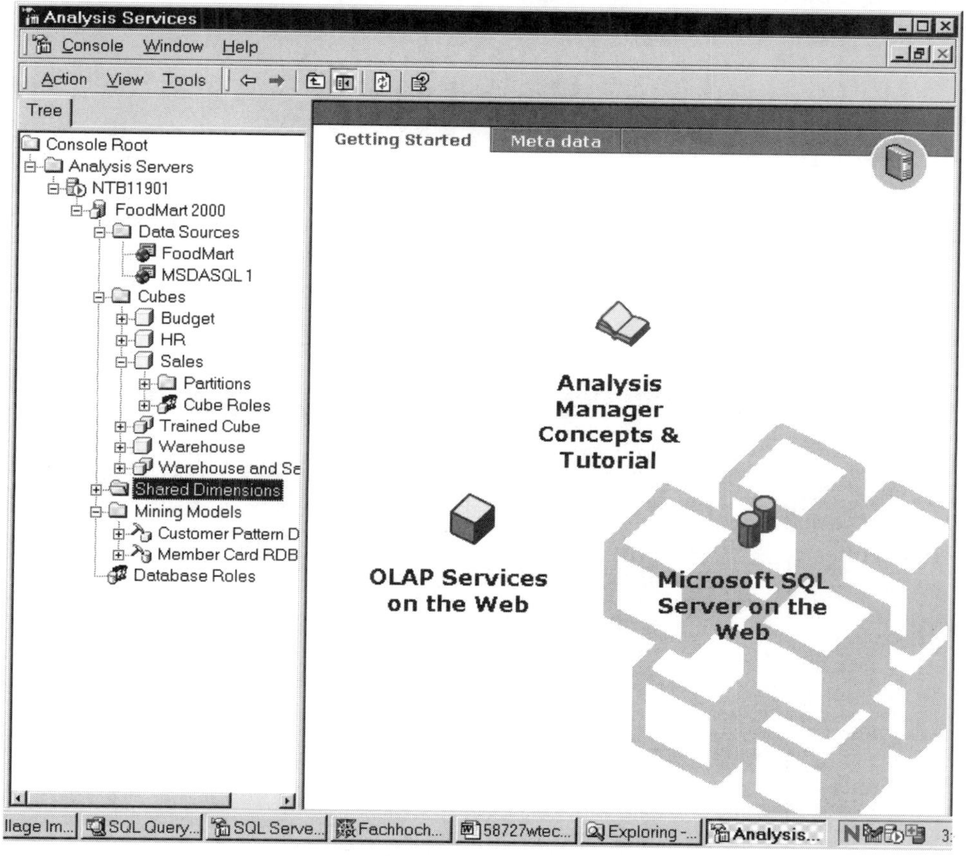

Figure 27-3. Analysis Manager tree structure

Figure 27-3 shows the sample database **FoodMart2000** with its parts. Beneath the database node there are five folders:

- Data Sources
- Cubes
- Shared Dimensions
- Mining Models
- Database Roles

The **Data Sources** subfolder contains information about the OLE DB provider, server connections, and security issues. To set up a data source, right-click the subfolder of the database and choose **New Data Source**. In the **Data Link Properties** dialog box, click the **Provider** tab (see Figure 27-4) and select the data you want to connect to. Additionally, click the **Connection** tab and choose the database from the list.

NOTE: Before you define the data source, you have to define the database. To define it, expand **Analysis Servers** in the Analysis Manager tree view, right-click the server, and choose **New Database**. In the **Database** dialog box, specify the name of the new database and optionally its description. (Setting up a data source, you define the source for all data that will be coming to your database.)

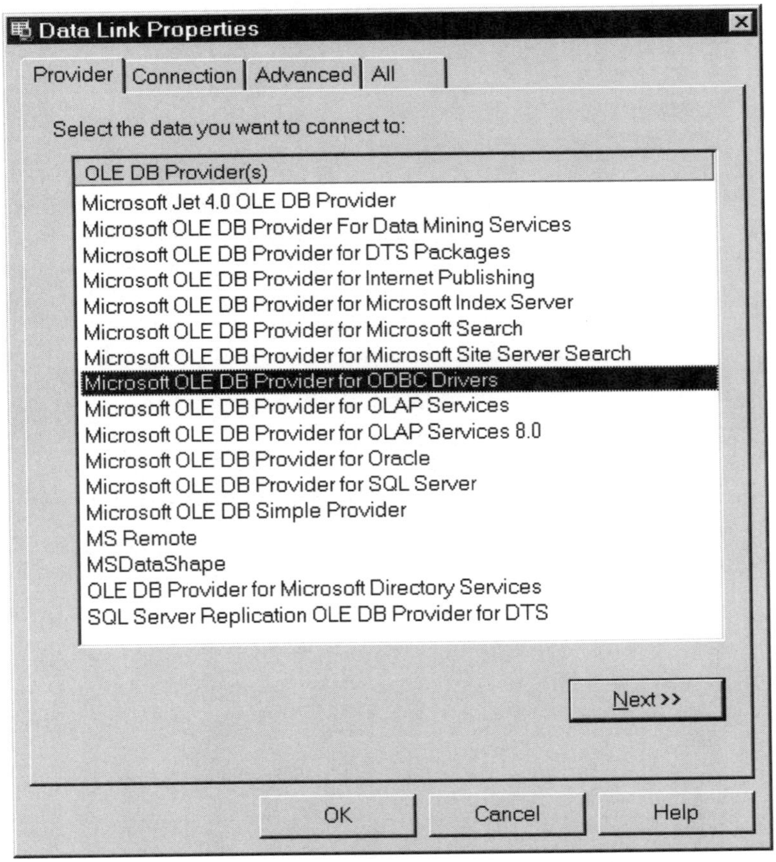

Figure 27-4. The Data Link Properties dialog box: the Provider tab

The next subfolder—**Cubes**—contains all cubes that belong to the database. For instance, the Analysis Server sample database (**FoodMart2000**) contains, among others, the **Budget**, **Sales**, and **Warehouse** cubes. Each cube contains **Partitions** and **Cube Roles** subfolders. The former specifies all partitions of the cube and the latter the security issues concerning that cube. (Both topics will be explained later in this chapter.)

The **Mining Models** subfolder allows you to create a data mining model using the Mining Model Wizard. These models are based on cube information and view the results as a new dimension or measure.

Besides the folders described above, there are two other folders: **Shared Dimensions** and **Database Roles**, which will be described later when we discuss the practical use of Analysis Manager.

Data Transformation Services

Data Transformation Services (DTS) is a general tool for transforming data from one or more source data stores to one or more target data stores. Besides data transfer, DTS allows transformation of data between the import and export processes. Another important property of DTS is that it imports data from heterogeneous sources (Oracle and MS Access, among others).

Because of all these properties, DTS is a tool of choice for an early phase in the process of building data warehouses, called the "data consolidation phase." In this phase, data is extracted from different sources and converted to an intermediate schema. After that, data is cleaned—that is, all extracted data is checked and different formats and types of the same data are unified. Finally, it is checked as to whether data meets already existing requirements. (For more information on this important tool, see Chapter 21.)

ANALYSIS SERVICES AND CUBES

A cube is a multidimensional structure that contains all or a part of the data from a data warehouse. Each cube contains the following components:

- Dimensions
- Members
- Hierarchies
- Levels
- Cells
- Properties

A dimension is a set of logically related attributes (stored together in a dimensional table) that closely describe measures (stored in the fact table). Although the term "cube" implies three dimensions, a multidimensional cube can have up to 64 dimensions. For instance, Time is the typical dimension that is part of many dimensional models.

NOTE: One dimension of a cube is the Measures dimension, which includes all measures defined in the fact table.

Member specifies each discrete value in a dimension. For instance, the members of a Product dimension could be: Computers, Disks, and CPUs. Member can be calculated meaning that its value is calculated at run time using an expression that is specified during the definition of the member. (Because calculated members are not stored on the disk, they allow you to add new members without increasing the size of a corresponding cube.)

Hierarchies specify groupings of multiple members within each dimension. They are used to refine queries concerning data analysis.

Cells are parts of a multidimensional cube that are identified by coordinates (x coordinate, y coordinate, z coordinate). That means, a cell is a set containing members from each dimension. For instance, consider a three-dimensional cube in Figure 26-4 that represents car sales for a single region within a quarter. The cells within this cube could be identified with the following coordinates:

- First quarter 1999, South America, Falcon
- Third quarter 1998, South Asia, Eagle

When you define hierarchies, you define them in terms of their levels. In other words, levels describe the hierarchy from the highest (most summarized) level to the lowest (most detailed) level of data. They are defined within a dimension to specify the contents and structure of the dimension's hierarchy. That is, the level definitions determine the members that are included in the hierarchy and their positions relative to one another within the hierarchy. For instance, if you sum the sales of cars by quarter, month, and day, each cell at these intersections would represent the total sales amount of cars for:

- Quarter (Q1, Q2, Q3, Q4)
- Month (January, February, ...)
- Day (Day1, Day2, ...)

Creating a Cube

Before creating a cube, you have to use the dimensional model and design a corresponding star schema. After that, you can use either Cube Wizard or Cube Editor to create a cube. The creation of a cube contains the following steps:

1. Identify a fact table from a data source.
2. Select all measures.
3. Define dimensions.

NOTE: To create a cube, use Cube Wizard. The wizard prompts you to identify all steps specified above.

In the first step, you identify the fact table from a data source. This is a simple step if you have already made a dimensional model of your database. In the next step, which is related to the first one, you must define the measures that are selected from the numeric columns of the fact table. (Cube Wizard selects and displays all such columns from the fact table.) Each measure can be atomic or combined. An atomic measure is identical to a column. A combined measure is specified with an expression that uses two or more columns from the fact table. (For instance, the Profit measure can be specified as the difference of the columns Sales and Cost.)

After you identify a fact table and choose its measures, you can define dimensions. This step is described later in this chapter.

Design Aggregations and Process the Cube

As you already know, basic data from the fact table can be summarized in advance and stored in intermediate tables. This process is called "aggregation" and it can significantly enhance the response time, because scanning millions of rows to calculate the aggregation on the fly can take a very long time.

There is a trade-off between storage requirements and the percentage of possible aggregations that are calculated and then stored. Calculation of all possible aggregations in a cube and their storage on the disk results in the fastest possible response time for all queries, because the response to each query is almost immediate. The disadvantage of this approach is that the storage and processing time required for the aggregations can be substantial.

On the other hand, if no aggregations are calculated and stored, you do not need any additional disk storage, but query response time will be slow because each aggregate has to be calculated on the fly.

MS Analysis Services supports Storage Design Wizard, which allows you to design aggregations optimally. To start the wizard, right-click the cube and select **Design Storage**. In the first step, you have to select the storage type for all precalculated aggregations (ROLAP, MOLAP, and HOLAP).

In the next step, you select aggregation options (see Figure 27-5). You can either determine the maximal amount of disk storage that should be used for precalculated aggregations or the performance gains you want to achieve. (The higher the percentage of precalculated aggregations, the better the performance.)

Storage Design Wizard supports, as the last step, processing the cube. Processing the cube means that the cube is populated with data. This step involves:

- Retrieving and storing the low-level data
- Calculating the aggregations
- Storing the cube in a multidimensional structure and/or relational tables

NOTE: Processing a cube must be executed when you first create the cube and each time you modify it. If a cube has lot of data and precalculated aggregations, processing the cube can be very time-consuming.

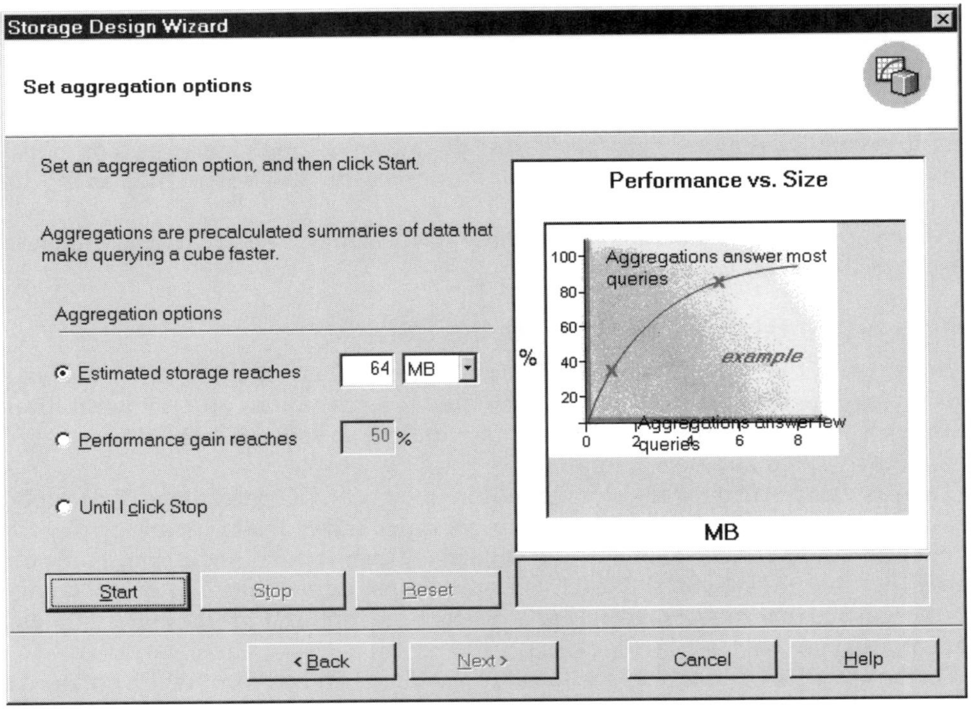

Figure 27-5. Storage Design Wizard: Set aggregation options

Editing a Cube

To edit a cube, expand the **Cubes** folder, right-click the cube you want to edit, and then click **Edit**. Figure 27-6 shows the **Budget** cube, which is edited in the detail pane of the Cube Editor. If you want to make any modifications to a cube, select the fact table and make your changes to **Dimensions**, **Measure**, **Aggregation**, **Field**, and/or **Units**.

Defining Dimensions

After you identify your fact table and choose its measures, you can define all dimensions. Defined dimensions can be used by one cube or by multiple cubes. For this reason Analysis Services supports two types of dimensions:

- Shared
- Private

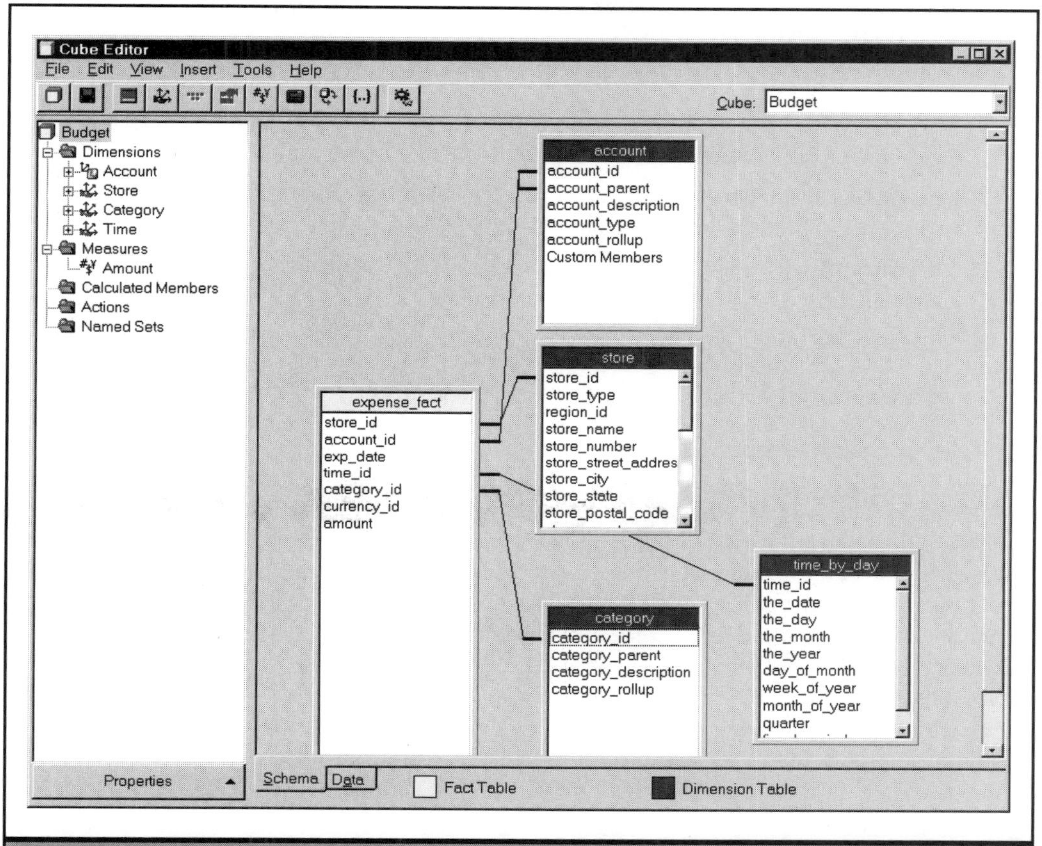

Figure 27-6. Editing the Budget cube

Shared dimensions (also called conformed dimensions) are dimensions that are shared among two or more cubes in the database. Typical shared dimensions are **Time**, **Product**, or **Customer**. A dimension can be created for use in an individual cube or multiple cubes. In the Analysis Manager tree pane, shared dimensions are located in the **Shared Dimensions** subfolder under the database in which they are created. For instance, **FoodMart2000** contains, among others, the following shared dimensions: **Category**, **Customers**, and **Store**.

Shared dimensions can be used within any cube in the database. By creating shared dimensions and using them in multiple cubes, you avoid the process of creating duplicate private dimensions within each of the cubes.

Private dimensions are created for an individual cube. In the Analysis Manager, private dimensions are found in the **Cube Editor** tree pane.

Creating a Shared Dimension

Before you create a shared dimension, you have to:

- Specify whether the shared dimension will be created from a star schema, a snowflake schema, a parent-child table, or from a virtual dimension.
- Identify the data source that contains the database objects (tables and columns) that define the shared dimension.
- Identify the dimension table(s) that contain the column(s) that you want in the shared dimension.
- Specify the levels that you want in the shared dimension.

To create a shared dimension you can use:

- Dimension Editor
- Dimension Wizard

To create a shared dimension using Dimension Editor, expand the database in which you want to create the shared dimension, right-click the **Shared dimensions** subfolder, select **New Dimension**, and click **Editor**. In the **Choose a Dimension Table** dialog box, expand a data source and select the dimension table(s) for the dimension. (To add multiple tables to the dimension, click **Tables** on the **Insert** menu and then use the **Select Table** dialog box.)

On the **Insert** menu, click **Level** to create levels in the dimension. (As you create each level, it appears in the tree pane.) In the **Select Column** dialog box, select the column on which the level is based, and then click **OK**.

NOTE: When defining a level, you could receive a warning message that the number of children is less than the number of parents. The reason for this message could be that you switched the levels in the level hierarchy or that you have the special case where the number of children is actually less than the number of parents. In the former case, delete the levels and specify the right hierarchy.

To save the dimension, click **Save** on the **File** menu, type the dimension name, and click **OK**.

To create a shared dimension using Dimension Wizard, expand the database in which you want to create the shared dimension, right-click the **Shared dimensions** subfolder, select **New Dimension**, and click **Wizard.** The Dimension Wizard has a few mandatory steps, which correspond to the general steps described above. All other steps are optional and depend on the type of the dimension you want to create.

Edit Dimensions

The Dimension Editor allows you to edit members of a shared dimension and all its levels. To open the Dimension Editor, you can either open the **Shared Dimensions** subfolder, right-click a dimension, and then click **Edit**, or open the **Shared Dimensions** subfolder, click a dimension, and click **Edit** on the **Action** menu.

The Dimension Editor has two views:

- Data
- Schema

The **Data** view displays the current dimension and its levels in a tree format. Clicking on the individual levels, you can expand (or collapse) them. Figure 27-7 shows the **Data** view of the **Customers** dimension in the **FoodMart2000** database. The **Schema** view displays the dimension tables with all its columns and joins specified by lines that connect the primary keys of the tables. Figure 27-8 shows the **Schema** view of the same dimension.

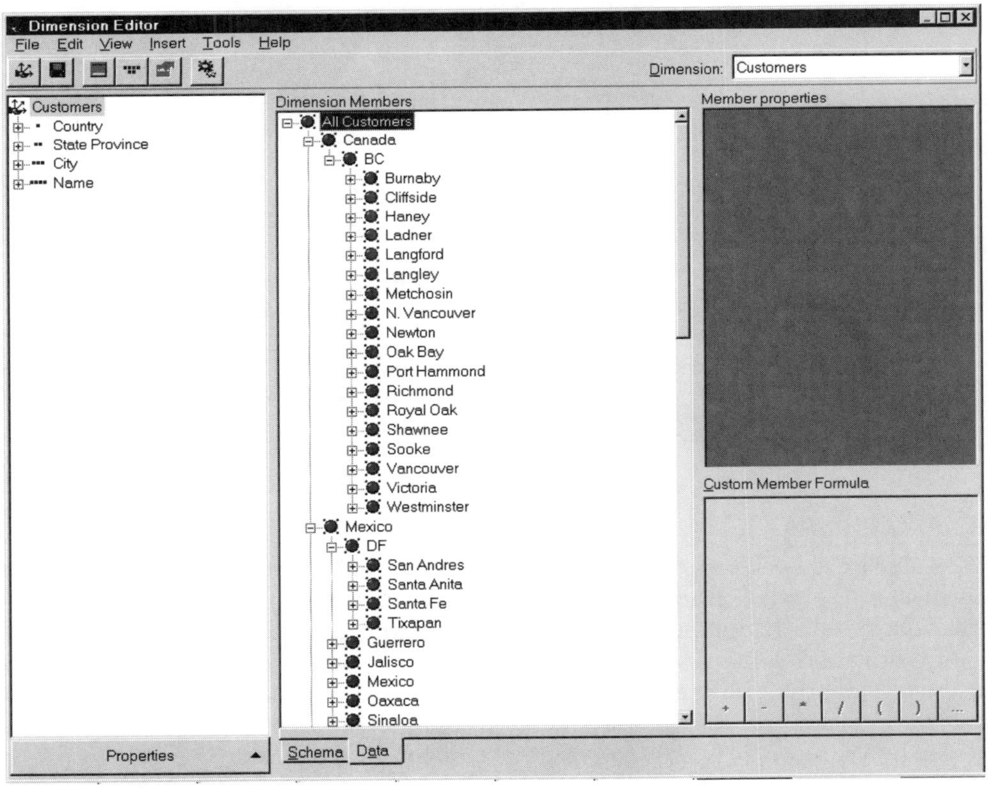

Figure 27-7. Dimension Editor: The Data view

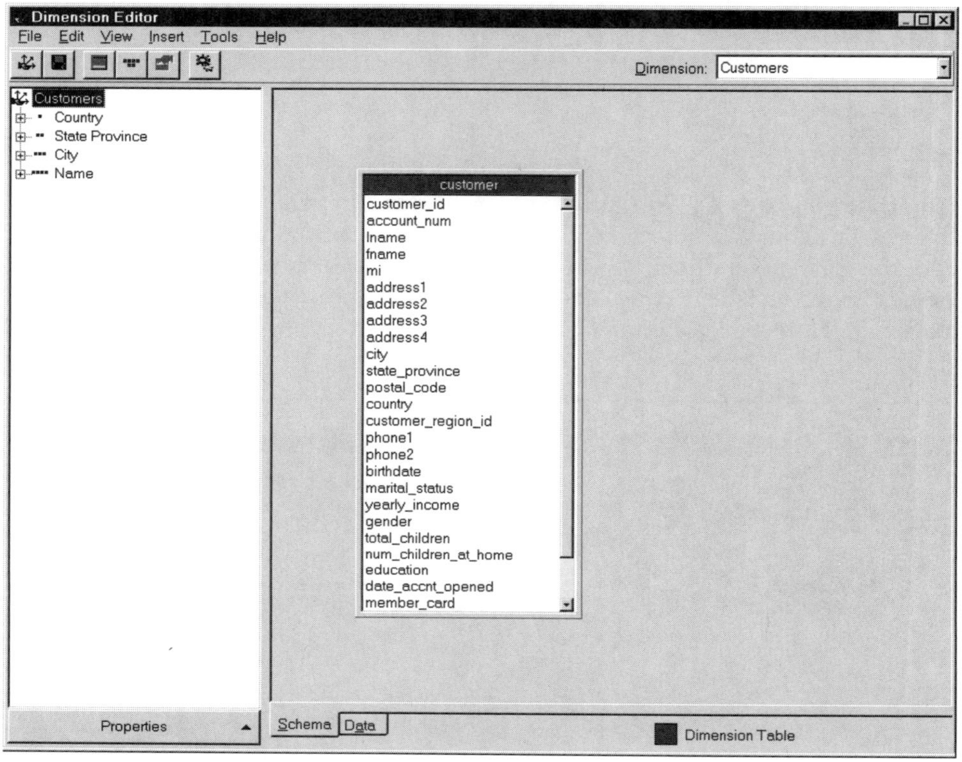

Figure 27-8. Dimension Editor: The Schema view

Security Issues

MS Analysis Services security issues correspond to the security issues of SQL Server. This means Analysis Services supports both general features—authorization and user permissions—as SQL Server does, but in a very restricted form.

Authorization defines which user has a legitimate access to MS Analysis Services. This issue is tightly connected to the operating system authorization. In other words, MS Analysis Services imposes user authorization based on the access rights being granted to the user by Windows NT/2000 or Windows 9*x* operating system.

You can use Analysis Manager to limit the special users that can perform administrative functions for Analysis Services. You can also specify which end users can access data and the types of operations they can perform. Additionally, you can control their access at different levels of data, such as the cube, dimension, and cube cell level.

Administrator security is controlled using the Windows group called OLAP Administrators. The authentication of end users is controlled during their connection to the Analysis server. Permissions of end users is managed using database roles and cube roles that are defined using Analysis Manager. (The notions of authentication and user permissions are defined in Chapter 12.)

A database role specifies a group of database users that can access the same objects of the database. Each role is defined at the Analysis Services database level and then assigned to cubes that the users in the role are permitted to access. You can perform limited changes to the role at the cube level. (A detailed discussion of security at each specific level—dimension, cube, and cube cell—is beyond the scope of this book.)

CONCLUSION

With its Analysis Server, Microsoft offers a set of data warehousing services that can be used by users for entry-level and intermediate-level data analysis. In particular, its ease of use through Analysis Manager, which is based upon the same console application MMC as Enterprise Manager of SQL Server, will give users an easy way to design, implement, and manage data warehouses and/or data marts.

The next chapter describes the client components of MS Analysis Services.

CHAPTER 28

Client Components for MS Analysis Services

All client components for MS Analysis Services can be roughly divided into three groups:

- SQL extensions
- Microsoft client tools
- Third-party client software

SQL EXTENSIONS

SQL Server offers some extensions to the SELECT statement that can be used especially for decision support operations. These extensions are as follows:

- CUBE operator
- ROLLUP operator
- TOP **n** clause

The first two operators—CUBE and ROLLUP—are used to add summary rows to the result of a SELECT statement with the GROUP BY clause. The TOP **n** clause provides the retrieval of the first **n** rows of a query result (usually sorted using some criteria).

CUBE Operator

The GROUP BY clause defines one or more columns as a group such that all rows within any group have the same values for these columns. The CUBE operator introduces additional rows called *summary rows* into the result of a SELECT statement. A GROUP BY summary row is returned for every possible combination of group and subgroup in the result. The following examples show how these operators can be applied.

Example 28.1 creates a table that is subsequently used for querying data.

▼ EXAMPLE 28.1

```
CREATE TABLE project_dept (dept_name CHAR(20) NOT NULL,
    employee_cnt INT NOT NULL,
    budget FLOAT NULL)
```

Example 28.1 creates a new table **project_dept** that contains the number of employees and budget of each project that is controlled by a department. The (possible) content of this table is given in Table 28-1.

Example 28.2 groups the rows of the **project_dept** table using two criteria: **dept_name** and **employee_cnt**.

dept_name	employee_cnt	budget
Research	5	50,000
Research	10	70,000
Research	5	65,000
Accounting	5	10,000
Accounting	10	40,000
Accounting	6	30,000
Accounting	6	40,000
Marketing	6	100,000
Marketing	10	180,000
Marketing	3	100,000
Marketing	5	120,000

Table 28-1. Content of the Table **project_dept**

▼ EXAMPLE 28.2

```
SELECT dept_name, employee_cnt, SUM(budget) sum_of_budgets
    FROM project_dept
    GROUP BY dept_name, employee_cnt
```

The result is

dept_name	employee_cnt	sum_of_budgets
Marketing	3	100000.0
Accounting	5	10000.0
Marketing	5	120000.0
Research	5	115000.0
Accounting	6	70000.0
Marketing	6	100000.0
Accounting	10	40000.0
Marketing	10	180000.0
Research	10	70000.0

The use of the CUBE operator is shown in Example 28.3.

▼ EXAMPLE 28.3

```
SELECT dept_name, employee_cnt, SUM(budget) sum_of_budgets
    FROM project_dept
    GROUP BY dept_name, employee_cnt
    WITH CUBE
```

The result is

dept_name	employee_cnt	sum_of_budgets
Accounting	5	10000.0
Accounting	6	70000.0
Accounting	10	40000.0
Accounting	NULL	120000.0
Marketing	3	100000.0
Marketing	5	120000.0
Marketing	6	100000.0
Marketing	10	180000.0
Marketing	NULL	500000.0
Research	5	115000.0
Research	10	70000.0
Research	NULL	185000.0
NULL	NULL	805000.0
NULL	3	100000.0
NULL	5	245000.0
NULL	6	170000.0
NULL	10	290000.0

Besides all rows from the result of Example 28.2, the result of Example 28.3 contains all possible summary rows. A GROUP BY summary row is displayed as NULL in the result, but it is used to indicate all values. For example, the row

```
NULL        NULL      805000.0
```

shows the sum of all budgets of all existing projects in the table, while the row

```
NULL        3         100000.0
```

shows the sum of all budgets for all projects that employ exactly three employees.

NOTE: Because the CUBE operator displays every possible combination of groups and subgroups, the number of rows is the same, regardless of the grouping order of columns.

ROLLUP Operator

In contrast to the CUBE operator that returns every possible combination of groups and subgroups, the group hierarchy using the ROLLUP operator is determined by the order in which the grouping columns are specified. Example 28.4 shows the use of the ROLLUP operator.

▼ EXAMPLE 28.4

```
SELECT dept_name, employee_cnt, SUM(budget) sum_of_budgets
        FROM project_dept
        GROUP BY dept_name, employee_cnt
        WITH CUBE
```

The result is

dept_name	employee_cnt	sum_of_budgets
Accounting	5	10000.0
Accounting	6	70000.0
Accounting	10	40000.0
Accounting	NULL	120000.0
Marketing	3	100000.0
Marketing	5	120000.0
Marketing	6	100000.0
Marketing	10	180000.0
Marketing	NULL	500000.0
Research	5	115000.0
Research	10	70000.0
Research	NULL	185000.0
NULL	NULL	805000.0

As you can see from the result of Example 28.4, the number of retrieved rows in this example is smaller than the number of displayed rows in the previous one. The reason is that the group hierarchy is determined by the order of columns in the GROUP BY clause. For Example 28.4, this means that the summary rows are displayed only for the first column in the GROUP BY clause: **dept_name**.

Example 28.5 shows that changing the order of the grouping columns can affect the number of rows produced in the result set.

▼ EXAMPLE 28.5

```
SELECT dept_name, employee_cnt, SUM(budget) sum_of_budgets
        FROM project_dept
        GROUP BY employee_cnt, dept_name
        WITH ROLLUP
```

The result is

dept_name	employee_cnt	sum_of_budgets
Marketing	3	100000.0
NULL	3	100000.0
Accounting	5	10000.0
Marketing	5	120000.0
Research	5	115000.0
NULL	5	245000.0
Accounting	6	70000.0
Marketing	6	100000.0
NULL	6	170000.0
Accounting	10	40000.0
Marketing	10	180000.0
Research	10	70000.0
NULL	10	290000.0
NULL	NULL	805000.0

Example 28.5 differs from the previous example in the order of the grouping columns. Because of this, the number and content of (some of) the displayed rows is different from Example 28.4.

NOTE: The aggregate functions combined with the DISTINCT option (COUNT(DISTINCT **column_name**), for example) cannot be used in combination with the CUBE or ROLLUP operator.

TOP n Clause

The TOP **n** clause specifies the first **n** rows of the query result that are to be retrieved. Example 28.6 shows the use of this clause.

▼ EXAMPLE 28.6

Retrieve eight projects with the highest budgets.

```
SELECT TOP 8  dept_name, budget
  FROM project_dept
  ORDER BY budget DESC
```

The result is

dept_name	budget
Marketing	180000.0
Marketing	120000.0
Marketing	100000.0
Marketing	100000.0
Research	70000.0
Research	65000.0
Research	50000.0
Accounting	40000.0

You can implement the functionality of the TOP **n** clause using the correlated query. Example 28.7 is equivalent to Example 28.6.

▼ EXAMPLE 28.7

Retrieve eight projects with the highest budgets.

```
SELECT dept_name, budget
  FROM project_dept t1
  WHERE 8 > (SELECT COUNT(*)
           FROM project_dept t2
           WHERE t2.budget > t1.budget)
ORDER BY budget DESC
```

The TOP **n** clause can be used with the additional PERCENT option. In that case, the first **n** percent of the rows are retrieved form the result set. The additional option—WITH TIES—specifies that additional rows will be retrieved from the query result if they have the same value in the ORDER BY column(s) as the last row that belongs to the displayed set. (This option can be used only with the ORDER BY clause.) Example 28.8 shows the use of the WITH TIES option.

▼ **EXAMPLE 28.8**

Retrieve six projects with the smallest number of employees.

```
SELECT TOP 6 WITH TIES *
  FROM project_dept
ORDER BY employee_cnt
```

The result is

dept_name	employee_cnt	budget
Marketing	3	100000.0
Research	5	50000.0
Research	5	65000.0
Accounting	5	10000.0
Marketing	5	120000.0
Accounting	6	30000.0
Accounting	6	40000.0
Marketing	6	100000.0

The result of Example 28.8 contains eight rows, because there are three projects with six employees.

MICROSOFT CLIENT TOOLS

You can use two Microsoft tools to analyze data:

- Excel 2000
- Analysis Manager

Excel 2000

Excel is a well-known spreadsheet tool that is part of Microsoft Office. With the newest version of Excel—Excel 2000—Microsoft delivers a large set of functions that are compatible with Analysis Services. (For example, Web-based access to data can be managed by MS Analysis Services and displayed using Excel 2000.)

You can use Excel 2000 to:

- Create cubes
- Analyze data
- Support mobile and off-site analysis
- Present data in a Web-based application

The description of Excel is beyond the scope of this book.

Analysis Manager

Analysis Manager is a component of Analysis Services that provides a way to access Analysis Servers and the metadata repositories that define multidimensional structures. As a client, you can use Analysis Manager to browse your data sources, shared dimensions, and security roles.

Browsing Data by Using Analysis Manager

Using the **Cube** browser, you will see how Analysis Manager can be used to browse warehouse data. We will use the **Sales** cube of the **Foodmart2000** database to show how you can drill up and drill down through the information in the cube.

Analysis Manager provides the **Cube** browser, which can be used to view and analyze the data of a cube. (The cube must be processed before you can view its data.) To start the **Cube** browser, expand the **Analysis Servers** folder (in the console tree of the Analysis Manager), expand your server, and expand the **Foodmart2000** database. After that, expand the **Cubes** folder, right-click the **Sales** cube, and then click **Browse Data** to open the **Cube** browser (see Figure 28-1).

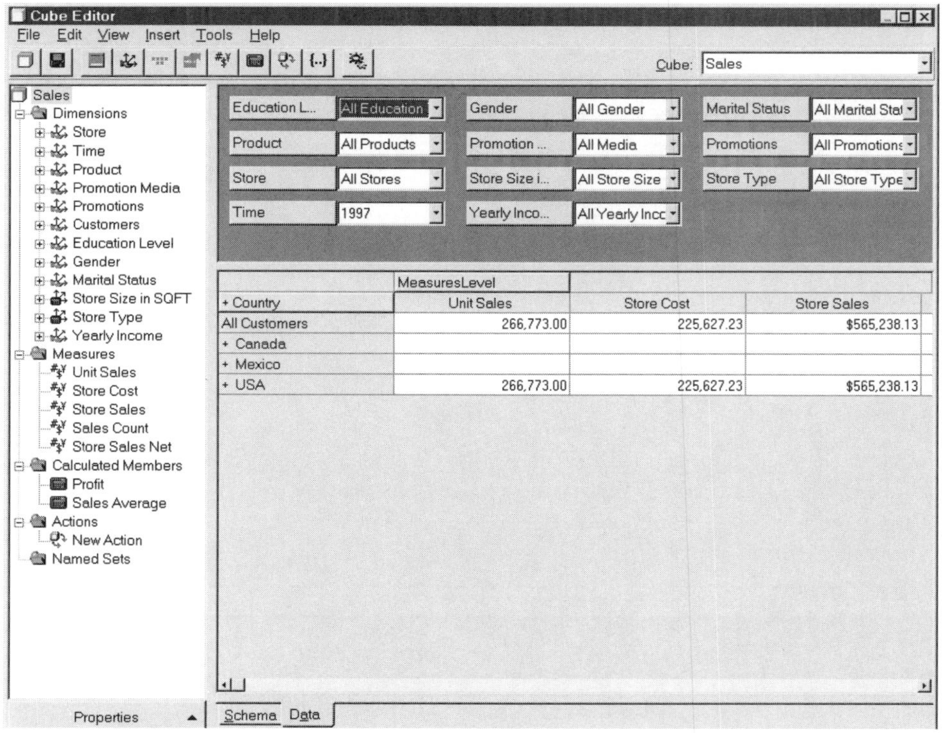

Figure 28-1. The **Cube** browser with the **Sales** cube

The **Cube** browser has two window parts. One part, called the slicer pane, displays the dimensions, while the other part (the data grid) displays the measures at specified levels. As you can see from Figure 28-1, the slicer pane contains 11 dimensions, while the data grid contains the dimension **Country** and the following measures: **Unit Sales**, **Store Cost**, and **Store Sales**. (There are also further measures, which are not shown with the figure.)

If you want to browse the cube data in the data grid by any combination of dimensions, you have to drag the dimension from the slicer pane to either axis on the data grid. (In Figure 28-2, the **Product** dimension is dragged from the slicer pane to the vertical axis of the data grid.) You can change the axis by dragging the column to the row or vice versa (see Figure 28-3).

One of the most frequently used methods of browsing the data in data warehouse is called drilling through the data. Of all existing drilling methods, the following two are the most important:

- Drilling down
- Drilling up

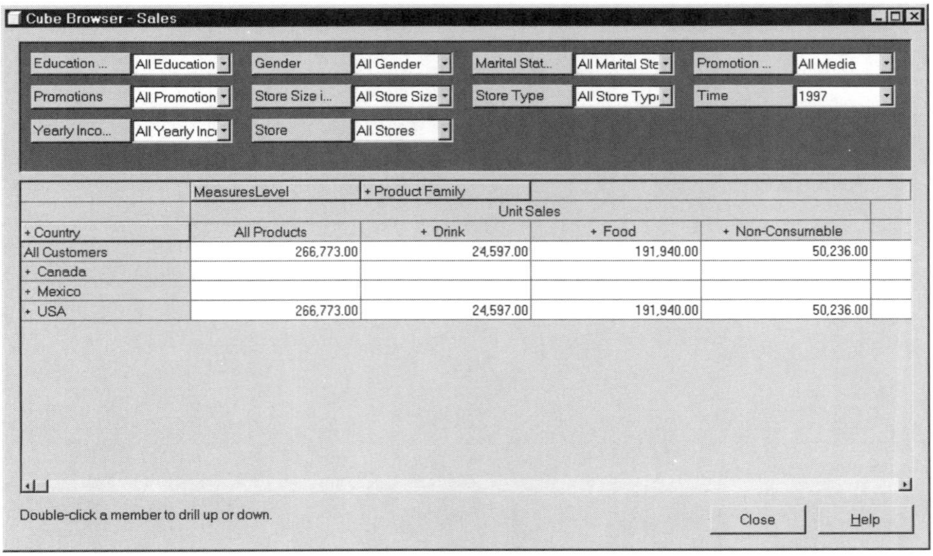

Figure 28-2. Browsing the **Product** dimension

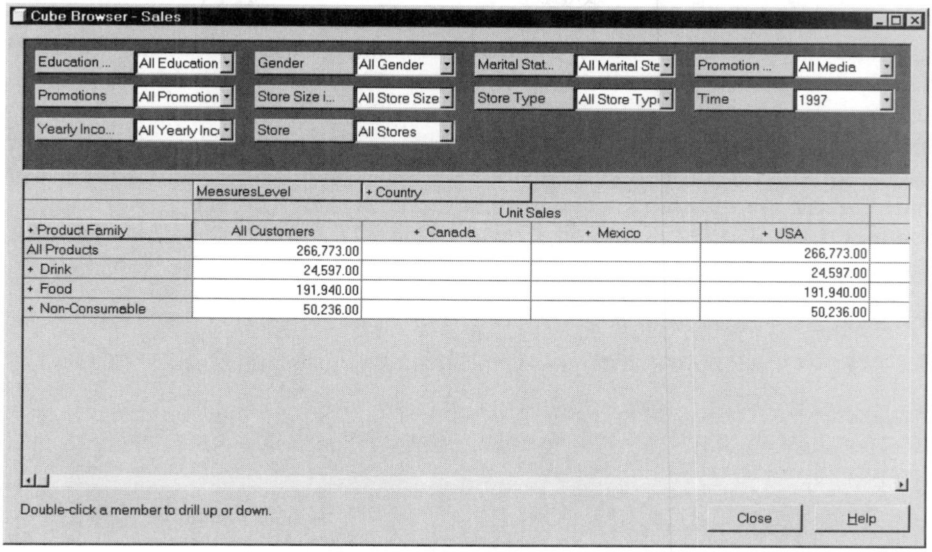

Figure 28-3. Browsing the **Product** dimension

When you drill down, you move down to sublevels of a dimension table to see additional details. For instance, for the **Time** dimension, you can first view the data for each year and then expand this dimension to see monthly, weekly, or daily data.

If you want to drill down using the **Cube** browser, double-click a dimension member on the data grid. The next level is expanded (if the member has a sublevel). The **Cube** browser expands only the member that you double-click.

Drilling up is the opposite process of drilling down, which is used to see fewer details. If you want to drill up using the **Cube** browser, double-click the extended parent level name in the data grid.

NOTE: Analysis Manager is primarily intended as an administration tool that should be used to specify databases, data sources, and storage options, as well as optimize query performance. For that reason you would more likely use Excel 2000 or a third-party analysis tool to browse the data in a data warehouse.

THIRD-PARTY CLIENT TOOLS

MS Analysis Services is a capability of data warehousing systems that allows you to perform analysis on huge amounts of data efficiently. Microsoft offers solutions for Analysis Services through the OLE DB for OLAP interface. OLE DB defines a set of interfaces for accessing different data types that are possibly located in several data stores. Third-party client solutions can be implemented using OLE DB for OLAP to communicate with MS Analysis Services and to allow users sophisticated data analysis using reports and ad hoc queries that they need.

The following companies, among others, offer client solutions for MS Analysis Services:

- ProClarity from Knosys
- Active OLAP Suite (AOS) from Application Consulting Group (ACG)
- Wired for OLAP from Appsource Corp.
- Platinum ERA Business Performance Suite from Epicor
- ECSDTool from Enterprise Computing Services
- Cizer Server from Cizer Software
- Max from Maximal Corp.
- BrioQuery from Brio Technology
- Comshare Decision from Comshare
- Seagate Worksheet from Seagate Software

NOTE: The necessary information about third-party client solutions can be found under http://www.microsoft.com/sql/productinfo

CONCLUSION

The available decision support systems come in three forms:

- Spreadsheet(s)
- Ad hoc queries
- Reporting tool(s)

Microsoft offers Excel 2000, which fully supports MS Analysis. SQL Server also supports several extensions for the SELECT statement that allow users to specify and execute ad hoc queries. For sophisticated queries and reporting, you should use one of the third-party solutions that communicate with MS Analysis Services using the OLE DB for OLAP interface.

This chapter closes the fourth part of the book. The fifth part describes how can you use different components of SQL Server to build solutions. Chapter 29 introduces you to one of most important new features of SQL Server 2000—XML support.

PART V

Building Solutions with SQL Server 2000

CHAPTER 29

XML Support

This chapter covers one of the most important new topics in SQL Server 2000—Extended Markup Language (XML). The introduction describes the World Wide Web, the existing markup languages, and the position of XML as such. The second part of the chapter shows you all the preliminary steps that you have to undertake before you can use Internet Information Server (IIS) to execute queries using URL. Finally, the different XML modes are discussed.

INTRODUCTION

In the last couple of years, the Internet made its way from the small network that was used exclusively by scientists to the powerful communication and information medium that is used by almost everyone. The Internet supports several services, of which the World Wide Web (WWW) is the most important.

World Wide Web

The World Wide Web has been gaining enormous importance as a medium, because it is used for many activities. The Web comprises all other Internet services (under the same user interface) and is therefore the most powerful Internet service of all. Generally, the Web has four parts:

- Web server
- Web browser
- HTML (Hypertext Markup Language)
- HTTP (Hypertext Transfer Protocol)

The Web server sends pages (usually HTML pages) to the network. A Web browser receives the pages and displays them on the screen. (Microsoft Internet Explorer is an example of a Web browser.)

You use HTML to create documents for the Web. This language allows you to format the data that is shown using a Web browser. The simplicity of HTML was one of reasons that the Web has gained such importance. However, HTML has one main disadvantage: It can tell you only how the data should look. In other words, the language does not allow you to gain any meaning out of the data.

HTML documents are text files that contain tags. Each tag is written in angle brackets (see Example 29.1). The most important tags are hyperlinks. You use hyperlinks to reference documents that are managed by a Web server. Those references build the network that spans the whole world. For this reason, it is called the "World Wide Web."

HTTP is a protocol that connects a Web browser with a Web server and sends the available pages from the former to the latter. If the pages contain another hyperlink, the protocol is used to connect to that Web server, using the given address.

XML and Related Languages

XML is a language that is used for the digital representation of documents. This language is related to two other languages:

- SGML
- HTML

Standard General Markup Language (SGML) is a very powerful markup language that is used for the interchange of large and/or complex documents. (A markup specifies special signs that are used either for formatting documents or to represent the logical structure of documents. LaTEX is an example of a (formatting) markup language.) SGML is used in many areas where there is a necessity for complex documents, such as airplane maintenance. As you will see in just a moment, XML is SGML light—that is, it is a simplified subset of SGML that is primarily used in the Web's world.

Hypertext Markup Language (HTML) is, today, the most important markup language that is used for the Web. Each HTML document is an SGML document with the fixed document type description. (For the description of fixed document type description, see the next section.) Therefore HTML is just an instance of SGML.

HTML has two important features:

- It is used only to format a document.
- It is not an extensible language.

HTML is a markup language that you can use to describe how the data should look. (On the other hand, this language offers more than a simple formatted language such as LaTEX, because its elements are generalized and descriptive.) In contrast to HTML, XML additionally describes the logical structure of a document.

HTML only uses a fixed number of elements. For this reason, you cannot use HTML suitably for particular document types. On the other hand, XML is an extensible language (as its name indicates). This means that you can use the language to define specific elements, attributes, and entities. (All these terms will be defined in the next section.)

XML—Basic Concepts

You use XML to digitally represent documents. To represent a document, you have to know its structure. For instance, if you consider a book as a document, it can first be broken into chapters (with titles). Each chapter comprises several sections (with their titles and corresponding figures), and each section has one or more paragraphs.

All parts of a document that belong to its logical structure are called *elements*. Therefore, in XML, each element represents a component of a document. (For example chapters, sections, and paragraphs build, among others, elements of a book.) Also, each element can contain other elements. (The parts of an element that do not belong to the logical structure of a document are called character data. For instance, words or sentences in a book can be treated as character data.)

All elements of a document build a hierarchy of elements that is called the tree structure of the document. Each structure has an element on the top level that contains all other elements: This element is called the root element. Also, all elements that do not contain any subelements are called leaves. (In the case of a book, the book itself is the root element, while paragraphs would be leaves.)

Each element can have extra information that is attached to it. Such information is called an *attribute* and it describes the element's properties. Attributes are used together with elements to represent objects (i.e., document types).

NOTE: Elements and attributes build the logical structure of a document. Besides the logical structure, each document also has physical structure. The physical structure of documents is built upon a series of characters. Each named series of characters is called an entity.

As you already know, XML allows the definition of a document's structure. You use document type definition (DTD) to define elements, attributes, and entities of a document. Therefore, each document can conform to a given DTD or not. (Each document that conforms to a given DTD is called a valid document.)

Besides the definition of a document's structure, formatting a document can be an important issue for those of you who do not want the Web browser, such as Microsoft Internet Explorer, to control the form of the document. For this task, XML supports another language called Extensible Stylesheet Language (XSL) that allows you to describe how the data of your document should be formatted or displayed.

NOTE: The style of a document is described as a separate entity. For this reason, each document without this part will use the default formatting of the Web browser.

All concepts until now belong to the general XML terminology. Microsoft introduced the specific concept of a template that describes a structured block of XML code that includes a batch (i.e., a group) of Transact-SQL statements. You use a template to access a SQL Server's data, which is then returned as an XML document. Each template is usually stored in a file. Template files can be put in the directory associated with the virtual root so that they can be executed using a Universal Resource Locator (URL). (The notion of a virtual root will be explained in the next section.)

Now that we have introduced all three relevant languages (DTD, XSL, and XML), let us take a look at an example. Example 29.1 shows the relationship between DTD, XSL, and XML, which are used to describe a catalog of products.

▼ EXAMPLE 29.1

DTD:

```
<?xml encoding="UTF-8"?>
<!ELEMENT catalog(product)*>
<!ELEMENT product(item)*>
<!ATTLIST product
```

```
  product_id CDATA #REQUIRED
  product_desc CDATA #REQUIRED>
<!ELEMENT item
  (item_no, price, size)*>
<!ATTLIST item
   gender CDATA #REQUIRED>
<!ELEMENT item_no (#PCDATA)>
<!ELEMENT price (#PCDATA)>
<!ELEMENT size (#PCDATA)>
```

XSL:

```
<rule>
 <target-element type="item_no"/>
 <!—you write here the formatting information for the item_no element -->
</rule>
 <-- you write here additional formatting for the other elements -->
```

XML:

```
<?xml version="1.0"?>
<?xml-stylesheet href="catalog.xsl" type="text/xsl"?>
<!DOCTYPE catalog SYSTEM  "catalog.dtd">
<catalog>
 <product product_id="soap" product_desc="Soap for men">
  <item gender="Men's">
  <item_no>SO1111</item_no>
  <price>2.99</price>
   <size>20</size>
  </item>
 </product>
</catalog>
```

NOTE: The DTD part of Example 29.1 must be stored separately in a file. This file is stored locally (using the SYSTEM option, as in the XML part of Example 29.1) or remotely (using the PUBLIC option).

The first part of Example 29.1 creates a document type definition (DTD) for a catalog of products. Element type declarations must start with the string <!ELEMENT, followed by the name of the element type being defined. (Every element in a valid XML document must conform to an element type declared in the DTD.) The first element declaration in Example 29.1 specifies the element named **catalog**. Each following element declaration specifies subelements of the previous element. For this reason, Example 29.1 has four levels: the root level with the **catalog** element, two subelements called **product** and **item**, and the leaf level with the elements **item_no**, **price**, and **size**. (Obviously, the **item** element is the subelement of the **product** element.)

Attributes are declared for specific element types using the ATTLIST specification. This means that each attribute declaration starts with the string <!ATTLIST. Immediately after that comes the attribute's name and its type. For instance, the **product** element has two attributes: **product_id** and **product_desc**, which have the data type CDATA. (The CDATA stands for character data and is the simplest type of attribute.) #REQUIRED tells you that the value for the corresponding attribute must be specified.

At the leaf level, we declare three elements: **item_no**, **price**, and **size**. All three elements are declared with the #PCDATA specification, meaning that these elements are of CHARACTER data type.

In the XSL part, you can define so-called template rules. During XSL processing, each element, character, and processing instruction in an XML document is processed by some template rule. In an XSL style sheet, each template rule is represented by an **xsl: template** element. For instance, the template rule for the **product** element would start with the following:

```
<xml:template match="product">
```

The last part of Example 29.1 shows the XML code that inserts a product into the specified catalog.

SQL SERVER AND XML SUPPORT

You can access SQL Server using a URL that specifies HTTP as the protocol. There are two ways to execute Transact-SQL statements:

- Directly through URL (using queries or stored procedures)
- Specifying a template

Before SQL queries or stored procedures can be specified at the URL to access SQL Server, a virtual directory must be set up on the computer running IIS. A virtual directory contains the information concerning a specific installation of SQL Server, including a database and security issues, such as login and password. (IIS Virtual Directory Management is the utility that creates the connection between the new virtual directory and a specific instance of SQL Server.)

NOTE: Virtual root is a synonym for virtual directory.

To set up a new virtual directory, you can use either of the following:

- The existing graphical interface
- The **regxmlss** utility

The following sections describe both features.

Creating an IIS Virtual Directory Using Graphical Interface

To start the graphical interface for IIS Virtual Directory Management, click **Start**, select **Programs**, then select **Microsoft SQL Server** and click **Configure SQL XML Support in IIS**. Expand the server, right-click the **Default Web Site** folder, and select **New** and **Virtual Directory**. The **New Virtual Directory Properties** dialog box appears (see Figure 29-1).

On the **General** tab in the **Virtual Directory Name** frame, enter the name through which you will access the database. In the **Local Path** frame, enter the full path to the directory that contains the files you want to make accessible. (In Figure 29-1, we enter the name of the sample database and the **D:\Temp\sample** directory.)

On the **Security** tab, select the authentication method you want to use to access data (see Figure 29-2). You can use either Windows NT or SQL Server authentication. (For more information on SQL Server authentication, see Chapter 12.)

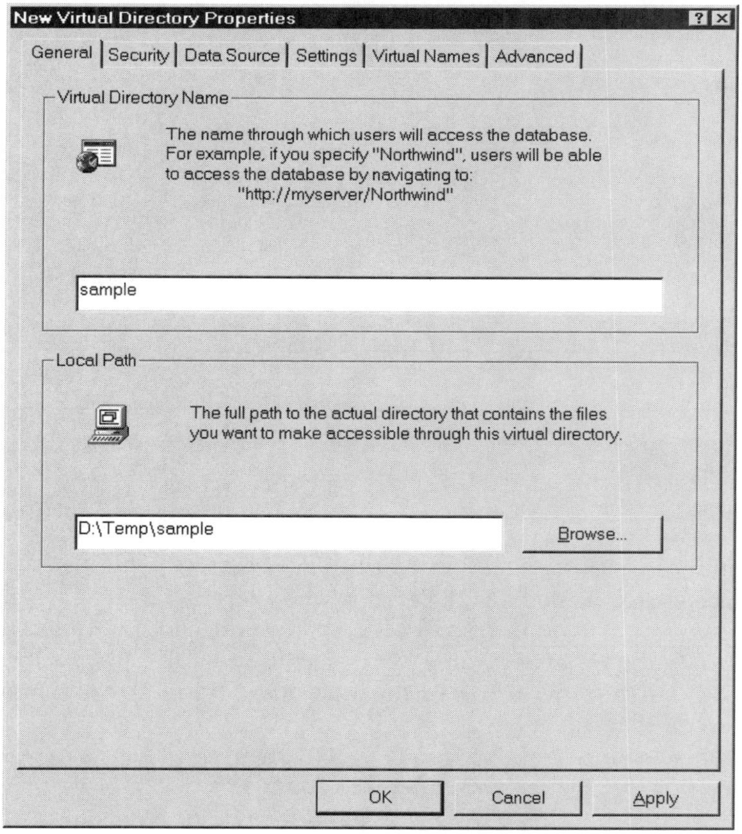

Figure 29-1. The New Virtual Directory Properties dialog box

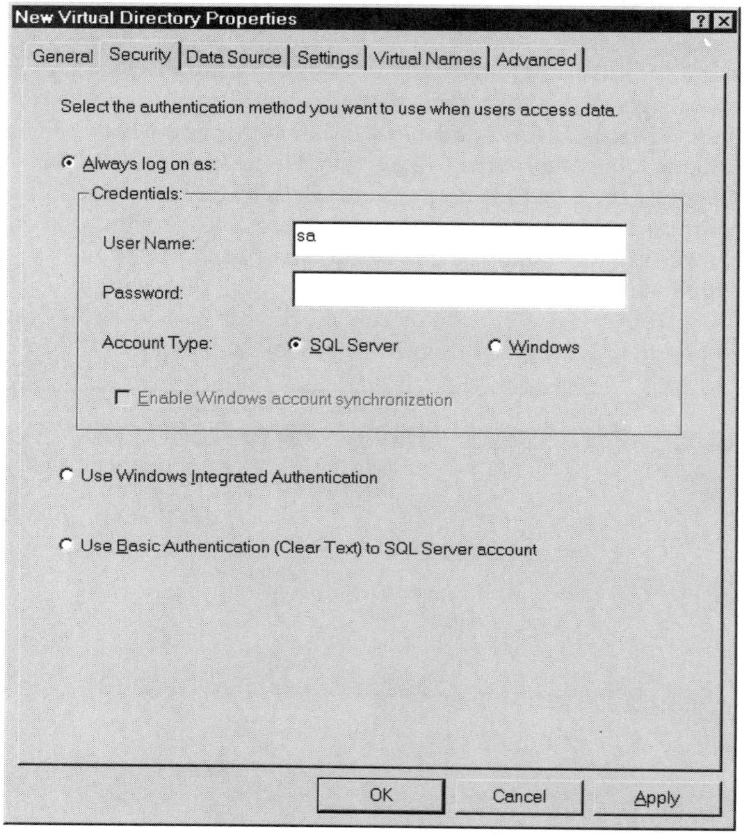

Figure 29-2. Security tab

On the **Data Source** tab in the **SQL Server** frame, you enter the name of the server that stores the data you want to publish. To browse for a server, click the **...** button on the right side of the field. In the **Database** frame, you select the default database for the specified SQL Server. Clicking the down arrow on the right side of the field, you can retrieve the list of all databases for that server.

The next tab—**Settings**—allows you to specify the type of access to SQL Server. The **Settings** dialog box (see Figure 29-3) has three options:

- Allow URL queries
- Allow template queries
- Allow XPath

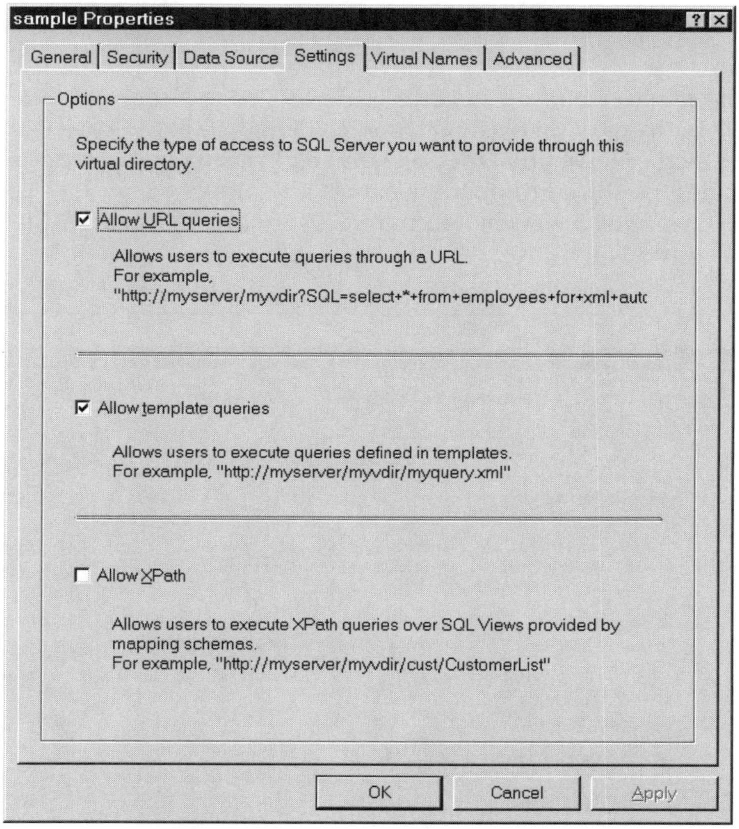

Figure 29-3. The Settings tab

The first option (**Allow URL queries**) allows you to execute queries through a URL. This is the most convenient way if you want to access SQL Server with a simple SELECT statement. You will use the second option (**Allow template queries**) if you want to access SQL Server through a URL with several SQL statements and want to avoid having to type all of them in a Web browser. The third option allows you to execute XPath queries over SQL views. (SQL Server 2000 supports a subset of the XPath language.)

NOTE: XPath is a graph navigation language defined by the World Wide Web Consortium (W3C) that can be used to select nodes from XML documents. You first use a mapping schema to define an XML-based view of the data in one or more SQL Server tables and views. You can then use XPath queries to retrieve data from that mapping schema.

NOTE: You should allow at least the execution of queries and templates, as is shown in Figure 29-3.

The **Virtual names** tab (see Figure 29-4) allows you to define the new virtual name and associate it with one of the existing types. To define the new virtual name (**queries** in Figure 29-4), click the **New** button (in the **Defined virtual names** frame) and enter the information for the type and corresponding path (see Figure 29-5). The IIS Virtual Directory Management transforms the given information in the corresponding URL.

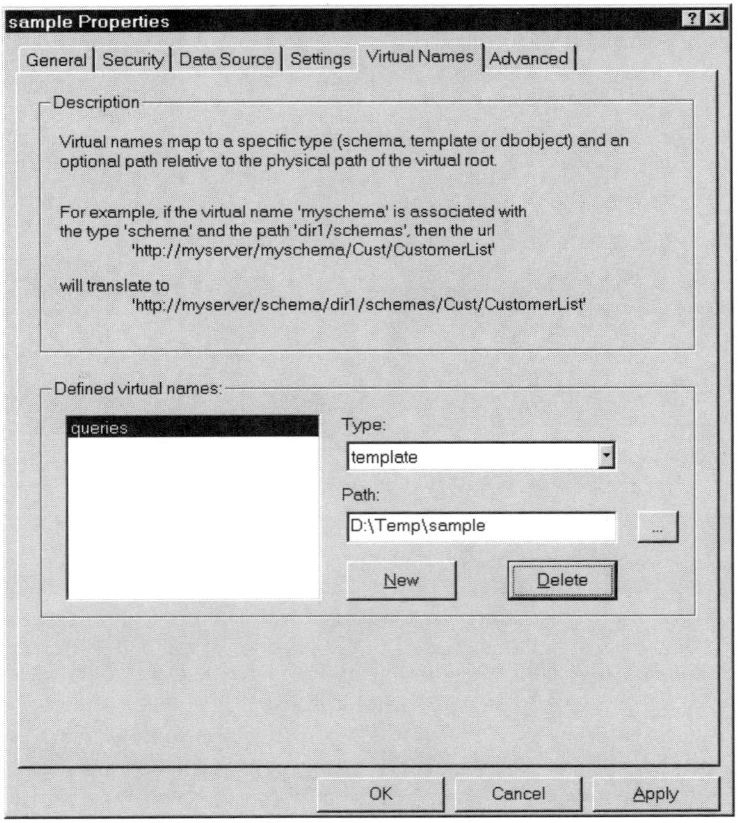

Figure 29-4. The New Virtual Directory Properties dialog box: The Virtual names tab

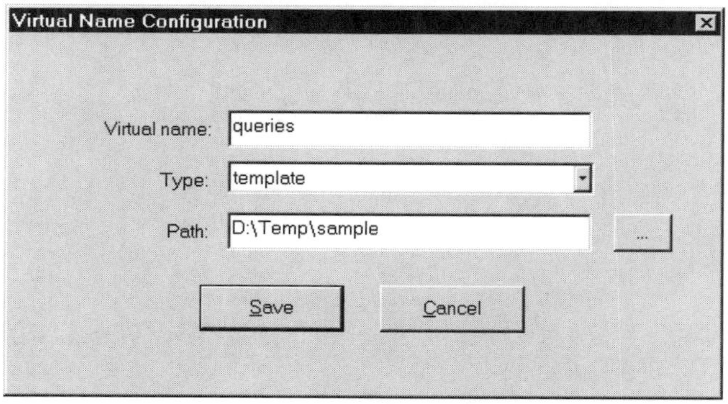

Figure 29-5. The Virtual Name Configuration dialog box

Creating an IIS Virtual Directory Using the regxmlss Utility

The **regxmlss** utility instructs IIS to create an association between the new virtual directory and a specific instance of SQL Server. (You can find this utility in the **Program Files\Common Files\system\OLD DB directory**.) After execution of the **regxmlss** utility, the **Register XML Server Extensions** dialog box appears, shown in Figure 29-6. This dialog box contains the same information that is explained in the section concerning the graphical interface.

The virtual directory created by the **regxmlss** utility points to an existing physical directory. This directory can store template files and other Web contents. (In contrast to the graphical interface, if the directory doesn't exist, the **regxmlss** utility creates the directory.)

Executing Queries Using a URL

SQL Server can be accessed directly with a URL (using SQL statements and stored procedures) or indirectly, using templates. You use the following syntax as the address in Internet Explorer to execute a SQL statement, a stored procedure, or a template:

```
http://iiserver/virtualroot{?sql=string | ?template=XMLtemplate} [{&param = value}...]
```

iiserver specifies the IIS server. (In our examples, the IIS server has either the specific name NTB11901 or the generic name **localhost**.) **virtualroot** is the name of the virtual directory you set. (In Figure 29-1, the name of the virtual directory is **sample**.) The address can contain either a Transact-SQL statement (**?sql = string**) or a template that is specified directly in a URL (**?template = XMLtemplate**).

param is either a parameter name or a keyword. The keyword can be **contenttype**, **outputencoding**, or **xsl**. Table 29-1 shows the meanings of these keywords.

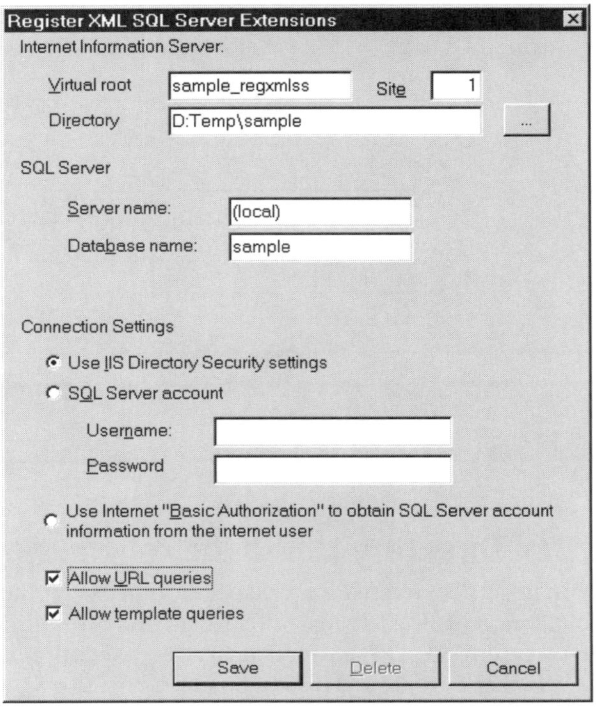

Figure 29-6. The Register XML Server Extensions dialog box

Parameter	Description
contenttype	Specifies the content type of the returned document. It describes the data fully enough that the Internet Explorer can pick an appropriate mechanism to present the data to the user.
outputencoding	Specifies the character set for the resulting XML document.
xsl	Specifies the URL to an XSL file that will be used to process the resulting XML data. (By definition, XSL takes two XML documents and produces a third. One of the input documents contains the data and the other contains the XSL processing instructions.)

Table 29-1. Parameters That Can Be Used to Execute Queries

The system allows you to store templates in a file. (That way, you can shorten the process of writing templates with several queries.) In this case, the URL syntax is a little bit different (**filepath.xml** specifies a file that contains the template):

```
http://iiserver/virtualroot[filepath]/filename.xml [?param =
value{&param=value}...]
```

As you can see from the above syntax, there are some characters (such as **?** and **&**) that have special meaning at the URL. Table 29-2 shows these characters with their meanings.

Examples 29.2 and 29.3 show two URL addresses using the SQL statement and the template stored in a file, respectively.

▼ EXAMPLE 29.2

```
http://NTB11901/sample?sql=SELECT+'<ROOT>';SELECT+emp_no+emp_lname+
FROM+employee+FOR+XML+RAW;SELECT+'</ROOT>'
```

The result is

```
<ROOT>
   <row emp_lname="2581" />
   <row emp_lname="9031" />
   <row emp_lname="10102" />
   <row emp_lname="18316" />
   <row emp_lname="25348" />
   <row emp_lname="28559" />
   <row emp_lname="29346" />
</ROOT>
```

Example 29.2 contains a URL address that accesses the SQL Server named NTB11901 using a query that retrieves rows from the **employee** table. (The description of the FOR XML RAW option, which is used in this example, will be given later in this chapter.)

Characters	Description
/	Separates directories and subdirectories
?	Indicates a period (.)
#	Indicates bookmarks
%	Used to specify special characters
+	Indicates a space (spaces cannot be used in URL)
&	Indicates the beginning of a parameter

Table 29-2. Special Characters

▼ **EXAMPLE 29.3**

```
http://localhost/sample/queries/simpleselect.xml
```

The result is

```
<ROOT xmlns:sql="urn:schemas-microsoft-com:xml-sql">
   <employee emp_no="28559" emp_lname="Moser" />
</ROOT>
```

Example 29.3 uses the filename **simpleselect.xml** in the directory **D:\Temp\sample** (see Figure 29-1) to access SQL Server with Transact-SQL statement(s) stored as a template in the file. (This example accesses local SQL Server—thus the name **localhost**.) The file **simpleselect.xml** has the following content:

```
<ROOT xmlns:sql="urn:schemas-microsoft-com:xml-sql">
<sql:query>SELECT emp_no, emp_lname
FROM employee WHERE emp_no = 28559
FOR XML AUTO
</sql:query></ROOT>
```

SQL Server XML Modes

When defining a query, you use the FOR XML clause to specify how the result should be returned. With this clause, you can specify one of the three following modes:

- RAW
- AUTO
- EXPLICIT

The general syntax for the FOR XML clause is

```
FOR [XML mode [,schema_option] [,ELEMENTS]]
```

> ***NOTE:*** The FOR XML clause must be specified at the end of the SELECT statement.

mode specifies one of the three options mentioned above. It determines the shape of the resulting XML tree. **schema_option** specifies that a schema should be returned. This option has two values: **dtd** and **xmldata**. **dtd** returns the schema and adds the root elements to the results. **xmldata** returns the schema but does not add the root element.

RAW Mode

The RAW mode transforms each row in the result set into an XML element with the generic identifier raw. Each column value is mapped to an attribute of the XML element, in which the attribute name is the same as the column name (see Example 29.2). (This is true only for the non-null columns.)

Example 29.4 shows the use of the RAW mode that is specified for the join of two tables from the sample database.

▼ EXAMPLE 29.4

```
http://localhost/sample?sql=SELECT+'<ROOT>';SELECT+department.dept_name,
employee.emp_fname+FROM+employee,+department+WHERE+emp_
no=28559+OR+emp_no=10102+AND+employee.dept_no=department.dept_
no+FOR+XML+RAW;SELECT+'</ROOT>'
```

The result is

```
<ROOT>
  <row dept_name="Research" emp_fname="Sybill" />
  <row dept_name="Accounting" emp_fname="Sybill" />
  <row dept_name="Marketing" emp_fname="Ann" />
  <row dept_name="Marketing" emp_fname="Sybill" />
</ROOT>
```

AUTO Mode

AUTO mode returns the result set of a query in a simple, nested XML tree. Each table in the FROM clause, from which at least one column appears in the SELECT list, is represented as an XML element. The columns in the SELECT list are mapped to the appropriate element's attributes.

Example 29.5 shows the use of the AUTO mode.

▼ EXAMPLE 29.5

```
http://localhost/sample?sql=SELECT+'<ROOT>';SELECT+department.dept_
name,%20employee.emp_fname+FROM+employee,+department+WHERE+emp_
no=28559+OR+emp_no=10102+AND+employee.dept_no=department.dept_
no+FOR+XML+AUTO;SELECT+'</ROOT>'
```

The result is

```
<ROOT>
<department dept_name="Research">
 <employee emp_fname="Sybill" />
 </department>
<department dept_name="Accounting">
 <employee emp_fname="Sybill" />
 </department>
<department dept_name="Marketing">
 <employee emp_fname="Ann" />
 <employee emp_fname="Sybill" />
 </department>
 </ROOT>
```

The result in Example 29.5 is significantly different from the result in Example 29.4, although the text of both examples is equivalent (except for the specification of the AUTO mode instead of RAW). As you can see from the result of Example 29.5, the result set is displayed as the hierarchy of tables **department** and **employee**. This hierarchy is based on the primary-key/foreign-key relationship of both tables. For this reason, the data from the **department** table is displayed first and the corresponding data from the **employee** table is displayed after that, at the lower hierarchy level. (The relationship between tables **department** and **employee** is called a 1:N relationship, because an employee works for exactly one department and one department employs zero or more employees. See also Chapter 1.)

NOTE: The ELEMENTS option in the FOR XML clause is specified, if the columns should be returned as subelements. (Otherwise, they are mapped to XML attributes.) This option is valid only for this mode.

EXPLICIT Mode

As you can see from Example 29.5, the result set in the AUTO mode is displayed as a simple, nested XML tree. If you want to specify the extended form of the result set, you have to use the EXPLICIT mode. With EXPLICIT mode, the return set is displayed as a universal table, which has all the information about the resulting XML tree. The data in the table is vertically partitioned into groups. Each group then becomes an XML element in the result set.

NOTE: You have to write a query in a specific way, so that the additional information about the desired nesting is explicitly defined.

Example 29.6 shows the use of the EXPLICIT mode.

▼ EXAMPLE 29.6

```
http://NTB11901/sample?sql=SELECT+'<ROOT>';SELECT+1+AS+tag,NULL+AS+parent,employee.emp_no+AS+[employee!1!emp_no],+emp_lname+AS+[employee!1!emp_lname!element]+FROM+employee+FOR+XML+EXPLICIT;SELECT+'</ROOT>'
```

The result is

```
<ROOT>
<employee emp_no="25348">
 <emp_lname>Smith</emp_lname>
 </employee>
<employee emp_no="10102">
 <emp_lname>Jones</emp_lname>
 </employee>
<employee emp_no="18316">
 <emp_lname>Barrimore</emp_lname>
 </employee>
```

```
<employee emp_no="29346">
 <emp_lname>James</emp_lname>
 </employee>
<employee emp_no="9031">
 <emp_lname>Bertoni</emp_lname>
 </employee>
<employee emp_no="2581">
 <emp_lname>Hansel</emp_lname>
 </employee>
<employee emp_no="28559">
 <emp_lname>Moser</emp_lname>
 </employee>
 </ROOT>
```

As you can see from Example 29.6, the EXPLICIT mode requires two additional metadata columns: **tag** and **parent**. (These two columns are used to determine the primary-key/foreign-key relationship in the XML tree.) The **tag** column stores the tag number of the current element, while the **parent** column stores the tag number of the parent element. (The parent table is the table with the primary key.) If the parent tag in the parent column is NULL (or zero), the row is placed directly under the root element.

Limitations on the FOR XML Clause

The FOR XML clause cannot be used with the following constructs:

- In a subquery (of the SELECT, INSERT, UPDATE, and DELETE statements)
- In a SELECT statement with the COMPUTE BY clause
- In a SELECT statement used as a part of a view definition

CONCLUSION

XML is a markup language that allows you to digitally represent documents. It addresses the need for semantic markup language. However, there is *no common set of classes*, which could be useful for most XML users.

The next chapter is the last chapter of the book. It discusses the full text search feature of SQL Server 2000.

CHAPTER 30

SQL Server Full-Text Search

This chapter describes the full-text search component of SQL Server 2000. After the general introduction you will learn how databases and tables are enabled for full-text search and how to populate full-text indexes. The final part of the chapter shows different ways to retrieve information from unstructured data after a full-text index is created and populated.

INTRODUCTION

Digital information can be stored in two different forms:

- Structured
- Unstructured

Structured data is usually stored in columns of relational tables. In contrast to it, unstructured data is primarily stored as text in the file system. For this reason, you will need different methods to retrieve information from unstructured than to retrieve structured data. Let us see which differences in the retrieval process exist.

In Chapter 5, you learned how to retrieve information from relational tables, using the LIKE operator, which compares column values with a specified pattern. This operation is very limited, because it can only match the given pattern. Also, a search with the LIKE operator can be very slow if a wildcard (percent sign or underscore) is used at the beginning of the pattern. In that case, SQL Server query optimizer uses table scan, even if an index for the column exists (see Example 10.9).

In addition to the LIKE operator, SQL Server allows you to retrieve information from unstructured data using its full-text search component. To allow full-text search, unstructured data, like structured data, must be stored in SQL Server tables. After that, you must create a full-text index to apply the advanced capabilities of the full-text search, such as searches for phrases in close proximity to one another.

SQL Server 2000 contains the full-text search engine that allows you the use of the advanced pattern matching. (The full-text engine runs as a service named Microsoft Search service.) The Microsoft Search service is available only in Standard and Enterprise Editions on Windows NT/2000.

NOTE: In contrast to SQL Server 7, where you install full-text search in a separate step, the full-text search engine is installed by default with a typical installation of SQL Server 2000.

FULL-TEXT INDEXES

Before you start the full-text search, you have to create an index for the column that contains the data to be searched. Full-text indexes differ in a number of ways from regular SQL Server indexes. If you take a look at Table 30-1, which shows the differences between

Regular SQL Server Indexes	Full-Text Indexes
Stored in the database and controlled by the database in which they are stored.	Stored in the file system, but administered through the database for which they are defined.
Many indexes per table allowed.	Only one full-text index per table allowed.
You can create indexes on every type of column except columns with TEXT, IMAGE, or BINARY data type.	You can create full-text indexes only on CHAR, VARCHAR, TEXT, BCHAR, and NVARCHAR data types.

Table 30-1. Differences Between Regular and Full-Text Indexes

a regular and a full-text index, you will see that the latter has a more complex structure, because it isn't stored in the database. For this reason, you have to first do several preliminary administrative tasks before the full-text index can be created.

NOTE: SQL Server 2000 allows you to search the textual part of columns with the IMAGE data type using image filtering. Image filtering allows you to index and query documents stored in IMAGE columns. The user provides the document type in a column that contains the file name extension. Using this information, the Microsoft Search service is able to load the appropriate document filter to extract textual information for indexing.

Before you can use the full-text index, the following administrative tasks must be done:

- Enabling a database for full-text indexing
- Enabling a table for full-text indexing
- Enabling a column for full-text indexing
- Creating a full-text catalog

All these tasks can be done using either SQL Server Enterprise Manager or system-stored procedures. We will first demonstrate the use of Enterprise Manager and then show how each step can be separately done using the corresponding system stored procedures.

Setting Up a Full-Text Search Using Enterprise Manager

Using Enterprise Manager, you can execute the administrative tasks explained in the last section. First expand the server, expand the **Databases** folder, and select the database you want. On the **Tools** menu, click **Full-Text Indexing**. This will start the Full-Text Indexing Wizard (see Figure 30-1).

After clicking **Next**, select a table form the drop-down list. (Remember that the table must contain at least one column containing character-based data.) After that, select a unique regular index for the table selected. (If the table has no such index, you will get the message "The selected table has no unique single column index on a column that does not allow NULLs.")

In the next step, the wizard selects all character-based and image-based columns from the table and shows them in the **Select Table Columns** dialog box (see Figure 30-2). Mark any columns that you want to be eligible for full-text queries. (Note that if you select several columns, the Microsoft Search service creates one composite full-text index for all selected columns.)

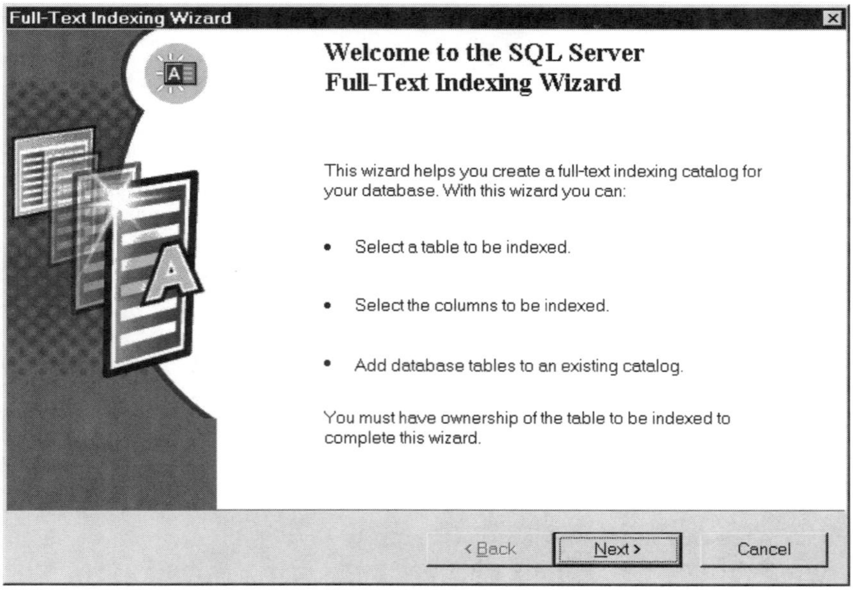

Figure 30-1. The Full-Text Indexing Wizard

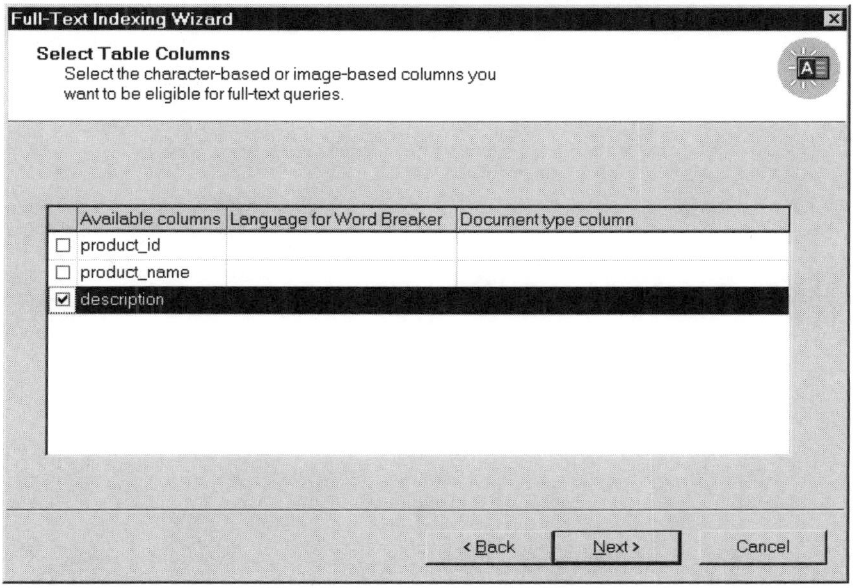

Figure 30-2. The Select Table Columns dialog box

In the last but one step, select a catalog (see Figure 30-3). You can choose an existing catalog or create a new one. (For the reasons described below, it is recommended to create a new catalog for each table of the database.) In the last step, you can optionally select or create a population schedule. (Population of a full-text index is discussed in the next section.)

NOTE: After the steps described above are executed, the full-text index is implicitly created. In other words, you do not have to use the CREATE INDEX statement explicitly. (This is the way some other full-text software systems create full-text indexes.)

Populating a Full-Text Index

The full-text indexes are activated on a catalog-by-catalog basis. When a full-text table index is activated, the table involved in the full-text index is identified. After that, index entries are built for all the rows in the table and stored in the corresponding full-text catalog. This process is called population.

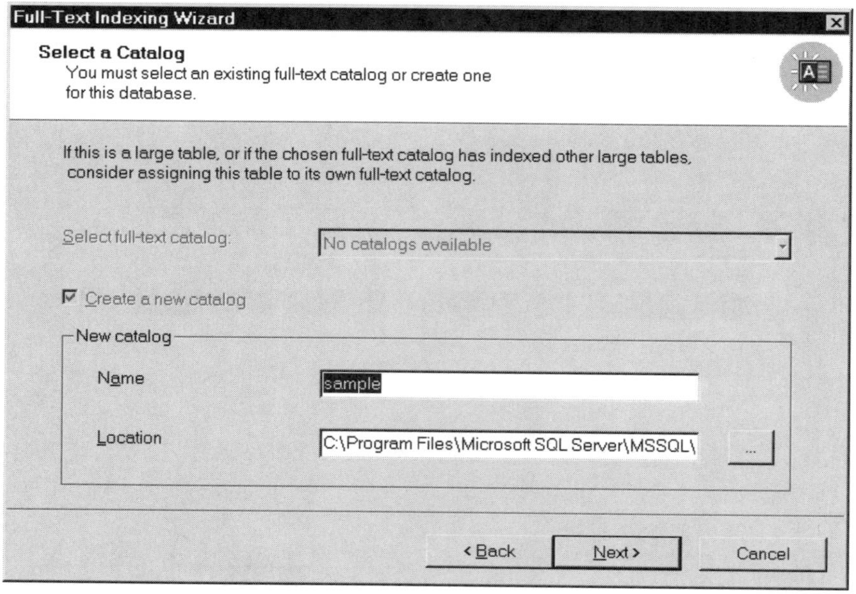

Figure 30-3. The Select a Catalog dialog box

During the population process, the Microsoft Search service eliminates so called noise words. *Noise words* (or *stop words*) are words that are ignored during the full-text search, because their relevance for the content of a text is low (or equal to zero). The practical meaning of this elimination is that the text becomes shorter and therefore the corresponding full-text index will need less storage memory. (Noise words are, among others, "a," "and," and "the.")

The population of a catalog can be twofold:

- Full
- Incremental

During the full population, all data stored in a full-text catalog is cleared and repopulated by building index entries for all the rows in all the tables covered by the catalog. (As you might have already guessed, a full population typically occurs when a catalog is first populated.)

NOTE: The system always performs the full population if the structure of the table is modified. This includes altering any column, index, or full-text index definition.

The incremental population adjusts only index entries for rows that have been modified since the last population. The benefit of incremental population is speed: It minimizes the time required to populate data, because the amount of index entries to be stored is considerably smaller than in the case of the full population.

NOTE: The incremental population can be performed only if the indexed table has a column of the TIMESTAMP data type. If a table does not have a TIMESTAMP column, only the full population can be performed.

In contrast to the previous version, SQL Server 2000 repopulates full-text indexes dynamically. This means that like regular SQL Server indexes, full-text indexes can be automatically updated when data is modified (added, updated, or deleted) in the associated table(s). Additionally, you can repopulate a full-text catalog in two ways: manually or using a schedule. With both of these methods, you can choose a full population or incremental population.

Because full-text indexes can consume a significant amount of disk space, it is important to plan their placement in full-text catalogs. The following guidelines should be considered when you assign a table to a catalog:

- Keep the full-text index as small as possible. (This can be done if you select the smallest column for your primary key.)
- If you are indexing a large table, assign the table to its own full-text catalog.

To populate a full-text index, open the **Databases** folder, select the database, and click the **Full-Text Catalogs** subfolder. In the detail pane, right-click the newly created catalog. Select **Start Full Population** and click **OK** after the population process is done.

NOTE: The full-text catalogs and indexes supported by the Microsoft Search service apply *only* to tables in SQL Server databases. The Windows NT/2000 Indexing Service provides similar functionality against operating system files. The Indexing Service includes an OLE DB provider that can be used by OLE DB consumers. SQL Server applications can access OLE DB provider for Indexing Service through distributed queries.

Enabling a Database for Full-Text Indexing

Besides Enterprise Manager, you can use the **sp_fulltext_database** system stored procedure to enable (or disable) full text indexing for a database. This stored procedure has the following syntax:

```
sp_fulltext_database [@action=] 'ENABLE' | 'DISABLE'
```

The ENABLE value enables full-text indexing for the current database, while the DISABLE value removes all full-text catalogs in the file system for the current database.

NOTE: If you want to disable a database for full-text indexing, you have to remove all full-text catalogs from the database.

Enabling and Disabling a Table for Full-Text Indexing

To enable (or disable) full-text indexing for a table, you can use the **sp_fulltext_table** system stored procedure. This stored procedure has the following syntax:

```
sp_fulltext_table [@tabname =] 'tabname', [@action =] 'action' [,[ @ftcat =] 'catname ',
                  [@keyname=] 'indexname ']
```

The **@tabname** parameter specifies the name of the table. The **@action** parameter defines the type of action that has to be performed. The values for this parameter are, among others, CREATE, DROP, and DEACTIVATE. The full-text indexing for the table is enabled using the CREATE option, while the DROP option disables this feature. The DEACTIVATE option deactivates the full-text index for the table. The **@ftcat** parameter specifies the catalog name where the Microsoft Search service catalogs the full-text index for that table. (The name of the catalog must be specified only for the CREATE action. For all other actions, it must be NULL.) The **@keyname** parameter defines a name for the index (for the CREATE option).

Enabling and Disabling a Column for Full-Text Indexing

To enable (or disable) full-text indexing for a column, use the **sp_fulltext_columns** system stored procedure. This stored procedure has the following syntax:

```
sp_fulltext_columns [[[@table_name] = 'tabname'] [,[@column_name =] 'colname']]
```

The **@table_name** parameter specifies the name of the table and the **@column_name** parameter defines the name of the column for which full-text indexing should be performed.

Creating and Removing a Full-Text Catalog

To create a full-text catalog, you can also use the **sp_fulltext_catalog** stored procedure that creates a full-text catalog. (You can use this procedure to remove an existing catalog, too.) The stored procedure has the following syntax:

```
sp_fulltext_catalog [@ftcat =] 'catname' , [@action =] 'action' [,[ @path = ] 'directory']
```

The **@ftcat** parameter specifies the catalog name. The **@action** parameter defines the type of action that has to be performed. The values for this parameter are, among others, CREATE, DROP, START_FULL, START_INCREMENTAL, and STOP. A new catalog is created using CREATE, while DROP removes an existing catalog. START_FULL and

START_INCREMENTAL start a full (i.e., incremental) population for the specified catalog, respectively. STOP stops index population for the given catalog.

QUERYING FULL-TEXT INDEXES

After the implementation of the full-text catalog and population of the corresponding full-text index, you can process different full-text search queries. For a given query, the Microsoft Search service determines which entries in the indexed column meet the full-text selection criteria. For each value that satisfies the selection criteria, it returns the identity of the row plus a ranking value. (The ranking value is used for the ordering of rows from the result set. The row with the highest ranking is displayed first.)

The following types of queries are supported by the Microsoft Search service:

- Searching for words or phrases
- Searching for words in close proximity to each other
- Searching for inflectional forms of verbs and nouns
- Searching for a word that has a higher designated weighting than another word

All of these query types will be shown in the following sections using examples.

Preliminary Steps

I'll use the **products** table to demonstrate full-text querying. Example 30.1 creates the table.

▼ EXAMPLE 30.1

```
USE sample
CREATE TABLE products
          (product_id CHAR(5) NOT NULL PRIMARY KEY,
           product_name VARCHAR (30) NOT NULL,
           description VARCHAR(4000) NULL)
```

Example 30.2 inserts the values in the **products** table.

▼ EXAMPLE 30.2

```
INSERT INTO products VALUES (1, 'MS Application Center 2000 ', 'This new
Microsoft product simplifies the deployment and management of Windows
DNA solutions within farms of servers. Application Center 2000 makes it easy
to configure and manage high-availability server arrays ')

INSERT INTO products VALUES (2, 'MS Commerce Server 2000 ', 'Commerce
Server 2000 is the fastest way to build an effective Microsoft online business. It
provides all of the personalization, user and product management, marketing,
closed loop analysis, and electronic ordering infrastructure necessary for both
business-to-business and business-to-consumer e-commerce. ')
```

The **products** table fulfills all requirements for building a full-text index. First, there is a column (**product_id**) with the unique index. (Remember that SQL Server implicitly creates the unique index for a column with the PRIMARY KEY constraint.) Second, all three columns of the table are character-based and can therefore be used to create a full-text index (see Figure 30-3).

Using either Enterprise Manager or system stored procedures, you have to create a full-text index for the **description** column and to populate the index. (This process is described in the previous sections.)

Microsoft Search service supports two predicates and two row functions that you can use to query text using a full-text index. These are as follows:

- The FREETEXT predicate
- The CONTAINS predicate
- The FREETEXTTABLE row function
- The CONTAINSTABLE row function

The following sections describe each of these predicates (i.e., functions).

The FREETEXT Predicate

The FREETEXT predicate is used to search columns containing values of the CHAR, VARCHAR, TEXT, NCHAR, and NVARCHAR data types that match the meaning in the search condition. Additionally, you can use this predicate if you want to find all words related to the word(s) in the search query.

Example 30.3 shows the use of the FREETEXT predicate for the given string.

▼ EXAMPLE 30.3

```
SELECT product_id, product_name FROM products
  WHERE FREETEXT(description, 'manage')
```

The result is

product_id	**product_name**
1	MS Application Center 2000

As you can see from Example 30.3, the FREETEXT predicate has two arguments. The first argument specifies the column that has be registered for full-text searching. (The alternative way is to specify the * sign if you want all columns that have been registered for full-text searching to be used.) The second parameter specifies the string that is searched in the specified column(s).

Example 30.4 shows the search for the related strings.

▼ EXAMPLE 30.4

```
SELECT product_id, product_name FROM products
  WHERE FREETEXT(description, 'fast solution')
```

The result is

product_id	**product_name**
2	MS Commerce Server 2000
1	MS Application Center 2000

Example 30.4 shows two things: the implicit use of the Boolean operator OR and the search for the words without the exact wording. Although the second parameter in the FREETEXT predicate in Example 30.4 looks like a search on the string "fast solution", it actually searches on one (or both) of two different strings, "fast" and "solution". (Therefore, the existence of several words in a search string means the use of the Boolean operator OR.) Also, neither the word "fast" nor the word "solution" appears in one of the rows. As you already know, the FREETEXT predicate searches for related words, too. The Microsoft Search service finds the word "solutions" (in the first row) and the word "fastest" (in the second one) and considers them as the related words to the words "solution" and "fast", respectively.

The CONTAINS predicate

The CONTAINS predicate is used to search columns containing character-based data types for exact matches and fuzzy matches. Additionally, it allows you to search for words and phrases, the proximity of words within a certain distance of one another, and weighted matches.

NOTE: The CONTAINS predicate provides significantly more functionality in a full-text search than the FREETEXT predicate.

Example 30.5 shows the use of the CONTAINS predicate for a search with a wildcard.

▼ EXAMPLE 30.5

```
SELECT product_id, product_name FROM products
  WHERE CONTAINS(description, ' "config*" ')
```

The result is

product_id	**product_name**
1	MS Application Center 2000

The CONTAINS predicate in Example 30.5 searches the **description** column for a word beginning with "config". The sign * is the wildcard of the CONTAINS predicate, which specifies any sequence of zero or more characters. Therefore, this sign has the same meaning as the percent for the LIKE predicate. (As you can see from Example 30.5, you need to use an additional pair of double quotes for the pattern with the wildcard.)

The CONTAINS predicate supports the Boolean operators AND, OR, and AND NOT. Example 30.6 shows the use of the AND operator.

▼ EXAMPLE 30.6

```
SELECT product_id, product_name FROM products
  WHERE CONTAINS(description, ' "manage*" AND "market*" ')
```

The result is

product_id	**product_name**
2	MS Commerce Server 2000

The query in Example 30.6 retrieves all rows that contain a word beginning with "manage" and a word beginning with "market".

Example 30.7 shows the use of the NEAR option that is used to match words close to one another.

▼ EXAMPLE 30.7

```
SELECT product_id, product_name FROM products
  WHERE CONTAINS(description, 'Microsoft NEAR management')
```

The result is

product_id	**product_name**
2	MS Commerce Server 2000
1	MS Application Center 2000

As you can see from the result of Example 30.7, the Microsoft Search service retrieves both rows, because both words ("Microsoft" and "management") appear in both rows relatively close to one another.

NOTE: The Microsoft Search service always returns the identity of the row plus its ranking value. The system uses the latter value to order the result set. (The result set of Example 30.7 shows that the rank of the second row is higher than the rank of the first one. This is obvious, because the words ("Microsoft" and "management") are closer to each other in the second than in the first row.)

The next example shows the use of the FORMSOF clause with the INFLECTIONAL specification.

▼ EXAMPLE 30.8

```
SELECT product_id, product_name FROM products
   WHERE CONTAINS(description, 'FORMSOF (INFLECTIONAL, fast) ')
```

The result is

product_id	product_name
2	MS Commerce Server 2000

INFLECTIONAL specifies that different forms of the string (plural and singular forms of nouns, comparative forms of adjectives, and various tenses of verbs) are to be matched. Therefore, the SELECT statement in Example 30.8 finds the word "fastest" as the superlative of the adjective "fast".

FREETEXTTABLE

As its name indicates, FREETEXTTABLE is a table that contains one or more rows for those columns that contain values matching the word(s) in the specified string. Analogous to the FREETEXT predicate, FREETEXTTABLE contains also such rows where values of the indexed column(s) do not exactly match the word(s) in the search condition. FREETEXTTABLE uses the same search conditions as the FREETEXT predicate, but has additional functionality: Queries using FREETEXTTABLE specify a ranking value for each row and can therefore display top **n** matches. (The FREETEXT predicate has also the ranking functionality, but always displays all matches.)

> ***NOTE:*** FREETEXTTABLE can be referenced in the FROM clause of a SELECT statement like any other user (or system) table.

Example 30.9 shows the use of FREETEXTTABLE.

▼ EXAMPLE 30.9

```
SELECT pr.product_id, pr.product_name
  FROM products pr, freetexttable(products,description, 'fast solution',1) ftt
   WHERE pr.product_id = ftt.[key]
```

The result is

product_id	product_name
2	MS Commerce Server 2000

The query in Example 30.9 joins two tables: the **products** table and FREETEXTTABLE. (FREETEXTTABLE has two fixed columns named **key** and **rank**, which can be referenced within the query to obtain the appropriate rows and use the row ranking values, respectively.) Example 30.9 is similar to Example 30.4, but their results are different: The specification of FREETEXTTABLE contains as the last parameter the number **n** (in Example 30.9, 1) that limits the result set only to the top **n** matches, ordered by rank.

CONTAINSTABLE

Like FREETEXTTABLE, CONTAINSTABLE is a table that returns zero or more rows. CONTAINSTABLE is used to search columns containing character-based data types for exact and fuzzy matches. Additionally, it allows you to search for words and phrases, the proximity of words within a certain distance of one another, and weighted matches. (CONTAINSTABLE uses the same search conditions as the CONTAINS predicate.)

Example 30.10 shows the use of CONTAINSTABLE.

▼ EXAMPLE 30.10

```
SELECT pr.product_id, pr.product_name
  FROM products pr,
  containstable(products, description, 'Microsoft NEAR management',1) ct
  WHERE pr.product_id = ct.[key]
  ORDER BY ct.rank DESC
```

The result is

product_id	product_name
1	MS Application Center 2000

The query in Example 30.10 joins two tables: the **products** table and CONTAINSTABLE. Analogous to FREETEXTTABLE, CONTAINSTABLE has two fixed columns named **key** and **rank**, with the same meaning. Example 30.10 is similar to Example 30.7, but their results are different: The specification of CONTAINSTABLE contains as the last parameter the number **n** (in Example 30.10, 1) that limits the result set only to the top **n** matches, ordered by rank. Also the ORDER BY clause contains the DESC option and therefore causes the display of the last ranked row.

CONCLUSION

SQL Server 2000 has a comprehensive set of components, which allows you (and your organization) to Web-enable an existing system. In this process, you can use the full-text search of SQL Server 2000 to implement the search engine for your Web applications.

The SQL Server 2000 full-text search component is based upon the Microsoft Search service. This service allows you to query words or phrases, words in proximity to each other, and inflectional forms of words (nouns, verbs, and adjectives). The Microsoft Search service acts only on documents that are stored in column(s) of a relational table. Before starting a query search, you have to create full-text index for the column(s) and to populate it. A full-text index is created implicitly after you enable the column as well as the table and database to which the column belongs. (This means that you do not have to execute the CREATE INDEX statement to create the index.)

The Microsoft Search service supports two predicates: FREETEXT and CONTAINS. Use the CONTAINS predicate, because it provides significantly more functionality in full-text searches than the FREETEXT predicate. Also, you can use two row functions: FREETEXTTABLE and CONTAINSTABLE. The functionality of FREETEXTTABLE and CONTAINSTABLE corresponds to the functionality of the predicates FREETEXT and CONTAINS, respectively. You should use one of these functions (instead of the corresponding predicates) in the case where you want to display only a subset of a result set in ascending or descending order of their ranking values.

APPENDIX A

Solutions

Chapter 1

▼ S.1.1

Data independence means that database application programs are not dependent on the physical structure of the stored data in a database (physical data independence) and that database application programs are independent of the logical structure of the database (logical data independence).

▼ S.1.2

The main concept of the relational model is a relation (i.e., a table). The whole relational model consists of only tables with one or more columns and zero or more rows. At every position in the table, there is only one data value.

▼ S.1.3

The **employee** table represents an entity, while the data for Ann Jones specifies an object (i.e., an instance of the entity).

▼ S.1.4

The **works_on** table represents the relationship between employees and projects. The difference from the other tables of the sample database is that it shows the relation between two entities, while all other tables each represent an entity.

▼ S.1.5

A. Yes, because it is unique.

B. Yes, because each title uniquely determines the corresponding ISBN.

C. Yes (there are no dependencies between the nonkey attributes, because there is just one).

▼ S.1.6

A. Yes, because all other columns are dependent on this one.

B. No, because of the functional dependency on the column **order_no**.

▼ S.1.7

The table **company** is not in any normal form, because the column **location** is multivalued.

▼ S.1.8

A. 1NF, because the column **city** is functionally dependent on the column **supplier_no**, which is the partial key of the table.

B. Using the following two tables:

- supplier1 (supplier_no, article)
- supplier2 (supplier_no, city)

▼ S.1.9

1NF, because the column C is dependent on the column B, which is the partial key of the table.

▼ S.1.10

This table is in 3NF, but its design is not well done.

Chapter 2

▼ S.2.1

Right-click the **Databases** folder and select **New Database**. Enter **test** in the field **Name**, enter the value **2** in the field **File growth – In megabytes** and **20** in the field **Maximum file size – Restrict filegrowth (MB)**. In the **location** column, change the path to **C:\tmp**. Do the same for the **initial size** column to change it to 10MB. Then click **OK**.

▼ S.2.2

Select the **test** database inside the folder **Databases** of your SQL Server. Right-click on it, select **Properties**, and choose the **Transaction Log** tab. Proceed with changing the values similar to Exercise 2.1.

▼ S.2.3

In the **Properties** dialog box of the **test** database, choose the tab **Options** and select **DBO use only**. Several DBOs can use the database if the option **Single User** is not activated.

▼ S.2.4

Right-click on the folder **Tables** inside the **test** database. Select **New Table** and enter the name of the first table (**department**). Then enter the column names with the corresponding data types. Proceed in the same way with all four tables.

▼ S.2.5

Click on the database **Northwind** in the folder **Databases** and select **User Tables**. All user tables of the database are now shown in the detail pane. Double-click the **orders** table to display its properties.

▼ S.2.6

It's not possible to create another database with the same name.

▼ S.2.7

Choose the function **File** in the main menu and select **Save as**. After that, change the destination directory, enter the new filename (**createdb**), and click **OK**.

▼ S.2.8

Either enter USE test and execute it inside the Query Analyzer's window or select the database from the **Database** select box in the toolbar.

▼ S.2.9

Select the **Northwind** database in the **Database** folder and enter SELECT * FROM orders. After starting the execution of the statement with F5 (or with the green button in the toolbar), press the red button to interrupt the current execution.

▼ S.2.10

Type Ctrl + T or click the arrow beside the **Execute Mode** button and select **Results in Text**.

Chapter 3

▼ S.3.1

The difference is in storage length and range of possible values.

TINYINT is stored in one byte with a value range from 0 to 255. SMALLINT is stored in two bytes with a value range from –32768 to 32767. INT is stored in four bytes with a value range from –2147483648 to 2147483647.

▼ S.3.2

CHAR is a string that can store up to 8,000 characters. It stores the amount of characters given by declaration. VARCHAR also can store up to 8,000 characters. However, the strings are stored with their actual length. Use CHAR when the data values in a column are expected to be approximately the same size. Use VARCHAR when the data values in a column are expected to vary considerably in size.

▼ S.3.3

SET DATEFORMAT ymd

▼ S.3.4

SELECT DB_ID('test')

▼ S.3.5

SELECT @@VERSION, @@LANGUAGE

▼ S.3.6

(01000101)
(11011111)
(00000110)

▼ S.3.7

A + NULL Result is NULL, independent of A
NULL = NULL Result is NULL
B OR NULL True, if B is true; otherwise, NULL
B AND NULL False, if B is false; otherwise, NULL

▼ S.3.8

By setting QUOTED_IDENTIFIER to OFF.

▼ S.3.9

Delimited identifiers specify special kinds of identifiers used to allow the use of reserved keywords as identifiers or table names that include blanks. (For instance, you need to use delimited identifiers to specify the table **order details** of the **Northwind** database in a Transact-SQL statement.)

Chapter 4

▼ S.4.1

```
USE master
GO
CREATE DATABASE test_db
        ON (NAME = test_db_dat,
        FILENAME='C:\tmp\test_db.mdf',
        SIZE = 5, MAXSIZE = UNLIMITED, FILEGROWTH = 8%)
        LOG ON
        (NAME=test_db_log,
        FILENAME = 'C:\tmp\test_db_log.ldf',
        SIZE = 2, MAXSIZE = 10, FILEGROWTH = 500KB)
```

▼ S.4.2

```
ALTER DATABASE test_db
        ADD LOG FILE (NAME=emp_log1,
                        FILENAME='C:\tmp\test_db.ldf',
                        SIZE=2, MAXSIZE=UNLIMITED, FILEGROWTH=2)
```

▼ S.4.3

```
ALTER DATABASE test_db
        MODIFY FILE
        (NAME = test_db_dat, SIZE = 10MB)
```

▼ S.4.4

The NOT NULL specification is necessary for all columns that are part of the primary key.

▼ S.4.5

dept_no and **project_no** are defined as CHAR values because they may also contain characters besides numerical values.

▼ S.4.6

```
CREATE TABLE customers (customerid char(5) not null,
                        companyName varchar(40) not null,
                        contactName char(30) null,
                        address varchar(60) null,
                        city char(15) null,
                        phone char(24) null,
                        fax char(24) null)
CREATE TABLE orders (orderid integer not null,
                        customerid char(5) not null,
                        orderdate datetime null,
                        shippeddate datetime null,
                        freight money null,
                        shipname varchar(40) null,
                        shipaddress varchar(60) null,
                        quantity integer null)
```

▼ S.4.7

```
ALTER TABLE orders
     ADD shipregion INTEGER NULL
```

▼ S.4.8

```
ALTER TABLE orders
     ALTER COLUMN shipregion CHAR(8) NULL
```

▼ S.4.9

```
ALTER TABLE orders
     DROP COLUMN shipregion
```

▼ S.4.10

After deleting a table with DROP TABLE, all data, indices, and triggers belonging to the removed table are also dropped. In contrast to that, all views that are defined using the table are not removed.

▼ S.4.11

```
DROP TABLE orders
DROP TABLE customers
CREATE TABLE customers (customerid char(5) not null
                        CONSTRAINT PRIM_CUST PRIMARY KEY,
                        companyName varchar(40) not null,
                        contactName char(30) null,
                        address varchar(60) null,
                        city char(15) null,
                        phone char(24) null,
                        fax char(24) null)
```

```
CREATE TABLE orders (orderid INTEGER NOT NULL,
                     customerid CHAR(5) NOT NULL,
                     orderdate DATETIME NULL,
                     shippeddate DATETIME NULL,
                     freight MONEY NULL,
                     shipname VARCHAR(40) NULL,
                     shipaddress VARCHAR(60) NULL,
                     quantity INTEGER NULL,
                     CONSTRAINT prim_ord PRIMARY KEY(orderid),
                     CONSTRAINT foreign_orders FOREIGN KEY(customerid)
                     REFERENCES customers(customerid))
```

▼ S.4.12

Right-click on **Diagrams** in the folder of the **test_db** database. Then choose **New Diagram** and select the tables **orders** and **customers**. Finish the wizard.

▼ S.4.13

It is not possible to insert the row, because of the referential constraint enforced in the CREATE TABLE statement (see S.4.11). SQL Server will print the following message:

"INSERT statement conflicted with COLUMN FOREIGN KEY constraint"

▼ S.4.14

```
ALTER TABLE orders
      ALTER COLUMN orderdate DATETIME NULL
ALTER TABLE orders
      ADD CONSTRAINT AddDateDflt DEFAULT getdate() FOR orderdate
```

▼ S.4.15

```
ALTER TABLE orders
      ADD CONSTRAINT limit_qu
      CHECK (quantity BETWEEN 1 AND 30)
```

▼ S.4.16

Creating the new data type:

```
sp_addtype western_countries, 'char(2) ', 'NOT NULL'
GO
```

Creating a new default-value for our data type:

```
CREATE DEFAULT western_countries_default AS 'CA'
GO
```

Bind the new default-value to our data type:

```
sp_bindefault 'western_countries_default', 'western_countries'
GO
```

Creating a rule for the allowed values for our data type:

```
CREATE RULE western_countries_rule
    AS @selection IN ('CA', 'WA', 'OR', 'NM')
GO
```

Bind the new rule to our data type:

```
sp_bindrule western_countries_rule, western_countries
GO
```

Now create the new table with the user-defined data type:

```
CREATE TABLE regions
    (city CHAR(25) NOT NULL,
country western_countries)
```

▼ S.4.17

```
sp_helpconstraint orders
```

▼ S.4.18

```
ALTER TABLE customers
        DROP CONSTRAINT prim_cust
```

That statement will not work, because the primary key constraint **prim_cust** is referenced by the foreign-key constraint defined in the **orders** table.

▼ S.4.19

```
ALTER TABLE orders
        DROP CONSTRAINT limit_qu
```

▼ S.4.20

```
sp_rename 'customers.city', town
```

Chapter 5

▼ S.5.1

```
SELECT *
        FROM works_on
```

▼ S.5.2

```
SELECT emp_no
        FROM works_on
        WHERE Job = 'Clerk'
```

▼ S.5.3

```
SELECT emp_no
        FROM works_on
        WHERE project_no = 'p2'
        AND emp_no < 10000
```

or:

```
SELECT emp_no
    FROM works_on
    WHERE project_no = 'p2'
    AND emp_no BETWEEN 0 AND 9999
```

▼ S.5.4

```
SELECT emp_no
        FROM works_on
        WHERE enter_date NOT BETWEEN
        '01.01.1998' AND '12.31.1998'
```

▼ S.5.5

```
SELECT emp_no
        FROM works_on
        WHERE project_no = 'p1'
        AND (job = 'Manager' OR job = 'Analyst')
```

▼ S.5.6

```
SELECT enter_date
        FROM works_on
        WHERE project_no = 'p2'
        AND Job IS NULL
```

▼ S.5.7

```
SELECT emp_no, emp_lname
        FROM employee
        WHERE emp_fname LIKE '%t%t%'
```

▼ S.5.8

```
SELECT emp_no, emp_fname
        FROM employee
        WHERE emp_lname LIKE '_[ao]%es'
```

▼ S.5.9

```
SELECT emp_no
        FROM employee
        WHERE dept_no =
        (SELECT dept_no FROM department
        WHERE location = 'Seattle')
```

▼ S.5.10

```
SELECT emp_lname, emp_fname
       FROM employee
       WHERE emp_no=IN
       (SELECT emp_no
       FROM works_on
       WHERE enter_date = '04/01/1998')
```

▼ S.5.11

```
SELECT location
       FROM department
       GROUP BY location
```

▼ S.5.12

If you use GROUP BY without any additional specifications (aggregates, HAVING clause), it is exactly like DISTINCT. (It divides a table into groups and returns one row for each group.)

▼ S.5.13

All NULL values belong to one group. (This is not exactly in accordance with the fact that each NULL value is a value per se, and cannot be compared with other NULL values.)

▼ S.5.14

COUNT(expression) takes an argument (i.e., a column or expression) and displays all non-NULL occurrences of that argument. COUNT(*) counts all rows, whether or not any particular column contains a NULL value.

▼ S.5.15

```
SELECT MAX(emp_no)
       FROM employee
```

▼ S.5.16

```
SELECT job
       FROM works_on
       GROUP BY job
       HAVING COUNT(*) > 2
```

▼ S.5.17

```
SELECT DISTINCT emp_no
       FROM works_on
       WHERE (Job = 'Clerk' OR emp_no IN
       (SELECT emp_no
              FROM employee
              WHERE dept_no='d3'))
```

▼ S.5.18

The inner SELECT statement can be used in conjunction with a comparison operator, such as =, if its result set has maximal one row (in this case, = may be used). The result of the SELECT statement in Example 5.18 has more than one row. Therefore, the comparison operator = has to be replaced with the IN operator:

```
SELECT project_name
  FROM project
  WHERE project_no IN
    (SELECT project_no FROM works_on WHERE Job = 'Clerk')
```

▼ S.5.19

Temporary tables can be used to store the intermediate result of a complex query.

▼ S.5.20

Local temporary tables are removed at the end of the current session, while the global temporary tables are removed at the end of the session that created the table.

Chapter 6

▼ S.6.1

```
SELECT *
      FROM project, works_on
      WHERE project.project_no = works_on.project_no

SELECT project.*, emp_no, job, enter_date
      FROM project, works_on
      WHERE project.project_no = works_on.project_no

SELECT *
      FROM project, works_on
```

SQL92:

```
SELECT *
      FROM project
      JOIN works_on ON project.project_no = works_on.project_no

SELECT project.*, emp_no, Job, enter_date
      FROM project JOIN works_on
      ON project.project_no = works_on.project_no

SELECT *
      FROM project CROSS JOIN works_on
```

▼ S.6.2

You need at least **N**-1 join conditions.

▼ S.6.3

```
SELECT emp_no, job
     FROM works_on, project
     WHERE works_on.project_no = project.project_no
     AND project_name = 'Gemini'
```

SQL92:

```
SELECT emp_no, job
     FROM works_on JOIN project
     ON works_on.project_no = project.project_no
     WHERE project_name = 'Gemini'
```

▼ S.6.4

```
SELECT emp_fname, emp_lname
     FROM employee, department
     WHERE employee.dept_no = department.dept_no
     AND (dept_name = 'Research' OR dept_name = 'Accounting')
```

SQL92:

```
SELECT emp_fname, emp_lname
     FROM employee JOIN department
     ON employee.dept_no = department.dept_no
     WHERE (dept_name = 'Research' OR dept_name = 'Accounting')
```

▼ S.6.5

```
SELECT enter_date
     FROM works_on, employee
     WHERE works_on.emp_no = employee.emp_no
     AND job = 'Clerk'
     AND dept_no = 'd1'
```

SQL92:

```
SELECT enter_date
     FROM works_on JOIN employee
     ON works_on.emp_no = employee.emp_no
     WHERE job = 'Clerk'
     AND dept_no = 'd1'
```

▼ S.6.6

```
SELECT project_name
     FROM project
     WHERE project_no=IN
     (SELECT project_no
     FROM works_on
     WHERE Job = 'Clerk'
     GROUP BY project_no
     HAVING COUNT(*) > 1)
```

▼ S.6.7

```
SELECT emp_fname, emp_lname
       FROM employee, works_on, project
       WHERE employee.emp_no = works_on.emp_no
       AND works_on.project_no = project.project_no
       AND project_name = 'Mercury'
       AND job = 'Manager'
```

SQL92:

```
SELECT emp_fname, emp_lname
       FROM employee
       JOIN works_on ON employee.emp_no = works_on.emp_no
       JOIN project ON works_on.project_no = project.project_no
        WHERE project_name = 'Mercury'
       AND job = 'Manager'
```

▼ S.6.8

```
SELECT emp_fname, emp_lname
       FROM employee
       WHERE emp_no IN
       (SELECT a.emp_no
       FROM works_on a, works_on b
       WHERE  b.enter_date=a.enter_date
       AND a.emp_no != b.emp_no)
```

▼ S.6.9

```
SELECT a.emp_no
       FROM employee_enh a, employee_enh b
       WHERE a.domicile = b.domicile
       AND a.dept_no = b.dept_no
       AND a.emp_no != b.emp_no
```

▼ S.6.10

```
SELECT emp_no
       FROM employee, department
       WHERE employee.dept_no = department.dept_no
       AND dept_name = 'Marketing'

SELECT emp_no
       FROM employee
       WHERE dept_no =
       (SELECT dept_no
       FROM department
       WHERE dept_name = 'Marketing')
```

SQL92:

```
SELECT emp_no
       FROM employee
       JOIN department
       ON employee.dept_no = department.dept_no
       WHERE dept_name = 'Marketing'
```

Chapter 7

▼ S.7.1

```
INSERT INTO employee values(11111, 'Julia', 'Long',NULL)
```

▼ S.7.2

```
CREATE TABLE emp_d1_d2  (emp_no INTEGER NOT NULL,
              emp_fname CHAR(20) NOT NULL,
              emp_lname CHAR(20) NOT NULL,
              dept_no CHAR(4) NULL)

INSERT INTO employee_d1_d2
       SELECT emp_no, emp_fname, emp_lname, dept_no
       FROM employee
       WHERE dept_no IN ('d1', 'd2')
```

or:

```
SELECT emp_no, emp_fname, emp_lname, dept_no
  INTO emp_d1_d2
FROM employee
  WHERE dept_no IN ('d1', 'd2')
```

▼ S.7.3

```
CREATE TABLE employee_three  (emp_no INTEGER NOT NULL,
              emp_fname CHAR(20) NOT NULL,
              emp_lname CHAR(20) NOT NULL,
              dept_no CHAR(4) NULL)

INSERT INTO employee_three(emp_no, emp_fname, emp_lname, dept_no)
       SELECT emp_no, emp_fname, emp_lname, dept_no
       FROM employee
       WHERE emp_no IN
       (SELECT emp_no FROM works_on
       WHERE enter_date BETWEEN '01.01.1998' AND '12.31.1998')
```

▼ S.7.4

```
UPDATE works_on
       SET job = 'Clerk'
       WHERE job = 'Manager' AND project_no = 'p1'
```

▼ S.7.5

```
UPDATE project
        SET budget = NULL
```

▼ S.7.6

```
UPDATE works_on
        SET job = 'Manager'
        WHERE emp_no = 28559
```

▼ S.7.7

```
UPDATE project
        SET budget = budget/10+budget
        WHERE project_no=IN(
        SELECT project_no FROM works_on
        WHERE job='Manager' AND emp_no=10102)
```

▼ S.7.8

```
UPDATE department
        SET dept_name='Sales'
        WHERE dept_no =
        (SELECT dept_no FROM employee
        WHERE emp_lname='James')
```

▼ S.7.9

```
UPDATE works_on
        SET enter_date='12/12/1998'
        WHERE project_no='p1' AND emp_no IN (
        SELECT emp_no FROM employee
        JOIN department ON employee.dept_no = department.dept_no
        WHERE dept_name='Sales'
```

▼ S.7.10

```
DELETE FROM department
        WHERE location = 'Seattle'
```

▼ S.7.11

```
DELETE FROM works_on
        WHERE project_no = 'p3'

DELETE FROM project
        WHERE project_no = 'p3'
```

▼ S.7.12

```
DELETE FROM works_on
        WHERE emp_no IN (
        SELECT emp_no FROM employee
        JOIN department ON employee.dept_no = department.dept_no
        WHERE location='Dallas'
```

Chapter 8

▼ S.8.1

```
- - This procedure inserts 9000 row in the table orders
declare @i integer
declare @customer_id char(5)
declare @shipped_date datetime
declare @freight money
set @i = 1
set @customer_id = 'ALKHE'
set @shipped_date = getdate()
set @freight = 100.00
while @i < 9001
begin
insert into orders (orderid, customerid, shippeddate, freight)
  values(@i, @customer_id, @shipped_date, @freight)
set @i = @i+1
end
```

▼ S.8.2

```
- - This procedure inserts 10000 rows in the table orders
declare @i int , @order_id integer
declare @customer_id char(5)
declare @shipped_date datetime
declare @freight money
set @i = 1
set @customer_id = 'ALKHE'
set @shipped_date = getdate()
set @freight = 100.00
while @i < 10001
begin
set @order_id =ceiling (rand ((datepart(mm,getdate())*100000) +(datepart(ss,
ETDATE())*1000)
            + DATEPART(ms,getdate())) * 100000000)
insert into orders (orderid, customerid, shippeddate, freight)
  values( @order_id, @customer_id, @shipped_date, @freight)
set @i = @i+1
end
```

Chapter 9

▼ S.9.1

```
CREATE INDEX i_enterdate
   ON works_on(enter_date)
   WITH FILLFACTOR = 60
```

▼ S.9.2

```
CREATE UNIQUE INDEX i_lfname
   ON employee (emp_lname, emp_fname)
```

A composite index can be used for index access for the leading part of the index. Therefore, there is a significant difference if you change the order of the columns in a composite index.

▼ S.9.3

An index that is implicitly created for the primary key of a table cannot be dropped using the DROP INDEX statement. It can be dropped only if you drop the constraint (using the ALTER TABLE statement with the DROP CONSTRAINT clause).

▼ S.9.4

During index access, only the rows that satisfy the search criteria of the query are accessed. This is, in most cases, an obvious advantage in relation to a table scan, where the system does not use an index. But besides this significant benefit, an index scan can have two disadvantages: In contrast to a table scan, SQL Server uses, for index access, smaller I/O units to read rows and therefore a number of read operations will be comparatively higher. The second disadvantage of the index access method (using a nonclustered index) is that data pages must be read repeatedly, because the rows to be selected are scattered on data pages.

▼ S.9.5

```
CREATE INDEX i_employee_lname ON employee (emp_lname)
```

▼ S.9.6

```
CREATE INDEX i_emp_name ON employee (emp_lname, emp_fname)
```

▼ S.9.7

```
CREATE INDEX i_workson_empno ON works_on (emp_no)
CREATE INDEX i_employee_empno ON employee (emp_no)
```

▼ S.9.8

```
CREATE INDEX i_department_deptno ON department (dept_no)
CREATE INDEX i_employee_deptno ON employee (dept_no)
CREATE INDEX i_department_deptname ON department (dept_name)
```

Chapter 10

▼ S.10.1

```
CREATE VIEW v_10_1
 AS SELECT *
 FROM employee WHERE dept_no = 'd1'
```

▼ S.10.2

```
CREATE VIEW v_10_2
 AS SELECT project_no, project_name
   FROM project
```

▼ S.10.3

```
CREATE VIEW v_10_3
 AS SELECT emp_lname, emp_fname
    FROM employee, works_on
    WHERE works_on.emp_no = employee.emp_no
    AND enter_date BETWEEN '06/01/1998' AND '12/31/1998'
```

▼ S.10.4

```
CREATE VIEW v_10_4 (first, last)
 AS SELECT emp_fname, emp_lname
    FROM v_10_3
```

▼ S.10.5

```
SELECT *
 FROM v_10_1 WHERE emp_lname LIKE 'M%'
```

▼ S.10.6

```
CREATE VIEW v_10_6
  AS SELECT project.*
    FROM project, employee, works_on
    WHERE project.project_no = works_on.project_no
    AND employee.emp_no = works_on.emp_no
    AND emp_lname = 'Smith'
```

▼ S.10.7

```
ALTER VIEW v_10_1
 AS SELECT *
 FROM employee WHERE dept_no IN('d1', 'd2')
```

▼ S.10.8

DROP VIEW v_10_3.

The DROP VIEW statement also removes the view v_10_4.

▼ S.10.9

```
INSERT INTO v_10_2 VALUES('p4', 'Moon')
```

▼ S.10.10

```
CREATE VIEW v_10_10
 AS SELECT emp_no, emp_fname, emp_lname, dept_no
      FROM employee
     WHERE emp_no  < 10000
     WITH CHECK OPTION

INSERT INTO v_10_10 VALUES(22123, 'Michael' , 'Kohn', 'd3')
```

doesn't work, because the employee number is greater than 10,000.

▼ S.10.11

```
CREATE VIEW v_10_11
 AS SELECT emp_no, emp_fname, emp_lname, dept_no
      FROM employee
     WHERE emp_no  < 10000

INSERT INTO v_10_11 VALUES(22123, 'Michael' , 'Kohn', 'd3')
```

works, because the employee number won't be checked.

▼ S.10.12

```
CREATE VIEW v_10_12
 AS SELECT emp_no, project_no, enter_date, job
    FROM works_on
    where enter_date between '01.01.1998' and '12.31.1999'
    with check option
UPDATE v_10_12 SET enter_date = '06/01/1997'
 where emp_no = 29346 and project_no='p1';
```

doesn't work, because the date does not belong to the years 1998 or 1999.

▼ S.10.13

```
CREATE VIEW v_10_13
 AS SELECT emp_no, project_no, enter_date, job
    FROM works_on
    where enter_date between '01.01.1998' and '12.31.1999'

UPDATE v_10_12 SET enter_date = '06/01/1997'
 where emp_no = 29346 and project_no='p1';
```

This UPDATE statement works.

Chapter 11

▼ S.11.1

```
USE master
SELECT filename from sysdatabases
  WHERE name = 'sample'
```

▼ S.11.2

```
USE sample
SELECT sysindexes.name
 FROM sysobjects, sysindexes
 WHERE sysobjects.id = sysindexes.id
 AND sysobjects.name = 'employee'
 AND sysindexes.indid = 1
```

▼ S.11.3

```
USE sample
SELECT COUNT(*)
 FROM sysconstraints, sysobjects
 WHERE sysconstraints.id = sysobjects.id
  AND sysobjects.name = 'employee'
```

▼ S.11.4

```
USE sample
SELECT sysconstraints.status
 FROM syscolumns, sysobjects, sysconstraints
 WHERE syscolumns.id = sysconstraints.colid
 AND sysobjects.id = sysconstraints.id
 AND sysobjects.name = 'employee'
  AND syscolumns.name = 'dept_no'
```

▼ S.11.5

The system procedure **sp_depends** uses the information that is contained in the system table **sysdepends**.

▼ S.11.6

```
SELECT syscolumns.name
FROM systypes, syscolumns
WHERE systypes.xtype = syscolumns.xtype
AND systypes.usertype = syscolumns.usertype
AND systypes.type = syscolumns.type
AND systypes.name = 'western_countries'
```

▼ S.11.7

```
USE northwind
SELECT table_name from information_schema.tables
WHERE table_type = 'BASE TABLE'
```

▼ S.11.8

```
USE sample
SELECT column_name, data_type, ordinal_position
    FROM information_schema.columns
   WHERE table_name = 'employee'
```

Chapter 12

▼ S.12.1

In Windows NT security mode, SQL Server exclusively uses NT user accounts, assuming that they already have been validated at the operating system level (trusted connection). In Mixed mode, SQL Server security works in addition to the Windows NT security.

▼ S.12.2

The login is used to allow a certain user to log into the SQL Server system, whereas the account is used to grant access to a particular database for a certain user or a role.

▼ S.12.3

```
sp_addlogin 'peter', 'abc', 'sample'
GO
sp_addlogin 'paul', 'def', 'sample'
GO
sp_addlogin 'mary', 'fgh', 'sample'
GO

use master
SELECT name FROM syslogins
```

▼ S.12.4

```
use sample
GO
sp_grantdbaccess 'peter', 's_peter'
GO
sp_grantdbaccess 'paul', 's_paul'
GO
sp_grantdbaccess 'mary', 's_mary'
```

▼ S.12.5

```
use sample
GO
sp_addrole 'managers'
GO
sp_addrolemember 'managers', 's_peter'
GO
sp_addrolemember 'managers', 's_mary'
GO
sp_addrolemember 'managers', 's_paul'

sp_helpuser 'managers'
```

▼ S.12.6

```
GRANT CREATE TABLE
      TO s_peter
GRANT CREATE PROCEDURE
      TO s_mary
```

▼ S.12.7

```
GRANT UPDATE ON employee(emp_lname,emp_fname)
      TO s_peter
```

▼ S.12.8

```
CREATE VIEW readnames
      AS SELECT emp_lname,emp_fname FROM employee
GO
GRANT SELECT ON readnames
      TO s_peter,s_mary
```

▼ S.12.9

```
GRANT INSERT ON project
      TO managers
```

▼ S.12.10

```
REVOKE SELECT ON readnames
      FROM s_peter
```

▼ S.12.11

```
DENY INSERT ON project
      TO s_mary
```

▼ S.12.12

The functionality of views in relation to the T-SQL statements GRANT, REVOKE, and DENY is limited, because with the former you can restrict only the access to one or more columns and one or more rows. (Using T-SQL statements, you can restrict operations on data, such as reading and writing.)

▼ S.12.13

```
USE sample
GO
sp_helpuser s_mary
```

Chapter 13

▼ S.13.1

```
CREATE TRIGGER tr_refint_dept
        ON department
        FOR DELETE, UPDATE
        AS
        IF UPDATE(dept_no)
                BEGIN
                IF (SELECT COUNT(*)
                        FROM employee, deleted
                        WHERE employee.dept_no = deleted.dept_no) >0
                        BEGIN
                                ROLLBACK TRANSACTION
                                PRINT "Transaction failed!"
                        END
                ELSE PRINT "Transaction succeeded"
                END

CREATE TRIGGER tr_refint_dept2
        ON employee
        FOR INSERT, UPDATE
        AS
        IF UPDATE(dept_no)
                BEGIN
                IF (SELECT department.dept_no
                        FROM department, inserted
                        WHERE department.dept_no = inserted.dept_no) IS NULL
                        BEGIN
                                ROLLBACK TRANSACTION
                                PRINT "Transaction failed!"
                        END
                ELSE PRINT "Transaction succeeded"
                END
```

▼ S.13.2

```
CREATE TRIGGER tr_refint_project
        ON project
        FOR DELETE, UPDATE
        AS
        IF UPDATE(project_no)
                BEGIN
                IF (SELECT COUNT(*)
                        FROM works_on, deleted
                        WHERE works_on.project_no = deleted.project_no) >0
                        BEGIN
                                ROLLBACK TRANSACTION
                                PRINT "Transaction failed!"
                        END
                ELSE PRINT "Transaction succeeded"
                END

CREATE TRIGGER tr_ref_project2
        ON works_on
        FOR INSERT, UPDATE
        AS
        IF UPDATE(project_no)
                BEGIN
                IF (SELECT project.project_no
                        FROM project, inserted
                        WHERE project.project_no = inserted.project_no) IS NULL
                        BEGIN
                                ROLLBACK TRANSACTION
                                PRINT "Transaction failed!"
                        END
                ELSE PRINT "Transaction succeeded"
                END
```

Chapter 14

▼ S.14.1

Transactions are used to keep the data consistent using its "all or nothing" property: Either all statements are (successfully) executed or none of them is executed.

▼ S.14.2

A distributed transaction needs a coordinator that coordinates the execution of all transaction parts on different servers. Also, you use the BEGIN TRANSACTION statement to start a local transaction and BEGIN DISTRIBUTED TRANSACTION to start a distributed transaction.

▼ S.14.3

Each Transact-SQL statement always belongs either implicitly or explicitly to a transaction. When a session operates in implicit transaction mode, selected statements implicitly issue the BEGIN TRANSACTION statement. This means that you do nothing to start such a transaction. However, the end of each implicit transaction must be explicitly committed or rolled back using the COMMIT (i.e., ROLLBACK) statement. An explicit transaction is specified with the pair of statements BEGIN TRANSACTION and COMMIT TRANSACTION (or ROLLBACK TRANSACTION).

▼ S.14.4

None.

▼ S.14.5

Using the global variable @@error.

▼ S.14.6

The SAVE TRANSACTION statement is used to execute parts of an entire transaction.

▼ S.14.7

The advantage of row-level locking is that it maximizes concurrency, because all other rows of the table that are stored on the same page can be used by other processes. On the other hand, it increases system overhead, because each locked row requires one lock (and you need many more locks if you use row-level locking instead of page-level locking). The advantage of row-level locking is the disadvantage of page-level locking and vice versa.

▼ S.14.8

Using the SET LOCK_TIMEOUT statement, a user can specify whether a transaction should wait or not for a lock to be released. Also, there are several options in the FROM clause of the SELECT statement that can be used by a user to influence the locking behavior of SQL Server (such as UPDALOCK, TABLOCK, ROWLOCK, and PAGLOCK).

▼ S.14.9

An intent lock is always placed at the next level in a hierarchy of database objects above the process it intends to lock. An X lock (i.e., S lock) is always used for the object that actually should be locked.

▼ S.14.10

The process of converting many page-level locks into one table lock (or many row-level locks into one page lock).

▼ S.14.11

READ UNCOMMITTED is the simplest isolation level and therefore allows the maximum of data inconsistency of all isolation levels. On the other hand, the advantage of this isolation level is that it allows the highest concurrency. The advantage of SERIALIZABLE is that there will be no data inconsistency at all when you apply this isolation level for a process. On the other hand, it decreases concurrency of the processes at most.

▼ S.14.12

A deadlock is a special situation in which two transactions block the progress of each other. (It is possible that several transactions cause a deadlock if the first transaction blocks the second, the second the third, and so on, and finally the last transaction blocks the first one.)

▼ S.14.13

SQL Server always chooses the process that closed the loop in a deadlock. Users can use the SET DEADLOCK_PRIORITY statement to choose the "victim" process.

Chapter 15

▼ S.15.1

An index page is identical to a data page except that it has only two parts:

- Page header
- Data space

(The row offset table does not appear at the end of an index page.)

▼ S.15.2

The only difference between these two utilities is that the **isql** utility uses DB-Library to communicate with the server, while the **osql** utility uses ODBC. You should use the **osql** utility, because features introduced in SQL Server 2000 and SQL Server version 7.0 are not supported for DB-Library applications.

▼ S.15.3

In the TEMP directory.

▼ S.15.4

Multiple instances have benefits in the following two areas:

- Dividing different database types. (The main purpose of multiple instances is to divide production databases, test databases, and sample databases into different groups to run on different instances.)
- Server consolidation. (Instead of having **N** machines to run **N** SQL Server systems, you can use one (big) computer and run **N** instances.

The disadvantage of multiple instances is that you need a very powerful computer to manage multiple instances.

▼ S.15.5

Multithreading specifies that several threads from different clients are scheduled and executed using one system process.

▼ S.15.6

Data load, backup and recovery, as well as query execution can be executed in parallel using SQL Server 2000.

Chapter 18

▼ S.18.1

The primary file group is by default also the default file group. The database administrator can set another file group to be the default file group using the ALTER DATABASE statement.

▼ S.18.2

The **sp_dboption** system procedure is a deprecated feature in SQL Server 2000. For this reason, you should use the DATABASEPROPERTYEX function to view database options.

▼ S.18.3

To modify database options, use either SQL Server Enterprise Manager or the DBCC command. The use of the **sp_dboption** system procedure is not recommended (see S.18.2).

▼ S.18.4

When the **autoshrink** database option is set, SQL Server implicitly shrinks the size of database files that belong to the database.

▼ S.18.5

No.

Chapter 19

▼ S.19.1

Expand the server, choose **Security**, right-click **Logins**, and select **New Login**. On the **General** tab of the **New Login** dialog box, type the new Login name (for example, **peter**). In the **Authentication** frame, select **SQL Server Authentication** and type the corresponding password. In the **Defaults** frame, select sample. The new login appears in the detail pane.

▼ S.19.2

In the **Database** folder, select the database. Right-click **Users** and select **New Database User**. In the **Database User Properties** dialog box, select the login name and type the new user name under it. In the **Database role membership** frame, select **public**.

▼ S.19.3

In the **Database** folder, select the database. Right-click **Roles** and select **New Database Role**. In the **Database Role Properties** dialog box, type the new role name (managers). In the **Database role type** frame, click **Add** to add user names. Select the user names that belong to the new role.

▼ S.19.4

Right-click the database and select **Properties**. On the **Permissions** tab of the **Database Properties** dialog box in the row with the user name (**s_peter**), check the boxes for the CREATE TABLE and CREATE PROCEDURE statements.

▼ S.19.5

Select the database and click **Users**. In the detail pane, right-click the user and select **Properties**. In the **Database User Properties** dialog box, choose **Permissions**. Select the table (**employee**) that you want to modify permissions. Select **Columns** and check the boxes for each row and column intersection that corresponds to the chosen column(s) (**emp_lname, emp_fname**) and the chosen statement(s) (UPDATE).

▼ S.19.6

In the **Database** folder, select the database and click **Roles.** In the detail pane, right-click the role (**managers**) that you want to modify. Click **Permissions** and check the box at the intersection of the **project** table and the INSERT statement.

Chapter 20

▼ S.20.1

The benefit of differential backups is that you save time in the restore process, because to recover a database completely, you need a full database backup and only the *latest* differential backup. If you use transaction logs for the same scenario, you have to apply the full database backup and *all* existing transaction logs to bring the database to a consistent state.

A disadvantage of differential backups is that you cannot use them to recover data to a specific point in time because they do not store intermediate changes to the database.

▼ S.20.2

It depends upon several factors, such as the size of the database, the number of modification operations, and so forth.

▼ S.20.3

There is no way to make a differential backup of the master database. (You can make only a full database backup of this system database.)

▼ S.20.4

One common technique is to configure database data files on a RAID 0 drive and place the transaction log and backups on a mirrored drive (RAID 1). If the data must be quickly recoverable, use RAID 5 for a database and RAID 1 for the corresponding transaction log(s).

▼ S.20.5

Automatic recovery is done by the system, while manual recovery must be initiated by the system administrator.

▼ S.20.6

The RESTORE VERIFYONLY statement.

▼ S.20.7

Using the full recovery model, no work is lost due to a lost or damaged data file and you can recover to any point in time. On the other hand, the corresponding transaction log may be very voluminous. Using the bulk-logged recovery model, you cannot recover to any point in time, but the corresponding transaction log is smaller because minimal log space is used by bulk operations. The simple recovery model provides the simplest backup strategy, but all changes, since the most recent database or differential backup, must be manually redone.

Chapter 21

▼ S.21.1

The BULK INSERT statement.

▼ S.21.2

The only SQL Server 2000 tool that allows transformation of the data (during data migration) is DTS.

▼ S.21.3

bcp Northwind..customers out customers.txt –c –t" | " –r"\n"

Chapter 22

▼ S.22.1

You can automate, among others, the following tasks: data transfer, backing up the database and transaction log, as well as maintaining indexes and data integrity.

▼ S.22.2

Create one job to back up your transaction log and specify two schedules.

▼ S.22.3

Create an alert on the SQL Server: Locks object counter.

Chapter 23

▼ S.23.1

A SQL Server error message contains the following parts: A unique error message number, a severity level number, a line number (which identifies the line where the error occurred), and the error text.

▼ S.23.2

The benefit of the Windows NT event viewer is that it marks all errors with a red stop sign at the beginning of the line. That way, you can recognize errors immediately. Also, the event log provides an additional component for the search for desired strings. On the other hand, the SQL Server error log contains only messages specific to the database system.

▼ S.23.3

The three most important columns of the **sysmessages** system table are **error**, **severity**, and **description**.

Chapter 25

▼ S.25.1

A primary key is required to uniquely identify the rows of the published table. All tables using transactional replication must explicitly contain a primary key.

▼ S.25.2

Partition tables and/or filter data, which you want to replicate.

▼ S.25.3

You can minimize update conflicts by limiting subscriber update capabilities to an appropriate subset of the data.

▼ S.25.4

Log Reader Agent searches for marked transactions and copies them from the transaction log on the publisher to the **distribution** database. It is used for transactional replications. The synchronization job between all sites is done by Merge Agent. It is used for merge replications. Finally, Snapshot Agent generates the schema and data of the published tables during snapshot replication.

Chapter 26

▼ S.26.1

OLTP systems have short transactions, many (possibly hundreds or thousands of) users, continuous read and write operations, and medium-size data. Data warehousing systems have a small number of users, a large amount of data stored in a database, and, after the load process, only read operations.

▼ S.26.2

The ER model is highly normalized, while the dimensional model is usually denormalized because it uses nonredundant data. Also, the ER model produces very complex database designs for large databases.

▼ S.26.3

Extracting specifies the process of loading source data from multiple, heterogeneous operational systems into a temporary staging area. Data transformation is the process of formatting and modifying data that is extracted from various sources to make the information more useful. Finally, during the load process, the cleaned data is loaded into the data warehouse.

▼ S.26.4

In a dimensional model, there is one fact table and many dimension tables (in a dimensional model). A fact table contains a very large amount of the data stored in a data warehouse (approximately 70 percent). Also, columns of a fact table are numeric and additive.

▼ S.26.5

The MOLAP structure offers the best query performance for data analysis, because the aggregations and a copy of the base data are stored in a multidimensional structure—allowing a high-speed query processor to retrieve data quickly. However, data in MOLAP is duplicated in the cube and consumes the most storage space.

The ROLAP structure allows you to use standard Transact-SQL statements to query the relational tables. It also eliminates data duplication and does not require extra storage space. However, the query performance is not as fast as with the MOLAP and HOLAP structures.

The HOLAP structure retrieves data in the cube quickly and consumes less storage space than MOLAP.

▼ S.26.6

Because of the large amount of data that is stored in a data warehouse. In that case, doing aggregations on the fly requires a significant amount of time.

Index

Symbols

A

B

C

D

E

F

G

H

I

J

K

L

M

N

O

P

Q

R

S

T

U

V

W

X

Z

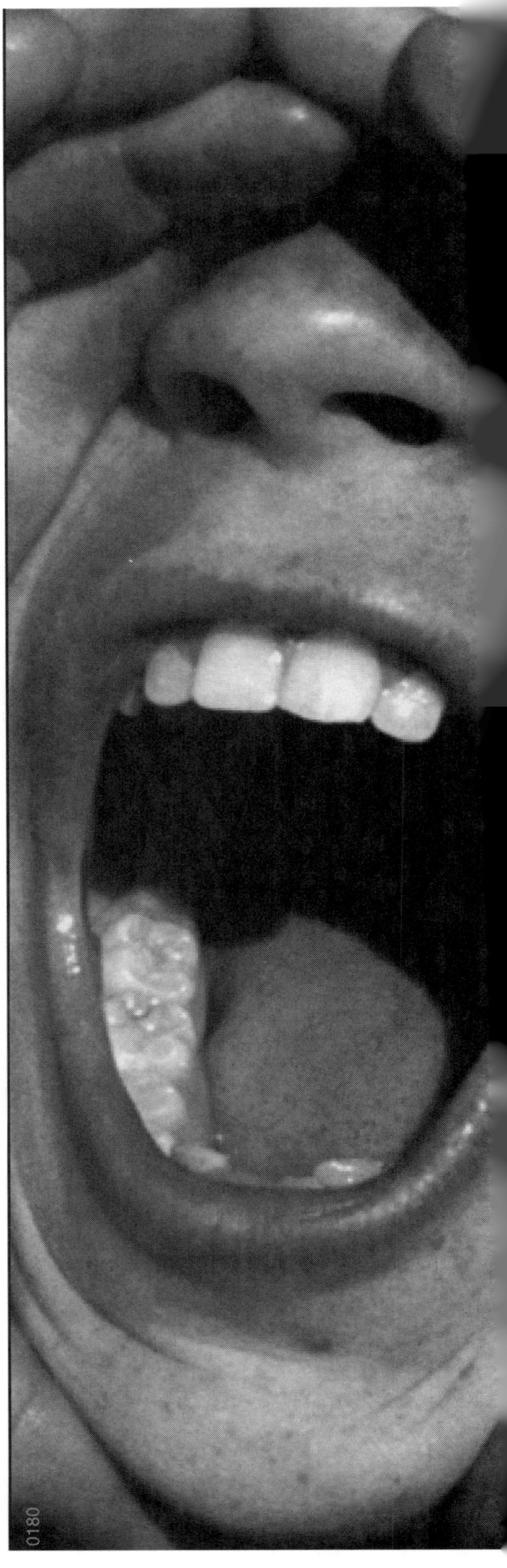

ABOUT THE CD

The enclosed CD-ROM includes SQL Server™ 2000 120-Day Enterprise Evaluation Edition.

Environment

Microsoft Windows®

Difference from Retail Product

Product Expires 120 days after installation. Restricted license rights.

System Requirements

- PC with an Intel or compatible Pentium 166 MHz or higher processor
- Microsoft Windows NT Server 4.0 with Service Pack 5 or later, Windows NT Server 4.0 Enterprise Edition with Service Pack 5 or later, Windows 2000 Server, Windows 2000 Advanced Server, or Windows 2000 Datacenter Server operation system
- Minimum of 64MB of RAM (128MB or more recommended)
- Hard-disk space required
- 95-270MB for database server; approximately 250MB for typical installation
- 50MB minimum for Analysis Services; 130MB for typical installation
- 80MB for Microsoft English Query (supported on Windows 2000 operating system but not logo certified)
- Microsoft Internet Explorer 5.0 or later
- CD-ROM drive
- VGA or higher resolution monitor
- Microsoft Mouse or compatible pointing device

This program was reproduced by Osborne/McGraw-Hill under special arrangement with Microsoft Corporation. For this reason, Osborne/McGraw-Hill is responsible for the product warranty and for support. If your CD is defective, please return it to Osborne/McGraw-Hill, which will arrange for its replacement. PLEASE DO NOT RETURN IT TO MICROSOFT CORPORATION. Any product support will be provided, if at all, by Osborne/McGraw-Hill. PLEASE DO NOT CONTACT MICROSOFT CORPORATION FOR PRODUCT SUPPORT. End users of this Microsoft program will not considered to be "registered owners" of a Microsoft product and therefore shall not be eligible for upgrades, promotions or other benefits available to "registered owners" of Microsoft products.

WARNING: BEFORE OPENING THE DISC PACKAGE, CAREFULLY READ THE TERMS AND CONDITIONS OF THE FOLLOWING COPYRIGHT STATEMENT AND LIMITED CD-ROM WARRANTY.

Copyright Statement

This software is protected by both United States copyright law and international copyright treaty provision. Except as noted in the contents of the CD-ROM, you must treat this software just like a book. However, you may copy it into a computer to be used and you may make archival copies of the software for the sole purpose of backing up the software and protecting your investment from loss. By saying, "just like a book," The McGraw-Hill Companies, Inc. ("Osborne/McGraw-Hill") means, for example, that this software may be used by any number of people and may be freely moved from one computer location to another, so long as there is no possibility of its being used at one location or on one computer while it is being used at another. Just as a book cannot be read by two different people in two different places at the same time, neither can the software be used by two different people in two different places at the same time.

Limited Warranty

Osborne/McGraw-Hill warrants the physical compact disc enclosed herein to be free of defects in materials and workmanship for a period of sixty days from the purchase date. If the CD included in your book has defects in materials or workmanship, please call McGraw-Hill at 1-800-217-0059, 9am to 5pm, Monday through Friday, Eastern Standard Time, and McGraw-Hill will replace the defective disc.

The entire and exclusive liability and remedy for breach of this Limited Warranty shall be limited to replacement of the defective disc, and shall not include or extend to any claim for or right to cover any other damages, including but not limited to, loss of profit, data, or use of the software, or special incidental, or consequential damages or other similar claims, even if Osborne/McGraw-Hill has been specifically advised of the possibility of such damages. In no event will Osborne/McGraw-Hill's liability for any damages to you or any other person ever exceed the lower of the suggested list price or actual price paid for the license to use the software, regardless of any form of the claim.

OSBORNE/McGRAW-HILL SPECIFICALLY DISCLAIMS ALL OTHER WARRANTIES, EXPRESS OR IMPLIED, INCLUDING BUT NOT LIMITED TO, ANY IMPLIED WARRANTY OF MERCHANTABILITY OR FITNESS FOR A PARTICULAR PURPOSE. Specifically, Osborne/McGraw-Hill makes no representation or warranty that the software is fit for any particular purpose, and any implied warranty of merchantability is limited to the sixty-day duration of the Limited Warranty covering the physical disc only (and not the software), and is otherwise expressly and specifically disclaimed.

This limited warranty gives you specific legal rights; you may have others which may vary from state to state. Some states do not allow the exclusion of incidental or consequential damages, or the limitation on how long an implied warranty lasts, so some of the above may not apply to you.

This agreement constitutes the entire agreement between the parties relating to use of the Product. The terms of any purchase order shall have no effect on the terms of this Agreement. Failure of Osborne/McGraw-Hill to insist at any time on strict compliance with this Agreement shall not constitute a waiver of any rights under this Agreement. This Agreement shall be construed and governed in accordance with the laws of New York. If any provision of this Agreement is held to be contrary to law, that provision will be enforced to the maximum extent permissible, and the remaining provisions will remain in force and effect.

NO TECHNICAL SUPPORT IS PROVIDED WITH THIS CD-ROM.